REX STOUT

Also by John McAleer

Theodore Dreiser: A Biography
Theodore Dreiser's Notes on Life (with M. Tjader)
Artist and Citizen Thoreau

REX STOUT
A Biography

JOHN McALEER

With a Foreword by P. G. Wodehouse

Little, Brown and Company—Boston–Toronto

Third Printing
T 10/77

The extract from Edna Ferber's letter on page 442 is
reprinted with the permission of Harriet F. Pilpel, Trustee
under Clause 8 of the Will of Edna Ferber.

LIBRARY OF CONGRESS CATALOGING IN PUBLICATION DATA
McAleer, John J
  Rex Stout.
  "A Rex Stout checklist": p.
  Includes index.
  1. Stout, Rex, 1886–1975—Biography.
  2. Novelists, American—20th century—Biography.
  PS3537.T733Z78   813'.5'2 [B]   77–24896
  ISBN 0–316–55340–9

Designed by Susan Windheim

*Published simultaneously in Canada
by Little, Brown & Company (Canada) Limited*

PRINTED IN THE UNITED STATES OF AMERICA

To Ruth
A sail, not an anchor

Contents

Book IV: A LIBERAL AWAKENING

Book V: THE YEARS OF CHOICE

Book VI: MINISTER OF PROPAGANDA

Book VII: CITIZEN OF THE WORLD

Book VIII: A KING'S RANSOM

Illustrations

(between pages 172 and 181 and 358 and 367)
Unless otherwise noted, the photographs appear through the
courtesy of Pola Stout.

The Todhunter family (Virginia Pretzfelder)

The Todhunter homestead (Virginia Pretzfelder)

Nathan Stout

Sophia Stout

Rex at six months

Stout's Mill (Natalie Stout Carr)

Rex's birthplace (Bud Ayres)

Clara Todhunter (From the Archives, Lilly Library, Earlham College)

Oscar Benjamin Todhunter (From the Archives, Lilly Library, Earlham College)

Hackberry Hall (Esther Doan Starbuck)

The Stouts, circa 1893

John Stout, circa 1899 (John W. Ripley, Shawnee County Historical Society, Topeka, Kansas)

Lucetta, circa 1920

John, circa 1918 (Natalie Stout Carr)

Police Chief A. G. Goodwin (John W. Ripley, Shawnee County Historical Society, Topeka, Kansas)

Lincoln School (John W. Ripley, Shawnee County Historical Society, Topeka, Kansas)

Rex on *Mayflower*

The Stouts in New York

Rex in 1916

Fay (Fay Koudrey)

The Stouts, 1920

Rex with Joe MacGregor and Harland Knowlton (Fay Koudrey)

Rex in Montana, 1926 (Fay Koudrey)

Rex, 1929

Foreword

Nobody who claims to be a competent critic can say that Rex Stout does not write well. His narrative and dialogue could not be improved, and he passes the supreme test of being rereadable. I don't know how many times I have reread the Nero Wolfe stories, but plenty. I know exactly what is coming and how it is all going to end, but it doesn't matter. That's *writing*.

Does the ordinary reader realize how exactly right those Nero Wolfe stories are? There are no loose ends. One could wonder why Sherlock Holmes, fawned on by kings and prime ministers, was not able to afford rooms in Baker Street — price at the turn of the century thirty bob a week including breakfast — unless he got Doctor Watson to put up half the money, but in Nero Wolfe, a professional detective charging huge fees, you can believe. Those orchids, perfectly understandable. He liked orchids and was in a financial position to collect them. He liked food, too. Again perfectly understandable. He refused to leave his house on business, and very sensible of him if his wealth and reputation were such that he could get away with it. In other words, there was nothing contrived about his eccentricities, purely because Stout knew his job.

But Stout's supreme triumph was the creation of Archie Goodwin.

Telling a mystery story in the third person is seldom satisfactory. To play fair you have to let the reader see into the detective's thoughts, and that gives the game away. The alternative is to have him pick up small objects from the floor and put them carefully in an envelope without revealing their significance, which is the lowest form of literary skulduggery. A Watson of some sort to tell the story is unavoidable, and the hundreds of Watsons who have appeared in print since Holmes's simply won't do. I decline to believe that when the prime minister sends for the detective to cry on his shoulder about some bounder having swiped the naval treaty and finds that he has brought a friend along, he just accepts the detective's statement that "This is Augustus So-and-So, who has been associated with me in many of my cases." What he would really do would be to ring the bell for the secretary of state and tell him to throw Mr. So-and-So out on his ear. "And I want to hear him bounce," he would add. Stout has avoided this trap. Archie is a Watson in the sense that he tells the story, but in no other way is there anything Watsonian about him. And he brings excellent comedy into the type of narrative where comedy seldom bats better than .100.

Summing up, I would say that there is only one Rex Stout, and if you think I am going to say "That's plenty," you are wrong, witty though it would be. I could do with a dozen.

P. G. Wodehouse

REX STOUT

Thomas Todhunter = Elizabeth Cockbain
(1577–1648)

Richard Stout = Penelope Kent Van Princin
(1615–1705)   (1622–1732)

William Todhunter =   Joshua Hoopes = Ann
(1625–?)   (1636–1723)   (1640–1678)

Peter Stout = Mary Bullen
(1654–1703)

John Todhunter = Margaret Hoopes
(c. 1657–1715)

John Stout = Sarah
(1675–?)

John Todhunter = Margaret Evans
(1715–?)

Edward   Catherine
Lanum   =   Power   William Ambler
(c. 1703–1765) (?–1778)   (c. 1745–1815)

Peter Stout = Margaret Cyfert
(1713–1802)   (1716–1799)

Isaac Todhunter = Eleanor Jury   Robert Power Lanum = Bathsheba Ambler
(1754–1821)   (1755–1839)   (1765–1821)   (1777–1845)

Mary
John   Woody
Atkinson = (1722–?)
(1766–?)

Charles Stout = Mary Noblit
(1742–1822)   (1746–1811)

Abner Todhunter = Elizabeth Job   Daniel McNeal = Mary Lanum
(1789–1871)   (1794–1866)   (1802–c. 1859) (1806–1890)

Ruth Atkinson John Nicholas = Regina
(?–1823)   Swingle   Hartman
                              (1788–1875)

Solomon Stout = Ruth Atkinson
(1787–1865)   (?–1823)

Amos Todhunter = Emily Elizabeth McNeal
(1818–1901)   (1828–1906)

Nathan Stout = Sophia Swingle
(1821–1908)   (1826–1912)

John Wallace Stout = Lucetta Elizabeth Todhunter
(1848–1933)   (1853–1940)

Winona May   John Robert   Walter Wallace   Juanita Lucetta   Ruth Imogen   Rex Todhunter   Mary Emily   Alice Elizabeth   Donald Phillip
(1876–1908)   (1878–1965)   (1880–1943)   (1882–1965)   (1884–)   (1886–1975)   (1888–1977)   (1890–1956)   (1896–1922)

Introduction

In the closing days of October 1975, when word came from rural Connecticut that Rex Stout, creator of Nero Wolfe and Archie Goodwin, had died at eighty-nine, readers around the world experienced an enveloping sense of loss, as though Wolfe and Archie had passed from the scene, too, in the company of their creator.

For more than forty years Wolfe and Archie had stepped with the times. When Wolfe first came on the scene, in 1933, he was kitchen-testing Prohibition beer. When last beheld, in the autumn of 1974, he was deploring the outrage of Watergate. But now the mirror which had given back Wolfe's image was broken. Readers would not again enter the brownstone on West Thirty-fifth Street to learn how Wolfe dealt with mankind's latest excursions and alarums. The bulwark that had been Wolfe's amazing perspicacity was gone — and so was Archie's reassuring banter. Or so it seemed.

Yet no one contends that Mr. Pickwick passed to extinction when Dickens died or that Huck Finn perished with Twain. The chronicle that celebrated Wolfe and Archie has been broken off, but the record of forty-two years, set down in seventy-two tales, survives. And, surviving, it will extend the existence of Rex Stout.

Those who knew Rex Stout best believe that he lives in his creations as well as through them. Rex's voice often is heard in Archie's utterances. At times, Rex was Nero Wolfe's identical twin. Certainly there existed within Rex the variegated potential he would have needed to have created Wolfe and Archie out of his own substance.

Geneticists tell us that we are the procession of our ancestors. If that is so then Rex Stout had a substantial legacy to draw on. Through his father, John Wallace Stout, Rex was descended from Penelope Van Princin, a colonial heroine who was scalped and disemboweled by Indians at Sandy Hook, New Jersey, in 1642, but lived to bear ten children and celebrate her one hundredth birthday; from Regina Hartman, who, late in the eighteenth century, survived nineteen years of captivity among the Indians, and from Solomon Stout, founder of Columbus, Indiana. Through his mother, Lucetta Todhunter Stout, Rex was descended from Mary Franklin, Benjamin Franklin's sister; from Elizabeth Maxwell, a kinswoman of Daniel Defoe's; and from an illustrious member of Pennsylvania's Colonial Assembly, Joshua Hoopes, from whom Hubert Humphrey also is descended. Additionally, both Stouts and Todhunters offered Rex a heritage of five generations of birthright Quakerism.

From the outset Rex Stout confronted life head-on. He began reading at the age of eighteen months. "I seldom had a book out of my hands when I was carrying him," his mother said. "It must have been that." His father was bookish too. John's mother thought his children went hungry because their dinner table always was so swamped with books they could find no place to eat. "Poor John," she said, "never has had anything but books and children."

When Rex was four Lucetta urged him to make a start on reading the Bible. She expected all her children to have read it through by their eighth birthday. "If you read three chapters a day," she reflected, "and five on Sunday, you could finish it in a year." Rex met this timetable, and, for good measure, read it through again, the next year. By the time he was seven he was a fifth of the way through his father's library of 1,126 books. Before he was eleven, he finished them. John, acting on the then accepted theory that a forward child should be braked, already had begun keeping Rex home part of every school term. Rex welcomed these interruptions. They gave him more time to read.

At ten Rex was exhibited around Kansas as a mathematical prodigy. At sixteen, he completed high school, the youngest member in a class of fifty-nine, most of whom were between eighteen and twenty-three. At nineteen he was keeping Theodore Roosevelt's accounts on board the presidential yacht, the *Mayflower*. At twenty-three he managed a hotel. At twenty-six he was a successful novelist. At thirty-one he was running a multi-million-dollar banking business. Between the ages of thirty-seven and forty-three he was, in quick succession, a publisher, a founder of *The New Masses*, a board member of the American Civil Liberties Union, president of Vanguard Press, an expatriate in Paris, and an avant-garde novelist, compared by critics in the United States and in England to D. H. Lawrence and William Faulkner. At forty-seven, he created Wolfe and Archie.

During World War II, Rex headed up a major portion of the American propaganda effort. In the years after World War II, as president of the Society for the Prevention of World War III and of the Authors' League, chairman of the Writers' Board for World Government, as treasurer of Freedom House, he was a champion of human liberties. Yet his writing continued. In all he wrote fifty-one novels and seventy-five novellas and short stories and saw his books translated into twenty-six languages, and sell more than 100,000,000 copies. During the last decade of his life he had more books in print than any other living American writer.

American Presidents, a British prime minister, a president of France, an Indian maharajah, a cardinal of the Vatican Curia, Nobel laureates, world-acclaimed nuclear physicists, psychiatrists, artists, and scholars read and admired his books. Yet Rex found time to build his own home, design and manufacture his own furniture, raise his own food, cultivate enormous collections of iris, day lilies, and begonias, double the membership of the Authors' Guild, come to the relief of hundreds of hard-pressed writers through his humane and discreet management of the Authors' League Fund, spread enlightenment to tens of thousands as chairman of Freedom House/Books USA, and bring about a major reform in copyright legislation benefiting all American writers. Rex knew how to use time to advantage. His own remarkable books were written down in finished form on first try and usually completed in thirty-eight days.

The success of the Wolfe stories has been attributed to several factors. "Like P. G. Wodehouse," says Donald Westlake, "Rex created a world." "If he had done nothing more than to create Archie Goodwin, Rex Stout would deserve the gratitude of whatever assessors watch over the prosperity of American literature," says Jacques Barzun. Kingsley Amis says Nero Wolfe is "the most interesting 'great detective' of them all." Many readers suppose that the characters make the series. Rex thought otherwise. He was right, as we shall see.

Ronald Knox believed we read detective stories because man is a puzzle-solving animal. Somerset Maugham said we read them because we like well-made stories. W. H. Auden said detective stories secularized the Grail quest. During World War II, British sociologists found that embattled Britons read detective stories because they liked to read about a world in which villains got their comeuppance and harmony was restored. They found support in the words of Lord Hewart, a Lord Chief Justice of England, who had remarked: "The detective story flourishes only in a settled community where the reader's sympathies are on the side of law and order." To this statement, Howard Haycraft, dean of American crime fiction historians, appended a significant insight: "Detection and the detective story definitely thrive in proportion to the strength of the democratic tradition and the essential decency of nations; while the closer governments approach legalized gangsterism and rule-by-force, the less likely we are to find conscientious criminal investigation or any body of competent detective literature."

The formal detective story is an allotropic form of the novel of manners. The novel of manners was designed to show that society is at its most secure and men happiest when they can find their identity in a stable order where the forms and manners governing their social obligations are fixed and to expose abuses which threaten that order. During its first eighty years, the detective story concentrated on instances in which the polite world repudiated behavior which went against the rules it subscribed to. Detectives themselves were gentlemen.

Then, in the early 1920's, an American author, Carroll John Daly, originated the hard-boiled detective story and murder forsook the vicar's rose garden for the mean streets which Dashiell Hammett and Raymond Chandler would celebrate in the years ahead. With this development the detective story jumped the banks of the novel of manners to run in the rapids of naturalism.

The hard-boiled detective is nomadic, seedy, hard-drinking, promiscuous, tough-talking and tough-acting. He has little formal education. Culturally he is illiterate. He mistrusts established institutions. Yet he is likely to be sincere, downright, just, and truthful.

To a genre which hitherto had justified its existence by justifying society, the hard-boiled detective proved a near fatal addition. In the nick of time, Rex Stout stepped in and saved it by creating a fiction which fused the best elements of both traditions.

Nero Wolfe is a "Great Detective" in the classic mold. Archie Goodwin is hard-boiled. The reconciliation was managed with care. Mark Van Doren noted: "Rex never subscribed to the theory that the detective must be a thug, a drunkard, and a lecher. He knew that the detective story must remain civilized. . . . That is what the literature of detection is all about; the protection of civilization by those courageous and competent enough to save it."

Through the hard-boiled detective story, Raymond Chandler, who followed Stout into the field, undertook to endow the genre with new seriousness. At the outset his rebelliousness illustrated his rejection of his own English social upbringing, but, after writing four novels, Chandler came to realize that the alliance between detective fiction and naturalism was an unholy one. In his last major novel, *The Long Goodbye,* he tried to reconcile the hard-boiled detective story with the novel of manners, which he now recognized as the true matrix of the detective story. His principal disciple, Ross Macdonald, completed this reconciliation after Chandler's death.

Rex Stout, like Chandler, had also been irritated by the simpering mannerisms of the orthodox detective story as it had come to be written by the early thirties. Recognizing, however, that the detective story had to be, by its very nature, supportive of the existing social order, Rex never repudiated that order. He drew on the strengths of hard-boiled detective fiction — its honesty, directness, social awareness, and idealism — to generate reforms, but, holding firm to the tradition of the novel of manners, he worked for peaceful change within the existing social order, rather than opting for that order's violent overthrow. To stand his ground and bring about a reformation within the genre was for Rex Stout much harder, of course, than renouncing the traditions of the genre altogether would have been. That he did stand his ground successfully and in doing so helped save the detective story from extinction is attested to by the eventual capitulation or eclipse of the leaders of the rebellion and by the perdurability of Rex's own stories, which, unlike most of the productions of the hard-boiled school, have not yellowed with age.

Rex's decision to work within the existing traditions of the detective story parallels the resolutions he had taken, after tempestuous encounters in the twenties with the radical left, to bring about meaningful reforms in society while working within the framework of the existing social order. The detective story was, for him, an advanced base from which he could promote realizable reforms. As he worked to save the genre, he was engaged in the larger labor of saving the existing social order which that genre shadowed forth, by urging on it, even as he upheld it, those reforms it had to undertake if it was to be healed of corruption and made fit for salvation.

For the fusion he effected, Rex exacted a price from both rebels and conservatives. His hard-boiled detective adheres to basic standards of decency. Archie Goodwin lives under Wolfe's roof and accepts Wolfe's values. In Wolfe's unorthodoxy Archie finds ample scope for his activist impulses, for Rex's classic detective does not have the conservative bias classic detectives usually display. Wolfe does not champion the establishment as a matter of course. He realizes that extremism of the right menaces civilization fully as much as extremism of the left does. When the establishment encroaches on fundamental human rights — even those of obscure citizens — Wolfe raises a mighty howl.

In the Wolfe saga, Rex Stout consistently gnaws more than one net. Even as he entertains us with a detective story, he attacks a wide assortment of social evils: fascism, communism, McCarthyism, racism, censorship, Madison Avenue, commercial radio; abuses in the law profession, the FBI, labor unions, the National Association of Manufacturers, and the publishing industry; exploitation of displaced persons; the Nixon government; and social pretense wherever found.

In his defense of values Rex Stout was not satisfied to limit himself to a morality-play contest between good and evil. Within his brownstone, Wolfe maintains a comic system of order that is overlaid on the heroic social order civilization depends on. Even as it entertains us, this comic order reaffirms the integrity of that heroic order, and gives to Rex Stout's stories a literary dimension that puts them at a further remove from sociological commentary, and mere crime fiction.

Conversely, the heresy which contends that Rex Stout's plots, and the commitment to order which they imply, are overwhelmed by his characterizations of Wolfe and Archie signifies a failure to come to grips with the essence of the characters themselves. Wolfe and Archie actually are extensions of their creator, and both relate intimately to his intrapsychic life.

Family environment is the matrix in which a child's personality develops. For Rex Stout that fact presented a problem. Despite their shared love of learning, his parents differed markedly from one another. John Stout was earnest, disciplined, set in his ways, possessed of a fine sense of indignation, and hot-tempered. Lucetta Stout was imaginative, receptive to new ideas, enthusiastic, fun-loving, hard to ruffle, aspiring, and stubborn. The Stouts were dark-eyed and dark-complexioned; the Todhunters, gray-eyed and fair-complexioned. Physically and mentally Rex was a Stout. In imagination, temperament, and outlook he was a Todhunter.

Normally a son's self-esteem is generated by his identification with a father whom his mother admires. When that admiration is lacking he finds a satisfactory self-image hard to achieve. During's Rex's boyhood John's fiery temper opened a wide breach between Lucetta and himself. Rex found this situation painful. Accordingly his normal movement toward individuation was obstructed.

While duties which kept John from home brought occasional relief, in the long run they exacerbated matters. Between 1901 and 1910, John was almost constantly away. In his absence Rex eventually succeeded to the role of decision-maker. He even managed family income. For the first time the Stouts were living in a well-regulated home (a brownstone at that). On John's return he was not reinstated as head of the family. Lucetta completed his humiliation by repudiating him. For the last twenty-five years of their life together, though they lived under one roof, by her choice they never spoke to one another except through a third party.

John Stout died, at eighty-six, in September 1933. A month later, Rex himself became a father for the first time. This confluence of events prompted Rex to reexamine his self-image.

The day after his wife returned home from the hospital with a daughter, Rex created Nero Wolfe and Archie Goodwin. In Wolfe, Rex created a surrogate father. To him he assigned many of John Stout's characteristics: brown eyes, dark coloring, discipline, earnestness, idealism, and a fine sense of indignation. On this figure he superimposed two substitute authority figures whom he had turned to earlier when normal gravitation toward his father was blocked — his mother's mother, the redoubtable Emily McNeal Todhunter, plump and lazy in her special chair, addicted to flowers, dictionaries, and atlases, an omnivorous reader, depended upon by her large family to adjudicate all problems; and Alvey Augustus Adee, scholar, sleuth, gourmet, bachelor, a model of efficiency, a master of the English language, the Second Under Secretary of State of the United States for thirty-six years, with whom Rex was thrust into intimate association during the time he served in the navy. (Photos of Adee show a bearded man who, significantly, looked as Rex Stout would look in maturity.)

In Archie Goodwin, Rex created a persona through whom he could approach Wolfe to continue his probing of the father-son relationship.

In many particulars Archie duplicated Rex Stout's self-image at that time. To Archie, Rex assigned the salient Todhunter characteristics: gray eyes, fair complexion, enthusiasm, curiosity, restiveness, a spirit of fun, and, as well, a birthplace, Chillicothe, Ohio, situated on the same tract of land where Todhunters farmed and prospered for a hundred years.

The dialogue between Wolfe and Archie is, in essence, a father-son dialogue. As the saga progresses, understanding grows between the two men. What is more remarkable, while the flow of Rex's traits into Archie gradually subsides, Nero Wolfe and Rex Stout come increasingly to share characteristics in common. Through Wolfe and Archie, Rex at last found a satisfactory self-image and slipped (though certainly not sheepishly) into Wolfe's clothing.

Nero Wolfe, then, is an amalgam of ideals brought together by Rex Stout in his search for an acceptable self-image. Small wonder that those close to Rex, including his wife and daughters, were at a loss to affirm his real identity.

Understanding himself was the greatest challenge Rex Stout ever faced, and, ultimately, he did attain a satisfactory self-image. For Rex this was essential. To offer himself as an advocate of a stable social order, while retaining no more than an obscure sense of his own identity, would have been to Rex fraudulent.

The biography of a literary man is but a pretext at biography if it does not show us how life materials contributed to the subject's art. It is not a pose for a writer to say he does not care to know how he has transmuted his experiences into art. If the process was too evident to him, that knowledge might well render him artistically impotent. But that knowledge need not be withheld from posterity. Indeed, only as we catch some sense of the subliminal process through which a writer has reshaped his experiences creatively are we able to take the true measure of his achievement. Our understanding of Wolfe and Archie is much enhanced when we realize that they sprang from the ordeal of Rex Stout's search for himself.

At the start of my labors I was told by Rex's long-time editor, Marshall Best, "Pray do not disabuse anyone of the idea that Rex Stout is God. I sometimes think so myself." I did not let myself be swayed by that petition. I sought no thesis there, either. Yet, as time passed, I came to realize that Marshall Best's appeal had validity. Rex had human failings, of course. But, taken in aggregate, they weighed little against his virtues.

Perhaps it was to my direct advantage that Rex Stout spent forty years using Wolfe and Archie to span the generation gap. I was separated in age from Rex by almost exactly the same number of years that had separated him in age from his father. Thanks to his skill at bridging such chasms (Wolfe, Rex told me, is twenty-four years older than Archie), we fell into an easy relationship with one another. He was forthright and open with me. He forbade no questions and I thought of none that, out of mistaken respect, I neglected to ask him. I did not consciously antagonize him, nor would I have known how to. If unwittingly I irritated him he must have borne my transgressions with good patience because I never knew about them. I was not a surrogate son but we were companionable and I was his confidant. He counted it an advantage that our friendship did not extend back into his prime years because he did not want my narrative tinctured with hale remembrances. He ate with me, something which, in later years, he rarely did with others. He saw me mornings, something he hated to do with almost anybody. He insisted that I ride on his stair elevator, and sit in his chair in his office, and sample his "fifty year old cognac." He found for me books I could not find for myself. He read from the Wolfe canon into my tape recorder. He showed me the scars he got in 1893 when his father's wagon overturned. He gave me the key to his pied-à-terre in Manhattan so that I would have an advance base from which to carry out research in New York. He gave me iris rhizomes, his palm prints, and a lock of his beard, and, after a time, when he decided that nothing stood in the way of true friendship between us, he inscribed his books and letters to me "with love." From a man wary of acknowledging affection (though not of feeling it), that counted for much.

During the last seven years of his life, putting aside a natural reluctance to talk about himself, Rex answered more than seventy-five hundred questions for me, either in writing or orally — a process that continued up to a few days before his death. He gave me access, without restriction, to his voluminous papers, to his office and current files, to his incoming mail, and to his library. At his invitation, his wife and daughters, his sons-in-law and grandchildren, sisters, nieces, and other kin, and a legion of friends explored with me every phase of his life from early boyhood to his years as gray elder.

This kind of help was essential. Though Rex wrote many thousands of letters, he wrote most of them on 5 1/2 × 8 1/2 notepaper and only one in a thousand (not excepting letters to intimate friends and his publishers) ever carried over to a second page. Some of his friends actually were ashamed to share his letters with me until I assured them he wrote long letters to no one. Indeed, Rex thought it peculiar that various of his contemporaries — Sandburg, Fitzgerald, Lovecraft, Chandler, to recall a few — produced massive accumulations of letters, squandering, as he saw it, energy they ought to have husbanded for creative work.

Most of Rex's letters contain quotable phrases. He seemed to shape his thoughts with his tongue, into pithy projectiles, and spit them out right on target. Yet none of the letters is autobiographical or in the least self-revelatory. That they do not contain glorious, ruminative swatches which, pieced together, would constitute an outline of his personal history is less a misfortune than might appear. When an author, with no clear intent of producing an autobiography, has, with almost masochistic intensity, laid bare, in random correspondence, various episodes in his life, the temptation is strong to accept these episodes as cardinal epiphanies and to structure his biography around them. Yet there is a likelihood that such revelations may have been composed subjectively and sponsored by random moods or situations, his search for authenticating touches for a character he is creating, or for the effect they might have on the intended recipient. For the unwary biographer a fabric of such confidences can be a winding-sheet.

If Rex Stout's correspondence is not a major source of information about his intimate world, neither did he keep diaries at any time in his life, prepare personal memoirs, or pour out his soul to selected confidants. To Rex all such confidences would have seemed a confession of inadequacy. By temperament he was the most private of persons. On that account, realizing as Poe did that exhibitionism is often the subtlest form of concealment, he sequestered information about himself only in the most public places. The truth is, Wolfe and Archie are the real repositories of information about Rex Stout's interior life — a cornucopia to the heedful.

"Any man who writes an autobiography thinks too damn much of himself," Rex told me. When he was with other people, he preferred to hear them talk about themselves and to get them to tell him what they knew. Yet it was very like him, once he had made a commitment to have his authorized biography written, to give himself to the task without stint. If he had not meant to, he would not have given permission at all. If he had not given this permission, only the most vaporous kind of book could have resulted.

In *Please Pass the Guilt* (1973), a client asks Wolfe, "How many things have *you* done that you wouldn't want everyone to know about?" Wolfe answers, "Perhaps a thousand." When I read that, I said to Rex, "I know a thousand things you've done that you wouldn't want everyone to know about. What shall I do about them?" He said, "Put them in. They'll probably be the most interesting things in the book." I did put them in, because I knew Rex always meant what he said.

During those last years Rex let me read his work in progress and handed copies of the manuscripts to me as soon as they were completed. Reading his work at those times provided rare opportunities to observe his mind under the stress of creation.

Few biographers can have had more complete access to the mind of their subject or fuller cooperation from others able to help. Many people went to exceptional bother — plundering their files, sitting for long interviews, preparing memoirs, traveling to my home in Lexington,

Massachusetts, to see me, opening their homes to me, writing letters, and chasing down facts — to supply information and needed clarifications, all because of the affection they had for Rex. During the seven years the book was under way, my correspondence on this project exceeded six thousand pieces of mail. What is more remarkable, the essential part of that material converges on a surprisingly consistent portrait of Rex Stout.

In old age Rex insisted that he had no philosophy: "If a philosophy is a settled idea of basic rules about human conditions and problems and how to handle them, I haven't got one. I never have had one. It keeps changing on me." Nor did he care to put his work under exacting analysis, or to know too clearly what portion of himself he had assigned to Archie and what portion he had assigned to Wolfe. Nonetheless, he conceded that their lives impinged on his at a thousand points. Part of my task was to identify these points of impingement.

In assuming the identity of Wolfe, Rex laid a heavy burden on himself. In everything that he attempted, he was a perfectionist. He was under a constant compulsion to come to firm conclusions about all problems that engaged his notice. Once he took a stand he was reluctant to reverse himself and almost never did. Sometimes, when he saw that he should back off from a stand he had taken, this need to stay locked into consistency was a source of true torment for him. In meeting the many commitments he assumed, he put himself under severe disciplines and held himself to them unswervingly, even when it meant paying the penalty of bleeding ulcers and chronic migraines. To his last days he saw himself bound by a "psychological necessity" to be no older than Nero Wolfe — fifty-eight — when he was with anyone. By some miracle of self-discipline, he again and again carried off this feat. Yet he saw that age, physically, was gaining on him. He learned to accept this. After all, Wolfe was a shut-in too. But wistfully, to the last day of his life, he regretted that it had to happen. As often as he felt he had gathered a reserve of energy he returned to his routines — writing, gardening, cabinetmaking, administrative work for the many committees he served, pretending that the infirmities of old age were a chimera.

Rex let me into the select company of those permitted to call Nero Wolfe by his given name. I never exercised the privilege because Rex himself never did. He arranged for Jill Krementz to photograph us together. He laughed robustly when Czarna, his beloved Labrador, switched masters and made herself my pet for the duration of the picture-taking. Sometimes, contrary to his usual practice, he sketched to me the plot of a story he had in mind. And when I would be heading off after a visit, he would stand in the drive to watch me out of sight and, at my final handwave, throw me a kiss from his fingertips, with the solemn dignity of a Grand Signor seeing off a favorite courier on a voyage to New Spain. All this had nothing to do with maintaining cordial relations with a biographer. It was just Rex. Who could be hard-boiled about a man like that? See for yourself. What was there to be hard-boiled about?

Rex believed that men transcend mortality, if at all, through the things they have done in their lifetimes. He would like to have known how succeeding generations would look on his work, but he believed no man could know with certainty the answer to that question. Unlike Conan Doyle and Agatha Christie, he never considered reporting the death of his detective hero. "I hope he lives forever," he said. He was even willing that the name of Rex Stout should drop from memory, if his creations lived on. In making that concession he was not courting oblivion. He knew his creations were part of himself.

Mount Independence,
Lexington, Massachusetts.
February 1977

In the Beginning

In 1892, a torrent of homesteaders, participating in the run for Chero-
kee lands, swept through the Wakarusa Valley, below Topeka, headed
south for the Indian Territory — now Oklahoma. Their route was the
trail marked out fifty years earlier by the Sac and Fox Indians, then
migrating westward to lands assigned them by Congress.

John Wallace Stout's forty-acre farm, two and a half miles from
Wakarusa village, lay along the Sac and Fox road, and John's five daughters and three sons, including six-year-old Rex, daily watched the endless flow of wagons moving southward. They tried to guess the point of
origin of the travelers: Green Mountain Boys from Vermont, Connecticut Yankees, Pennsylvanians and New Yorkers, and Buckeyes from
Ohio. The New Englanders were the easiest to pick out. They had extra
horses, spare axles, wheels, mattocks, and helves, an ample supply of
food, and clean cooking utensils. Though respectful, they said little and
offered no sugary tidbits to the children as other travelers sometimes
did when they replenished their water supply from John's well, which,
with its brace of wooden buckets, stood within inviting view of the road.
Yet, whatever their demeanor and circumstances, all the homesteading
travelers seemed bolstered by their prospects. Years later, Rex still kept
a vivid memory of them, lined up, set to continue their journey, and of
the crack of gunfire that signaled their dawn departures.

The next spring many of these same homesteaders reappeared, heading back now on the route which they had followed westward. There
had not been enough land for every settler. Their money and stores
exhausted, their horses dead or traded, they struggled along, often in
makeshift ways. Rex would never forget their heartbreak, or the vehe-
ment curses they aimed at a government that had not kept its promises.

Many of the failed homesteaders had emaciated dogs with them. The
older Stout boys, Bob and Walt — fifteen and thirteen that July —
despite parental cautions, took in a dozen of them, and a blind filly.
They planned to kill rabbits and prairie chickens to feed the dogs, a
resolve that soon left them low in ammunition, and footsore. Incessant
dogfights exhausted John Stout's patience. He shot the dogs. Then, to
inculcate the lesson, he gave the boys the job of burying them.

From a window, their pensive, freckled, nine-year-old sister, Ruth,
watched while Bob and Walt dug the burial pit. Ruth never had favored

the menagerie. She did not even like dogs. Still, her tears were plentiful. Then, her grandfather, Nathan Stout, a gentle Quaker, called to her from across the room, "Ruth! Come look!" She went, and from his window saw that a sunflower she had planted had opened to the sun. Her face lit up. "Thee was looking through the wrong window," Nathan told her.

Rex's reaction to his brothers' plight was matter-of-fact. He saw in it the lesson of the homesteaders reaffirmed: before you take on anything, you should know what you are getting into.

A further episode involving the homesteaders completed Rex's course of instruction. One morning John and Walt had hitched up the spring wagon. But the horses were skittish. The strange caravans wending past had made them quick to shy. When they bucked and John dodged clear of their flailing hooves, Rex decided to act. He scampered up into the wagon and grabbed the reins. But the horses were past controlling. They flew down the road in headlong fury, dust billowing from under the wagon wheels. Trudging homesteaders lurched out of their path. Yelping hounds scurried into culverts. Rex put all his resources into the battle of checking the runaways, but about a mile north of the farm the wagon overturned, pinning his leg under it.

A dozen years later, when he entered the navy, Rex's enlistment record would cite, as his most readily identifiable characteristic, a scar which began on the front of his left thigh and slashed across his knee, to continue on down his calf.[1] If ever Rex needed a tangible reminder of the risks run in taking on insuperable odds, he had only to consider this scar. Lesser men would have been intimidated by such graphic evidence of what presumption had brought them to. Rex never was. Nor did his scar make him battle shy. It merely made him wary of going into battle unprepared. And it served well as a token of his lifelong abhorrence of chaos, and his pertinacious efforts to see reason prevail in the governance of human affairs. Over the next eighty years, Rex would many times repeat his feat of seizing the reins to stay the flight of runaway horses.

With one difference. His resourcefulness would match his resolve. He would not again be overturned.

BOOK I

Heritage

1.

Rootstock and Genes
— The Stouts

Rex Stout is, for all his irony and occasional dogmatism, that very rare being, a good man. His tradition is Quaker; and he reflects the practical benevolence that sect has always held to be essential to civilized living. He is a natural leader of men, not merely because he has unusual reserves of energy, but because the integrity of his character draws other men and women to him naturally.

— CLIFTON FADIMAN

In the late summer of 1642, Penelope Kent, an English Dissenter living in Amsterdam, married a native Hollander named Van Princin. Both were just twenty and soon afterward sailed for New Amsterdam, where they hoped a long and prosperous life awaited them. The voyage was a bad one. During the fifty-eight-day crossing the ship was battered by frequent storms. Finally, off Sandy Hook, New Jersey, winds piled it onto rocky shoals, and the voyagers were compelled to come ashore in treacherous dories. Nor was that the whole of their ordeal. When they landed Indians set upon them. A rain of tomahawk blows felled Van Princin. Penelope, stripped and senseless, was left for dead on the beach. A scalp lock had been taken, her left shoulder hacked, and her abdomen slashed so that loops of bowels protruded. Hours later, when she regained consciousness, Penelope found herself alone with her young husband's corpse. She made her way to the margin of the woodland and crept inside a hollow tree. There, as the days passed, she kept herself alive by munching fungi and lumps of sap.

A week later one of the Lenni Lenape, an old man pursuing deer, found Penelope when his dog scented her refuge. Seeing merit in her pluck, the Indian bound up her wounds with tree withes and took her to his village, where his squaw tended her until she recovered her strength. Months later he paddled her to New Amsterdam. There she was given shelter by a Dissenting minister, the Reverend Mr. Applegate. Although Penelope never again had full use of her left arm, she was thankful to be alive and did not dwell on her misfortunes.

Even in those turbulent times, when General Kieft's reckless policies brought open warfare between the Dutch settlers and the Indians, Penelope was admired by many for her fortitude. One of her admirers was Richard Stout, a native of Nottinghamshire serving in Kieft's guard. He was the son of John Stout, a prosperous yeoman, and his wife, Elizabeth Gee.[1]

Ten years earlier, after a quarrel with his father, who had wanted him to marry for money, Richard had left home and shipped on board a man-of-war. Before deserting this ship in New Amsterdam, in 1640, Richard served on it for seven years. On New Year's Day, 1644, Richard at last had his way and married for love when he took Penelope Van Princin for his bride.

Until 1648 the Stouts lived at Gravesend. Then they moved to Monmouth County, New Jersey, where they founded Baptist Town (later called Middletown). There they prospered, raising ten children, and harvesting bountiful crops of tobacco on lush farmland. By 1675 Richard had 750 acres under cultivation. Probably no word of this success carried to John Stout in Nottinghamshire, but he was well commemorated in the New World, nonetheless. Richard and Penelope named their first son John and their fifth, Jonathan.

In 1683, at Shackamaxon, Richard, now something of a man of affairs, was present at the peace conference between Tamenand, astute chief of the Delaware, and William Penn. When he died, at ninety, in 1705, Penelope caught his excellence in a single line, "I was never unhappy with him."

Peter Stout, Richard's third son, was past fifty when his father died. At twenty he had married Mary Bullen; their son, John, was born at Middletown in 1675. Three years after his grandfather's death, John left Middletown and settled at Dragon Swamp in Delaware, where he built a cabin and took a wife, Sarah. John's son Peter was born at Dragon Swamp on 14 April 1715, in ample time to be a part of the statistical workup which shows that Penelope had 502 descendants before she died in 1732 at the age of 110. "All these sprang from one woman," one mourner said, with biblical awe, "and she as good as dead."[2]

Two generations of Stouts scarcely had moved out of reach of Penelope's leading strings. Peter, however, belonged to a new age. In his early twenties he struck down into Pennsylvania, to Lancaster. In Lancaster he met and wooed Margaret Cyfert. Margaret was German-born and a firm Quaker. In 1739 Peter joined the Society of Friends and married her.

Peter's next remove took him across the Susquehanna, in 1744, to Warrington, in York County. Charles, the second of the seven children Margaret and he would raise, and the one who would continue the line we are following, was two at this time.

Despite his earlier moves, Peter Stout's distinctive history did not begin till 1762, when, at the age of forty-seven, he left Pennsylvania with his wife and children and traveled hundreds of miles, through rugged country, to Snow Camp, a flourishing Quaker settlement founded a dozen years earlier in the Piedmont area of North Carolina. With them the Stouts brought certificates commending them to Cane Creek Monthly Meeting. Just south of Cane Creek, Peter and Margaret lived and managed their plantation through the remaining years of the century. Peter died in 1802, at eighty-eight, outliving Margaret by three years. The stone that marks their grave tells us that they were "Quaker Leaders for 40 Years." In Quaker annals, Peter is always identified as "Peter the Quaker," a title that singles him out for his zeal.[3]

Five years after his family had settled in the Piedmont, Charles Stout married Mary Noblit. Like himself, Mary had lived most of her life in York County, Pennsylvania. Mary's father, John Noblit, was of French Huguenot descent and had come to America from Ireland with Irish Friends, about 1728.[4] In 1737, Noblit and his wife Ann joined the new settlement at Newberry, in York County, and there he prospered. When he died in 1748, an inventory of his estate put its value at £250, including his "purse and apral" valued at £10 and a "still & vesals" worth £12.

John Noblit left seven children. Abraham, the eldest, stayed at Newberry and became a judge of the York County courts, in 1761. The next in age, Thomas, served in the French and Indian War, and was with Wolfe, in 1759, at the siege of Quebec, where he was wounded in the same action in which Wolfe fell. The name Wolfe thus was coupled with that of Rex Stout's forebears before it was coupled with his own.

Mary, John Noblit's youngest child, was two when John died. In 1763, her mother, now remarried, took her with her to North Carolina, where they were received by Cane Creek Monthly Meeting. Mary was twenty-one when she married Charles Stout. During the next twenty years she bore him ten children.

With Solomon Stout, the youngest of Charles's and Mary's children, the modern history of the family begins. Solomon carried the Stout dynasty into the Northwest Territories and, with the help of five wives in as many decades, begat children in such numbers (no fewer than seventeen), that in old age he seemed to those around him a patriarch of biblical stature, not only allied to an entire community by ties of blood, but progenitor of the social order which sheltered them. The pattern which Richard Stout had set was repeating itself, save that Solomon found no one wife with the stamina of Penelope Van Princin. If Rex Stout saw himself as the natural protector of the society he lived in, the instinct may well have been a part of his genetic inheritance.

Mary Marshill, a member of the Marshill family from which Herbert Hoover was descended, was Solomon Stout's first wife. They were married in 1807. In 1810 she died in childbed. Solomon's grief came at an uneasy time for Quakers in North Carolina. In the days when they first came to Cane Creek (1751), John Woolman, the Quaker social reformer, had come among them awakening in them a repugnance to slavery. Many of them subsequently bought slaves and freed them, only to see them gathered up by traders and resold. Through the years they were ridiculed and overtaxed. The War of 1812 added to their burdens. They were reviled for refusing to bear arms. In the first half of the nineteenth century nearly six thousand Quakers forsook their North Carolina holdings and moved on into Ohio and Indiana, where slavery, by the Ordinance of 1787, was forever prohibited. Solomon Stout was one of these. In 1814, on 10 February, he took a new wife, Ruth Atkinson. The Atkinsons were Quakers too, and Ruth's mother, Mary Woody, was from a Quaker family which has left its name in Quaker annals in North Carolina through every generation from that time to the present.

Early in 1815 the Solomon Stouts made their way to neighboring Salisbury, where Boone's Trail, known also as the Cumberland Gap Road, had its origin. With other Quakers, including Solomon's cousin John, his wife, Elizabeth Moon, and her sister, Lurany, they went northward through the Gap, into Kentucky, moving onward then through Mount Vernon to Louisville, and, at last, into Orange County, in southern Indiana, where they offered their certificates to Lick Creek Monthly Meeting in November 1815. The journey of eight hundred miles had been long and often broken. The covered wagons, pulled by horses or oxen, were loaded with all they had dared to take, and the able-bodied, women as well as men, had walked most of the distance.

The John Stouts stopped at Paoli, Indiana. Solomon, lured by rumors of the fertile plateau at Flat Rock Creek, pushed on another hundred miles, to build his cabin close by awesome mounds left by the pre-Columbian Mound Builders, in the celebrated Haw Patch, a prehistoric lake bottom, said to be the finest land in Indiana, and much prized because, in a land of forests, this large tract stood, cleared by nature, and ready for settling and planting. Of necessity Solomon came there as a squatter. Statehood still was a year away. The Indian wars had ended and the Indians themselves were withdrawing across the Mississippi, but Indian title to the lands here would not be extinguished until 1818. No sale of them would occur before 1820.

Not yet thirty, Solomon Stout was a leader of men. In 1821 Bartholomew County was organized and he was elected one of the three county commissioners to preside over its functioning. During the next four years his partners changed annually, but Solomon held his post. He was a natural-born administrator. Under his order Columbus was founded and designated the county seat. Forests were felled and those buildings, including a courthouse, put up which the requirements of the county demanded. Today Columbus is not only the home of the world's largest manufacturer of diesel engines, Cummins Engine Company, but thanks to an enlightened program of redevelopment which has seen

Pei, the Saarinens, and others put their talents at the disposal of Columbus, the city Solomon founded is known as "the Athens of the Prairie."[5]

In 1824 a dramatic reversal of fortunes befell Solomon. By a state law his duties as commissioner passed to the county justices. Next, a survey showed that his cabin stood on the site reserved for school purposes. Finally, Ruth, who for a decade had shared his hardships and his dreams, had died on 30 September, giving birth to their fifth child. Her death followed by one day the second birthday of her youngest son, Nathan, who, in his maturity, came to be his father's mainstay and, still later, an inspiration to two younger generations of Stouts, including his grandson, Rex, upon whom his serene authority made an ineradicable impression.

Solomon went on with life. Before 1825 was over he was a father again, this time of a daughter, Ruth, born to his third wife, Lurany Moon. Moreover, vacating his ill-fated cabin, he moved down to the southeastern corner of the new county, to Sand Creek township. There he bought 190 acres on Sand Creek, on the Driftwood Fork of the White River. By 1827 he had in his employ many men making rails at 25 cents per hundred, or hired on at $50 per annum.[6]

At forty-seven, the same age his grandfather had been when he led his family into the promised land of the Piedmont (and the same age his great-grandson, Rex, would be when Rex launched the series of books that brought him fame), Solomon began the most ambitious undertaking of his life. On the south bank of Sand Creek, at Seymour, just fifty yards from the point where Bartholomew, Jennings, and Jackson counties join, he built a gristmill, four stories high, supported by stone pillars. To run the mill by waterpower he built a dam of logs and driftwood, filled with dirt and rocks. An overshot waterwheel operated the mill. Burr-type grinders and large hollow stones ground the grain. From the outset the mill was a success.

Only one thing jeopardized Solomon's prosperity. A notebook he kept tells the story: "June the 30th 1846 High Water — November 9th 1847 Do."

The mill held, but wives came and went. Lurany died in 1835, to be succeeded by Penelope Cry. Each bore Solomon a family. In 1845, Clarissa Swingle became the fifth and final wife of Solomon. With her Solomon raised his last family — children younger than many of his grandchildren. A widow, Clarissa was thirty-one when she married Solomon. In November 1846, Sophia Swingle, her niece by her first marriage, married her stepson, Nathan Stout.

The Swingles (Swengels then) reached America from Germany, on the *Samuel,* in 1740. They settled first in Pennsylvania, then moved on to Ohio. In 1814, John Nicholas Swingle married Regina Hartman who, tradition relates, was captured by Indians in early childhood and lived nineteen years among them. At the time of her marriage Regina was twenty-six. In the mid-1840's the Swingles had come to Sand Creek from Circleville, Ohio, by covered wagon, with their cousins, the Overmyers.[7]

On 2 February 1848, Clarissa gave birth to Solomon's son David, who preceded into the world by just two months his nephew, John Wallace Stout, born to Sophia and Nathan on 8 April and named for another uncle, then serving with the United States Army in Mexico.[8]

By 1850 operation of the mill had passed largely into Nathan's hands. In this period Solomon and Nathan took an active role in the affairs of the Underground Railroad, a lifeline for runaway slaves which, under the general management of a Piedmont Quaker, Levi Coffin, extended from North Carolina into Indiana, and beyond. Solomon lived to see the Civil War end, not dying until November 1865.

In his executive skill, organizing zeal, abhorrence of injustice, and ability to put adversity behind him, Solomon continued a pattern of conduct set earlier by Peter, his grandfather, which would extend to succeeding generations.

As late as 1881 Nathan still put his trust in the mill. Known to one and all as "Uncle Nathan," he was reported in January of that year to have bought a purifier to make fancy brands of flour. Then, early in March, a freshet all but ruined the ford. Nathan had had enough. The next January he sold the mill and farm for $3,000. In February, he auctioned off his personal property, and, with Sophia, went to live with his son John, a move that would put him on the scene when Rex Stout was born, four years later, in 1886.

The mill stood till 1912. On 21 February in that year, the worst blizzard in fifty years swept across Indiana. A day later torrential rains fell and the White River rose five inches an hour. Shifting ice knocked a stone pillar from beneath the building. On 26 February ladders were being used to rescue grain through windows when a second pillar gave way. The next morning, with a sigh that sent people running from their doors, the mill toppled into the creek.

At Sand Creek now a few stones still lie under the water, the only reminder of Solomon's glory.[9]

2.

Rootstock and Genes—
The Todhunters

My paternal grandfather once explored the family past. He turned up a
knighted John Ambler, an attorney to Queen Charlotte, and was much
encouraged; but on digging deeper found only farm labourers. I would
sooner have been related to Rex Stout, however distantly, than to that
undistinguished lawyer.

— ERIC AMBLER

The children of Amos Todhunter were beset with a restiveness which
struck their neighbors as odd. They were compulsive hankerers. They
wanted to go, to see, to do, to be better than anyone at everything. In
Ohio's Perry Township Quakers had predominated from the first period of its settlement, early in the nineteenth century. Three generations of Todhunters had found contentment on the same farm there.
They had donated land for the school and Walnut Creek Meeting
House, and when they died had slumbered in apparent bliss in nearby
Walnut Creek Cemetery, the deed to which was likewise a gift from
their hands. Nothing in the Todhunter inheritance quite explained the
antic moods of Amos's children.

John, the first Todhunter to come to America, was born on old New
Year's Eve, 24 March 1657, the son of William Todhunter of Gardhouse,
a farm west of the village of Threlkeld in Cumberland. William, born
in 1625, was the son of Thomas Todhunter (1577–1648) and Elizabeth
Cockbain; and his father was Anthony Todhunter, who died in 1616. All
had been Cumberland people and lived in the rugged border region
between England and Scotland that gave rise to the calling that gave
them their name, tod-hunters, hunters of foxes — not a sport, but an
earnest undertaking. Foxes killed many sheep each year and men were
paid good bounties to kill them. Early prints show the tod-hunter in
Scottish bonnet, plaid, and trews, the dress of the border region.[1]

At thirty, John Todhunter left Threlkeld and came to America. He
arrived in Pennsylvania with the first wave of English settlers and
situated himself at Westtown, near West Chester — then a wilderness

fully the equal of his native bourn. Probably religious dissension drove John from home.

Westtown was a Quaker settlement. John found himself well suited to his environment and his neighbors and around 1703 married Margaret Hoopes Beakes, widow of Abraham Beakes and daughter of Joshua Hoopes, one of the most eminent Quaker elders of colonial Pennsylvania. John's alliance with this extraordinary family may well have endowed future generations of Todhunters with an enhanced range of attributes.

Joshua Hoopes himself came to America by way of provocation. He had spent the first forty-eight years of his life in Yorkshire, in Skelton-in-Cleveland, his birthplace, where contemporary records describe his family as "people of account." Joshua was past forty when, in 1677, he and his wife Ann were fined ten shillings for being present at a Quaker meeting held at the home of his brother Tobias. Though Joshua was not then a Quaker, this challenge to his freedom of conscience was enough to make him one.

Joshua sailed to America on the *Providence* in 1683, settled in Makefield, Bucks County, Pennsylvania, and was received into membership in Falls Monthly Meeting. He was a member of it through the remaining forty years of his life. The meeting often was held at his house. Joshua was elected thirteen times a member of the Colonial Assembly of Pennsylvania between 1686 and 1711. He died in 1723, at eighty-eight. Joshua's son Daniel served in the assembly also and sired seventeen children. Through him Joshua became the forebear of numerous distinguished educators, physicians, astronomers, botanists, business leaders, and public servants (including J. Reuben Clark, Under Secretary of State under Coolidge, and Hubert H. Humphrey). Through their common descent from Joshua Hoopes, Hubert Humphrey and Rex Stout were sixth cousins twice removed.[2]

Margaret and John had two children. The first, Sarah, died young. The second, John, was born in 1715. That same year, on 20 June, at fifty-eight, his father died. Eight years later Margaret herself died. John then came under the care of his Uncle Daniel, who had extensive land holdings at Westtown. In 1739, after marrying Margaret Evans, he settled in nearby Whiteland, where he and she raised nine children. In 1767, when John was fifty-two, he moved with his family to Leesburg, Virginia. There, though they affiliated with Fairfax Monthly Meeting, two of his sons, Braham and Jacob, joined the Revolutionary army when the war against England began.

Of John Todhunter's children, however, we are interested chiefly in Isaac. Isaac was thirteen when the move to Virginia was made. Twenty years later he joined Daniel Boone on his second migration to Kentucky. With him went his wife, Eleanor Jury — whose family was prominent in Quaker annals in what later would be West Virginia — and their three young sons. Abner, their fourth son, the great-grandfather-to-be of Rex Stout, was born in 1789, during the family's Kentucky sojourn. When Abner was five, Isaac moved his family to Lost Creek, Tennessee. For ten years they stayed put at Lost Creek. Then, in the spring of 1804 Isaac sent his older sons, Richard and Isaac II, on into Ohio, to scout prospects there. Richard and Isaac squatted on a small prairie, site of present day Leesburg, in Highland County, and sent word back that the land promised much. The first year there they raised a patch of corn to support the family. In December, Isaac and the rest of his household joined them. With her, in her butter churn, Eleanor brought some apple trees, and a pecan tree the family had carried all the way from Virginia.[3] Rex Stout's great affinity for trees had a long tradition behind it.

In the spring of 1805 Isaac bought 1,200 acres known as the Massie Survey — part of the original site from which Nathaniel Massie took land for Chillicothe. This land was on Walnut Creek, in the southwestern part of Perry township. Half of it he sold to the Ellis brothers, Thomas and Mordecai, who had come on from Lost Creek with their families at the same time the Todhunters did. The Ellises were originally from Virginia too. Both families remained neighbors throughout the rest of the century. and eventually were related by ties of blood.

The Todhunter farm lay about halfway between present day East Monroe and New Martinsburg and not far from Chillicothe, then the seat of government. There, according to Rex Stout, Archie Goodwin was born in a year that does not matter because Archie is never more than thirty-four.

Ohio had been organized as a state in 1803 and within the decade had been the scene of major Indian uprisings. Even in the period in which the Todhunters made their settlement, negotiations with the Indians for cession and purchase of Indian lands were continuing, and outbreaks of violence similar to those which led to the Battle of Fallen Timbers, at Maumee, in 1794, were feared.

These circumstances give sober coloring to an episode in which Abner figured in the autumn of 1805, when he was sixteen. One day, after Isaac's cabin was built, Isaac and Eleanor and the older boys went to neighboring Greenfield for winter supplies. Abner was alone at the cabin with his younger brothers, Jacob, Jury, and John, and their sister Margaret, when he saw six Indians in war paint, bearing down on them on horseback. The Indians sprang from their horses, strode to the cabin, and entered as the thin muster of gaping children shrank back. With Quaker calm, Abner invited the warriors to sit down. Then he put before them the best that the Todhunter larder held and stood aside, leaving them to enjoy their meal without distraction. When the Indians were done eating, one of them got up and came toward him. He tapped Abner's shoulder with solemn insistence. "White man good," he said.

"Feed Indian." The Indians thereupon mounted their horses and rode away into the woodlands. In after years the story was retold as one of the finest moments in Todhunter history.[4]

In 1812, Abner built his own cabin on land set off for him by his father, and the following summer, on 29 July 1813, he married Elizabeth Job, a bride at nineteen. Elizabeth was said to be related to Daniel Defoe, author of *Robinson Crusoe*.[5] The Jobs came to America from Cheshire, with Penn's Quakers, in the 1680's. They came to Ohio in 1807, from Winchester, Virginia, where they had extensive landholdings. Andrew Job, Elizabeth's great-great-grandfather, was high sheriff of Pennsylvania's Chester County, from 1697 to 1700, giving Rex Stout a bona fide law enforcement official among his ancestors.

Abner and Elizabeth named their first son, born 18 February 1818, for Amos Milton, Elizabeth's uncle. Abner and Elizabeth would have eight children in all, four sons and four daughters.

Between 1853 and 1855, Abner built, on the same land his father had given him, a substantial homestead to house those of his family who still remained with him. There his granddaughter, Rex Stout's mother, Lucetta Elizabeth, and her ten brothers and sisters passed their childhood. Theirs was an ample domain. As a girl, Lucetta could stand on the hummock behind the farmhouse and, looking in every direction, see nothing but Todhunter land. As behooved their status, when Perry Township was organized in 1845, her uncle, Jacob Todhunter, was one of the two judges appointed to oversee the first election, and her father, Amos, was one of two town clerks.

The Todhunters were not trailblazers by inclination. Their successive moves had been dictated not by restiveness or a nomadic itch. They advanced westward seeking a place where they could live in contentment, according to their beliefs, and where they could, by earnest labor, know the fruits of prosperity. The families they intermarried with had similar backgrounds and similar convictions — that is, until Amos Todhunter, in 1848, married Emily Elizabeth McNeal. That marriage made all the difference to the Todhunters.

At the outset, there was an uproar. United to his bride by her uncle, Reverend Richard Lanum, a Presbyterian minister, Amos was condemned by Walnut Creek Monthly Meeting for marrying "contrary to discipline." Two years later, Walnut Creek was stunned anew when Emily's sister, Alice (Alison) Matilda, married Levi Ellis, scion of that Thomas Ellis who had come to Walnut Creek with the Todhunters. This marriage also was solemnized by the Presbyterian Richard Lanum. Many must have wondered what arcane powers the McNeal sisters had that they could overturn the convictions of two birthright Quakers, each with four generations of Quakerism behind him. For the answer to that question we must briefly travel back in history.

In the *Minute Book of the Common Pleas Court,* Fayette County, Ohio, the following entry appears under the date 21 July 1835:

Mary McNeal, a married woman, applied in open court and on the testimony of witnesses heard touching this matter, it is ordered and adjudged that the said Mary McNeal do have and retain guardianship, custody, and care of her two infant, small children, Emily and Alison Matilda McNeal. And that Daniel McNeal, the husband of said Mary be and he is hereby restrained and enjoined from taking said female children from or out of the possession & custody of said Mary McNeal.[6]

In her deposition at that time, Mary affirmed that Daniel Wilson McNeal had been guilty of desertion and "great violence of character." Mary, called "Polly" by family and friends, then was living at Washington Court House, a town a few miles north of the Todhunter farm. Mary had married McNeal, a schoolteacher from Pennsylvania, in Ross County, Ohio, on 23 May 1827. She was nineteen; he was twenty-four. Neither was Quaker. Although the Reverend Richard Lanum later would describe James McNeal, Daniel's father, as "of fine gentlemanly bearing & a true patriot," Daniel himself was a sorry catch. Mary's troubles began almost at once. She was just eight months married when she gave birth to twins, Emily Elizabeth and Amelia Jane, on 28 January 1828. Two other children soon followed, James Scott and Alison Matilda. But Daniel McNeal was a malcontent. Several times he "dragged Mary and the children back and forth between Ohio and Pennsylvania in a rough spring wagon." Indeed, Alison was born in Pennsylvania on one such visit.

The strain of these rugged trips across the Alleghenies told on his family, and Amelia and James sickened and died. On Mary's final visit to Pennsylvania, McNeal's parents told her to stay with her family when she got back to Ohio, because McNeal was restless and would be happy no place for long. She took that advice and began to support herself at tailoring. McNeal then abducted the children, taking them to Hillsboro, in neighboring Highland County, where he was living with another woman. That was in 1835. To support Mary in her restraining action during the hearing that followed, her brothers, Will and Lewis, went to Hillsboro and sought out McNeal's cabin. Lewis rode up in front. Will rode through the trees to the back. While Lewis called out the woman to make inquiries and conversation, Will crawled through a high window, got the girls, put them on his horse, and took them to the courthouse, dirty and unkempt as they were. Thus exhibited, they were given into Mary's custody.[7]

For some years, Mary lived in a log cabin on a farm near Greenfield, not far from Walnut Creek. Amos Todhunter sold corn to the landowner. When he delivered it he met the McNeals and soon after offered them use of the original log house on his own land. From there Mary conducted her tailoring business.

Amos Todhunter had taught school. Learning that Emily and Alison McNeal had advanced only to the fourth reader, he undertook to educate them himself. The sprightliness of Emily's mind delighted him and he fell in love with her. A curious document relating to his courtship survives. Observing the proprieties, he had written to Daniel McNeal, in Jay County, Indiana, where he was then living, in 1847. McNeal's reply was sealed with wax and hand delivered:

Yours of 20^t July came to hand a few days since in which you avow your affection for my daughter and ask my assent to your union. I must own that your frank, candid manner has prepossessed me much in your favor, but you will no doubt sympathize with a Father's feelings if I should hesitate a little in encouraging a union between you & my daughter, seeing you are a total stranger to me and I am without reference as to your character *etc.* I durst not trifle with the obligations I owe my child and, placed as I am, can neither encourage nor discourage you at this time. . . . I . . . will take it as a favor of you to give me refferences [sic]. . . . My young friend think it not unkind in me to hesitate in this matter for you may yet be a parent and will be better able to appreciate my feelings on this occasion.[8]

While McNeal's correctness and scruples must equally fascinate us, we cannot overlook his reference to Amos's "frank and candid manner." It would be a source of strength to the Todhunters throughout their marriage, and a beacon to their children.

Emily had given birth to five of their eleven children before she made up her mind, ten years after she married Amos, to become a Quaker herself. From what we know of her, she probably made a careful study of the subject in the interim. When leisure offered, she was never without a book. One might ask if it was Amos's skill as tutor that accounted for Emily's scholarship, or if the potential had passed to her through her scapegrace schoolteacher father. Still another explanation offers. For that we must go back into Emily's family history.

Mary (Polly) Lanum was the daughter of Bathsheba Ambler and Robert Power Lanum [Lanham]. The Lanum ancestors had come to America from Scotland and had settled in Maryland, in Piscataway Parish, Prince Georges County, close by the Potomac. The first of Edward Lanum's sixteen children was born in 1723 and the last in 1765. Edward died before this last child, Robert Power Lanum, was a year old. The census of 1776 shows that Robert then was living with his half-sister Rachel and her husband, Richard Bryan, the only father he ever knew. (Thirty-six years later he named his own youngest son Richard Bryan Lanum. The Lanums scrupulously preserved family surnames as given names, a fact of some importance to this history, as will develop. People of diminished means, they clung to what they had, and to one another.)[9]

Something brought Robert Lanum down into Virginia, to Loudoun County. There, on 3 May 1798, he married Bathsheba Ambler, and there lived out his life obscurely. The only words we have from him are those he spoke to Bathsheba on the last day of his life, 24 January 1821, as he lay on his death bed: "Take the children to the state of Ohio, or some other *free* state, for the slavery question will give this country great trouble some day." Remarkable words to be spoken then by someone who was not a Quaker and who had himself been a slave-holder, and, for that reason, all the more cherished by his Quaker descendants.

Robert and Bathsheba Lanum were Emily and Alison McNeal's grandparents. Nothing in their Lanum heritage suggests that their distinctiveness came from that source. Our attention, therefore, narrows to Bathsheba Ambler Lanum, the widow with ten children, ages twenty-two down to seven, to whom Robert left a remarkable mandate, an honest reputation, and little else.

William Ambler, Bathsheba's father, was born in 1744. He was orphaned young, and the first work he did was to split rails and carry them on his shoulders, to build fences. The Reverend Richard Lanum, his grandson, said William was in Boston in 1775, and present at the Battle of Bunker Hill. In Boston he married Benjamin Franklin's grandniece, the granddaughter of Mrs. Robert Homes, Franklin's sister Mary. Their daughter Bathsheba was born in February 1777. To commemorate their Franklin alliance, Robert and Bathsheba named their first child, born 16 March 1799, Elizabeth Franklin Lanum. Elizabeth, in turn, named her first child, born 18 March 1823, Mary Franklin Waldron. Since the 1770's, the family, with the exactness of ritual, has passed down through the female line a tall case clock, a vest, and a nightcap, all of which once belonged to Franklin himself. Their present owner, Mabel Todhunter, has had them for eighty years. With them came a slip of paper enumerating the previous owners: "Bathsheba, Polly, Emily, Clara."

After Robert Lanum's death, Bathsheba, heeding his advice, set out with all ten of her children, crossing Virginia and the western regions of the state by the Kanawah Route, into Ohio to Fayette County, where she lived the rest of her life, dying there in 1845. She seems to have been one of Rex Stout's most remarkable forebears.[10]

BOOK II

A Prairie Boyhood

3.

Cabbages and Kings

Both Mr. Stout and myself are descended from Joshua Hoopes. Even without that kinship, I would have admired Rex Stout for his amazing career and many contributions to American life. He is truly a remarkable man. He has one United States Senator who is an avid fan of his.

— HUBERT H. HUMPHREY

On 6 August 1884, the Indianapolis *News* and the Indianapolis *Journal* both reported that "Professor John W. Stout, formerly Superintendent of Public Schools at Tipton and Greenfield, but lately from Kansas, has bought the Noblesville *Republican-Ledger* of W. W. Stephenson, and assumes possession Friday next." The *Journal* said further: "Professor Stout is an accomplished gentleman and scholar, and a simon-pure Republican who will make the *Republican-Ledger* a boon for Blaine and Logan and the whole Republican ticket." A man named Puntenny was joint purchaser.

John and Lucetta Stout came to Noblesville from Girard, Kansas, where Ruth, their fifth child, had been born on June 14. John had been superintendent at Tipton in 1878 and at Greenfield in 1882. His friend and kinsman David Overmyer had moved to Kansas that same year, and David's account of the state's attractions induced John to follow him there. Since Girard was a publishing center and Kansas was good to its editors — later putting more of them in the governor's chair and in the Senate than any other state in the Union — John Stout may have gone to Girard to begin his new career in publishing. No one now remembers.

Noblesville began as a town in 1823. It was named for Lavinia Noble, fiancée of Josiah Polk, one of the founders. Tradition has it that when Josiah spelled out her name in his garden, with cabbages, Lavinia threw him over. The town survived this repudiation and by the time John Stout took up the job of editor at his office in what is now the City Hall Block, on Maple Street, it was a prospering Republican stronghold, serving many small farms and a population of twenty-six hundred.[1]

The house John leased for his family, at 1151 Cherry Street, was within easy walking distance of his office. In muddy weather, in winter and in the wet springs, the sidewalks were shod with wood planking, but fine elms, beeches, locusts, and tulip poplars gave a sequestered content-ment to life in Noblesville which, to the Stouts, must have seemed a welcome alternative to Kansas, where the wind blew day and night and trees were scant. The house had been built nine years before, by Daniel Craycraft. It faced north, toward the White River, which at this point snaked in close to the public square and was less than nine hundred yards from the Cherry Street house. This was the same White River which fed Sand Creek, where John's family had lived for seventy years. The Indians had called it Wapahani, meaning "white water," its most memorable characteristic.

For the time being the Stouts found the house ample for their needs. The children were small, and sleeping them several to a room pre-sented no problems. The congeniality of the setting was ample compen-sation for any inconvenience they felt.

In the spring of 1886, Lucetta was pregnant with her sixth child. The ground was ablaze with magenta (locally called rosebud), and dogwood bloomed in every dooryard. Lucetta, who gardened all her life with a dedication that might have confounded a Nebuchadnezzar, was philo-sophical about her pregnancy. Spring was the season in which new things began to grow. Besides, she had had a baby every even-num-bered year since she was married. It was time for another.

The day Rex Stout was born, Wednesday, 1 December 1886, the tem-perature at 7 A.M. was twenty-four. By late afternoon it had dropped to seven. An hour before midnight, it hovered just a degree above zero. Snow had fallen in the morning, as the cold front advanced, but by midmorning the skies had cleared. In early afternoon, with no pro-phetic intent, "the wind shifted and blew briskly N. to NW."[2] So local weather records tell us. With the ground lapped in ermine, Rex was born as the thermometer plummeted, and the way was open for No-blesville to supplant its legend of cabbages with a legend of a king, as became its fine-sounding name.

More than fifty years later, visiting Rex at his hilltop home in Con-necticut, Lucetta, then eighty-six, watched her youngest granddaugh-ter, Rex's two-year-old Rebecca, squirming in her high chair. Rebecca worked a foot free and propped it on the tray of the chair. She looked satisfied.

"Rebecca is going to be a lawyer," Lucetta declared.

Rebecca's mother laughed.

"What did you think Rex would be when he was that age?" she asked.

Lucetta countered with a question of her own.

"Have I ever told you why I named him Rex?"

"No," her daughter-in-law replied, "I don't think so — "

"When he came out," Lucetta said, "he came out like a king."[3]

Puntenny had left the paper and now John found a new partner, named Montgomery. Things looked encouraging. In January a gas well came in at Noblesville, the first of many, and there was promise of a local boom, no one anticipating what electricity would do to the gas industry a decade later. But in the summer Montgomery took his money out of the paper and, some said, John's money too, and left town.

It was a summer of absurdities. One day, Bob and Walt, ages nine and seven, drove a goat and goat cart up the long flight of stairs to their father's office. The 900 block was in an uproar. A famous visitor, James Whitcomb Riley, getting shaved at the barbershop across the street, stepped out, lather and all, to watch the fun.[4]

Without financial backing there was no holding on in Noblesville. On 12 August 1887, John sold the paper and prepared to move back to Kansas, where, David Overmyer assured him, prospects for advancement were now unlimited.

Rex was not yet a year old when his family left Indiana. In later years he would say he left at the age of one because he could not stand Indiana politics. The years did not change things much. In 1961, Tom Neal, the editor of the Noblesville *Republican-Ledger,* reported that Midwesterners could accept Rex's fictions more readily than his politics. Yet four years later Neal wrote Rex to say that the paper wanted to run a feature article on him. Rex wrote back: "How I wish I could show my father your letter!" He had no wish to gloat. He knew merely that his success would have been a balm to ease one of John's many disappointments.

The many peregrinations of the Stouts as John Stout sought to advance himself during the early years of his marriage might easily have been a source of major disorientation to his children had not Lucetta Stout been an exceptional woman who sought to give them values which made changes of situation a matter of small consequence to them. Their upbringing was left to her and it was her norms that prevailed. The influences brought to bear on Lucetta in the period of her own formation, and the way in which she responded to them, in keeping with her own distinctive temperament, had much to do, of course, with the precepts and outlook which she passed on to her children.

Abner Todhunter gave each of his children a farm, or the cash equivalent, when they married. But Amos, when he married Emily McNeal, had stayed with his parents. Lucetta, the third of Amos's eleven children, was born on 27 February 1853. About that time the older Todhunters built the larger house and all moved into it. Abner was then sixty-four. Two years later, his wife, Elizabeth Job, was felled by a stroke. Paralyzed in mind and body, she was bedridden till her death in 1866. Abner died on 2 December 1871. From 1855 to 1866, Emily cared for the invalid and for Abner's brother and sister, Aaron and

Rebecca, both retarded. She also gave birth to eight more children, including twins, Layton and Clayton, born the year of Elizabeth's death.

Lucetta Stout's chief remembrance of Abner was of someone who told her it was greedy to help yourself to more food than you could eat — advice which, fortunately, he had refrained from giving his Indian guests back in 1805.

There was always a hired girl. One, Kate Dill, lived with the Todhunters for years. When Kate married Tom Snider, who helped Amos with the heavy farm work — Perry township was corn and hog territory — "Mother Todhunter," as everyone called Emily, gave them a nice wedding in her parlor. And there was Ann Wood, a black woman with several children, who lived in Polly's old log cabin on "Upper Farm" and did the washing and heavy housework.

Most of all there was Jack Gantz, whose role in the household was unique. Jack Gantz came to them in the early days of the Civil War. He was seventeen and had run away from a Southern family where he had been personal slave to the daughter of the household. He stayed on, raised all the Todhunter children, and looked after them with boundless affection. He became their "Uncle Jack" and a real member of the family. Jack always ate with the Todhunters. Once, when a visitor from the South saw Jack take his place at the table, he called Amos aside. "I can't sit down to eat with that . . . that . . . ," he sputtered. Amos was instantly understanding. "No . . . I guess thee can't. Now which would thee rather do — have thy dinner in the kitchen forthwith, or eat in here after we are done?"

Amos was the most exemplary of Quakers, stern and unyielding but so kindhearted he would not kill a mouse with young. Instead of spanking his daughters, Amos shook their skirt tails. He had a reputation for never being taken in a trade, but one day he came home with a spavined horse for which he had traded a fine cow. Everyone thought it was a great joke on Amos, but, in fact, he had made the swap with a poor man who had seven children and no money.

Amos knew thrift, to be sure, and though he was the largest stockholder in the Citizens' National Bank at Hillsboro, and chairman of its board of directors, he still bought muslin and calico by the bolt as the cheapest way of supplying his daughters with dressmaking materials. His nephew, Daniel Webster Ellis, said Amos was so tight that he went around the fields picking from the underbrush and fences wool the sheep had rubbed off. Since Daniel himself was fabled for thrift, this must have been notable behavior.

But Amos's prudence extended in all directions. Oldtimers in Clinton County remember the aspiring politician who solicited Amos's support. Amos listened with perfect attention and then said: "I am not going to vote for thee. If thee are as good as thee say thee are, thee don't belong in politics." In addition to his example and precepts, Amos left most of his children his height (he was taller than average), and the formidable Todhunter nose.[5]

Emily not only managed her household, she managed Amos. A neighbor commented later, "I'd back Emily one thousand percent for being the one to pass on real character and family traits worth tracing — she was, to my mind, the head of the house." At Emily Todhunter's insistence, eight of her children (all but one of the nine who lived to maturity) went to college. The older ones — Lavinia, Oscar, Lucetta, Alice, and Clara — went to Earlham, one of the first coeducational colleges in America. It was a Quaker school in Richmond, Indiana, one hundred and thirty miles from home. Laura, Bessie, and Layton went to Wilmington. Only Lucy (whose hearing was seriously impaired) chose to skip college.

In 1884, Amos moved his family from New Martinsburg to an imposing brick house which stood facing the entrance to the campus of Wilmington College, in Wilmington, Ohio, another Quaker institution, which had begun operations in 1871, taking over from Benjamin Franklin College, which had failed. The house, built originally as a residence for Franklin's president, was called "Hackberry Hall" because of a large hackberry tree which grew on its west side. It duplicated, on a reduced scale, College Hall, across the way.

Amos had sent his other children away to college. He said he was going to keep the younger ones with him. The house had eleven rooms, a huge attic, an elegant open stairway, and a little twisting backstairs down to the kitchen area. It faced south, on six acres. On the east side were apple trees. Two big elms and an ash were east of the front walk. The best of the furnishings, including Franklin's tall case clock, came along with the Todhunters from New Martinsburg. But Emily saw to it that the appointments of the new house were in keeping with the setting. There was a fine dinner service of Haviland Limoges, with a tureen large enough to hold soup for all eleven Todhunters and Uncle Jack. There was a fine mahogany four-poster, so magnificent that fifty years later, Lucy, looking at it, would say, "This will always mean my parents." Emily also had one of the first sewing machines — now in the Wilmington College Museum — one of many things which dispose Wilmingtonians to remember Emily as someone "responsible for a number of innovations in and around Wilmington."[6]

Lucetta Todhunter began her studies at Earlham in the fall of 1869 and spent her last term there in the spring of 1874. She maintained a ninety-five average. The president of Earlham then was Joseph Moore, who had trained at Harvard. The total enrollment was not much over two hundred students, and Moore communicated to most of them a sense of the transcendental vision he had brought back from Boston.

Yet Moore did not think God would give men by inward illumination those truths which they could know through the exercise of their intellects. His legacy to Earlham was a statement of goals summed up in twelve words: "Yearning for honesty, sincerity, broader outlook on life, finer and harder tasks." And he enjoyed quoting Agassiz's words: "None of our preconceived and favorite theories will ever affect the truth." Moore was a naturalist, like his great teacher Louis Agassiz, and often took his students over to Elks Creek to dig for brachiopods and trilobites or other specimens of the Upper and Lower Silurian strata. But most of all, he taught them to look within themselves, and to be themselves at all costs.

As a Todhunter, Lucetta found that that posed no problem. "There are seven Todhunter girls," sister Alice would say, "three pairs and an odd one." Each prided herself on being the odd one. Typical was Lucetta's idea of money: if you had it, you spent it. If you didn't, you got along without it. During her first term at college she read a novel, *Eric,* which she thought her sisters would enjoy. Having no money to buy it for them, she copied all four hundred pages in longhand. Even Amos, though he embraced the old Quaker view that fiction was frivolous, was so touched by her solicitude that he consented to read it. When he laid down the last page, he reviewed the book with soulful succinctness: "If it had been so, it would have been a pity." In later years, though she was not a great giver of presents, when Lucetta took a liking to a book she would buy half a dozen copies and give them to people with whom she wanted to share the experience. In this habit she became the prototype of Mrs. Rachel Bruner in *The Doorbell Rang.*

When Lucetta returned to Earlham for the fall term, in 1871, Alice came with her. With them they brought two thick English woolen shawls useful for sleigh rides, long carriage rides, or extra bed covering. "Cetta," as her friends called her, loaned so much of her wardrobe that soon she had nothing to wear. Alice, always decisive, gathered the clothes, locked them in their bell-topped trunk, and carried the key.

On their outings the girls visited Richmond to hear Frederick C. Douglass speak, explored the night skies at Earlham's observatory, or, on Earlham's fine court, played croquet, a game Lucetta played fiercely till past eighty.[7] Her enthusiasm was contagious. Her children came to think of croquet as their favorite sport.

Lucetta's brother, Oscar Benjamin, graduated from Earlham in 1872, and for the next two years taught at Azalea, in Sand Creek. In 1874 he paid Earlham a visit, bringing with him a young man his own age — John Stout from Sand Creek, then teaching at Elizabethtown, Indiana.[8] Lucetta and her friends challenged them to a spelling bee. After many rounds only two contestants remained, Lucetta and John. Although the Stouts later would tell their children that no words could be found which neither could spell, the Todhunter aunts confided that

Lucetta had spelled John down. A year later, on 22 July 1875, she completed her conquest by marrying him.[9] At the service she wore a wreath of fresh orange blossoms in her hair. For Emily Todhunter, whose dealings with plants went on at a preternatural level — she kept hordes of cyclamen blooming through the winter — supplying fresh orange blossoms for her daughter's wedding would have posed no problem.

4.

John and Lucetta

He had that marvellous quality of a good politician — but mostly of a good friend — certainly Rex never did it with political intent — of when he was talking to you, making you feel you were the whole center of his attention. He'd say, "How are you?" You'd say, "Fine!" And he'd say "No, I mean how *are* you?" Great fella —

— KATHERINE GAUSS JACKSON

John Stout was five years older than Lucetta Todhunter. He had gone to the district schools in Seymour and, in the summer, worked along with his younger brother, Solomon, at Nathan's mill. When his cousin, David Overmyer, went off to Ashby (later DePauw) to study law, John decided to be a lawyer too. He read law in Benjamin Harrison's office in Indianapolis, but then decided he would rather teach.

John had arresting good looks. He stood six feet tall and held himself ramrod-straight. He had blue-black hair. His chin was short, but he grew a spade beard, which gave him a force that went with his piercing eyes, his booming basso, and his sharp temper. As a teacher John moved about, improving himself, and toting with him his many books. One of his pupils in the early years of his marriage was Booth Tarkington, the future novelist. A lasting friendship sprang up between them.

After their marriage, the Stouts lived first at Seymour. There Lucetta, in 1876, was granted a certificate to Sand Creek Monthly Meeting. That same year their first child was born, on May first. They named her Winona May, and called her "May." Winona is an Indian word for firstborn daughter.

The progress of the Stouts over the next few years can be followed by the birth records of their children. John Robert (called "Bob"), born at Tipton, where his father was superintendent of schools, in 1878. Walter and Juanita, born in Greenfield, in 1880 and 1882. Ruth, Girard, Kansas, 1884. Rex, Noblesville, Indiana, 1886. And then came the return to Kansas, where they would live for the next twenty years and where the last three children would be born.

Lucetta, at five feet eight, was typically Todhunter. She held herself severely erect and taught her children that good posture went with good character. Her hair was blond, her eyes gray, her skin noticeably fair. She had the prominent Todhunter nose. None of the Todhunter girls was good-looking. But Lucetta was impelled by an enthusiasm for ideas and for life which gave her face a fascination which would have made beauty seem an impertinence.[1]

Amy Overmyer, David's oldest daughter, knew Lucetta for more than sixty years. When Lucetta died, Amy wrote the Stouts: "The desire for wider understanding was basic in your mother's nature. Her curiosity about everything from 'Hudson's Laws of Psychic Phenomena' to 'Solar Biology' persisted till the end."[2] Rex told me: "She was thirty-three when I was born and already had five children, but she spent many evenings reading. Her favorites included the Bible, Emerson, Jane Austen, Jefferson, Mark Twain, and Thackeray." On the farm she read in the parlor or kitchen, because the bedrooms were cold. She kept a pan of cold water and a washcloth at her elbow. When one of the children interrupted her, she would take out time to wash his face. They let her be. "New Thought, Theosophy, Swedenborgianism," Ruth says; "nothing was too radical or absurd for Mother to consider." Once when John and his friends were scoffing at the idea of manned flight, Lucetta looked so provoked one of them said, "I suppose you can picture all of us sailing around in the air someday, like birds?" Lucetta's shrug was unmistakable — "Why not?"

Lucetta was that rarest of mortals, a completely natural person. She was a nonconformist but without self-consciousness and without aggressiveness. She was one of a kind, but none of her actions was undertaken with the desire either to shock or impress. Once a decision was taken she felt you should act on it even if the whole world thought you were out of step.

If Lucetta never looked down on anyone, neither was she apt to look up to anyone. Unlike John, who kept Lincoln and several others on pedestals, she admired no one for his heroic deeds, though she might admire the deeds themselves. Told once that Zebulon Pike, discoverer of Pike's Peak, was a descendant of Richard and Penelope Stout, she said, "If he hadn't found it, someone else would have."

Knowing that we cannot justify arrogating to ourselves a freedom we deny others, Lucetta never deplored the conduct of anyone else. Once, in Topeka, a neighbor became the target of ridicule because of her noisy outbursts. Lucetta merely said, "I'm sure she's doing the best she can." Finally the woman was taken away in restraining straps after she tried to murder her children. Lucetta's comment was, "Isn't it too bad she had to go so far before people realized she was to be pitied rather than blamed?"

Although Nathan Stout built a cottage on the farm for Sophia and himself, and they lived apart from John and Lucetta, the two women saw much of each other. That could have meant trouble had Lucetta been the in least vulnerable, because Sophia was peppery, complaining, all business, and a compulsive housekeeper. When Sophia went anywhere with Nathan, who was gentle and ambling, she was always half a block ahead of him. When she overdid her nagging, he had one unfailing rebuke. "Sophie," he would say, "thee has said enough." That would silence her for the rest of the day.

At eighty-eight Rex said of Sophia: "She was slender, small; around five two, and weighed one hundred and ten pounds. Small face, black darting eyes. Everything fast, quick — movements, eyes, speech, decisions. If I walked over to their cottage around nine or ten of a Saturday morning, she would ask, 'You going to be here to eat dinner with us?' I would say, 'Well, I could be.' She would put a kettle of water on the stove, dash out to the yard, catch a hen, behead it, scald it, pick it, cut it up, and put it on to cook. The whole operation would take about nine minutes."[3] Rex had Sophia's chicken and dumplings in mind when, in a celebrated passage in *Some Buried Caesar,* he introduced Mrs. Miller's fricassee with dumplings, served at the Methodist tent at the Crowfield Fair — the masterpiece, also, of a sharp-tongued woman. "I must have eaten it fifty times," Rex told me. "No one else's has ever compared to it."

Unlike Sophia, Lucetta seldom expressed her views. One of her few dicta ran, "Never praise or blame anyone, including yourself."

And Lucetta got along with no promises, no threats, no emphases, and few punishments. Since John was absent from home much of the time, it was her conception of order that prevailed. The fact is, when John was home, his ungovernable outbursts of temper so terrified his children that their appreciation of her methods was much enhanced. Once, Mrs. Overmyer, who was of Vermont stock, urged Lucetta to be sterner with her children. "Oh, Mrs. Overmyer," little Amy heard her say, "they'll never be children but once."

When her children were performing chores, Lucetta seldom interfered with them or hurried them. Ruth Stout remembers that if your job was filling the kerosene lamps, upon which the family depended for light, Lucetta, without saying a word, was capable of making you feel that, but for you, everyone would have had to sit around all evening in darkness. To solve the problem of disorder, articles left where they did not belong were dated a week ahead and put in a discarded icebox. There they stayed till the expiration date, unless the owner wanted them badly enough to pay a fine to get them. Wheedling never occurred to the children as a feasible alternative to meeting Lucetta's terms. Her "noes" were final.

If voices were raised, Lucetta might say, "Rex, run outside and see if you can find a nice little switch. It might come in handy if anybody should get naughty." If she heard someone crying she would say, "Must you cry so hard? Let's see how softly you can cry." It would become a game to let the sobs grow fainter and fainter till they ceased. A favorite stratagem, if strife seemed imminent, was to give each disputant a cloth and put them on either side of a glass door, to wash the panes. They'd begin by making faces at each other. In no time they'd be giggling.

Lucetta's restraint taught tolerance. "It's hard enough to behave creditably yourself," she would say, "without telling others what to do or not do." Or "I've never understood how anyone manages to despise another person. For one thing, it must require a tremendous amount of conceit."

Emersonian optimism suffused Lucetta's thinking. The phrases "If only I" and "I wish I had" were unknown to her. "Don't fret," she would say; "sometimes your worst luck turns out to be your best." Asked once to teach a Sunday school lesson, she chose a text that contained the essence of her philosophy: "In all thy getting, get understanding."[4]

A major influence on Lucetta's theories for conducting her own life and raising her children, was a book, *Solar Biology,* by Hiram Butler, brought to her notice by her brother Oscar in 1889.[5] Butler said his book would "enable parents to know just what business their children are best adapted for, and how to educate them. . . ." As a Pisces, Lucetta would find herself described by Butler as independent, thoughtful, just, and sensible, as "acquisitive of knowledge from every quarter," possessed of "fine intuitions relative to the raising of children," and predisposed to gardening and inspirational thinking. She was all these things.

Aries were described as "thinkers, natural lovers of scientific thought, reason, philosophy, and of educational pursuits." John was an Aries. Where signs adjoined, a man marrying a woman in the sign above his must be governed by her. Pisces is above Aries. (Perhaps Lucetta kept this fact to herself.)

Rex was a Sagittarian — "natural-born executives . . . bold, fearless, determined, and combative." Butler was right about Rex. He also made telling hits on the others. We can only guess how great a part Lucetta herself played in bending the natures of her children to fit Butler's formulations.

A friend, struck by Lucetta's individualism, once told Ruth: "Do you realize that if your mother wasn't so thoroughly good, she would long ago have been locked up either in jail or in an insane asylum?" In truth, at times even her family found Lucetta's extraordinary self-sufficiency a dubious blessing. She seemed to need no one else. She was so wary of showing admiration or affection that her children all but stood on their heads to impress her. She remained unimpressed.

"God damn it," Bob would say about Lucetta after her death, "I could kill that woman for the things she did to our family." Yet he cried too when he recalled her strength and serenity. Natalie, Lucetta's firstborn granddaughter, summed her up in these terms: "Grandma was brainy. But she was as cold as hell."

Jack Gantz and Polly McNeal (who lived with the Todhunters till her death in 1890) practically raised Emily Todhunter's children for her. Without her parents' resources, Lucetta had had to create her own leisure time. She did it by handling her children with almost clinical detachment. By making herself in many ways inaccessible to them she quickly made them self-sufficient. Her methods produced an independent, precocious family. But the future would show that, in some ways, the results attained came at too high a cost.

5.

Stout Traits—Todhuntery Ways

Rex Stout has the admiration and respect of everyone who has met him.

— MARC CONNELLY

The Kansas-Nebraska Bill, enacted in 1854, stipulated that the vote of
the majority would determine whether Kansas came into the Union as
a slave or a free state. Congress probably expected a contest. It got
something more: a crusade. The extremists of the nation, unwilling to
leave "popular sovereignty" to chance, flocked to Kansas to incorporate
their convictions into law. From Missouri and the South came a flood
of immigrants bent on voting proslavery politicians into territorial
office. New England Abolitionists responded with the Emigrant Aid
Company, an agency which quickly dispatched 3,000 settlers to Kansas
and induced another 10,000 to follow. There was strife when the two
elements met, but the Abolitionists won out. In 1858 Kansans rejected
a proslavery constitution. In 1860 Kansas was admitted to the Union as
a state in which slavery was forever prohibited.

With victory, the influence of New Englanders in Kansas affairs did
not wane. Quite otherwise; for the next thirty years they dominated
Kansas politics. Their efforts to bring to pass the moral government of
the world brought in swarms of Mennonites, Quakers, and others, who
shared that goal. A constitutional amendment banning the sale of intox-
icating beverages induced many worldly settlers to move elsewhere.
Kansas became an entity unique among states west of the Alleghenies:
a political Puritan commonwealth. The motto the state chose affirmed
its moral rule: *"Ad astra per aspera"* (to the stars by the hard ways). In
the middle of the next century, a great Kansan, William Allen White
(himself the grandson of Quakers who came to Kansas to cast their lot
with freedom's cause), said ruefully, "We Kansans remain essentially
New Englanders — essentially a Puritanical type."

Such was the Kansas the Stouts moved to late in the summer of 1887.
John Stout went to Kansas with definite expectations. He hoped to
improve his fortunes in a hospitable and moral environment. He was
justified in thinking Kansas offered him such an environment and such

an opportunity. The state was riding a boom that was now at its perihelion. It was host to eighty-seven railroad companies. As of 30 June 1887, it had 6,549 miles of track, a third of which had been laid during the twelve months just ending. That same year several new western Kansas counties were organized. Building was going on in every city and township. Ninety-three miles of the new Eureka Irrigating Canal had been constructed. Drought and grasshoppers seemed a thing of the past. Crops were bountiful. At Ellsworth a salt vein had been discovered. And eastern Kansas rejoiced in the discovery of natural gas. Furthermore, 1887 was the year in which Kansas women won the right to vote in municipal elections.

The Stouts were preparing to settle in the environs of Topeka. The capital of Kansas, Topeka likewise had come into the most prosperous period of its history. In 1880 the population of the city had been less than 15,000. In mid 1887 it exceeded 39,000; 10,000 of this increase had occurred since June 1885. Real estate transfers in Topeka during the first five months of 1887 totaled $7,641,867, a jump of more than $6,000,000 over the total for the same period in 1886. Plans had been approved for the main building of the state house and funds found to give Topeka its own pleasure dome — a hotel, a botanical garden, an observatory, and an artificial lake — in the western reaches of the city. John Stout seemed to have chosen well a place of nurture for his young and ample family.

On their return to Kansas, the Stouts stayed for several weeks in Topeka, while John weighed his prospects. Then, for the winter, they moved to Bellview, an outlying district so close to the city that they could look across the prairie and see it probing the skyline, like a western Camelot, as indeed it was, with its grandly conceived broad thoroughfares, its two opera houses, its majestic new statehouse, and other public buildings. The Overmyers were living in Bellview, and David, though in Republican Kansas little was promised in the way of rewards from the electorate, was rising to prominence in the Democratic Party. John Stout himself was a rock-ribbed Lincoln Republican. Yet politics could make no inroads on their friendship. What mattered to both was that they were facing together the challenge of this new life. Their loyalty to one another gave Rex powerful illustration of the bond of goodwill which can join two men in faithful alliance, a pattern useful to him later as a writer.

In the spring of 1888, with a down payment jointly advanced by Nathan and Amos, John bought a forty-acre farm just outside Wakarusa and eight miles beyond Bellview. The plan was that John would teach and Nathan run the farm. In the school year 1888–1889, John taught in District 61, Bellview. The next year, he taught in District 72, and then in District 40, Wakarusa, in its white, two-room school house. Each morning he was off to the schoolhouse early to get a fire started in the potbellied iron stove. He was a stern, effective teacher who, despite his love of literature and history, saw math as his best subject. In 1892, John became principal of the Wakarusa schools, a job which kept him at his desk nine months of the year. In 1895 he was appointed superintendent of schools in Shawnee County, the district in which Topeka itself lay. His office was in Topeka and the family saw him thereafter only on weekends. Customarily he visited each school in the district thrice annually. At first he filled out the unexpired term of his predecessor. Then he won election on his own.

Each morning John set out before the household was astir. It fell to him as chief school officer to create or alter school districts, certify teachers, conduct programs for upgrading instruction, keep statistical records of schools under his supervision, confer with school boards, supervise educational activities in the county, and give assistance to the state superintendent.[1] In a period of rapid population growth, none of these duties could be handled routinely.

With John heavily committed, Lucetta found it a matter of survival to establish a domestic agenda which saw each of her children assigned certain tasks. Lucetta determined these services according to willingness to obey and fitness. Thus Rex never was expected to milk the cows; his hands were too small. That was Bob's and Walt's job. Once, when they forgot about the milking for two days, John took up a stick to thrash them. That was one of the few times he raised a hand against his children, and little Mary was so appalled she rushed out and began kicking him. Mary was the great empathizer in the family.

One of Ruth's jobs was to "carry in the cobs" — dry corncobs, fine for starting fires in the stoves. Rex's chores included filling the kerosene lamps and trimming their wicks, getting the kindling in every evening, keeping the back porch clean, setting rat traps, opening and closing the screen door when they were chasing out flies, putting back in the bookcases books that had been left lying around. Egg gathering was another of his jobs. He told me: "I always ate one raw as I gathered." And he helped with the weeding and hoeing, and shucked corn. The first money Rex made was from Bob and Walt, who liked to lie under an apple tree and read Wild West stories. When he was not yet five they paid him a nickel to hoe a row of corn and a penny if he saw John or Nathan coming. Their pet name for him was "Brose" (rhymes with "rose") — Rex wasn't sure why they called him Brose, but remembered that Bob started it. When guests came, Rex would be sent out to pick another two quarts of peas, or more corn, to accommodate the appetites of the visitors.

In winter, as he grew bigger, Rex helped cut ice on the creek for the icehouse, a small stone building that stood just outside the back door. This ice, preserved under sawdust, was their guarantee of fresh fruits and vegetables through the winter. Seventy-five years later, David

Hicks Overmyer still could recall the taste of the delicious watermelons which came out of the Stout icehouse at Christmas.[2]

The Stouts sold muskmelons, watermelons, and strawberries. The rest of what they produced, the family itself ate. There were plenty of bullhead holes around Wakarusa, and catfish in the river, and the fish the boys caught were a welcome addition to the family diet. Bob and Walt did a lot of rabbit hunting. Rex did too, as soon as he was big enough. Sometimes, if they were lucky, they brought home a prairie chicken.

One way Lucetta managed with the children was to follow the "each one teach one" method. Juanita was an extra mother to Mary, as Ruth was to Elizabeth, "Betty," who was born in 1890.

But May, the oldest child, was a true second mother to them all. Bob and Walt nicknamed her "Old Trustworthy" — an implied reproach for being so reliable and giving them too high a standard to measure up to. Without making a point of it, May assumed a generous share of the duties as she grew into adolescence, and Lucetta fell into a sisterly relationship with her. Lucetta had cut the children's hair. May began to do it as soon as she showed aptitude for it. In one area, however, her resourcefulness lagged. Like Lucetta, she did not sew well. Here Juanita came to the rescue. In her, Polly McNeal's skill with the needle returned in profusion.

Apart from reading, Lucetta's principal recreation was working in her flowerbeds. She was at them from early spring until the ground froze. She was a sorceress with plants. Her geraniums bloomed on through the winter. Sometimes, at the approach of frost, she brought marigolds and petunias indoors and kept them blooming. She had a passion for gourds. The more grotesque they were, the more they appealed to her. Her lilac hedge was one of her favorite accomplishments. Years later, in her eighties, she planted one just like it at Ruth's place in Connecticut. She had her own language for plants. A languishing plant she spoke of as "dauncy," and she knew how to restore it to vigor.

At eighty-five, Bob Stout wrote, "Father never said 'Thee little You thee' when he scolded. He had other words and was never very generous."[3] This Bob said in sorrow rather than resentment because he knew John's success in life had fallen beneath his expectations.

And there were other goads to his bad temper, such as the normal frustrations and anxieties that went with feeding and clothing nine children on a school superintendent's salary, and a Teutonic preference for discipline and system which Lucetta's permissive and flexible arrangements, without — one assumes — conscious design, quietly contradicted. His punctiliousness is illustrative. Lucetta was casual about adhering to time schedules. If John was going to the theater, he had to be there not at curtain time but at door-opening time.

Bob agreed with Rex that a sense of fairness was one of John's most conspicuous virtues. Although Quakerism was not to him the source of strength it was to Lucetta, he did hold himself to the rule that he would punish no child for a misdemeanor before the accused had had the chance to muster every argument he could think of in his own defense. This was John's way of cooling off. The ratiocinative feats and occasional sleight-of-hand which Nero Wolfe engages in were foreshadowed in Rex's early appearances before his father's tribunal. When the alternative was a switching, albeit with a twig of his own choosing, Rex found he was capable of amazing feats of tergiversation. Before he was eight he could talk the tongue out of a shoe, giving to his arguments such emotional conviction that John usually bowed to them. On one occasion, in 1893, John arrived home in his buggy just in time to see Rex glissading down a haystack, a prohibited recreation on a busy farm. "I saw thee," John began ominously. "No, thee didn't," Rex answered, in tones every bit as lowering.

"He kept at me," Rex told me, "for what was probably about ten minutes but which I firmly think was two hours; I think because he was fascinated by my performance. He had been looking straight at me as I came down, and he knew I knew it. I would give eight dollars and thirty-five cents (inflation) to know what I said." When the thwacking came, it was lackluster. Rex had been too beguiling for John to administer it with enthusiasm. Such triumphs, of course, led Rex to experiment with other uses of argumentation. Ruth says that one of the two mean things Rex did to her in childhood was to persuade John once that it was his turn to read *The Youth's Companion* first when most certainly it was hers.

From his earliest days as a writer Rex would enjoy putting his debater's wiles to work. He liked nothing better than carrying his hero to an appalling impasse at the end of one chapter, only to extricate him with ease at the start of the next. These exercises anticipated the far more intricate conundrums which would fall to Nero Wolfe.

Rex thought his father was "very unsure about how to deal with girls." If his daughters were afraid of him, he was, "in a way, afraid of them." Gruffness became his shield. He was irritable and exacting with them. On those rare occasions when he sought to sport with them, he was apt to assume the role of bear — growling and embracing them with a rough bear hug. Ruth says they found it thrilling — shudders aplenty and goose bumps guaranteed. Those familiar with John's mother found her "prejudiced and opinionated." When John chose a wife he picked someone who was Sophia's reverse. Moving between two such extremes, John might indeed have found women an enigma.

John's daughters, moreover, falling so much under their mother's instruction, were Todhuntery in their ways. When Ruth was ready to enter high school, John said to her, "I like to have you think for yourself, but just once in a long while can't you think like somebody else?" Only Juanita was predictable. She was attractive, sociable, and warmhearted, and had no urgent curiosity about ideas. She was the only one of the Stout girls to become a mother and conventional housewife. Sometimes her husband, Wally Roddy, would say, "Nita is the only normal one in the bunch."[4]

Rex would have some of his father's difficulty in understanding women. Ruth Stout does not think Rex has characterized women as well as he has men. The kind of women he liked best and drew best were objective and analytical. "Dad understands women to a point," his daughter Barbara said, "but then it stops. As long as a woman's behavior is easily analyzed, he has no problem. As soon as it becomes too emotional, then understanding fades away." When his longtime friend, historian Margaret Leech Pulitzer, died in 1974, Rex described her to me in terms fitting an ideal he respected: "Quick and sharp mind, good judgment, wide information, accurate and effective use of words." In his early fiction, his portrayals of women conversing without a man present fall short of total conviction. Whether by design or chance, the Wolfe format relieved him of this dilemma, since Archie as narrator, observer, and/or participant always is present. "Dad gets a funny look on his face when he's stuck talking with a scatterbrained woman," Barbara said. "They bore him stiff. If they're good-looking it helps some. But only briefly."

Lucetta set no limits on John's encyclopedic mind. On a visit to Wakarusa, her sister Laura was amused when Lucetta answered all her appeals for information with the refrain "I'll ask John." "You say that all the time," Laura said. "You won't know anything if John dies first." Lucetta laughed in the hardy Todhunter way that was one of her legacies to most of her children. "I don't know much," she said, "but at least I know where to go to find out things. If John dies first, I'll have to hunt up another source of information."

The truth is, John and Lucetta did not have much in common, and the years accentuated their differences as the children matured and seemed more and more like Lucetta. In time John left the field of education and traveled as a salesman, while Lucetta, increasingly free of the duties that went with child-rearing, found herself able at last to go about to lectures of every kind, feeding her inexhaustible curiosity. In later years Juanita said her parents were as poorly matched as any two people could be. Rex thought Juanita went too far. "They differed greatly in temperament," he conceded, "but I think their basic attitude toward life and their fellow beings was quite similar, though expressed and acted upon differently."

This we do know. As time passed, a pall of silence settled between them.

Ironically, those differences of temperament that separated John and Lucetta, combined to bring their children to a state of completeness neither of them could attain.

John offered reason, cultivated literary tastes, commitment to duty, and fierce loyalties. He gave meticulous attention to details. To him routine was a part of discipline. He liked a good argument. In these things Rex resembled him.

Lucetta offered imagination, responsiveness to new ideas, a discriminating scepticism, solicitude for human needs, curiosity, aspiration, hankering, scope, and a basic faith in the ultimate triumph of virtue. She was innovative. She brought enthusiasm to everything she did. In these things Rex resembled her.

Qualities onerous in isolation can be a legacy when combined.

6.

Everything Alive

Mr. Stout, in the face of violent competition, has created the most interesting "great detective" of them all.

— KINGSLEY AMIS

Wakarusa was platted in 1868 by agents from Williamsport, Pennsylvania, and was at first called Kingston, a name even more apt than
Noblesville for someone called Rex. But when the Santa Fe Railroad
announced plans to come through the area, the agents decided the new
town would do better on the Wakarusa River, so they moved the town
a mile and renamed it. Wakarusa came into existence with a ready-
made history. Not only had the Sac and Fox camped there in the 1840's,
but on 26 November 1855, the celebrated "Wakarusa War" had been
fought close by, between proslavery and free-state forces. Legend reports that the Wakarusa got its name when an Indian maiden undertook
to wade it. Stepping into a sink hole in midstream, she cried out
"wakarusa," meaning "hip-deep." Kansas historians put limits on this
translation. The maiden's choice of words was apt, and the word itself
without vulgarity in the Indian tongue. Yet rendered literally in English, it would give offense to some ears. As one who was never afraid to
wade into controversy and to account for himself forthrightly, Rex Stout
elected for a vigorous rendering of the term.[1]

Unlike those who had preceded him, John Stout had no great issues
to resolve when he settled at Wakarusa. Maybe he thought he had quit
the struggle and that he and his children would live out their days there
in peace. If he did, he was wrong, but certainly, as the environment of
their childhood, Wakarusa offered the Stout children a bower of contentment which, in maturity, gave substance to their dreams of a better
world.

Of buffalo and antelope at Wakarusa there were none. They had
moved on. Coyotes were there, but more often heard than seen. Yet
there was much for future remembrance — the prairie locusts (billions
of them), their music on late summer afternoons an entertainment
which Rex never wearied of, and the Kansas sky, bluer than the sky in
other places, and the billowing clouds, whiter by far. Around the farm-

house were haystacks, big walnut and cottonwood trees, three cherry, ten apple, four peach, two pear, two quince. Fifty yards in front of the house there was a great apple tree. John took an apple with him to the Grange and came home and said it was a Baldwin. Thereafter they called the tree "Old Baldy."

Only local trains stopped at Wakarusa — two a day. The railroad passed half a mile from the house. When the sun was not too hot for his bare feet, Rex often crossed the fields to look for loose spikes and to watch the trains go by. Less than a mile from the house were twenty acres of woodlands, where black walnuts predominated. "I spent thousands of hours there," Rex told me, "looking at everything alive, animal and vegetable, playing hide-and-seek, robbing birds' nests, trying to find truffles (which I had never seen), gathering hickories, or bushels of black walnuts, shooting at squirrels with slingshots, or using them to make life tough for prairie dogs, swinging down from the tops of high saplings, collecting leaves." Other places to visit included the Stone Arch Bridge (which looked as though it had spanned the Avon in Shakespeare's boyhood), and Stony Lonesome, a favorite picnic spot on the Wakarusa. There was a natural ford there and the creek ran clear over great stones. At that place the stream level descended an impressive six feet in a hundred yards, earning the site the alternate name of Wakarusa Falls.

Yet Wakarusa was not quite another Eden. The clapboard house had just six rooms. Rex shared a room with his brothers. The wind blew constantly and the windows were loose. Lucetta finally made little wedges to stop them from rattling.

Those early years passed over Rex lightly. The snapping brown eyes, the unusually high forehead, apparent even at six months in his first photograph, gave a promise of precociousness quickly confirmed. When the Stouts moved to Wakarusa, in the spring of 1888, Lucetta was four months pregnant.[2] Because of that fact and the many new chores of farm life, Lucetta had less time to give to Rex. When she needed to rest, books again became her refuge. To share in his mother's world, Rex began to read too — at eighteen months. "After I was two," Rex told me, "I started saving my money to buy my mother a gift. On my third birthday, I gave her a book." He was allowed to read any of his father's books that took his fancy. In his fourth year he read not only the Bible, he read Macaulay's *Essays* and some of the *History*, forming an attachment that never waned. He identified Macaulay as a major influence on his own style: "He had a wonderful way of making a point in a few words." Mercifully, he felt no urge to reproduce Macaulay's rolling, periodic sentences.

One day Rex counted his father's books. He never forgot the figure: 1,126. May Stout started to catalogue them once. Among them she counted 95 histories. One day, when Rex was four, May found him making marginal notes on page 866 of Gibbons's *Decline and Fall of the Roman Empire*. Perhaps that encounter caused her to think he needed a change of direction. She read *Little Women* aloud to him. Bob contributed too. He gave them melodramatic readings of Kipling and Dickens.

John's library contained Bacon's *Essays*, the *Novum Organum*, and *The Advancement of Learning* — in Latin as well as in English. One day Rex made a beginning on Latin by comparing the two texts word by word. He got into Emerson, too, and read Woolman, and George Fox, whose grammar irritated him. Between the ages of seven and twelve he read all Shakespeare's plays and memorized all the sonnets. At eighty-six he still could quote them, letter-perfect. Shakespeare's word sense overwhelmed him. He said that that fact influenced him prodigiously. In the Nero Wolfe tales Shakespeare is quoted far oftener than any other writer. Rex's library still has his father's twenty-volume Harvard edition of Shakespeare and ten-volume Bibliophile edition of Macaulay.

But Rex did not detour around boyhood. Curled up under Old Baldy in summer, or snug in the kitchen, evenings and in winter, he read hour after contented hour. He read Bulfinch's *Mythology* and Plutarch's *Lives.* (Achilles became one of his heroes.) He read *The Arabian Nights* and *Robin Hood,* and in Snyder's Grove played outlaw, shooting crude arrows. He read *Lorna Doone* — "more than once" — and *Swiss Family Robinson* — "only about five or six times." He read *Little Lord Fauntleroy* — "at least ten times." Rex would say later: "My earliest, and therefore presumably deepest, opinion of Britons was based on the two compatible facts that the dastardly redcoats had brutally massacred my forebears and that only the sweet and noble character of an American boy could transform an English lord from an ogre into a human being. If Little Lord Fauntleroy were available now I'd pack him off to the Kremlin, but I suspect they would eat him raw."

Rex read *Uncle Tom's Cabin* several times, too. He read *Vanity Fair* and *Barry Lyndon*. He read *Ivanhoe* and *Quentin Durward* and a dozen more of Scott's novels. He read Cooper, Kipling, Dumas and Stevenson and loved them all. Hugo's *Les Misérables* was a favorite. He read *Tom Brown's School Days* and *Peck's Bad Boy, Tom Sawyer, Huckleberry Finn,* and *In His Steps* by his fellow Topekan, Charles M. Sheldon. He read Franklin's autobiography, but did not rate it near the top. He read *Robinson Crusoe,* by that other collateral forebear, Daniel Defoe, and readily identified with Defoe's gospel of self-reliance. In a pantheon of their own, he housed Old and Young King Brady, Nick Carter, and Frank Merriwell. "God," he once said, "I thought Frank was a wonderful person."

Other writers have romped with imaginary playmates in childhood. Rex had none. "With so many right there in my house," he explained, "there wasn't room for an imaginary one." Nor was there much room for hobbies. He collected arrowheads but found only a dozen. At ten he assembled a collection of more than a hundred birds' eggs, "many kinds, including owls' and chicken hawks'."

Rex learned to swim in Wakarusa Creek when he was five. It was safe. Once though he saw a raccoon drown Charley Hanna's dog "by getting the dog by the throat and holding it under."

A "slippery" offered all the Stout children major enjoyment. This was a steep slope without vegetation, at the edge of the creek. Naked, they slid down it into the water. It was soon mud and as slick as lard. Riding a slippery was not a sport for the fastidious.

Of skating, Rex recalled, "My third, fourth, and fifth winters I skated on a pond on Charley Hanna's farm (next to ours), without skates. My sixth winter I had one skate, which I found. My seventh, eighth, and ninth I had a pair. My tenth and eleventh I skated on Shunganung Creek, near Bellview. That ended it." Toys, as such, were a rarity for Rex. "It isn't easy to have favorite toys when you have eight brothers and sisters. I loved my pair of stilts — if that's a toy."

At Christmas, save for small items put in stockings hung by the fireplace, each child got one gift. It was put at his place at the table and was apt to be something practical. "There was no such thing as a Christmas tree in Kansas. In winter no green things were available."

None of the Stouts was musical. Rex was in high school before music interested him. But among the Todhunters there existed a well-developed tradition for family entertainments, which Lucetta fostered now in her own household. Together in the evening or when bad weather kept everyone indoors, they played charades, Congress, Twenty Questions, hide-and-seek, or the game they liked best, run sheep run. The family also had its outdoor sports: croquet and horseshoes. Again, everybody played. For years pitching horseshoes was one of Rex's major passions. Once he threw eight successive ringers.

Baseball was not played at Wakarusa, although later Rex became an avid fan. But in any sport Rex felt he had to excel. Whenever he lost he always called for a rematch. Invariably he won these. He seldom lost at croquet. Scudder's croquet manual was invoked incessantly, to bring about hairsplitting decisions. "When the cry went up 'Get the Bible,'" Rex said, "Quaker household or not, it wasn't Holy Writ we wanted. It was Scudder."[3]

Rex had his first pet crow in the summer of 1891. He took it from the nest, fed it worms, and trained it to come at his summons. Some summers he trained as many as four crows. They would stay till late autumn.

On the periphery of Rex's childhood menagerie was Shawnee Belle, the blind filly which Bob and Walt had accepted as a gift from failed homesteaders, and Lulu, Walt's jumping pig. Shawnee Belle's time was short. She fell into a ravine and, with Bob directing rescue operations, the younger children hauled her out with a rope. She seemed exhausted. Betty, then four, was the first to realize that they had choked her to death.

Walt's Lulu was basically a lonesome pig. She was the only pig the Stouts had and always was jumping out of her pen and running home to her brothers and sisters, a quarter of a mile away. The cry "Walter, your pig is out again" became a familiar one in the Stout household. One day when Walt came home from school, Nathan said to him gently, "Come along with me. I want to show thee something." The other children threw their books on the grass and trooped after them. The pen Walt had built was five feet high on the roadside, but only three feet high on its other three sides. "Walter," Grandpa Stout said, "have thee considered this? Because Lulu always runs down the road every time she gets out doesn't mean that she has to jump out of the pen on the road side. If thee wants to keep her in, thee must build up all sides."[4]

Though short of stature, Bob had the Todhunter nose and eyes and the Todhunter compulsion to want "to be better and do better than anyone in the world, at whatever he did." He was confident, articulate, enthusiastic, and generous. He was argumentative. He was also easily hurt but quick to forgive. He was splendidly mindful of his clothes and his grooming. He prized cleanliness. All his life the sight of dirty fingernails vexed him, even as it would Rex. Bob's moods were mercurial. He was an original thinker but had no patience for detail. He was an omnivorous reader but so impatient of study that he quit school after the eighth grade. A natural-born actor, he could have sold slingshots to the Pentagon. His manner was assured, and his lively curses, as genial as they were frequent, broke down restraints and enveloped both the wary and the willing in a tranquilizing effulgence. His assumed hardihood made even his faux pas seem part of his charm — "Let's put a catamaran in that story — what is a catamaran?"[5] He was a leader but needed trusted lieutenants to carry him through to victory. He succeeded at many things but probably never considered himself a success. The restlessness of the Todhunters was in him. He moved from goal to goal, looking for something he never found. Many of the things he initiated prospered because he consigned them to capable hands. Acting alone, he would have let them perish. Bob was proud of his kinship with Franklin and in time built a magnificent Franklin collection and became president of the International Benjamin Franklin Society. In the diversity of his interests he resembled Franklin, but he clearly lacked Franklin's steadfastness.

Unlike Bob, Walt Stout was without ambition. He had Sophia's eyes but Nathan's temperament. He was undemanding, unselfish, and droll.

Latent in him, however, was the Todhunter compulsion to achieve. It bothered him that he had done nothing with his life. (He also quit school after the eighth grade.) He had never liked to read but had enjoyed watching the reactions of his brothers and sisters when May or Bob read to them. On his eighteenth birthday he announced: "I'm a man now, and I'm not going to read anymore."

Once Bob and Walt took Rex with them on a fishing trip to the Marais des Cygnes River, where they caught a sixty-pound channel catfish and accidentally shot two holes through the bottom of a preempted boat. They had borrowed two white mules for the journey but came back with only one. The other had rolled in a wild mulberry patch and, emerging streaked with purple, had been shot by a simple minded farmhand who mistook it for a wild zebra. John Stout had had to make good the loss.[6]

When Rex was eight he was one night carrying two pails of milk home from a neighboring farm when Bob and Walt, disguised as specters, rose up out of a clump of bushes by the roadside. In his panicky dash for safety Rex lost one pail altogether and slopped half the milk out of the other. When he found out he had been the butt of a joke he never again credited preternatural occurrences.

One day when Rex was seven he decided that the din and disorder of the Stout household was more than he could take. So he made up his mind to leave home and set out on the dusty road leading away from the farm. He had to walk only three hundred yards along that twisting trail to be out of sight of the little shabby clapboard house. When he got to that point he halted. The only world he had known lay behind him. A thought entered his head. Everyone would be so lonesome without him. He came to a heroic resolve. He couldn't do that to them. He spun around and hurried back to the family he had almost left heartbroken, pleased to think of how much grief he had spared them.

There was no Friends Meeting in reach of Wakarusa. Nor did the Stouts have any Quaker neighbors. John and Lucetta said "thee" to one another, but seldom to the children. They did not say Quaker grace before meals. Lucetta was staunchly religious all her life, but John, although he clung to Quaker forms, was not. The children were not raised as active Quakers. On Sundays they went by spring wagon to the Presbyterian Church, the only church in Wakarusa. And a few times they attended Methodist camp meetings at Snyder's Grove. Lucetta seldom accompanied them.

Eighteen ninety-three was the year Rex injured his leg when he tried to stop his father's runaway horses. "It shattered my right leg," Rex told me; "it busted the skin all open." He said further: "A funny thing happened about that leg. The local doctor, the county doctor, was taking care of my difficulties, probably handling it properly, for a doctor. But the damn thing seemed to take a long time healing. There was a black woman who lived locally — a magnetic healer. To me she was an old woman, so she probably was forty. She weighed about two hundred pounds. She was just about as black as anybody could be — Aunt Lucindy. I don't know her other name. I've completely forgotten whom she lived with or what she did for a living. I know she lived in the neighborhood and we knew her. She heard about my hurt leg and she came over to our house several afternoons, in a horse and buggy, and she sat with me and stroked my leg, and hell, it got better — well in three days. What those people have who have what you'd call a healing power, I don't know. Do some people have something like that? I don't think there's any question about it. I think they do."

Between the ages of five and nine Rex attended District 40 school, the white two-room schoolhouse, a mile and a half from the farm. In that interval at least three Stouts were in attendance at all times, and during the last year and a half, from January 1895 to June 1896, five were there, including May, who was their teacher.

The next fall the District 40 school became a Stout monopoly when John became superintendent of schools, a job which put May and her school under his direct supervision. Ruth Stout says that May let her study anything she wanted. When she was ready she would raise her hand, go up and be tested, then go back and study some more. With students belonging to eight grades all studying in one room, perhaps no other plan would have worked as well. Yet with someone as precocious as Rex in the room, the teacher who allowed complete freedom of expression did so at her own peril. Indeed, Rex may have put to rout his first teacher, Lizzie Tice. Rex had a quick, definite answer for everything — whether he knew the answer or not. One day Lizzie asked Rex what color the ocean was.

"Pink," Rex answered.

"Wrong," Lizzie said. "Blue."

He asked her if she had ever seen the ocean. No. But her book said it was blue.

Could we be sure that the man who wrote the book had seen the ocean? And so the argument went, not only that day, but during subsequent days. Meanwhile Rex went burrowing in John's books for a passage that said the ocean was pink. He found none but did find some which said it was gray or green, or wine-dark. His clincher was a photo of the Pacific at sunset. Definite pinkish hues lay upon its waters. The class felt Rex had made his point.

Rex injected more drama into District 40 school when, in the third grade, he penned a smoldering love letter to Mabel Vawter, two years older than he was. Mabel ran weeping with it to the teacher. Rex remembered that episode as his first show of literary talent. In sly tribute to the girl who opened his eyes to this potential, Rex, several times through the years, introduced into his books characters who are named Vawter. The Hibbards and Snyders of Wakarusa also find cognominal counterparts in his books.

Rex found in his father's books many things which contradicted accepted opinion in the Great Plains. They guaranteed him a never diminishing supply of points for classroom controversy. At home he was hardly less disputatious. Once May said to him, "Rex, I left my scissors on my bed. Will you get them?" He came back and said they weren't there. May said they had to be. He checked again and insisted they were not there. "They must be," said May, and rose to get them. They tumbled from her lap. "Oh, Rex, I'm sorry," she began. "Don't be sorry," Rex snapped. "It's just that I like people to be sure whether they know or not." Before Rex was ten, he heard Juanita telling a friend, "Rex has more willpower than any one person has a right to."

Rex walked both ways to school, as did the others. Sometimes he would come early to fire up the big iron stove for May. In one corner of the room there was a water bucket and tin cup so the pupils could quench their thirst at recess. There was a big cottonwood tree just outside the schoolhouse, and under it, at recess, the students played crack-the-whip, skip-rope, mumblety-peg, run sheep run, and pom-pom-pullaway, which was also called dare base. They ran footraces, too, and shot marbles.

A big attraction was their own personal rattlesnake den — a small ravine about three hundred yards north of the schoolhouse, with a pile of rocks in it. Killing snakes there was a school sport. This exercise led to Rex's first vivid encounter with death. He told me: "When I was about seven or eight, I was with Charley Whipple, a boy about my age, when he was bitten during recess. He and I killed the snake. He ran all the way home, about two miles, which was of course the worst thing he could do. He died five or six days later." This episode was in Rex's mind when, in his first Nero Wolfe story, *Fer-de-Lance,* a man is murdered when pierced with a minute dart tinctured with snake venom, and Wolfe himself is menaced by a deadly snake concealed in his desk by the murderer.

Rex's years at District 40 school were drought and depression years in Kansas and these problems led to the Populist revolt, which swept the Democrats into the Kansas statehouse, in 1894. In 1892 and 1893, John's monthly salary was $40, $15 less than it had been in 1891. In 1894, John was made principal of the two-room schoolhouse at Wakarusa, where the older children were enrolled, and his salary increased to $75. When he was appointed superintendent in 1895, the *Western School Journal* said of him: "He is a successful teacher, mature in years and judgment; is active, enthusiastic and full of energy. He will make an excellent superintendent." His salary then increased to $1,000; the salary of the mayor of Topeka was $100 less. May's teaching brought in another $40. All at once the Stouts were affluent.

7.

Hackberry Hall

I shall never forget my excitement on reading *Fer-de-Lance*, sprung like Athena perfect from the Jovian brow, fresh and new and at the same time with enough plain familiar things in scene and setting to put any reader at his ease. That in my mind is Rex Stout's secret, and with each new Nero Wolfe it has jelled more perfectly.

— WALTER D. EDMONDS

In 1892 a phase of Stout activities began which was to have remarkable consequences. A traveling acting company, the Powell family — father, mother, and small daughter — gave an evening's entertainment at the Wakarusa schoolhouse. None of the Stout children had seen anyone act before. For days afterward they were stunned, convinced nothing so wonderful ever would come their way again. Finally Lucetta said, ever so casually, "Why don't you children do that Powells' show for Papa and May and me?"

The Powells had presented a tragedy. In their half-starved condition their performance had carried great conviction. But what the Stout children lacked in desperation they made up for in enthusiasm. They gave the play again and again until Lucetta, undaunted by Quaker traditions, made a further suggestion: "If you're bored doing the same show each time, why not think up some new stories of your own?" Thus was launched the practice of "having scenes," as they described it, the single most important tradition to develop within the Stout family. During the next twenty years the family put on several score plays and staged literally hundreds of tableaux. The custom of annual Christmas skits, in which the whole family participated, would continue till 1929. Sometimes the plays were improvisations, but by preference they were scripted in advance. The children became not only actors, but playwrights, directors, scenic and costume designers. Lucetta remained available as technical adviser. Thus when they wanted footlights, she suggested a row of candles, with John, Bob, and Walt standing by to douse any fire that might result.

Usually they dramatized an episode from a book they had read — *The Light That Failed, Little Women, Uncle Tom's Cabin* — or offered scenes from a temperance melodrama. Scripts were prepared by Ruth and Rex. Since Rex's scripts tended to be short and to the point, when his plays were being given, Ruth, as a precaution, wrote an extra playlet. As playwright Rex served his literary apprenticeship. He told me, "Between the ages of six and twelve I must have done dozens and dozens and dozens of them." Only Juanita never performed. Her skill with the needle destined her to the role of wardrobe mistress. Rex always preempted the role of villain, but Mary was, by common agreement, the family's outstanding performer.

Ruth found a happy carry-over in her personal life. She was flattered when teachers told her she overdramatized herself. She remembers that "having scenes taught you how to pretend to be annoyed." She found herself yearning to conquer the stage in New York, and London and Paris. Bob even took a tentative step in that direction. In April 1896, the Topeka *State Journal* said of a local production, "Robert Stout, who played the part of Joe Morgan in *Ten Nights in a Barroom*, played the delirious part so well that it made one feel chilly."

Did Rex ever think about earning his living as an actor? "No," he told me, "nor did I ever consider sitting on flagpoles." Successful as they were, the theatricals at Wakarusa were only a curtain raiser to productions launched when the Stouts moved to Bellview, in 1896, and enrolled the Overmyer children in their company.

In the summer of 1893 Lucetta went to Chicago to the World's Fair. With her she brought Ruth, nine, Rex, six, and Mary, four. They stayed three weeks with the Stevenses, old friends of John's, who lived a mile from the fairgrounds. There they met Lucetta's sisters, Bess and Clara, who had come up from Wilmington. Rex remembered only one thing about this visit. He had sat on a flight of steps and cried. A passerby stopped to ask the reason. "I'm lost," Rex said, between sobs. Just then Lucetta appeared in the doorway behind him. Rex had been sitting on the Stevenses' steps the whole while.

From Chicago the travelers went on to Wilmington. En route the train passed through Chillicothe, a town the Todhunters had known well for ninety years. The name rang pleasantly on Rex's ear. "Like Wakarusa," he said, "Chillicothe is a funny word, without being silly — like Kalamazoo or Oshkosh."

Hitherto Rex had seen little of his mother's family. Alice and Lucy had visited Wakarusa, but usually when Lucetta wanted to see her family, she went home to Wilmington. Hackberry Hall, in contrast to the tiny Wakarusa farmhouse, seemed vast to Rex. And to encounter his mother's traits duplicated several times over in her Todhunter kin gave him great satisfaction.

At the center of the household was the remarkable Emily McNeal Todhunter. Bob would remember her as "plump and lazy in a fascinating sort of way." Her hair was snow white, the color in her cheeks high.

She sat much of the time, but always in her special straightback chair (she loathed rockers) from which she adjudicated all family problems with astonishing prescience. There was always a book in her hands. On a stand beside her a mammoth dictionary lay, perpetually open. When she came to a word she did not know, she looked it up and learned its meaning, pronunciation, and etymology.[1] With houseplants she was a sorceress. Quite possibly Emily was the first "genius" Rex ever saw. Who can think that the evocation he gave us later of Nero Wolfe, plump and lazy, in his special chair, a stand at his side bracing an unabridged dictionary, and a book in hand, plus his special skills in handing down judgments and raising flowers, did not draw substance from this encounter with his extraordinary grandmother?

One effect of the Wilmington visit on Rex was immediately apparent. On his return home he became absorbed with the dictionary. This enthusiasm persisted. At eleven, he was crowned spelling champion of Kansas, Nebraska, and Illinois by John Macdonald, editor of the *Western School Journal*. And he knew the meanings as well as the spelling of the words he learned. In his first serious novel, *How Like a God* (1929), Rex drew on his own adolescence for details touching the early life of his protagonist, Bill Sidney. At one point Bill is traumatized when a teacher tasks him with faulty word usage in a poem he has written. Mortified, he destroys the offending verses.[2] Rex insisted that this episode was not autobiographical. His sister Ruth agrees. Even as an adolescent Rex revered words too much to use them haphazardly. His infatuation with words would persist for a lifetime. He assured me that it was his unvarying practice to look up words he did not know when he encountered them while reading. There is no reason to doubt him. In the 1920's a Stout employee told a guest, "We don't need a dictionary in this house. We have Mr. Stout." In the last year of his life, his secretary reported, "He hides the dictionary on me. When I can't spell a word, he spells it for me."[3] Let there be no mistake about it, in Rex the verbal Emily found her true continuator. In some furtive moment a look of understanding must have passed between them.

Of Emily Todhunter's four sons, by 1893 just one remained. Horace and Clayton died young. Layton, who in 1888 had graduated with top honors from Wilmington College, had drowned the next year when his canoe capsized on Lake Cayuga. Two months before he died he had been granted a second degree, at Haverford. Oscar Benjamin, the remaining son — the brother who had introduced Lucetta to John — had gone for six years to Earlham and in 1872 had taken his degree as a classics major. For two years he taught at the Friends School in Azalea. The following three years he was a partner in the Friends Publishing House, New Vienna, Ohio. He then joined a publishing firm in Cincinnati. In 1883 he was state secretary for the Society for the Prevention of Cruelty to Children and Animals, and editor of its publication, *Hu-*

mane Educator. Meanwhile he announced himself as a freelance writer, became chairman of Earlham's Alumni Loaning Fund Committee, Alumni Association treasurer, a member of the executive board, and, as leader of an abortive revolt, was an unsuccessful candidate for a place on the board of trustees.

Oscar often visited the Earlham campus where he gave lectures on an improved curriculum. For *The Earlhamite* he wrote two articles, one on the history of Brazil, the other "Is It a New Science?" which lauded Hiram Butler's solar biology and quickened Lucetta's interest in the subject.[4] At the time of Rex's visit, Oscar was enrolled in Cincinnati's Hygeia School of Chiropractic, where he earned a degree before the school shut down in 1899. Presently, during a period of boom in southern Nevada and Mexico, Oscar became a broker specializing in mining investments. He grew rich, but then grew poor again, buying his own stocks. He spent his last years as an attorney for Burnett House, in Cincinnati, where he died in 1926.[5] Oscar was well read and droll. Sometimes, sporting with his initials, he referred to himself as "O Beautiful Todhunter." "He was intelligent, and lovable," Rex told me, "but unable to make anything go for him." Oscar never visited Emily without bringing another cyclamen for her collection. Rex thought Emily might have spoiled him because she had lost her other sons.

Mary Lavinia — "Veenie" — was two years younger than Oscar. She went to Earlham, too. She married Enos Barrett, was active in Quaker good works, wrote verse for local farm journals, served on many civic committees, and was for many years chaplain of the Ohio State Grange. Her son Leslie extended her hankering for fulfillment by becoming a traveling actor.

Alice, three years younger than Lucetta, was the most dynamic Todhunter. After studying at Earlham, she taught at Walnut Creek School and organized debating societies. To shock the old Quakers, she bought a green velvet riding habit with brass buttons and rode the wildest horses she could find. She took a correspondence course in taxidermy and displayed the results in her room, which the family called "Purgatory." When lecturers sponsored by the district teachers' association came and spoke about far-off places, Alice decided to be a lecturer. She told Amos she wanted to go out West. He said he would not have a penny from him for such an unheard-of thing. So Alice earned the money teaching school at Leesburg and East Monroe, and in 1880 left home for San Francisco. Prudently she packed in her trunk a large kitchen apron.

In San Francisco Alice took a job with a Nob Hill family and became supervisor of the Chinese help. She held the keys, doled out supplies, and kept careful watch. She wrote a lecture on San Francisco and its Chinese and moved on to Salt Lake City, where she was hired to teach the children of some of Brigham Young's in-laws. Holding to her purpose, she read and looked and listened, and wrote a lecture on Mormonism. For good measure she wrote one on intemperance, too. Then she headed for Colorado.

In Denver, Alice placed an ad in the newspaper and got a job teaching two boys at a stage stop on the Blue River, high in the mountains, a locale even today remote. She helped run the kitchen and made a point of eating with the stage passengers, keeping the conversation going so they wouldn't eat too much. She rode to the mines on the ore wagons and galloped about the mountains, to the amazement of the miners, on the most spirited horses the region could supply. To Earlham she wrote back saucily, saying that she was situated at a Colorado hotel and "in charge of dishwashing — a task which I perform merely for exercise and recreation."

On her travels Alice noticed that many women had trouble making clothes that fitted them well. Dressmakers were few in the West and the era of ready-made clothes still lay in the future. She perfected her own cutting system, patented it, and set up a dressmaking school in downtown Denver. Here she married Robert Burnett, a security guard on trains transporting gold ore from the mines. Burnett died in May 1893, three weeks after the Burnetts' daughter Adda was born. Alice's sewing business now became her livelihood. She did not sew well, but her cutting system sufficed. She also opened a kindergarten. Busy as her days were, ever avid for ideas, she went to lectures every night. "I was practically raised on Eugene Debs's knee," says Adda.

In 1905 Alice married J. J. Bradley, a Populist who served several terms in the Colorado legislature.[6] She lived on till 1929. Adda penned a suitable epitaph for her when she wrote: "My mother always met life head-on, and was unafraid."[7]

Clara and Laura came next among the Todhunter girls. Clara was a dedicated worker in a small mission in Clarktown, Wilmington's ghetto. The Franklin memorabilia passed to her, and from the Reverend Richard Lanum she gathered data for a family history. Laura, who graduated from Wilmington, visited Alice in Denver late in 1893, stayed on to teach school there, and married Charles Geiger, a young civil engineer.

Bess took advanced degrees at Bryn Mawr and the University of Chicago and taught Greek and Latin at Wilmington, prior to her marriage to Frederick Ballard, Commissioner of Heat and Light for Cleveland. Eventually she published a history of the Todhunters. Her son, Willis Todhunter Ballard, also became a writer.[8]

Lucy, the youngest Todhunter, married Frank Whinery, Deputy Sealer of Weights and Measures at Wilmington. In later years the Whinerys renamed Hackberry Hall "Loma Vista," and boarded college girls. In 1920 they sold the house to Wilmington College.

While visiting Wilmington, Rex met his cousin Howard Ellis, Alice Matilda McNeal's grandson. Howard later became personal attorney to both Cardinal Stritch and Colonel Robert R. McCormick. McCormick never realized, when he ran editorials and cartoons traducing Rex, that Ellis was Rex's second cousin.[9]

On this visit Rex acquired his first bona fide fan. He was introduced to Lucetta's cousin Henry Todhunter and Henry's wife, Belle Ann Haines. Belle Ann liked Rex and in August, when she gave birth to a son of her own, called him Rex. Rex Todhunter lived to be eighty-two but never met Rex Todhunter Stout.[10]

Rex's Wilmington visit came at the last possible time for him to see his mother's family as a happy, prospering unit. In late August, the treasurer of Amos's bank staged a "cashbox elopement" with the bank's funds. The bank failed and the aggrieved Amos voluntarily divested himself of many holdings, including the farm at New Martinsburg, to make restitution to those whose trust had been betrayed. Although Amos's dignity never lessened, his circumstances were much reduced.

The visit beyond the confines of the Wakarusa Valley put Rex's mind in sharper focus. He now had other people besides his own family to relate to. His encounter with Jack Gantz was especially fruitful. Rex's only previous experience of men of other races had been of the tall, gaunt, and pensive Indians who paused at the Stout farm on their way to the territories. While "he had felt the detachment of their alien wisdom," he had had no real contact with them. In the summer of 1894, Jack came to visit the Stouts and stayed two months. During that time he took Rex as his special charge, roaming with him in the woods and fields. "For that summer (and perhaps longer)," Rex told me, "he had me convinced by what he said and did that black people were wiser and cleverer than white people. Not that he said that, and I doubt if he thought it. He impressed me as strongly as anyone I have ever met. If I could meet again one person out of my past, it would be Uncle Jack — to learn why I was so impressed by him." A decade later, Tod Ballard, living in Cleveland, was similarly impressed when Jack spent two weeks with the Ballards. "We all looked on him with real affection," says Tod, "and the kids on the Heights couldn't get it through their heads how I could have a colored uncle."

After the Todhunters moved to Wilmington, Jack continued to live with them but took a job as janitor at the college. There the affairs of the college absorbed him. A local paper said: "He often knew more than the best students knew, and the Faculty and the President were fortunate indeed if they knew as much about what was going on around the College as Jack knew." In 1906, when the older Todhunters both were gone, Jack went to work in the statehouse, at Columbus, at the invitation of a former Wilmington student, W. H. Miller, then assistant attorney general for Ohio. Jack was a Lincoln Republican. When a Democrat became governor, Jack was told he could stay if he changed his politics.

"I change for no man," he said. Miller found him a job as custodian at the state university. One year, after he donated money to Wilmington for its new gymnasium, two thousand people at commencement stood up and gave him the Chautauqua salute.[11] Jack died in Columbus in 1922.

Jack was, without a doubt, an "Uncle Tom." The fact remains, Jack gave Rex Stout, and many another man, a lifelong respect and admiration for blacks. From his early years in New York, Rex shrugged off the epithet "nigger-lover." Several black friends — Ethel Waters, Paul Robeson, and Jimmie Harris, a high school teacher in Brooklyn — visited his home often. When Rex came to write of blacks, as early as *Too Many Cooks* (1938), he portrayed them without a trace of condescension, and he was quite as familiar as Wolfe was, in that era, with the poetry of Paul Laurence Dunbar.[12]

Once in 1967, at dinner at Marian Anderson's house, Rex found himself seated next to Jackie Robinson. Robinson was stiff in his exchanges until Rex began to talk about the role his grandsires, Solomon and Nathan Stout and Amos Todhunter, had played in the Underground Railroad. And he spoke of his Uncle Jack. Robinson's attitude softened. "Uncle Tomism" was never mentioned. To Rex, Jack Gantz was one of the boasts of the human race. Robinson understood that.

8.

Mr. Brilliance

Rex Stout as a person seems closer to Archie than to Nero. But surely the brain that created the masterly plots of the series cannot be too far from the brain of Wolfe who solves them.

— HOWARD HAYCRAFT

From his arrival in Topeka in 1882, until his death twenty-five years later, David Overmyer was a beacon in Kansas public life. Orator, idealist, champion of human rights, he was soon known as "the student and scholar of the Topeka bar." In 1884 David had taken his seat in the Kansas Legislature as an Independent. In 1888 he was Democratic candidate for Congress from the Fourth District. Later came his candidacy for governor, in 1894, and for the Senate, in 1901. In the latter campaign he was the candidate not only of the Democrats, but of the Populists and the Silver Republicans. In 1906, he missed being elected attorney general by a mere handful of votes.

David's public life, apart from his formal campaigns, was yet more remarkable. At his suggestion, in 1890, the People's Party, which had developed out of the Farmers' Alliance, designated itself the Populist Party. The term was of his coinage.[1] William Jennings Bryan respected David's judgment and on several occasions came to Topeka to consult with him. On one such visit Rex perched on Bryan's knee for an hour while the Great Commoner, in melodious tones, reviewed current politics with David and John. Rex was so mesmerized by Bryan's voice that for a day or two after, out of earshot behind the barn, he tried to imitate it. The following year, at the Democratic National Convention at Chicago, Bryan asked David to give the speech nominating him for the presidency. David declined. Bryan was thirty-six — too young, David thought, to have his candidacy taken seriously by a majority of the electorate.

David's family had come to Sand Creek from Ohio, by covered wagon, when he was two. David worked on his father's farm there till he was nineteen. Despite his prominence in Kansas and in national public life, he did not stray from his simple origins. A few years before his death, the Topeka *Daily Capital* reported: "Nobody ever saw Overmyer loafing about the hotels at night. With his family and his books he spends his evenings and his Sundays, and these associations give him the mental and the moral and the physical strength which makes him a recognized power in public affairs."[2]

Although David had a temper fully as fierce as John Stout's, the two cousins never fell out. To their children they seemed like brothers. David so esteemed John that he sent his two oldest children, George and Amy, to District 40 school and later to Wakarusa school to have them under John's instruction. During the eight years the Stouts were in Wakarusa, the two families visited constantly. At Christmas, one year the Overmyers would be guests of the Stouts; the next, the Stouts would be their guests. This custom continued even after the Stouts became neighbors of the Overmyers in Bellview, in Tecumseh Township, in 1896, and later, when both families moved into Topeka. Because of this regular contact, young David, though two years younger than Rex, became Rex's closest friend. David said of their visits: "It was a delight to spend the days at Stouts'. Rex and three of his sisters, Ruth, Mary, and Betty, sat on the big sofa with sister Grace and me. Then we covered our laps with the big buffalo robe and played sleigh riding. Rex, of course, was always the imaginary driver and held the imaginary reins."[3]

Every year, on the Fourth of July, Kansas Republicans held a major rally at Wakarusa, at Snyder's Grove, the four-acre tract which Jonas Snyder had set aside for general recreation. Throughout Rex's childhood the Fourth was always the occasion for an all-day celebration at the Grove. There they listened to patriotic speeches and enjoyed a great community picnic, which lasted till sundown. John Stout chaired the event annually. In 1894 that tradition posed a dilemma. The Populist revolt was under way. The Republicans wanted the best rally ever, and, to allow more planning time, scheduled it for 7 September, the eve of the election. John was named chairman. And then the bombshell burst. The Democrats, by acclamation, chose David Overmyer as their candidate for governor. John's throes of conscience went unrecorded, but he saw his duty and did it. Six trains were needed to handle the people who came out from Topeka. The hamlet of 200 was host to 10,000. It was a day of public triumph and personal agony for John. Ruth remembers that it was a day of personal agony for her too. She had new shoes. After she had been going barefoot all summer, her feet hurt. Finally she got Juanita to switch with her.

In the election that followed the Democrats captured the legislature, but not the governor's chair. Did John vote against David? "Surely not!" Rex said.

The same year that saw David denied the governorship saw Rex denied his kingship. A classmate, Tom Leslie, said to him, "My father says 'Rex' means 'king.' But you're not a king. You're only a duke." For the next ten years Rex's friends called him "The Duke."

As the end of summer approached, in 1894, Nathan and Sophia Stout decided to leave John's farm to live with their daughter Mary and her husband, Bailey Wickersham, in Western Springs, a Chicago suburb.[4] Nathan, now seventy-five, was growing old for farming and knew it. For the younger Stouts, however, he had been something of a father surrogate (he was available much oftener than John was), and the news of his impending departure left them devastated. Rex protested angrily, but to no avail. On the day they were leaving he hid himself behind the barn and prayed for hours (or so it seemed to him) that Nathan would change his mind. Then May found him and told him they had gone. "I stood up," Rex remembered, "and looked up at the sky. 'You son-of-a-bitch,' I said. Because He had taken my grandfather, I was off God for good." No other single event in Rex's childhood was as traumatic for him as Nathan's departure was. Though he saw Nathan again from time to time before his death a dozen years later, he could not shake the conviction that he was dead.

Eighteen ninety-four left a crowd of other memories as well.

Walking home from Sunday school one September afternoon, Rex made a mistake that taught him that logic and word precision are not the only resources a sensible man needs to carry an argument. He also needs foresight and swiftness of foot — at least if his argument is with a bull. Rex had a three-mile walk back to the farm. To save steps he cut through Whipple's prairie pasture. When he was two hundred yards from the fence, Whipple's big black longhorn bull took after him. Mart Whipple had said the bull's horns were three feet long. Rex leaped and scooted. Borne on a brisk west wind, the dust of the bull's pursuit billowed past him. His shirt torn, his back clawed by barbed wire, Rex tumbled to safety into a ditch alongside the road.[5]

This episode was Rex's immediate source for the celebrated opening of *Some Buried Caesar,* in which Wolfe and Archie are pursued across a pasture by a massive bull. Rex himself thought this episode forced but necessary and was glad he could supply verisimilitude from his own memories of his contest with Whipple's huge black longhorn.

One day that same autumn, Rex asked for a nickel. Since there was nothing in Wakarusa in October that a boy could spend a nickel on, John thought the request absurd and told Rex so. To get a rehearing Rex put the family's whole financial structure under analysis. Since at meals his father and mother often talked over the allocation of John's income, Rex already had the basic facts to go on. Presently he disclosed that his father's daily income came to sixty-six nickels, plus three cents over. For ten people that was God's plenty.

In November that year, a stray dog bit Rex on the nose. The wound had to be stitched. And in December, John, May, and Rex all got typhoid fever. Weeks passed before John was strong enough to work again. Believing fevers should be starved, Lucetta put the invalids on reduced rations. That led to an episode which Rex, in later years, would often recall with glee. Before Lucetta realized he was convalescent, he was ravenous. One night, at supper, the kerosene lamp flickered out and the family was left sitting in pitch blackness. When John got the lamp going again, the family gaped in astonishment. From the big bowl which stood in the center of the table, a trail of molasses extended out, directly to Rex. The inductive powers of Sherlock Holmes were not needed to account for it. During the interval of darkness Rex had grabbed up a great hunk of salt-rising bread and plunged it into the molasses, and there he sat now gluttonously devouring it. Rex remembered it as his greatest moment as a gourmet.

For the period just following, owing to John's beneficence, a close chronicle exists of the activities of the Stouts. Late in 1894 John gave $25 to a young friend, Arthur Capper, to help him buy the *North Topeka Mail*, a weekly magazine. Capper, who was the nephew of the lieutenant governor and would himself be, in the future, a United States Senator, from this small beginning ultimately would control a publishing empire. Capper was as loyal a friend as he was able a businessman. He soon began publishing almost weekly notices about the Stouts. His notices on them in 1895 amounted to a virtual journal touching the major events of their lives. On 11 January, an account of John's resumption of teaching, after his illness; on 25 January, news that Robert Stout had written a play, *Pro Tem*, which would be performed, at no charge, in Wakarusa; in February, news that John was one of the three members of Wakarusa's township board. In March, Bob had debated affirmatively at the Lyceum on the topic "Resolved: That Natural Talent is Superior to Education." In April, Bob was announced as a delegate elected by the Republican Club to the convention being held in Topeka. In June, May was attending an Institute in Topeka. Then came two stark announcements. The first, on 21 June: "Mrs. J. W. Stout is quite sick." The second, on 28 June: "Mrs. J. W. Stout is quite sick with erysipelas." That same issue carried the happier news that John had announced as a candidate to succeed W. H. Wright as superintendent of public instruction for Shawnee County. The *Mail* declared: "The people of Williamsport township will support him almost to a man, and they will consider it an honor to crown him with the laurels of superintendentship."

In the weeks that followed, Lucetta's illness and his own candidacy gave John little time to think about the farm, now in the care of his sons. By early August, the *Mail* confirmed that John would take over the duties of county superintendent in mid-September. A thousand details called for his attention, beforehand. Then one day he thought of the crops his sons had been tending through the summer. Bob Stout describes what followed:

He walked back to the little rise of land behind the barn and as he stood there it was the only time in my life I ever saw my father cry. It was possible to see the entire farm from where he stood and all he saw was millions of morning glory blossoms. We two farm kids had had no supervision all summer. We had planted the corn in the spring and we had set out the sweet potato plants — we had done some cultivating. Then it rained for days and days. Morning glories were a weed menace in those days in Kansas and when a vine climbs the tender growing corn stalk it isn't long before you can't even see the corn and you can't remove the vine with a regular plow cultivator. It must be pulled by hand and if you had a thousand hands you couldn't pull up and untwine millions of morning glories.[6]

The morning glory crisis sealed the fate of the farm. In September the *North Topeka Mail* — now the *Mail and Breeze* — reported that John had purchased "a fine new buggy." He needed it, to take him into the far reaches of Shawnee County, out of sight of his morning glory harvest.

That winter John showed where his true interests lay when he gave a paper on 6 March, at the Berryton Farmers' Institute, on the topic, "Literature for the Farmer." Perhaps he was hoping that some of his listeners would have better luck blending the two interests than he ever had. In February, Sophia and Nathan Stout came to the farm for a visit. They came for a final strategy session on what was to be done. Lucetta confided to Sophia that she was three months pregnant. That fact probably helped them to a decision. In June 1896, the Topeka *Daily Capital* reported that the farm had been sold to John H. Stephens, who would take occupancy at the end of summer.

On 14 August 1896, Donald Phillip Stout, the last of the nine Stout children, was born. Donald had a tumor under his right arm and, for several weeks, had to be hospitalized in Topeka. Lucetta stayed with him and thus was not at the farm in mid-September when the family moved to Bellview. She was glad to be spared the general excitement.

Sentiment and opinion had varied when talk of giving up the farm first began. For Bob and Walt it seemed a liberation. As Bob wrote, almost seventy years later: "Farm life is rarely exciting for impatient boys. It is necessary to wait too long for everything. Nothing ever grows fast enough except weeds. Too many things are seasonal and too often there is something wrong with the season." Bob's plan now was to open a coal and feed store, with Walt, on East Eighth Street, in Topeka, as soon as Walt finished eighth grade in the spring. May was teaching at Rice School, east of Topeka, and boarding nearby. The move pleased her. Her family would be closer. Juanita loved people and good times. She cared nothing for farm life.

The younger children had a harder time sorting out their feelings. To Ruth it meant saying good-bye to the home she knew best — to the schoolhouse, the haystack, the walnuts and cottonwoods, Old Baldy, the lilac hedge, the cherry and peach orchards, the slipperies and the Stone Arched Bridge. For her, their departure held a lot of heartbreak. For Rex, there were positive things to think about. Bellview, half again as big as Wakarusa, was only three miles from the center of Topeka.[7] Five cents would take you into town where you could borrow all the books you wanted from the public library, and maybe, sometimes, visit the Grand Opera House and see a real play. "I suspect, too," Rex told me, "that we all welcomed the chance to know more people."

With the horses Dan and Beck pulling the spring wagon, the trills of larks and song sparrows rising from the fields, the sweet wind blowing the grass in the hay meadows as they passed, the day of transfer was one of glad excitement. Like the homesteaders, the Stouts were retracing their steps from their point of farthest penetration; but it was no rout. They had had their farm childhood and now the world called them. Nearing ninety, Rex would look back and say: "Wakarusa! I doubt if anyone has ever had a more satisfactory early boyhood than mine there."

Moving gave the children a grown-up feeling. Lucetta saw this and smiled when Ruth, as spokesman, told her that they had decided not to call their parents "Mama" and "Papa" anymore. It sounded too farm-like. Henceforth it would be Mother and Dad.

Six of the children (Walt, Juanita, Ruth, Rex, Mary, and Betty) enrolled together at District 61 school — Belvoir School, better known as the East Hill School. This schoolhouse, set up to handle eight full grades, had four classrooms and an enrollment of eighty. Even so, the principal, Mr. Martin, who with his wife taught most of the classes, saw that Rex differed from the others. That was apparent from the first day, when he asked Rex to recite something from memory. Rex had begun on Macaulay's *Lays of Ancient Rome* and, two hundred lines later, was still declaiming when Martin broke in to tell him that that sufficed. After that he referred to Rex as "Mr. Brilliance," (though, Ruth thought, with some pique). A moody man, Martin at times was close to open warfare with his pupils. When he found he could not show up Rex in the classroom, he took him on in the schoolyard.

The occasion was Rex's recess marble racket. Enlisting the help of two classmates, Jack Chase and Fat Byers, Rex formed a corporation. In one side of an empty cigar box he cut a hole about the size of a silver dollar. Inside the box, on the side opposite the hole, he attached a bicycle bell. A marble rolled for a distance of five feet, with enough accuracy to go through the hole and ring the bell by striking it, entitled the boy who rolled it to a bonus marble. Any marble that failed to ring the bell was pocketed by the corporation. When Martin saw what was going on, he confiscated the box and called the full enrollment of students into assembly, first graders as well as teenagers. A long harangue on gambling followed. For his finale, Martin raised the offending cigar box over his head and cried out, "This is what I think of gambling!" He hurled the box to the floor where it burst apart with a splintering crash. The bell jangled and marbles bounced in all directions. "Now, Rex," Martin said, "you and Vern and John come pick up this mess."[8]

The showdown with Martin came finally when he settled his anger on Fanny Neale, who was eighteen and retarded. Fanny had been left in the same grade year after year. One day Martin snapped at her because she couldn't name the bones of the forearm. Since Fanny never knew the right answers anyway, the others knew Martin was in a strange mood. At dismissal time he pushed Fanny upstairs ahead of him into the loft. Rex and Charlie Hawks tiptoed up after them. When the boys came down again, Charlie looked scared, but Rex looked furious. "I had never," Ruth says, "seen anything as mad as Rex's eyes." Martin was whipping Fanny with a real whip. When Mrs. Martin heard Fanny's cries she came out of her room. Her color drained away. She went in again and shut the door behind her.

That afternoon the older students met at Stout's house. At Ruth's suggestion they agreed on psychological warfare. They wouldn't look at Martin. They wouldn't smile. They'd say "I don't know" to all his questions. This plan was put in operation the next day. For good measure, Walt and Art Hibbard got themselves put out of class for shooting paper wads. They went to Martin's yard and wrung the necks of his four best Leghorns. Four days were enough to show Martin he was beaten. He promised never to repeat his action.[9]

Martin may not have known about the home theatricals the Stouts engaged in, but he must have suspected something. One day he called Ruth aside and told her, "You are very dramatic and you go to extremes in everything you do. It isn't good to be too much that way. Think about it." That night Ruth told her diary: "I am an extremist, who goes to extremes in everything I do. It isn't very good. I'll try to get over it as soon as I understand a little better what it means."

The first Christmas at Bellview had seen a spectacular advance in drama-making among the domestic players. Grace Overmyer — "Tatie" — was Ruth's special friend. She and David had taken roles in several previous Stout productions but, being neighbors now, they were able to carry out a program more ambitious than anything they had essayed before. That year it was the Overmyers' turn to visit the Stouts. The fine dinner in prospect notwithstanding, excitement centered on the "scenes," already several weeks in rehearsal. The major production of the day would be an excerpt from *Uncle Tom's Cabin*, but several skits were ready as well. One was a scene from grand opera in which everyone got murdered except David. Since everybody in grand opera died sooner or later, David obliged by killing himself as the curtain fell.

His father and John liked this and insisted on a second run-through. They were ready for a third when Rex said that their mother had taught them that it was a good thing to know when to quit.

The second skit offered two scenes which contrasted a good man's home with a drunkard's home. Rex played the father in the good man's home and one of the drunkard's children. Heavy stress fell on the absence of books in the drunkard's home. "Oh, I wish I had a book," Tatie and Betty kept crying out, with a pathos that would have melted a publisher's heart. Ruth thought her final line was particularly good. She was the drunkard's oldest daughter, and about to succumb to a beating he had given her. "Oh dear," she said, "I'm so tired and lonesome." For a finale, the whole cast sang "Lips That Touch Liquor Shall Never Touch Mine."

The Stowe excerpt centered on Eliza's flight across the Ohio. Ice floes were simulated by books scattered across the dining room floor, encyclopedias and Bartlett's *Quotations* representing the big blocks, the smaller blocks a selection of desk dictionaries which John had given the children for Christmas. Ruth, the terrified Eliza, plunged from one reference work to another, with Donald clutched in her arms, while hot in pursuit came the menacing bloodhounds, played by Rex and David, who were covered by sections of old carpet and barking hoarsely. "I was really scared of those dogs," Ruth insisted, eighty years later; "they barked so loud."

For an epilogue, pieces of furniture — a low footstool, a higher footstool, a chair, a low table, a higher table — were arranged across the room to form a flight of stairs. The whole cast, littlest ones first, slowly ascended the steps single file, the last, the tallest, hobbling along on canes. As they climbed, they sang:

> *Climb up, ye little children,*
> *Climb up, ye older people,*
> *Climb up to the sky.*[10]

The day was a smash. Ruth, Grace, and Rex would grow up to be writers, David to be a celebrated painter. All would live more than fourscore years. Yet it is doubtful that any of them ever surpassed the sense of unmitigated happiness they felt on that day when they performed to the unstinting praise of their elders, united in talent and affection.

During the first year in Bellview, word began to travel about in Kansas educational circles concerning a remarkable prodigy found at the East Hill School. Mr. Martin had discovered that Rex was a rapid calculator. Standing Rex with his back to the blackboard, or sometimes blindfolding him, Martin would write random numbers, six across, four tiers of them, on the board, and then, slipping off Rex's blindfold, would ask him to give the total. Within five seconds Rex would call out the answer. He was never wrong. His father spoke of this curious ability to John MacDonald, who earlier had acclaimed Rex's spelling prowess. MacDonald found the performance fascinating and took Rex along with him on a tour of Kansas schools.[11]

For Rex this feat was an uncomfortable business. He had no idea how he did it and, for someone with his commitment to logical methods and system, that was unsettling. It hurt his ego, also, to be exhibited as a *lusus naturae*. Fortunately his parents sensed his uneasiness. They removed him from the exhibition circuit. His gift continued to be talked about, but gradually the notoriety attaching to it subsided. Throughout his life Rex never added a column of figures incorrectly. He found it literally impossible to be in error. And he became an excellent book-keeper, though he never understood why: "It was just a kink," he told me, "the same thing that makes a Bobby Fischer. Or a Hank Aaron or Joe DiMaggio. They can hear the crack of the bat and move at once to where the ball will be."

Gradually the gift for rapid calculating disappeared. "I think I consciously lost it," Rex said, "because I didn't like it. I turned to words instead of figures. I'd always loved words."

Rex's love of words was upheld by his reading. As had been true at Wakarusa, at Bellview he had his favorite reading places — the side porch or his own small (10′ × 10′) room. When he was eleven he finished reading all John's books, a feat he accomplished by reading five books a week. Of the eighteenth-century writers, he read Addison and Steele, Swift, Pope, and Johnson. Nero Wolfe has been called Johnsonian, and the description pleased Rex, but he knew Johnson chiefly through Boswell's *Life*. He never reread him. But he did go back to Pope again and again. "Pope," he said, "is the wittiest versifier who ever rhymed . . . a nasty little man who wrote perfect verse."[12] Other writers whom he read then and later were Chaucer, Erasmus, Montaigne, and Bunyan.[13] He found Chaucer a struggle then. In his fifties the difficulties vanished. For Montaigne he found his greatest affinity. The attachment never would languish. He told me: "Montaigne is always assured and positive without ever being pretentious. And of course I nearly always agree with his ideas and feelings about people and their conduct."

Among novelists, George Eliot and Hardy were favorites. Dickens, Trollope, and the Brontës were not.[14] *The Human Comedy* and *Anna Karenina* stood first in his esteem. Tolstoy's hold on him would never slacken. Of Meredith, he said: "I thought he was wonderful. *Rhoda Fleming* and *The Egoist*. I suspect I would still find him very readable." He thought Wilde's *Picture of Dorian Gray* "rather silly, but a good stunt." Yet he found Wilde "sharp, smooth, always readable." He said too: "I read much of Swinburne; for reading aloud he is unsurpassed. I also read much of Beerbohm, the sharpest thorn on the bush." At eighty-seven Rex reread *Zuleika Dobson* and found its appeal undiminished.

For Verne, Wells, and Rider Haggard, Rex had a youthful enthusiasm. An interest in Tarkington began when he read *The Gentleman from Indiana* at thirteen. The success of John Stout's former pupil gave his books an added luster in the Stout household. More than that, seeing success strike at close range, Rex then first began to think of literary success as something possible for himself. Indeed, he was already storing material for future use, for he was also, in this period, devouring Poe, Wilkie Collins, and Conan Doyle. Even as Dupin's ratiocinative aloofness anticipates Nero Wolfe's method and shut-in status, Sergeant Cuff's passion for roses, in *The Moonstone,* presages Wolfe's affinity for orchids.

Rex's friendship with David Overmyer, himself a boy of fine talents, was fortunate. In his eighties, David still kept by him several books Rex had given him in boyhood, as a mark of friendship and to stimulate curiosity — such books as Guerber's *Story of the Thirteen Colonies* and a popular history of Troy. Yet theirs was not a bookish alliance. Indeed, a pattern in friendships was set here which continued through Rex's lifetime and is admirably re-created for his readers in the bonding alliance of Wolfe and Archie. The ties with the Overmyers identify it as a tradition handed up from Rex's pioneer inheritance, when survival itself often was contingent upon such interdependencies.

David said, "It seemed to give Rex pleasure when as a young boy he had made a little money and could take me riding on a tandem, rented at the bicycle store. More than once we enjoyed such a thrill as we pedaled up and down Quincy Street, from one end to the other, as casually as though we owned the whole thoroughfare."[15]

Rex's income for such treats came from odd jobs he did. For two summers, at Bellview, he was a cowherder, herding ten or twelve cows, belonging to neighbors, back and forth to a pasture two miles away. His last year in Bellview Rex had an afternoon paper route, delivering the *State Journal.* Thanks to Bob, who bought a new bike and gave Rex his old one, Rex was able to go about by bike delivering his papers. For a while, after he got it, he was followed home from school daily by anywhere from fifteen to twenty classmates who wanted rides.

One of Rex's friends, Jimmy Whitestone, had no head for books at all. Jimmy's mother took in washing to support her large family after her husband abandoned her, and survival, not education, was Jimmy's chief concern. Once while visiting the Stouts, Jimmy stole Rex's mittens. After that he stopped coming to the house and avoided Rex at school. When Lucetta understood the situation, she gave Rex a commission prototypical of commissions Nero Wolfe later would give Archie Goodwin. "Bring him here," she said. Rex was not sure he could manage it. "You're resourceful," Lucetta said. "You can bring him if you make up your mind to." That afternoon, Rex came home with Jimmy in tow.

"How cold your hands look," Lucetta said to Jimmy. "Why didn't you wear mittens?"

Jimmy looked away.

"I don't have any," he said.

"What about Rex's, that you took? It'd be a shame if you lost those. They'd be so nice and warm for you."

Jimmy wanted to say he didn't have them, but he couldn't. Lucetta seemed so understanding.

"Did you lose them?" she persisted.

"No."

"Well, you mustn't be afraid to wear them when you come here again. We know how cold a person's bare hands can get."

She found a warmer coat for him before he went home. As he started out, she caught one of his hands in hers and said,

"No child should have to go without mittens in cold weather, and it's not your fault, or your mother's, that you've had to. But you might get in trouble if you take other people's things without asking, so if you need something else, come tell me."[16] Lucetta set high standards for Rex. Nero Wolfe never would handle a confrontation better.

Rex was eleven when he had his last fistfight. It was with Homer Emery, a boy bigger than himself. Rex tagged him out at second and Homer began shoving, and then slugging. Then he picked up a rock and threw it. Several rocks got thrown till finally Rex caught Homer above the ear with a rock the size of a duck egg, and dropped him. "He bled some," Rex told me, "and I swore off." He resolved never to give way again to his temper. Through the rest of his life the episode continued to sear his Quaker conscience. He often referred to it.

Bellview offered few chances for exploring the unknown. Predictably, therefore, when Juanita fell ill with symptoms we now recognize as those of mononucleosis and seemed to get no better under the care of a local doctor, Lucetta turned again to Aunt Lucindy, the magnetic healer. Upon learning Juanita's symptoms, the black healer gave her a potent brew of herbs, which soon set her on her feet. Magnetism was not needed. Lucindy also treated Ruth's ankle. Magnetism, but mostly psychology (Ruth had been using her ailment to dramatize herself), took care of that problem too. Aunt Lucindy was an astute judge of moods. Later, Mrs. Overmyer owned amazement that Lucetta would patronize a magnetic healer. "Someone has to try out the new things that come along," Lucetta explained, "otherwise the world wouldn't move forward at all."

9.

Know-It-All in Knee Pants

Rex Stout's novels are "abstracts and brief chronicles of the time." They are
about New York, about America, about people anywhere, everywhere. Go
back to the earliest ones and you are right there in the world of the thirties;
read on through the canon and you move with the times. The constant is
Rex Stout's style, ironic, brilliantly economical; the change is in the relationships, and in the climate of the world he describes.

— MARY STEWART

While her children were being maneuvered through the hazards of
childhood and adolescence, the fortunes of Lucetta's family in Wilmington were sinking. The heavy losses Amos Todhunter suffered with the
collapse of his bank could not be overcome. The one whom the tragedy
touched most was Clara, then nearing forty. When her depression failed
to lift she was sent, at the suggestion of her brother Oscar, to a Cincinnati sanatorium. Anxious days followed when she wandered away from
her keepers. When she was found, Emily and Amos insisted on taking
her home again. Her condition had been diagnosed as melancholia
dementia. She had to be kept under a constantly watchful eye. Then
came a final chapter which might have been spawned in the Faulk-
nerian dusk.

The end of harvest time, a week yet till Allhallows' Eve, and just a
week since Clara's fortieth birthday — Saturday, 24 October 1897, a fine
autumn day. Across the road at the college a crowd had gathered for
football. The wind was brisk and carried the cheers of the spectators
across the campus to Hackberry Hall. The old hackberry itself was
losing its leaves with every gust and even the bugs that swarmed about
hackberries every fall had dwindled in numbers. Adjacent to Hackberry Hall was the house of J. B. Unthank, president of Wilmington. In
the cellar, Unthank's only son, six-year-old Russell, was striking matches. Then he set his cotton waist afire. He ran to the yard and tried to
pump water on himself. Wind whipped the flames. His cries brought his
mother, who was badly burned herself smothering the fire. Word
passed quickly among the neighbors. The Todhunters hurried to the
scene to give what help they could.

Clara Todhunter found herself alone. With quiet cunning she took a roller towel from the linen closet. Then she entered the coal house and, standing on a box, swung the towel over a beam, seven feet above the floor. She was tall, like her sisters, and the job was done in an instant. Now she put the end of the towel around her neck and swung off from the box. When the family missed her a hurried search began. Alice, home on a visit, was the first to enter the coal house.

On Tuesday morning at eight, Professor Wright conducted Clara's funeral at Hackberry Hall. Then, at ten, he went down the way to conduct services for Russell Unthank. The Wilmington papers said of Clara: "The cause of her mental trouble is attributed to the heavy loss her father sustained by the collapse of the Citizens' National Bank. Miss Todhunter was, until about a year ago, a young woman of exceptionable mind and attainments."[1] When Lucetta went back to Topeka after the funeral she brought with her Clara's Bible, which her mother now entrusted to her.

Clara's death and the general eclipsing of the Todhunters, apparent now on this visit home, weighed on Lucetta. She had been through twenty years of childbearing and she was weary. She took to her bed — the only time in her life when she would do that, till her final illness more than forty years in the future. Many dogs ran loose through the neighborhood, and their barking seemed more than she could bear. The family shifted about in anguish as night after night delirious exclamations carried from her room: "The dogs! The dogs! Please, I can't stand the dogs." For Bob and Walt, who still had their shotgun, duty was clear. In less than a week, nine neighborhood dogs were dead. In court, after their lawyer accounted for their rampage, the judge commended them and dismissed them with no penalty.[2]

Two doctors from Topeka looked at Lucetta. They seemed vague about how to proceed. John went in his buggy to Wakarusa, for old Doc Taylor, who had seen them through nearly a decade of ailments. Within a few weeks Lucetta was caught up again in the concerns of her family, the pressures that had distressed her forgotten.

In January 1899 the Stouts moved into Topeka. Kansas was in the grip of the worst winter in memory and it seemed absurd for John to live so far from the courthouse, where his office was, and for Bob and Walt to be so far from their coal and feed store. The move had to come soon, anyway, because in the fall Ruth and Rex were starting high school. Most of the entering freshmen would be, like Ruth, sixteen or older. Rex would enter at thirteen.

Newcomers always express surprise at the width of Topeka's streets. The planners had laid them out like Parisian boulevards. Rex was unimpressed: "Our pasture was wider." Sour grapes, perhaps, because he missed David. But that problem would have a speedy remedy. The Overmyers were moving into town, too, in the spring.

Rex completed the final term of the eighth grade, at Topeka's Lincoln School, three miles from the new Stout home on Quincy Street. Again there would be long walks to get to school and home again. Elizabeth Schnemayer, seventy-three years later, recalled the arrival of Ruth and Rex at Lincoln School. Snow was falling and the day was bitterly cold. Yet the newcomers seemed not to mind. There was something special about them, Elizabeth decided — they had "a kind of theatrical presence." And why not? They had had enough practice at it.[3]

With his burgeoning scepticism and love for an argument, Rex quickly became the scourge of his Sunday school class at the First Congregational Church, at Seventh and Harrison in Topeka. The teacher, like most Sunday school teachers, a coerced volunteer whose duty it was to pass along intact the record of Holy Writ, saw his goal as realized if his pupils could repeat what he had told them. Yet when he told the story of the miracle of Cana, Rex scoffed. No one could change water into wine. To the next class Rex brought a statement signed by five apothecaries which affirmed that the feat could not be duplicated even in the best equipped modern laboratory. He meant the document to serve as the basis for a lively debate and was outraged when the scandalized teacher gave him no chance to plead his case. The incident is recalled in *How Like a God,* with certain embellishments, when Bill Sidney reports that he reduced his Sunday school teacher, Mr. Snyder, "to a cold and speechless fury" by pitting against his account of the Cana miracle the arguments which the elder Sidney, a druggist, raised against it. On that account Snyder quit his post. Some feats are best left to the imagination.

On 3 March 1900, the *Daily Capital* reported: "Superintendent Stout has just received the latest thing in maps. It is an elevation map of the United States and shows relative heights of every point in the country." As a refuge it was not exactly the equal of Nero Wolfe's massive Gouchard terrestrial globe, but for John the map must have been a source of gratification as he saw spread before him those unknown regions he had visited only in books. Life in Topeka did have some satisfactions, of course. Among his friends were C. F. Menninger, M.D., future founder, with his sons, of the Menninger Clinic, Arthur Capper, and William Allen White, whom Rex met several times when he conferred with John, on visits to Topeka. The friendships with Capper and White were reminders, nonetheless, that John had not forgotten his dream of being a successful editor himself.

Once, soon after the family moved into Topeka, John tried to change his image. He shaved off the beard he had worn as long as the children could remember. It had hidden a receding double chin. When he came beardless to a meeting at school, some of the teachers grinned. The next

day John said he had visiting to do in Western Kansas. When he returned he again had a beard. In 1901, John gave up his superintendency
and went on the road for the *Encyclopaedia Britannica.* He thought he
could earn more, and he wanted to see more of the United States.

Among John's children the same restiveness was showing itself. Walt
had gone to Denver to see what opportunities offered there. Bob made
visits to Chicago, Denver, and New Orleans. When Bob came home he
noticed that the family had to shift sleeping arrangements. Everyone
was good-natured and uncomplaining but he felt he was in the way.
One night he overheard his parents talking about the struggle to cover
expenses. The room was chilly, and Lucetta, thinking he had fallen
asleep in his chair, had put a shawl over his shoulders. They talked on,
and he listened. They knew he had money from the sale of the coal and
feed store, but neither felt it would be fair to ask him to pay more into
the house than the others. Bob's savings came to $255. The next day he
closed out his bank account and put $100 in his wallet for fare to New
York and for living expenses. The remainder he slipped into a folded
tablecloth where he knew Lucetta would find it. At noon he bought an
excursion rate ticket to New York. In one hand he carried a small
suitcase, in the other, a graphophone with a morning glory horn. In this
inauspicious fashion he made the move which, before the decade was
out, would see all the family, save May, follow him to New York and into
an assortment of adventures so varied and marvelous that a history of
the twentieth century in America might be written around them.[4]

May also had left Kansas. Lucetta had enlisted her in The Home
Defenders, a temperance group formed by Dr. Eva Harding to support
Carry Nation's militant assault on strong drink. Dr. Harding was vice
president of the Shawnee County Homeopathic Society, of which C. F.
Menninger was president. Carry Nation herself was an occasional dinner guest in the teetotaling Stout home and, in 1901, May and Ruth
joined her in a dawn raid on a pair of downtown saloons. To their lasting
disappointment, only Carry was arrested. They were distressed to see
her being led away, laughing and joking with the constables. Ruth came
home nursing a gash in her index finger, made by flying glass, and taking
as much pride in it as the Student Prince would have taken in a saber
nick.[5]

As their friendship deepened, Dr. Harding urged May to become a
doctor herself. In 1901, with some financial help from Dr. Harding, May
began studies at Herring Medical College in Chicago. When she completed the two-year program there she returned to Topeka, where she
enrolled in the medical department at Washburn College. She graduated from Washburn in 1905.

While May was at Herring, Ruth wrote her long letters telling her
every detail of their lives. At Rex's suggestion, as she finished each sheet

she passed it around the table for the others to read. "That makes us feel as though we've written to her too," Rex explained.[6]

Juanita fell in love so often that Lucetta gave her, on her twenty-first birthday, Clara Todhunter's Bible, in which pointedly she inscribed the words "True love is the love of love,/And not a love of the pleasures of love." Unlike Juanita, May was finding it hard to yield her heart to anyone. Twice she became engaged and twice broke the engagement off. The second time, she went to Denver for a month, to see if she would miss her fiancé. She didn't.

The records of the Lincoln School show that during the term he was there, as a twelve-year-old competing with sixteen- and seventeen-year-olds, Rex had an 86 average, and stood in the top rank.[7] In the summer of 1899, he worked in the general offices of the Atchison, Topeka, and Santa Fe Railroad, as an office boy. This was better than cowherding, yet he found it odd to pass the summer indoors. Office life is reported without sympathy in Rex's fiction. From the beginning he found it unattractive. In the fall, he entered Topeka High.

Rex said he went through high school without bothering to study much. Yet in a class of fifty-nine, competing with students who were, on the average, three years older than he was, he functioned without difficulty. He earned grades of "Excellent" in algebra, trigonometry, and chemistry, "Good" grades in Latin and economics, but only "Fair" grades in rhetoric.

Unlike Ruth, who published short stories in the *State Journal*, Rex published nothing while in high school. His interest then centered on what other writers had done. He found it easier to conceive of what went on in the mind of an Isaac Newton than in the mind of a Shakespeare or a Michelangelo. Shakespeare had submitted himself to the discipline of the sonnet form. Michelangelo had accepted the restrictions imposed by the odd shapes and curvatures of each of the panels he filled in the Sistine Chapel ceiling. Yet the resultant works seemed free of all binding laws. How did such artists triumph over the difficulties that confronted them? Later Rex would see the formulaic nature of the detective story and the limitations imposed in following a series detective with strongly marked habits through more than seventy tales, as an exercise through which he could address himself further to the unraveling of this same mystery.

Throughout high school, though none of his classmates wore them, Rex wore knee pants. He was small, he had a supply of them, and the Stouts had no money to buy him long pants. Far from feeling compromised, he cultivated a smug composure which suggested he gloried in his attire. To some, accordingly, he was "a know-it-all in knee pants," to others, "an intellectual snob." To Helen McClintock and her friend

Harriet Stanley, the governor's daughter, who were in his physics class, Rex seemed fascinating. "He spoke seldom," Helen said, "but when he did it was worth listening to."[8]

In October 1901, Rex was tried out at quarterback on the varsity football team. "Once was enough," he told me. "I weighed around a hundred and fifteen." His sports continued to be croquet and horseshoes. For shorter intervals he shone at dominoes and pocket billiards.

In his junior and senior years, Rex was captain of the debating team. "Rex," said David Overmyer, "was always a first-class persuader." Handling such spirited topics as "Resolved: That Anticipation Is More Enjoyable than Realization," Rex was invincible. But this skill held some hazards. One classmate remembers, "Cockiness in arguments did little to enhance his popularity." And Rex's persuasive powers had a way of getting his friends into trouble. Once, after reading Hornung's *Raffles,* Rex weighed the feasibility of taking up thieving for a living. He convinced Ralph Byers that they had the wits to be successful at it. Rex told me that they came home from their first excursion with an assortment of neckties, handkerchiefs, and pipe cleaners that would have won them ranking as Fagin's first- and second-draft choices. Ralph's recollection was that they moved about the first store they entered with such sinister intent the owner chased them out and threatened to tell their fathers what they were up to. Perhaps Ralph's memory was at fault. Surely the resourceful creator of those masters of subtle detection, Wolfe and Archie, could never have handled so ineptly a routine thieving assignment.

In his senior year, Rex and his two best friends, Herbert Clark and Tinkham Veale, were involved in a more public escapade. That year Topeka High had a football team so formidable that none of the local high schools was willing to take them on. Finally the University of Kansas agreed to put its second team in the field against them on 1 November. For Topekans, this was the game of the century. When Topeka High won it, jubilation was general.[9] Sharing in the excitement, Rex, Tink, and Herb strung up a victory banner across West Eighth Street — from the high school to the steeple of the First Presbyterian Church. Not only did this engineering feat go unappreciated but the three aerialists spent the night in jail. This was Rex's only stay behind bars and there is no way of endowing it with significance. He slept soundly through the night and was released when he awoke.

During Rex's high school years, the family theatricals, done in collaboration with the Overmyers, grew in scope, professional finish, and popularity. Soon the performers were charging admission, a penny at first, then five cents. They offered seating arrangements, out-of-doors, for fifty people and had to give repeat performances to accommodate all those who wanted to see their productions. Grace Overmyer was thrilled to overhear her mother telling a friend, "Those children are really quite remarkable; they are superior to many professionals we see here. And the plays they write are surprisingly good."[10]

For a time, the Stouts had two boarders, a Mrs. Dale and her young daughter, Dorothy. Mr. Dale had abandoned them, and they were destitute. More than fifty years later Rex received a letter from a lady on the West Coast. The former Dorothy Dale, she wondered if he was the same Rex Stout with whose family she had lived, in hard times, in Topeka, in 1902. She wrote: "I never knew people were supposed to have fun till I lived with the Stouts. It amazed me to discover that there were people who considered life as something to be enjoyed. Why Mary and Elizabeth actually set the alarm to get up early each morning to get their chores done, so they'd have more time to play!" She concluded, "The shows in which you always gave me a part were like visits to fairyland to me. Those experiences changed my whole life." At least one Dorothy did not have to leave Kansas to find Oz.

The fun in the Stout household was not always so wholesome. Once Rex bet Ruth a box of candy she could not go for a week without eating. Ruth took the bet. After three days she felt strangely weak. One of the boys at school asked Rex what had happened to his sister's voice. He said it sounded "far away." Ruth's fast was into its fourth day when May found out what was going on. She told Ruth she must eat and said she would pay for the candy. Ruth refused to give in, so May put the matter before Lucetta. "I knew about it," Lucetta admitted, "but I've been counting on Ruth to act sensibly rather than dramatically." Ruth capitulated, but insisted on buying the candy herself, though it wiped out her savings.

The chance to see plays acted by professionals was a source of major stimulation to Rex and Ruth. Many good shows reached Topeka. The first such production Rex saw was *Katherine and Petruchio,* starring Otis Skinner.[11] That was in 1900, at Crawford's Opera House. Twice a year Rex went to Kansas City, where he stayed overnight with a Wickersham cousin. He went primarily to see plays that were not coming to Topeka. There, in 1903, he saw William Gillette as Sherlock Holmes. Smitten with Gillette's memorable portrayal of Doyle's "great detective," the next night he was in the audience again. In just this same interval he was absorbed in his first reading of a work that was to become one of his lifelong favorites, Cervantes' *Don Quixote.* Was it chance that sixty years later critics assessing Rex's Nero Wolfe stories would find in them a subtle blend of details reminiscent of the Holmes stories and Cervantes' satiric masterpiece?

10

Dramatic Interlude

Rex was such a marvelous companion. From that elegant bearded counte-
nance forever shone the lively curiosity, naïveté, enthusiasm, and even
exuberance of a boy. He was a remarkably sophisticated man, but sophistication never dimmed his excitement at the world. All his efforts to become an
old curmudgeon fell on barren ground. He remained adorable. When I used
to meet him occasionally, ambling down some avenue in New York, I always
felt happy. He was one of the things in that transitory city that did not
change and I set store by that.

— MARGARET COUSINS

Amos Todhunter died, at eighty-four, on 3 June 1901, at Hackberry Hall.
More than ever, now the thrust of Lucetta's life was toward her children. Lucetta had brought Ruth with her to Amos's funeral and returned to Topeka by way of Chicago, so that she might leave Ruth (now
seventeen) with the Clarence Wickershams, who had two-year-old
twins and wanted live-in help.

Ellen, Clarence's wife, was self-centered, irritable, and a penny-
watcher. One day, Clarence asked Ruth how she came to have so many
holes through the white dots in her red gingham skirt. Ruth explained:
"I noticed one day that there are just as many dots in my dress as days
I have to stay here. The holes are the days that have gone. Every night
I punch a new one, with a pin. Sometimes I can't wait till night. I punch
after lunch."

In August, Lucetta again visited Ohio. On the way home she stopped
to see Ruth. "I want to go home with you," Ruth whispered. "All right,"
Lucetta said. Ellen was annoyed. She wanted Ruth for another month.
Lucetta was matter-of-fact. "It's too bad. But Ruth is homesick. This
couldn't possibly be as important to you as it is to her."

The others, too, could always count on Lucetta's understanding.
Once Juanita dated two beaux at the same time. Neither knew about
the other. Sometimes she came and went by the window to avoid seeing
them together. "Oh, how you trust your children," Mrs. Overmyer said.
"If I don't, who will?" Lucetta replied.

How ardent a suitor can you be when you are still in knee pants? The
subject never seemed a problem to Rex. While still living on the farm
at Wakarusa, he had spent an ample share of his time with his eye glued

to a knothole in the back of the barn, watching the couplings of the farm animals. He wrote several stanzas later to record this phase of his inquiries into Nature:

> *How dear to my heart is the sex of my boyhood*
> *When fond inhibitions release it to view!*
> *The stallion, the gander, the sow who so coy stood,*
> *The old boar displaying his bore good as new!*
> *The rooster maintaining his amorous toehold,*
> *His feathers erect and his comb flaming red,*
> *The buck in the wood as his eye o'er the doe rolled,*
> *The old oaken knothole in back of the shed!*
>
> *The old oaken knothole, the fairly smooth knothole,*
> *My personal knothole in back of the shed!*
>
> *The bull pawed and snorted in arrogant fancy,*
> *His proud apparatus unsheathed like a sword,*
> *While Uncle Pierre, who no doubt was a nancy,*
> *Threw stones at the thing and appeared to be bored.*
> *The turkeys, the sheep — oh, how well I remember*
> *The numberless times they were lovingly wed!*
> *Suggesting in season, from March to November,*
> *The old oaken knothole in back of the shed!*
>
> *The old oaken knothole, the fairly smooth knothole,*
> *My personal knothole in back of the shed!*
>
> *The jackass attempted a full double ration*
> *By trying to bray and beget both at once;*
> *The dogs filled the night with the howls of their passion,*
> *The hounds and the mongrels, the mastiffs and runts.*
> *You are waiting, perhaps, for a line on the milkmaids.*
> *In vain; not for me; I remember, instead*
> *Of the pleasures in which it is said that their ilk trades,*
> *The old oaken knothole in back of the shed!*
>
> *The old oaken knothole, the fairly smooth knothole,*
> *My personal knothole in back of the shed!*

Rex had just one comment on this major verse effort: "I like 'sow who so coy stood' — five consecutive monosyllables with o's, no two pronounced alike." He added: "Jim Thurber liked it too."

Starting in his sophomore year, Rex went to the school dances and became adept in the waltz and two-step. Ruth saw herself as a party-giver extraordinary and gave what she deemed "highly original and sensational parties." Usually she came dressed as Little Eva, despite her height. At one of her masquerades, Mary and Rex dressed alike — in Rex's clothes. Since they were the same height and both had dark eyes, dark hair, olive complexions, they had the satisfaction of being followed around most of the night by other guests who could not figure out which was which. Most often Rex had a bona fide date. Sometimes he rented a boat, or a horse and buggy, and took out Pearl Wilson or Dorothy Marshall. Despite the buggy rides, when he was fifteen Dorothy jilted him, a new experience for his ego. For two or three years he dated Juanita Lord. Ruth says that Juana, as she was called, "was more fun than almost anyone I've ever known." Juana was a redhead and towered over Rex. She was not beautiful. But Rex liked her because she was "witty, skeptical, and articulate." In 1967, after Rex underwent ulcer surgery, Juana wrote to Ruth to ask after him. She had not seen Rex for sixty-one years. She was then past eighty, and a shut-in. "I started to write Rex a note but decided not to," she said. "It might have bored him. Give him my love."[1]

Sue Rodgers, the daughter of Alphonso Rodgers, whose murder, by a housebreaker, in 1889, had led to Topeka's only lynching, was Juana's stepsister. Although Sue was four years older than Rex, he was smitten by her, too. He guarded the secret well. On 4 May 1957, when he sent Sue — then Susan Rodgers Durant — a copy of his newly published *Three for the Chair,* he inscribed it: "To Sue with love, Rex. On May 4 1904, I decided that Sue Rodgers was the prettiest girl in Topeka (possibly she still is) and it would have been a great thrill to have dared to give her something with my love. At last I dare! Rex Stout."

Ruth herself was moonstruck over Rex's friend Joe Lodge. But Joe seemed never to suspect it.

In 1902, the Stouts moved to a larger house, at 900 Madison Street in Topeka. Their next door neighbors, a couple in their thirties, with three children, were Roman Catholics. That was not an era in which Quakers and papists fraternized. "There was no hostility or friction," Rex told me, "but there was no rapport. There was no fence between the yards, but everyone was constantly aware of the line." In the new house Rex at last had to himself an ample room, about 10' × 16'. He did much of his reading there, yet when the weather was nice he often carried his book to the front porch or, when he craved companionship, to the dining room.

A few weeks before his graduation, in May 1903, Topeka High's newspaper, *The World,* dazzled its readers with an electrifying bulletin — "Have you seen Rex Stout lately? Long pants!" Ruth says that some of the bigger boys had threatened to tar and feather Rex if he showed up at graduation in short pants. But the threat was not a factor. Lucetta wanted him to have a new suit for graduation. At sixteen he was too old to buy a suit with knee pants.

The last month at Topeka High featured a series of climaxes. On 22 May, the seniors presented their class play, *Striking Oil.* The next day the Topeka *Capital* reported that an audience of nearly seven hundred had attended it and that "The part of Lord Duttonhead was well played by Rex Stout."

On 29 May the seniors held their Class Day exercises. Rex, as Class Poet, read an original poem. The *Capital* reported that Rex, in his poem, "said little about his own class but delivered a number of hard 'slams' on the other classes, especially the juniors between whom and the seniors there has been the sharpest rivalry all year."[2]

The same issue of the *Capital* that reported the Class Day exercises carried a banner headline: "4,000 Topekans Driven from Home." May had been a month of heavy rains, and, as Class Day exercises were ending word passed that the Kaw was rising rapidly. The class of "naughty three" went together to the bridge to see what was happening. Even then no one realized that a disaster was taking shape which would cause their class to be remembered as "the flood class." That night hundreds of homes on the North Side were washed away by the torrent, including the homes of seven members of the graduating class. The Baccalaureate service was canceled and graduation itself postponed a week because the City Auditorium, where the ceremonies were scheduled to be held, was filled with refugees and supplies. On 12 June, a much abbreviated program was held in the school assembly hall. No programs, few flowers. Several girls wore borrowed dresses because they had lost everything in the flood. There was no yearbook either. The contents (including Rex's class poem) had not survived the inundation.

The next September, equipped with letters from his father to two professors at the University of Kansas, Rex went over to Lawrence. No one seemed interested in a boy with no money who wanted to go to college, even if he was the whiz kid of Topeka High's flood class. Rex talked with some of the students. He decided he was not sorry he was not one of them. From what he could see, he already knew more than most of them anyway.

Rex now became an usher at Crawford's Opera House, which had been a Topeka landmark since 1881 and was described by F. W. Giles, Topeka historian, in 1884, as "one of the neatest playhouses to be found in the country." With its upholstered chairs, Brussels carpeting, French plate mirrors, silk and lace curtains, Crawford's was called the "Parlor Opera House" of the West. L. M. Crawford owned a string of opera houses across Kansas which gave him control of the Kansas–New Mexico acting circuit and assured Topeka audiences of top-run attractions.

During the next two years Crawford's became Rex's university. Some of the productions, of course, were merely popular favorites of the era, such as *The Two Orphans, The Power Behind the Throne,* and *Lady Audley's Secret.* But he also saw Maud Grainger and Robert Mantell in *Romeo and Juliet,* James O'Neill (Eugene O'Neill's father) in *The Count of Monte Cristo,* Blanche Walsh in Tolstoy's *Resurrection,* productions of *Pinafore* and *The Mikado,* and many of the greats of the era, including Modjeska, Maurice Barrymore, John and Georgianna Drew, Tom Keene, the Shakespearean Ranter, Rose Coghlan, and Marlowe and Sothern.

Although it was a major source of culture, ushering was not a major source of income. Thus when his friend Wally Roddy, who was a clerk at the Knights and Ladies of Security, offered Rex a job as bookkeeper at the People's Ice & Fuel Company, he took it. An intimate family situation offered itself at the People's Ice & Fuel. Wally's mother ran the office. Her chief assistant was her sister, Emma Sands. Wally was dating Juanita, and was soon to be Rex's brother-in-law. But Rex did not need family ties to hold the job. Although his knowledge of bookkeeping was limited to a one-semester course he had taken at Lincoln School, he found he had a natural affinity for it. It was a pleasure to decree order.

At seventeen Rex sold a poem to *The Smart Set* for twelve dollars. The poem propounded a legend. A Breton priest is found dead in his cottage, his hand clutching a locket which holds a fair curl clipped from the head of his true love. On his bosom sits a twitching lizard. Rex never had seen a Breton and never had spoken to a priest. Nor had he given lizards any more than casual notice. Imagination was an ample provider.

We are dependent on Rex's memory for knowledge of this poem's existence. He kept no copies. And *Smart Set* apparently filed its copy away with materials bought but never used. The sense of rapture which acceptance gave him fast disappeared when he realized he would not see the poem in print. Disgruntled, he made a bonfire of all the poems he had written up to that time, a sheaf of sonnets included. Several years would pass before he would again use his pen to court the muses. Then, characteristically, he would mend his career at the point it had been broken, selling his measures to *Smart Set* and preening with contentment as each appeared in print.

At seventeen, Rex's disappointing encounter with *Smart Set* was not the only experience he had which gave him a sense of his finiteness. He tried boxing — "barely long enough to own a cheap pair of gloves" — and concluded that in a crisis his survival would depend not on his fists but on his fleetness of foot. Although Lucetta at all times wore pinned to her dress the little white bow of the W.C.T.U., Rex, in this

period, gave liquor a try too. With his friend Tom Leslie, he emptied
a bottle of Virginia Dare wine. Both got sick. And on a visit to St. Joseph,
Missouri, after he spent his return fare to see Otis Skinner again as
Shylock, he rode a freight train home — a distance of nearly two hundred miles. "It damned near killed me," he said. "It's very painful, very
difficult, riding the rods."

During his last weeks in Topeka, Rex had his first encounter with
virtuoso detective work when he figured prominently in what posterity
may call "The Case of the Missing Crank." In 1904 he bought himself
a fine Victor disk graphophone with a morning glory horn.[3] He built up
a collection of nearly a hundred records. In April 1905, the record player
and records were stolen from the Stout home at 423 East Eighth Street.
But the thief left behind the crank that operated the machine. On 5
May, the Topeka *Capital* and the Topeka *State Journal* reported that
the Santa Fe Watch Company had been visited by a man who wanted
a crank for a Victor graphophone. Alonzo Thomas, the proprietor,
remembering the theft, told the would-be customer he would place an
order for one. He took the customer's name — Arthur Walker —
and address, and afterward alerted the police. That night, detectives
Betts and Ross visited Walker's home on East Tenth Street, recovered
Rex's graphophone and records, and took Walker into custody. He was
charged with grand larceny. The *Capital* reported that Chief A. G.
Goodwin treated the station house to a grand concert which included
"El Capitan" and other Sousa marches, and such sentimental favorites
as "Just Break the News to Mother" and "Only a Bird in a Gilded Cage."
The *Capital* suggested that "if the graphophone is left there for three
days it will be worn out." That hint sufficed. Rex came by next morning
to collect it and to shake hands with Chief Goodwin, who then, quietly,
and without either handshaker being aware of it, stepped into the pages
of literary history.

The real-life Goodwin has a claim to fame all his own. He was the first
policeman anywhere to use an automobile in police work — a Veracity.
He was also Grand Exalted Leader of the local Elks Lodge. That doesn't
sound like Wolfe's Archie.[4]

What the "A" in Chief Goodwin's name stood for does not matter.
None of his contemporaries knew. To one and all the Chief was always
"A. G." — which isn't far from "Archie."

Born in Peach Orchard, Kentucky, in 1863, Goodwin, a bachelor, had
been a crack telegrapher for the Santa Fe Railroad, and a grain broker.
He was over six feet tall and weighed more than two hundred pounds.

BOOK III

The Nomadic Years

11.

The *Mayflower* Years

Haven't you studied chemistry? Don't you know the air we breathe is composed of oxygen, nitrogen, and odium?

— REX STOUT

The Stouts did not go sullenly forth from home when they went. Like the troubadours dancing across the face of Europe in the Middle Ages, they sprang forth in a glad greeting to life. All were dreamers, all yearned to fulfill themselves in some wonderful way. Horatio Alger never had been much read in their household. That scarcely mattered, since what Alger wrote about was not rags to riches but rags to respectability: the Stouts already had respectability. What each of them longed to do now was to climb a hundred pinnacles and gain the summit of each. Like their pioneer forebears, they could do many things well. To survive, the pioneer had had to be able to build, to plant, to teach, to plan, to innovate, to improvise, to propagate, to harvest. The Stout heritage impelled them in the direction of universal accomplishment, propelled them out upon the world. Lucetta and John found their stewardship over their remarkable children drawing to a close.

The autumn after her graduation, Ruth Stout came home one day with exciting news for her mother. A bizarre opportunity had come her way. She had answered a newspaper ad and an unmarried, thirty-five-year-old man who had a fake mind-reading act had offered her the job as his confederate. They would travel about the country together. She would see many new places. Ruth's setness of purpose was a legend in the family. Indeed, once she bought a book on willpower. When Lucetta saw it, she said, "Oh, Ruth, do you really need more willpower?" She did not try to deter her now. In fact, she seemed to fall in readily with her plans. She even set Juanita to work making a gray evening dress which Ruth would need for the act. The closest she came to voicing any misgivings was when she told Juanita, "I wouldn't make it too low in the neck, if I were you." When Dr. Eva Harding, May Stout's possessive friend and benefactress, heard about Ruth's plans she was aghast. She reminded Lucetta that Quaker tradition was against stage performances. Lucetta said times were changing. Finally Eva asked if Ruth was not running grave moral risk in going off with an unmarried man twice her age. Lucetta said, "If I've been such an inadequate mother that at nineteen Ruth can't be trusted to behave well without me hovering over her, then nothing I can do or say would be of much help."

Before Ruth's moral upbringing could be put to the test, Bob Stout came home. The previous July, in Hoboken, New Jersey, he had gotten married. His wife was Irish and a Roman Catholic and had gone to school to the Mesdames of the Sacred Heart. They were married before a priest. Lucetta was undismayed. Esther Boyce — or Tad, as Bob called her, because she was "no bigger than a tadpole" — was spirited and attractive and quick witted, and the family took to her warmly.

During his absence Bob had acquired a new talent as well as a wife. On the train to New York he had found a book on chiromancy, written by a Frenchman named Beaucamp. In New York Bob supported himself analyzing palm prints. He soon had twelve solicitors working under him and presided over his team attired in a Prince Albert coat, wing collar, dress shirt, striped gray trousers, spats, patent leather shoes, and silk hat. When Bob married Tad, Tad and he set out for Topeka, reading palms as they went in order to earn living and travel expenses.[1]

Bob deplored Ruth's plans. He did not think they were grand enough. She would do better, he said, if she went back to New York with Tad and himself. If she wanted to be an actress, that was the place to be. He was sure she could earn her way, as they would earn theirs, reading palms. There was just one thing to remember: "Be careful never to say anything that would give a person a setback." Ruth liked the idea. On her last night in Topeka, her friends gave her a surprise party. They insisted the Stouts give a few last scenes. "One word," says Ruth, "and we were off."

Bob's plans miscarried. Christmas was at hand. People were not spending money on palm analysis. Tad and Bob went on ahead. Ruth stayed behind, in Kansas City, working as a nanny, till she had enough money to entrain for Indianapolis. There she got a job as a long distance telephone operator. She decided to make no further move until she could mature her plans. The range of Ruth's aspirations made this course a wise one. Actress, writer, diva, dancer, artist — she wanted to be all these things. She thought there was nothing she could not succeed at. Each day raised a vision of new and shining possibilities.

The course of Rex's ambitions paralleled Ruth's. The urge to go forward in myriad directions was, after all, a Todhunter compulsion. Books, the theater, and the ventures which already had drawn other members of the family from home stirred in Rex a plenitude of expectations. He saw in Topeka no prospect of realizing them. Whimsy may have at times impelled Ruth and Bob, but Rex looked on his ambitions with sober earnestness. Regimen and pride would not allow him to trust his future to chance spins of the wheel of fortune. His panache itself required something more of him than a haphazard setting-out.

When Rex weighed his prospects he decided to join the navy. Youth since the start of human history has been beckoned forth from home by the call of the deep. Even Richard Stout had run away to sea. But Rex did not see himself joining in any rites of passage hornpipe. The navy would offer him opportunities to extend the range of his accomplishments. He would meet people beyond the rim of his present world. He would travel. But most of all, he believed that in the navy, rid of money cares, he could confirm his own potential.

On 12 July 1905 Rex went to Pittsburg, Kansas, where the navy had a recruiting crew, and sought to enlist. To his dismay, he was rejected. The chief master-at-arms told him to try again when he was rid of his tonsils, which were inflamed. Rex had three dollars in his pocket. He found a young doctor who agreed to take out the unseaworthy tonsils for two dollars. Although the doctor had no surgery of his own, beneath his office there was a barbershop. The barber let him use one of his chairs, after hours. The tonsils came out readily enough but afterward Rex looked so much like a veteran of recent battle action that the barber bribed him with a quarter to go elsewhere to convalesce. Rex lay most of the night in a vacant lot. In the morning he again presented himself to the chief master-at-arms and was accepted without further delay.

Fifteen new enlistees were being shipped to the Brooklyn Navy Yard. Rex was the youngest, but the others had enlisted as coal-passers so Rex was put in charge. All papers were given into his keeping, including vouchers for meals in the dining car. When the steward saw that Rex controlled the vouchers, he told him he could eat what he liked. The menu offered a choice of dishes which hitherto Rex had savored only in his imagination. He selected a meal that would have made Henry VIII loosen his waistband. But when the meal arrived it was King Midas whom Rex identified with. He couldn't eat. His tonsils had come out three days before. He was still at the milk and gruel stage of his convalescence. He edged back to his berth out of sight of his amused charges and cried with frustration.[2]

Rex had enlisted as landsman for yeoman. The yeoman school to which he was sent was on board the *Hancock*, a ship permanently moored in the Brooklyn Navy Yard. That was his home during his first six weeks in the navy, before he was transferred to the *Franklin* at Norfolk when the yeoman school moved there. In that interval Rex undertook to satisfy himself on several points. He checked out the color of the ocean. Though blue and green predominated, it was many tints and hues. He was disappointed to find it so indefinite after the trouble he had taken earlier to settle the matter. It was also too flat. Later, he wished it was still flatter because, once he put to sea, he found that even a moderate roll made him seasick.

On his first leave Rex had several things to check out. He began with the Flatiron Building, then the tallest building in New York. From the top of it he could see the whole city. Next: "I went across to the New Jersey Palisades and pretended I was Lucien de Rubempré, the hero in *Les Illusions Perdues.* I had read about twenty of Balzac's novels; my father had a set." He also had some cultural explorations to undertake. He had read a life of Beethoven and decided he liked classical music, although he had never heard any. A visit to the Philharmonic satisfied him that he did like it. He went to the Met and found he liked grand opera too.

At yeoman school Rex was taught navy bookkeeping. After two months, a request came from President Theodore Roosevelt's yacht, the *Mayflower,* for a pay-yeoman. Rex's schooling had another month to run, but Chief Petty Officer Trigere, who was in charge of the school, picked Rex for the assignment. Rex had rescued Trigere's dog when it fell off the *Franklin.* That gained Rex points. But the crucial factors were his bookkeeping competence and mental alertness.

Not only was the *Mayflower* a place where the President came to take his ease; it provided a secure and relaxed environment where Roosevelt could meet with cabinet officials and other high members of government as well as with distinguished private citizens and foreign visitors. It was 183 feet long, and could do 20 knots. It had a crew of 145. It already had served several Presidents, and the festive atmosphere that sometimes existed on board had drawn predictable comments. Grover Cleveland told William Allen White: "What infernal lies they told! Said that I was drunk aboard the *Mayflower.* That was their favorite slander."[3] Roosevelt supplied no occasion for such criticism. He liked a well-run ship and his officers saw that he got it. Even Rex, who had a compulsive interest in order, thought there was too much "spit and polish" discipline aboard. The chief instigator was the executive officer, Lieutenant Chauncey Shackford. The officers of the *Mayflower* later would furnish Rex models for his constabulary.

During his first eight months aboard the *Mayflower* Rex usually was seasick. Then, "it just quit." During that time, with the paymaster's approbation, he began sleeping in the pay office on a roll-up mattress. He ought to have been sleeping below deck in a hammock. The chief boatswain's mate resented this breach of regulations by Yeoman Stout but could do nothing to prevent it. While the mate fumed, Rex gloated. He gloated too, to learn that his problem was not unique. Roosevelt was also a poor sailor. Once, going through the Windward Passage in a howling hurricane, Roosevelt had had to stay flat for eight hours. Rex matched him hour for hour. On a later occasion Roosevelt sailed to Panama on the battleship *Indiana,* rather than the *Mayflower,* because the heavier ship could be depended on to pitch less.

One officer aboard the *Mayflower*, Lieutenant (Junior Grade) G. J. Rowcliff, was unspeakable. Rex told me: "He was an invariable stinker. He was supercilious even with veteran CPO's, and the crew's hope that he would fall overboard was unanimous." Rex conceded that Rowcliff was the real-life double of Lieutenant George Rowcliff, the obnoxious police officer in New York's Homicide South, who, after a battle that raged over decades, finally was given his all-time comeuppance in *Please Pass the Guilt* (1973).

One of Rex's duties on the *Mayflower* was to audit the bills which Roosevelt incurred giving parties, receptions, and banquets on board, and to decide whether the food, champagne, and cigars should be paid for out of the President's own purse or out of a fund Congress set aside for official functions. Rex himself sometimes got to sample the presidential provender because he was on excellent terms with the Chinese cooks and stewards who supplied Roosevelt's table.

Inevitably, Rex's presence on the *Mayflower* put him in the company of many of the notables who were the President's guests. Though curious about them, he could talk with Taft, or Roosevelt himself, and not be overawed. Lucetta's Quaker precepts had done their work.

The Roosevelts often used the *Mayflower* for trips along the coast: Boston, Philadelphia, and New York. Even if Rex had had an exalted opinion of Roosevelt, experience would have altered it. The sight of Roosevelt strutting about the decks of the *Mayflower*, his aides scampering to keep pace, stayed in Rex's memory. In *Golden Remedy*, written nearly twenty-five years after Rex left the navy, he causes one man, about to join another in a walk, to say: "I'll go along. If I can keep up! I'm no T. R."[4]

Rex did not find Roosevelt unreasonable. On one occasion when the crew and junior officers put on an entertainment for Roosevelt and his guests, the President found himself being mocked by a clever mimic. He led the laughs. When he did get angry, provocation was ample. That happened once when a drunken sailor walked in on a midnight conference and sought to make him a gift of a squealing pig. And again, when a guest began bestowing intimate pats and pinches among the cabinet wives.

Only once was Rex himself the target of presidential wrath. In the spring of 1907 the *Mayflower* carried out a naval review on the James River. Cruisers and battleships lined up and fired twenty-one-gun salutes as the *Mayflower* steamed past. Roosevelt, flanked by his staff and senior officers, stood on the bridge, raising his top hat to each ship as a prelude to its salute. While this maneuver was under way, Roosevelt's two young sons, Quentin and Archie, ages nine and twelve, were in the keeping of Rex and his closest navy buddy, Yeoman Wallace W. Whitecotton — a non-Morman from Provo, Utah — who ran the ship's canteen. Their job was to keep the boys entertained below deck. This they managed effectively for a time by catching fleas and imprisoning them in matchboxes with the promise that they would glue threads to them and make them drag about the matchboxes as though they were miniature coaches. Unhappily, their own engrossment with this activity surpassed that of their charges. The boys disappeared. Quentin made his way to the bridge, watched until his father doffed his topper, then snatched it and scampered below deck with it, where he hid with his prize till the review was concluded. In Roosevelt's opinion Rex and Wallace merited the darbies, but he let them off with a verbal rebuke.

Occasionally the men themselves set an example for mischief which Archie and Quentin could only stand in awe of. At a Caribbean port several of them smuggled on board ship, under their jackets, a total of nine monkeys and twenty parrots. Rex told me: "Wallace Whitecotton and I took two parrots and a monkey aboard. We traded cigarettes for them — ten cigarettes for a parrot and twenty for a monkey." When the *Mayflower* was a hundred miles at sea, this assortment of wildlife was given liberty. The last of the menagerie was not rounded up till ten hours later.

Fate had chosen to put under Rex's observation, in the expansionist era, the man most responsible for the character of that era. In the future Rex's instincts would place him always close to the pulse of events, so that in his own history the history of his times could be read. Yet in Theodore Roosevelt, Rex Stout found no pattern of conduct which he cared to follow, unless perhaps, in his speech. Rex came out of the navy with an un-Quakerish talent for swearing in a loud voice — profanely but never obscenely — and the habit would stay with him for a lifetime.

Roosevelt saw himself as a patron of letters. At various times he heaped accolades on Edwin Arlington Robinson, James B. Connolly, Ernest Thompson Seton, and Rudyard Kipling. And he invited Sir Arthur Conan Doyle to come to America and be his guest at the White House. Rex Stout was not influenced by Roosevelt's preferences. He had read too much before coming into the navy, for that. In fact, he scorned the judgment of a man who had dismissed Thomas Paine as "a dirty little atheist." Roosevelt was apt to leave books lying around on the *Mayflower*, and Rex "swiped four or five detective stories" — works by Anna Katharine Green, Israel Zangwill, and Godfrey Benson. He doubted that their influence on him amounted to much. Rating the Presidents, Rex placed Roosevelt "in the first ten, but not the first five."

During his time on the *Mayflower*, Rex put in twenty-thousand miles at sea. That included four visits to Puerto Rico, two to Guantánamo — though not during maneuvers — and visits to Havana, the Canal Zone, French Guiana, Barbados, Port-au-Prince, Martinique, and the Argentine coast.[5] "We once stopped," he said, "I forget why, at a little town on the Florida coast called Miami." On a visit to Havana, Rex procured a supply of Carbajal cigars, acquiring a taste which his pocket-book, for many years after, would not allow him to indulge. In 1907, the *Mayflower* honored a Mardi Gras at New Orleans. It supplied the sole occasion in Rex's life when he was "really owled." He told me: "Tuesday afternoon I went ashore in uniform. Wednesday, at noon, I awoke in an elegant bedroom, clad in a Mother Hubbard."

Rex's most spectacular extraterritorial adventures in the navy occurred at San Pedro de Macorís, Santo Domingo, in 1907. When Wallace Whitecotton told him that flamingos brought top dollar in New York zoos, Rex decided they should take some home. For about three hours, one afternoon, covered with burlap, Rex lurked behind a boulder in the surf, just outside San Pedro, waiting for a flamingo to make itself available. When he at last caught one by the leg, the bird used its claws and beak to cut deep gashes in his hands and face. Only by engulfing the bird in his burlap did he save his eyes and his prey. That night, when Walter and he, "bloody with scratches and bruises," tried to smuggle their prize on board, they got stopped at the top of the gangway.

Another day, nemesis again sought out Rex in Santo Domingo. He took a detail ashore to buy fresh vegetables for the crew. Whitecotton came along. They bartered well. For example, they got three hundred fine big avocados for seventy-five cents. Their quest took them a couple of miles inland where rebels were actively pursuing an uprising. When they passed a group of the rebels taking their ease in a ravine below the road, Wallace tried out a few Spanish curses, lately acquired. The rebels seemed to take no notice of him. Shortly afterward, however, Rex saw one of them, gun in hand, peering at them around the corner of a shed. Wallace chucked a green banana at him. The rebel fired and the bullet caught Rex in the left calf. Back on the *Mayflower*, the ship's doctor, Lieutenant Karl Ohnesborg — on whom Taft's daughter Helen had a crush — found that the bullet had missed the bone.

Rex had no recollection of carrying orchids back to the *Mayflower* from various Caribbean ports of call, although he had no doubt that he saw orchids for the first time while on *Mayflower* duty. Even if he was not laden down usually with monkeys, parrots, or flamingos, when returning to the ship, he would not have brought an orchid on board. He told me: "I have never been especially interested in orchids."

Had there been some way of cultivating orchids on board ship, nonetheless, Rex might have been tempted to try because he had found someone who could wear an orchid and dominate it. On one of the *Mayflower*'s visits to New York, he had gone to a Broadway show, *Winsome Winnie*, starring the lovely soprano Julia Sanderson. Julia was just emerging into a prominence that would keep her in starring roles on Broadway for a quarter of a century and on radio as a starring performer for many years after that. Rex wrote her "an elegant mash note." Julia was charmed and accepted his invitation to dinner. Their dinner dates became the high points of his subsequent visits to New York. One of his gifts to her was a copy of Omar Khayyam's *Rubáiyát* which he had had bound in white leather with her name printed in gold leaf on the cover. At eighty-eight Rex would say, "My memory of her dainty loveliness is still vivid." Julia, at eighty-six, told me, "I recall a charming young boy. I was his 'dream-girl.' He told me of his love in both verse and prose."[6]

Among photos taken on the *Mayflower* is one of Rex wearing a football uniform complete down to cleats. An M is prominent on his jersey. The photo was taken in the ship's pay office. The football career which he had not had at Topeka High had come his way in the navy. In the fall of 1906, the *Mayflower*'s football team won nine of the thirteen games it played, most of them against teams representing other Navy ships. Rex played end. The Washington *Post* ran his picture and acclaimed him "the best end in the Navy."

Horse racing gave Rex his moment of greatest trial in the navy. Acting on an inside tip, the crew of the *Mayflower* got together a purse of $1,100 to bet on a long shot in a steeplechase at a Maryland track. Rex was sent to place the bet. At the track he made fresh inquiries, which convinced him the horse was anything but a sure winner. He did not place the bet. For three-quarters of the race, the horse showed its heels to the other horses. Then, at the last barrier, the runaway long shot fell and broke a leg. When Rex returned each man his original investment, one and all applauded his discretion. For his part, he knew he had, by the skin of his teeth, escaped a keelhauling. His education had taken a giant step forward.

Rex's best source of income in the navy was card playing. To Quakers playing cards were "the devil's picture book." But Lucetta Stout, finding no harm in them, had let her children play cards at will. In the navy, Rex at first had amused himself with solitaire. Then he found that whist was his game. Rex's immediate superior, Lieutenant Graham Montrose Adee, paymaster of the *Mayflower*, was the nephew of Alvey Augustus Adee, Second Assistant Secretary of State and the true power in the State Department. Graham and Rex got on well. "He was competent," said Rex, "but I did all the work. It took an average of around thirty hours a week." Several times Graham took Rex to dinner with him at Alvey's house. Alvey, a published Shakespearean scholar, took a liking to the young yeoman who could quote Shakespeare's sonnets by heart, and taught him whist. Rex told me: "One day he came to lunch on the *Mayflower* and insisted on playing whist in the wardroom with Graham, an ensign whose name I have forgotten, and me. Of course that was against regulations, but Commander Andrew T. Long, who commanded the *Mayflower*, liked Alvey A. Adee and permitted it. Alvey did this several times, and the second time he wrote 'Pay Clerk' on a piece of paper and pinned it on me. A pay clerk is a warrant officer and on a ship too small to have a warrant officers' mess, a warrant officer ate in the wardroom. The Chief of Naval Operations was not notified that I had been made a pay clerk."

As far as whist playing went, Rex's unofficial pay clerk rank bothered no one. The *Mayflower* had seven commissioned officers. Once Adee set the precedent, Rex regularly made up the eighth for two tables of whist. His salary was $26.20 a month. At whist, in an average month, he picked up another $150.

In terms of his own intellectual growth, Rex's friendship with Alvey A. Adee was more important than his encounters with Roosevelt. Adee was Second Assistant Secretary of State for thirty-six years and could have risen higher had he not chosen to stay in that post. Adee shaped the character of the State Department and gave continuity to its operations. A bachelor, he read constantly and for recreation sought the company of his nieces and nephews. When the pressure was on, he slept on a cot in his office. Perhaps it was Alvey's sleeping habits that disposed Graham to let Rex sleep in the pay office. But that was not the only point of likeness between Rex and the eccentric diplomat. Adee had a powerful addiction to exact word choice. During his time in office he wrote thousands of State Department memos and communiqués. Few documents came from the department which did not pass under his hand. Although he introduced the typewriter into the State Department and sent out the first diplomatic documents typed by any government, the style of all State Department documents, by his decree, was kept scrupulously pure. Moreover, Adee had a genius for summing up lengthy documents in one succinct paragraph. Further, he was a mathematician and the editor of an annotated text of *Hamlet*. His genius, his reclusive ways, his omniscience, his splendid table — "It seemed elegant to me," Rex told me, "but I was young and hungry" — and pronounced preferences all impressed Rex, and reinforced the direction in which his own mind moved.

Of Adee, Rex said: "He was quiet, articulate but not gabby, pleasant, well read and well informed. Ninety percent of my time with him we were playing whist." Adee was not only a purveyor of standards which Rex could wish to uphold, he augmented the image of genius Emily Todhunter had given Rex and supplied details which, sifted through Rex's creative consciousness, would in time contribute to his portrait of Nero Wolfe.

While Rex was cleaving the Caribbean, or chasing after the President's hat, or cutting the deck for a round of whist with the Second Assistant Secretary of State, things had not stood still in Topeka. Rex's brother Walt had married Gertrude Cathers and was traveling for the Calumet Company. Juanita Stout and Wally Roddy, with whom she had eloped early in October 1906, now were living with Wally's mother and aunt.[7] Mary, Elizabeth, and Donald still were at home with Lucetta. But Mary was working for the *Capital* and Elizabeth was in her senior year in high school and making plans to go to Washington, D.C., to nursing school. John, still selling the *Britannica*, was home rarely.

May seemed to be the one member of the family committed to Topeka. She was in practice with Dr. Harding and in popular demand as a lecturer. In November 1906, the *Capital* gave two columns to a lecture, "The Relation of Food to Health," which she delivered before the Indian Creek Grange. A photograph of May accompanied the article. In her talk May deplored food faddism but cited its rise as proof of new public awareness of the importance of diet. She suggested that most health problems would cease if people would fletcherize (the practice of masticating food thoroughly, promoted by Horace Fletcher, a New York physician). She drove home her point with a startling paraphrase of John Philpot Curran: "Eternal vigilance becomes the price of rational mastication." Chewing had found a powerful new champion.

The fall of 1906 found Ruth still in Indianapolis. Bob, ever restive, was in Canton, Ohio, where, the previous July, his wife, Tad, had given birth to a daughter, Natalie, the first Stout grandchild. Ruth several times had written to Lucetta urging her to move the rest of the family to Indianapolis. Abruptly, in midautumn, Lucetta went, taking Donald with her but leaving Betty in May's care, so that she could finish out her senior year at the high school. Mary promised to join them in January.

The move to Indianapolis put Lucetta within easy run of Wilmington and her mother, at Hackberry Hall. But this advantage was one she enjoyed only briefly. Emily died on 19 December.

The Wilmington press would, with admiration, recall Emily Todhunter as a "stately" woman, dressed always in "soft gray" in compliance with Quaker custom, and surrounded invariably by "the flowers she loved." Her funeral was held on Friday afternoon, 21 December. The next morning she was buried beside Amos at Walnut Creek. After a hundred years all that remained of the Todhunters at New Martinsburg was their dust moldering in that bit of ground they had given to the Lord when their bright day of promise was new.

When Rex got word of his grandmother's death he asked for and was granted a leave extending through the holidays. He went home to Topeka. There, in the last days of the old year, he gave an interview to the *Daily Capital*, which, with a photograph, was spread over three columns of the front page of the paper on 13 January 1907. The headline, "TOPEKA BOY CRUISES WITH PRESIDENT," was followed by five subheads: "Rex Stout is on Yacht *Mayflower*," "Is in the Paymaster's Office There," "HE AUDITS THE BILLS," "Decides Who Shall Pay for Drinks," "Sees Much of the Roosevelt Family."

In a later era, Rex's chattiness would have earned him a transfer to the Aleutian winter patrol. In that happy day, the story probably went no farther than Topeka. Rex had discussed the President's champagne bills. He had revealed that the President was a poor sailor. He had rehearsed the peccadillos of the Roosevelt children.

Rereading the interview nearly seventy years later, Rex laughed. "What a damn fool I must have been," he said. "Why did I say those things? I was still in the Navy."

Rex was determined to let Topeka know he was prospering. In the interview, he spoke of his prowess as a member of the *Mayflower*'s football team. He identified the embroidered gun cannon on the sleeve of his jacket as an insigne showing he had qualified in marksmanship as a gun pointer. He explained that while on temporary duty abroad the battleship *Illinois* he used his friendship with the officer in charge of heavy gun target practice, to get clearance to aim one of the six-inch guns. Out of five targets, he hit four, a percentage of eighty, which entitled him to the rank of gun pointer. Rex's subsequent recollection was that this story itself was pure embroidery.[8]

Rex further identified himself to the Topeka interviewer as the ranking enlisted man on the *Mayflower*. This carried prerogatives. "Every year," he told the interviewer, "the crew of the *Mayflower* gives an elaborate ball in Washington, using the huge ballroom in the Washington Navy Yard." "This ball," he said, "is one of the social events of the season at Washington. Every member of the Congress, the President, heads of departments, foreign ambassadors, etc. are invited. . . . The President leads the grand march." He himself, he revealed, would head the receiving line at the *Mayflower* crew's next ball, in the coming March.

Some of Rex's former classmates now were studying law or medicine, or preparing for careers in teaching, in government, or the church. Others were emerging to prominence in prospering family businesses, or dreaming of great harvests if only Nature did its part. Some of them (amused, no doubt, that Rex's precociousness had carried him no further) had wondered why "Mr. Brilliance" had settled for the anonymous life of a mere yeoman in the United States navy. Rex's disclosures to the *Capital* interviewer were meant to disconcert all such sniggerers. Few of them would have heard of Baron Munchausen.

But the visit home was an occasion for stocktaking for Rex also. Before leaving Topeka he made a nostalgic visit to the site of the Crawford Opera House. On the morning of 29 September, the building had been destroyed by a natural-gas explosion and fire. His alma mater had vanished.

With Rex gone back to the navy and the holidays ended, Mary was ready to join her mother, Ruth, and Donald in Indianapolis. She spent her last day in Topeka with the Overmyers, at their Quincy Street home. Early in December, the elder David had had pneumonia, to which was added the complications of chronic diabetes. By 28 December he felt well enough to walk to the Auditorium to hear Bryan speak and to confer with him afterward. A relapse followed a few days later. But now he was on the mend again. That day he had received visits from three judges, from members of the secretarial staff of the state Democratic headquarters, and others. And he ate a hearty meal with his family, and with Mary and May. May and Dr. Harding had been attending him through his illness. He was affable as he saw Mary off, and Grace and May, who were accompanying her to the station.

When May and Grace got back to the house at 8:30 P.M., they found Mrs. Overmyer distraught. David had gone into the bathroom and had not come out. When she called he didn't answer. At May's urging, young David broke in the door. May found her patient sprawled on the floor. All vital signs were gone.[9] The day May was born, David had celebrated his twenty-ninth birthday. Now, at fifty-nine, he was dead. How quickly life goes by, May thought. Doors seemed to be closing all around her. In the same hour Mary and Mr. Overmyer had gone out of her life by different exits.

On 8 July 1907, while the *Mayflower* was visiting New York, Rex asked permission to buy his discharge, an option open to men who had served at least two years of their four-year enlistment. In his application he said he had wanted to go to law school when he completed high school, but that his father had balked, "saying he was unable to pay the expenses of a course, and that he intended having [Rex] learn the ranching business on his ranch at Richland, Kansas." That fate he had escaped by joining the navy. Now a letter had come from Rex's brother Bob, in which he declared that he was willing to pay Rex's expenses through a law school in Cleveland, provided Rex could obtain his discharge from the navy in time to attend a summer preliminary.

The letter, Rex told me, was, in its entirety, an exercise in fiction. Yet it served its purpose. The skipper, Commander Long, gave his approval and described Yeoman Stout as "an excellent man," who had met his duties "honestly, faithfully, and cheerfully." Indeed, his health record for the two years and twenty-four days he served in the Navy showed he had not been on the sick list once during that interval. On payment of the sum of $80, Rex was released from the *Mayflower* at New York, on 5 August.

While in the Navy, Rex, unlike many sailors, never had himself tattooed. "Tattoos," he told me, "are too immutable." That verdict paralleled his estimate of the navy. The narrow cycle of events possible for the *Mayflower* seemed fixed and ineradicable. He wanted to know the world on his own terms.

On 4 September 1907, Commander Long wrote a two-page letter to the Secretary of the Navy. The subject of the letter was Rex Stout. As his last official act in the navy, Yeoman Stout had entered in the receipt cash book, opposite the names of men down for monthly money, substantial boosts in pay. The money was paid out before Graham Adee realized what had happened. When the discovery was made, there was pandemonium on board the *Mayflower* — just the kind of confusion, in fact, that every serviceman dreams of leaving in his wake. Rex's explanation for what he had done needs no elaboration. "I was thumbing my nose," he told me. The years would mellow him some. In 1973, he was pleased when, sixty-six years after he left the navy, Roy Stratton, husband of novelist Monica Dickens, wrote to tell him that he had been made an honorary member of the Yeoman School Alumni Association. Just possibly the honor would have come sooner had his fellow yeomen known he had cooked the books in 1907.[10]

12.

Logic and Life

Nero Wolfe is only one of the reflections of Rex's remarkable makeup. In many ways he is a road-company Leonardo. He is an autodidact, whose general knowledge of literature, music, history, and politics is on a level superior to that of many professors of the subject. He is one of the half dozen best conversationalists I have encountered. He is probably one of the ablest propagandists since Tom Paine. I have no doubt he could turn his hand to almost anything that the occasion required. Like his pioneer ancestors, he is a practical generalist, as skillful with his hands as he is versatile with his brain.

— CLIFTON FADIMAN

The day Rex left the navy, he took a train to Cleveland, where Bob was assistant sales manager with the May Company, Cleveland's biggest department store. His compulsion to bring harmony to the world by the suasions of reason given impetus by his years under navy discipline, Rex decided now that he wanted to study law after all. As a lawyer he would "be in a good strategic position for abolishing all injustice everywhere." Sympathetic to his aims, Bob got Rex a night job, as a window dresser with the May Company, to leave his days free. His solvency thus assured, Rex began to read law at a law office on Euclid Avenue. He stayed at it for just two months. Being a lawyer, he decided, was "much too low-down a profession for an honest man." Time would mellow this view. "I really have no antipathy toward lawyers," Rex told me; "it's just that the nature of their profession makes nearly all of them overly cautious and pernickety."[1]

When Rex stepped out of the law office on Euclid Avenue, he stepped into Louis Klein's tobacco store, a few doors away. There he was taken on as a salesman. Klein told Rex to smoke as many cigars as he wanted to. He liked contented employees. Klein did not reckon with the taste for Carbajals which Rex had acquired in Havana. When he took inventory at the end of the month he thought he might have to file for bankruptcy. To defend his conduct Rex summoned forth all his skills as a master debater. But this was not a mere matter of who slid down a haystack. Logic was on his side. Klein wasn't. He was fired.

Fresh disaster struck early in the new year, when Bob collapsed from overwork. Pneumonia developed, and for days he was delirious. Rex now revealed a hitherto unsuspected potential. He was a genius around the sickbed. Though Bob and he would later be estranged, Bob always remembered Rex's dedication through that harrowing time. "He never left my side day or night," Bob said. "He nursed me a teaspoonful at a time." When Bob was convalescent, for hours on end the two brothers told one another stories — not merely accounts of their experiences, but stories in which the storyteller's art played a part. "I have always been a better than average oral storyteller," Rex conceded.[2]

Advised by the May Company's Dr. Prince never again to bind himself to a job that had confining hours, Bob moved his family on to New York, ready to make a start at something else. Rex had taken a job as bookkeeper with the Cleveland Street Railway Company, so he stayed behind. His job was to process transfers and conductors' reports. He was one of four men who did this work. He was not ten minutes on the job when that quirk in his nature which impelled him to summon order out of chaos told him he would be perpetuating an absurdity if he didn't put the work he was doing on an efficient basis. The transfers had to be sorted. If they were kept in order to start with, one man could do everything. The human hurt that could result from his plan never entered into his calculations. He told his boss, "You are paying four of us now to do this job. That's a hundred and twenty dollars. If I do it alone, will you double my salary?" The boss liked the idea and fired the other three bookkeepers. Rex was honestly surprised when the men he had reorganized out of their jobs waylaid him that night as he was walking home in the winter dusk and beat him up. That ended this adventure as a time and methods engineer. He was afraid to go back to the office again.

At this point, Rex put his own conduct under review. He concluded that other men generally did not share his capacity for indulging in and acting upon feats of inexorable logic. He could work still for the ultimate triumph of order, but he must never again forget to allow for the limitations which bound the intellects of others.

From Cleveland, Rex now set out on a rambling tour that took him through several states before he joined Bob and Tad in New York in the summer. He worked as he went. For three weeks he was a bellhop in Indianapolis. For another three weeks he was a motorman in Springfield, Illinois. For two weeks he worked on a tugboat at Norfolk, Virginia. He stayed no place long because no place held for him the appeal New York did.

Rex was back in New York only a short time before he saw a way to make a start on his writing career.[3] A presidential election was in the offing and Taft was the Republican nominee. When Rex read that Taft was visiting New York and staying at the Hotel Manhattan, he went to the *World* building and told the Sunday editor he had access to Taft and to Tom Loftus Johnson, Cleveland's famous reform mayor, who was also in New York and was a front runner for the Democratic nomination. He said he could procure authentic palm prints of both men, and supply character analyses based on the prints, if the *World* would publish them. The editor agreed and Rex spent his last few dollars on paper and camphor. With each sheet carefully smoked with burning gum of camphor, he went to the Manhattan and sent up word to Taft that former Yeoman Stout, of the *Mayflower,* wanted to see him on urgent business. Taft received him and, with gusto, clapped his hand into the sooty mess. Then he urged the other guests in his suite to give Rex a souvenir handprint. Rex barely salvaged the carbonized sheet needed for Johnson's print. With the two essential prints in custody, he put together his Sunday feature, taking care to assure readers that both men were kind, capable, and good to their mothers. The *World* paid him two hundred dollars. He knew that his ingenuity, not his prose, brought him this windfall. But he had an article in print. That was something.[4]

Even as Rex was experiencing this modest upturn in fortune, on another family frontier tragedy was building. In May 1908, shortly after her thirty-second birthday, May Stout visited the family in Indianapolis. Mary, then nineteen, was ill and local doctors were making no progress toward a cure. May recommended diet changes and the invalid soon was recovering. But May herself was unhappy. Their patients preferred her to Dr. Harding, and Dr. Harding resented it. The younger Stouts never had liked Dr. Harding and had made it a game, when talking about her, to call her "all kinds of names always trying to use the word 'hard.'" Juanita wrote Lucetta now: "Everyone in Topeka is talking about how Dr. Harding is going to ruin May's career if she can."

In Indianapolis, May said merely that she thought Dr. Harding would use the excuse of her absence to end their association. She talked of going into nursing. Finally, she asked Ruth to get her a job with the telephone company. Ruth refused. She did not want May to abandon her medical career. Pursuing her usual policy, Lucetta did not intervene. May misunderstood. She thought the family was washing its hands of her. Sensitive and upset, she went back to Topeka. As she had foreseen, Dr. Harding dropped her. To complete her isolation, she resigned from the Topeka Board of Health. She then enrolled for courses at Chicago Medical College, thinking that new responsibilites would help her regain her self-confidence. But Chicago was in the grip of a heat wave. After a few oppressive days there, she changed her plans and went to Denver to be with Aunt Alice. In Denver May wrote constantly. The stack of penciled sheets in the old bell-topped trunk grew and grew. Once she said darkly, "All Todhunters think they can write but none has been successful." (That was true even of Lucetta. "She liked to write," Rex told me. "I don't know if she ever offered anything for publication. She wrote me long letters when I was in the navy, but I didn't save them.")

One day May's topic was poisons. She told her teenage cousin, Adda, that she had read widely on the subject. She said that when one was really through with life it was not a bad idea to find a way out. She knew, she said, of a poison impossible to detect. She told Adda she felt she had been idle too long and should do some nursing. But her health troubled her. Her hands and face were breaking out in large brown spots.

At noon, on the last day of September, Alice found May senseless on her bed. Alice ran a block and a half down Broadway for Dr. Thulin. He found May dead of heart failure.

May once had visited Fairmont Cemetery in Denver, with Adda, to see the Gothic chapel there, which Uncle Bradley — a stonecutter by trade — considered his best work. She read many of the inscriptions on the markers, and said, "The only thing I would want is 'God Knows.' " She was buried at Fairmont. Bradley himself fashioned her stone. His eyes were wet as he cut the words "God Knows Best."[5]

Topeka papers reported May's death four days later. The announcement was made by Dr. Harding, to whom Betty Stout, without comment, had forwarded Alice's telegram. The *Journal* reported that May had been "a woman of unusual physical vigor."[6]

13.

A Brownstone in New York

Rex Stout has been one of the great pleasures of my last half century. He is, of course, *sui generis*. One of the most extraordinary human beings I have ever had the privilege of knowing.

— JEROME WEIDMAN

In 1965, when Rex Stout touched eighty, Jacques Barzun said in tribute: "Archie is the lineal descendant of Huck Finn. . . . Not since Mark Twain and Mr. Dooley has the native spirit of comedy found an interpreter of equal force."[1] Barzun's assessment was not farfetched. An ardent Twainian from boyhood, Rex himself surmised that, in some fashion, he fell within the Twainian tradition. Early in 1909 that influence possibly was quickened. Booth Tarkington was in New York and invited Rex to join a friend and himself for lunch at Delmonico's. When Rex got there he found that Tarkington's other guest was Twain. To his disappointment, however, Twain and Tarkington had just one topic: the new copyright law. It satisfied neither of them. Rex could not have cared less.

Forty-five years later, a President of the United States, with Rex at his elbow, would sign into law copyright legislation which Rex had taken a major role in steering through Congress. While Rex carried away from the Twain-Tarkington luncheon none of the clear directives he thought might come from it, it had been, after all, a fecundating experience. Who can put limits on the growth that began then?

Early in October 1909, Ruth got a letter from Rex. He had been working as a bookkeeper for *Phamaceutical Era and Soda Fountain* at eighteen dollars a week. Discovering that the magazine's advertising man was making eighty a week, he began bringing in advertising on his own, for extra income. When the adman found out, Rex was bounced.

A pattern was emerging. Rex was losing jobs not because of want of zeal but because of want of restraint. In the business world, apparently, it was dangerous to think for yourself. The last paragraph in Rex's letter, however, was the one that really held Ruth's attention: "If you and Mary can manage the train fare," it read, "bring Mother and Donald and come to New York. Only let me know a few days in advance so I can reserve a table for dinner. Which shall it be: Sherry's or Delmonico's?"

Before the week was out the Indianapolis Stouts told the furniture company to come to repossess its furniture, and moved from their apartment into one large room, where they went back to living Kansas-style, bathing in a washtub. They did not want to wait a minute longer than they had to, to get to New York. "Christmas in New York" became their rallying cry.

Over the next seven weeks not a nickel was spent without turning it over twice. Austerity worked, and on a dark Saturday afternoon, on the last day of November, the train that brought the last of the Stouts out of Indiana pulled into Penn Station. Bob and Rex were there on the platform, waiting. The next day Rex would be twenty-three. Looking back sixty-five years later, Ruth said: "I felt a strange little stab of pain when I looked at Rex, for that chubby little fellow, whose hair needed pulling every now and then, was gone forever. Here was a good-looking young man who would never, whatever difficulty arose, yell 'Shut up' at you. You could bet on that. They called me by my childhood nickname, Poof, which somehow made me want to cry."

When they left the depot, the new arrivals turning their heads this way and that, Bob and Rex looked as proud as if New York had been built to their specifications. Mary's eyes narrowed to dark pinpoints.

"It isn't as wonderful as I thought it would be," she said.

"You can't see it all from here," Rex said.

Bob and Rex had found a furnished apartment for the family at 8 Morningside Avenue. The house was a brownstone, and Lucetta, sitting in the window, would have in full view a park across the street. "It was hard to imagine Mother without some green growing thing at hand," Bob explained. Yet something else green and essential was lacking. They had rented the apartment without a cent to pay for it — and the rent was fifty dollars a month. They had bluffed the agent. Rex had produced his wallet with a flourish only to slap his thigh in annoyance a moment later. "Damn it," he said, "I left my money home." Bob trumped that. "I even left my checkbook at home," he said with astonishment. But the time was at hand when the landlord would be looking for his payment. Rex had signed on as a bookkeeper again and now urged Ruth to take a similar job, "because bookkeepers make more money than secretaries." Ruth protested. She had no head for figures. "Stall when you come to something you don't know," Rex said, "and I'll explain it to you at night." At that point Donald whispered to Ruth, "Tell them what you've got sewed in your corset."

"We saved a little money for New York," Ruth admitted.

"How much?"

"A little over fifty dollars."

Bob and Rex said nothing, but stood up, as though on cue, came across the room to where Ruth and Mary were sitting, and knelt before them. Bob took Mary's hand. Rex took Ruth's. And they solemnly kissed them. Then they got up and found their chairs again in silence.

Before the end of December, Bob got together enough money to move his family into 6 Morningside — the brownstone next door. Rex settled in at Number 8. At this time the Stouts adopted the practice of referring to their houses by street number.

John Stout had been told of the move to New York and had promised to join the family quickly. John was not a good drummer. He was sure he could find something better to do in New York. And so their ranks almost were reformed.

Early in January, Mary got a job with the advertising department of *The New York Times* and Franklin Simon hired Ruth as a ledger clerk. Rex wanted to know how much Ruth would be paid each week. She hadn't asked. He was disgusted. With one accord the family agreed Rex should handle finances. Each Monday Ruth and Mary got carfare for the week. Each day they got twenty-five cents for lunch. Rex held himself to the same budget. This arrangement continued even when John joined them after a few weeks and went to work for a trust company in Jersey City.

Although their means were limited, the Stouts had survived other lean times. For weekends, just as Josiah Franklin had done with his large family, they prepared in advance an agenda of topics for discussion. And on Sunday nights, at dinner, they amused themselves with extemporaneous speeches on unannounced topics, or read aloud short articles or poems on topics chosen the previous Sunday.[2] Donald wrote a funny poem on food which Rex sent to Franklin P. Adams, who printed it in his column in the *Evening Mail,* a precursor of his "Conning Tower." Lucetta's pieces were so unusual that Ruth wanted Rex to send some of them to F. P. A., too. "They're too different," Rex said. "Mother doesn't think like other people. And she's cryptic. Even if F. P. A. got what she was talking about, he'd darn well know his readers wouldn't."

"I always know what she's getting at," Ruth said.

"Don't kid yourself," said Rex.

Their family shows became more important than ever. One night they gave a play at Bob's apartment. The audience sat in the living room. The dining room was the stage. To come on stage Ruth had to pass down the hall and enter the dining room by a side door. As she came along the corridor she was reviewing her lines. There ahead of her the rug was ablaze from a hot ash Bob had dropped. She stepped over the fire and continued on her way. She was on stage declaiming her lines when Bob called out, "There's a fire in the hall!" "Oh, yes," Ruth said, "I saw it when I came in."

On Sundays, by agreement, the icebox was well stocked and everyone ate when he pleased. In that way they all had a free day and got a lot of reading done. One Sunday, thrilled with *The Brothers Karama-zov*, Ruth sighed as evening approached. "My Sunday is almost over," she said. "So is everybody's," Rex said coldbloodedly, and returned to his Macaulay.[3]

At Morningside Avenue Rex saw more of his father than he had in years. In their period of separation Rex had come to manhood. Spirited discussions on the topics of the day now regularly took place between them. Politically, of course, their views were antipodal, and John often fired off letters to the newspapers supporting positions Rex spurned. Yet, at times, John seemed almost eager to have Rex's good opinion.

Ruth, in this period, also became aware of John's desire to hold the good opinion of others. One night, when the heating failed at the evening school where she was giving volunteer time, she brought home a black pupil. When John saw him, even though he was confined to a chair with an infected foot, he pulled himself painfully erect to greet him lest the visitor think he was showing lack of respect.

There was in fact a reason for John's almost morbid reluctance to give offense. His position in the family following his return was distinctly anomalous. When John rejoined his family in 1910, he was ending an exile which, save for brief visits, had lasted nearly a decade. In the interval, Lucetta and the children had learned to cope without him. Moreover, in his absence, that series of major decisions had been taken which had seen the family reestablish itself at last in New York City, a thousand miles and more away from Topeka. On his return John was head of the household in a titular sense only. Goals and ventures were decided upon without reference to his views. This was not astonishing. John never had shown much aptitude for family leadership, even in Topeka. And his decade of absence had been a lost decade in which he had scored no successes. At sixty-three, John was not equipped to pick up with life at the pace it was lived in New York City. In a sense, he had become a ward of his children.

But that was by no means the whole story. John's place now on the periphery of active family life was assured by his curious relationship with Lucetta. Lucetta had been skeptical when John had taken up life as a drummer. Like an Eastern sadhu, he had gone off in middle life for a decade of wandering. During that time he had sunk to the ignominious role of peddling eyeglass lenses. In his absence the burden of decision making, touching the lives of their children, had devolved on Lucetta. Not relishing it, she had stood aside to let events follow their own course. She believed now that her oldest daughter's tragedy could have been averted had fewer responsibilities fallen to her and had John been home to counsel May when her fortunes sagged. After May's death Lucetta stopped speaking to John. His interlude of freedom had come at a cost she could not forgive. She did not resume speaking to him when, once again, he was under the same roof with her. This cruel punishment continued, without remission, until John's death, at eighty-six, in 1933.

John's chastisement, which he bore meekly, complicated his relations with his children. They knew the matter was nonnegotiable with Lucetta and made no attempt to persuade her to relent. By way of compensation, they were quick to commend John's natural dignity, integrity, and devotion to learning. All things considered, however, this amounted to little more than a polite charade contrived to support the illusion that John's self-respect was intact. And it was played out always against the background of Lucetta's uncompromising frigidity — "Ask your father if he'd like another slice of beef." "Tell your mother, no, thank you, I've had my sufficiency."

For Rex this struggle was a source of continuing anguish. How did a fruitful dialogue develop between father and son, when the father had been ousted from his natural place, and the son, by default, had become de facto usurper of some of the father's prerogatives? This crisis came too late in Rex's life to be designated oedipal, but the difficulties it produced were nonetheless genuine and far-reaching. Indeed, they may have contributed to Rex's own wariness, in the years immediately ahead, about choosing a wife and accepting the role of fatherhood.

14.

Literary Apprenticeship

Rex Stout is the epitome of the careful writer. There aren't many of those around these days.

— THEODORE BERNSTEIN

In July 1910, a fire broke out at Number Eight after midnight. Rex was there but could save little from his tiny bedroom. Most of John's books were lost as well as Rex's own library and Lucetta's family papers. Among the books Rex especially lamented the loss of was the copy of the *Maxims* of La Rochefoucauld from his father's library, which he had read and revered in his teens. Although the fire was kept to two rooms and no one was hurt, many things that linked the Stouts to their old life had perished.[1] More than ever they were in a time of new beginnings. But at least those beginnings would be something they would be undertaking together. Walt and Trude had moved to New York from Topeka, and now Juanita wrote to say that all the Roddys were coming to New York to live with Wally's grandfather in Brooklyn.

In the spring of 1910, Rex had taken a job as a barker on a Manhattan sightseeing bus, which began its run from Times Square. It was good training, because visitors soon were coming in from Topeka eager to see the sights with the Stouts, and Rex was able to exude a sense of proprietorship which suggested that he knew every facet of the city's history back to the days when it was the setting for Richard Stout's courtship of Penelope Van Princin.

Among those who showed up that summer was David Overmyer, who had come to New York to study for a year at the Art Students' League. David brought news of Grandma Stout, who was living in Los Angeles with her daughter, Mary Wickersham. Both now were widows.[2]

David took a room with a fellow artist, a short distance from Number Eight. Rex came by often to see him. Sometimes Rex would be wearing an expensive, soft felt hat. A theatrical flair for clothing seemed to have passed from the Swingles down through the Stouts. At Sand Creek, Sophia's brother Charlie, when in his cups, unfailingly dressed up and announced that he was going to the opera. Both John and Bob had found that fashionable attire could work to their advantage in business. One day Rex entered David's fifth-floor room, to discover him staring soulfully out an open window. Feigning contempt, Rex scaled his elegant hat at him. David ducked. The hat spun out the window. "Rex rushed back down the five flights of stairs to recover it," David said, "but he never saw it again."[3]

In that same eventful summer, Rex sold to *The Smart Set* a four-line poem, for which he got ten dollars. When it was published in November, he submitted two more poems, both of which would be published in *Smart Set* in the course of 1911. The first poem, "In Cupid's Family," was a quatrain, and disclosed that Pity's kinship to Love is that of "poor relation." In the second, "Cupid's Revenge," in two nine-line stanzas, the narrator relates that he had taken for his own view Democritus's contention that love between the sexes is "all a joke." He laughed at friends who thought they were in love. Then he fell in love himself. But Cupid made him squirm. The girl he wanted had treated his love as a joke.

The last of Rex's trilogy of love poems, "The Victory of Love," was cast in the form of a dialogue between Love and Philosophy, a blank verse playlet of seventy-one lines, which, unlike the other two poems, owed more to early English "body and soul" dialogues than to Latin verse. Here Love and Philosophy contend for a Soul pledged to Reason. Love vanquishes Philosophy, then confronts the annexed Soul:

> *Courageous thou hast been? Prepare to fear!*
> *In quiet thou hast lived? Thou now*
> *Shall boil in fury!*
> *Thou hast known the placid happiness*
> *Of peaceful contemplation, quiet thought;*
> *But peace and quiet never more shalt know,*
> *And in the days to come shalt measure well*
> *Delights of Paradise and pains of Hell.*[4]

The next poems which Rex sent to *Smart Set* were rejected and not preserved by him, so we don't know what stages he would have added to his Love epic had he been encouraged to continue. Yet that portion of it which survives is enlightening. It begins with a philosophical inquiry into the nature of love, moves to that stage at which Love baffles Reason, and finally to that stage where Love puts Reason to rout. In *Golden Remedy* (1931) Rex would choose as protagonist a man whose passions are short-circuited by Reason — the person he might have been himself had he not learned to make important concessions to Nature and to adopt the pose that Reason is an illusion for some men all of the time and for all men some of the time. Rex's correspondence with Sheila Hibben in 1930 affirms that the problem Love presents in seeming to force a choice between itself and Reason continued to fascinate him, though at the personal level he had long since resolved it.[5] The trio of *Smart Set* poems showed Rex taking on this problem at the theoretical level, and realistically predicting how the struggle must go.

For Rex himself, however, love still lay several years in the future — "I dated four or five girls whose names I have forgotten except Claire Dowsey. I saw her frequently for two or three years because she sang many good songs — a lovely soprano. Nothing serious. Evidently I had decided to make no commitments." Possibly he thought his own reasoning powers would let him subjugate Love to his terms. Certainly he saw no prospect of renouncing his own commitments to Reason. Nero Wolfe would embody Reason kept intact at the expense of full humanity — by eschewing emotional commitments. In that sense Wolfe embodies a position Rex weighed and rejected. As earlier, in Cleveland, he had learned that he must allow for want of Reason in other men, so now Rex understood that he must allow for the presence of emotion in himself.

Possibly Rex's resolve, at this stage of his life, to go on with his probing of the twin enigmas of Reason and Love, was a rationalization designed to hide, even from himself, a caution which family experience had implanted in him. John Stout was twenty-seven when he had married. Even though he sired nine children in the ensuing twenty-one years, his active commitment continued to be to his bookish interests, and these finally became the haven he withdrew into when life withheld the rewards his ambitions sought. In time, as Rex well knew, John's conflicting allegiances had made a shambles of his marriage.

Rex's siblings furnished him a further hard lesson. Bob, Walt, and Juanita had married without making provision for the future. Now all were struggling to catch up. Obviously marriage produced complications which men who set high goals for themselves, as Rex had done, could ill afford. His cultural needs also impeded Rex's progress toward marriage. There was still much he wanted to know about and experience. In the years just ahead he would spend his income on concerts, operas, the theater, sports events, fine restaurants, fine holiday resorts.

Of course all of Rex's reasons for thrusting marriage into the future could be reduced to one basic statement: living haphazardly offended his sense of order.

The *Smart Set* interlude did induce Rex to take a self-inventory. Just enough happened to make him realize that he had to determine in what direction he would henceforth move. He could not go on postponing major decisions. Thus, early in 1911, he set out on a period of nomadism which would see him working in a dozen states in as many months and as a wayfarer visiting curious sites in a score of other states. He struck out roots nowhere. All the while, his mind was turning and shaping events in shifting configurations as he sought a pattern to please him.

Rex was not a vagrant (or "tramp bookkeeper"), as some reports have described him. He was always respectable, never broke, and earned his way. For two weeks he was a plumber's assistant in Pittsburgh. For a month he worked on a shrimp boat out of New Orleans. In New Mexico, east of Santa Fe, on a Navaho reservation, he sold baskets and blankets. He was a pueblo guide in Albuquerque and in Colorado Springs gave the spiel on a sightseeing bus. A bellhop in Spokane, a cook in Duluth, he sold books in Chicago and Butte. He was a ledger clerk in Helena and Laramie, and in St. Louis a hotel manager.

Rex's hotel job was the most substantial job he held during this time of wandering. It was a small, residential hotel, with rooms for sixty guests, most of them either sedate, retired gentlemen or clucking dowagers. To make a favorable impression, Rex laid out $4.50 to rent striped pants and a cutaway. That, his self-assurance, and his evident meticulousness gained him a favorable reception. Since, in fact, he knew nothing about managing a hotel, he took the elevator man and the head telephone operator into his confidence. Both found his coup amusing and agreed to help him. The operator — middle-aged, maternal, and protective — knew the business cold at the administrative level; the elevator man knew equally well its physical operations. When Rex had enough money to leave for New York, after two months, it was not an imposter who left, but a man who knew his job from the ground up. Of this roustabout period Rex said: "I never had any adventures, but I had a lot of episodes. It was not only a good preparation for a writer, but also for life."

When Rex got back to New York he went to work again as a bookkeeper, for the Milbury Atlantic Supply Company. He wanted to put aside money so he could take a room and begin writing in earnest.

Meantime family resources were increasing. The family found roomier quarters at 364 West 116th Street, west of Eighth Avenue. This house, like its predecessor, was a brownstone. It had four floors, a basement kitchen, and a walled-in garden. It was just half a block from Morningside Park. Lucetta had found it. When she called their rental agent and told him to stop looking, he was perturbed. Blacks then were moving into the adjacent side streets. "There's a very undesirable element moving into that section of town," he told Lucetta. "I'm not interested in the element," Lucetta said; "I'll be concentrating on the park."[6]

The rent was higher at the new place and it had more rooms to fill, so when new furniture was bought, including a player piano, there were times when the family stretched the interval between payments. Rex usually covered the gap with a plausible letter. Once a bill came from the piano dealer with a note which read: "Dear Mr. Stout: Will you please send us your check for this amount, or one of your witty notes, telling why you can't? We don't much care which." Thus, hidden from posterity, the name of an anonymous dealer in installment plan furniture stands first on the rolls of Rex Stout's admiring readership.

Having a bigger house meant that the Stouts now could receive friends and kin in comfort. Uncle Oscar Todhunter, looking more than ever like the twin of Chauncey DePew, came for an extended stay. He was now, he disclosed, a Christian Science reader. Adda Burnett came from Denver on a visit. Adda introduced them to Ed Carlson, a young, barrel-chested tenor whose father owned the biggest ice cream factory in Denver. Ed, who was seeking a singing career in New York, was Rex's age. They became boon companions and for six years, until Ed joined the army when the United States entered World War I, went together to operas and concerts. Rex told me: "Asked what man, in all my life, I have most enjoyed being with, I would probably say Ed Carlson. He was as close to faultless as anyone I have ever known." Something of Ed's irrepressible good-naturedness found its way into Rex's characterization of Archie Goodwin.[7]

Another visitor to the Stout household who caught Rex's notice during this interlude was Eugene Manlove Rhodes, a friend of Ruth's. Rhodes wrote stories on the American West for the *Saturday Evening Post*.[8] Finding him pleasant but ordinary, Rex concluded that if Rhodes could make his pen pay, then he could too. Acting on this conviction, early in 1912 he quit his job and began writing in earnest. He sent two stories to *Short Stories* magazine and sold both, for eighteen dollars apiece. To celebrate, he bought Ruth a gold lorgnette.

Short Stories was a Doubleday publication. Initially Rex was content to appear there and in *Lippincott's Monthly* and *The Black Cat*, respectable slicks of the second magnitude. Soon, however, *All-Story* was to monopolize his output. *All-Story* was a Munsey magazine, and in 1912 Frank A. Munsey was the man for the aspiring writer to throw in with. The pulp fiction magazine, then sending shock waves through the publishing world, had originated with Munsey, who began his published career, in 1882, with forty dollars in his pocket, but was able, when he died, in 1925, to leave twenty million dollars to New York's Metropolitan Art Museum.

Beginning with *Argosy*, which he printed on cheap, rough wood-pulp paper, Munsey undersold the popular slicks, such as the *Saturday Evening Post*, *Collier's* and *Everybody's*, and, by the early 1900's, lifted its circulation past the half-million mark. When Street & Smith entered the pulp field with *The Popular Magazine* and *People's Magazine*, Munsey countered with *All-Story* and *Cavalier*. By 1909, the combined monthly circulation of his pulps approached two million. When the enterprise of his competitors began to erode that figure, the innovative Munsey converted *Cavalier* to a weekly and merged it with *All-Story*.

Munsey's weeklies were a success. Although they sold for a dime, an average issue contained 200,000 words of fiction. Often a complete novel appeared in a single issue. Promoted as "family" magazines, they repudiated "tiresome descriptions and baffling dialects." Action, blended with romance and the unexpected, was their special point of excellence.

To prosper, Munsey needed a major talent pool to draw on. He got it by paying writers immediately on acceptance. Among those who achieved recognition through his magazines were O. Henry, Edgar Rice Burroughs, Ludwig Lewisohn, Zane Grey, Octavius Roy Cohen, Max Brand, Ben Ames Williams, Fannie Hurst, Faith Baldwin, Mary Roberts Rinehart, James Branch Cabell, Damon Runyon, Upton Sinclair, and Rex Stout.

By the close of World War I, pulps began to specialize. The multifaceted *All-Story* had had its day, and was merged with *Argosy*. But Rex Stout had come into Munsey's ranks in time to serve a strenuous apprenticeship and to share in *All-Story*'s span of renown.[9]

"Excess Baggage" was published in *Short Stories* in October 1912. Frank Keller, a brash young drummer for a furniture company, is his own narrator, and tells his story with lugubrious candor. Over a period of a dozen years Frank had become the "Secret Sorrow" of some girl in nearly every town along the Hudson River route, from New York to St. Albans. Women, to Frank, were "the most delightful creatures in the world," but none would ever ensnare him. Then he met a Vermont charmer and married her. Now came Frank's glorious comeuppance. Dreiser, in *Sister Carrie*, had compared his drummer, Charles Drouet, to a butterfly. Rex uses the same term to describe Frank. It's a hard reputation to live down. On his next run upriver, everywhere Frank alights he finds some woman waiting for him. Only by putting up at obscure hotels, where he is unknown, can he avoid temptation and hold to his vow to be faithful to his wife. But fate has a lesson in store for him. A Poughkeepsie dealer sends his pulchritudinous niece back to New York in Frank's keeping. Although the niece is forward and vulnerable, Frank, with the aid of apt thoughts from Tennyson, stays true to his wife. But just as the girl is expressing her grudging admiration for his fidelity, his wife spots the couple and is convinced Frank is perfidious. The narrator's idiom, economy, and pace presage the future narrative gifts of Archie Goodwin.

For the situation around which "The Infernal Feminine" develops, Rex went to his own experience. Arnold Stafford, a young lawyer just newly committed to practice, dispatches a mash note, quite as correct and disarming as Rex's note to Julia Sanderson must have been (could it be the same note?), to Betty Blair, a popular musical comedy soubrette whom he has just seen in her latest success, *Winning Winona.* Miss Blair pens a gracious reply and offers to meet Stafford after her Friday performance. At this point fiction takes over as Rex explores a theme he would remain constant to for many years. Stafford thinks of himself as a creature of reason, not emotion. Yet as soon as Miss Blair and he are settled at dinner at the Vanderbilt, he sheds his "cold logic." On a surge of emotion "his heart speaks." He promises to "do anything, go anywhere" for her. With "a cool, calculating eye" the soubrette procures pen and paper and asks Stafford to sign a petition supporting female suffrage. Stafford's infatuation instantly expires.

In December of 1912 Rex published his first crime story — "A Professional Recall" — in *The Black Cat.* His protagonist, Dudd Bronson, is a con man. Three things predispose us to Dudd. As first-person narrator of his own exploits, he speaks with beguiling candor. Second, he has a disarming addiction to malapropisms. And, finally, his victims, two lawyers, are made vulnerable by their own avarice. The double sting at the close is made possible by the emotion of greed routing reason. A fine exemplar of the trickster (or *Till Eulenspiegel*) archetype, Dudd reminds us that Archie Goodwin has elements in his nature which link him to that tradition.

The next month Rex was in *The Black Cat* again, with "Pamfret and Peace," a prophetic vision of the future — and a curious one for a man who would devote his later years to the cause of world peace. Pamfret is a damned soul. After passing sixty years in hell, he is restored to life by Satan, in 1970, as a reward for unspecified services. Pamfret finds himself in a world at peace — but it is a world where peace is maintained by rigid laws and rigid vigilance. He elects to return to hell. Even then Rex knew that a stable social order achieved through forfeiture of basic freedoms came at too dear a price.

At Christmas, in 1912, Rex decided he needed to get away for a while if his writing career was going to get the increased scope it needed. Early in the new year he went to Burlington, Vermont, and took a room in a boardinghouse run by a Mrs. Vail. Mrs. Vail's baked beans were good enough to turn up in an article which Rex wrote for *The American Magazine* forty-four years later. From Mrs. Vail he learned that cooking went by instinct. He disclosed: "By exhaustive interrogation and surveillance, I learned she boasted no secret ingredient, or selection of ingredients. . . . I had to go deeper and I did. She was an artist. Knowing that all beans are not alike, she soaked each batch, not a certain number of hours, but until they looked and felt right. . . . Every detail of the whole process was determined not by rule, but by some inner calculation. Sometimes she left the oven door open a crack for the last two hours, and sometimes she didn't, and when I asked her why, she would only say, 'It's the smell.' "

Mrs. Vail was a good influence for a young writer to be touched by. Her feat of "inner calculation" challenged Rex to aim for new subtleties in his art. Reason set standards and goals but the actual process of creation could not be blueprinted in advance or made to conform to rules. As a writer, Rex never would work from an outline. When an idea came into his head, he would leave the basic ingredients to soak "until they looked and felt right." The nuances of his art came only with the act of writing itself.

In late winter Rex came back to New York with four new stories and the start of a novel, *Her Forbidden Knight*. Before the year was out he would have the stories and the novel in print, and another novel, *Under the Andes*, finished and ready for publication. His stories would be seen that year in *The Black Cat, Short Stories, Lippincott's Monthly, All-Story*, and, to his particular satisfaction, *Smart Set*.

Now he rented a three-room apartment at 311 East Twenty-ninth Street, where he lived alone and wrote in the afternoons and at night. For Rex mornings never were right. Ruth told me he tacked a sign on his bedroom wall: "Christ Has Risen. Why Can't You?" Furthermore, he would leave the alarm clock at the point in the room farthest from his bed, then set up between bed and clock an obstacle course of toppled chairs, tables, and trunks, hoping that by the time he had dodged around them to shut off the alarm he would be enough awake not to want to go back to bed. It seldom sufficed.

In April 1913, "A Companion of Fortune" was published in *Short Stories*. It is set in Rome, and its protagonist, Arthur Churchill-Brown, is an attaché at the British legation. An elegant, mildly irresponsible young diplomat, Churchill-Brown is hoodwinked by two lady visitors who, with quiet resourcefulness, help to bring him to maturity. In due time, in Wodehousean fashion, he makes the proper admissions that he has been "a silly ass," and "jolly fool" who "never did anything worthwhile in [his] life," and the women are satisfied that he has been tamed enough to become the husband of one of them. Even then Arthur's ordeal is not quite over. He is "afraid of his mother" and will not act without her approbation. Even that is not denied him. The girl he loves has been traveling incognito. She is an heiress and quite acceptable to Lady Churchill-Brown. Pace and ambience — Arthur and his lady love tour the Borghese and talk "in hushed tones of Gabriele d'Annunzio" — lift the story slightly above the mundane.

On 4 May 1913 Rex was again the subject of an interview in the Topeka *Capital*. "Writings of Ex-Topeka Boy Win Approval N.Y. Editors," read the caption to the story. In his first year as a writer, the

Capital said, Rex had sold fourteen stories. It said further: "Mr. Stout has had a variety of experiences from which to draw the material for his stories. . . . He has laid the scenes of his stories in New York, Paris, Porto Rico and country towns, and has portrayed diplomats, naval officers, the men and women of the underworld, clerks, 'society' and 'the middle class.' " The interviewer stated that Rex had visited numerous European as well as Caribbean ports, while serving on the *Mayflower*. Rex's fiction-making sometimes spilled over into interviews.

When asked how he had "happened to go into the work of writing stories," Rex replied: "I didn't happen to go into it, unless you consider that phrase a proper substitute for irresistible attraction. I always had it in mind" — even then, he had the debater's habit of taking another's words and handling them with gingerly disdain. He concluded his answer with a sailor's metaphor: "I merely waited till I thought myself close enough to a landing, then jumped." A substantial part of the interview is an excerpt from a letter written to an unidentified Topeka friend (Juana Lord), advising her how to earn her living by her pen in New York.[10]

The *Capital* fixes the start of Rex's writing career as January 1912. It discloses also that in April 1913 he was putting securing touches on a 70,000-word serial which he had already sold. This was *Her Forbidden Knight*, which began appearing in *All-Story* the following August.

"A White Precipitate," one of the briefest of Rex's stories, appeared in *Lippincott's Monthly* in June 1913. A story with a surprise ending, it is, in its tight construction and singleness of purpose, more reminiscent of H. H. Munro ("Saki") than O. Henry. It relies so heavily on dialogue that it is nearly a playlet. Bernard and Paula Reynolds, six months married, have come to a crisis in their marriage. She construes his attention to business as proof that he has married her for her money. Their marriage is a partnership joining his brains to her wealth. Then Bernard shows her the *Morning News*. Her fortune has been swept away. She is penniless. He is glad. He still wants her. Now she must realize he has always wanted her for herself. Bernard is a type Rex approves of — clear-headed, unemotional in a crisis, a man who will use his brains, not to manipulate the emotions of others for pecuniary advantage but to get on honestly in the world.

"The Pickled Picnic" — *The Black Cat*, June 1913 — pits a son who is guided by his emotions against a father who is dominated by his reason, a combination which would become a regular part of Rex's repertoire. James Hamlin decides to go into ward politics to champion the interests of the people against the "industrial pirates." He expects his father, Cyrus Hamlin, to bankroll him, although Cyrus is one of the industrial pirates he is opposing and he has lately antagonized Cyrus by leading a successful strike to unionize one of his mills. Hamlin's day in politics is brief. When he tries to substitute a program of uplift lectures for the ward's annual picnic his constituency evaporates. Better worlds are not built by nincompoops.

"The Mother of Invention" came out in August in *The Black Cat*. William Marston, profligate son of a rich father, finds himself broke in Paris after a summer of high living. His angry father refuses to wire him passage fare home. Under pressure Marston shows he has his father's business acumen. He assumes identity as "Jules Mercade," Parisian palmist, and causes a friend in Philadelphia to paint Mercade's name, profession, and address, in lavish red letters, on the Liberty Bell. The desecration is world news and "Mercade" is arrested in Paris and remanded to America. There Marston is released as the victim of mistaken identity. He is home in time to start the fall term at Harvard, his financier father elated that Bill has at last used his head.

Her Forbidden Knight began appearing in *All-Story* in August 1913 and ran for four months. Despite the hint of naughtiness the title conveyed, Lila Williams, the story's heroine, is a chaste young girl without seductive aspirations. Though alone in the world, Lila has many protectors. She works at the Lamartine Hotel, off Madison Square, as a telegrapher. Several habitués of the hotel's bar and billiard room appoint themselves her guardians. The group consists of Pierre Dumain, palmist; Tom Dougherty, ex-prizefighter; Bub Driscoll and Harry Jennings, actors; Billy Sherman, a newspaperman; and Sam Booth, a typewriter salesman. A latecomer to the group is John Knowlton, occupation unknown. Lila is amused to have a "tenderloin gang" as chaperon, and playfully dubs them her Erring Knights. The awkward chivalry they display gives the story a mock-heroic texture, but basically it is a quasi-mystery, making the point that all good men in America are not found in the West. To underscore this thesis, Rex's villain in *Her Forbidden Knight* is a Midwesterner.

The knight of the title is John Norton, alias John Knowlton, a purveyor of counterfeit currency. How Norton came to follow this calling, and how he wins Lila's love and the goodwill of the other knights, is the main business of the narrative.

To give substance to *Her Forbidden Knight* Rex drew upon his own memories and experiences. As a tyro Rex was grateful for such resources and made no effort to hide them. He moves about the Lamartine with comfortable authority. Rex's pattern was the hotel he had managed in St. Louis, and as events there had flowed around the telephone operator at her switchboard, so here is Lila, at her telegraph, much the center of things. The cigar counter, another nerve center at the Lamartine, gathers verisimilitude from Klein's of Cleveland, where Rex had served his perilous apprenticeship as a clerk.

Knowlton falls in love with Lila when he goes to her desk to send a telegram. When Rex describes him initially he is, in fact, describing his brother, Bob Stout: "He had a very ordinary face and figure, though the former was marked by an unusually genial and pleasing pair of gray eyes, and bore an expression of uncommon frank good nature." Bob's wife, Tad, had been a Western Union clerk. Bob had been sending a telegram when he first met her. Then and there he had fallen in love with her. Like Bob, Knowlton grew up on a farm in the Midwest. There the resemblance ceases. Rex now moves back in family history, and scrambles facts. Knowlton is from a small Ohio township and has come to New York after being falsely accused of embezzling money from a bank. (Twenty years earlier an embezzler had caused the collapse of Amos Todhunter's bank in Ohio.) Rex puts something of himself into Knowlton too. As part of his ritual of courtship, Knowlton, like Rex Stout, gives his ladylove books published in de luxe editions.

In Amanda Berry, Lila's capable, warmhearted, and resourceful landlady, Rex re-creates his aunt, Alice Bradley — even to the initials. Despite her walk-on part, Amanda, "a legion in herself," is the best-drawn character in the novel. That fact was not lost on Rex. Amanda became the precursor of several later characters in his stories, most notably the formidable Hattie Annis in "Counterfeit for Murder." Commanding women in Rex's fiction often would be Todhunter women.[11]

Two details in *Her Forbidden Knight* were meant to amuse Rex's family. Pierre Dumain, French palmist and clairvoyant, while following Bob's old line of work — chiromancy — seems suspiciously like Joseph Poulin, "Pauline," a stage hypnotist who had caught the fancy of Rex's sisters and Tad, both in Topeka and New York. Also, Lila, wondering how to dispose of a packet of counterfeit bills, asks herself if she should "place it on the floor of the hall and set it afire?" Had she done so, and Ruth Stout had come upon it, no doubt Ruth would have stepped over it and continued on her way.

Her Forbidden Knight, in a few particulars, anticipates the Wolfe series. Police detective Barrett is a crude anticipation of Inspector Cramer. Amanda's house is an "old-fashioned brownstone." At his place on West Twenty-first Street, Dumain gives sumptuous dinner parties. Sleuthing falls to lawyer Siegel, who has Wolfe's skill at cross-examination and plotting charades. There is praise also for "sweetness of facts."

Although *Her Forbidden Knight* is apprentice work, it does forecast Rex's later success with characterization, at least in the secondary characters — Dougherty, Dumain, and Amanda Blake — who submit better to management.

Most of the action in "Méthode Américaine" — *Smart Set*, November 1913 — takes place in Parisian restaurants. (At this stage of his career Rex favored hotels, restaurants, and places of public entertainment for action scenes; he had had little opportunity to observe fashionable people in more domestic situations.) His target here is the masculine ego — the extremes men of alleged intelligence can go to to maintain their

reputations before the world when, in truth, inward terrors have van-
quished them.

Pierre Dumain, drama critic for *L'Avenir,* and Lamon, a German
playwright, contract for a duel. The combatants are to be masked.
Dumain trades on this advantage to hire a stand-in, then goes to an
obscure restaurant (La Tour d'Ivoire, no less), the windows of which
command a view of the field of combat. There he finds Lamon, who had
yielded to the same temptation. For a final irony, both have hired as
their proxy the same American fencing master. How amused he must
be at this evidence of the low stage to which manly virtue has fallen in
modern Europe. For further proof of their poltroonery, Rex's "duel"
protagonists cannot even plead the intoxications of love as an excuse for
their conduct. The duel had been occasioned by an alleged matter of
head rather than of heart — a hostile review.

Much of Rex's initial writing income was spent on the opera, symphony, and ballet. From 1911 to 1915 he saw Caruso and Toscanini nearly
every time they appeared. He saw Nijinski every time he danced in
New York, and each time was awed by the dancer's spectacular leap in
Spectre de la Rose. The renowned Metropolitan Opera contralto Louise
Homer took a liking to Rex. Once she brought him with her to a rehearsal of *Martha.* After singing "M'appari" Caruso shook his raised fists
and cried, "I will never be an arteeste!" Louise told Rex, "He thinks he
phrased badly." Through Louise's intervention Rex was briefly the
pupil of Herbert Witherspoon, the Met basso who was destined to be,
at the time of his death in 1936, the general manager of the Met. Rex
recalled: "When Witherspoon saw her again, two months later, at a
luncheon at the Musicians' Club, he said 'All right, I want to report on
this Stout person. In his voice he has nine beautiful notes but no two
are juxtaposed.' "

Thwarted musicians figure in several of Rex's novels — *How Like a
God, Seed on the Wind, Golden Remedy,* and *The Broken Vase.* In the
Nero Wolfe story "Bullet for One," a Met tenor loses his voice and then
is murdered under the passive gaze of a bust of Caruso.[12]

15.

Underground Novelist

One modest observation occurs to me that may not have been remarked by everyone who is concentrating on the larger target (if one may so refer to Nero Wolfe): It always seemed to me that his narrator and sidekick, Archie, was a creation worth noticing in his own right. Unlike nearly all such characters, who are by dull (or unimaginative) tradition only sycophantic nonentities, whose considerable stupidity serves by contrast to enhance the apparent brilliance of the Great Man, but which often makes one wonder why the G M ever put up with them, Goodwin has his own personality, can carry out an assignment with intelligence and efficiency, and is not incapable of occasional irreverence towards some of the affectations and grandiosities of the boss. Which I found a most refreshing change from the usual formula in this genre.

— Leslie Charteris

When Rex was not writing, he was reading. He read William Dean Howells, Frank Norris, and Jack London, found Howells "pedestrian," Norris "a good reporter," and London "readable, competent, lively — a born storyteller with a limited range and not much intellect." Fielding's *Tom Jones* and *Jonathan Wild* he admired. *Moby-Dick* he found "amazing," but he thought *Typee* and *Omoo* "third-rate." Emily Dickinson came to him as "a lovely whisper." He read Galsworthy's *Forsyte Saga*, Rolland's *Jean-Christophe*, and Gottfried Keller's *Green Henry*. He read Shaw's plays, prefaces, and polemical pieces, and adjudged Shaw "the most agile word man of the century, and close to the wittiest, but, as a thinker, shallow and superficial." He tried Kant's *Critique of Pure Reason* but came away convinced it was unreadable. Nietzsche he categorized as "a good poet of the second rank, who wrote in prose." Goethe he dismissed as "the most overrated writer who ever wrote." Despite his own descent from Cyferts, Swingles, and Hartmans, Rex, through much of his adult life, was intransigent in his detestation of all things German. If he realized that his own passion for discipline and order was Teutonic, he never acknowledged it.

Rex revered Dostoyevsky. From *Crime and Punishment* he went on to *The Idiot*, to *The Brothers Karamazov*, to *A Raw Youth*. One paragraph sufficed to tell him how Dostoyevsky felt about Raskolnikov. Great writers, he realized, involve themselves in the difficulties of the people they write about, a feat then beyond him. Now he was dealing

with made characters, their parts and moods fabricated to enable them
to operate according to plan in the situations they found themselves in.
He wondered how Tolstoy created Natasha; and Conrad, Lord Jim.
"Huck Finn is a created character," he decided, "and Anna Karenina
is, too. So is Tarzan, just as much as Huck — of course on a different
literary level."

Edgar Rice Burroughs's success in creating Tarzan was, in fact, of
more than passing interest to Rex. *Tarzan of the Apes,* Burroughs's first
Tarzan story, was published in *All-Story,* in October 1912.[1] The event
was at once hailed as a literary landmark. That same month, Rex Stout
had published his first piece of fiction, "Excess Baggage," in *Short Stories.* No one seemed to notice. Since then Rex had gained some ground
but he knew that the secret of creating a character, as Burroughs had
created Tarzan, still eluded him.

Late in June 1914, at the invitation of Robert Hobart Davis, Munsey's
fiction editor, Burroughs came on to New York from Chicago to plot his
future course with *All-Story.* Strange to relate, when Davis brought
Rex along to have lunch with Burroughs and himself at the Brevoort,
at Eighth Street and Fifth Avenue, conversation centered not on Tarzan but on *Under the Andes,* a novel Rex had written the previous
summer and had published in *All-Story* in the February just past.
Under the Andes was Rex's one excursion into the lost-world subgenre.
It took two American brothers and a gorgeous international adventuress into a subterranean kingdom inhabited by the misshapen descendants of Incas who had retreated there in the sixteenth century to
escape European tormentors. Rex's immediate sources of inspiration
had been Ludwig Lewisohn's *Cave of the Glittering Lamps,* published
in *All-Story* three years earlier, and George Allan England's *Darkness
and Dawn,* published a year after that in *Cavalier.* The Morlocks of H.
G. Wells's *Time Machine* had, of course, supplied Rex a model for his
degenerate race of subhumans, even as they supplied George England
one for his. But Rex was careful to point out to Burroughs that he had
modeled his adventuress on the notorious Lola Montez, on whose sensational career he had fully informed himself. Burroughs said he admired
Rex's story for its vigor and assured style, but his interest in it went
beyond politeness. He had already sold *All-Story* a novelette, *The Inner
World,* about Pellucidar, an underground world of his own contrivance,
and, after some expansion, it was now ready to appear in *All-Story* as
At the Earth's Core. Davis was urging him to produce a sequel. Not
being partial to the scientific romance, Rex was prompt to disclaim any
further ambitions in that area. When Burroughs's tale was well received, he turned his success to good account. Between 1914 and 1963,
he published six more Pellucidar novels.[2]

Burroughs was not the only person to take notice of *Under the Andes.*[3]
A Rutgers anthropologist who read the story wrote Rex a three-page

letter congratulating him on his knowledge of ancient Inca civilization. Since Rex had written his tale without researching it, he found that surprising news indeed.

"A Tyrant Abdicates," the first of a batch of eight short stories which Rex published in the year World War I began, appeared in January in *Lippincott's*. His protagonist here, Mrs. Coit, a New York rooming-house keeper, rules as a tyrant over her boarders. Embittered by the failure of her own marriage, she is especially scornful of young love. Her reign of bitter reason ends when she effects a reconciliation between two young boarders who have had a lovers' quarrel. Rex's long-standing admiration of O. Henry is out in the open here.

"The Pay-Yeoman," published that same January in *All-Story*, is a companion piece to "Rose Orchid," published the following March. Both stories grew out of Rex's term of service on board the *Mayflower*. Both deal with the sympathetic reactions of American naval officers who stumble upon deserters in the Puerto Rican back country. In each story the *Helena* is sent to "Porto Rico" to relieve the *Chester*.

The protagonist of "The Pay-Yeoman," Paymaster Garway Ross, is an amiable fellow modeled on Graham Adee. Indeed, something of Adee may have gone into most of the wealthy, easygoing young men who appear in Rex's early stories. And perhaps Ross's surprise upon discovering that James Martin, his trusted pay yeoman, has made off with eight thousand dollars from the office safe was paralleled by Adee's discovery that Rex had given pay boosts to his shipmates in his last days in the navy. Ross knows he has brought his troubles on himself. He has been lax. He knows, too, that he probably will be dismissed from the navy if he reports his shortage to his superiors. Accordingly he covers it from his own funds and charges up his misfortune to experience.

Then, by chance, Ross learns of Martin's whereabouts. He isn't sure quite how to handle it, since he is not truly vindictive. And just as well. When he visits Martin's plantation, he finds that Martin is dead, and his ignorant, chronically nagging mother is his chief survivor. Jimmie had stolen to try to bring her some happiness, but without success; she found too much satisfaction in her bitterness. All Ross's vague, hostile emotions toward Jimmie seep away when he realizes what Jimmie's life must have been. His original high opinion of Jimmie is vindicated. He knows Jimmie now with heart as well as head, and has also a better opinion of himself. His head had not failed him after all. Jimmie was, as Ross told Mrs. Martin, "a good boy."

Under the Andes, published in February 1914, was the most ambitious of the early Stout fictions. Its defects are glaring and predictable. Like Burroughs, Rex, at this stage of his career, belonged to the "slaughter-house school." Once his protagonists find themselves among the subterranean Incas, it is race war. Centuries of living away from the sun have turned the Incas into shrunken black trolls — speechless brutes, naked, hairy, ugly, begrimed, and gross in their personal habits. They are Yahoos incarnate. And Paul and Harry Lamar match their hostility with lusty butchery. The reader loses count of the successive battles in dark caverns in which the Lamars leave Inca corpses piled head-high. Although they are in perpetual darkness, and usually without food and sleep, the scratches, flesh wounds, and contusions the Lamars receive are but the concern of a moment, and heal promptly without attention. A mouthful of raw fish or a handful of water seems all either needs to be replenished in vigor and intellect. The ending of nearly every one of the twenty-four chapters is a cliffhanger. Raging torrents, human sacrifice, earthquakes, primeval beasts, all have their chance to bring the Lamars to destruction. All fail. The terrified shrieks of the French courtesan, Desirée Le Mire, reverberate through the endless caverns with the persistence of a sound track in a carnival spook house. One can see the author improvising on the spot to extricate himself from dilemmas he has wrought.

A beneficent fortuity accompanies the Lamars on their adventures. When they need a raft, a whale with a buoyant backbone swims into their cavern. The happy stroke of good fortune for which they had been yearning a moment before is never withheld. Throughout their adventures, the dialogue and conduct of the three interlopers, when dealing with one another, has a stiff propriety, meant, no doubt, to emphasize their superiority to their reluctant troll hosts. (" 'Your spear,' I gasped, 'Quick — they are upon us!' ") Paul's gallantry, even in desperate circumstances, is awesome. With a solid wall of spear-toting Incas advancing on him, he can pause to massage Desirée's fingertips with a caressing kiss.

While Rex needed a twelve-year layoff to recover from some of the pulp trade habits he acquired in this era — it looked as though the hackberry had not fallen far from the tree — *Under the Andes* nonetheless had virtues which prefigured his later successes. The pace of the work was excellent. Even when Paul Lamar leases a yacht — a yacht nearly the size of the *Mayflower* — to take Harry and Desirée on a South American cruise, Rex does not pause to display his knowledge of the management of such a vessel. A paragraph suffices. Only when they are navigating the subterranean river does he draw upon his sailor's lore and then with strict attention to the developing action. In speaking of the way the Incas have adapted to their environment, even to the extent of building a spiral stairway — a feat unknown to their aboveground antecedents — Paul Lamar observes that the true artist "bows to his material." In his own capacity to make such adjustments, Rex already was exercising a talent which would see him utilize later, to its full potential, the strictly defined terms by which Nero Wolfe governed the conduct of his life from the moment of his first appearance.

Readers of *Under the Andes* got better value than they met with usually in adventure tales. Apposite allusions are made to *Tom Jones* and *Childe Harold*, and to Balzac, Voltaire, Congreve, Kipling, Aristotle, and Socrates. Porthos, Les Marana, Francesco Colonna, and Albert Savarus are mentioned with a familiar ease that must have sent many readers hurrying to the reference shelf to mend gaps in their erudition. Epigrams are administered in acceptable doses. Of mountain climbing, Paul says: "The exaltation at the summit hardly repays you for the reaction at the foot."

Although Paul carries the humor of the story, Rex allows himself some amusement. Desirée, who turns men into swine, is called "Le Mire." The Inca king still answers to the title "Child of the Sun." In a passage designed to amuse Tad and his sisters, Ruth and Mary, Rex has the fugitives pursued hotly through the caverns by a hypnotic dragon who all but routs reason with his fatal allure. Their favorite stage personality — Pauline, surely?

Both in his function as first-person narrator and in his asides, Paul Lamar prefigures Archie Goodwin, even though he says, "I certainly lack the training of a detective." Paul lacks Archie's ease of utterance too. Archie would never quip so formally, "I am satisfied that they [the Incas] were incapable of vocalization, for even the women did not talk!" Nor would he hold with Paul's attitude toward women, for through Paul Rex perpetuates his debate on Love versus Reason. This topic gives *Under the Andes* its sustaining interest. Paul first meets Desirée in France. She is a woman driven by a compulsive need to conquer every man's heart. But Paul, a cynic, emerges unscathed. To revenge herself on him, Desirée elopes with his callow young brother, Harry, who is also his ward. Paul overtakes them in Colorado Springs, then a mere outpost in the West. Wolfe watchers will be astonished to learn that Desirée, at Colorado Springs, on a visit to a humble eatery, tries to order *oeufs au beurre noir*.[4]

Throughout the novel the brothers maintain a restive relationship with one another, their natural affection blunted by the game Desirée plays with both. When they are not physically separated they are apt to be emotionally estranged, so that reunions and reconciliations between them happen constantly. Curiously, as Paul holds to his fatuousness, Harry grows in strength and authority. In the closing phases of the story, Harry supplies the more effective leadership. Love bestows on him a fortitude which Reason does not impart to Paul. With the veneer of the world on him, the best Paul can offer are such lines as "a man owes something to the woman who carries a room for him" or "I myself was in no mood for talk; indeed, I scarcely ever am in such a mood, unless it be with a pretty woman or a great sinner." Occasionally, however, the struggle for survival brings the two brothers into a state of genuine comradeship. At times, the Stout brothers themselves seem

Rex's model, as when he speaks of "bursts of genuine laughter, dissolv-
ing their vicissitudes."

While his ordeals mature Paul, Desirée also undergoes a transforma-
tion. Ultimately she is a Penelope Van Princin, resourceful in her struggle against a hostile environment. When Paul and she are ready to
acknowledge their love for one another, they have, through hardship,
been purged of the weak traits they had acquired in an effete civilization. But Rex does not find his resolution in that uplifting development.
As they are escaping, an Inca spear pierces Desirée's throat; the brothers alone escape, both more mature now because of what love and
sacrifice have taught them.

Yet Rex does not settle for that ending either. Harry later denies that
any such adventure ever befell them. Paul seemingly has imagined it
to bring himself to reconcile Love and Reason. Earlier Paul had said,
in terms Hemingway later would make into a code: "If looking death
in the face, a man can preserve his philosophy unchanged, he has made
the only success in life that is worth while." It is Paul's glory that in time
of peril he renounced his philosophy when he found it did not suffice.

"Secrets," the first story Rex wrote which can be called a detective
story, appeared in *All-Story* on 7 March 1914. Although it is told in the
first person, the protagonist, Moorfield — "one of the most conscientious men at the New York bar" — seems a precursor not of Archie
Goodwin but of Perry Mason. One quaintness does show itself. In his
rolltop desk Moorfield keeps a picture, seemingly an aesthetic depiction
of conjugal love, which is placed to catch the eye of prospective clients.
Their reactions to it he finds a reliable index of their character —
knowledge essential to him as a criminal lawyer. Moorfield prides himself on his intellect. In fact he is known as "the coolest and least impres-
sionable lawyer" in New York. Ironically, a lady client, Lillian Markton,
outwits him by using his desk picture to bring about his full and shameful failure.

Moorfield relates: "Her voice, her face, her figure, filled my thoughts
to the exclusion of all else. My dry light had deserted me, and I found
myself swimming, or struggling rather, in a sea of sentiment and emotion." In retrospect, he concedes: "How little, after all, do we shape our
actions by reason, when once the senses feel their strength! The light-
est perfume of a woman's hair is sufficient to benumb the strongest
brain. . . . "

Moorfield is so certain Lillian did not take $50,000 which she has been
accused of taking he stakes his reputation on her innocence. Moreover,
he is ready to ask her to marry him. Then Lillian drops around to his
office to retrieve the $50,000. On her initial visit she had hidden it
behind his desk picture. Because Moorfield cannot expose her without
making himself look ridiculous, he has to let Lillian get away with her

theft. Humiliated by her success in using his heart to defeat his intellect, Moorfield embraces lifelong bachelorhood.

"An Agacella Or" — *Lippincott's,* April 1914 — records an instance in which women have the tables turned on them, though by Fate rather than masculine wiles. George Stafford is typical of Rex's early male protagonists — a foolish, all but imbecilic, young heir. While vacationing at an elegant Berkshire resort hotel, George is mistaken by Mrs. Gordon Wheeler for the incognito Earl of Woodstock. She thrusts her daughter Cecily at him. George is married to Cecily before Mrs. Wheeler realizes her blunder. No credit goes to George for this social coup. Reader satisfaction comes in seeing head outsmarted by heart — the formidable Mrs. Wheeler undone by her own excess of ingenuity.

A Prize for Princes, at 85,000 words, is the longest of the early Stout novels. It ran in *All-Story's* five May issues in 1914. With what must be regarded as remarkable prescience on Rex's part, in view of the assassination of the Archduke Ferdinand at Sarajevo on 28 June, this story reaches its climax with the assassination of a reigning Balkan prince by an anarchist.

Once again the protagonist is the Harvard-educated playboy son of an American millionaire. With characteristic myopia, Richard Stetton begins his adventures by rescuing from a Balkan convent, which is about to be the scene of a mass rape by rampaging Turkish invaders, the one woman there who might have relished an orgy: the magnificent Aline Solini. Born a Russian peasant, Aline is fleeing from Vasili Petrovich, the husband whom she has tried to poison in circumstances similar to those Nero Wolfe would later recall in speaking of his own wretched marriage. Cynically, ruthlessly, Aline uses Stetton to advance her ambitions. Nowhere has Rex created a lover more blinded to reality by the exhilarations of love or more susceptible to feminine deceptions. Nothing can convince him of Aline's true character. He is told: "She is that most dangerous thing in the world — a woman with the face of an angel and the heart of a demon. Beware."

Time and again Stetton is confronted with evidence of Aline's true nature, but his caution is readily routed by her persuasiveness. After one confrontation, "he was haunted by a feeling that he had made a fool of himself, but the memory of her caresses and her assurances of love drove it back into the unexplored recesses of his brain — in his case, a not inconsiderable area." When it looks as though Aline is handing out her favors to several other men, though keeping him — who has given her a fortune — at arm's length, we hear that "he had that evening, for the first time, begun to fear — as he expressed it to himself — that he 'was being worked for a sucker.'" With his usual stress on the ability of the sense of smell to rout reason, Rex notes Stetton's repeated ravishment by the odor of perfume which wafts from Aline's hair. Perhaps that is why Nero Wolfe raises scentless flowers.

In fairness to Stetton, Aline is no amateur. Throughout the courtship she rids herself of enemies with poisoned apricot tarts, poisoned envelopes, poisoned swords. Indeed, the court of Louis XIV might have profited from a course of instruction from her. If Stetton has early "given up all attempts at finesse with Mlle. Solini," that fact reflects no great discredit on him. She prides herself on the skill with which she "manages men." She uses the seasoned General Nirzann and sends him to his death. She conquers the heart of the Prince of Mariso and becomes his bride, though women have been his pastime for forty years. Petrovich himself, though twice her age, and equipped with a brilliant mind which has carried him far, repeatedly is outmaneuvered by her. We should not be too scornful of Stetton, therefore, when, already the victim of a thousand of her deceptions, he sets out for New York to get two million dollars for her from his father. Yet we must keep our scorn for his folly in underestimating Petrovich's intelligence — the mistake that brings death to Aline and himself.

While Stetton is pursuing the dubious prize that is Aline, his friend, the German diplomat Naumann, is courting Aline's ward, Vivi Janvour. The convent-bred Vivi is as angelic as Aline is demonic. And Naumann seems to possess the reasoning powers Stetton lacks. By repeated warnings and demonstrations he undertakes, without avail, to show Stetton Aline's real character. Yet even he falters when he matches his logical powers against the naïve Vivi's. When Vivi challenges his assertion that Schopenhauer has destroyed Christianity for all thinkers, "he avoided utter annihilation only by demanding, in the middle of the argument, that he be served with tea."

In this first venture into the Balkans, whence Nero Wolfe would emerge twenty years later, Rex seemed less interested in laying groundwork for future narratives than in approaching the world he had met in the works of Turgenev and Dostoyevsky. Petrovich is forcefully drawn. A sense of the Russian heritage of Aline and General Nirzann also is managed with some success.

Objections may be raised. For example, why does Petrovich have such difficulty finding Aline when her Cinderella marriage to the prince must have put her picture in every newspaper in Europe? But even in an anti-Graustark world, fantasy must have its place. What is remarkable is that, after a few attempts at sketching the spoiled sons of the rich, Rex had moved with confidence to the large canvas *A Prize for Princes* supplied him.

16.

The Heart Has Reasons

One of my husband's most cherished tributes was Mary Stewart's statement
that when she came to the U.S. the two men she particularly wanted to meet
were Archie Goodwin and Anthony Boucher.

— PHYLLIS BOUCHER

Of Mrs. Sam Rossington, world-weary at thirty-two, we read, "Agatha's
fluttering brain was seldom long disturbed by anything so uncomfortable as thought."

"Out of the Line" — *All-Story*, 13 June 1914 — records Agatha's encounter with her moment of truth: a rendezvous she has long avoided.
Ten years earlier Agatha had been asked to choose between love and
security. She loved John Carter. She didn't love Sam Rossington. But
John had no money and Sam did. So she married Sam. Her marriage,
which ended after seven years, with Sam's death, had been for her a
period of "malodorous disillusionment." For Sam she had been a mere
acquisition, a plaything. Aimless pleasures had deadened thought for
her. Now even their capacity to divert her was waning. Selfishness had
done its work. She had no friends. Even her personal maid was a stranger to her. "I have never taken the trouble to know you," she told the
girl. Sam had said she was "unsympathetic." She saw that she had been.
And now her superficial life had left her spiritually empty.

To give her life new direction, Agatha decides on a unique birthday
party for herself. At midnight she hands out greenbacks to vagrants
waiting in a bread line. For her it is an emotional binge. She and her
beneficiaries shed mutual tears. Then, to her astonishment, John Carter
turns up in the line. He had kept his word and gone "straight to the
devil," after she had gone to the highest bidder. She manages a near
swoon and extracts from John a promise to come to her, later that night.
John obliges but a change of heart cannot undo past mischief. Rex
resisted the easy triumph of a happy ending. John is anything but
gallant. He says: "The Man you're looking for died ten years ago —
you know best who killed him." For good measure, he adds: "You are
not the Atha I loved — you are not Atha at all. My life is not the only
one you've ruined." With that, he walks out on her. Once reason had

overruled her heart and she rejected John. Now, by a neat reversal of fortune, John has paid her back in kind.

The contention that mind and heart sometimes are damaged irrevocably when one of them is given unlimited sway would also be the subject of Rex's next short story, "The Lie" — *All-Story,* 4 July 1914 — though there, by relinquishing coincidence as a resource, he made a substantial gain in sophistication. Thomas Hanley, protagonist of "The Lie," offers himself to the world as "a man without a heart." By hard work he has become the owner of a lumber mill. To his own conduct and to that of others he has applied strict Puritan criteria. He was thought to be incapable of emotion. Then, at forty, he fell in love with Marie Barber. Marie's acceptance of him is pragmatic. She is flattered to catch the eye of a man who has found no one else interesting — "In addition, she had a mother, and he owned the best business in Burrton." But Marie was a fair bargainer. She did not suspect the intensity of her husband's feelings for her. He kept his emotions too well locked up for that. But she adapted to his ways and even bore, with patience, the "business like questions" he put to her when she told him she was carrying his child.

But here his cold logic got the better of him. When she tells him she wants a daughter, he says, "Why certainly not . . . it must be a boy." Hanley "could not understand how she could fail to realize the necessity that there should be a son and heir to perpetuate his name and carry on his business." He continued to hold his emotions in check — his wife never suspected his true feeling for her nor did he suspect that she would like him to be more demonstrative. The trap he fell into was one Rex himself had narrowly skirted. We are told: "He had ever found his own mind thoroughly capable of supporting itself, and could not realize the existence of a soul that required to be fed from without." Marie gives birth to a son, but the ordeal carries her to the edge of the grave. The doctor asks Hanley to tell her she has borne a daughter. For love's sake he denies his own code and tells the doctor's lie. This merciful deception awakens within him an unsuspected tenderness. Rex tells us: "It is a painful thing to find one's heart at forty, and delightful."

But then the doctor comes and tells Hanley, in the cold way his manner always has invited, that Marie has died. Hanley's morality and emotions rage together in confusion. He thinks God has punished him for betraying his code. He flings himself down beside Marie's corpse, embracing her and "sobbing like a woman." His parched nature is inundated — "The floodgates that had been closed for a lifetime burst suddenly." The season is spring, a time of new beginnings. In that fact there is hope for Hanley, even in his anguished state.

"The Lie" is the finest of Rex's early stories — his most mature and complex exploration of the agony that possesses the human heart when

it is made the servitor of reason. For its situation "The Lie" looks back
to Hawthorne and Chekhov. For management of that situation it looks
ahead to Dreiser's *Free* and Anderson's *Winesburg, Ohio.*

"Target Practise" [*sic*] written in October 1914, and published the
following December, looks with disdain at the great war which had
broken out the previous summer. The narrator is an American correspondent who had visited a French army hospital looking for a story.
The story he found is a blend of Rex's favorite themes — the conflicting
loyalties of two brothers and the usurpation of the intellect by the
emotions.

Again the name Dumain is used — this time for the doctor who is the
narrator's cicerone on his tour.[1] But the story is of the Bonnot brothers,
Joseph and Théodore, born in German Alsace and separated in childhood. Joseph, the elder, grew up in Paris. Théodore grew up in Frankfort. When the war broke out Joseph was sent to a coastal fort at Toulon.
There he is joined by Théodore, who reveals that he has fled Germany
to escape conscription. Excitement at Toulon is feverish. Joseph would
observe: "The men at the fort eat like hogs, like wild beasts, and they
yell around all night, and the officers smile and say it's the fighting
spirit." A mania takes hold. Joseph says: "Day after day we had heard
nothing but France, France, France, until I believe everyone in the fort
was crazy." This atmosphere worked on Joseph's sensibilities and made
possible the disaster which followed.

Joseph discovers that Théodore is a spy. Was his loyalty to his brother
or to France? Wily Théodore tries to exploit Joseph's fraternal feeling
to win his complicity. The sound of his fellows singing the "Marseillaise"
as they march to noon mess, at just that moment, has greater impact,
however. Joseph feels his "heart bursting within" him. He resolves to
unmask Théodore. He vacillates, uncertain what course to follow. He
is almost relieved when he thinks Théodore has escaped. Then he finds
him hiding inside No. 3 gun. The gun is due to be fired. Joseph undergoes a mental crisis: "Suddenly my head grew hot, as though my
brain were on fire; and then, quite as suddenly, I felt cool and calm as
ice." He lets the gun be loaded and fires it. Then his "brain seemed to
be on fire again." But before he died he told the reporter: "I am of no
nation: I am Joseph Bonnot. . . . I love my brother Théodore, but I hate
war and I hate all nations — *all.*"

Bonnot is an enigma. He sees his choice as between blind loyalty to
his family and blind loyalty to his country. No third alternative, based
on reason, offers. The fact is, Joseph's rage is as much sponsored by his
realization that Théodore "had tried to make a fool of" him as by his
fidelity to France. First, he is heartbroken because his fraternal love was
not reciprocated in equal measure. Then he is heartbroken because, in
his wounded pride, he had overreacted to the discovery. Patriotism is
merely the pretext in the name of which he has acted. He even kills

himself for the wrong reason. He should have died cursing not patriotism but his own vanity and want of a cool head.

Two stories Rex published in *All-Story* in 1914 appeared under the *nom de plume* of Evans Day: "Rose Orchid" (28 March) and "The Inevitable Third" (25 April). While Rex published four other stories in *All-Story* that year, as well as two novels, that was just part of the overexposure problem that necessitated use of a pen name. Both Ruth and Bob had sold stories to *All-Story;* both these stories appeared in the 11 April issue — Ruth Imogen Stout's "Volatile Essence"[2] and J. Robert Stout's "Windows of Darkness."[3] Nonetheless, if they thought they were starting a Stout literary dynasty, they were disappointed. Bob's second and final story, "Cherries," was carried in the 8 August issue.[4] Since that was the week World War I broke out, by then even his attention was centered elsewhere. Ruth's second and final appearance in *All-Story* came three years later.[5]

Only Bob's "Cherries" need engage our attention here. It is written in dialect, reflecting Bob's admiration for James Whitcomb Riley. Mrs. Sarah Ellis, the first-person narrator, is a thoroughgoing individual. Sarah had been a Stillwell before her marriage, which apparently was a lot like being a Todhunter, because the Stillwells had "hankerin's" few other people had. Like Alice Matilda McNeal, Sarah has married an Ellis. She lives on a farm in Sycamore Valley, Ohio, but much of the story takes place in New York City, where she has gone to visit a married daughter. Yet when she reminisces of home it is of Stony Lonesome and Six Mile Creek — Wakarusa landmarks. Sarah had a sister Laura who once had such a hankering for a black silk dress she wrote to her Congressman asking "where she could get enough black silk worms to make a silk dress, bust thirty-six." (The Congressman sent her the dress.)

Sarah's hankering is on a larger scale. She wants to bring home a hansom cab. And she does, too. Her husband is appalled but has sense enough not to go against a Stillwell hankering and has a happy wife as a result. There is a lot of Lucetta in Sarah, but Bob went back a generation earlier for touches authenticating the kind of rapport that existed between Sarah and Henry. They are modeled on Amos and Emily Todhunter. Bob's boyhood visits to Wilmington had left impressions which time had not diminished.

"The Inevitable Third" deals routinely with boredom in marriage. The other Evans Day story, "Rose Orchid," is indebted to Rex's tour of duty on the *Mayflower*. Its protagonist, Lieutenant Commander Brinsley Reed, is modeled on Lieutenant Commander Chauncey Shackford, the *Mayflower*'s executive officer. Shackford had been a martinet. Reed is a martinet, too. "Bag and hammock inspection and fire drill twice a week. Abandon ship three times a month; and when he can't think of nothing else it's general quarters. For a seagoin' hat it's ten days in the brig. And brasswork. . . ." Thus the seamen describe Reed. Thus Rex describes Shackford.

Reed sees himself in these terms: "Stern, passionately fond of authority, conscious of but one code of morals and of conduct, and supremely happy in his power and ability to enforce it. . . ." This again is Shackford as he was. But a metamorphosis was needed, and Rex effected one. While on assignment to San Juan, Reed goes to visit a boyhood friend at the village of Rio, twenty miles away. Yet all he can think about is such matters as "the disgraceful condition of the pay store-room at the last Sunday inspection." Despite the threat of a cloudburst, he sets out by himself to return to his ship. Torrential rains overtake him. His pony stumbles and, in the ensuing fall, Reed's arm is fractured. He convalesces at a mountain cottage occupied by a native girl and a navy deserter, James Moser. While the beard Reed has grown and his civilian clothes keep Moser from recognizing him, Reed weighs his course of action. But the loving intimacy of the young couple mellows him. Rita is as lovely as the armful of rose orchids she has gathered to adorn the cottage. "Lieutenant-Commander Reed, for the first time in his life, had emotions." When he returns to the ship, he prepares an order for Moser's arrest. But a rose orchid he has carried home with him and hidden in a drawer of his desk reminds him that there is more to life than his Blue Book of navy regulations. He destroys the order and leaves the deserter unmolested. Once again, the man of reason learns that the heart, as well as the head, must be given its due.

17.

Crime Fiction

> Those who like the detective story as Jacques Barzun defines it have special reason to be grateful to Rex Stout, of course, because a considerable body of work such as his, with its consistent ingenuity and fine craftsmanship, raises the whole standard of the genre a further notch above the mundane.
>
> — ERIC AMBLER

For twenty years Robert Hobart Davis was fiction editor of the Munsey magazines. Sam Moskowitz describes him as "one of the greatest American fiction editors of all time, respected and, because of his great heart and human warmth, loved throughout the magazine and newspaper industry."[1] As a discerner and encourager he had no equal. When Tom Metcalf, editor of *All-Story,* almost aborted the Tarzan series by rejecting *The Return of Tarzan,* it was Davis who got Burroughs to return to Munsey's. It was Davis who launched Rex, bringing him along, as a pivot writer, in tandem with Burroughs.

Nothing Rex submitted was rejected, and for each story he got a penny a word. When he decided on a story idea, he went ahead with full confidence, never troubled by thoughts that it could be better. The stories were published just as they came from his typewriter. Later, when he scrutinized them in print, a cliché, an imprecise word, or faulty pronoun would leap out at him and bring a moment of remorse, but he did not grieve deeply. His competitors did not outshine him and Davis raised his payment, in stages, to two and a half cents a word, a sum Burroughs had to scrap to get.

To provide copy at the pace expected, Rex could not be expected to write masterpieces. He wrote when he needed money, spent it, then wrote again. He spent his earnings on baseball games, concerts, operas, and plays. Davis paid him $1,800 for *Under the Andes.* Within six months Rex was back with *A Prize for Princes,* because the money had run out. Some weeks his output topped twenty-five thousand words.

Sometimes Rex was uneasy about the novels. The discipline that governed the short story was not there. Yet a slack performance passed muster and brought in more money. The discovery, he afterward concluded, had been a bad one. Years later, Nero Wolfe would tell a visitor, "Nothing corrupts a man as deeply as writing a book, the myriad temptations are overpowering." In his first writing career Rex yielded to most of them.

Although the stories Rex wrote in this period were published during six successive years, disillusionment set in fairly early. He kept no copies of these stories. He did not see them as anything to boast of. By my count, Rex wrote in this period thirty-two short stories and four novels, all published in an interval extending from the fall of 1912 to the fall of 1917. Four short stories were published in 1912; six stories and one novel in 1913; nine stories and two novels in 1914, the peak year. In 1915, the count dropped to nine stories. In 1916, Rex published two stories and a novel. The novel, at least, had been written in 1915. Two stories were added to the total in 1917, before a twelve-year silence descended.

Several factors accounted for this quick halt to a career which, at first, seemed to be keeping pace with that of Burroughs. In his personal life he had incurred new responsibilities; to meet them he had embarked upon a practical business venture of sizable magnitude. These facts in themselves were not crucial in his decision to withdraw from his career as magazinist. He had reached some brave conclusions. First, the kind of life he was living was not getting him anywhere. Write a story, grab the check, spend it. He was faring no better than a compulsive gambler. Sometimes the money was gone before he had a chance to redeem his laundry. He was getting rid of it as though it was tainted. That thought led him to a second conclusion: the stories were not a true expression of the whole of his potential as a writer. If he was to be a serious writer, he decided, he needed a bankroll of half a million. Then he could work on his own terms and have access to that cultural stimulation which he craved.

Several further stories from the false dawn of Rex's writing career invite our appraisal as apprenticeship work which forecast his later themes and later attributes as a literary craftsman. "Their Lady" (1912), the first of his published stories, might have come from the portfolio of Damon Runyon. It recounts the happy ascent of a manicurist anonymously launched on a career of respectability by an assortment of Broadway hoodlums. Shaw's *Pygmalion*, which appeared that same year, may have been the most immediate influence, but the New York flavor seems to derive from the New York tales of Alfred Henry Lewis, to whom Runyon himself owed a debt.[2]

Thematically, "If He Be Married" — *All-Story*, 16 January 1915 — harkens back to the Horatio Alger era, which held aloft ideals not destined to survive in the new world the great war was bringing in. It is a slight tale. The dream of success has brought Carl McNair to New York. After a few months, he settles for a job as bookkeeper in the garment district. And there he would have stayed had he not, in a reversal of the Cinderella myth, caught the eye of the daughter of an illustrious financier. She gets him a job in her father's office and inti-mates that she wants him for a husband. After a token struggle he capitulates. Though to be wooed and won is damaging to his ego, he does not protest overmuch. After all, she has met his price. He will have what he wanted.

"Baba" — *All-Story,* 30 January 1915 — is slight too. But Edward Be-sant, the story's hero, is at least a man of action. Besant has been pursu-ing Sylvia Herrow for two years, with just enough encouragement to keep his hopes alive. When at last he sees that straightforward wooing will never win Sylvia, he devises a charade. Using the device of the faked letter — later so useful a weapon in Nero Wolfe's arsenal — he invites Sylvia to think he has given his heart to someone else. Then she wants him. By using his head, he has his heart's desire. Like its predecessor, this story seems apprenticeship work.

"Warner & Wife" — *All-Story,* 27 February 1915 — is a 12,000-word novella, a companion piece to a second novella, "Justice Ends at Home," published in December 1915. While it impinges on the genre of crime fiction, the tale focuses too much on the hero's struggle to master his wife for us to categorize it under that heading. Indeed, Rex finds more enjoyment here developing the nuances of his characters — especially those of Timothy D. Warner — than he did in any other story done in this period. Lora Warner, Timmie's wife, was not the beneficiary of the same subtle attention, possibly because she is not a sympathetic character.

Timmie Warner, a redheaded elf, had met and married Lora when they were classmates in law school. Four inches taller than Timmie, Lora is one of the "New Women." She sets up her own law practice in Granton, and scores a success. Where Granton is, we are not told. But at its outskirts lies "the Wakarusa Road," with its lovely country scenes. Rex had not forgotten.

Lora soon is thought to be the best lawyer in Granton. Timmie offers her no competition. No clients come to his office, and he meets the expenses of the household out of his inherited income. The bustling Lora treats him as she might an amiable pet. In fact, he is far more essential than she is willing to let herself believe. Timmie works up her cases and provides her with the insights she needs to win them.

Timmie tolerates her egocentricity until she tells him she does not have time to give him children. Then he acts. He leaves her on her own and lets her lose a case. Rumors circulate that Timmie has always been her brains. To squelch the rumors, Lora gets Timmie assigned to "the Holdup Suit." They will be representing opposing sides. Lora is not worried. Timmie has no case at all. But Timmie finds one and wins it. In the process, he asserts himself with such handsome authority that Lora, in effect, is wooed by him successfully a second time. Her tears flow, signifying the reappearance of her emotional life and the replenishment of her heart. Henceforth they are to be law partners and bed partners and — one gathers — parents.

Timmie Warner is Rex's first try at portraying a man of genius. Timmie, like Nero Wolfe, will not exert himself to exercise his genius except under compulsion. Normally he prefers to play cards — a recreation he shares in common with A. A. Adee. Like Adee, also, in times of crisis Timmie sleeps on a cot in his office.

The companion story to "Warner & Wife," "Justice Ends at Home," is an indisputable crime fiction story. A lazy lawyer has a prominent role in this tale too, but Rex provides him with an energetic assistant, thus making this story an obvious forerunner of the Nero Wolfe stories. But "Warner & Wife" must be remembered as the first link in the chain. It announced that the creative talents which would culminate in the creation of Nero Wolfe, were astir.

"Jonathan Stannard's Secret Vice" — *All-Story,* 11 September 1915 — features a detective named Pearson. But Pearson's role is perfunctory. Vera Stannard hires him to learn the reason for her husband's frequent absences from home. The Stannards have been married for twelve years. Stannard is a scholar and a traditionalist. He has written books which dwell on the subtleties of Homer and articles which heap scorn on the movie industry. That he is unfaithful is improbable, but what else is Vera to think? Presently Pearson makes his report. The austere critic is human after all. During the eight days he has been under observation, he has been to seven movies — elapsed viewing time, twenty hours and two minutes. Despite his announced conviction that "the cinema . . . appeals only to the lowest function of our mentality," the cerebral Jonathan needed some balance in his life, and the movies were supplying it.

Pearson is not to be ignored. He is droll and entertaining and romps through his part. He wants refinement — "I take it that Mr. Stannard is one of them serious guys. Moody and a kicker." But he knows his job and is quick to understand. He is amused at the turn his inquiries take, and plays out the suspense with Vera when he reports: "In my judgment your husband is the finest example of a *Dr. Jekyll* and *Mr. Hyde* I have met in my professional career." After confronting Stannard, his parting shot is Goodwinian: "You'll have to excuse me for hurrying off like this, but I got a date to go to the movies."

"Santétomo" — *All-Story,* 25 September 1915 — is another of the husband and wife stories which, like the young playboy stories, form a group among Rex's *oeuvre* of the early period. Santétomo is a Japanese seneschal, who had been with Henry Brillon through the last ten years of his bachelorhood. When Henry married Dora Creval, Tomo came along, as part of the household. Dora found him creepy. Only Henry's attachment to Tomo, who once had saved his life, kept her from pressing for his dismissal.

Matters are resolved when the Brillons, accompanied by Tomo, go to the Rockies on a holiday. The Brillons are testy and take it out on poor Tomo, who accepts their unwarranted rebukes with admirable stoicism. Finally Brillon grows inattentive and puts the car over a precipice. He scrambles to safety, but Dora and Tomo end up in the branches of a scrub oak, suspended over the abyss. The branch they cling to cannot hold the weight of both. For Brillon's sake, Tomo drops to his death. In the last look that passes between them, Dora realizes that Tomo hates her but has elected to die to give her back to someone whom they both love. By his sacrifice she understands the shamefulness and unreasonableness of her racial bias. The fineness of Tomo's sacrifice consumes her pettiness and she never tells her husband that Tomo had died, not to save her, but to spare him.

The only Asians Rex had known before writing "Santétomo" were the cooks and waiters on the *Mayflower.* But scorn for race prejudice had been with him from earliest remembrance. "Santétomo" was the first of many statements he would make through the years in support of racial justice and understanding.

"Justice Ends at Home" — *All-Story,* 4 December 1915 — is 20,000 words long and divides into seven chapters. With it Rex moves a giant step closer to the creation of Wolfe and Archie. Timothy "Timmie" Warner of "Warner & Wife" is a lawyer, lazy but clever. Simon "Simmie" Leg of "Justice Ends at Home" is a lawyer too, both lazy and slow-witted. On the face of it, Simmie seems at a farther remove from Nero Wolfe than Timmie is. But Timmie has to act on his own and Simmie is provided with a resourceful dogsbody, Dan Culp — his aspiring office boy. Lacking Leg's credentials, Culp has to work through his employer. He manages him much as Archie manages Wolfe when he gets interested in a case of which Wolfe wants no part. Like Archie, Dan is alert, resourceful, and good-natured. Unlike his bachelor boss, he has an eye for a pretty girl. He is a milk drinker. And he does all the running about, working up the evidence. Unlike Archie, he does all the brain work, too. With constant prodding Simon cooperates, but Simon has no ideas of his own and is totally dependent on Culp's wits to win acquittal for his client.

With "Justice Ends at Home" Rex made a major breakthrough. He had invented the resourceful Watson. Ironically, he had left the new Watson's companion in detection back in "Warner & Wife." Timothy Warner and Dan Culp acting together as a team — a lazy, brilliant sleuth assisted by an energetic, resourceful dogsbody — would have constituted a fair anticipation of the team of Nero Wolfe and Archie Goodwin. Rex almost had the idea within his grasp.

If Rex had found his dual protagonists in 1915, they may have operated out of a law office. He had hit upon the idea of lawyer-as-detective before either Arthur Train or Erle Stanley Gardner. But, by 1933, when Rex created Wolfe and Archie, Mr. Tutt and Perry Mason were well established in the public eye. Thus Wolfe and Archie escaped being tied to courtroom rituals. British crime fiction offers an earlier instance of barrister-turned-sleuth, in the person of Arthur Morrison's Martin Hewitt, who came upon the scene in 1894. But Morrison's detective, though stoutish in appearance, was Holmesian in performance, and offered Rex no pattern.

"Justice Ends at Home" is a true detective story, the only indisputable one Rex wrote before *Fer-de-Lance*. When Judge Fraser Manton appoints Simon Leg to defend William Mount, who is charged with the murder of Elaine Mount, his wife, Leg is dumbfounded. He believes Mount is innocent but has no idea how to win his acquittal. Culp, with Leg's grateful approval, gets things into motion.

Rex later would define logical thinking as "the ability to consider a problem without introducing the extraneous." Like his creator, Culp possesses this ability to a remarkable degree. Working from a carefully thought out agenda, Culp soon has made a shrewd surmise about the true identity of the murderer. Neither Leg nor the reader is made privy to this surmise, though hints are supplied. But conjecture is not evidence, and there Culp meets his greatest frustration. Mrs. Mount had left her husband and, for several years prior to her murder, had been the mistress of a prominent citizen, whose name has been kept out of the case. Pressure through him has led the police commissioner and others to give Leg no more than token cooperation. Essential to Leg's case is the testimony of Patrick Cummings, janitor at the apartment house where Elaine Mount had been stabbed to death. But Cummings is missing and the police are not interested in finding him.

When Culp learns that Cummings is an avid moviegoer, he has letters sent to ten thousand theaters, asking that the managers flash on the screen the message that there is a phone call for Cummings. A $5,000 reward is guaranteed to the man who holds Cummings for Culp. Leg supports this search and pays out close to $10,000 to see it through. Cummings is found in Albany and brought back just in time to save Mount from the chair. The true culprit proves to be Judge Fraser Manton himself, who, when his guilt is exposed, fells Culp with his gavel. The melodramatics of that courtroom scene are so spectacular one sees why Rex avoided courtroom scenes thereafter. From there he had nowhere else to go.

The liveliness of Dan Culp seen in contrast to the exasperating inertia of Simon Leg supplies this story its true center of interest. Like Adee, like Warner, Culp even sets up a cot in his office to be on the job twenty-four hours a day, when the pressure is on. With creditable shrewdness he tells Leg he believes Mount is innocent because Mount has said he had agreed to take back his wife and live on the money her infidelity had brought her. "No man would make up a thing like that about himself, even to save his own neck," Culp says. This exchange follows:

"So you're a student of human nature, are you, Dan?" "Yes, sir. I'm just beginning. I've had very little experience, but there's something else just as good. The people who say experience is the best school don't know what they're talking about. Most people could learn more about human nature in one week by studying Montaigne's *Essays* than in a lifetime of observation, because hardly any one knows how to observe. . . . You remember, sir, it was you who told me to read Montaigne."

"Yes, I believe I did. . . . I never got much out of him myself."

"No, sir; I suppose not."

Dan explains why his suspicions had centered on Judge Manton. Manton himself had picked Simon to defend Mount. He could only have done that if he wanted a conviction. "You've been awfully good to me, sir," Dan says, "but you hadn't had a case in ten years, and you certainly are a bum lawyer."

In the story, Dan twice repeats a line from Montaigne: "The passions smothered by modern civilization are doubly ferocious when awakened." A judge should be the embodiment of virtue and reason. Yet Manton had murdered Elaine in a fit of passion and in a fit of passion strikes down Culp. More than that, he had been willing to let Mount die for a crime he himself had committed. Attributing to Manton the logic of Dostoyevsky's Raskolnikov, Dan surmises: "He probably said to himself, 'What does this broken-down creature amount to compared with a man like me — wealthy, intellectual, cultured, of high position?' " Seduced by lust and pride, Manton becomes first the prisoner of his emotions and then the prisoner of his intellect.

In concerning himself with the difficulties man's instincts raise when he tries to impose civilization's compact and induce head and heart to interact harmoniously, Rex here has moved to new ground. The struggle now is not so much, as he had suggested before, one that arises out of man's unwillingness to use his intellect, but one that finds him contending against seething compulsions that are striving to engulf him and from which no man is immune.

The Great Legend, the last novel Rex wrote for *All-Story* — January 1916 — is set in Troy. The story opens in the ninth year of the siege. Rex's encounter with the *Aeneid* had stood him in good stead, although he took his revenge for the hours spent construing Virgil's epic by portraying Aeneas as a man of small consequence. The narrator of the story is Idaeus, a Trojan Kesten, secretary to King Priam. The familiar bonding pattern is present in his attachment to Phegeus, his blood brother, and to Cisseis, his best friend. But when Phegeus is killed, Idaeus flees the battlefield without trying to recover his body. Much later, when Cisseis falls in battle, Idaeus not only returns with his body; he carries his severed head under his arm. Between the two events much has happened to elevate Idaeus to manhood.

Idaeus, a self-professed agnostic and skeptic, is habitually a victim of his emotions. "Love . . . fires my brain," he says. And when it does, he behaves like a fool. In contrast, the women he loves, Helen of Troy and Hecamed, daughter of Arsinous, King of Tenedos, use Reason to manipulate men.[3] Idaeus believes that "indecision is the worst weakness in a man" — a view Rex shared — yet his affairs of the heart leave him in a constant state of indecision. Despite his lovesickness, he has a bold imagination. When Priam sends him as emissary to the Greeks, offering conditions for peace, he improvises a condition of his own — that the Greeks make a gift of the Delphic oracle to Troy — so that the Greeks will reject the offered terms and his courtship of Helen can continue. He also contrives the death of Achilles, and slays Paris.

Gradually Idaeus comes to prize "Helen's quick brain" above her physical charms. And Hecamed finally agrees to be his wife, after she has played Petruchio's game in taming him. He asks her which did she think was the greater man, a philosopher or a warrior? Again Reason is victor. They flee burning Troy and Idaeus lives out his days as a shepherd-philosopher with the wise Hecamed at his side.

By focusing on the struggle between reason and emotion, Rex was able here to sketch the historical background economically. Enough is said to carry conviction. Only rarely do we raise an eyebrow, as when Menelaus is described as "a tall, anemic chap," or Idaeus confesses to having "the very deuce of a time," or to taking a "much needed bath." He does in fact bathe as often as Archie Goodwin, a practice apparently as rare among detectives as it is among warriors. In handling of background, Rex profited as much from Shakespeare's history plays as from *Ben-Hur.* The characters are decisively drawn. Even a half-century of Hollywood's encroachments on the matter of Greece and Rome have not reduced this narrative to obsolescence.

"It's Science that Counts" — *All-Story,* 1 April 1916 — was an amusing tale with which to follow *The Great Legend.* Rex's editors thought so, at least. They introduced it with a boxed announcement which read: "There were fights a plenty in *The Great Legend,* which we published recently. But not one of them can equal Mr. Stout's conception of the fight in this story. Mr. Stout wrote it just to show that he knows other things besides Greek archeology — one of them being human nature."

Although "It's Science that Counts" is mock-heroic, it invites more direct comparison with "Méthode Américaine" than with *The Great*

Legend. The setting is an Ohio village — Holtville — and the antagonists are Jone Simmons, who runs a hardware store, and Notter, the new clerk at the general store — both middle-aged. Both boast of their scientific skill as pugilists, only to find themselves, quite against their expectations, booked for ten rounds as the main event at the Merchants' Association Annual Picnic. When the Ladies' Reading Circle lodges a protest, it is overruled. This is not to be a "brutal, inhuman and degrading exhibition of the lowest instinct in man," as they fear, but "a scientific exhibition." The children of Holtville must learn that there is more to fighting than hair-pulling and kicking.

Just before the encounter is to take place, Simmons panics and slips away to the woods. A moment later, he finds himself face to face with Notter, who has fled the scene also. Hot words pass between them and there, unobserved, they engage in a kicking, hair-pulling free-for-all which would have brought a blush of shame to the lowliest village brat. The contest ends only when Notter is knocked senseless when he hits his head against a tree. Just then, Pete Boley, who had promoted the fight, comes upon the scene. The villagers assume that the two had engaged privately in their scientific encounter to spare the women and children the sight of a bloody spectacle. Magnanimously, Simmons allows that Notter was strong, but claims that his own superior boxing skill had been decisive. "It's science that counts," he reminds his auditors.

Thematically this story relates to the others of the early period. Ruled by their instincts, men are, like children, primitive and savage in their encounters. Being neither Troy nor Paris, Holtville is a fitting setting neither for tragedy nor bitter irony. Simmons and Notter have their true shame hidden from their friends. A polite myth is given continuance. Civilization in the American Middle West moves ahead on its grand and glorious upward course. A victory of the passions is recorded as a victory of the intellect.

Rex's earlier visit to the Far West gave him the resources needed to portray a bona fide nobleman of nature — Rick Duggett, "the best roper in Eastern Arizona." Rick is hero of "The Rope Dance" — *All-Story,* 24 June 1916. One fact sets Rick apart from most other men: "He never did anything by halves." He knew his mind, and when he came to a decision he saw it through. The original nobleman of nature, he is a natural oddity because of his serene self-assurance, forthrightness, and basic decency, when he comes to New York to spend $818 he has won in a roping contest in Arizona. His manly western ways make native New Yorkers seem the waste products of an ailing civilization.

When a sharper separates him from his money, Rick gives the New York police a pleasant shock: "No use writing anything down, because I'm not making any holler. I've always had a theory that if a man can't take care of himself he's not fit to have anyone else do the job." Rick gets taken on at Broadway's "most famous cabaret" as partner in a rope dance done with his lariat. No one is proof against his amiable frankness. His clear thinking seems to spring from pureness of heart. He is that rarest of all mortals, a man in good working order — a one hundred percent healthy specimen — head and heart interacting in perfect harmony. Fate cannot stand against such a man for long. Nor does it. The act is a success. Rick falls in love with his partner who, by happy chance, is as innocent as Tarzan's Jane. The sharper who had fleeced him visits the cabaret. Rick lassos him and gets back his bankroll plus a $130 bonus.

Several of the later stories Rex wrote during his first writing career were fitted together with skill and patience. Characterization and dialogue were wrought with more care, and humor replaced stiffness as though, finally, he was enjoying what he was doing. He seemed more interested in people than in conveying to his readers a sense of his broad cultural background. And he had come to realize that his insights into human nature were more plentiful when he moved the action out of the drawing room and into the rural world he knew best.

Rex's two final early stories were published in 1917. "An Officer and a Lady" — *All-Story*, 13 January 1917 — is a neat exercise in roles reversal. A veteran housebreaker, betraying by sentiment, is put to rout by an eight-year-old-girl who is cold and calculating and as steely nerved as a veteran pathologist. "Major" Wentworth is active in the World War I preparedness program at Miss Vanderhoof's Academy and can shoot nine straight centers from the hip. She owns: "I've never got a man on the run, but I'd love to have a crack at one." All this is dismal news to Bill Farden. Bill knows how to look after himself. He has just chloroformed the burly Scandinavian cook and bound and gagged the Major's father but, as he looks at the sleeping child, he marvels that "a creature could be so utterly helpless without thereby incurring the contempt of a strong man." He has a lofty thought: "Perhaps after all physical force [is] not the only power worth having." A moment later the Major has the muzzle of a "mean-looking little revolver" aimed one inch above the apex of his heart. If they gave a course in sentiment at Miss Vanderhoof's, it's clear that the Major hadn't enrolled in it. She learned about the misfortunes which had befallen her father and the cook with chilly detachment. "I shall have to revive Hilda, if it is possible," she says. "I have my doubts on the subject. She refuses to keep herself in condition." Of her father, she says: "To put it mildly he is a weakling. . . . If you have gagged him scientifically he may have ceased breathing by now. In one way it would be nothing to grieve over. . . ." She then releases Bill, not out of compassion but to dramatize her conviction that the penal system needs an overhaul. When she asks Bill to salute her, upon dismissal, she goes too far. As he runs off, he calls back over his shoulder, "Go to hell."

A child has no business having a clinically analytical mind. A thief has no business having a warm heart. The travesty that results is intentional. "An Officer and a Lady" is a parable dealing with the absurdities which befall those who let heart or head take total control of them.

"Heels of Fate" — *All-Story*, 17 November 1917 — the final story of this first phase, concerns a murder that will go undetected. The narrator is a country lawyer. He influences events, but Dal Willett, who makes the essential decisions, is the true protagonist. Willett, who owns the local livery stable, is a man to whom people turn when they need advice. He has "a sharp knowledge of humans and understanding of them."

John Hawkins and his daughter, Janet, settle on a local farm. John, though past fifty, is a hard worker and makes the farm prosper, though it never has prospered before. People respect him for it. Janet blooms under the spell of farm life and soon has many suitors, including Dal Willett himself. When she marries a young farmer, Roy Nelson, everyone wishes them well. Then a slick and sinister fellow, Nosey Gruber, comes to town and begins to harass old John. When the narrator realizes the man is a blackmailer he persuades John to open up to him. Janet had been to prison. John had engineered her escape. The blackmailer threatens to tell the authorities of her whereabouts. The matter is referred to Dal. Dal's affection for Janet stirs his sense of outrage. Cogitation brings him to an impasse. "It's a case of only two alternatives," he says, "and both of them impossible." John could neither pay nor refuse to pay. Willett prepares a charade. Hawkins is told not to answer Gruber's phone calls. After a few days the tension is unbearable. The lawyer knows Willett has a plan but cannot figure out what it is.

The end comes suddenly. Gruber goes to Willett's stable to get a rig to go out to Hawkins's farm. Willett directs him to the back of the stable where he keeps Machiavelli, a vicious stallion with a kick that has "the force of a dozen sledgehammers." The iron-shod hooves lash out "like a shot from a cannon," and John Hawkins is rid of his antagonist.

Rex's first writing career was variegated and rich in promise. He had anticipated Burroughs with a lost-world novel. He had anticipated Sherwood Anderson in his study of the twisted lives of rural Americans and Arthur Train in his creation of a lawyer sleuth. As a novelist he had traveled to the Andes, the Balkans, and ancient Troy, and did not seem outside his range. He had portrayed socialites, fortune hunters, playboys, sailors, lawyers, businessmen, landladies, warriors, aristocrats, charlatans, soubrettes, farm maids, dowagers, termagants, career women, feminists, children, a cowboy, a Japanese manservant, an actress, a burglar, all with more than passable success. He had found a subject of universal appeal and limitless possibilities — the contention of heart and head. He had advanced his skills in architectonics, characterization, dialogue, pace, and style. He had prepared the way for Wolfe and Archie.

A good beginning.

BOOK IV

A Liberal Awakening

18.

Melons and Millions

Rex Stout is at the very top of that list of writers I keep, whom I never, never read — from being afraid I'll start copy-catting, a vice we're all subject to. And yet of course I do read him — peep at him, from not being able to resist — and regard Nero Wolfe as one of the master creations, as well as an inspiration. And Rex is inspiring too. Long may he reign!

— JAMES M. CAIN

Donald Stout inherited more of Lucetta's individualism than any of his brothers and sisters did. While still in grade school he skipped classes to spend his days at the vast Zoological Park in the Bronx, running errands for the keepers. Donald never had lived on the farm, a melancholy fact since no one in the family loved animals more. When Lucetta found that he wanted to work with the big animals and to go to Africa some day to capture them for zoos, she let him quit school to work at the zoo full time. One day he brought Frank Buck home to lunch. Adventure was strong in Donald. When World War I broke out, he signed on as a stoker on a cattle boat bound for England. He came back on the same boat.

The other Stouts had been busy too. Three of Juanita's four children, Walter, Juanita, and Roger, had arrived by 1913, and she was adding to the Roddy income by designing and making clothes for Best's.[1] Betty worked as a nurse at Columbia Presbyterian Hospital. The Todhunter plainness had not found her. On occasion she was mistaken for Ethel Barrymore, then the toast of Broadway. A friend recalls, "She had the sweetest, rather low and slow, comforting voice I have ever heard." When she cried or was tired she looked even more beautiful. Several of Rex's heroines, including Phoebe Gunther in *The Silent Speaker*, possess this enviable attribute.

Betty often was asked to go home with rich patients, when they were discharged, to continue their nursing care. When she contrasted their life-styles with those of her charity cases, she left Columbia to go into social work. After a time she had to go back to conventional nursing; she was giving all her money to her hardship cases. When Bob's daughter Natalie almost died of diphtheria in 1911, Betty stayed with her day and night till recovery was certain. In gratitude, Bob gave her a diamond ring. She didn't speak to him for weeks afterward.

The theatricals continued. One year the Stout family players put on a complete vaudeville show. When they had the show put together, they realized they were stuck for a finale. Lucetta offered to provide one, but it was to be her secret. "How will we know when to draw the curtain?" Rex protested. She smiled. "You'll know," she said.

John started off the show with a prestidigitation routine. He had two hats on two tables on opposite sides of the stage. Under one was an apple. After much arm waving and muttering of incantations, he announced that the apple now was under the other hat. He did not show that it was, however. "The real trick," he said, "is to get it back where it was in the first place." More gestures and incantations and the hat was lifted, disclosing the apple. John beamed. "I wasn't at all sure I could do it tonight," he said, "but I succeeded." He bit into the apple. "Um-m-m," he murmured as he strode from view, "Northern Spy."

At last the curtains parted for Lucetta's finale. The couch on the stage, the audience saw, had been made up as a bed, with sheets and a pillow. Close by, on a nightstand, were a few toilet articles and a glass of water. Lucetta, in nightdress, robe, and bedroom slippers, was seated at a table. She removed her hairpins, and gave her hair a few strokes with a brush. Then she stood up, removed her dentures, and slid them into the tumbler. She turned toward the bed and began to slip out of the robe. She glanced at her audience. "Good night," she said in a tone of firm dismissal. Rex and Bob tugged the curtain shut.

In 1915 the Stouts moved from 116th Street to 414 Central Park West, a brownstone which looked out on the park. That same summer Bob moved his family to the Hotel Marseilles, at 103rd Street and Broadway, while he weighed the prospects of finding a home for them in the suburbs. He now had three children, Natalie, Jay, and Winona.

Nineteen fifteen was not wholly a happy time for Ruth. She fell in love with Ed Carlson. When she realized Ed did not love her, she turned on the gas one afternoon and lay down on her bed to await the end. As the minutes ticked by, she thought of Ed's ruddy face and jolly ways and reflected on how unhappy he would be when he found out what she had done. She saw she couldn't do that to him. She turned the gas off and threw open the windows. Nathan's words came back to her: "Thee was looking through the wrong window." And so she had been. Her happiest years lay ahead of her.

When he reached twenty, in 1916, Donald went to Montreal to join the Canadian army. Though deaf in one ear, he passed the physical. When he found out that army discipline did not suit him, however, he stopped hiding his affliction and the Canadians decided to release him. For Donald the prospect was as good as the reality. He deserted and came home. That did not suit Lucetta. She took him back to Canada and stayed on until his release was duly processed. The Canadians accommodated her at a visitors' guest house. One Sunday morning, in the midst of a dress review, she walked up behind the company commander and prodded him between the shoulder blades. "Stand up straight, sonny," she said. "How you ever got to be in charge with posture like that is beyond me." Within a week she was back home with Donald.

That summer, Ruth's high school friend Ethel Chapman came to New York to take courses at Columbia. Ethel and another teacher from Topeka took a furnished apartment near the university. Their summer in New York was to supply hints to Rex nearly twenty years later when he wrote *O Careless Love,* which recounts the adventures of several teachers from the "Lincoln School," in Curran City, Kansas, who come to New York for summer courses. But that was not the most important consequence of their visit. While Ethel was in New York, her mother, Margaret Chapman, and a cousin, Fay Kennedy, came on for a visit.[2] During their stay Ruth invited them over to 414 for breakfast. An invitation was extended also to Aaron J. Stout. A. J. was not related to John, but had taught science and mathematics to both Rex and Ruth at Topeka High and was now the principal there. He was in New York to complete work on his doctorate at Columbia.

Ruth decided that breakfast should begin with muskmelons. She wanted the best so she called East Twenty-ninth Street and asked Rex to come to breakfast, too, and to bring the melons. She knew Rex had selected hundreds of them from their melon patch back in Wakarusa, in his boyhood, and that he was an infallible judge of the caprices of that moody fruit.

Other factors too subtle for communication also were at work that morning. Rex remembered Fay Kennedy. One of his friends in high school had been Fay's brother Ralph. But Fay was six years younger than Rex, so in those days she was merely Ralph's kid sister. At first it seemed as though Rex still thought of her that way. During breakfast he made a cynical remark about the absurdity of falling in love. "By gosh," he said, "I'd never be caught doing anything as inane as that." "I wish I could be there when it happens," A. J. said. A. J. evidently was a persuasive wisher.

When Fay left, Rex left with her. She was going back to Topeka the next day and he did not want her to waste her last day in New York riding around on the wrong subway train. Or so he said. Ruth and Mary found that odd. Usually Rex did not fuss over such things. Fay was impressed, too, by his solicitude. Rex thought it would be fun to show her something of New York if she could extend her stay. She remained in New York another week. Before she left, Rex proposed to her and she accepted. Truly, as Benjamin Franklin had long before observed, "Men and melons are hard to know."

Bob Stout later would describe Fay as "the little, innocent Kansas farm gal." She was smart-looking, practical, good-natured, soft in manner, and unobtrusive. She was more the Rita of "Rose-Orchid" than the Hecamed of *The Great Legend.* Trust and admiration shone in her gray eyes. She would not compel a man to indecisiveness. She would leave it to Rex to shape their world. Fay's father had been a yardmaster for the Atchison, Topeka, and Santa Fe, a man accustomed to sending trains and people to their proper destinations — a useful education for Fay, since now she would be married to a man who liked to point people and events in the right direction.

On 1 December 1916, Rex turned thirty. On 16 December Fay would be twenty-four. There was an exchange of letters on what the new year would hold for them. Within a few days Rex set out for Chicago. Accompanied by her brother Ralph, Fay set out for Chicago, too. Rex and she were married on 16 December at the office of the county clerk, Cook County, by Circuit Court Justice Dean Franklin.[3] From Chicago they went on to Pittsburgh, where they put up at the Hotel Schenley.

Theirs was a combination wedding and business trip. Bob had a new idea he wanted to share with them. He had no taste for details. If the idea was to work, these would have to be Rex's concern. In the midst of the deliberations, Fay decided it would be fun to have a spoof wedding picture taken. She draped herself in curtains taken down from the windows and gripped a clump of greenery that looked as though it had been cropped from a pot in the lobby. But the look of adulation in Rex's eyes was not counterfeit. Idaeus the Trojan could not have surpassed it.

Bob Stout had an inventive mind. One day he might weigh the feasibility of removable shoe buckles, another, of paper cups — before either product had been marketed. He enjoyed selling ideas off the top of his head and did it superbly. "He could sell the Brooklyn Bridge," his daughter Natalie says, "but he was capable of buying it back at a loss." He believed in his dreams and shared the excitement they engendered. Nonetheless the esurient demands of paperwork repelled him. "J. R.," says Frances Cox, his longtime personal secretary, "worked harder to get out of working than anyone I could imagine." He liked to stand at the head of things, to remind himself that they had begun with him, but he needed a practical man to put his product on the market. Once, joking with Walt, he said, "If someone invented a new game, Walt would want to know if he could play it sitting down." Walt came back: "And Bob won't play at all unless he can be president."

The year 1916 found Bob selling reference books for Dodd, Mead. He was an aggressive salesman. One customer, to whom he tried to sell encyclopedias, told him, "I already have a set." Bob told him, "Your fire's getting low. Use it for firewood." In September that year, Bob made a routine call on a Mr. Galloway, superintendent of schools in Carbondale, Pennsylvania. Galloway was convalescing from surgery, and Bob called on him at his home, about noon. Forty years later Bob re-created the scene: "We sat on the porch of his old Dutch residence built very close to the street. School had let out for midday lunch and several of the children called to Mr. Galloway and told him the amount of money they had in their school savings accounts. It was Tuesday, and Mr. Galloway told me that each Tuesday morning deposits in any amount were accepted from the children under a plan he and the local banker had set up. The object, of course, was to teach money management by the actual practice of thrift."

Several weeks later, at Williamsport, Pennsylvania, Bob was visiting the high school and the principal invited him to say a few words to the students in the assembly hall. Carbondale flashed into Bob's mind and in an instant he was off and galloping, talking to them about Galloway's plan: "Saved money is happy money. It has only one real value, of course, and that is its spending value. But when put to good purpose, saved dollars are laughing dollars." At that moment the Educational Thrift Service was born in Bob's mind. Williamsport had to wait awhile for ETS, but then and there Bob sold himself on it.

Now came the task of setting up the machinery to make the dream a reality. That's when Bob sent for Rex. Before Rex could join him, however, Bob outlined his plans to another book salesman, William E. Loving, and together they persuaded the school superintendent and the board of education in Morris, New York, to authorize installation of a Bank Day in the Morris public schools. They showed Rex a contract from a local bank. The bank had agreed to accept the deposits and to pay them for installing the plan and for needed supplies. But they had no plan. For ownership of one-third of the business Rex agreed to devise one.

In his room at the Schenley, in the days that followed, Rex worked out the method by which the ETS would function.[4] The plan was not evolved over weeks and months. Just as he would do when he wrote the first Nero Wolfe story, Rex designed at the outset a structure fully articulated and able to absorb strain and stress. In every particular it was superior to other school banking systems then in use. It was efficient, economical, and effective. That would please the banks. It was well serviced and educational. That would please the schools. It was theft-proof. It was mistake-proof. That would please the depositors.

The most striking features of the plan were the coupon book and substitution posting, both new ideas and widely copied afterward. Each child had his own passbook, which he kept. When he made a deposit on Bank Day — also called Opportunity Day — it was made on a blue coupon in his book, which was then torn out and put with his deposit in his deposit envelope. It showed the amount of deposit and the new balance. A white carbon copy of the transaction remained in his book. At the bank the accounts would be kept on the coupons by a substitution-posting system. The preceding coupon was removed from the bank's file and the new coupon substituted for it. That was the only bookkeeping entry made. "This," said Rex, "was the main point, because it made it possible for the banks to handle thousands of miniature deposits without prohibitive cost." The balance sheets were segregated into units of two hundred accounts each, automatically confining errors to limited areas. All the banks had to do was hold the money. ETS would install the system, service it, provide the passbooks, and attend to all the paperwork. The banks would pay ETS so much per child per year.

Bob took the title of president of ETS. Rex became secretary and director of installation and maintained hair-trigger control. Nothing escaped his attention. He introduced mutiple-head numbering machines to print the books. He prepared more than one hundred and fifty separate forms for teachers and students. He originated the "goldenrod files" — slips of that color which carried data about a particular town visited — the bank officer to be in touch with, the school superintendent, most interested teacher, and other data.[5] When clipped and folded, these files reduced to convenient 4 × 6 slips. Trained service people — eventually sixty-five of them — installed the system. A member of the team spoke at the school assembly. Weekly summaries of the school's banking activities, in comparison with other schools, were sent to the principal. Stamped postcards were supplied for teachers to send in criticisms, complaints, or suggestions. "Bank Day Tomorrow" cards were supplied teachers, for Monday displaying. Cash prizes were awarded schools with the best records. The teacher who came closest in guessing the amount his school deposited in a given week received a ten-dollar gold piece. Five hundred dollars in award money was distributed among those schools which met quotas on their first Bank Day. When a school had one hundred percent enrollment, a group picture of the entire student body appeared in the ETS *Gazette,* a paper of tabloid size sent out monthly to thirty thousand school teachers. Buttons were given to everyone in a class that reached one hundred percent enrollment. A collotype picture of Franklin and Lincoln, for the assembly hall, was sent to schools fully participating. Letters were given to the children urging them to set goals and to earn and save for them: "If you buy that bike with your own money, it's yours. No one can tell you what to do or not do with it." On the passbook envelopes, this line appeared: "A penny saved is a good example for the other 99 cents." Annual visits were made to each school to review the effectiveness of the system, and to the banks to announce new short cuts and/or to explain improvements.

Rex himself prepared the detailed job description for getting out the *Gazette* and wrote most of the contents. In addition to the *Gazette,* ETS publications included a series of pamphlets carrying such titles as "Thrifty Angus," or "My Favorite Grandparent." They told of the boy

who went barefoot to school all winter to keep his shoes new for graduation. And of the seventy-year-old man who had saved nothing through
life and now confided, "They are waiting for me to go."

To the banks Rex emphasized that ETS was a form of self-advertising.
A bank that had twenty thousand passbooks in homes throughout one
small city was getting a lot of publicity. To the schools Rex emphasized
other benefits of the program. It was well coordinated with math, spelling, and civics. Ten minutes was all the time it took from a teacher's
schedule. The children enrolled were eating less candy and chewing
less gum. The young depositors themselves were reminded that some
of those enrolled in the plan had put aside money for college or to set
themselves up in business. In hard times, especially in mining areas,
ETS savings were all that some families had. Yet no emphasis was ever
put on the amount saved. Deposits could be as little as a penny a week.

Rex also invited banks and schools considering ETS to solicit the
views of those already enrolled. Numerous testimonials from bank
presidents and school superintendents found their way into his files.
Bankers often singled out Rex's "personal ability and qualifications" for
commendation. They praised the efficiency of the operation and its
complete workability, and said it exceeded their expectations.

While Rex was making certain that ETS delivered what it promised
and that enthusiasm for the program did not wane, Bob, Bill Loving,
Will Semple, "Doctor" Watson, and others trained for this purpose,
went on the road to secure more accounts. They had one basic plan of
procedure. They would first secure a franchise from a board of education to establish a plan of saving and thrift in its schools. Then they
would find a local bank to act as depository and pay the costs. Rather
than let the advantage go to their competitors, most banks accepted the
program with alacrity.

Bob never forgot the advice Andrew Mellon gave him after a successful meeting in Pittsburgh. Mellon, then United States Secretary of the
Treasury, suggested that on Bank Day metal cabinets should be placed
in the money-collecting cars, the cabinets to be covered with Vaseline
and their handles removed. When the cars returned to the bank with
the money, the handles could then be reattached.[6] Actually, the money
was taken to the banks by school principals or appointed aides, in
padlocked bags. The plan worked well. No ETS deposits were heisted.

Resourcefulness was a much prized virtue among ETS personnel.
Once when Doctor Watson sent his card in to a bank president he heard
the busy executive say, "Don't want to see him — give him this." The
secretary came out and handed Watson a nickel. Watson whipped out
another card and said crisply, "I owe him this. They're two for a nickel."
A bellow came from the president's office: "Send that damn fool in here.
I want to see him." He bought the system. On a visit to Dearborn, Bob
tried to interest Henry Ford in ETS. He sat on the porch rocking with

Henry and said, "People would do better if they knew how to manage what they've got." Henry agreed and said he liked the idea of promoting thrift. That was as far as it went.

Quick to realize that a business which dealt with bankers and school superintendents had to maintain a visible prestige, in the first year of operation Bob took four offices on the twenty-third floor of the Woolworth Building, then New York's tallest building. His own office looked out on the Hudson and commanded a view of ocean liners coming and going and of the sunsets on the Jersey side. A splendid blue Chinese rug, eighteen by twenty-four feet, covered the floor, and later, two fine Doten-Dunton desks were acquired from the office of Josephus Daniels, when Daniels stepped down as Secretary of the Navy. Rex had a working office, half the size of Bob's. John was given an office of the same size. The staff worked in the remaining room, a large bullpen with ten desks. In the summer of 1922 alone, six hundred and forty-two superintendents, principals, and teachers visited the ETS offices. None carried away the impression that ETS was a shoestring operation.

19

Pied Piper of Thrift

Rex Stout is truly *sui generis*. And I can think of few men so widely loved by their colleagues. Rex has an astonishing combination of creative juices and ruthless realism. His business sense, tax insight, mastery of accounting, and stratagems as a committee chairman have always surprised and delighted me. His chipper manner and mischievous mind make any visit with him memorable.

— LEO ROSTEN

In the early years of ETS Rex was less needed in New York than in the towns and cities that had adopted the program. During the school year, Fay and he were on the road much of the time, setting up installations. Fay had excellent secretarial skills and was able to give much practical assistance. They traveled about in a Model T Ford, Rex's first car, and in the first two years alone visited more than a hundred towns and cities.

In the summer of 1917, Fay and Rex went west to visit Fay's family in San Francisco. They camped out all the way. In Colorado they climbed Pike's Peak — by auto, though in *Under the Andes* the Lamar brothers climbed it on foot. Mountain climbing was not one of Rex's enthusiasms. Anyway, he had already climbed Pike's Peak the hard way — verbally.[1] On this same vacation they visited a Navaho Reservation in Arizona. At Tuba City, a trading post, Rex met an old Indian, Joe Two Trees, who had learned arithmetic by watching the trader make out sales checks from across the counter. He "could write columns of figures upside down and add them, rapidly and accurately" — a feat even an erstwhile rapid calculator could admire. Unpredictable performances always amused Rex. The turn of mind that can accommodate itself to such whimsy pleased him.

At Tuba City Rex worked hard to get on close terms with a Navaho Indian so he could "talk turkey" with him: "I made it by expressing my appreciation for the loveliness of his wife's back as she sat weaving at a loom before their hogan. I finally got him to tell me why Indians avoid white men: because we smell bad."

While in California, Rex made a visit to Hollywood. He saw enough.

He never repeated the visit. He also made a brief trip to Baja California
— the one and only time he went to Mexico.[2]

When Rex and Fay got back to New York, they found that Ruth had
opened a tearoom in Greenwich Village. The previous December she
and a friend, Kitty Morton, had started "The Wisp" — the Village's
second tearoom. When the Wisp failed to bring in enough money to
support them both, they flipped a coin and Kitty took sole possession.
Ruth's new tearoom was located in a dilapidated building in Sheridan
Square. The rent was twenty-five dollars a month. It was gloomy. The
kitchenette was tiny. But it reeked with atmosphere. Russell Speakman
Lindsay, a lady artist from Topeka and a friend of Fay's, helped Ruth
decorate. Fay did, too. And Rex wrote a couplet of welcome to hang
over the door:

> *What liquor promises, tea bestows —*
> *Good cheer, good converse, and repose.*

Rex had just one admonition: "For God's sake, don't name the place 'To
a Wild Rose' or something wishy-washy like that!" Ruth picked a name
by shutting her eyes and stabbing the dictionary with her index finger.
It would be "The Klicket."

Ruth was thrilled about the venture but naïve about her environment
and about the practical side of running a business. She soon had half a
dozen regulars who lounged in the Klicket and borrowed money from
her. Sometimes she had difficulty holding out eight dollars to pay room-
and-board money for a nearby flat, which she shared with a friend.
Dudley Digges was her next-door neighbor and John Barrymore lived
just around the corner. Ruth was in the Village eight months before she
saw a prostitute. "My God, that's Ruth," said Kitty. "Eight months in the
Village and she thinks that's the first one she's seen."

One afternoon Ruth was reading in the rear yard when she heard
someone come into the Klicket. "Friend or customer?" she called out.
"Friend, I hope," came the reply. She went in to see who it was. "I'm
John Barrymore, and I'm thirsty," said the visitor. He ordered black
coffee for six and drank all six cups. While he worked on the coffee, Ruth
brought out a copy of *Hamlet* and asked him to read her favorite
passage, "This above all. . . ." His voice thrilled her so that she found
it hard to put her mind on what he said. When the coffee was gone, he
stood up.

"How long have you been in the Village?" he asked.

"Eight months."

"How old are you?"

"Thirty-three."

He shook his head slowly.

"I've seen everything," he said. Then, with sober majesty, he repeated the first three lines of Polonius's advice to Laertes. Without another word to spoil it, he left.

Once when Fay and Rex came by, Ruth told them how she had started out the night with a bare larder. By serving toast to customers who had not ordered it, she had taken in seventy cents. With that she had bought half a cake, butter, and cocoa, which she sold at a profit to her next customers. By ten o'clock she had the larder full again. Fay was aghast. Why on earth hadn't Ruth called her? She would have come over with some money.

"It doesn't work like that," Rex said. "This way you keep your self-respect. It's fun the way they do it." Ruth thought he sounded wistful. He was making a go of ETS, but she doubted that he enjoyed being tied into business the way he was.[3]

Ruth gave up the Klicket in the spring of 1918. For its furnishings she got $4.50. She did not think of it as a failure. For one thing, through it she had met Alfred Rossiter, the man she would marry eleven years later.

World War I gave ETS some anxious moments. War Savings Stamps began to compete for the pennies of school children. Then, early in 1918, with polite firmness, the Treasury Department asked ETS to convert the children's balances into savings stamps, if they requested it. This plan, Rex saw, was a good compromise. It would keep the organization together. At the same time, it would help the war effort. For the duration of the war, ETS promoted the sale of saving stamps and Liberty Bonds. Although the organization was run on a nonprofit basis, expansion continued. When the war ended, ETS had been established in more than two hundred communities. Armistice Day found Rex at Memphis, Tennessee, working on a new installation. "Fay and I," he told me, "got uplifted at the home of the vice president of the Bank of Commerce and Trust Company." The armistice was good news for ETS, too. Business soon was booming.

In 1917, Bob had moved his family to Waldwick, New Jersey, to a three-hundred-year-old house coincidentally occupied, through most of its history, by successive generations of Stouts. With his strong sense of family, the association was, for Bob, irresistible. The road curved as it passed the house and many autos misjudged the turn. One day, in 1919, Douglas MacArthur piled into a tree on the front lawn. Bob rushed out and collected MacArthur for cocktails and dinner while the car was being repaired.[4]

Presently, Bob bought the splendid home of sporting goods tycoon Henry C. Lee at nearby Ridgewood. There, through the 1920's, the Stouts gathered for holidays and for their annual Christmas theatricals. Rather than everyone bringing presents for everyone else, with ETS efficiency each bought one thing of general usefulness, with each person taking a present according to the number he drew. One year Lucetta drew the last number. At Donald's suggestion — passed in whispers among them — no one picked the one package which obviously was a quart of whiskey. So Lucetta got it. Knowing her firm teetotaling convictions, everyone wondered how she would deal with her gift. The answer was not long in coming. "Here," she said, handing the bottle to young Walter Roddy, "take this out to the yard. I bet you can break it with your new air rifle."

In the early spring of 1919, Rex was in Wilkes-Barre, Pennsylvania, to make an installation. At noon he was walking on South Main Street when a man stepped up to the pedestrian walking ahead of him and shot him through the heart. That was the only time Rex saw murder committed. Like Archie Goodwin coming upon an unannounced corpse, Rex did not linger.

Later that same April, Fay and Rex came in off the road. He had trained others to handle the installation work and now it was time to follow up, from his office at the Woolworth Building, new ideas which he had for the program, and to apply his prosperity to the attractions New York offered. Fay and he took an apartment at 11 West Eighth Street. Bob's daughter Natalie remembers being impressed with the drapes. They were made of silk.[5]

The success of ETS meant that the Stouts could see Europe if they wanted to. Lucetta had no desire to go. Ideas, not places, interested her. To John, who knew England through his history books better than most Englishmen did, the prospect was overwhelming. In the summer of 1919, with Betty along for company, he set off on a three-month tour of the British Isles and the Continent. For a bon voyage gift, Natalie gave him a copy of Gray's poems and got him to promise to sit under the yew at Stoke Poges and read the "Elegy" aloud. On their return, Betty confirmed that John fulfilled his promise to the letter, indifferent to the gaping astonishment of conventional pilgrims.

In the years when the Educational Thrift Service was coming of age, Rex's mind constantly was reaching out to new interests. During the early days of United States involvement in World War I, he had walked out on a British lecturer whom he thought excessive in his traducement of the Germans. Analyzing his own behavior afterward, Rex saw that he had a moral obligation to reach informed convictions about vital issues of the day and, if it became necessary, to act on them. In 1919, when Eugene Debs was imprisoned, Rex followed with sympathy the efforts of William Allen White and Oswald Villard to procure his release, and signed two appeals drawn up to effect that end. At this time he also became interested in the socialist theorist Scott Nearing, first attending his lectures, then reading his books, then making his acquaintance. But at that stage of his life these concerns of necessity had to be peripheral. He was now committed more than ever to ETS for Bob and he had bought out their partner, Bill Loving, and assumed half-and-half ownership of the business. Loving was a supersalesman, no doubt about it, but ETS was not the right business for him. For one thing, he had had his picture taken with one-hundred-dollar bills protruding from the pockets of his checkered weskit. More and more, ETS was becoming a family business. Old John Stout was traveling, visiting schools and banks — a perfect assignment for John because it brought him again into an administrative relationship with children. His natural dignity reenforced his fitness. He specialized in intimate, paternal talks in grammar schools. Preaching thrift, he would pick the youngest, prettiest tot from the assembly, call her to the platform, lay his hand on her head, and launch into his inspirational discourse.

Walt also was on the road selling the system, and, in the office, Mary and Betty dealt with the volumes of paperwork. Tad's sister Stella worked with them. Eventually Juanita Merle Roddy joined them, and Natalie and her husband, Wallace Carr, fresh out of Dartmouth. Natalie and Wally went on the road, giving a heavy Franklin emphasis to their appeals.

In a sense, Franklin was another family member of the firm. As president of the International Benjamin Franklin Society, Bob was well publicized in the role — the president of a thrift savings program, paying homage to the apostle of thrift himself. One day the papers might carry a picture of J. Robert Stout placing a wreath in front of Franklin's statue in Printing House Square; on another, they might show him presenting a citation from the Franklin Society to Thomas Alva Edison. For one of the society's exhibits, Franklin's nightcap, passed down in the family for eight generations, was brought on from Wilmington, a coup which pleased Bob more than if he had procured the loan of the *Mona Lisa*. His secretary, Frances Cox, was likewise the secretary of the International Benjamin Franklin Society and edited the society's *Gazette*.

Helen May, a beautiful, honey-colored blond, with hazel eyes, began her ten-year association with ETS in 1923. Looking back fifty-two years later, she recalls:

On a cold morning in January 1923, Rex Stout interviewed me for a clerical position with ETS. I was nineteen years old, timid, and scared stiff. Rex's courtesy and kind manner soon put me at ease. During the interview, he asked me to remove my hat and then looked at me intently for several seconds. I resented this, but he hired me so I decided to overlook it. Later I found out that he wanted to see if I kept my hair neat. A very short time later I became the bookkeeper, and continued in that position until I left ETS to marry.[6]

Charlotte Foucart later had the same experience. Rex told me: "I can't judge a prospective employee with her hat on." Helen May continues:

> Rex Stout was in the office every day. . . . He was very orderly. No matter how busy he was, the papers on his desk and on the large table at his back were always neatly arranged.
>
> In his dress he was meticulous and seemed to prefer tweeds. He was always patient, considerate, thoughtful, and even-tempered in his daily life at the office. He told a story about having had a violent temper in his youth. The realization of its violence came to him one day when he lost control of it. He swore then that he would never lose it again. During the years I knew him, he had it well under control.

Although she had not seen Rex for nearly forty-five years, Helen found that his books brought him vividly to mind:

> As I read, I had trouble detaching him from the characters. He was dashing around the City in taxis; driving to Westchester and Long Island; locating boats on Long Island Sound; or doing whatever the fast pace of the story called for. These associations were especially evident when I read *Double for Death*. In my judgment, Tecumseh Fox gives an excellent portrayal of the real Rex Stout — his brilliant mind, his alertness, his crispness of speech, and his fast decisive action. Here you have the author himself in action.

Of the Nero Wolfe story "Kill Now — Pay Later," Helen says:

> Most of the action takes place in a suite of offices in a tall building. I am sure Rex Stout had the ETS offices on the twenty-third floor of the Woolworth Building in mind. I was amused and surprised to find that the description of the office receptionist was that of Frances Cox, J. Robert Stout's private secretary. It was perfect, from her little mannerisms to her fox neck piece. She was most attractive, tall, stately.

Charlotte Foucart, Rex's secretary for several years at ETS, says: "Rex was always disposed to give one time for explanations and was as quick as all get-out in anything he undertook. He had a fine brand of humor."[7] Sometimes he let Charlotte use his season's ticket to the New York Symphony.[8]

ETS held out many inducements to its employees to do their work well — an extra week's salary at Christmas, alternate Tuesdays off if you got to work on time, an outing once a year to the Ridgewood Country Club (of which Bob, of course, was president), and, once a year, lunch at a fine restaurant, followed by a matinee of a first-run show.

Though other thrift systems pirated ETS methods, none could match the efficiency Rex insisted on and got. By 1925, 432 cities, in more than 30 states, had adopted the system, and 3,000,000 children were en-

Amos and Emily Todhunter and Family, 1873

Amos and Family at Todhunter Homestead, New Martinsburg, Ohio, 1875

Nathan Stout

Sophia Stout

Rex at six months

Stout's Mill

Birthplace of Rex Stout, Noblesville, Indiana

Clara Todhunter

Oscar Benjamin Todhunter

Hackberry Hall

John and Lucetta and family, circa 1893

John Wallace Stout, County Superintendent, circa 1899

Lucetta Todhunter Stout, circa 1920

John Wallace Stout, circa 1918

Police Chief A. G. Goodwin, circa 1905

rolled. In Pittsburgh, under an earlier plan, in 23 years 11,000 students had saved $140,000. Under ETS, in 6 months 75,000 students saved $370,000. In Port Jervis, New York, 1,400 saved $15,000 in a year. In Dayton, Ohio, 23,000 students saved $100,000 in one term. Newspapers in Memphis reported that in black schools 79 percent of the students had enrolled. In Rhode Island, 7 cities adopted the plan simultaneously. The first week it took fifty-two clerks to prepare passbooks and verify them. In Indianapolis, E. U. Graff, the superintendent of schools, declared ETS superior to all other plans. Graff had written books on school savings and, during World War I, had directed the educational thrift program for the state of Indiana.

Saluting ETS subscribers in 1922, Rex declared: "To the men and women in the schools and banks who have assisted us during seven years to bring order out of chaos and to make universal, popular, and successful what was isolated, stagnant, and contemned, we make the obeisances of appreciation and gratitude." Rex insisted later that in the ETS years he wrote "37,826 business letters, and nothing for publication," but his rhetoric here suggests that the disciple of Addison, Macaulay, Montaigne, and La Rochefoucauld had not yet laid waste his powers in getting and spending.

The return to New York opened the way for Rex to sift through his storyteller's consciousness an expanding knowledge of the good life. Fay and he dined often at the Brevoort, famed for its chef, and at Louis Martin's, which, Rex told me, came to mind when he was asked to identify Rusterman's, the restaurant to which Nero Wolfe extends enlightened patronage.[9] Few Stout readers realize that the visiting Kansans in *O Careless Love* dine at Rusterman's before the restaurant comes into the Wolfe series. In the summer of 1920, Rex's palate was further instructed when he stayed at Quebec's Château Frontenac for two weeks and there discovered the merits of claret.

Early in the summer of 1921 Fay wanted to go again to California, this time to visit her aunt's ranch in Los Angeles. When Ruth said she would like to go, too, Rex begged off. He disliked southern California and there was plenty going on in New York that interested him. On their way west, Ruth and Fay stopped off in Topeka. Ruth had not seen Topeka since she had left home to seek her fortune, seventeen years before. One afternoon, Fay's aunt, Margaret Chapman, drove her out to Wakarusa. The farmhouse and barn were gone. So was the lilac hedge. Old Baldy was still there, but sadly neglected. Yet things could have been worse. In fact, they did become worse. Fifty years later, the site was occupied by an automobile junkyard.[10]

Meanwhile, Rex was relishing his stay-at-home holiday. One night, in the back room of the Washington Square Bookshop, on Twenty-eighth Street, he listened enraptured for three hours while Theodore Dreiser and H. L. Mencken exchanged views with crusty vigor. The owner of the celebrated bookshop was Josephine Bell (not to be confused with Doris Bell Collier Ball, M.D., the English detective story writer whose pen name is Josephine Bell), who had been a neighbor of the Overmyers in Topeka. Rex had known Josephine since he was thirteen and she was eleven. Josephine and her husband, Egmont Arens, lived in the rear of the shop. A few years later they were divorced and Egmont married Ruth Chrisman. In the years that followed, Egmont was to become one of Rex's steadfast friends, though Fay and he would continue to cherish Josephine's friendship as well.[11]

On 2 July 1921, Rex, accompanied by Bob, was in Jersey City to see Jack Dempsey defend his title against the French challenger, Georges Carpentier. The fight, staged out-of-doors at Boyle's Thirty Acres, drew a crowd of 90,000. Gate receipts were $1,626,580, marking the first time receipts for a boxing match went over the million-dollar mark. Carpentier was knocked out in the fourth round.[12]

But it was still High Culture that claimed Rex's greatest support. Through the early 1920's he kept up an active schedule of theater-going. He saw Eleanora Duse in three performances at a theater on Central Park West. He took Ruth and Mary to the Met's production of *Carmen.* He saw Isadora Duncan several times. His verdict: "Not well trained or disciplined, but she had fine presence and personality, much invention, and sometimes imagination." But nothing could or would usurp in his favor the place he allotted John Barrymore's 1922 production of *Hamlet.* If he could have called back just one evening at the theater, it would have been that one.

Visiting the Village, Rex formed friendships with Floyd Dell and Rockwell Kent. Although Kent's politics went farther to the left than Rex cared to go, Rex found that no barrier to their friendship. He thought it would have been futile to argue with Kent about it. "Let an artist keep to his business and forget ideas," he said.

Asked at eighty-eight what he missed most out of his past life, Rex said: "Moving around on my feet; theater, concerts, ballet; meeting new people, ball games at the park; sex; baked beans."

Ironically, since Rex had given up writing, his circle of literary friends and acquaintances had enlarged. Through Oswald Villard he met Carl and Mark Van Doren. His friendship with Mark would become one of the closest friendships of his lifetime. Through Carl, a friendship ripened with Ford Madox Ford. Despite Ford's stutter, Rex found him the best talker he had ever met. Often their topic was Joseph Conrad. There had been a rift in Ford's friendship with Conrad, but in the past they had collaborated and Ford continued to hold him in esteem. When he realized that Rex accorded Conrad first place among contemporary novelists, Ford urged him to write to Conrad. Rex did write and Conrad answered with an invitation to Rex to come visit him. In 1922, in the early spring, Rex was Conrad's guest at Oswalds, near Canterbury, for six days. Of his visit, Rex told me: "Conrad didn't talk a lot, but in a curious way the things he said were more intense and interesting than the things others say. He was almost squat — kind of pulled together. His gestures were all small — with a finger rather than an arm. At lunchtime his voice was strong, vibrant and a little halting — unsure. But when he came down at six o'clock after a hard afternoon's work of writing one hundred and seventy words his voice was high and querulous. He was a hell of a good listener. He had an interest in anything anyone would say." Conrad was working on *The Rover* and understandably preoccupied. And his health was failing. Yet he was considerate and encouraging. Before Rex left, Conrad gave him an inscribed copy of *The End of the Tether.*

Conrad's impress is heavy on four of the five novels Rex wrote in the five years before he began the Nero Wolfe series. In a sense, the series did not escape the Conradian influence either. Latent in most of Conrad's work, and conspicuous in the books written after his breakdown, is the view that women are disgusting. This view obsesses the protagonist of Rex's third psychological novel, *Golden Remedy.* The book's title comes from the brand name of a V.D. nostrum which the protagonist has recourse to in young manhood. Years later he notices that his daughter's perfume has the same odor. The inference is unmistakable — women and disease are one. Hair fetishism — where a woman's long hair, envisaged as an illusory phallus, arouses in the male a castration anxiety — likewise is common both to Conrad and Stout. One wonders if the mannish Dr. Eva Harding, who had "destroyed" Rex's proxy mother, Winona May, made accessible to him a theme which parallels a major Conradian motif.

Writing of Conrad's misogyny, Bernard C. Meyer says: "Like his fictional seafaring characters Conrad undoubtedly saw in the exclusively masculine community of life at sea a bulwark protecting him not only against the threat of physical annihilation in general but against the dangers associated with romantic entanglements in particular."[13] As an erstwhile sailor, Rex would be sensitive to the emphasis Conrad gives to "the exclusively masculine community of life at sea." Similar logic leads Nero Wolfe to set up his brownstone seraglio in which orchids — demanding, effete, and in constant need of pampering — figure as surrogate concubines, outrageous but controllable. In his own life, Rex would escape this problem. His exploration of it in creative fiction does not constitute for him, as it did for Conrad, a corrective revision of painful reality. But he understood it, and he saw it was the one problem which the wholly cerebral Wolfe could handle only in the Conradian way.

Borys Conrad, Joseph's son, tells us that when his father wanted to exercise his intellect unmolested, he would retreat to his garden and, imagining himself in the safe and inviolate environment of a ship, stride back and forth within its defined precincts — a captain pacing his quarterdeck.[14] Perhaps at Oswalds, as Rex watched Conrad in his garden, he caught and stored this sense of his conduct in his subconscious — thrift savings which he would withdraw a dozen years hence, the interest compounded, when he placed Nero Wolfe within his confining quarters.

20.

Civil Libertarian

Rex Stout has all the attributes of a good business man–author. He knows the market and the value of his work. He has imagination. And he is a cool-headed negotiator.

— IRWIN KARP

The success of the Educational Thrift Service owed much to the ability of the Stouts to work together as a family. In point of fact, as their prosperity grew, their family spirit quickened. One evidence of this was their Christmas festivities, which continued with innovations. An engraved silver loving cup now was awarded to those who put on the best skit. And it was decided that gifts for the adults should be handmade. The first year that that was done, Rex won the most applause when he gave John a yellow silk nightshirt which he had made himself. That same year, those living at 414 regaled the others with an inverted seance. The participants were the spirits of the departed, trying to communicate with the real world. Lucetta was a trapezist in white tights. Mary and Donald paired off as Bacon and Shakespeare. (The scene ended with a dispute raging between them over which of them had written the plays; the insults they hurled at one another all were apt quotations from Shakespeare.)

This look at death from the other side had a melancholy epilogue. Before another December arrived, Donald had stepped through the barrier to join May in that world the others could not reach. Death came with scant notice. Donald had the merry Todhunter ways and seemed robust. His love of the out-of-doors and his liking for physical exercise seemed his guarantee of well-being. Morning and evening he ran in the park. His views about physical culture were antipodal to those of Rex, who dismissed the term with Neronian disdain: "A verbal absurdity. What's cultured about it?" One night in February 1922, Donald was at the theater with Tad and Bob when he began hemorrhaging. Tests showed he was deep in the grip of tuberculosis. "I think he may have been running, trying to get away from that crazy family of his," said his niece, Natalie, only half in jest.[1]

Donald was sent to a sanatorium at Saranac Lake, where his condition worsened steadily. In his last weeks, before his death on 30 August 1922,

Lucetta all but lived at the hospital. Her positiveness and her efforts to bolster other patients made Donald's doctors and nurses think she did not realize he would die. She was alone with him when the final crisis came. She called in the doctor and stood by the bed while he worked over his patient. When the doctor groped for words to tell her he was gone, she told him, "Donald won't breathe in this world any longer."

"Why couldn't I have saved him for you?" the doctor lamented.

"Oh, but I haven't lost him," Lucetta said.[2]

Despite its value to him as a ready route to affluence, if ETS had not had redeeming social value as a purveyor to the young of the idea of managing their money prudently, Rex might not have stayed with it as long as he did. "I certainly wasn't cynical about it," he told me; "I approve of thrift and solvency." But business never could engross him. Of businessmen he said: "I admire and respect them, yes, but I have no fondness for them. I keep my fondness for other kinds of people. I think it's probably what their main interest is. A man whose main interest is that can't be a very interesting person. A valuable person — sure. We can't get along without them. But not a very interesting person."

In Rex's fictions, businessmen are faintly caricatured, their preoccupation with a few ideas indicting them as men of narrow understanding. Even as a writer whose sales would go past the one hundred million mark, and whose books would appear in twenty-seven languages, Rex never would retain an agent, or even an accountant to figure his income tax. He looked after these matters himself, with complete competence, in odd moments, grateful to escape an agent's importunities to turn book writing into a business enterprise. Those close to him would find him sensible in money matters, but conscious of money only as something that left him free to live as he chose. Even as he captained ETS, he looked elsewhere for self-realization.

Not until the 1930's would Rex build High Meadow and provide himself a miniature realm which he could preside over on his own terms. But even in the early years of ETS his eyes were cast toward the Brewster-Danbury divide. He first went to Brewster, New York, along the Connecticut border, in the summer of 1919 as guest at Gage Hill of William Nyland and his wife, Ilonka Karasz, *New Yorker* cover artist. In 1922 he rented a farmhouse at the foot of the hill — the second oldest house in Putnam County. It belonged to Adelbert Salmon, whose family had lived there since the eighteenth century. At that time Rex was first introduced to Adelbert's son, Harold, who was destined to become the Archie Goodwin of his household through the next half-century. From 1922 to 1927, the Salmon farmhouse was to be Rex's chief haven from the harassments of New York City. Farming was still a while in the future for him. But he got back to croquet and horseshoes. And he found peace being in the midst of a growing, green world.

Another summertime venture in this era also had far-ranging results. In the summer of 1923, Rex and Fay went to California to see Fay's family again. En route they visited Glacier National Park, the Grand Canyon, and Yosemite. For Glacier Park Rex felt an instant affinity. It figured conspicuously in his vacation plans during the next several summers. As a writer, he found Glacier Park a resource from which he could seek replenishment for more than forty years.

By 1924 Rex was able to run ETS almost as an avocation. Increasingly his attention was taken up with the activities of the liberal intelligentsia, among whom he found many friends in New York. One of those who knew him best in those years was Morris Ernst, attorney for the American Civil Liberties Union — the man who would guide the *Ulysses* case through the courts. Ernst said of the strategy by which Rex governed his conduct in those years:

As a man of business experience, Rex was an oddity in our circle. He was important to all of the people in that part of the culture in New York. . . . He was riding no hobby horse. Without propaganda, he stimulated the others in the group — a man of quiet, unspectacular influence. He didn't convert people, like Scott Nearing, or have them marching in parades, like Norman Thomas. He never went out on a picket line. . . . He was secure enough financially — with his home and his hobbies. He didn't need to exhibit himself. . . . He was much more self-sufficient than the people he went with. He had a rare sense of inner security. . . . Rex didn't need others to complete himself. . . . He didn't need to go where the crowd was. He never went around to get guidance from his friends — to find out how they were voting, how dealing with some current issue. You couldn't count on him to go along with the liberal line. He wouldn't jump on board because everyone else was backing Norman Thomas or Al Smith. Many of the others were fighting momma and poppa, striking out against the conservatism of their own families — fighting their past. Rex had none of those problems. He was supremely his own man.[3]

Rex's liberalism was no aberration. All that happened in the 1920's was that his attitudes became visible to the people who were bent on shaping the direction our society moved in. Rex remained himself. Others did not influence Rex; Rex influenced them. His personal authority both baffled and intrigued them. Those who tried to challenge it made no headway against it. He was not susceptible to manipulation. Musing about Rex as he found him then, Scott Nearing says, "He was a pretty determined kind of fellow."[4]

In the field of liberal politics, Rex applied the same kind of efficiency he had used to foster ETS. These people said they wanted a better organized world. He was ready to support those activities which would move them toward that goal. But he could act only from his own convictions. He saw that the motivations of many of his new friends were uncertain. Rex soon was picking and choosing his spots in the liberal movement. He probed it like a muskmelon. What was too soft, too unyielding, or off in scent, color, or flavor, he passed by.

One of Rex's liveliest friendships in this period was with Egmont Arens, his Washington Square Bookshop acquaintance, now his neighbor on West Eighth Street. Egmont was an artist, and later would pioneer streamlining in train design, but in seven years he already had had many careers in New York — as bookseller, editor of the original *Playboy,* art editor of *Vanity Fair,* officer of the Pratt Institute of Art, Manager of the People's Symphony Concerts, editor of *The Philadelphian,* and founder of the Flying Stag Press. In 1921, with two friends, he had sailed the twenty-one-ton schooner yacht *Diablesse* to Europe. In prior times he had been a cowboy. Egmont was an amiable madman. He liked Rex and sought his friendship aggressively. Rex enjoyed Arens but could not share his emotional approach to life.

Rex's objectivity perplexed Egmont. He campaigned to make inroads on it. Thus on 4 April 1924, he wrote Rex:

It's not very easy to talk to you, because you are so careful, so covered up, so walled about, and one never knows whether the things you say are spoken for the benefit of strengthening the wall, or are the voice of the you within. As I have come to know even this little of your real self, I've often wondered why you bother so about the wall. The real you is so adequate and complete and fine and to-be-loved, that I'm amazed that you keep that part of you so hidden.[5]

Despite his restraints, Rex soon joined Egmont in bringing out a de luxe twelve-volume edition of Arthur Machen's translation of Casanova's *Memoirs,* a book barred from the United States because of alleged erotic content. The idea originated with Egmont, but Rex took no convincing. Censorship would have his lifelong repugnance.

The plan was that Rex would finance the undertaking — which he did, to the sum of $24,000 — and that Egmont would handle the details of publication. This Egmont did with verve. He asked Havelock Ellis to write an introduction. When Ellis demurred, Egmont, undismayed, asked Arthur Symons to do it. Symons obliged. Egmont then got Arthur Machen himself to supply a new preface. Egmont's efforts did not stop there. He hired Edmund Wilson to read, and correct as required, the whole of the text. Rockwell Kent was asked to prepare twelve illustrations. Egmont, calling himself "Eggface the Pirate," further plotted to have Kent, then abroad, transport to Mexico the remainder of an earlier English edition of the *Memoirs,* so that they could control the market without competition. The scheme called for having Rex and himself fetch the books in Mexico and smuggle them back on a chartered yacht, by way of the Gulf. In Egmont's mind, the thought that they might be intercepted by coast guard ships patrolling for bootleggers only added zest to the caper.

Rex seemed to catch some of the excitement. When Egmont wrote to outline the plan to Rex, who was in California — at Glendale, to visit Fay's family once more and to fish the mountain streams — Rex wired back: "GEE BUT I FEEL ADVENTUROUS." In a follow-up letter, he extrapolated:

Perhaps we could get them in from Mexico by airplane or submarine. Or — I have now learned to pack mules, and no doubt we could creep through some mountain passes down there, by night, with knives in our teeth and canteens filled with goats' blood at our saddle pommels. In the meantime you could be cruising the Gulf of Mexico to keep the navy off. Hell's bells I feel murderous.

Rex's letter was followed by a cable from Rockwell Kent: "WILL DO IT. DEAD BROKE. WIRE MONEY FOR EXPENSES." Kent thought that Rex and Egmont wanted to market the English edition itself. Twenty years later, in his autobiography, *It's Me O Lord,* he wrote: "Happily for me and for its backers, that crazy enterprise was translated into a bona-fide American edition of the work, to be illustrated by me and privately distributed." Seeking isolation in Vermont, Kent spent the fall and the winter reading the books and studying up on eighteenth-century manners and dress so that his drawings would be historically beyond reproach. His meticulousness brought him greater profits than he himself foresaw. From then on, for years to come, illustrating books was to be his chief source of income.[6] The originals of Kent's illustrations of the *Memoirs* were turned over to Rex after the book was done.[7]

Despite the comradeship the Casanova venture sponsored between them, Egmont still felt that Rex set limits to their friendship. "I have never tried so hard to reach anyone," he complained, "and been so unsuccessful as I have in your case." He insisted that their intellects complemented one another and speculated on what the results would be if their best elements were mingled to produce "a composite wonder-man." He said they would be better off if he had some of Rex's prudence and Rex had some of his foolhardiness. But mostly he hid his exasperation behind a mocking, incessant persiflage. Habitually he addressed Rex as Silenus — the foster father of Bacchus — and urged him to give vent to a satyr's passions. When Rex took a trip, a letter from Egmont followed, informing him: "Ruth [the second Mrs: Arens] has some magenta garters. You will enjoy snapping these on your return." Rex humored him to the extent of occasionally signing his letters Silenus, or sometimes just "Si."

The way Rex held Egmont to practical considerations involved in their publishing venture suggests that theirs was a Tom Sawyer–Huck Finn alliance — with Egmont freely fantasizing and Rex seeing to it that commonsense had the decisive voice in all their counsels. Casanova's *Memoirs* appeared as an "Aventuros" publication. Leatherbound it sold at $300 a set; in cloth, at $150. There were fifteen hundred sets in all.[8] Rex had gone into this enterprise as a quixotic thrust at the censor, prepared to lose half his investment. In fact, he made a profit. Earlier he had written to Egmont, "I suggest for our second venture a thin paper edition of *India's Coral Strand,* with a foreword by Mahatma Gandhi." Now he could say, "Why not?"

Edmund Wilson was paid generously for emending the text of the *Memoirs.* Although it quickened his own amorous activities, he did not give his employers the satisfaction of knowing that. In fact they thought he cast a cold eye on the project and its sponsors. Rex told me: "Bunny and I met several times while the edition was under way. We didn't like each other." Years later, in 1945, Wilson deprecated Rex and the whole genre of detective fiction in a series of *New Yorker* articles. Rex then replied: "Edmund Wilson, the critic who walks like a man . . . ate green apples when a child, and can't go for a walk in the country now, to get more green apples, because his brow gets caught in the telephone wires."[9] When Wilson died, in 1972, Rex commented: "I knew Bunny for fifty years. He'd criticize, of course. I would have been disappointed in him if he didn't. He was a scholar who was also a good writer, but he had no feeling at all for a straight job of storytelling."

Throughout the nineteen twenties Ruth Stout was running her brother Rex a close second as the adventure-seeking member of the family. Rex, quite innocently, had been the start of it all. Back in 1919, on his recommendation, she had read an article in *The Nation* on the right to strike. She took it to heart and urged four girls whom she worked with at Franklin Simon to walk off the job until they got a pay raise. When all five were fired, Ruth reported the results to Oswald Garrison Villard, grandson of William Lloyd Garrison and editor of *The Nation.* Villard offered her a job with the magazine, if she knew shorthand. She did not and did not want to learn it, either. Her experience with the strike had awakened her social conscience and she wanted to do something meaningful. About then, the occasion arose for her to pay her first income tax. She wondered if, as a Quaker, she should pay the money when it might be used for military expenditures. She sent a wire to Rex, who was then in Scranton, setting up another ETS unit: "DO I BELIEVE IN INCOME TAX?" Rex sent back a one word reply: "YES." Nero Wolfe's stoical acceptance of the income tax was no afterthought on Rex's part. Ruth decided she had more thinking to do and took a job with the publishing house of T. Y. Crowell.

At about this time Ruth's romance with Fred Rossiter went into a long night of eclipse and she was feeling dispirited. Rex intervened. "If you want a new enthusiasm," he said, "you ought to go hear Scott Nearing." So she did. At the start she was not too clear about Nearing's teachings, but his voice, his smile, and his personality held her. That was just after Christmas, in 1920.

Ruth thinks she would have been attracted to Nearing even if she had not needed a hero badly at the time she first became aware of him. She soon realized that his concern for people beckoned her in the very direction she had been groping. But she was not cut out to pursue her ideals in the abstract. She admits: "I couldn't enjoy myself if I couldn't drag in something personal and, if possible, dramatic and warm." Accordingly she signed up for several of Nearing's courses at the Rand School and began a campaign to be noticed by him. The campaign went well. By August 1921 she was on his payroll as a member of his office staff at the Rand School's Camp Tamiment, at Bushkill, Pennsylvania. At last she really got his notice when she told him that the proofreading of his books — he had already published twenty of them — was "sloppy." She offered to take on the job. Had she known that Nearing did his own proofing, she would not have brought up the subject at all. But she was right, and Nearing knew it and put her to work on the galleys of *The American Empire.*

In September, when the camp closed, Ruth volunteered to prepare transcripts of Nearing's extemporaneous lectures on current events, for the New York *Call.* She did not tell him she knew no shorthand. Anyway, she reasoned, she had three weeks to learn it. Fay, who had excellent clerical skills, thought she was out of her mind. Even a veteran stenographer would find Nearing's rapid-fire delivery an all but insurmountable challenge. But Ruth was adamant, so Fay coached her. And when the series began, in late September, she came along with her to help take notes. Moreover, Lucetta, John, Mary, Betty, Donald (who would be dead before the year was out), and Russell Lindsay all were in the audience too — all pledged to listen carefully and to help later to reconstruct what was said. A hysterical week followed but Ruth finally came up with a transcript which Nearing approved of. Later efforts came easier. Ruth soon was handling all the details for his lectures and debates.[10]

For Scott, a surprise bonus of his friendship with Ruth was his friendship with Lucetta. The first time he came to dinner, Ruth and Mary left him in the living room with her while they saw the meal through its final stages. Scott's laughter carried to them repeatedly.

"What do you suppose Mother's saying?" Mary asked.

"There's no telling," Ruth said.

During dinner Scott made a point that would have brought an audience out of its seats with applause. Lucetta reached over and patted the forty-year-old Scott on the arm.

"Tut, tut, sonny," she said, "you've got a lot to learn." After that, he was her slave. (At ninety, Scott would say of Lucetta: "She was a person in her own right. She was positive, but not peppery. She had her own ideas — own standards of conduct. She was definitely a person.")

One day in the spring of 1923, Ruth sat engrossed in Dostoyevsky's *Notes from Underground* when Lucetta said to her, "Since you're so fond of Dostoyevsky, why don't you go see his country?"

"I'm stone broke," Ruth said.

"The man who's directing Quaker relief in Russia used to go to school to me," Lucetta said. "Suppose I write and ask if you can go along?"

Before she half-realized what was happening, Ruth was on the Quaker relief team, Rex and Fay were there on shipboard presenting her with a brocaded dressing gown as a bon voyage gift, and she was off on a year's visit to Russia, where, she fondly hoped, she would learn enough Russian to read Dostoyevsky in the original. But the Russians were so eager to learn English that she gave them English lessons instead. Ruth was past fifty before she was able to read Dostoyevsky in his own language.

Ruth had gone to Russia at a historic moment. In January 1924, Lenin died. She went to his funeral. Never had her sense of drama been so satisfied.

As soon as she got back from Russia, Ruth resumed her duties as Scott Nearing's secretary. One of the first things she did was to arrange for Scott to debate Bertrand Russell at Carnegie Hall, on 25 May 1924. For moderators, she rounded up Samuel Untermeyer and Benjamin A. Javits, brother of Jacob Javits. The topic was "Can the Soviet Idea Take Hold of America, England, and France?" Scott took the affirmative side.

Rex had an aversion to staged debates and avoided them as a matter of principle. Yet he wanted to meet Russell. Ruth handled that too. She brought Russell around to Rex's apartment, on Perry Street, for high tea. In Rex Russell found a lively intellectual sparring partner. Over the next five years, until Rex went to Europe, whenever Russell was in New York, he came by regularly for dinner and conversation. One night when they were having dinner together, their minds ranged over English literature. They talked of the Mediterranean origin of the usual Gothic villain in English novels. Rex asked: "Why is it that whenever there is a character of Latin extraction in a novel by an Englishman, even if the novelist is obviously sympathetic with the character, between the lines there is always a note of condescension?" Russell's brow corrugated. "They gesticulate," he announced, "and we can't bear it."

Of Russell, Rex told me: "In 1926 he was fifty-four and world-famous; I was forty and merely an American businessman who could answer his thousands of questions about my country and fellow citizens, and could (and did) supply vast quantities of fresh caviar, which he loved. And apparently he liked me. There wasn't much we never talked about. Once he spent hours trying to define and describe to his satisfaction, precisely, the difference between the operation of his mind and mine that made me incapable of understanding the general theory of relativity."[11]

Russell was one of the few men in the world who could hold Rex in awe. Years later, in the spring of 1940, he was Rex's dinner guest at High Meadow. Of that occasion Egmont Arens afterward reported: "I'd known Rex more than twenty years and never saw him at a loss for words. He was informed and intelligent and he showed it. But that night he was like a little mouse at a feast of cats — silent and attentive and bright eyed and quietly pleasant. And all of a sudden I realized, By God, Rex is scared! He really was scared. I was surprised and kind of touched."[12]

During World War II, when Russell sent his children to America, on his instructions they visited Rex.

In the summer of 1923, on their visit to Glacier National Park in Montana, Rex and Fay had taken a week-long packing-in trip inside the park with two park employees, Joe MacGregor and Harland Knowlton. In 1924, determined to roughleather it for a longer time, Rex sent instructions to Joe and Harland to buy sixteen horses — four to ride and twelve to pack — and the equipment needed for an extended stay in the mountains south of the park.

Joe, who had grown up in the Flathead, guided the party to a spot on the Flathead River, near the Whitefish range. There, in the South Fork of the river, on the first day of his vacation, Rex landed a sixteen-pound rainbow trout. The only other game he went after was young blue grouse, which at that time of the year lived chiefly on huckleberries. Rex never had tasted their equal. In later years, at High Meadow, he put chickens on blueberries, with gratifying success. Nero Wolfe fell heir to this same hankering.

Joe MacGregor, who always identified himself as "Mrs. MacGregor's son Joe," was young then but already an original. He enjoyed local fame for his sourdough pancakes, irreverently referred to by everyone as his "circles of torture." The piquancy of his idiom amused Rex. Of a local rapscallion, Joe said: "The lightning sure don't use too good a judgment it lets things like that live and kills good pine trees and stuff." Of a venerable squaw, he commented: "Her face looks like it has wore out seven bodies." Joe continued to be a great favorite with campers at Glacier Park, till his death in 1971. Once, when he saw a newspaper photograph of Rex standing with President Eisenhower and an assortment of writers in the Oval Room at the White House, he wrote Rex: "I liked that picture, but there was a hell of a lot of other livestock in the same pen." Joe supplied confirming touches to several characters in Rex's novels.

In 1925, Rex persuaded his brother Walt and Will Semple, who

worked for ETS, to join Fay and himself when they went again to
Montana. In February he began firing off ETS-type memos to Joe and
Harland. One list enumerated thirty-three items, including a calendar
("A fine item," said Joe), brooms ("For the birds," said Joe), scales and
a ruler for weighing and measuring fish, a mirror ("Another 'bird' item
for mountain men of the hairy kind," said Joe), and an alarm clock ("For
why?" asked Joe, "You always let it unravel clean to the end").

Rex's glossings on his lists give us a look at his organizational mind in
peak form:

I'm having a hole for the stove-pipe made in the cook-tent, 4 feet back from
the door, and 3 feet in from the wall on the left as you go in. Is that correct?

We will bring a rifle with 22 longs. I understand that you are going to bring
the heavy rifles with which we will shoot moose, elk, deer, lions, grizzlies, tigers,
camels, wolves, and elephants. Is that correct?

I have ordered the cook-tent 14 by 14, with a 4-foot wall. The fly is to cover
the tent entirely, and is to extend 6 feet in front. Is that all right?

For my personal use I would like to have a pure-bred Arabian with green ears,
a purple tail, and a pink belly. Please advise. Fay says she wants a wild untamed
mustang.

Rex also made other preparations for his second Flathead incursion. He
had thirty books "bound in tough leather for the rough going on pack
horses."

The campers were on their way in early June. They ate Joe's smoked
fish and circles of torture, and Harland's trout deal. They fished and
hunted and helped the rangers contain a small forest fire. Rex listened,
probed, observed, and stored. When he wrote *Forest Fire*, seven years
later, he had no need to research his subject. Nor was any research
necessary when he portrayed Montana types in *The Rubber Band*, "The
Rodeo Murders," and *Death of a Dude*.

On his earlier visits to Montana Rex had been a dude receiving instruction. In 1925 he was veteran host and guide. But, in one particular,
the wilderness mastered Rex. He discovered that "it was very lovely not
to shave," and returned to New York wearing a bristling beard. At that
time beards were enough of a novelty to make anyone who wore one
the butt of lively abuse. But Rex, having gone through high school in
knee pants, was impervious to criticism. He liked his beard and he kept
it. He told me: "All this furor over beards on the young men today is
silly. Wearing a beard or not wearing one is purely subjective. If any
man wants to permit the hair that nature put there to grow, what right
has anyone to comment, let alone condemn?"

In a jacket essay written for Reginald Reynolds' *Beards*, Rex insists
that he did not grow a beard to embroil himself in controversy, but
merely "to beat the shaving rap."[13] That factor cannot be discounted,

but, for Rex, the prospect of spirited arguments on the subject must have been a major inducement to keep it. Bob, for one, did not welcome it. Old John Stout's beard was no problem at ETS headquarters. He was nearly eighty now, and had the look of a patriarch. But what would conservative bankers and academics think of this second beard? Would they wonder if Rex had crawled out of the Village? To confound them, Rex gave his beard elegant styling. Its appearance would leave three generations of interviewers fumbling for words.

Even with his time split among social, cultural, ideological, and business interests, Rex retained his common humanity. When Larry Pope, who was on the road for ETS, took a wife, Rex found a job for her in the office and then gave Larry close-by installations so that he could be in New York on weekends. When the Stouts went to Montana in the summer of 1925, Rex let the Popes use his apartment. With the apartment came Boris, Fay's Angora cat. Forty years later Pope confessed to Rex: "We soon learned that the bathroom was the perfect place with its tile floor and walls to clean up after a shedding Angora in midsummer. Before you returned he had learned that his domain was among the nickel pipes, and we wondered if you ever became curious why Boris wished to spend so much time in the john."[14]

In late August 1925, Rex spent a week with Morris Ernst on Nantucket. There the artist Boardman Robinson wanted to sculpt his head. Rex would have to go to Woods Hole for sittings. He said no. In several of Rex's stories, sculptured busts, including one of Benjamin Franklin, are used for murder or mayhem. In his first serious novel, *How Like a God,* the protagonist crushes the skull of his victim with a bust of himself. In the first novel of all, *Her Forbidden Knight,* a bronze figure is wielded with murderous intent. Clearly Rex had ambiguous feelings about graven images.

21

His Own Man

Rex Stout has been a solid American institution — comparable to Jack
Dempsey, O. Henry, Lindbergh, Bix Beiderbecke, Mark Twain, and Mom's
apple pie — for as long as I can remember. It has been my privilege to have
had him as a friend for thirty years.

— H. ALLEN SMITH

In 1920 Roger Baldwin had founded the American Civil Liberties
Union, for which Morris Ernst and Arthur Garfield Hays served as
general counsel. Early affiliates of Baldwin's included Scott Nearing and
Oswald Villard. Perhaps the beard made the difference, but whatever
it was, by the autumn of 1925 these liberals had decided that Rex's
courtship was concluded. Without overtures from Rex, Baldwin appointed him to the Board of the ACLU's powerful National Council on
Censorship and, soon after, nudged him into the League for Mutual Aid.
Next came an appeal for funds for a new magazine, *The New Masses*,
which described itself as "primarily a magazine of arts and letters for
the masses."[1] Egmont Arens had been appointed to the executive
board, as had been Hugo Gellert, James Rorty, Mike Gold, John Dos
Passos, and John Sloan. William Carlos Williams, Babette Deutsch, and
Robinson Jeffers had promised early contributions. Rex had money
coming in from the Casanova edition and reinvesting it seemed to him
a good idea. To get *The New Masses* started, he contributed $4,000. He,
too, was then appointed to the magazine's executive board.[2]

Simultaneously Rex was recruited into another venture: the Vanguard Press. When Charles Garland of Boston inherited $918,000, he
established with it the American Fund for Public Service, better known
as the Garland Fund. Specifying that his fund be used to promote
left-wing causes, Garland named Roger Baldwin and Scott Nearing as
trustees to administer it.[3] Roger and Scott decided to use a portion of
the fund to found a publishing house, which would, Scott told me,
"bring out books unlikely to find a publisher of leftish tendencies."[4]
They called it Vanguard Press and offered Rex the job of president.

Rex accepted the post and held it until 1928, when the Garland
subsidy ran out and James Henle bought the firm. Even then Rex's
association with Vanguard did not end. As late as 1931, he was still vice

president of Vanguard, under Henle. But really, in the early years, the person who ran Vanguard was Jacob "Jake" Baker, Rex's vice president. That was a matter of necessity. Until the close of 1926 Rex was active in the affairs of the Educational Thrift Service. He lacked time to run a publishing house. Yet Rex was not a figurehead. He helped choose the books that went on Vanguard's list. Roger Baldwin, at ninety-one, would remember: "Rex was always the decisive man at meetings; had a sensible view and expressed it; rarely argumentative but quite persuasive. Sometimes he could be explosive."[5]

Rex did, in fact, get on well with Baker, and their friendship continued long after both had left Vanguard. Jake's Labor Day visits later to High Meadow, the house Rex would build in Connecticut in 1930, were for many years a tradition both men cherished, even after Jake's politics swung far to the right.

During Rex's presidency, Vanguard brought out one hundred and fifty titles, with heavy emphasis on reprints, ranging from *Erewhon* to Henry George. Three of Scott Nearing's books were on the list. Another four of Nearing's books, including his prophetic *Black America* (1929) appeared during the period of Rex's vice-presidency. In that same interval, Rex's first three serious novels, *How Like a God, Seed on the Wind,* and *Golden Remedy,* came out bearing the Vanguard imprint.

Of the three liberal affiliations Rex made in 1925, Vanguard alone lasted with him. Only at Vanguard was he in a position to shape policy. That fact was crucial with him. Of the ACLU he said: "I have approved of about eighty percent of its positions and actions. It has done much good and little harm." Yet Morris Ernst suspected that Rex was irked at various positions the ACLU took: for example, the right of a fool to express himself, under the first amendment, even when such expression is detrimental to the common good.[6] Rex seldom went to ACLU board meetings. When his term ran out it was not renewed.

Rex's separation from *The New Masses* was not managed with the same ease. At first things went well. Ruth Stout, who helped to get the magazine under way, even to the extent of tapping Clarence Darrow for a hundred-dollar contribution, was picked to be the magazine's office manager, and when Rex moved from 11 West Eighth Street to a penthouse apartment at 66 Fifth Avenue, in mid-January 1926, the executive board held some of its meetings there. In the magazine's second issue, June 1926, Mike Gold had written: "What I deny is that I, or anyone else, demands of young Americans that they take their 'spiritual' commands from Moscow. . . . Let us forget Moscow in this discussion. Let us think of America, where you and I have spent the better part of our lives."

That meant nothing. After a few issues appeared, Rex saw "that it was Communist and intended to stay Communist." He won Sloan, Rorty, Eastman, and Arens to the same conviction. For about six months he battled to turn the magazine back to its original commitment. When he saw he was making no headway, he quit. "It took more than a year," Rex told me, "and three letters from my lawyer, to get them to take my name off of the listing of the executive board." Indeed, it did not come off till the June 1928 issue. That same issue also carried news of Egmont Arens's resignation as editor and Michael Gold's emergence as actual editor of the magazine. Even then, Rex's and Egmont's names were not removed from the masthead but merely dropped into the magazine's crowded list of contributing editors. They did not disappear from that listing (nor did the names of Edmund Wilson, Lewis Mumford, and Genevieve Taggard) until September 1930.

Contributions made by Rex and Egmont to *The New Masses* during the four years when their names were linked to it seem to have been scant. Egmont's name was signed to six pieces. Rex's name was signed to none.

In the fall of 1926, Ruth resigned from *The New Masses,* too.[7] The editors seemed to her "like so many Lord Bountifuls." She says: "The masses, whom they were trying to uplift, were really an unknown quantity to them. The middle-aged, tired-looking elevator man, whom they saw hundreds of times in the course of a few months, scarcely existed for them except as a part of the machinery of the elevator."

When a friend of Rex's, Jack Kaplan, bought the old Macmillan building at 66 Fifth Avenue in 1925, he had offered to build a penthouse for Rex, to Rex's specifications.[8] "And of course," Rex recalled, "I gladly specified." One of the things he specified was an enormous living room, with a cathedral ceiling, though it did not occur to him what a magnet such a room could be.

Initially the penthouse was a splendid refuge. Rex gave Ruth a key and, in the late afternoon, she went there to rest and read or to hold quiet conversations with Fay. Then a change came. No matter how early Ruth got there, someone else already was there. It could be Jake Baker, or Jimmie Harris and his wife — a black couple, both high school teachers in Brooklyn — or Freda Kirchwey, the *Nation*'s managing editor, Lawrence Langner, founder of the Theatre Guild, and his wife Armina, or Robert Sherwood, John Dos Passos, or Paul Robeson, or Josephine Bell and her new husband, Chase Horton; not to mention Egmont and Ruth Arens, and others from *The New Masses.* Number 66 "had become a day and a night club, free for all." Ruth says: "It had come gradually. And by the time it was there, in full swing, it was too late to do anything about it."

There were frequent dinners and parties. The rugs were rolled back and dancing went on with scarcely a break. When everybody was friendly and sober at the start of the evening, it was pleasant, Ruth remembers. But as the night advanced the men began to paw indis-

criminately, and the women notched conquests with the dead earnestness of hired guns. "Rex," says Ruth, "neither drank nor danced much,
but spent most of his time near the Victrola, changing records." Or he
sat talking quietly with someone like Joseph Wood Krutch, Thorstein
Veblen, or Norma Millay, Edna's sister, who was an actress at the Neighborhood Playhouse.[9]

Sometimes they took a look at New York nightlife. Rex told me: "One
evening, when Carl Van Vechten took eight or nine of us to the Cotton
Club in Harlem, two of the party were Ethel Waters and a dashing
young black named Earl Dancer, whom Ethel had a crush on. Earl
danced for more than half an hour with a very pretty mulatto girl, and
when they separated and Earl headed for our table, Ethel, who was
seated next to me, rose, walked across to the girl, hauled off and swung
at her jaw, knocked her flat, walked back to us and sat, perfectly calm."

When there was a party Ruth usually stayed overnight. She hated the
trip uptown to her own place, in the early hours of the morning. At one
party, when she was sitting there wishing the guests would thin out so
that she could go to bed, Jake Baker came and sat with her. "Angel,"
he said, "for Christ's sake, go home! Carry Nation must have turned
over in her grave a hundred times tonight!"

"What a way to live," Ruth said. "What does he get out of it?"

"He gets experience. Information," Jake said. "Look at his face."

That was in fact true. For three hundred a month in rent, Rex was
getting a million-dollar education. In his penthouse Rex was learning as
much about the ailments of the modern world and the people who were
trying to lead the way to a healthier society as Whitman had learned
about the spirit of America in the Civil War hospitals. In the Gatsby
pattern, he put on his Sulka shirts and Brooks Brothers suits each day
and threw open his doors to his guests. He took them out on the Hudson
on his thirty-six-foot cabin cruiser, the *Jurgen*. He joined their theater
parties. He sat on their boards. But mostly he probed, causing them, by
skillful arguments and calculated thrusts, to react and disclose. One
night Max Eastman leaped out of his chair and shouted to his wife,
"Come home. I won't stay in the same room with anyone who talks like
that about Plato."

Taking advantage of his rooftop elevation, Rex went in for gardening
in earnest at the penthouse, successfully growing a score of different
flowers and vegetables. Edna Millay was impressed. She invited him out
to Steepletop, her farm at Austerlitz, New York. When he came she
showed him first her personal flower garden, a profusion of some two
dozen kinds of flowers, without a single weed. Then she showed him a
second garden, a profusion of milkweed, ragweed, wild asters, and
goldenrod. "In the first garden," Edna said, "I make all the decisions
and don't let Nature interfere. In this one Gene and I plant seeds in the
spring and early summer, but from there on nature makes all the deci-

sions and we don't interfere. The question is, which is handled better, which is more attractive? I simply can't decide, and I do want your opinion."

Rex told her that one was a sonnet sequence; the other *vers libre.* "But, of course," he told me, "what I said wasn't the point."

Edna, in fact, had put to Rex the central question coming out of all this stormy exposure to the troubled people who were trying to rid the world of its troubles. He had dodged it because he knew the beauty of a discipline that could bend to its materials. But here was the real issue: did men, when they did not truly understand what they were attempting, do more harm than good with their interfering? Were not the best rules the rules Nature formulated?

If there were those who drew strength from Rex, there were others from whom he drew sustenance. In 1924, in Montana, he had torn the meniscus in his right knee when his horse, frightened by a black bear, had run him into a tree. A trip to the Poconos in the early winter of 1926, where he tried skiing, convinced him it was time to have something done about it. Not that he wanted to take up skiing. "I decided that it was fun only for experts," he said, "and I didn't want to spend the time required to become an expert." In the spring, Rex's knee was operated on at Presbyterian Hospital.[10] One morning Ethel Waters arrived in nurse's uniform and specialed him for the day.

Despite his interest in the arts and the world of ideas, there were businessmen activities which Rex had to participate in also. One day he went to a Rotary Club luncheon with his brother Bob. The two speakers that day were Field Marshal French and Babe Ruth. Rex was given the seat next to Ruth. Since Rex had in his head as much information about baseball as a sports encyclopedia would have, they had no problem communicating. "Of the two speakers, both poor," Rex told me, "Babe Ruth was the less poor."[11]

In May 1926, Rockwell Kent came to Rex with a proposition. "I want to go to Ireland for awhile to paint," he said. "If you give me $300 a month for a year, when I get back from Ireland you can have any two of the paintings I do while I'm there." Rex agreed to the proposal on the spot. In his autobiography, Kent says: "Through the generous help of Duncan Phillips of Washington, and Rex Stout, it was with sufficient money in the bank to take care of my multiple obligations and ourselves for one long summer that Frances and I set sail for what was to be, for me, four months of uninterrupted work. . . ."[12]

Kent spent this interlude in the isolated valley of Glenlough, in Donegal. There he painted wild scenes of Ireland's Druidic past. "Be gorr, they're turrible," gasped an Irish cottager when he saw them. A painting of a naked, hermaphroditic youth, stretched out before a cromlech, passively waiting to be sacrificed, was one of the two Rex chose. The other was of a turbulent stretch of the coastal hills. Through the years, these two works — done in days which Kent later would recall as among "the very happiest of all [his] life" — have hung at High Meadow in the alcove where Rex always took his ease.

On 1 December 1926 Rex turned forty. That morning, at the Woolworth Building, he took the elevator up past ETS, clear to the tower. Standing alone, he spat four times — north, south, east, west. Then he went down to Bob's office and told him he wanted to sell him his half of the business. Fifteen years later, Robert Van Gelder wrote of Rex in *The New York Times:* "One has the impression that he has lived more and worked less than the majority of his peers." That freedom began for Rex on his fortieth birthday.

Rex's separation from ETS strained his relations with Bob. Under the written agreement drawn up between them, Rex would receive a percentage of the gross income of ETS for twenty years. That came to $30,000 in an average year. In addition, certain sums were set aside providing for Lucetta and John, and some shares signed over to Ruth and Mary. Bob, who handled best the ceremonial aspects of ETS, greeting visitors, placing wreaths, organizing Franklin exhibits, promoting the concept of National Thrift Week, felt that Rex was running out on him. After some hesitation, he asked Walt to take over Rex's job.

But Walt was not Rex. He was lost between his expansive older brother and his purposeful younger brother. Bob charmed people by a ruthless rudeness. Walt's sole expletive was "God a'mighty." He was gracious and gentle. The social graces seemed naturally his. He was thoughtful. His beautiful wife, Gertrude, a woman of quiet dignity, put no pressure on him. For her, it was enough that he should follow his natural bent. Walt went along with events without trying to influence them. Frances Cox, Bob's secretary, once set her wastepaper basket ablaze. By the time she realized it the offices reeked with smoke. Walt came around and calmly opened the windows. "That's all right," he said mildly. "It will burn itself out."

The family held one common opinion about Walt: he was "one of the sweetest, most lovable guys in the world." The trouble was, as Rex knew, it is not the nature of businessmen to be lovable. Actually, Walt's mildness cloaked a deep sense of insecurity. Once, while drinking, he crawled out on the window ledge at a hotel in Scranton. "I'm the only one in the family who's never done anything with my life," he told Wally Carr, who dragged him back in. Lucetta never knew of his periodic visits to Brown's sanatorium, to be dried out.

Nineteen twenty-seven was a year of milestones in the family. Walt replaced Rex. Betty left ETS and went back to nursing. Lucetta took up Dr. William H. Bates's eye relaxation exercises, at seventy-six, and threw away her glasses. In the summer, with Bob along, she visited her sister Alice in Denver. On the way home, she attended the first annual Todhunter reunion, in Wilmington. She was invited to give the benediction opening the meeting. Her sister Lucy squirmed. Lucetta was so different. There was no telling what she might say. Lucetta stood up, "I give thanks in all things," she said. "Lord!" Lucy murmured. "So do I!" That same year Lucetta played her one and only game of golf and went around the eighteen holes in the low nineties, beating the best score Ruth had ever made. And in 1927 Ruth took her to the Adirondacks, to a resort hotel. The first two days she played croquet. On the third day they found her, after breakfast, on her knees in the garden, weeding a flower bed. That fall, Bob took her to the annual banquet of the International Benjamin Franklin Society. Frances Cox had brought her mother and introduced the two women, who were of an age.

"So you've had nine children?" said Mrs. Bellman.

"Yes. Do you have others besides Frances?"

"I lost a little boy at six, with scarlet fever," said Mrs. Bellman, with a sigh.

"If I had lost a child like that," Lucetta said, "I'd never have forgiven myself."

In 1927 Ruth Stout assumed command, in New York, of an enterprise feeding left-of-the-center printed matter to Scott Nearing and Sam Krieger as they traveled throughout the United States and Canada. In three years time she would get several hundred thousand books and pamphlets into their hands as they needed them. No evangelical tractarian society could boast of a more zealous worker. Every so often Scott proposed to her, but Ruth's noes were firm. She believed in Nearing's work, but she did not want to be Mrs. Nearing.

Rex had his commitments too. He participated in lengthy group discussions convoked by Morris Ernst to consider the Sacco-Vanzetti case. In July 1927, with Heywood Broun and Dorothy Parker, he spent two hours with Arthur Hays Sulzberger trying to persuade him to bring *The New York Times* over to the side of the condemned men. Sulzberger remained unpersuaded. When the executions were carried out, on 23 August, the *Times* stood its ground.

Just a dozen weeks before that, on 1 June, Lizzie Borden had died at Fall River, Massachusetts, thirty-four years after being acquitted of the ax murder of her parents. With memories of that case revived by Lizzie's demise, many had been quick to say that the Borden case was one more proof that Massachusetts courts dealt out strange justice. Rex was not among them. He believed in Lizzie Borden's innocence. Later, Archie Goodwin would allude often to Lizzie Borden. In *Not Quite Dead Enough* he says, "I doubt if I could inspire even Lizzie Borden to murder." And in *Might as Well Be Dead,* he says, "I wouldn't drink

gin and ginger ale to get the lowdown on Lizzie Borden."[13] Clearly
Archie had not arrived at Rex's state of certitude about Lizzie's innocence.

In December 1927, Rex and Fay set out for Europe on a trip that kept
them abroad until the following November. Before they sailed, Albert
A. Tilney, president of the Bankers Trust Company of New York,
helped Rex select the "right" stocks for his portfolio.

22

Expatriate Novelist

Nero Wolfe and Dr. Sam: Johnson are brothers under the skin. The great dictionary-maker, with his flair for sesquipedalian terms, meets his match in Wolfe, the great dictionary-reader, who imperiously passes sentence of banishment on verbiage he contemns. Nero and Sam:, brought face to face, might have disputed for victory; but they would have respected one another.

— LILLIAN DE LA TORRE

Their travels in Europe took the Stouts first to England, where, in London, Rex lingered long in the Abbey.[1] They made a day's visit to Stratford, and a visit to Ayot Saint Lawrence to look in on Bernard Shaw. For Rex, the greater thrill came in visiting the dead playwright, not the living one. "Shaw was one of the cleverest men that ever lived," Rex said, "and I just can't stand him; he was such a goddamn smart aleck." An encounter that did mean something to him was his lunch with G. K. Chesterton, at the Savoy Grill. Chesterton's appreciation of good food alone would have been persuasive, but Rex had great admiration for the Father Brown stories and for *The Man Who Was Thursday*. When Rex, at eighty-six, reread *The Man Who Was Thursday*, he decided that it was "damn silly." But his admiration for the Father Brown stories never wavered. "They are very ingenious," he told me. "It's too bad he handled Father Brown the way he did. He didn't have to make him so damned esoteric. That wasn't necessary. He could have told the stories without going to that length. Still and all, they're damned good stories."[2] Detective fiction was not their only topic. "He thought I knew too little about revelation," Rex said, "and I thought he knew too much." Rex was sorry GKC had not brought Father Ronald Knox along to lunch. Knox had done several detective stories and Rex had enjoyed their wit and ingenuity.

In Paris, the Stouts took an apartment at 44 boulevard Henri Quatre, built, they were told, on the exact spot where Rabelais had lived. Paris then was teeming with expatriates. Although Rex never classed himself as an expatriate, he had friends among them and fell in with them easily. He went a dozen times to Gertrude Stein's salon in the rue de

Fleurus, usually in the company of Whit Burnett, Ludwig Lewisohn, Adolph Dehn, or Robert Sherwood. Hemingway was there, and Thornton Wilder, and sometimes James Joyce. Rex saw nothing of Fitzgerald or Anderson.[3]

To Rex, Gertrude Stein was more amusing than any of her guests. He thought she looked like her Picasso portrait. Joyce was an enigma. He spoke seldom and poorly and "sounded either like a poet or a stuttering half-wit." And "When he listened he gave the impression of not hearing a word you said." Rex read *Ulysses* that year and thought it the best novel written in the twentieth century. Forty years later, he revised this estimate: "It's spotty," he told me; "parts of it, when he was prancing, are barely readable. The Walpurgisnacht chapter is marvelous, and a few other chapters are very fine." Rex liked salons no better than table groups. "I was bored," he said, "by all the straining to show off."

The friends Rex saw most often in Paris were Dehn, Lewisohn, and Burnett. Fay and he dined often with Thelma and Ludwig Lewisohn at their apartment on the Left Bank and reciprocated by taking them to dinner at three-star restaurants of Paris, where Rex lost his heart to *cordon bleu* food.

One night when Rex was their guest, the Lewisohns invited Thomas Mann and his daughter to dinner. Over dessert, with more presumption than discretion, Rex launched at Mann a calculated taunt. "It's not in the German temperament," he said, "to produce great writers." Mann looked thunderstruck. Then his daughter intervened: "That's all right — Papa is half Brazilian."

Rex and Adolph Dehn spent long hours together at the Louvre and at the little galleries Rex might not have found for himself. One night, at a bistro, Dehn propounded a question — "What woman in history would you most like to spend the night with?" "Catherine of Russia," Rex said. Thereupon a man six feet five rose up from the adjoining table and stood looking down at Rex. "You know about the Great Catherine," he said. "Come and have a vodka." It was Chaliapin.

One of the few pictures in the small office at High Meadow, where Rex did all his writing after 1931, is a large pen-and-ink drawing of Rex, which Dehn did as Rex worked in his garden.

Another good friend encountered in the Paris interlude was Elliot Paul. Like Rex himself, Paul was full-bearded. Rex found Paul "highly intelligent, quick-witted, and wonderful company." He told me:

One winter night he and Whit Burnett and I dined at a café that was a hangout of a bunch of right-wingers (out of curiosity), got into a rough brawl with some habitués, and were arrested. We were taken to the station and charged, but Elliot so charmed the officer in command with a long discussion of police procedures in various countries that he went and had a drink with us, and let us go.

Burnett himself re-creates another night in Paris which Rex and he spent in the company of Alvah C. Bessie:

> Bessie, at the time, was hale and beardless, but Rex was bearded to the knees, could, indeed, the saying is, have used his great dark beard for pajamas. But he didn't. He rested it on the table and sat back surrounded by *demi blondes* of Würzburger or Spatenbräu and told us his plans for his first Broadway play. When he had got done telling his plans, he never wrote a line of play, having said all he wanted to say; he went straight home to the Place de la République, and wrote his first novel, *How Like a God.* At the time he had no idea what a sensational mystery story writer was there being diverted by serious fiction; Nero Wolfe and all his orchids and clues were far in the future.[4]

Rex, of course, did not shackle himself to a writing desk immediately upon reaching Paris. He was in Europe to experience as well as to create. Whit Burnett recalled that one Sunday Rex joined Martha Foley (soon to be Mrs. Burnett) and him for a day's cycling at Fontainebleau, on a bicycle supplied them by a great-grandson of Brigham Young. At Fontainebleau they found the French army carrying out equestrian maneuvers. Rex stopped to watch. A horse reared and a young lieutenant was spilled from his seat to the amusement of his comrades and the dismay of his colonel. The lieutenant thought the bicycle had caused the horse to take fright. Burnett suggested that the war-horse, disciplined though it was to confront with composure the uproar of battle, had been plunged into panic by the sight of Rex's "handsome black beard."[5]

The maneuvers at Fontainebleau were not Rex's only reminder of Europe's tempestuous history. No other historical figure is so often mentioned in the Wolfe saga as Napoleon, whom Rex regarded as "the ablest and most interesting of all the great egomaniacs." One day Rex went to the Invalides and spent some time staring down at Napoleon's tomb. A dozen years later, Adolf Hitler would stand on the same spot.

At a Parisian flea market, Rex bought a cane. "It's a nice feeling carrying one," he told me, "though I never have understood how anyone could carry one without a crook." By temperament Rex was more inclined to the shepherd's crook than the scepter. He carried a cane for several years thereafter. But the change France worked on his dietary habits was more far-reaching.

For a starter he made a gourmet's tour of the provinces. He went to Mont-Saint-Michel, where he tried the island's Mère Poulard omelet. At Caen, he gorged himself on *tripe à la mode,* which Nero Wolfe later would pronounce "one of the great dishes of the world." At Castelnaudary, in the south, for four days he ate his fill of *cassoulet Castelnaudary*

— a casserole of baked beans with a variety of meats. It gives a pedigree to Rex's palate to say that he acquired it in France. But the predisposition was already there — perhaps as early as the day he plunged his mother's salt-rising bread into the molasses pot. What France did was give direction to a preference already well established.

Europe also nurtured a second interest — one that could not be gratified in America: the contemplation of the ruins of ancient civilizations. In Arles Rex explored the Roman ruins. Then, by way of Dubrovnik — the nearest he would ever get to Nero Wolfe's Montenegrin homeland — he went on to Greece. During seven days in August, alone, he walked ninety-five miles from Athens to Thermopylae. He found there no battle scars but a green and pleasant valley. From Greece he crossed over to Africa. From Tunis, he went to visit the site of ancient Carthage. "I walked around awhile," he told me, "picking flowers where Carthage had been."

Another experience left less pleasant memories: "I was tailed by a middle-aged Arab, in Bou-Saada, for two days. I think he was just hoping that I, a nonbeliever, would fall and break my neck." When Elliot Paul, years later, wrote *Waylaid in Boston* (1953), his opening scene found a group of men debating whether or not Rex Stout knew how difficult it was to tail anyone unobserved.[6] Rex had told Paul about the incident at Bou-Saada, of course. And Paul was having quiet fun at Rex's expense. "He's right," Rex admitted. "No one can follow anyone for long without being noticed."

In Casablanca Rex visited a carpet factory. There he saw the loveliest child he had ever seen, a girl, not more than twelve. The heavy work she was doing made him pity her. When he left he bought a box of dainty petits fours for her and sent it in by the foreman. The man returned to inform him: "She says, tell you in one year she will be old enough for you to have her."

For Fay, Rex brought back to Paris from Cairo a gold headband too heavy for her to wear. He told me: "The damned thing must have weighed three pounds. Stupid!"

After being at home a month at the end of 1928, Rex was off again to France, in December. Tourism was less his purpose this time. He gave Belgium a week, Italy two weeks — not missing the ruins of Pompeii — and, on a quick visit to Spain, saw a bullfight in Figueras. One night in January, Hemingway and he, after an evening at the Deux Magots, decided to see if the sun also rises over Chartres. With Thelma Lewisohn and Martha Foley, they set out in a taxi at one A.M. Halfway there the driver braked the car to a halt, pitching them out of their seats. He had run down a rabbit. He tucked his victim under the seat, to be dealt with later with what recipe one could only imagine. When they reached Chartres, he tallied the fare. It was 900 francs. From that sum he deducted 60 francs for the rabbit. Hemingway roared. Rex paid the fare.

Rex was now in Paris to write. At the three-room apartment at 44 boulevard Henri Quatre, he began *How Like a God* in February 1929 and finished it in March.[7] Since he trusted his own logic, his first version of a story was always the final version. And so it was this time. He wrote in longhand. His style was rapid and incisive, reflecting the assurance with which he wrote. Later, when the book appeared, critics commended him for choosing a functional style which caught "the irresolute character of his hero, and the restlessness of a great city in the twentieth century." They did not realize that the style reflected the writer, who was anything but irresolute. It was a style that would fit well the Nero Wolfe stories and make creditable the New York milieu in which the action of those stories so often unfolds.

As he wrote, Rex read the manuscript, chapter by chapter, to Ludwig Lewisohn, at Lewisohn's insistence.

The structure of *How Like a God,* which is intricate, was decided on beforehand, and names were chosen for the principal characters. The narrative itself was left to unfold as the book was written. Rex insisted that then, as always, he left it to his subconscious to work out the nuances of plot and characterization. (Midway through the book, his protagonist, Bill Sidney, is visited at his office by his son. Rex was well into the scene when suddenly he leaped out of his chair. "Jesus Christ," he said, "I didn't know he had a son.")

How Like a God had not sprung from encounters with literary people or from the perusal of manuscripts which passed across Rex's desk at Vanguard. To be sure, Rex read Hemingway, Wilder, Dos Passos, Floyd Dell, Ronald Firbank (whose *Prancing Nigger* he regarded as the most completely amoral book he had ever read), Joyce, and others whom he met both in New York and Paris, but he never had lost his appetite for omnivorous reading. During the ETS years he had read much of the best the age produced. He read and reread Henry Adams's *Education* and *Mont-Saint-Michel and Chartres* and thought they were both beautiful and wonderful. Proust, on the other hand, was "nothing but a good writer"; most of what he wrote was "horribly dull." Gide, like Proust, wrote well, "but his mind was fuzzy." Faulkner's "thinking and feeling were singsong." Rex liked Anderson's *Winesburg, Ohio.* He thought the concinnity and dialogue of Hemingway's *The Sun Also Rises* were excellent, but found the content "adolescent." Though technically deft, Hemingway was "a man of few ideas." Eventually Rex decided: "Hemingway never grew out of adolescence. His scope and depth stayed shallow because he had no idea what women are for. I think he was a latent homosexual and hated himself for it." This supposition, which Rex found he shared with Christopher La Farge and Leslie Fiedler, gathers substance now from José Luis Castillo-Puche's disclosure, in *Hemingway in Spain* (1974), that Hemingway, in later years, was as jealous as a woman might be in the same circumstances, when others tried to share the friendship of Spanish bullfighters he had attached himself to.[8]

Rex read Veblen's *Theory of the Leisure Class,* then reread it. He admired it. Yet he thought Thoreau wrote well but said little: "Thoreau loved pronouncements. His famous statement that 'the mass of men lead lives of quiet desperation' is of course nonsense. Of the twenty men you know best, of how many is that true?" Conversely, he thought Dreiser had something to say, but said it badly: "Dreiser had no style. One of the essentials of style is an excitement with words as words — and Dreiser lacked that." Evelyn Waugh, Rex set upon a middle ground: "He handled words extremely well, and I agreed with some of his positions, but his conviction of his connate superiority to almost everybody crippled him."

Rex read a subscriber's copy of T. E. Lawrence's *Seven Pillars of Wisdom* and reread it twice more. It belonged "on the shelf of the very best." Time would erode that view somewhat, but, at eighty-eight Rex still thought it "a wonderful writing job." He also read William Bolitho's *Twelve against the Gods,* three times. He read Aldous Huxley's *Crome Yellow, Antic Hay,* and *Point Counter Point.* Huxley "had an interesting mind and was always readable." Yet Rex thought Huxley had erred in supposing that "the troubles and mistakes inherent to our imperfect world can and should be corrected." Rex was beguiled by Sinclair Lewis — believing his "plain and unaffected style or approach" cloaked a clever and worthwhile mind even though critics were impressed more by the obscurity of Virginia Woolf. To Rex, T. S. Eliot "wasn't a poet; he was a second-rate thinker and a fourth-rate feeler." Yeats was "the great poet of the century."

The first reviewers of *How Like a God* discerned a debt to D. H. Lawrence. Rex had read *Sons and Lovers, Women in Love,* and *The Plumed Serpent,* yet Lawrence did not stand high in his favor. He said: "Freda Kirchwey asked me to review *Lady Chatterley's Lover* for *The Nation,* and wouldn't print what I wrote because it wasn't enthusiastic enough for her. I have never reread it, but if I did I would probably be even less enthusiastic. Lawrence was a highly talented writer, especially on growing things and scenery. But he had a midget intellect completely dominated by an obsession."

Rex saw that the traditions of the novel were under heavy assault and followed the experimentation with enough interest to contribute innovations of his own. He had read Krafft-Ebing ("a poet trying to be a scientist"), Freud, Jung, and Ellis. At the outset, as he sought to individuate his characters and to refine their motivations, the influence of contemporary psychology on his work would be evident. At the same time, he put under scrutiny various psychological factors which had influenced his own life and behavior. From these he drew hints for his fictions. Not until he created Wolfe and Archie, however, would the psychological state of his principal characters become essentially autobiographical, and there these elements are so successfully assimilated, readers do not think of them as psychological explorations at all. Thus Karl Menninger says:

> One thing I like about Nero Wolfe is that he never dives into the realm of psychiatry; all of his murderers seem to be quite "normal people" who are over-tempted by the circumstances of everyday life. Somebody steps on their toes, or threatens to get ahead of them and impulsively they act. He never pretends to believe that murderers are mostly sick.[9]

Although Rex's murderers are always responsible for their acts, in the first of the Wolfe novels, written when Rex still was close to his own interlude as psychological novelist, he did occasionally mold a character's behavior around a disturbed psyche. Thus Paul Chapin, the crippled protagonist of *The League of Frightened Men,* is addicted to glove fetishism, and marries the personal maid of the woman he loves — to fulfill a masochistic yearning for ignominy. Possibly such characterizations were intended to counterpoint Rex's unannounced probing of his own psyche.

As an *avant-garde* novelist Rex seemed preoccupied with characterization, structure, and technique. Yet his true preference was for the storytellers — Conan Doyle, Maugham, H. G. Wells, and Wodehouse, whom he found "witty, wise, and wonderful." He disputed Galsworthy's avowal that "characterization is plot." He thought that a declining interest in storytelling imperiled the future of the novel. Some of his reviewers suspected as much. Beneath the experimentalist they saw the storyteller trying to get out.

When Rex and Fay returned to the United States from Paris in the spring of 1929, they went to live at the farmhouse at Brewster, New York. Fay was not keen on country living, but Rex was. It felt good to be settling into a writing career again, and to be free of the omnipresent illuminati that had clung to him in New York. In 1927, Rex had bought eighteen hilly acres behind the Salmon farmhouse. They extended right across the New York state line into Connecticut and Danbury township. He decided now to build a house there, modeled after a palace belonging to the Bey, which he had seen at the outskirts of Tunis.

This same interval also found Ruth Stout striking out in new directions. Back in the days of the Klicket she had fallen in love with Fred Rossiter. But Fred was already married. They decided to give his marriage another chance and Ruth dropped out of his life. In 1927 the marriage broke up anyway. Fred saw Ruth again and they took an apartment together. In the meantime Ruth had altered course in pursuit of her career goals. She had finally acted on Oswald Villard's long-standing offer and had gone to work for *The Nation*. There her penchant for drama soon found an outlet. Early in 1928, the Daughters of the American Revolution, acting in concert with the Key Men of America, issued a blacklist of persons who, because of their "subversive" views, should not be allowed to address meetings of the two organizations. Among those listed were Eleanor Roosevelt, Fiorello La Guardia, William Allen White, Morris Ernst, Clarence Darrow, Arthur Garfield Hays, Freda Kirchwey, and Oswald Villard. Those thus signalized were as much amused as they were appalled. Some who failed to make the list were incensed, Heywood Broun particularly so. Broun's indignation gave Ruth the idea of running a Blacklist Party for *The Nation*. Never did her party-giving genius hit upon a more congenial concept. Villard at once organized a Blacklist Committee, consisting of Ernst, Hays, Darrow, and Kirchwey. Invitations were sent to President Coolidge, Governor Alfred E. Smith, and Mayor Jimmy Walker of New York. Those on the DAR's "Roll of Honor" were urged to come and bring with them relatives who were assumed "to be at least slightly tinged from association with [them]." The Committee was deluged with telegrams from people who lamented their failure to qualify because they had been left off the DAR's list. A thousand people, including the spurned Broun, came to the party at the Level Club on 9 May 1929. Broun said he had a stupendous time.[10] The Blacklist Party actually put *The Nation* in the black, for the first time in its history. "It was," quipped Ruth, "the only party *The Nation* ever backed that it made money on."

The next month Fred Rossiter's divorce became final, and a few days later Ruth and he exchanged vows before a justice of the peace, at Danbury. At the farmhouse, Rex and Fay gave them a wedding breakfast. Not long afterward they took a house in nearby Redding, where they would be Rex's neighbors through the long years ahead.

Fred's first wife accepted the inevitable. She was a fine cook. Ruth, she knew, was a wretched one. Often, thereafter, she invited Ruth and Fred over for dinner. She hated to think that Fred was going hungry.

Ruth was forty-four when she married, and thoroughly independent. At her insistence, they had left the words "love, honor, and obey" out of their wedding ceremony. She kept her maiden name, too, a fact her rural Connecticut neighbors found perplexing. Asked by visitors where Ruth Stout's house was, they were apt to say, "Oh, yes, that's the woman who lives with Fred Rossiter."[11]

Lucetta, of course, knew Ruth was living with Fred in the period before his divorce. She did not object. Her own experience had taught her that some marriages were unworkable. Ruth had stayed out of Fred's life for seven years. To Lucetta that seemed a fair trial. When another divorce impended in the family, Lucetta, having seen Ruth through her ordeal, would take this new crisis in stride.

Rex's plans for his new life were, of course, tied in with the fortunes of his new novel. He did not have to wait long for results. Vanguard published *How Like a God* in August 1929. In *The Nation* Clifton Fadiman wrote: *"How Like a God* has an air of maturity about it few American first novels possess." Burton Rascoe greeted Rex as "a new novelist who is certain to command much attention from now on." Vanguard supplied a publicity photo of Rex which "revealed a remarkable resemblance to D. H. Lawrence." Acting on that hint, the *Herald Tribune*'s William Soskin praised Rex for "avoiding the emotional splurging of Lawrence." Others lauded his "glowingly articulate" exploration of "the dark regions of sex psychoses." As "a brilliant conception of modern human psychoses," his protagonist was accounted superior to Spandrell, Huxley's protagonist in *Point Counter Point.*

How Like a God's technical innovations were twofold. First, it pioneered a new technique for handling interior monologue. Second, it subordinated chronological time-relation to a relation of a significant action-sequence. The first effect was achieved by telling the story in the second person singular. Opinion was divided about the merits of this innovation. Compton MacKenzie hailed it as "a brilliant technical device which combines the intimacy of the first person with the detachment of the third." Yet Fadiman thought it an affectation.

The second innovation was more controversial. The story is told while the protagonist is mounting the stairs to kill his mistress. As he climbs he reviews the circumstances of his life that have led him to this moment. Reviewers were reluctant to concede that so much could pass through a man's mind in so brief a span of time. It would have suited them better if Bill had been trapped alone in a stalled elevator, with half a day to inventory his past. Nonetheless, some approved. Rascoe thought "his shuttling of memory, without confusion, a triumph of skill." The *Times* said: "In spite of the lack of sequence in the narrative the author succeeds in building a complete picture of a life." William Soskin suggested that Rex had made of time "a system of punctuation." Lewis Gannett found the method "really very natural," since what we learn of people does not come to us "chronologically, like a set biography, but piecemeal." The confusions usually found in the involuted tale were lacking. Rex had slipped between the "mechanical directness of realism" and the "vagueness of expressionism," to tell his story with freshness and clarity.

Rex had to wait awhile to get the English reaction to *How Like a God.* It was not published in England till late in 1931, a year after English readers had been introduced to Rex's second serious novel, *Seed on the Wind,* published in America in 1930. Reverse-order publication produced ludicrous results. British reviewers commended this "second novel" as a distinct advance over *Seed on the Wind.* Yet enough good things were said otherwise to offset that blunder. In the *Daily Mail* (3

November 1931), Compton MacKenzie wrote: "It is a magnificent piece of work, and proves Mr. Rex Stout to be a considerable figure in contemporary American literature." In a dispatch to the New York *Sun* from London (December 1931), Peter Quennell said that its merits surpassed those of *Sanctuary*, William Faulkner's newest novel.

By concerning themselves with the book's psychological properties rather than its technical precosities, British reviewers stole a march on their American counterparts. The preoccupation of the latter with Rex's craft had, of course, signaled their reluctance to take up his "sordid" subject matter. This dilemma was hinted at by the St. Louis *Globe Democrat* when it conjectured, with more leniency than most of the others showed, that a writer with Rex's mastery of forceful phrase and dramatic episode "could write a novel that might leave in the mouth a taste of honeydew melon rather than one of decayed cabbage."

In *The New Masses* (November, 1929), however, Valentine Konin did discuss the book without coyness:

Its characters are not people. . . . Millicent . . . is the basis for the whole structure of bourgeois life, and is characteristically introduced in the book in connection with soiled underwear and abnormal gratification of pederastic tendencies. . . .
Sister Jane is no more a character than the whole radical movement. Bill is a relic of the business man's illegitimate impulse towards freeing himself from the stench of commercial and sexual degeneration into which he has become so closely drawn.

Konin scores points with his assessment of the book's sexual content, but his insistence that the book is primarily an allegory of the class struggle cheats his remarks of much of their effectiveness.

In its barest essentials, this is the plot of *How Like a God*. Bill Sidney's mother, who has few domestic skills, delegates the upbringing of her younger children to her oldest daughter, Jane, who is efficient and maternal. For this much of the story Rex relied on his own family history. He told me that his sister May — "the typical efficient older sister — efficient but not at all officious" — had supplied him his model for Jane. Much of what follows in the story, however, sprang from Rex's own inventiveness. Bill forms an oedipal attachment to Jane with consequent incestuous, but unrealizable, longings. He fails to mature emotionally and at college falls prey to the sexual overtures of Millicent Moran, the ten-year-old daughter of the campus laundrywoman. What services Millicent renders are not disclosed, though clearly she is the aggressor — an unmistakable precursor of Nabokov's Lolita. Rex told me: "Fellatio was not specified because the situation and its outcome might result from any persisting sexual act other than copulation which is morally repulsive to a participant. Also, of course, in storytelling omission is often more effective, and better art, than description."

Ironically, by engaging in a fistfight with a classmate, Dick Carr, when the latter makes a remark about Millicent — "insulting her innocence" — Bill brings himself to Carr's notice. Carr takes him into the Carr family business. Bill prospers and marries Carr's sister, Erma. The marriage is a consolidation of business interests. Erma is worldly, selfish, and promiscuous. She cannot mother Bill as he requires. Meanwhile Bill is haunted by past sexual confusions, compounding those already noted. As a teenager he had been seduced by his Sunday School teacher, Mrs. Davies, a woman his mother's age. She had used him to have the child her husband could not give her. Later Bill had courted Lucy Morris, a girl his own age. In Lucy Bill had sought a wife who would mother him. Lucy sensed that there was something unnatural about Bill's love for her, and rejected it.

When Jane marries, even though her marriage postdates his own, Bill sees himself as a rejected child and his misogyny bursts into the open:

> Any man who expects to get anything from a woman is a fool. . . . Essentially they're barbarians, animals, they'll tear you to pieces in an instant and think nothing of it, like a jackal, and then lie down and stretch and lick themselves, and expect to be patted by the next one that comes along. It's too bad they don't do it literally, devour you, then it could happen only once.[12]

Bill wonders if even Lucy would have betrayed him. He is plagued further by memories of his sordid sessions with Millicent. Millicent had hated to be called Millie. She had run to him when he called her "Mil." She is indeed a millstone hung about his neck, especially when she seeks him out in New York and resumes their old relationship. He is repelled by her, yet mesmerized by her sexuality.

Millicent dominates *How Like a God.* Forty years later Rex could see that, beyond question, he had derived Millicent from Mildred, the female protagonist of Somerset Maugham's *Of Human Bondage,* yet when he drew her the debt was not apparent to him. What he overlooked, however, was not missed by Burton Rascoe. In *Plain Talk* (December, 1929) Rascoe made this record of parallels:

> Mildred and the Millicent of *How Like a God* are as much alike as two peas. . . . Both of them are physically unattractive; they have pale, greenish, anemic complexions; their lips are thin and colorless; their bodies are scrawny; they are untidy; they are illiterate, stupid, and phlegmatic. . . . Both . . . are natural born liars. . . . They are both unfaithful and both are caught in infidelity. . . . And, finally . . . the power of Millicent over Bill is too great for him to resist, just as the power of Mildred is too great for Philip to resist.

Rex rated Maugham as "one of the five or six best storytellers (in English) of this century." He admired *Of Human Bondage* when it first appeared, in 1915. In 1960 he reread it and was satisfied that it "held up."

By many individuating touches, Rex made Millicent an unforgettable specter in his league of frightful women. "This dumb drab insect," munching candy, jaws chomping "methodical as some automatic engine of destruction," sets up a revulsion not easily dismissed. We are told: "She seemed entirely devoid of opinions even regarding food."

While *How Like a God* is a book of many ironies, Rex reserves his greatest irony for the title. When Bill staked Paul, his son by Mrs. Davies, to art studies in Paris, the young man thanked him by sculpting a bust of him. When Erma saw it, Shakespeare's lines came to mind: "What a piece of work is man! . . . /In action how like an angel./In apprehension how like a god!" She was amused. Paul had made his father masterful. The bust mocked him. Emotion, not reason, governed Bill.

When Bill moves the bust to his love nest, even Millicent senses its absurdity. She suggests he vent his wrath against it since its self-assurance reproaches his inadequacy. Even then he lacks the will to act on his own. The bust, which portrays him as he would like to be, becomes his surrogate. He uses it to crush Millicent's skull. This quasirejection of his oedipal dependency is illusory. The deed done, he phones Jane. He is running to mother.

Both Gannett and Rascoe speculated on the autobiographical content of *How Like a God*. Gannett suggested that Bill's rise to affluence was a form of wish-fulfillment for the author. Rascoe thought the murder "autobiographical" and that it signified some renunciation which the author wished to make but could not hold himself to. Gannett's conjecture, of course, had no validity, since Rex already was prosperous and had, by his own choice, turned his back on the pursuit of further riches. But Rascoe's speculations cannot be dismissed so simply.

Rex had no Millicent in his life. But he had had a Jane. And he was stumbling through oedipal confusions. May's tragic death had deprived him of his proxy mother. One result of that loss had been a strengthening of his ties with his actual mother. Yet this was not accomplished without a sense of guilt. To align himself with Lucetta implied repudiation of his father, from whom Lucetta was estranged. Marriage did not diminish that problem. Fay, too, was drawn to Lucetta. Often, only partly in jest, she told friends she could never give up Rex because she was too fond of her mother-in-law.

Only by lessening his dependency on his mother could Rex have drawn into a closer relationship with John. Although Rex understood this and saw that it was desirable, he could not bring his emotions under the yoke of his convictions. To that extent he did resemble Bill Sidney.

For Rex, who prided himself on being at all times accessible to reason, that was a true humiliation.

The murder with which *How Like a God* ends left some reviewers puzzled about how to categorize the book. They spoke of it as a "blend of mystery, sex-psychology, and straightforward-narrative." They said it had "the suspense of a mystery story." They even called it "a psychological mystery story." Some thought the murder should be omitted altogether. Fadiman argued: "The suspense in which the reader is held as he tries to guess which of the five women 'you' are to murder is of the detective-story order, and accordingly unworthy of many of the author's carefully conceived psychological nuances." MacKenzie acknowledged its kinship with crime fiction but, with British tolerance for the genre, suggested that his compatriots might do well to raise themselves to Rex's standards. *"How Like a God,"* he said, "makes the average English detective yarn look like a cross-word puzzle filled in with red ink."

Gannett supplied an interesting insight. A death at the end of the book gave "geometric perfection to the patterns of real life." Yet in life that seldom occurred. Life "goes on and on and on, until the individual is adjusted to its inevitabilities." He concluded: "The truest novels admit the rareness of neat solutions."[13]

Rex, of course, liked neat solutions. It was his bookkeeper's imperative. Even then, while he was scoring a *succès d'estime* with *How Like a God* — the book which the critics could not classify — while he was signing over the dramatic and movie rights to Lewis E. Gensler, and there was talk of an imminent Broadway production, he was pointed toward the field in which he would enjoy his greatest triumph as a writer. Detective fiction did not merely tolerate "neat solutions," it compelled them.

BOOK V

The Years of Choice

23.

Squire of High Meadow

Rex Stout has had much the same impact on his game as Casey Stengel had on baseball; he knows it *all,* he probably invented most of the rules, and when he is on the field no one need watch anyone else.

— THOMAS H. GUINZBURG

The new writing career of Rex Stout was taking shape in a rapidly changing world. He had taken a pied-à-terre at 33 Perry Street, in the Village, in the late summer of 1929, but early in October began his second psychological novel, *Seed on the Wind,* and did much of the writing at Gage Hill. At the end of October the stockmarket crashed. With it went most of the money he had earned in ETS years. "It took me one bottle of wine to adjust to the news," Rex told me. Nonetheless, he understood that there were serious prospects to be weighed. Although, under the agreement he had made with Bob, he was to continue to receive $30,000 a year, even that was uncertain. In a true depression, school children would drop out of ETS by the tens of thousands. Bob, moreover, had a new interest. He had founded the North Jersey Trust Company, at Ridgewood. There was no guarantee that he would make the effort to save ETS if the crisis deepened. Nor was *How Like a God* making Rex a fortune. His royalties at the end of six months came to less than $700. If he was to prosper, his second book would have to realize the promise the critics saw in the first.

The day after Thanksgiving, 1929, Rex wrote Egmont Arens declining to participate in a literary workshop. He stated the hard facts: "I am rarely through before seven in the evening, including Sundays and holidays. Just a goddamn fiction factory."

By March the book was done and he was making preparations to build his house. It would be more the product of self-labor now than he had foreseen. On 22 March he rapped out a quick message to Egmont: "Marshalling my forces in preparation for a career as a Master Builder."

High Meadow, which lies partly in Putnam County, New York, and partly in Fairfield County, Connecticut, is about midway between downtown Brewster and downtown Danbury, and fifty miles above New York City. The mailing address is Brewster because the road to the house begins there. The house is 1780 feet from the road and 1600 feet across the line, in Connecticut.

Gage Hill is the established name of the hill to the south of which Rex's hill is a continuation. It is one of the long slopes to the south of the Berkshires. Behind the house it rises to an elevation of 1,091 feet. The house itself is set at about 1,000 feet, and faces a broad ten-mile run of meadows, trees, and hills. Across several ranges, landmarks on the west bank of the Hudson, forty-five miles away, can be discerned. Standing on the roof terrace over the living room, Rex would point toward Pauling, a locale where several well-publicized conservatives lived, and say: "One of the reasons I bought this hill was I thought this was a perfect place to mount a 105 howitzer. I figured I could pot them from here."

Before breaking ground, Rex took eight months to study the fundamentals of house construction, with the help of a selection of government pamphlets, bought at ten cents apiece. Unable to visualize drawings or blueprints, he made a plywood model of the house he wanted. He made six more models before he was satisfied. He then submitted the plans to architects A. Lawrence Kocher and Gerhard Ziegler for verification and was guided by their technical information and advice.

Rex's final model was of a fourteen-room, flat-roofed, U-shaped house built around a garden court and adjusted to the hillside site — exterior walls of concrete cast in place with Van Guilder steel molds, two walls, in fact, each four inches thick, tied together with light steel rods at intervals of two feet, and with a continuous air space intervening. It was to be one story high except for the two-story wing containing guest rooms, studio, service, workroom, and office. The living room would have two levels and would be higher in back, to conform to the slope of the hill. A roof terrace above it would be the central feature of the front facade. A slight curve to the right wing of the house would afford a view of the orchards.

Rex literally was the Master Builder. Professionals knew "too many shoddy shortcuts." They would have plumped for their own "just-as-good" proposals. Besides, speaking as a true Todhunter, Rex told me, "It wouldn't have been any fun if I had it done for me."

For the work, he signed on nine men, none of them experienced, and "three and a half boys." Rex explained: "One boy was just eight. There wasn't a lot he could do. But he did find things to do. He did help." Veenie Todhunter's son, Leslie Barrett, a vaudeville actor left idle by the Depression, surprised Rex and himself by hanging, expertly, all forty-one doors.

One of the things Rex had studied beforehand was cement mixing and pouring. He himself made the large masonry blocks in a mold. These were "laid up" by Harold and Orrie Salmon, the sons of Adelbert Salmon, Rex's erstwhile landlord. (For the next forty-five years Harold

Salmon would be Rex's man-of-all-work — Rex's "Archie" in the eyes of local people. Another teenager who stayed on through the years was Paul Ruffles.)[1] Even though local help was putting up the house, its alien sprawl shocked Yankee sensibilities. Rex's neighbors referred to it as "the monkey house."

Although Rex came to the job with no engineering or carpentry skills, he found out what had to be done and did it. He took all the plumbs and levels and sights. When problems of construction arose for which neither the manuals nor the experts had answers, he solved them himself. Several times he had metal braces and fittings made to his specifications to answer specific needs. He laid the teak floor in the living room, the oak floors in the other rooms, and the tiles. He did all the interior cabinetwork, including waxed chestnut cabinets in the kitchen. He built the kitchen counters, including the sink cabinet. "It was a hell of a job," he admitted, "to fit that so it would be even." He put in the cork walls of the studio. He built the bookshelves. And eventually he filled the house with flawlessly constructed furniture — beds, tables, desks, dressers — which he designed and made himself. Only the pamphlet on plumbing defeated him. "I knew damned well I'd better not monkey around with that," Rex told me. He also indulged in the extravagance of hiring a stonemason to build the off-center fireplace in the living room, and an electrician to do the wiring.

Fred Swenson, for fifty year Rex's neighbor on Milltown Road, remembers well the building of High Meadow, because he owned the building material yard from which Rex bought most of the materials he needed. "Rex," he says, "was indefatigable." Swenson recalls that Rex's rampant beard dramatized, in those days, his presence in rural Brewster and Danbury. He says: "One day Rex approached my wife and our five-year-old son on Brewster's Main Street. The boy grasped my wife's arm and said excitedly: 'Mom! Look! Here comes Jesus Christ!' "

Painting High Meadow, Rex used color to emphasize the third dimension. Walls that served as a background to terraces were painted a light gray. Terminating wall faces were painted black. Blues and white also were used. Red lead on the window frames served as trim. Doors facing the outside were orange-red.

Fifty feet from the front terrace, near a two-hundred-year-old maple, Rex poured cement for a swimming pool, formed in the shape of an ellipse. The Bey of Tunis had had a eunuch well, marking the point in the courtyard beyond which eunuchs could not venture. Rex elected for the pool instead. He advised me: "There weren't enough eunuchs around here to make it worth the bother to sink a well." Asked if the elephantine Wolfe might be High Meadow's eunuch, Rex said, "Emphatically no."

At the end of seven months, at a cost of $40,000, Rex had the house he wanted in the place he wanted it. "Nobody could trample on me," he said, "and I didn't have to have curtains on the windows. I want to see out of the windows. That's what windows are for." In January 1933, High Meadow was the subject of an illustrated article in *The New York Times.* Models of it, the *Times* said, were then on diplay at the exhibition of modern architecture being held at the New School for Social Research. High Meadow, the *Times* said, was a trend-setter. In July 1933, the *Architectural Record* ran a seven-page feature on High Meadow, illustrated with twelve photographs and two blueprints. Most of the experts, but not quite all, seemed satisfied. In 1935, Frank Lloyd Wright was Rex's guest. Wright looked the place over, then told Rex, "I'd like to build a house here."

The 10 × 14 room to the left of the stairs on the second floor of the two-story wing was the room Rex had built for his office. It did not look out on the broad valley and distant hills, but on the garden court. Rex thought too much grandeur would be a source of distraction. As it turned out, his office became a command post. Rex admitted: "The door from the living room to the front terrace was supposed to be a front door. That was a miscalculation, because all arrivals are by car and end at the rear of the house. As a result, the door from the passageway to the court is really the front door." Rex never looked out the window while he was working; still, he stayed subtly in touch.

A palpable atmosphere existed at High Meadow just as it did in the brownstone at West Thirty-fifth Street. In maturity Rex was determined to have the efficiently functioning home he had longed for in childhood. High Meadow was simultaneously a bastion and an ambuscade. Here Rex reigned. He had his routine, his family, his flowers, his books, his own vegetables and fruits, and, when he chose, he could, on his terms, confront the world. To his friends, High Meadow was his "country seat." To himself, it was the center of his world. There, touching the earth, he renewed himself. Deer roamed his woodlands. Flowers caressed his hillsides. Fruits and berries and vegetables sprang in abundance from the land to grace his table. A faithful dog ran at his side. And he commanded the birds of the air. What more had Xanadu to offer? Except, of course, a sacred, subterranean river.[2]

On 21 August 1930, while High Meadow was still abuilding, Rex received a telegram from William Soskin: "BOOK IS MARVELOUS," it read; "CONGRATULATIONS ON INCREASING MATURITY." *Seed on the Wind* was in the hands of the reviewers and about to appear. A few days later Mrs. Bernard DeVoto wrote Rex: "I think you have done a splendid piece of work. Your complete detachment from emotion pleases me very much. My husband, who is entirely too critical of American fiction, for once agrees with me." The first reviews also were supportive. Lewis Gannett thought "a brilliant first novel" had been succeeded by "a better second novel." He found the plot — the story of a woman who had five children by five men, though married to none of them — "a little preposterous," but marveled that Rex's art "makes you believe in the preposterous." The Philadelphia *Inquirer*'s Howard Rockery said *Seed on the Wind* put Rex in the front rank of important American writers.

On 19 September, at his huge basement apartment at 16 West Tenth Street, Soskin gave a party to honor Rex and Lynn Riggs, author of *Green Grow the Lilacs*. The long guest list included Ford Madox Ford, William Rose Benét, Henry Seidel Canby, Nunnally Johnson, Brooks Atkinson, and Sydney Howard. Doffing his rustic identity, Rex adroitly slipped back into the role he had played when the doors of his Fifth Avenue penthouse stood open to the world. Forty-five years later Lawrence Blochman would recall: "I can still see Rex reclining on a bed, a glass in his hand, his beard very black and lustrous, holding forth to a bevy of admiring young women sitting on the floor around him."[3]

Soskin later gave *Seed on the Wind* a further boost by choosing it, along with Faulkner's *As I Lay Dying* and Maugham's *Cakes and Ale*, as one of the year's best books. But in November, Christopher Morley told *Saturday Review* readers that the book was being neglected. "If it were by a Russian or a German," he said, "what a fashionable halloo there would have been." He insisted further: "It churns up the emotions and instigates all sorts of anxiety. . . . It is brilliantly and cruelly unique." Morley followed up his encomium by asking Rex to have dinner with him at Keen's Chop House. A warm friendship came of this encounter. Rex told me: "Kit's lasting admiration of *Seed on the Wind* was immoderate." Thereafter they got together two or three times a year for dinner and conversation. When Morley founded the Baker Street Irregulars in 1934, he asked Rex to join. In a sense, therefore, Rex's celebrated parody, "Watson Was a Woman," done for the Irregulars, was a by-blow of his novel about polyandrous matriarchy.

On 5 February 1931, Kennerley published *Seed* in England. An advance copy, sent by Kennerley to Frank V. Morley (Christopher's brother), had drawn warm praise: "It is bigger than anything Hemingway has done though there's a similar ease in the writing. More than anybody else, in his ability to select, and in his feeling generally, Stout reminds me of Remarque."[4] Morley urged Kennerley to send copies to Herbert Read, H. G. Wells, and T. E. Lawrence. Whether Read and Lawrence read the book is unknown. Wells gave his copy to his French mistress, with results that will be reported in their place.

Norman Douglas thought *Seed on the Wind* was "the kind of book we need right now." In the *New Leader*, Mrs. Bertrand Russell (Russell's second wife, Dora Black) said it was one of the best books of the year and wrote Rex several letters about it. Havelock Ellis also opened a correspondence with Rex on the subject.[5] And Morley Kennerley (who with his brother, Mitchell Kennerley, Jr., ran the Kennerley publishing house) jubilantly wrote to tell Rex that the militant birth control advocate Naomi Mitchison, undismayed by the heroine's appalling fecundity, had found the book admirable. Indeed, she thought it showed such an acute grasp of feminine psychology she wondered if Rex Stout was a woman, a remark sure to have provoked bushels of merriment later among the Baker Street Irregulars had it become known.[6]

The word from Britain helped some. The decision of the Irish Free State to ban the book helped more. In May, Walter Winchell gave it a boost in his column in the *Daily Mirror,* in the same paragraph in which he saluted Bing Crosby's vocalization of "Wrap Your Troubles in Dreams." In June, in the *Nation,* Joseph Warren Beach placed Rex in the company of Woolf, Wolfe, Dos Passos, and Faulkner, as a disciple of Joyce.

Critics who had limited themselves to comments on the technical merits of *How Like a God* went on the offensive when they read *Seed,* excoriating virtues they had praised before. It was just "another stunt in technique." The story was told backward. "I'm Yorkshire, not Chinese," cried one critic. They found the book "sex rampant." They described it as "a novel in which disgustingness and silliness are mingled in equal parts." They spoke of the author's "tortured efforts at psychoanalysis." They found the book to be "without moral or aesthetic justification," or, as Frank Swinnerton said, "without object and without quality." Isabel Patterson, who had singled out *How Like a God* as the most loathsome book of the previous summer, thought *Seed on the Wind* still worse. *The New York Times* said it was "little more than a clever Greenwich Village dream." It had about it "a cloak of seeming profundity and sophistication masking what in essence is a shilling shocker."

Gladys Graham's dissenting opinion in the *Saturday Review* was refreshing. To her, Lora Winter's "understanding fecundity" was "a pleasant relief in these days of hard, glittering heroines for whom sterile experience is the end and aim of their accelerated lives." She said further: "Lora . . . has about her the modernism that permits a woman to direct her life a little way along the long way that she wishes." Gladys Graham here might be describing Lena Grove, the earth mother of Faulkner's *Light in August.* But that book had not yet been written. As a goddess of fertility, a symbolic demiurge, Lora may well have been in Faulkner's mind when he created Lena. He was familiar with Rex's works, and enjoyed them.[7]

Sylvia Lynd said: "Lora's occupation is having babies. Sometimes she has one for love and sometimes she supplies one for spot cash." The shallowness of this assessment is typical of the poor grasp of the story shown by those scandalized by it. Though the involuted form of the novel withheld an explanation till the end, Rex did finally account for Lora's behavior and make it, if not defensible, then at least comprehensible. As a teenager Lora became pregnant by a boy whom she loved and hoped to marry. She herself had been conceived out of wedlock and on that account her father had been compelled to marry her mother. Theirs had been a hateful marriage, and her father's feelings toward Lora were, as a result, ambivalent. He resented her for tying him to a woman he despised. He loved her because she had qualities he would like to have found in a wife. When Lora's child is born her father delivers it, and kills it. By this act he is simultaneously punishing her as the cause of his unhappy marriage and rebuking her for loving someone else. When Lora realizes what he has done, she leaves home. To spite him she then embarks on her career of childbearing, sending to him, with each arrival, a telegraphed birth announcement and photographs. She is unaware that he had killed himself the day after she left home. When Lora finally learns of her father's death, predictably she renounces all men and resolves to devote herself to the welfare of her children.

Though Lora's relentless childbearing had been intended as a calculated rebuke to her father, prudish reviewers singled out one of her pregnancies for venomous assault. For a settlement which provided for her other children, she had borne a child for Lewis Kane, a kindly Jewish businessman, married but hitherto childless.[8] Since love was incidental to her purpose all along, her arrangement with Kane carried her to no new depths of degradation. Moreover, it saved her other children from want. These facts meant nothing to the reviewers. They could forgive motherhood by whim; motherhood by contract they found intolerable.

Alone among the critics, British poet and novelist Richard Aldington (*Sunday Referee*, 8 February 1931) raised good and sufficient objections against *Seed on the Wind:*

The novelist relies entirely upon his wits and invention, never upon his imagination and intuition. . . . Every objection is foreseen . . . but it is all *trop voulu*. The author fails to convince me that his situation as one reconstructs it must inevitably work out as it does. It is not a defect of construction, but a defect of method; one might almost say of humanity. This book is the homunculus in the bottle, the synthetic product without the vitally necessary vitamins, a full-sized oak in *papier-mâché*.

Seed on the Wind was, in Aldington's opinion, a work of the intellect, done without inspiration. This, indeed, was the kind of misstep which Rex, with his analytical mind, might make. He could no more write from an outline than he could build a house from a blueprint. But in those days when he was building plywood models of High Meadow and writing *Seed on the Wind,* had he in fact held himself to a preconceived plan for the book? "Possibly I did," Rex told me.

In the reviews of *Seed on the Wind* there was an undercurrent which nudged Rex in a new direction. Mary Ross mused, "Somewhat in the manner of a detective story . . . *Seed on the Wind* untangles the skeins involved." Sara Harrison said: "The tale has all the suspense and sensational quality of a perfectly constructed mystery story." Gladys Graham agreed. All were reaching for the point Aldington would make explicitly — Rex's analytical mind dominated his material.

Rex might have surmised that the critics were trying to tell him to follow up his natural potential and realize himself in the compatible genre of the detective story. But time had still to pass before he saw the wisdom of that course.

24.

A Literary Farmer

If I had to say what I most admired about Rex, it might well be his exquisite professionalism. After all, he's been married to Nero and Archie for forty years now. Speaking both as a wife and a writer, I can appreciate the extraordinary and creative interest in life that has kept his relationship with his heroes so fresh. This is the *inside* of true professional craft — the repeated choice to do again well what one has done well before. It isn't easy. Most series go stale rather fast. It is Rex's vast concern in the fascinating details of our common human life that makes his work so exceptional. Curious! He's like a bird dog on the scent when he suspects there might be something new to learn.

— ELIZABETH JANEWAY

In early April 1931 the *Herald Tribune* observed that, a few days before, several writers had gathered at The Meeting Place to greet visiting Russian author Boris Pilniak. Those present included Sinclair Lewis, Heywood Broun, Bill Soskin, and Rex Stout. Asked to address the group, Rex, to their delight, "pictured the horror that would result if reviewers could review lives as they do books." He had reason to be in fine fettle. He had just finished *Golden Remedy,* his third psychological novel and the first of his books to be written in his new house. By early May, Henle had read it and had written to Rex, "It's the best thing you've done and a darn good book." He was having a contract drawn up.

"But my God," Henle exclaimed, "what about Sumner?"[1] He meant John S. Sumner, who headed up the New York Society for the Suppression of Vice and had cast his nets wide to ensnare, among others, Dreiser, Branch Cabell, and the Roman poet Horace. *Golden Remedy* had not been written to sooth Sumner, and Henle, fearing a showdown, asked Morris Ernst for his opinion. Ernst was reassuring. "I doubt very much if the book will be attacked," he said, "and if it is attacked, I am confident that I can sustain it. . . . For purposes of complying with the obscenity statutes, there is no change that need be made."[2] Ernst did, however, suggest a few changes on the grounds of taste. Rex adopted none of them, and Henle doggedly insisted, "I still feel in my bones that we are in for a fight."[3] Publication was set for late August.

Through the summer, Rex and his forthcoming book were mentioned in the New York papers almost as often as the Stouts used to be mentioned in the North Topeka *Mail and Breeze.* On 7 June the New York *American* told its readers, in "Titles and Tattle," "Rex Stout has another novel this Fall, *Golden Remedy.* He doesn't care whether he makes money on it or not. . . . He wears a brown beard and a hickory shirt and lives like a country squire in Brewster. . . . He quit being a reporter to make a fortune in banking so he could write what he darned please, and is doing it." On 6 July the New York *Mirror* said: "Rex Stout, the millionaire author and publisher, has a pool on his Brewster, N.Y., estate in which guests are not permitted to wear bathing suits." On 7 July the *Herald Tribune* revealed that Rex had finished *Golden Remedy.* On 5 August, it reported that he had finished correcting proof. On 17 August, the same paper was back with yet another Stout story: "Rex Stout, author of *Golden Remedy,* which Vanguard will publish next week, is lamenting the loss of his pet crows, Alice and Hamlet. Alice went wild after tasting applejack at a neighbor's farm. Hamlet was presented to Mr. William Soskin . . . who took him to Long Island. Hamlet did not like Long Island, or Mr. Soskin's books, and disappeared."

Now that life at High Meadow was settling in to a comfortable procedure, Rex was indeed rearing crows again. There was one change in his methods, however. He no longer dug worms for them. He had made the fortuitous discovery that they liked canned dog beef just as well. Usually he let them join him for breakfast. Once, when John Stout was visiting High Meadow, Rex heard him crying out in panic, from the terrace, where he had gone to eat his breakfast. Rex found four junior-sized crows swooping about John, their wings agitating like vibrators. When Rex vouched for him, they withdrew.

Hamlet came close to being Rex's most memorable crow. A distinctive crown of feathers behind his ears made him identifiable, even at a great distance. Rex told me:

"Hamlet was the smartest non-human creature I've ever known. Every morning, all summer, after the middle of July, I'd get up, dress, and go to the kitchen. I'd take a piece of bread, put a bit of baloney on it, put it on my shoulder, in the open area by the garage. Hamlet would be perched somewhere in the vicinity — on a branch or on the fence. The minute he saw me come out of the garage, he'd start up, five hundred, six hundred, eight hundred feet — way up. And he'd stay up till I looked up and called 'Hamlet! Hamlet!' The second I called, he'd start down. He'd come down in beautiful, graceful circles, land on my shoulder, and eat the baloney and bread."

One last item made the news before *Golden Remedy* fell into the hands of the critics. Several papers reported, on 20 August, that Rex had lately been stopped by a policeman when he ran a red light. Scowling at Rex's beard, the cop asked, "Are you on your way to a barber?" "Certainly," Rex said. "Okay," the cop told him, "go ahead."

This interlude of anecdotal homage ceased on 26 August when Bill Soskin published his review of *Golden Remedy* in the *Evening Post*. Soskin did not like Marvin Trask, Rex's most Conradian protagonist. Marvin once had thought "that love was beautiful and that some day its beauty would come to him." But experience forced him to conclude "that love's inexorable formula contained the poison that destroyed beauty; however fiercely and desperately you might embrace it, it corroded in your arms, so that you released it in disgust and shut your eyes on its ugliness." The book affirmed Marvin's "impotence in embracing beauty," Soskin conceded, but he did not think we should generalize from that. After all, Marvin brought little to his romantic relationships.

Soskin suspected that Trask was enunciating a thesis which Rex himself upheld, that it reflected a recent change in his domestic situation. The facts were these.

Fay had watched the construction of High Meadow without enthusiasm. Until she was twenty-four, she had lived prosaically in Topeka. For her, New York had been breathtaking. Her friends there now were legion, and she cherished her visits to the city's theaters and art galleries. To her, living with Rex at Danbury had about as much appeal as living with Caesar in Transalpine Gaul would have had. She did not hide her feelings. During the week she stayed in New York. She went down to Connecticut on weekends. Even then she enjoyed Poverty Hollow, Ruth's farm at Redding Ridge, far more than High Meadow. Poverty Hollow was swarming always with attractive guests from New York. It was the penthouse all over again. The good old days were back. The Depression and High Meadow had never happened.

For Rex, the Gatsby era was over. He no longer had either the funds or the fancy for it. He was bent now on realizing himself as a writer, and the new environment he was creating was an essential resource — a physical embodiment of the inner consistency he sought and advocated. He needed daily the gratification of discernible results. Without being conscious of it, he was already establishing those routines which would supply verisimilitude to the scheduled existence of Nero Wolfe.

Fay could not see why so much should be sacrificed to Rex's writing ambitions. His books were not a source of income. He should have been satisfied with his modest successes and renewed his search for gratification in some other direction. After all, during fourteen years of marriage such hit-and-run cultural enthusiasms had been their common diversion. The thought of permanent immurement at High Meadow, while Rex puttered with plants, hammered furniture together, and wrote obscure novels which few people read and fewer people understood made her shudder. During the ETS years she had worked at his side and worked hard. Indeed, Rex told Egmont Arens: "Everything I have and own belongs as much to Fay as to me, maybe more. She worked as hard as I and is at least as responsible for our success." If they had had to go back to those days, she could have done it, difficult though it would have been, but there seemed to be no role for her in the life Rex was evolving.

Later Fay would become an artist and have a full and rewarding life that complemented Rex's own. That career lay some years in the future, however. Now she saw herself as incidental to his plans. She sought to make him jealous by letting him think her attention had shifted else-where. That merely widened the breach. Pride told her that Rex was no longer essential to the life she wanted. With Rex's assent she asked Morris Ernst to arrange a divorce. Quite naturally, Bill Soskin thought *Golden Remedy* was a chronicle of the bitterness and disillusion Rex must be feeling at the breakup of his marriage.

When Marvin Trask arrives in New York from Nebraska, he is an idealistic young man who wants a singing career. He falls short of this goal and becomes the manager of a concert bureau. But a second ideal — the attainment of perfection in love — persists. His business supplies him a steady flow of candidates and he moves from woman to woman, hoping he will find spirit, body, and mind in beautiful conjunction. He never does. Disenchantment deepens: "It was all ugly, a dirty joke from beginning to end . . . nothing but vulgarity and distaste and disgust."[4] He probes his dilemma: "There was something wrong with him; or rather, and more likely, there was something wrong with women. That wasn't it either. Here was the truth: there was something wrong with what you did with them."[5] He could see no difference between Rabelais slaking his lust with a scullery maid and Tristan fulfilling his soul's yearning with Isolde. Women had qualities he could admire, but "unanimously and utterly they failed in the one function in which nature had given them a monopoly." The ideal perished in the attain-ment. "A hag not yet possessed is immortal Helen; Helen known is no better than a hag."[6] In fact, Helen, as Rex had portrayed her in *The Great Legend,* barters sex for advantage. For a time Marvin seems to have found his ideal when he courts and marries an unspoiled country girl, Lydia Brooke. Yet soon her touch is poison to him. Many of Rex's friends besides Soskin must have thought that Fay had sat for Rex's portrait of Lydia.

In its releases Vanguard did not account for Marvin's state of mind. Readers were told: "Whether Marvin Trask is to be called a shrewd little philanderer or the tragic victim of malign circumstances; whether he represents the triumph of indifferent nature or merely a comical hypersensitivity to the mean little accidents at which heroes laugh; these are points of the puzzle on which your judgment is perhaps as good as his — or worse, or better."

In point of fact, Rex had accounted for Marvin's confusions. Marvin's mother had died giving birth to him. His father had hated him for killing her. In Marvin's mind, his father's love for his mother became an inaccessible ideal. Because he was responsible for destroying that union, he punished himself by destroying every union he himself attempted.

In this same book, Marvin's sister-in-law, Ruth Brooke, is destroyed by her relationship with her father. When she was a child, her mother died. To comfort her, her father had taken her into his bed. As a result, in maturity she could have only a shunamitic relationship with a man. She dies a suicide.

The problems of Rex Stout's characters in his psychological novels consistently are rooted in their relationships in childhood with their parents. Through the problems posed in these novels, Rex was already probing his relationship with his own parents. These explorations would prove preliminary to the major exploration he would undertake when he started the Wolfe series.

Rex's interest in Marvin's sexual frustrations, however, was more literary than personal. His own early cerebral interest in the enigma of love, reinforced by his readings in contemporary psychology and in Conrad, naturally drew him to the topic. The debt to Conrad is shown further in Marvin's fascination with his wife's uncoiling hair and his gesture of kissing his secretary's ankles. Foot and hair fetishism are plentiful in Conrad, as Bernard C. Meyer indisputably shows in *Joseph Conrad: A Psychoanalytic Biography* (1967).

Marvin's zeal in setting up love nests likewise mirrored no taste of Rex's own, as, in later years, readers of *Too Many Clients* could logically infer. Rex assured me: "The kind of necessity, desire, need that requires a man to support a love nest, I don't have at all. I'm not contemptuous of love nests as such. I accept the fact that some men can't live satisfactorily unless they have that kind of arrangement, but I'm not that kind of a man. Therefore my sympathy for it is not the same as it would be if it was something that I myself required. For the man who needs it, it's not a weakness — but it's too bad he has to waste so much time."

On the topic of mistresses, Rex was no less explicit: "Have I ever kept a mistress? Webster II on 'mistress': '3A: A woman with whom a man habitually cohabits unlawfully as his paramour.' Under that definition my answer is no. All of my extramarital episodes have been comparatively brief and enjoyable and have left no scars. No details will be supplied." Keeping a mistress, as a recreation, did not outrage Rex's sense of decency. The logistics of the practice did seem to offend his sense of order.

That Rex had been weighing for some time ideas dealt with in *Golden Remedy* may be educed from Egmont Arens's letters to him in this period. On 12 April 1929, Egmont had written him: "Spring is just around the corner, and there's a rainbow in her vagina. That's as good an explanation of violets and daffodils as I've heard, and it ought to have double significance to a man who is beyond sex. BEYOND SEX. What a name for a book!" When *Golden Remedy* came out Egmont wrote:

> Your protagonist never breaks the system of his habit, never alters the pattern of his behavior, never revolts against the conditions of his defeat. But I think of the three books this is the least savage. The author seems to have abandoned some of the keenness of his hostility to human warmth and happiness. He allows himself at least a covert suspicion that there may be some other fruits of intimacy than bitterness. Behind the books is the person who wrote them and whom I love. These books are the fierce sledgehammers with which he is smashing his own habit pattern.[7]

Golden Remedy was not innovative. That fact, coupled with the book's controversial theme, exposed Rex to the full glare of hostile criticism. In the New York *Sun,* under the caption "The Sex Boys in Carnegie Hall or — Giving Our Sex-Life the Omaha-Ha," Laurence Stallings leaped to the attack. "Marve is a sad one, a scientific one," he said. He implied that Rex shared Trask's impotence: "One doubts that Mr. Stout is moved at all, even though he occasionally flares up in the Laurentian manner about sex." The *Saturday Review* identified the book as three hundred pages "containing practically nothing else" but descriptions of "the mechanics of copulation."

H. R. Pinckard's review in the Huntington, West Virginia, *Herald-Advertiser* was captioned "Sex Dominates Latest Novel by Rex Stout." Only the style kept *Golden Remedy* from being "one of the most blatantly oversexed novels of the last ten years." Added Pinckard, "Don't give it to Aunt Lucy for Christmas." Nonsense. Rex's Aunt Lucy would have taken it in stride.

One thing Pinckard said must have occurred to other reviewers, too — "If Marvin were not so utterly masculine, he might be tainted with the bacillus of perversion, so powerful and instinctive are his emotional revulsions to women whom he has seduced." Is a man who is sexually repelled by women consequently sexually attracted to men? That would be the dilemma Rex would deal with next, in *Forest Fire.*

As the year ended, it looked as though *Golden Remedy* was going to get a reprieve. *The New York Times* saw Marvin as "a symbolic figure of man's refusal to admit his inevitable defeat at the hands of nature." Moreover, Rex had scored a gain. The book was "greatly superior in clarity and precision to Mr. Stout's earlier work. . . ." On 22 December, Bill Soskin apologized to Rex for taking the book "too seriously." Perhaps that handsome gesture piqued Laurence Stallings. On 30 December, Stallings told New York *Sun* readers: "*Golden Remedy* is a minor minorpiece."

In the closing pages of *Golden Remedy* Rex had taken a gratuitous swipe at the socialists: "What they're really interested in is words and ideas. Not things, and not people. What is a worker to them? He's a word, an economic unit, a political atom; but in reality he's none of these things, he's a man."[8] No doubt this passage goaded a few reviewers to acts of reprisal, but *Golden Remedy,* even without that, seemed to rub just about everybody the wrong way.

In the days ahead the rural press would spread the word that *Golden Remedy* was "sex obsession in its most unrelieved form." For all practical purposes, the jury was back with its verdict by year's end. Rex had written his first flop.

The chronicler of misogyny could not have cared less. Leaving poor Marvin to deal with his inhibitions as best as he could, Rex himself was wallowing in no slough of despond. He had fallen in love again.

The adjustments that had to be made as Americans moved out of the roaring twenties into the sobering thirties had broken the harmony of many marriages. Egmont Arens's second marriage had failed, too. In the aftermath Ruth had married Lewis Gannett. There were no deep estrangements. All were friends and continued to be friends. Rex, in fact, had grown as close to Lewis as he was to Egmont. Everyone liked Lewis. Indeed, after the realignment had taken place, Egmont wrote to Rex: "Mother dropped in to see us from Oregon on her way to visit Ruth and Lewis. She feels that Lewis is a fine son-in-law-in-law."[9]

The Gannetts also had elected for country living. Cream Hill, at West Cornwall, Connecticut, was their haven from the harassments of New York. Often on Sunday afternoons, before returning to the city, they stopped at High Meadow to see what progress Rex was making in subduing his eighteen acres. One Sunday when they came by, they had the Hoffmanns with them, Pola and Wolfgang. Wolfgang was the son of Josef Hoffmann, the famous Austrian architect. Pola, born Pola Weinbach, in Stryj, Poland, in 1902, had studied in Hoffmann's Kunstgewerbe Schule in Vienna, and in the Wienerverkstätte, and was on her way to becoming one of the foremost designers of wool fabrics in America.[10] Her marriage to Hoffmann was shaky. He was frightened at the thought of having a family. She wanted one. In Rex she saw someone much like herself. High Meadow, she sensed, was a statement Rex had made about himself. She could relate to it. She stood on the terrace and let her eye travel over the functional lines of the fine house hugging the hillside, with its ample roof terrace, meandering conservatory, and sun-filled gardens. "Very nice," she said. "Very nice. Of course copied after Poland." The lovely face radiated assurance. Even then Rex half-suspected that the Bey of Danbury had found a bayan to share his pleasure dome.

25.

Stout Fellow

My friendship with Rex Stout over the years has done more than produce in me a feeling of respect for the man. I love the guy.

— NORMAN COUSINS

In mid-November 1931, Rex Stout wrote to the United States Department of Agriculture requesting information about the work of the Forest Service. The questions he asked about the family life of rangers and about methods of fire control in the forest reserves of Montana show that *Forest Fire*, which would not be completed until the following August, already was taking shape in his mind. The Forest Service forwarded a selection of manuals and pamphlets and a useful glossary of terms on fire control. Later, when the book came out, the service ordered two hundred copies.[1] Eyebrows must have been singed at ranger lookouts across the land as readers discovered that the hottest flames that burned in *Forest Fire* were those of human passion. No copies were returned for refunds, however.

On 15 December Lewis Gannett told *Herald Tribune* readers: "Rex Stout has shut himself up on Gage's Hill, Brewster, to write a novel which, he explains, is 'about two men and a woman.'" Even as *Forest Fire* was conceived and begun, the drama of love was unfolding in Rex's personal life. In February, Fay and Rex were divorced. In the meantime the Hoffmanns had separated. Now Pola and Rex moved quickly toward an understanding. Just one thing made Pola hesitate. "I knew," she told me, "that at times I would be — not perfect, something that Rex cannot tolerate." Finally she decided to run the risk and told him she would marry him. "He seemed happy then," she said, "but spoke no more of marriage." After a couple of weeks the suspense became unbearable. "I have no wish to seem indiscreet," she said, "but do you still intend to marry me?" Rex raised his left eyebrow in astonishment. "It's understood," he said.

As befitted a prospective bridegroom, Rex, in this period, had a night out with the boys — predictably, an unusual one. Winston Churchill was then making an American lecture tour. One night in January he was a dinner guest at a private club which Egmont Arens belonged to. Mindful that Churchill was a two-fisted drinker, the Club laid in a generous stock of bootleg bourbon with the set goal of getting him drunk. Egmont invited Rex to come see the fun. Rex went and found about thirty men on hand. "At half-past one," Rex said, "eight or ten of them were out, another dozen or more couldn't articulate, and Churchill, who had drunk as much as anyone, was sipping bourbon and discussing Sherlock Holmes with me and three other men." "I lasted the distance," he conceded, "because I hadn't drunk much." He remembered fondly: "Churchill knew the Holmes stories fairly well and thought them 'perfect entertainment.'"

In May 1932, with the half-completed manuscript of *Forest Fire* in his luggage, Rex headed west with Pola. At Reno, awaiting Pola's divorce decree, Rex wrote the rest of the book. Then, in the closing days of August, they went on to Glacier Park. There, for safekeeping, Rex gave his manuscript to George Edkins, the postmaster, and with Joe MacGregor and Harland Knowlton along again to supply the fine points of woodcraft, took Pola into the mountains for a three-week packing-in trip. The party camped about ninety miles southwest of the park, on Shafer Creek. Thirty-six years later, in *Death of a Dude,* Pola would recognize as their Shafer Creek camping site the quiet spot in the Montana mountains where Nero Wolfe bathes his feet. "Nero Wolfe could never climb up there," she expostulated. "That doesn't matter," Rex said; "I could."

Pola had a special reason for remembering Shafer Creek. There, on horseback, with Joe and Harland as witnesses, Rex and she exchanged marriage vows. "Who am I now?" she asked. "Pola Hoffmann or Pola Stout?" "Pola Stout, of course," Rex told her. Yet by his preference the legal ceremony would come later.

On the way home, Rex stopped at Topeka. With Pola he toured the site of the farm at Wakarusa. This was the last visit he ever made to Kansas.

When Jim Henle of Vanguard read *Forest Fire* he was enthusiastic. On 25 October he wrote Rex concerning the book's protagonist: "I think Stan Durham is, by all odds, the best character you have created — the fullest rounded, the most interesting, the most consistent (psychologically) and the most convincing."[2] Though Henle wanted to publish the book, Rex hesitated. John Farrar, of Farrar & Rinehart, wanted to publish it, too, and thought it would bring in a good deal of money. That was a factor Rex now had to take into account. As the economic depression deepened, ETS revenue was dropping and Bob wanted to be released from the agreement that guaranteed Rex $30,000 a year. Rex saw his point and called it quits. Then, in November, he signed with

Farrar & Rinehart. Farrar welcomed him on their list "with all force and fury." He was certain great things would come of their alliance.

At Christmas, Dreiser's bibliographer, Vrest Orton, wrote Farrar:

> I hear that you are going to have the honor of publishing Rex Stout's next book. May I send you my most enthusiastic congratulations! In my humble opinion you have got a winner here. He is, I think, one of the white hopes . . . he will be as good as Faulkner for collections, make a bigger dent in American literature than Hemingway and sell better than either of them.[3]

Rex had other reasons for being in good cheer that Yuletide season. On 21 December, Pola and he were married at a civil ceremony at High Meadow. Rex picked the date. He explained: "December twenty-first is the shortest day of the year, and has the longest night."[4]

On Stan Durham, protagonist of *Forest Fire*, Rex's Casanovan logic would have been wasted. Stan is chief ranger of Montana's Middle Branch District. As a fire fighter he has no equal. He prides himself on his cool head. His one rule is "Never be in a position where you have to decide what to do now, that must always have been decided an hour ago."[5] But Stan's one love is the forest. He is forty-five, married, the father of a grown son, yet he relates poorly to women. He no longer sleeps with his wife, who thinks of him as a "snub nosed gelding" and occasionally turns to other men for solace. Quite unexpectedly, without realizing what is happening, the unrequited Stan forms an incipiently homosexual attachment for Harry Fallon, a young summer helper.

The unsuspecting, theatrical, yellow-haired Harry is stalked also by Dorothy Fuller, a "dudine" who sees the forest as a logical place in which to hunt a husband. She is twenty-nine to his nineteen. Dot begins by camping in the woods near Harry's station, then moves into his cabin when she injures her foot. Although Harry's innocence persists, Stan thinks Dot is Harry's mistress. In a jealous rage, which he construes as righteous indignation at a ranger who has disgraced the service, Stan undertakes to drive the "lovers" out of the forest. A major forest fire, set by Dot's carelessness and paralleling the emotional conflagration she has ignited, brings the story to its climax. In a disordered attempt to reassert his slumbering masculinity, Stan tries to rape Dot. He is prevented from carrying out his intentions by his wife, who, with motivations fully as contradictory as those which would govern the behavior of Margot Macomber in Hemingway's "The Short Happy Life of Francis Macomber," shoots him. Harry perishes in the forest fire. The women survive unscathed. In none of Rex's stories is woman as predator more blatantly portrayed.

Farrar & Rinehart's advance promotion of *Forest Fire* was frankly exploitative: "This novel rips aside the film of normality covering the deranged mentalities of sexually-starved people living in a circumscribed, primitive environment. . . . In the forest reserves of Montana, the emotions and deep inhibitions of four people were tinder as dry as the trees themselves one waterless summer . . . thrown together, they struck forth a spark which brought tragedy to two of them, which made the forest a red-mouthed inferno." A slump in book sales called for desperate measures.

The first day of publication, 13 April, brought a telegram from Charles G. Norris, congratulating Rex on "a strong upstanding book engrossingly told and admirably written." It also brought a cautionary letter from John Farrar. The Depression was strengthening. Book sales were down to half of what they had been the previous spring.

One of the most revered myths of American national consciousness has been the romantic view that men are ennobled by life in the wilderness. The Turner thesis, with its stress on pioneer experience in the American West as the force which had created a great and noble people, had been accepted by many as the formalized statement of an undeniable fact. Most readers of *Forest Fire*, therefore, were ready for a story of idealized love in the pinewoods. Stan Durham was a New Englander by birth; Harry, an Easterner, the son of traveling actors; Dot, a city girl from Chicago. By every reasonable expectation, life in the wilderness should have elevated them in mind and heart. Reviewers, therefore, were either perplexed or scandalized by *Forest Fire*. They found here an authentic new world which fiction writers had not dealt with before. Stout's forest was real. His forest fire was real. The rough and unaffected language of the rangers, the homely incidents of their daily lives, all carried conviction. To talk of forbidden sexual desires awakening in such an environment seemed a desecration. It was wrong to take a nobleman of nature — the stern, efficient, hard-driving chief of the rangers — and twist his psyche with homosexual yearnings. Even *The New York Times* was displeased: "If the Zane Grey public is so misled by the title as to purchase *Forest Fire*, it will be sorely disappointed. The familiar ingredients are, to be sure, all there. The scene is laid in the wild forest reserves of Montana; it is peopled by robust he-men." But Rex had not followed through in approved fashion. "Despite the intimacy here shown with the great outdoors, he has written once again a drama of contorted psychology, of strange, dark impulses." The *Times* concluded: "His emphasis on abnormality in this instance seems misplaced and strained."

Bill Soskin (*New York Evening Post*, 13 April 1933) assessed the problem with amusement and satisfaction:

Rex Stout's new novel, *Forest Fire*, will never attain the large and solvent popularity that attends the Zane Grey fraternity of woodsmen. The virile noblemen of Mr. Stout's Montana forests have the physique and enough of the routine bravery to qualify as American heroes; but they are touched with that suggestion of introspective examination which makes them anathema to God's-country-and-heart-throb readers . . . a tricky arrangement of chromosomes lies beneath the defensive virility of these he-men of the West. . . . The average reader, I am afraid, will find it queer.

The *Herald Tribune*'s Mary Ross cannily suggested that Rex's actual theme was not Stan's sexual confusions but "the destructiveness of rejected emotion." Stan, she argued, had ceased to live long before Harry and Dot entered his forest reserve. She did not find the book's ending melodramatic. A tragic outcome was inevitable and the crisis of the fire served well both as a convincing physical manifestation of the emotional situation the story is built on and the inevitable rebuff to a man who had made fire fighting a surrogate for dealing with the fire storm of passions that blazed within him.

Harry Hansen's widely reprinted review in the New York *World-Telegram* typified reviewer orthodoxy. He was disappointed that the book was not another glorification of the West. The best passages were those which described the heroic efforts men make to contain forest fires. The book's melodramatic ending moved it "out of the realm of a psychological study into that of a thriller."

T. S. Matthews told *New Republic* readers that Rex was "much too temperamentally cheerful" to write a tragedy. This point had validity. *Forest Fire* was finished at a time when Rex was well satisfied with life. His state of mind may have taken the edge of conviction from the tragic denouement of his story.

Whereas other reviewers felt Rex had overlaid his natural setting with a transparency of abnormal psychology, the *Saturday Review* asserted that he had done the reverse. He had made fiction out of abnormal psychology: "The narrative surface is always tightly stretched over a skeleton of laboratory principles." The reviewer resented the strangeness Rex found in the souls of his characters, as though Harry would have been more convincing if his self-consciousness did not keep him from expressing his emotions, and Dot more real if her cynicism did not defraud her of emotional experience, and Stan truer to himself if he understood the reasons for his sexual confusions. For all his grave concern over imagination in art, the reviewer was disappointed because Rex had not done a piece of "straightforward writing" about the American West, reiterating Rousseauvian clichés.

One important aspect of *Forest Fire* escaped reviewers. If Stan, without fully understanding himself, courts Harry — brings him flowers and food, conspires to sleep under the same roof with him, to fondle his clothes, and watch him undress — Harry, in like measure, entices Stan. Perhaps Harry does not realize that the bobbing bear-grass plume he wears in his hat will become for Harry a beckoning phallic symbol or that the cuspidor he fills with sawdust and places before the juiceless

Stan will emblemize for Stan his own impotence, but he likes to place his hand on Stan's knee and admits that he does. He strikes postures which make him look attractive and enjoys stirring in Stan an admiring response. He admits he does not know how to use a woman sexually. He admits that feminine psychology baffles him. In short, he is readier for a homosexual than for a heterosexual encounter. Harry, now, could be as Stan had been twenty-five years earlier. Harry says:

"The truth is, I'm a poor judge of women. I'm not exactly afraid of them, but I never know what they're up to. I don't mean just sex . . . they always act as if the world had begun only that minute. . . . What you've got to go on from is not what has already happened, or what has been said and agreed upon, but the state of her own mind at that particular moment. That's the only reality and the only record she pays any attention to."[6]

When Harry outlines this thesis to Dot, she says he has borrowed it from an old sage. And well she might. None of Rex's characters comes as close to explaining the quandary "the analytical male" is put in by "the intuitional female."

Their national experience found the British better able to deal with the sexual concerns Rex wrote about in *Forest Fire*. The Cambridge *Daily News* thought Rex had created "characters whose virility and queerness attract in a remarkable way." The *Sunday Times*, Johannesburg, found the story "psychologically sound and beautifully written." Peter Quennell, in the *New Statesman and Nation*, did not find Rex's presentation of Stan's dilemma convincing. Yet he offered extenuation: "One of the difficulties of portraying homosexual love, even when, as in this instance, it does not aspire beyond sentimental infatuation, is the comparative absence of literary precedent. . . ." The crime fiction historian and writer Julian Symons read *Forest Fire* in 1933. In 1974, Symons said of it: "The book has stuck in my memory where thousands of others have been washed away."[7]

Forest Fire was the only one of Rex's serious novels not to be compared to a detective story by a reviewer. Nonetheless, in 1948 an appeal came from a broadcasting station in Salisbury, Southern Rhodesia, "for permission to use *Forest Fire* in a program in which famous detective stories are outlined." Rex gave permission without turning a hair. "Gee," he told Marguerite Reese of Farrar & Rinehart, "I've been wanting to do something nice for Salisbury, Southern Rhodesia all my life. . . . They can use *Forest Fire* . . . without emolument."[8]

While reviews of *Forest Fire* were piling up, other notices were reaching Rex. The day after the book came out, Egmont Arens wrote: "I see that you have written the story of my life. It ought to be a good seller. Anyhow, congratulations." Rex replied: *"Forest Fire* is not the story of your life; I'm going to wait to write that until after you've written mine, so I'll know what to say." On 5 May, John Farrar wrote to say that Aldous Huxley had told Van Gelder of the *Times* that Rex Stout was one of his "first admirations among American authors." On 25 May, en route to England aboard the *Statendam,* Huxley himself wrote Farrar: "I liked Stout's *How Like a God,* the only one I've read . . . thought it a very fine treatment of an exceedingly terrifying theme." That news was sent to Rex, too. It was a useful palliative then, because in between the Huxley bulletins Stan Rinehart had broken the news that *Forest Fire* was another victim of the Depression. It was not selling. That was ironic. *Forest Fire* was the most vital of Rex's serious fictions.

Even as *Forest Fire* was being assessed by the critics, one of its predecessors brought Rex unexpected notice. In April 1932 he had received an urgent appeal from the editor of *Forum,* Henry Goddard Leach. H. G. Wells was on his way to America and Leach had spoken to him by ship's radio. Wells wanted to meet Rex while he was in New York. Leach suggested lunch at his place on West Twelfth Street. Rex was flattered. The luncheon, however, presented a sobering revelation. Wells took Rex into a corner where they could be alone. The name Odette Keun came quickly into the conversation. Odette had written to Rex from Paris to say how much she liked *Seed on the Wind.* A flurry of letters had passed between them. What Rex did not know was that Odette was Wells's current mistress. Wells was not interested at all in Rex's books. "What he did want to know," Rex told me, "was who in hell this American son of a bitch was who was writing to his mistress."

In late July Soskin told readers of a visit on Saturday, 22 July, to High Meadow: "Talk was of Hervey Allen's *Anthony Adverse. . . .* Rex thought that any book hailed with the superlatives that were thrown in Hervey Allen's direction should at least survive the present season and live for some five or ten years." Soskin doubted that *Tom Jones* itself would live for ten years in an era in which turnover in ideas and tastes was so fast. "Rex agreed that that was generally true," said Soskin, "but added that if a book appeared today which had the originality and the richness in relation to our own age which Fielding's had in his day the book would certainly survive." He suggested that *Ulysses* was such a book. The day ended with "a superb meal" cooked by Pola and Chase Horton and served in the garden to the accompaniment of some lively discussion on good cooking. Even then, perhaps, the first glimmerings of Nero Wolfe were taking shape in Rex's mind. In ten weeks' time, confronting his Underwood in his L-shaped office, Rex would set down on paper the first lines of *Fer-de-Lance.* Maybe that night's discussion gave him the idea to provide Wolfe with a Fritz Brenner and a gourmet's appreciation of good food.

The next week Soskin reported that on Sunday, 30 July, he had pitched horseshoes with Rex and Whit Burnett at High Meadow: "The Stout-Burnett combination from the Middle West walked off with the honors." Nothing of this encounter found its way into the characterization of Wolfe. Horseshoes? Pfui.

26.

Lazy Bloodhound

Rex Stout is one of the half-dozen major figures in the development of the
American detective novel. With great wit and cunning, he devised a form
which combined the traditional virtues of Sherlock Holmes and the English
school with the fast-moving vernacular narrative of Dashiell Hammett.

— Ross Macdonald

On 7 August 1933, John Farrar wrote Rex telling him that Faber &
Faber would publish *Forest Fire* in England and wanted an option on
his next two novels. "As for the next two novels," Rex replied on the
fourteenth, "to horse! Though I don't suppose even Trollope could
write in the saddle." Had circumstances required it, Rex no doubt
would have found a way to write on horseback. After all, he had been
married there. And the fact was, he now stood in need of further
income. Pola was expecting their first baby in October. That prospect,
indeed, had led Rex to do some hard thinking. "To write profound
things about the human soul," he decided, "your feelings about it have
to be very deep, very difficult, as Dostoyevsky's were, or Melville's, or
Balzac's." He told himself he was not that kind of person. Forty years
later he still held the same opinion: "I could have been like Steinbeck
or H. G. Wells. Just another one of the good ones. But when you're
making serious comment on people and their behavior, you have to put
part of your soul in the work. I thought, if you're merely good and not
great, what's the use of putting all that agony into it?"

"While I could afford it," Rex said, "I played with words because I
loved words and loved to put them together in ways that pleased me."
Now he had to use his pen to bring him income. Since reviewers said
his novels often rang melodious changes on the brazen flanks of detective fiction, he decided to try his hand at writing detective stories. After
all, nothing sold better. Besides, detective stories got to some definite
place, and that, to his mind, was what stories should do.

In later years, speaking on copyright reform before the congressional
Ways and Means Committee, Rex cited the compromises financial need
compels many writers to make — settling for the security which jobs in
television, advertising, and the movie industry offer.[1] Yet he did not see
himself as someone who had capitulated to the lure of ready money:

"There was no thought of 'compromise.' I was satisfied that I was a good storyteller; I enjoyed the special plotting problems of detective stories; and I felt that whatever comments I might want to make about people and their handling of life could be made in detective stories as well as in any other kind. I think the detective stories I've done are the better stories, except maybe *How Like a God*. That's a good story. Or rather it isn't so much a good story as it is a good character — the study of a man."

At the end of August 1933 Rex visited John Farrar at his office at 237 Madison Avenue. He had an idea, he said, for a detective story. He outlined his character of a lazy sleuth with a brash young aide who did his legwork. At that stage the idea did not differ markedly from the one used eighteen years earlier in "Justice Ends at Home," when he brought together Simon Leg and Dan Culp. But its potentials interested Farrar, who told Rex to go ahead with it.

Rex returned to High Meadow with a clear plan of action. Pola's pregnancy still had six weeks to run. Once that event was safely past, and his family settled around him, he would begin writing. The period of grace proved fortuitous. On 8 September John Stout died, at eighty-six, and Rex found himself entered upon an emotional inventory that would have a wide-ranging influence on his understanding of himself and on his work as a writer.

In old age John Stout had maintained his commanding dignity. With his snow-white thatch, trim white beard, and ramrod posture, he was an impressive figure as he took his daily walk in the park across the way from 414 Central Park West, where Lucetta, Mary, and he had a sixth-floor apartment. As always he held himself to schedule, consulting the pocket watch he had carried for sixty-two years to meet punctiliously the commitments he set for himself. The cane which he had carried for style had come into practical use as age diminished the steadiness of his gait. But he was not visibly dependent on it. Indeed, he still saw himself as something of a dandy, a fact which had its drawbacks, as the secretaries who worked for ETS could attest. John had a heavy hand with talcum powder. The girls guessed that he doused himself with about a pound of it every day. When he visited the ETS offices he was enveloped in so highly perfumed a scent that they experienced attacks of vertigo when he came close.

If John's fastidiousness and vigor lasted, his temper had lasted too. He was forever firing off letters to the *Times* protesting neglect of trees and shrubs in the park, the lack of sufficient trash containers, or the discourtesy of minor functionaries. Twice he was taken into custody for thwacking with his cane people who had jostled him in the subway. His granddaughter Natalie can remember her mother rushing to her father and saying, "Grandpa has been arrested in the subway," and Bob clamping his hands to his temples and groaning, "Oh, God, not again!"

One day in 1932, in the early fall, John came upon a produce peddler whipping a fallen horse. John berated him, and when the man, to spite him, put new fury into his blows, John leaped into the street, cane poised menacingly. A cab swinging in to discharge a passenger struck him. His right leg was fractured above the knee. Weeks of hospitalization followed before he returned home. He was a bed patient for nearly a year before a stroke ended his life. The nurse who attended him told Rex later that John often had said to her, "Nurse, what's the right time?" To please him she had consulted his old watch on the dresser and told him the time. Shortly before he died, he called out the same question. "The right time is eight o'clock, Mr. Stout," she replied. John considered this awhile. Then he said, "I wonder what the *wrong* time is?" After a lifetime of proud punctuality, John had decided the right time really did not matter. He was in a good frame of mind to face eternity.

John was buried at Ridgewood, beside May and Donald — his oldest and his youngest.

The venerable pocket watch passed to Bob, as the oldest son. Rex's legacy consisted of books and one curious item, the yellow nightshirt he had made for his father at Christmas several years before. The gift had been an act of atonement. One night, while staying at his parents' apartment, he had worn to bed a yellow nightshirt belonging to John. He had ripped it as he slept. John was overwhelmed to realize that Rex had gone to the bother of making a nightshirt to replace the one he had ruined. He thought it was one of the nicest things anyone ever had done for him. Now the nightshirt came back to Rex. It occupied an honored place in his personal dresser till the end of his life. Mere fetishism does not account for the literary use to which Rex presently put this cherished garment.

On Thursday, 5 October 1933, Rex became a father when Pola gave birth to a seven-pound daughter. "I'm glad it's a girl," he wrote Egmont Arens on the ninth. "She won't go to war, and she'll never be strong enough to sock me in the jaw."

If they had had a son, Pola had wanted to call him Todhunter. Rex had agreed. The only thing he had insisted on was that they should choose a three-syllable name, which he thought hit the ear best when combined with a one-syllable surname. Pola left it up to him to name their daughter. He decided on "Barbara."

The same week that he selected a three-syllable name for his daughter, Rex tried out another three-syllable name for the protagonist of his new novel. (One of the few things Rex did before he began a story was to draw up a list of the names of the principal characters.) "Nero Wolfe" — it was "simple but odd." People would remember it, just as they remembered the name Rex Stout. Rex meant "king." Nero had been an emperor. Stout meant "bull." Wolfe meant . . . well, "wolf." A wolf had suckled the founders of Rome. Nero had seen Rome burn and had rebuilt it. The name had a nice inevitability about it. Rex began writing about Nero Wolfe on Wednesday, 18 October, the day after Pola and Barbara came home to High Meadow from Danbury Hospital. Rex, in 1937, would commemorate that date by telling Gilbert Gabriel that each year he began writing a Nero Wolfe story on 18 October. That was not literally true. To confuse matters further, Archie celebrates his birthday on 23 October.

Since boyhood Rex had read hundreds of detective stories. In the decade of the twenties he had kept up with Doyle and Chesterton and had found varying degrees of amusement in Ronald Knox, S. S. Van Dine, Sayers, Edgar Wallace, Christie, Baroness Orczy, R. Austin Freeman, Earl Derr Biggers, and H. C. Bailey. Later he had read Hammett. But he entered their ranks without special preparation. The decision once taken, he read nothing on criminology or detective science. Nor did he visit any police courts, cultivate stalwarts of the law, or those afoul of the law or in durance vile. He chose a milieu he knew because he "wanted to avoid the stiffness of a researched setting." He could not remember where he was when the idea of Nero Wolfe struck him: "In a chapel, no. In a whorehouse, no. But there are lots of other places." But he was certain he did not begin by thinking of Nero Wolfe as a series character. He said that that possibility was raised only after the story was in John Farrar's hands. Farrar believed Rex's memory played him false here. He was sure Rex envisaged Wolfe as a series character from the start.

When would-be writers asked Rex how to get a mystery started, he was apt to tell them, "Apply the seat of the pants to the seat of the chair, and go." Evidently that is what Rex did when he wrote *Fer-de-Lance*. Before Christmas he delivered the completed manuscript to Farrar. In 1933, Hervey Allen's *Anthony Adverse* had secured Farrar & Rinehart's reputation as a publishing house. Yet to make the book marketable John Farrar had had to rewrite it almost line-by-line. *Fer-de-Lance* was phenomenal. It required no editing. Farrar told me later: "Rex is the kind of author publishers dream about. He would block out a certain number of months in which to write a Nero Wolfe book. He would start work on a certain date. And with uncanny precision would finish the book on a specified date. And turn in a manuscript in perfect order."

But Farrar's enthusiasm was not immediately shared by others. He had begun by offering the book to the *Saturday Evening Post* for serialization. On 29 January, the associate editor, Graeme Lorimer, sent back the manuscript, commenting: "The detective is a novelty even if his assistant is Watson's first cousin. We don't feel, however, that the emotional relationships of the characters are sufficiently gripping to hold a serial audience. . . ." If Lorimer had deplored the method of the murder or the melodrama of the closing pages, his dissatisfaction might have been comprehensible. In view of the subsequent popularity of Archie and of the interplay between Archie and Wolfe, we can only conclude Lorimer was having a bad day.

At this stage the book still lacked a title. While working on it, Rex had thought of it merely as "the Nero Wolfe story." By mid-January 1934, Farrar and he were tossing titles at one another with no success. John's first suggestion is not remembered, and that may be just as well, because Rex did not care for it. "I don't like that title," he wrote from High Meadow on 27 January. "Please let me not like it." He offered several alternate suggestions: "Nero Wolfe — Midsummer Chore"; "Nero Wolfe — Summer Chore"; "Nero Wolfe — Midsummer Charade"; "Nero Wolfe — Summer Charade"; "Bloodhound as Artist"; and "Lazy Bloodhound." "What about them," he asked; "any good?" By now, at least, Rex was reconciled to launching a series, for he continued: "The idea would be to use a similar style for the titles of subsequent Nero Wolfe stories, which would serve to differentiate them at a glance from my epics, genre pieces, blank verse dramas, and problem novels." No doubt about it, Rex was ebullient.

On 1 February, Farrar wrote Rex that he still was looking for a title. "The salesmen don't like the 'Charade' business," he said, "as they think it is too light in tone." The next day he wrote to Gertrude Lane of *The Woman's Home Companion:* "I am sending you herewith the manuscript of Rex Stout's Mystery Story which I talked to you about. I think it is a corker. . . . All of us who have read it here feel that we can go out and sell a great many copies of it. . . . Rex Stout is a mature man with a very fine mind. He will go on doing this sort of thing. We have no title as yet. I think quite obviously 'Nero Wolfe' should appear in the title somehow." That same day, the manuscript, bearing the title *Fer-de-Lance,* was sent by messenger to Miss Lane. Across Farrar's covering letter a penciled notation read *"Fer-de-Lance* (new title)." Thus the book which the *London Times* later would put on its list of the "One Hundred Greatest Mystery Stories," got its title. Its subtitle, "A Nero Wolfe Mystery," affirmed its identity as one of a series.

The snake which gave the first Nero Wolfe novel its title was not selected from an encyclopedia, as some accounts allege. Rex found it in "Dick Donovan's" (J. E. P. Muddock's) "The Problem of Dead Wood Hall," a *fin-de-siècle* British mystery in which "the fearful and deadly Fer de lance" is cited in the same paragraph in which Donovan discusses the use of poison-tinctured mechanisms which can inflict a fatal scratch or puncture wound — the actual method by which death is induced in *Fer-de-Lance.*[2]

The idea of using a golf course for the setting of the murder may have been suggested by Agatha Christie's *Murder on the Links* (1923) or

Ronald Knox's *Murder at the Viaduct* (1926), both of which feature golf course killings. At one point in *Golden Remedy*, Marvin Trask had deliberated murdering his girlfriend, Nell McDonnell, on a golf course, when he found out that she was homosexual.

Where Nero Wolfe and Archie Goodwin came from is something less easily ascertained. Through the years Rex professed not to know:

Wolfe was born, he wasn't synthetic. I didn't have to sit down and decide What color will his eyes be? Well, they'll be brown. How much will he weigh? How will he walk? What expressions will he use? He was born. A born character arrives completely created. Nero Wolfe just appeared. I haven't the faintest idea where he came from. I can't answer any "why" questions about him. I don't know a thing about him. He does what he pleases. I really don't know who he is and I don't give a damn so long as he's an interesting guy. I know this must sound phony, but it isn't. I never have had to ask myself one question about Nero Wolfe. He just does what he does. Wolfe, Archie, the brownstone — I haven't the slightest idea how I thought of them.[3]

In September 1935 Alexander Woollcott phoned Rex and invited him to dinner at the Lambs' Club. Until then the two men had never met. Woollcott wanted to meet Rex because he had just read *The League of Frightened Men* and was convinced the character of Wolfe was modeled on himself. He cited the circumstantial evidence. First, he was fat (254 pounds!), brilliant, and absolutist. Second, in 1933, Edna Ferber had publicly ridiculed him as "that New Jersey Nero who thinks his pinafore is a toga." Third, he had annexed the Nero identity by publishing, in the spring of 1934, a book entitled *While Rome Burns*. Rex assured him he was mistaken. Aleck was not impressed. He was certain Rex had found in him Wolfe's prototype and, so far as he was concerned, the matter was not open to further discussion. In fact, aided and abetted by Rex's friendship, as time passed, he settled into the role with contentment. In later years, to add to the legend, he always addressed Jo Hennessey, his factotum, as "Archie."

Rex, of course, assured interviewers that he himself was not Wolfe. Some of them took him at his word. In 1937 Gilbert Gabriel commented: "The difference between them is so huge and so uncompromising I can hardly understand how Wolfe can be a hero to his own author."[4] Thirty years later Alfred Bester reaffirmed Gabriel's verdict: "There is absolutely no resemblance between him [Rex Stout] and Wolfe, either in appearance or character."[5] Alva Johnston, who wrote a profile of Rex for the *New Yorker* in 1949, had a theory which contradicted this view: "When Stout started writing mysteries, he had no idea of patterning his fat detective after himself. The autobiographical note came in unexpectedly. Even today, Stout will not admit that he and Nero Wolfe are identical twins."[6] Johnston said also: "Nero is a unique personality because Stout is. . . . Nero can tackle a problem from forty angles because Stout is a man of forty occupations, avocations, and hobbies."[7]

For a further complication, those closest to Rex saw Rex in Archie as well as in Wolfe.

Margaret and John Farrar announced a consensus: "We both believe that Rex is both Wolfe and Archie — Rex is a many-splendored and many-sided man and he could speak through either character."[8] Marshall Best, who for many years would handle Rex's manuscripts for Viking, said: "Rex is much like Nero in mind and manner, even though there's a good deal of Archie in him."[9]

Mark Van Doren, with whom Rex formed his most enduring friendship, said: "Archie is Rex himself. They are identical in brightness, in cockiness, in learning, in hatred of sentiment, in directness and sharpness of speech. I often hear Rex talking between Archie's sentences, or for that matter in them. Both are impatient of fools and pompous persons; both know how to recognize brains and genius in others. . . . There are times when Nero equals Rex."[10] Jacques Barzun insisted: "Rex in the chair at a meeting of the Authors' Guild Council is Nero to the life."[11]

Pola Stout thinks that through the years Rex was both Wolfe and Archie but that, in the closing phase of his life, both were subsumed into a personality truly his own. His daughters saw Archie as his spontaneous self and Wolfe as his achieved self.

Rex told me he knew that Wolfe and Archie did not exist wholly apart from himself. "A created character," he conceded, "responds to something in the writer. I suspect my subconscious has a very strong feeling toward them." This concession was a major one.

Although Rex had a fair idea of where Wolfe and Archie came from, he chose, with good reason, not to inquire into the mystery too deeply. He believed that the artist who analyzes his art runs the risk of banishing it, especially if such an inquiry necessitates immoderate introspection, as would have been true here. Wolfe and Archie are, in fact, extensions of their creator. Both relate intimately to Rex Stout's intrapsychic life. In the space of a brief month Rex lost his father and became a father. As a new father, newly deprived of a father, he regretted that his own self-image owed so little to John, the authority figure it should have exemplified. During the final decade of John's life Rex had come to understand better his father's value and his worth. He was sorry that that relationship now was broken off. Then he realized that it need not be, that through the characters he was creating for John Farrar, it could be extended.

In Archie Goodwin Rex created a persona who embodied his existent self-image, which, because of Lucetta's all but exclusive sovereignty over him in his period of maturation, was strongly Todhunterian in orientation. To Archie Rex assigned the predominant Todhunter characteristics — gray eyes, fair complexion, charm, brio, curiosity, wit, and a youthful vision of life. In Wolfe Rex created a surrogate father. To him he assigned those characteristics which he did share in common with John Stout — brown eyes, dark complexion, discipline, earnestness, idealism, and a fine sense of indignation. This figure he superimposed on those surrogate authority figures which he had turned to earlier when he found John wanting — Emily McNeal Todhunter and Alvey Augustus Adee. Through Archie and Wolfe, Rex now would be able to continue exploring the father-son relationship.

At the start of the Wolfe saga the dialogue between Archie and Wolfe is, fundamentally, a father-son dialogue. As the saga advances, understanding grows between them. Remarkably, while the flow of Rex's traits into Archie gradually slackens, Nero Wolfe and Rex Stout come, more and more, to take on each other's characteristics — characteristics of a Stoutian kind. With Wolfe as John Stout's proxy, Rex eventually was able to right an ancient wrong and to recast his self-image in his father's likeness.

Again we must revert to the yellow nightshirt which Rex made for John Stout and which returned to Rex's possession just at the time he got *Fer-de-Lance* under way. Yellow is Nero Wolfe's favorite color. He wears yellow shirts and yellow socks, always. His bed linen is yellow. His pajamas always are yellow. For Krafft-Ebing sleepwear fetishism emblemized metamorphosis — death and rebirth. Perhaps, in Rex Stout's subconscious mind, the yellow nightshirt (a symbol of reconciliation offered by Rex to John, and accepted by John) represented a chrysalis into which he could withdraw and from which he could reemerge with a new identity: that of the original wearer.

Some critics, remarking the harmony that flows between Wolfe and Archie (despite occasional clashes), have speculated on the existence of an unacknowledged — though implied — father-son relationship. At the very least, their solicitude for one another in time of danger suggests that Archie has found in Wolfe a father image, and that Wolfe sees in Archie the son he never had.[12] With recognition of Rex's personal, father-son relationship to the characters, these affinities become wholly comprehensible.

Archie Goodwin's early ties link him to Rex's Todhunter antecedents and to the world of Rex's boyhood. Archie was born in Chillicothe, Ohio, and spent his boyhood on a farm there. Chillicothe is situated on the same tract of land where Todhunters farmed and prospered for a hundred years, and where Lucetta was born and grew to maturity. (In *Too Many Women*, a private investigator would report to Mrs. Jasper Pine that Archie's birthplace was Canton, Ohio. Rex thought Mrs. Pine — who was the kind of person who supposes money can buy anything — got what she deserved: "Of course Archie was born in Chillicothe.

I don't know how he got Mrs. Pine's dick misinformed.") In Archie's boyhood home there was a picture of harassed travelers in a storm-battered sleigh, tossing their baby to the wolves, as a delaying tactic. The same picture hung in the Stout farmhouse at Wakarusa — with what traumatic impact Rex did not recall, though certainly if John Stout put in place this portrayal of an unnatural father feeding his infant to *wolves,* the situation abounds in Freudian implications.[13]

Archie says his father, Titus Goodwin (namesake of a Roman emperor brought to prominence by Nero and later occupying his throne), is dead, but his mother is living. At the time Archie wrote that, Rex too was fatherless but still had his mother.

Rex was inquisitive, reliable, resourceful, and loyal. He had a ready wit. He had a good memory for names, faces, facts, and details. He was an adept bookkeeper. When occasion warranted he could be tart, scep-tical, critical, and sardonic. He had a native pugnacity to which his wit gave sizable relief. He always had time for little people — secretaries, receptionists, cabbies — and had good rapport with them. "I never look on them as furniture," he told me, "but see them as human beings — and human beings are interesting."

Rex was an independent and fastidious dresser. He wore colored shirts even when they were not in fashion. He disliked button-down collars, even when they were in fashion. He had an enlightened palate, yet he liked corned beef and was a milk drinker.[14] When he drank hot beverages he liked them served at moderate temperatures.

He was an expert, confident driver, but did not like to talk while driving. He liked opera and the theater. He never missed a play starring the Lunts. He was an ardent Giants (and latterly Mets) fan and would lay odds as readily as a bookie. He went to prizefights occasionally. He enjoyed fishing trips and Montana holidays. He played billiards and chess. He saw Greenleaf and Baldwin play pool at the Strand. He liked dogs. He carried a pocketknife at all times.

Rex disliked television, noiseless typewriters, and long phonecalls. He disliked drawers left partway open. He disliked southern California.[15]

Rex required nine hours' sleep. When he went to bed he fell asleep instantly. He disliked having his sleep interrupted. He solved problems in his sleep. In the morning he did not come alive until after breakfast, a meal he preferred to eat alone.

Archie Goodwin shares all these characteristics with his creator.

Archie says he was "born neat." Rex said he, too, was "born neat, and remained so except for a year or two, when [he] was twelve or thir-teen."

Archie has, in his bathroom, a copy of Paul Chabas's *September Morn.* "There was one at Perry Street," Rex told me. "Fay bought it." Making a quick guess, Rex estimated that he had fallen in love at first sight at least seventeen times. Archie probably could top that figure, but then Archie is free to play the field, and forever thirty-four.

In self-assurance and utterance Rex was Neronian.

Asked if he would have been surprised at forty to know what he would accomplish in the years ahead, he said, "I doubt it; I have never felt inadequate." Asked if he scorned money, Rex said, "You couldn't be more wrong. Money has supplied me — and supplies — most of my comfort, much of my leisure, and a fair share of my pleasure."

He spoke his mind plainly.

"Automation? I sneer at it."

"Motorcycles? I sneer at them, too."

"Rum and Coca-Cola? Undrinkable."

"Rye bread? Insults the palate."

"Mortician? What does it mean? Specialist in death. For a thug it wouldn't be bad at all."

"How dependable is my memory? My subconscious memory is exceptional — replete and exact."

Told that Clifton Fadiman had pegged his IQ at "185 or better," Rex said, "Kip should know."

Only on the subject of home freezers was he furtive: "I have one but would rather no one knew about it. Wolfe has an upright freezer, too, but don't tell anyone."

Rex Stout disliked loud noises, bells and chimes, telephones, trains, cats, television, movies, plastic-covered furniture, bare floors, spray cans, paper dishes, unemptied ashtrays, fastened manuscripts, speed reading, being read aloud to, and people who quote.[16] He disliked people on vacations, and practical jokes. He disliked interruptions, truisms, timetables, credit cards, and waste. He disliked discussing business at meals or in automobiles. He disliked pressure cookers, doughnuts, jellied consommé, canned soups, ice water. He disliked dandruff and pug noses. He disliked unctuousness, genteel manners, babbling women, and men who marry money. He did not like to sit facing a window or hearth fire ("too distracting"). He did not like to carry things. Under his roof, "contact" was not a verb. He loathed Webster's *Third International Dictionary*. Nero Wolfe shares all these aversions.

Rex was no less allied to Wolfe in his preferences.

He breakfasted alone. He drank his coffee black. He ate fowl fattened for him on blueberries, and prepared *oeufs beurre noir* to perfection. He eschewed highballs before meals. He preferred the look and feel of silver table cutlery and the performance of stainless steel. He sharpened his own knives and pencils. When he untied a package he did so patiently and precisely. He liked crossword puzzles and chess.

Rex had a desk made of arcwood, a small study table made of massaranduba, a piece of petrified wood for a paperweight, a thin strip of gold for a bookmark.[17] So does Wolfe.

Rex's library was the size of Wolfe's library: between eleven and twelve hundred books (the size of John Stout's library in Rex's boyhood). He read the books Wolfe read, often books written by his own friends: Mark Van Doren, Clifton Fadiman, Christopher La Farge, Louis Adamic, Elmer Davis, Jacques Barzun, Merle Miller, Christopher Morley, John Hersey, Lewis Gannett, Laura Z. Hobson, John Gunther, William L. Shirer, John Roy Carlson, Bruce Catton, Robert Sherwood, Oscar Hammerstein II, Gilbert Gabriel, Herblock, and Alfred Rossiter, Ruth Stout's husband. After reading Jane Austen both men were compelled to renounce their previously held conviction that a woman could not write a good novel. Rex reread the same books Wolfe reread — Shakespeare, Macaulay, Polybius, Erasmus. Both men removed More's *Utopia* from their shelves after investigating the case against Richard III and concluding that More had maligned him. Both prized copies of Brillat-Savarin's *Physiology of Taste* and Fowler's *Modern English Usage*.[18] Rex thought that the English language needs another pronoun.[19] Wolfe thinks so too. Like Wolfe, Rex was a horticulturist and knew the Latin names of everything he grew.

"In this respect, Rex and Nero are alike," Ruth Stout said. "They think what they think and its a waste of time to try to change them." Rex admitted he had a naturally sceptical turn of mind. He disliked ready-made answers. He believed men have free will and the reasoning power to make a right choice. When he had a problem to solve he gave it his full attention. He disliked jumping to conclusions but seldom delayed coming to one. He would not let sentiment dissolve judgment. A decision once taken, he stood by it, sometimes trapped by his own consistency. He gave of affection warily. He liked to meet people at eye level. He was a liberal. He was an agnostic.[20] He esteemed the black race and world government. For the sake of truth and justice he readily relinquished his comforts and even his home. In all these particulars Wolfe duplicates his behavior.

At High Meadow Rex hung three pictures on the wall of his living room: one of Einstein, one of Shakespeare, one of an unwashed coal miner — the latter an oil painting, the gift of the artist, Zoltán Sepeshy. These, he told visitors, signified man's three primary attributes: intellect, imagination, and muscle. On the wall of his office Wolfe hung three pictures: Socrates, Shakespeare, and an unwashed coal miner. "Man's three resources," he explained, "intellect, imagination, and muscle."

Rex had a few aversions and preferences which Wolfe does not share. He disliked air conditioning, haggling, breakfast in bed, and morning appointments.[21] He liked airplanes, electric blankets, and geraniums.[22] These divergencies are not crucial. Some of them were decreed, no doubt, by Wolfe's foreign upbringing, elected shut-in status, and calculated eccentricity. Of more interest are those idiosyncrasies Rex had which he never assigned to Wolfe. He disliked physical culture, sunbathing, going barefooted, and drinking from a can. He did not like to be visited when he was sick. He liked his meals served on a heated plate. He did not carry insurance. Surely we can infer that Wolfe shares these characteristics. Rex did, however, have two others which Wolfe may have found puzzling. For forty years he used only uncirculated paper money.[23] And he had an intense dislike of bad smells. He told me: "The sense of smell has always been important to me. I am probably more keenly affected through my sense of smell than my sense of sight. It is a more immediate thing."

Nero Wolfe is the same age John Stout was when Rex Stout left home to seek his fortune. Archie Goodwin is the same age Rex Stout was when he found his fortune. Chance did not decree this parallel. By locking his characters into those ages, Rex was able to concentrate his focus on those periods in his lifetime most crucial to his understanding of his relationship with his father.

Possibly, if Pola Stout had borne Rex a son in October 1933, Rex might have accepted a reversal of roles (a device he relished as a storyteller) and sought, in the cultivation of his relationship with his son, to eradicate vicariously the failure of his relationship with his father. But Pola had borne a daughter. His family believes this circumstance was fortunate. They think any boy would have had a hard time of it being the son of Rex Stout. Rex would have expected too much of him. Rex's readers may count themselves fortunate too. If Rex had become the father of a son, in October 1933, he might have found no need to create Nero Wolfe and Archie Goodwin.

Consider further: in *Fer-de-Lance*, Oliver Barstow's wife unjustly despises him. Barstow, born 9 April 1875, dies in 1933, at fifty-eight, victim of a would-be patricide. In 1933, John Stout died at eighty-five. John's birthday fell on 8 April. In 1875 he had married Lucetta. The Stout family was implanted in America when Richard Stout became estranged from his father, John Stout. Richard later expiated for psychic patricide by naming two of his sons for his father. In using Nero Wolfe to avenge Barstow was Rex Stout, three hundred years later, following in the footsteps of Richard Stout?

27

Mystery Monger

In writing of crystal excellence, Rex Stout has made a world I like to revisit; it's our own world, seen in clear. He has done what I'd have sworn wasn't possible. He has written — how many? I don't know for sure — detective stories centered on the same brownstone house and the same people, with recognizably the same "discovery scene" at the end, but he never repeats himself. He is a very good writer indeed. And fifty years from now, I can imagine as many pilgrims hunting for the old brownstone house in West 35th Street as go calling today in London's Baker Street. Vivat Rex!

— MARY STEWART

In March 1934, *The American Magazine* bought the serial rights to *Fer-de-Lance* for $2,500 and told John Farrar that it would appear in the fall, abridged, in one installment. The editor, Sumner Blossom, thought Wolfe "rich in magazine fiction possibilities," and, a few days later, over luncheon, projected plans with Rex for Wolfe's continued existence. To John, Rex reported that Wolfe, to celebrate the occasion, "is going to indulge in a case of imported beer."

Farrar's attention shifted now to the movie rights. Several Hollywood studios were interested. Rex himself wanted Charles Laughton to play Wolfe, but Laughton was then tied into other commitments. Some years later the two men met. They talked about the Wolfe stories. Rex told me: "He had read several of them. A motion picture producer had asked him to do a series of Nero Wolfe movies, and he had said he would agree to do one but would not commit himself to a series. Of all the actors I have seen, I think he would have come closest to doing Nero Wolfe perfectly."[1] John Farrar had other ideas. For the role of Wolfe he had "hit upon a man called Nigel Bruce." In retrospect the choice is amusing. Bruce afterward became fixed in the minds of millions of theatergoers as the Watson of Basil Rathbone's Sherlock Holmes series.

When Walter Wanger came into the negotiations, he insisted the part be offered to Alexander Woollcott. Wanger apparently saw a resemblance between Wolfe and Woollcott before Woollcott himself did. When Columbia pictures bought the screen rights to *Fer-de-Lance* for $7,500, and secured the option to buy further stories in the series, it was thought the role would go to Walter Connolly. Instead Edward Arnold got it. Columbia's idea was to keep Arnold busy with low-cost Wolfe films between features. Two Wolfe movies presently were made by Columbia, *Meet Nero Wolfe (Fer-de-Lance)*, and *The League of Frightened Men*. Connolly did portray Wolfe in the latter film, after Arnold decided he did not want to become identified in the public mind with one part. In both films, Lionel Stander portrayed Archie Goodwin. Stander was a capable actor but, as Archie, Rex thought he had been miscast.

While the groundwork was being laid for the Wolfe series, Rex's pen had been active again. He had written *The President Vanishes*, a tale of political intrigue set in Washington, D.C. A timely novel, which portrayed the dangers in the United States of a fascist takeover patterned on Hitler's takeover of Germany, it was sold at once to Hollywood. As a forerunner of such books as Allen Drury's *Advise and Consent* and Fletcher Knebel's *Seven Days in May* it has a readily comprehensible appeal.

Although *The President Vanishes* postdated *Fer-de-Lance* among Rex's productions, it preceded *Fer-de-Lance* into print by five weeks, being published in hardcover on 17 September 1934. *Fer-de-Lance*, under the title *Point of Death*, appeared in *The American Magazine* on 24 October, and as a book two days later. *The President Vanishes* was published anonymously. Rex had recalled the widespread speculative curiosity anonymity had engendered when, in 1880, Henry Adams concealed his authorship of *Democracy* (the prototypical novel in that genre which probes the Washington scene) and wanted to see what it would do for his book. As he had hoped, rumor circulated that the book was a *roman à clef* written by someone high in the nation's councils. Sales were good. President Stanley found his original in the chief executive of Kansas, William Eugene Stanley (1899–1903), whose daughter, Harriet, had been Rex's classmate. Otherwise, none of the characters in the book has a real-life counterpart. Not until 1936, when he began to take an active role in national affairs, did Rex acknowledge *The President Vanishes* as his own.

Prompt publication of *The President Vanishes* was decreed by the speed with which Hollywood, recognizing its contemporaneity, had transformed it into a movie. By early November, even as he was negotiating for the screen rights to *Fer-de-Lance*, Walter Wanger told Farrar that *The President Vanishes* was ready for previewing. The film, which Wanger produced and William Wellman directed, had a strong cast, including Edward Arnold (the future Nero Wolfe, who here played the Secretary of War), Paul Kelly, Jason Robards, Sr., Charley Grapewin, Rosalind Russell, Sidney Blackmer, and Andy Devine. Forty-two years later, paired in a revival with Robert Penn Warren's *All the King's Men*, it could still stir audiences. For the initiated the film supplied a hint of the tale's authorship. Placing a glass of dark liquid before President Stanley, Mrs. Stanley said, "Here's a new stout for you to try."

Rex now was writing at an accelerated pace. In October 1934, he began *The League of Frightened Men.* At the end of six weeks, he delivered it to Farrar. He had found rhythms which would enable him, for many years, to produce a novel in thirty-eight days and a novella in a dozen days or less. Though even then Sumner Blossom was urging him to do some short Wolfes which might "help build the character," only when World War II made major encroachments on his time did he capitulate and write "Bitter End," the first of thirty-nine Wolfe novellas. In nineteen months, between October 1934 and April 1936, Farrar & Rinehart would publish five novels by Rex, three of them Wolfe novels. Even Farrar's lawyers would be bewildered by the pace of his output.

Reviewers gave *Fer-de-Lance* a cordial welcome. The *Saturday Review* called it "great stuff." On 28 October, two days after publication, Isaac Anderson reviewed it in the Sunday *New York Times.* Though reluctant to credit Wolfe's genius, Anderson made amends with Archie: "The author has done a clever bit of work in making the narrative style employed by Archie correspond so exactly to his character and attainments as they are revealed in little touches here and there throughout the book." Right off, Archie had stolen a major reviewer out from under Wolfe's nose. There was to be no helping this. But it was no misfortune. If you bought Archie, sooner or later you would buy Wolfe, too. There was no other way to go.

That was all the encouragement Rex needed. Wolfe had survived the journey of creation. And with Archie at his side, his prospects looked bright. Meanwhile, other signs, unknown then either to Rex or his publisher, augured the success of the series. Justice Oliver Wendell Holmes died on 6 March 1935, at ninety-four. During the last year of his life he read *Fer-de-Lance.* After his death, a marginal note he had made was found. Carl Van Doren got hold of it and showed it to Rex. It read, "This fellow is the best of them all."[2] Another early and steadfast admirer was William Faulkner. Carvel Collins, whom Faulkner picked as his literary executor, says: "Among the detective fiction Faulkner read — and it was of considerable quantity — he especially liked that by Rex Stout. One of Mr. Stout's novels which was singled out was *Fer-de-Lance.*"[3]

January 1935 found many of the questions asked about the first Wolfe book being asked now about the second. The title was debated, and serialization, and screen rights. Rex had called the book "The League of the White Feather." Under that title Sumner Blossom read it and complained that it was not as well done as *Fer-de-Lance.* Under that title it was sold immediately afterward to the *Saturday Evening Post,* for $7,500. Bruce Gould of the *Post* told Farrar that he hoped Rex would "prove to be one of our big authors." He said further, "We would be

very happy if Nero Wolfe should become the *Post*'s 'Charlie Chan.' "[4]
Yet Gould balked at subtitling the book "A Nero Wolfe Mystery." Farrar told him they had used the phrase to describe *Fer-de-Lance* "knowing that there would be a series of these stories." Gould was unmoved.
"Let Nero Wolfe make a good impression on our readers before using
such a subtitle," he insisted. He balked at Rex's title, too. In June 1935,
a five- part serialization of the story began in the *Post* under the title
Frightened Men. Farrar & Rinehart released it on 14 August as *The
League of Frightened Men*. "What a superb title," said John Dickson Carr, never suspecting the painful process of evolution that produced it.[5]

In 1933, when *Who's Who* asked Rex to supply data for an entry in
its forthcoming edition, Rex wanted to say that his career had not begun
yet. At forty-seven most men do not feel that their life's work lies in the
future. But most men are not descended from Solomon Stout, Joshua
Hoopes, John Todhunter, or, for that matter, Ben Franklin, all of whom,
at that age, had their best years ahead of them. Within a few months
Rex had an inkling of what was in store for him. On 31 March 1934,
Egmont Arens wrote him: "I am quite excited about these books you
are writing. There are rumors going around that the book that is now
at Farrar & Rinehart is going to make a killing. When that kind of rumor
gets around among the critics even before the book is printed, it is good
news."[6] When Rex's protagonists had been people who defied society,
his novels had attracted only modest notice. Success was not withheld
when he moved to the side of those who guarded the ramparts. He had
been running with the hare when he should have been hunting with
the hounds.

Yet even as he was finding himself as a writer, Rex was fulfilling
himself in other ways: as father, gentleman farmer, cabinetmaker,
stonemason, landscape architect, cook, apiarist, hen man, dairy farmer,
and iris fancier. Todhunter hankerings had been the bane of Oscar,
Clara, May, and perhaps even Bob, as they struggled to realize themselves in many directions and found themselves overwhelmed by seeming conflicts. Perhaps because of his remarkable capacity for self-discipline, Rex's new activities merely gave scope and depth to his
philosophy and his art.

As a farmer Rex had had to begin at the beginning. With Nathan's
departure, when Rex was only seven, first-class farming had ceased at
Wakarusa. No matter. Rex liked to find things out for himself, anyway.
Typically, he learned fast. Ruth Stout's gardening methods eventually
would bring her worldwide fame, yet Ruth says: "Rex was a good gardener before I started. I knew nothing about it, then." In fact Rex
reconciled her to the hankering she had to grow things. She had felt

guilty about it. What of her old resolve to do something for humanity? "Can you do anything more fundamental than to raise food?" Rex had asked her. "Even Einstein has to eat."

Rex was stubborn enough to win arguments even with nature. When a friend told him that rows on an ear of corn always are even-numbered, he cut a row from several young ears, then let them grow to maturity. As he anticipated, on some of them the surviving kernels concealed the mutilation. Thereupon he sent several odd-rowed ears to his omniscient friend, to bring him down a peg. For two years running, he took top prize at the Danbury Fair, for producing the heaviest pumpkins. He had force-fed them with a solution of milk and sugar, intravenous-fashion, with a saturated lampwick inserted into the vine. One weighed a hundred and ten pounds. Though mammoth, they were no more edible than gourds. These were stunts. Rex knew he had taught Nature nothing. To deal with something as truthful as Nature was salutary.

There was joy, too, in working with his hands. Both Ruth and Rex had the beautiful hands of their father, but whereas John's hands were suited to no manual skills, they realized in theirs that potential through which the Todhunters had expressed themselves in gardening, in sketching, in fine needlework. "Rex had the pioneer's gift for the practical," Morris Ernst said. "While others theorized, Rex accomplished. None of them had any manual gifts. They were limited by their dependencies. He could follow something through to its conclusion."[7]

Rex extracted his own honey. He planted his own fruit trees: six varieties of apple, six of peach, three pear, two cherry, one apricot, one quince, and, eventually, a fig tree. By grafting, he inverted the chemistry of one of the peach trees and produced peaches the size of grapefruit. He grew five varieties of grapes, three of strawberries, and fifty kinds of vegetables and herbs, including shallots, a special favorite of his. He designed a screen stand on which to wash just-picked vegetables, and a box stand to simplify raspberry picking. He grew tulips by the thousands. One night in 1938, deer ate 3,000 of them — in 60 varieties.

"I admire flowers for their form, color, and habit of life," Rex told me. "As each season brings its blossoms, I think, 'Ah, these are the best.' " Yet he found irises the flower that gratified most his inner need for harmony. In a thirty-by-three-foot stretch of ground he would plant irises in various gradations of blue, ranging from delicate Azure Skies at one end to somber Black Hills at the other, using as many as fifteen varieties to play out this "Rhapsody in Blue." He said: "The same thing is possible with yellows, pinks, reds, and blends. You couldn't even begin to do that with any other flower." Eventually he cultivated one hundred and ninety-one varieties (mostly bearded, but some Siberian and some Dutch), each adopted only after exacting periods of probation. Hemerocallis (the day lily), of which he had a hundred and three varieties, came next in his favor.

In *The Second Confession*, Arnold Zeck tommy-guns Nero Wolfe's orchid rooms. If a Zeck had menaced Rex's garden and he had time to protect only one species of plant, which would it have been? "The iris," Rex admitted.

Rex's most exotic plant was not of his own cultivation. He told me: "In 1923 Josef Hoffmann gave Pola a sprig of mimosa on her birthday, January eighth, and said, 'You should have a tree of mimosa on your thirty-third birthday, the perfect age for a woman, when you will be most beautiful.' On 8 January 1935, when Pola turned thirty-three, a truck showed up at High Meadow, in a snowstorm, with a twelve-foot-high mimosa tree, in full bloom — the gift of Josef Hoffmann."

Rex thought the city was no place for pets. He made up for that at High Meadow by surrounding himself with a veritable menagerie — cows, chickens, the inevitable crows, a macaw called Nero, and Sheila, a Chincoteague pony, named for the daughter of the gift-giver, Jake Baker. Interest in Sheila would diminish when she kicked Rebecca in the face when Rebecca was four, shattering her cheekbone. There were, as well, two Dalmatians, Warp and Woof, and a mongrel, Czarna, half-airedale, half-Newfoundland. *Czarna* is Polish for "Blackie," or "Nero." She lived for twelve years and was Rex's all-time favorite among his pets.

When winter encroached, and "when no writing job was on," Rex worked at cabinetmaking. In 1930, Henry Ford sent to New York a shipload of logs from Brazil — massaranduba, brazilwood, and arcwood. Rex bought some and had them lumbered. From the arcwood he made his desk; from the massaranduba, a dressing-table for Pola and a study table for himself. "As a cabinetmaker," he told me, "I am not advanced, but meticulous." The designs of others seldom satisfied him. He found most beds too high or too low. He liked drawers sectioned to keep scarfs distinct from gloves, socks distinct from handkerchiefs. He liked a separate sliding tray for each shirt. He disliked handles. "A perfectly constructed drawer," he said, "must have an invisible groove to the exact measure of my instructions, so that I can open the drawer without hunting for the groove, and without breaking a fingernail." He made most of his furniture from American walnut, "a lovely, lovely wood to work with."

Once Wolfe's gourmet tastes were established, Rex found he had an image to maintain. He had no intention, of course, of increasing his weight to two hundred and eighty-three pounds, to please his public. Indeed, he told me, "From the age of twenty-five to seventy-seven I never weighed less than a hundred and forty-six or more than a hundred and fifty-three." But he did think it incumbent upon himself to be knowledgeable about foods and nimble with his skillet. That involved some conniving, since his own tastes ran to plain cooking. For breakfast he always had "oatmeal with plenty of sugar and cream." For a main meal he was content with finnan haddie, steak, or sausages, or broiled kidneys or sweetbreads, both of which Pola cooked "to a king's (or a duke's) taste." For dessert he settled for fruit or cheese. Eggs were the one food he experimented with extensively. "I'll bet I've cooked eggs four hundred and nineteen different ways," he told me. Pola used to groan when Rex would be away for a few days and friends would ask, "How are you getting on, without Rex to do the cooking?" She could count on one hand the times Rex had cooked dinner during the years of their marriage.

Of course Rex kept up a good front. For public consumption he went through the motions of becoming a member of the Society of Amateur Chefs and had his picture taken, in chef's garb, carving a turkey, while Ben Irwin Butler, founder of the society, Walter Slezak, and the writer Achmed Abdullah (Alexander N. Romanoff) stood around him savoring choice morsels. The group proposed to meet on Thursday evenings, the maid's traditional night out. Rex's publishers thought the society was a great idea. Rex was affiliated with it just long enough to have his picture taken for the publicity release.

Much of Rex's cooking was summertime cooking, out-of-doors — brook trout broiled on the grill, chickens roasted on the spit — done while awed guests looked on. His incessant basting, accomplished with a long feathery wand of his own devising, which he dipped into a sauce also of his devising, never failed to hold them spellbound. On the first Sunday of October 1935, eighty friends converged on High Meadow for Rex's most spectacular cookout: roast suckling pig. Rex remembered: "Harold and I made two seven-foot troughs of hardware cloth to hold the charcoal for roasting the pigs, and he turned the spit, with plenty of help from guests." The porkers made savory eating, and Rex's reputation as a gourmet chef was secure forever after.

To be sure, Rex did bring a fine appreciation to good food and drink. He was a true oenophile. To watch him savor wine was itself an education. His friends insisted that he could identify vintage and year without consulting the label. "No," Rex said, "no one on earth can." The wines he liked best were claret, white Burgundy, especially Montrachet and Chablis, and, among champagnes, Dom Perignon. Reflecting on what he would like to eat for his last meal, if that circumstance ever offered, Rex stipulated, "Fresh caviar with sour cream, grilled pompano, broiled young woodcock with fresh young peas, endive, Camembert."

For all his wide-ranging activities, writing remained central to Rex's life at High Meadow, for it was the income his books brought him that made all his other activities possible.

In the summer of 1935, Rex set up a pyramidal tent "under a very old, very large, and very fine white oak about two hundred yards downhill from the house," and there he wrote during the hot days. The family knew it was all right to disturb him "if really necessary," but usually he was left to himself. For seven years the tent was his summer office. As his daughters grew they sometimes brought him lemonade or cold tea, but they knew they were not to trouble him otherwise.

In August 1935, perusing the *New York Times* review of *The League of Frightened Men,* Rex met with the phrase "Rex Stout was a legitimate novelist before he took up the trade of mystery monger." He sought redress in verse. On 21 August, under the caption "Apologia Pro Vita Sua," the *Times* wrote, "Rex Stout, whose mystery novel *The League of Frightened Men* has served as the basis of a United Front of highbrows and mere readers of *The Saturday Evening Post,* explains himself as follows:

Once I lived in humble hovels
And wrote a few legitimate novels.
Now, tiring of the pangs of hunger,
I ply the trade of mystery monger.

Murder, mayhem, gun and knife,
Violent death, my staff of life!

I wrote, though eating not bewhiles,
Of fate profound and secret trials.
Now — calmed the empty belly's fury,
I write of guilt and trial by jury.

Suspense, excitement, thrills, suspicion,
Sources of excellent nutrition!

I took men's souls on bitter cruises,
Explored the heart and necked the Muses.
But now to me I say: poor critter,
Be fed, and let who will be bitter.

Clues, deductions right and wrong,
O Mystery! Of thee I mong!"

28

Commander over the Earth

I travel a big part of the time, and sometimes find myself feeling lonely in some swank hotel in a strange city. Then happiness is finding a Nero Wolfe story that I haven't read, on the news-stand. Finding an unread Nero Wolfe story brings a sudden rush of gladness. It's like finding a couple of wadded-up twenty-dollar bills in a pair of pants you haven't worn since that crap game at Eddie's last fall.

But be sure you are in a really first-class hotel when spending an evening with Nero Wolfe. These stories are not only some of the most entertaining detective stories in the whole literature, but they are also about food. Nero Wolfe is not only a genius, he is a gourmet. To read a Nero Wolfe tale all the way through without eating, smacks of masochism. It's enough to make one eat a pine tree.

— EUELL GIBBONS

There were no great comic creations either in Rex's early fiction or in the "legitimate" novels with which he announced his return to writing. But, somehow, he came to the task of writing his first detective story equipped with a robust sense of humor.[1] How it developed is itself a mystery. Apparently it was always there, but while he had aspirations as a serious writer he had been reluctant to give it free rein. To be sure he had read most of the contemporary humorists. And he had always held Twain in favor. But, except for occasional Wodehousian sallies in the earlier stories, he shows no apparent debt to any of them. About all that is certain is that he did serve a brief, adulatory apprenticeship to Donald Ogden Stewart. He did not even try to deny it. "God," he said, "Stewart wrote some awful good verse." Fortunately, for sake of the reputation of the Wolfe saga, Stewart's influence was limited to a few recreational pieces, especially those exercises which Rex contributed in 1935 to Farrar & Rinehart's *Bedroom Companion,* a poem and two articles, including the lead article, "So You're Going Out for a Record."[2]

"On My Bashfulness" is a shameless parody of Milton's sonnet "On His Blindness." The narrator laments that he is too shy to do more than mix drinks at parties at which women topple into bed with every aspiring seducer with a readiness that would have confounded Casanova. It then occurs to him that the liquor he serves helps make the game go.

The subtitle of the lead article is "The Compleat Philanderer." An essay on the art of being a successful amorist, it owes no more to Izaak

Walton than his sonnet does to Milton. When the reader encounters such phrases as "a gyneolatry case" and "Receptivity quotient," however, he can see Rex has written a parody of his own fastidious ways of dealing with a problem.

The second essay, "Love among the Editors," satirizes the slick magazines: *The Sunday Morning Pillar* and *Jollier's Weekly*. A successful contributor explains how he reshapes reality to write romantic fiction for these magazines. For example, in a slick story a stockbroker marries the right girl, reforms his life, and raises five wholesome children. In real life, says Rex, the fellow moved three girls into his penthouse and married none of them. Thus — with "minor glosses" — slick writers reshape reality to please their editors.

Rex's ribaldry spilled over into further poems, which might have found their way into a second *Bedroom Companion* — had there been one.[3] "In and Out," for example:

> *What the burrow is to the rabbit,*
> *And the key-hole is to the key,*
> *What Rotary is to the Babbitt,*
>   *Thou art, my love, to me!*
>
> *What the coin-slot is to the nickel,*
> *And the dove-cote is to the dove,*
> *What the glass jar is to the pickle,*
>   *Thou art to me, my love!*
>
> *What the target is to the arrow,*
> *Or, if you prefer, to the dart,*
> *What the courtroom is to the Darrow,*
>   *To me, my love, thou art!*
>
> *What the channel is to the river,*
> *What the kennel is to the chow,*
> *And the home garage to the flivver,*
>   *To me, my love, art thou!*
>
> *What concrete is to the air-drill,*
> *What hard wood is to the screw,*
> *And frozen ground to the hare, still,*
>   *To me, alas, are you!*

Andrew Marvell's "To His Coy Mistress," with its wheedling tone, was better calculated to rout restraint, but in affairs of the heart Rex had no illusions about masculine dominion. And what a marvelous time he was having spoofing the bawdy lyric itself.

"Offering from a Good Fairy" shows a similar want of seriousness on the subject of the battle between the sexes:

Woman! Essential creature! Oh, that I
Could adequately sing my gratitude
To Helen, who for years has cooked my food
To Anne, who irons the sheets on which I lie!
I offer homage to them all: to Grace,
Who dusts and sweeps — ah, what I owe to her!
And Cynara, my best stenographer —
For me no man can take a woman's place.
And when the day is done and night is here,
And shadows beckon to the tender passion,
Silent and soft the women disappear,
Leaving me to my sweet exotic ration,
And so to you! But you must know, my dear,
I'm fond of women, too — after my fashion.

For these lines Nero Wolfe could have only a double "pfui." He would scorn a household dependent on women for its maintenance. He would find it improbable that women, let into a man's household in such numbers, could play so discreet and useful a role.

In the character of a true, but droll-spirited, wooing swain, Rex, in yet another poem, chided Keats for an alleged slip in phrasing:

Ope at Night

"And there shall be for thee all soft delight
That shadowy thought can win,
A bright torch, and a casement ope at night
To let the warm Love in!"
                              — Ode to Psyche

I am not one to cavil at John Keats,
Nor pedant I, to call a spade a spade,
But beauty has her rights, and truth entreats
We leave her not entirely in the shade —
Even us poets. And so I must complain
Of that word "casement." What a careless bard
To label thus that soft inviting nest
Which in its welcome overwhelms the guest!
Softened he leaves, entering however hard,
Coming and going, only to come again!
Many great singers have its virtues told,
    And sung its pregnant praises,
With epithets both beautiful and bold,
    And fond descriptive phrases.

It has been called — to choose from many a few —
The trap of Venus and the devil's chute,
The flower unfolding for the precious dew,
The cave where female bandits take their loot;
L'allée couverte d'amour, a tube, a tunnel,
The orifice of Aphrodite, a funnel,
The moral maiden's moat, the Grand Canal,
The castle in the wood, the virgin's cell,
The fort where "shall not" only waits for "shall,"
The road to heaven and the slide to hell;
And even, by one who knew it well, forsooth,
    The pit of man's abasement!
But surely, Keats, nor beauty 'tis nor truth
    To call the thing a casement.

For Rex, the emotions associated with carnal love so blatantly contradicted the concept of man committed to the rational ideal that intellectual fun at the expense of sex, and at the expense of masculine vanity, was a temptation he could not forgo.

Rex published a non–Nero Wolfe novel, *O Careless Love*, on 4 November 1935. Ostensibly a romantic novel done in the light manner of the slicks, *O Careless Love* actually satirizes the genre — no small feat, since the *Saturday Evening Post* itself bought the story and serialized it in its September and October issues. A major object of quest in the novel is a schoolteacher from Kansas, Carola Smith — an unpresuming sex goddess. Herbert Tinkham, a pompous middle-aged lawyer, pursues Carola to New York. Though Tinkham bears a conspicuous resemblance to Rex's high school friend, Tinkham Veale (who had become a prosperous Topeka attorney), skillful, universalizing touches lift him above point-by-point parallels. A younger swain, Bill Updegraff (the surname appears again in "Black Orchids"), also pursues Carola. Bill does not quite fit the stereotype of the magazine romance hero. Indeed, at one point Bill says he had dreamed "that he was standing, naked, on a high platform in the middle of a cornfield at home, and millions of lovely women, little ones, not more than five inches high, were sitting all over the corn-tassels swaying in the breeze, with pads and pencils, drawing pictures of him." Of Carola, we learn: "She is the quintessence of Sex. . . . It is the music of her body. . . . It is a flowing of the sex harmony." This diagnosis is not given by a Broadway seducer, but by one of her traveling companions, Emily Kurtz. Emily's pragmatic decision to marry the cast-off but affluent Tinkham puts romantic love at a far remove. Equally surprising is Victoria Rant, the oldest of the three teachers who have accompanied Carola to New York. Victoria has made the trip in order to read Joyce's *Ulysses*, unobtainable in Kansas. When she does read it, she brands it "Victorian." Victoria, the most engaging character in the book, has a Neronian mind set. To resolve a crisis she convokes an assembly of those involved, and carries it off with a fine charade.

Carola marries no one at all. For the Fox Film Corporation, at least, that fact killed the story. For solace, Rex could cite the Boston *Transcript*'s verdict: "A logical and clever end, thus proving himself an able storyteller."

A song, "O Careless Love," had given Rex his title. His daughters say that when they were growing up, Rex on occasion would burst into the song's refrain. It was a song Ethel Waters several times had sung to him privately.[4]

Fay, the first Mrs. Stout, recalls Rex working on *O Careless Love* during the time of their marriage. It does, in fact, have mannerisms in common with his earlier work and it would be logical to think of it as a transitional piece. Rex was certain, however, that it was published soon after he wrote it. Possibly he had written it earlier and revamped it before publishing it in 1935. If so the episode would have been without precedent. Nonetheless, *O Careless Love* is not up to the standards Rex had arrived at in the mid-1930's.

A second slick romance, "It Happened Last Night," published in *The Canadian Magazine* in March 1936, also reads like apprentice work. For a happily married young husband, Lurton Morrow seems to be going to a lot of trouble to meet another woman. At last we find out why. Lurton designs ladies' suits. She is a buyer. That was one way around the code of the slicks. Let the reader think the worst. Then show him that his mind has been in the gutter. Possibly this story and *O Careless Love* lack Rex's assured touch because he was out of his element. He was not at ease writing about a woman's world.

"It Happened Last Night" was not the only Stout story of this era in which Pola's professional world of fashion and design served as a background. *The Red Box* (1936) involves murder on the premises of an eminent ladies' fashion house. *Red Threads* (1939) transports us to a locale where fine fabrics are woven.[5] From 1934 to 1938 Pola, working on hand- and power-looms, created collections for such designers as Molyneux and Valentina, and designed an extensive group of coordinated woolens for Otterburn Mill, Ltd. Rex had enjoyed following all stages of her work. Evidence of that interest survives in the attention he gave to the attire of his characters, male as well as female, especially Archie. Barbara says: "It was fun hearing Dad over dinner discussing with my mother ensembles and bra sizes and such to get the facts he needed for something he was writing."[6]

When, in 1935, a manufacturer backed out of an oral agreement with Pola, Rex got his one moment to shine in court. Rex told me: "Pola sued,

I testified, and in cross-examination the lawyer said to me, 'You have written and had published many thousand words of fiction. For writing fiction the most important thing is to have a good imagination, to make things up. Isn't that true?' I replied, 'No, not the most important. A good memory is the most important.' Pola won the suit. I have always been proud of that reply."

The third Wolfe novel, *The Rubber Band*, was written in the fall of 1935. When *The American Magazine* bid for it, Rex wrote Albert Benjamin III on 15 October, explaining that John Farrar was his agent — "So, if you are still interested in the fat scalawag, will you communicate with Farrar?" But John already had sold the story to the *Saturday Evening Post* for $15,000. Expressing thanks for the check, Rex told Stanley Rinehart on 27 December: "I refuse to consider it as a Christmas present. I wore out a whole typewriter ribbon writing that story." The hardcover edition was released on 9 April. Reviewers were enthusiastic. Yale's perdurable William Lyon Phelps called it "a work of art." Christopher Morley said: "The whole affair is brilliantly handled and gives complete satisfaction." Isaac Anderson thought it "the peak of his achievements." To Will Cuppy, Wolfe was "the Falstaff of detectives."

The Rubber Band has a heroine, Clara Fox, but Nero Wolfe does not hide his male chauvinism in dealing with her. To her he says of women: "When they stick to the vocations for which they are best adapted, such as chicanery, sophistry, self-adornment, cajolery, mystification, and incubation, they are sometimes splendid creatures." But he sets a precedent by letting Clara sleep under his roof. To her the brownstone is a revelation. In grudging admiration, she says: "This house represents the most insolent denial of female rights the mind of man has ever conceived. No woman in it from top to bottom, but the routine is faultless, the food is perfect, and the sweeping and dusting are impeccable. . . . I can't overlook this challenge. I'm going to marry Mr. Wolfe."[7]

In this tale a rubber band snapped against a telephone simulates the report of a pistol and sets up an alibi for a murderer. Rex thought up the idea himself and checked it out with Egmont Arens. Whether Egmont snapped a magenta garter is not known.

The fourth Wolfe novel, *The Red Box*, was done in the spring of 1936, began appearing as a serial in *The American Magazine* in December, and came out in hardcover on 15 April 1937. Its running indictment of the Calvinist mentality — a theme first broached in *The Rubber Band* — affirms Rex's expanding social awareness. In both books a cautious Scot prompts this commentary. Here, also, Wolfe uses as a detecting resource his knowledge of language, an asset he will rely on in several future cases. And here again female characters pitting themselves against Wolfe supply dynamic tension. The evil genius of the ruthless Calida Frost is one thing, the independence of her "daughter," Helen, another. For Helen, Wolfe has respect: "It is a pleasure to earn a fee from a client like you. You can come to a yes or no without first encircling the globe."[8] A further insight into Wolfe's understanding of women comes in his comments on Lawrence of Arabia. Lawrence held the Arab tribes together because his "personal attitude toward women was the same as the classic and traditional Arabian attitude." Wolfe explains further: "The central fact about any man, in respect to his activities as a social animal, is his attitude toward women; hence the Arabs felt that essentially Lawrence was one of them, and so accepted him."[9]

Of Wolfe's aloofness from women, Kingsley Amis has written: "What are we to make of this avoidance of the fair sex . . . ? Could there be something a bit . . . you know . . . ?"[10] Asked to assess Amis's quasiconjecture, Karl Menninger wrote on 22 May 1973:

I took the problem up with my wife who is a very discerning reader. We are both fem libbers. She suggests that Wolfe's avoidance of the fair sex (on the detecting side, of course) may represent only a case of occupational handicap; Sherlock Holmes, Hercule Poirot and several others seem to have been similarly constituted (parthenogenesis?).[11]

Wolfe himself says he shuns women not because they fail to arouse him but, quite otherwise, because they stir dangerous emotions, which imperil the life of the intellect. Archie has noted that Wolfe often will have an attractive lady visitor placed where he can observe a well-turned calf. If we may believe Wolfe, he was married once and his wife tried to poison him. His wariness of women seems to date from that time. He says his orchids are his "concubines." Orchids, gourmet cookery, and avoirdupois — these seem to be the things which insulate him from, and constitute his defense against, and his alternative to, active sexual expression.

Sir Hugh Greene says: "The relations between Nero Wolfe and Archie Goodwin are even more intriguing than the crimes they solve together. Did they ever in their early days get into bed together and find it less exciting than food?"[12] Rex showed signs of exasperation when this point was raised with him but roared with laughter when Alan Green said of an Australian reader who broached the topic, "He's just self-conscious because he's a down under man."

The Wolfe-Archie relationship may be seen as an illustration of "bonding" — of those male alliances which go back to the origins of human society when its survival depended more on the values demanded in the hunt, such as endurance and camaraderie, and joint support, than on man's reproductive affinity for women. For Wolfe and Archie, as detectives engaged in the hunt, and in safeguarding the social order, a relationship that follows the bonding pattern is both natural and practical.[13]

At this point in Rex's career, John Farrar asked him to come up with a new detective to spell Wolfe. Two Wolfes a year created the risk of overexposure. Yet John wanted "to keep the serial market moving." In the fall of 1936, Rex obliged with *The Hand in the Glove*, introducing a lady detective, Theodolinda "Dol" Bonner. Superficially, Dol is the female double of Wolfe. Because her fiancé jilted her, she hates all men. Later, in some of the Wolfe stories, Dol turns up as an operative in Wolfe's employ. She is not memorable, yet one episode in *The Hand in the Glove* rates a footnote in history. In 1949, ex-Communist Whittaker Chambers made his sensational disclosure about "the pumpkin papers" — important microfilms which, for safekeeping, were allegedly hidden for a time in a pumpkin. In *The Hand in the Glove*, Dol discovers important evidence concealed in a large melon. Readers have wondered: "Did Mr. Stout foresee Whittaker Chambers? Or did Mr. Chambers read Mr. Stout?" Chambers may have done just that. In *Witness*, his autobiography, he recalls having lunch with Ruth Stout, "the sister of the mystery writer, Rex Stout."[14]

Thanks to Rex, the Danbury-Brewster locale was becoming murder country. Among Pola's friends was Frances Lockridge. One day the Lockridges visited High Meadow for a barbecue. They were impressed with the lively state of Rex's lawns, unaffected by a prolonged drought. Under the grass Rex had laid a distribution system. Every blade was well watered. The Lockridges talked it over afterward. If Rex could afford to do that, then there was money to be made in writing detective stories. That same night they blocked out their first Mr. and Mrs. North murder story. That's the legend. Richard Lockridge says it isn't quite true:

We first knew Pola and Rex when we were spending weekends, and summers, in a cabin at a place called Lost Lake, a few miles from Rex's hilltop house. . . . If one could have that sort of place by writing mystery novels, writing them, I thought, might be something worth trying. . . . Frances started a mystery and got blocked. I couldn't help with the block. We worked out a new one, using the Norths, who had been around for some years in *The New Yorker*.[15]

On 13 December 1936, Rex made a signed appearance in *The New Masses*. Purdy, the protagonist of "A Good Character for a Novel," is a Shavian industrialist with a Wodehousian capacity for amiable inconsistency. He will sack a scrubwoman for splashing his shoes, and then reflect that she was probably so exhausted she did not realize what she was doing. Yet he will not rehire her. He can see the other fellow's point of view, but he makes no decisions that might tell against his pocketbook.

This parable comes to a tantalizing climax when one of Purdy's factories is shut down by a strike. With "bold and firm" decisiveness he hires professional goons to break the strike. He tells himself: "I can see their side of it. I can even understand those goddamn agitators. I can see how a man of that type will say, 'You listen to me, boys, and we'll make that bastard Purdy sign on the dotted line.' " But one of Purdy's goons mistakes him for an agitator and clubs him to death.

Purdy is a portrait of Henry Ford himself. Ford had used goon squads to block the efforts of his employees to unionize. Like Purdy, Ford said he deplored paternalism, yet he could not understand why his workers were not content to be guided by his decrees. Purdy's fate draws attention to an industrial despotism which a Democrat should repudiate as readily as a socialist. In later years Rex's critics would cite this story as proof of his Communist ties. Yet, in substance as well as form, it reiterated the parables of Jesus, and would have been an appropriate feature in an evangelical weekly.

In the summer of 1936, Rex agreed to let Egmont Arens name him as his daughter Patricia's guardian in the event fate deprived her of a father. Egmont used the occasion to discuss her upbringing: "She knows how to get what she wants even now — and her method of getting it is sufficiently winning to constitute a mild form of racketeering. More power to her in that!"[16] Rex demurred: "Might it not be suggested to her that she should be ready to accept her duties as well as to take advantage of her privileges?"

With gusto, Egmont had paid passing tribute to Pola: "Either too much charm, laid on too thick, or spread on too thin are faults in a woman. But when integrated as part of the working equipment (as in Pola Stout) it's a delight to have under the same roof." Several months later, Gilbert Gabriel enlarged on this topic for *Saturday Review* readers. He hailed Pola as "designer, stylist, weaver, almost his [Rex's] match in multifarious activity." Gabriel saw Rex as "a dictator over dog and goat and vasty rows of vegetables . . . a commander over the face of the earth." He saw Rex as Crusoe, the redoubtable castaway. But Crusoe had no helpmate at his side, nor was he a "hearty parent." Rex, Gabriel concluded, lived "more of a majesty's life . . . than a hermit's."[17]

In February 1937, Rex refused an invitation from Egmont to join Jake Baker and him for dinner in New York. He explained: "We can leave Barbara all right, but not the one who is going to be born in April and is already kicking to get out. It might succeed right in the middle of the party, and then where would we be, with only two return tickets to Brewster?"[18]

Although *The Red Box* appeared as planned in April 1937, there was a slight delay with the other Stout production expected that month. Rebecca, Rex's second daughter, did not arrive till 4 May. Rex's friend Dr. Nathaniel Selleck made the delivery. Dr. Selleck — "Than" — was apologetic. He thought Rex had wanted a son. "Rex made the whole thing perfectly right," Than said later. "Oh, that's not any problem," Rex had said. "Do you realize how those girls are going to take care of me when they're fifteen or sixteen, and I'm an old man?" Pola was equally reassured. Standing at the foot of her bed, Rex said, "Pola, it's a girl! I looked at it, and I looked and I looked. And it's a girl!" Rex didn't need a son. He had Wolfe and Archie.

In June, Rex wrote Egmont: "How is your idealism getting along? Mine has a sore finger but its heart still beats." About this same time he told Gilbert Gabriel that he hoped to get back one day to the deeper themes of his four psychological novels. Yet Gabriel admitted: "There is nothing in the confession that implies he has not put all possible expertness, all available inspiration, into every one of his several chronicles of Nero Wolfe and Co. . . ."[19]

That summer Rex carried out the biggest construction job he had undertaken since he built High Meadow. He mixed and poured tons of concrete, to make suitable settings for his flowers. Yet not before he had finished a fifth Wolfe novel — *Too Many Cooks* — a book which *The New Yorker* would single out as "By far the best of Mr. Stout's books."

The Gabriel interview, in the *Saturday Review*, appeared about the same time *The Hand in the Glove* came out: mid-September. The book itself got a tepid review in the same issue: "Dol Bonner, if attractive, is minor league." In October, the English publisher Cassell declined to take it up. Offering an explanation which Dol Bonner might have found ungallant, H. Aubrey Gentry explained: "We are, as you know, having a fight to get him across with his Nero Wolfe stories, and we feel that if we draw Dol Bonner across the trail, then so much longer will it take us to make a success of him [Rex] from the Nero Wolfe point of view." With heady abandon, Adelaide Sherer, of Farrar & Rinehart, wrote Cassell on 29 October that Rex had just finished up "the first book in a possible third series" with Inspector Cramer as hero. This was *Red Threads*, then called "Dressed for Murder." She disclosed further that *Too Many Cooks* would begin appearing in *The American Magazine* in the coming spring. This pile-up of Stout books routed Cassell. It relinquished the series to Collins, which would sell more than twenty million Nero Wolfe books over the next thirty-five years.

BOOK VI

Minister of Propaganda

29.

King's Gambit

I have had the pleasure of reading some of Mr. Rex Stout's books and I have much enjoyed them.

— ANTHONY EDEN, EARL OF AVON

I have enjoyed a great many of his books. Archie is a splendid character to have invented and his first person remarks and descriptions are always most entertaining to read. I must also reveal that greed and the general enjoyment of food is one of my main characteristics and the descriptions of the meals served and prepared by Nero Wolfe's cook have given me a lot of pleasure and a great wish to have occasionally tasted these suggestions myself. Perhaps for that reason, I particularly liked *Too Many Cooks.*

— DAME AGATHA CHRISTIE

Too Many Cooks would vindicate both Gilbert Gabriel's assertion that Rex was giving his best to the Wolfe novels, and Rex's own assertion that his idealism was not dead. Its tribute to the black race remains compelling proof that reason is a surer weapon than emotion. As David Evans remarked: "Rex cleverly strikes a blow for human freedom so subtly the reader never realizes he is being enlisted for a point of view in the process of enjoying a detective story."[1]

When Adelaide Sherer asked Rex if he wanted to do anything to *Too Many Cooks* before it was set up, Rex replied, on 7 March 1938, "Yes I do, I want to rub it against the manuscript of *Gone With the Wind* on the chance it might catch something. Nothing else."[2] He also registered his amusement at an item of news Adelaide had passed along to him: "As for the Italian publishers who wrapped some books in sheets of *La Lega Degli Uomini Spaventati* [*The League of Frightened Men*] by Rex Stout — if they must show off, have they no old illuminated parchments they can use for wrapping paper?"

A follow-up letter, on 16 March, acknowledged Adelaide's news that Collins would be Rex's new publisher in England: "Of course I am pleased — though a close observer might have perceived on my lips a bitter smile, with a lurking hint of pathos, as I read of the royalty provision after 10,000 copies are sold. Who do they think I am, Maggie Mitchell?" No soothsayer was there to tell Rex that his English sales alone would one day surpass the combined sales of *Gone With the Wind.*

That same month, as serialization of *Too Many Cooks* was getting under way in *The American Magazine,* Rex finished up work on the next Wolfe novel, *Some Buried Caesar.* For this book, critics would go beyond the superlatives they had used for *Too Many Cooks:* "Stout's best . . . unbeatable." . . . "Stout working at top form." . . . "this book . . . goes a long way to make Rex Stout a literary figure." Rex later would tell a Toronto interviewer that *Some Buried Caesar* was his favorite among his works.[3]

With completion of *Some Buried Caesar,* Rex was in a state of high expectation. *The American Magazine* was making plans to send him, together with Gene Sarazen, golf's first quadruple-crown winner, on a tour of a dozen American cities in the East, South, and Midwest: Boston, New York, Philadelphia, Atlanta, Cleveland, Akron, Cincinnati, Louisville, Detroit, Chicago, Minneapolis, and St. Louis. The tour would coincide with the *American*'s serialization of *Too Many Cooks.* Heading it up was Albert Benjamin III, associate editor of the magazine. It was Benjamin, an Annapolis graduate, who edited and abridged all of Rex's stories published in the magazine between 1934 and the summer of 1941, when he was recalled to active service. Benjamin also supplied titles for the magazine versions of the stories. One of his titles, *Too Many Cooks,* was retained for the hardcover edition.

On 30 March John Farrar wrote Benjamin for particulars of the tour. Farrar felt that if they knew what Benjamin was contemplating "in the promotion of Mr. Stout and the stout Mr. Wolfe," they could synchronize their promotion of the book, to everyone's advantage. On 1 April Benjamin wrote: "Rex was in here the other day and seems very enthusiastic about it and especially about the publicity and promotion we are giving him during said vaudeville tramp."[4] As for the road show, Benjamin explained that an *American* editorial luncheon would be given in each of the cities visited. This year *Too Many Cooks* would be a major benefactor:

> We always have special menus at these affairs — menus that tie in with one book. This year . . . the menu is being made up from *Too Many Cooks.* As souvenirs for the luncheon, we are having a small box in the shape of a book. The outside cover will be a reproduction of the opening spread of *Too Many Cooks* in the March issue. Inside will be the menu of the luncheon and then, on separate cards, will be printed all of the recipes appearing in the story.[5]

The *American*'s spring tour was perhaps the most famous promotional show in publishing history. It was indeed a traveling road show, comprised of actors, actresses, and models as well as well-known writers or subjects of articles which had appeared in the magazine. The cast was transported in a chartered Pullman; there was a baggage car for the scenery, and a revolving stage — the first of its kind. The show was scripted by Borden Chase, the Hollywood writer and novelist.

Two Powers models accompanied the tour: Suzanne Shaw, a blonde, and Lillian Eggers, a redhead — both statuesque. Benjamin says: "In those days a man with a beard was an unusual specimen and Rex's growth of hair on his face not only was the butt of many comments, it intrigued the two models, who, in off-stage moments, especially on train rides, took delight in braiding and twisting Rex's beard."

As well as engaging in patter with Gene Sarazen at each luncheon, in each city Rex played a round of golf with him, presumably on the theory that he knew all about golf because he had committed murder on a golf course in *Fer-de-Lance*. Rex felt about golf as he felt about skiing. Not having the time to learn to play it well, he would do better not to play it at all. Of the 216 holes he played with Gene, Rex won 8. These he won fair and square. Gene made no concessions to duffers. "Golf," Rex reminded me, "was his life."

Too Many Cooks was published on 17 August. To celebrate, Rex went to the Adirondacks on a fishing trip. He was on his way back to High Meadow when the great 1938 hurricane struck, on 21 September. Only once had he seen a worse storm and that was the hurricane he had ridden out in the Windward Passage, aboard the *Mayflower*. Pola and he spent the night in New York. "The next day," he told me, "it took us four hours to drive to High Meadow on account of things like fallen trees." Throughout New England the storm felled more than a million trees. Damage went above the half-billion mark. But High Meadow, protected by the brow of Gage Hill, was intact.

Rex accepted natural calamities. Man-made calamities were another matter. In Europe, the Munich crisis was building. Rex had read *Mein Kampf* and thought it the most immoral book ever written. When the betrayal of Czechoslovakia was announced on 29 September, he felt physically ill. He found he was incubating an ulcer. He quit cigarettes and went on a bland diet. But this was mere tokenism, and he knew it. All his apprehensions converged on a clear conviction. It would be immoral to limit his vision to the Arcadian haven he had created at Danbury — and do nothing to combat despotism. Cost what it may, Hitler had to be brought down. He made up his mind to have a part in making it happen. As soon as he did, his sense of well-being returned.

Wolfe often would forsake his claustral indulgences to welcome a thorn for justice and truth. Munich showed Rex that the thorn must be his, too. Rex now stepped out from behind his fictional characters, to become a defender of the social order he believed in, and the nemesis of those agencies that menaced it.[6]

The increased tempo of Rex's writing activities had anticipated the time when he would have to exchange pen for halberd. He no longer had income from the Educational Thrift Service. His writing now maintained his family, the establishment at High Meadow, and Pola's brilliant venture into textiles. Nineteen thirty-nine was Rex's *annus mirabilis* as a novelist. From birthday to birthday, in 1938 and 1939, he published five novels — *Mr. Cinderella* (1 December 1938), *Some Buried Caesar* (2 February 1939), *Mountain Cat* (27 July 1939), *Double for Death* (3 October 1939), and *Red Threads* (1 December 1939) — in hardcover.[7] Another, *Over My Dead Body*, the seventh Wolfe novel, appeared in *The American Magazine* in September.[8] In this book Wolfe is, for the first time, identified as a Montenegrin. Rex admitted: "I got the idea of making Wolfe a Montenegrin from Louis Adamic. Louis told me that Montenegrin men are famous for being lazy. He said, in fact, that you can't get a Tsernogore to do anything." Rex said that everything he knew about Montenegrins he got either from Adamic's book *The Native's Return* (1934), or from Adamic himself.[9] In *The League of Frightened Men* Wolfe himself reads *The Native's Return* but says nothing about his own Montenegrin origins.[10] Wolfe's assertion, in *Over My Dead Body*, when queried by an FBI man, that he was born in the United States, later would become a notable crux in Wolfe scholarship.

The eighth Wolfe novel, *Where There's a Will*, was written in the fall of 1939, and set for spring release.

Rex had become a wonder of the publishing world. Even an emergency appendectomy, done at Danbury Hospital on 31 July, did not check his pace. He was soon home and off to visit Aleck Woollcott at Bomoseen Lake in Vermont. There they would play fierce games of croquet and plot their strategy for dealing with Hitler, who appeared ready to march into Poland.

Activities mounted through the fall. As a frequent guest on the radio program "Information, Please!" Rex was gaining a big following. The program host, Clifton Fadiman, and he explored together their common animosity toward Hitler and ways of translating it into action.[11] Rex at this time made his first contacts with Leon M. Birkhead, a Unitarian minister, who in 1937 had founded the Friends of Democracy to combat extremism of the right and left. (In the late 1920's, as Sinclair Lewis's houseguest, Birkhead had fed Lewis data for *Elmer Gantry*.)

Until the spring of 1940, Rex worked through the New York office of the Friends of Democracy, attacking the right wing America First Committee, and urging preparedness, the lifting of the arms embargo, and lend-lease.[12] George Merten, a former civil servant of the state government in East Prussia, then working in New York with the British Secret Intelligence, says of Rex's activities in this interval: "Rex Stout deserves honor and credit for exposing himself at that time for a cause which was not too popular in influential, especially corporation, quarters."[13]

In April 1940, Rex spoke at Smith College urging a step-up in United States aid to Britain. After his talk he had tea with the then acting president of Smith, Mrs. Dwight Morrow, Colonel Lindbergh's mother-in-law, and Claude M. Fuess, author of a new book, *Calvin Coolidge: The Man from Vermont.* Fuess recalled that when Mrs. Coolidge was gathering papers for his perusal, she produced one batch of her husband's letters from a humidor. "I knew Coolidge was dry," Rex said, "but I never knew he was so goddamn dry they had to keep his letters in a humidor."

On 9 April, when the Germans swept into Norway and Denmark, William Allen White hurried to New York, where he met with Clark Eichelberger, executive secretary of the Union of Concerted Peace Efforts. In September 1939, Eichelberger had persuaded White to accept chairmanship of the new Nonpartisan Committee for Peace. Now, together, they decided that a committee should be formed to help the Allies in all ways "short of war." At a luncheon at the University Club attended by White, Eichelberger, John Farrar, Elmer Davis, Harold Guinzberg, Rex, and others, the Nonpartisan Committee was reborn as the Committee to Defend America by Aiding the Allies. Again White was chairman; Rex was a charter member. When Hitler invaded the Low Countries on 10 May, the committee sought mass support. It got it. By 1 July, it had three hundred local chapters.

National headquarters of White's committee was in New York City. That fact was to become a problem for White. The nucleus of the New York chapter was the Century Club or "Miller Group," under the nominal leadership of Francis Pickens Miller, their executive secretary. Membership of this group included Ulric Bell, William Agar, Elmer Davis, John Balderston, Henry R. Luce, Robert Sherwood, Dean Acheson, Allan Dulles, Admiral W. H. Standley, George Field, Barry Bingham, James B. Conant, Harold Guinzberg, and Joseph Alsop. All went beyond White in believing in direct military intervention. If they did not advocate it openly, that was because they did not yet dare to. White was afraid their advanced demands would wreck the committee. He told a friend, "The New York committee is my hair shirt." White held on while the group promoted giving destroyers, fighter planes, torpedo boats, munitions, lend-lease, food, and credit to Britain, but hostile mail from isolationists at last unnerved him. In January 1941 he retreated to the post of honorary chairman, and in April, when his committee advocated convoys to get supplies to Britain, he withdrew from it altogether.

Rex relished the militancy of the Miller Group and supported its campaigns. When the New York chapter of White's committee experienced yet another rebirth, as the Fight for Freedom Committee, Rex, at the invitation of Ulric Bell, was one of its sponsors.

Even as Rex's political awareness reached out to embrace the international scene, so did his writing career. His books were beginning to appear in foreign languages with increasing frequency. In November 1939 he complained goodnaturedly to Adelaide Sherer when an Italian publisher failed to forward copies of two Wolfe books newly published in Italy:

I'm mad at Mondadori of Milan,
Alliterative anger, see it scan.

While Hitler was overrunning France, *Where There's a Will,* the last Wolfe novel to appear till the world was at peace again, was serialized as *Sisters in Trouble* in *The American Magazine.* On 10 June it came out in hardcover. Indicative of Rex's new interests, the action in *Where There's a Will* reaches into high places. Indeed, the victim is the brother-in-law of the United States Secretary of State.

Unlike previous Wolfe novels, *Where There's a Will* was illustrated. Readers were given the opportunity to study the six snapshots from which Wolfe got the clue that enabled him to solve the mystery. There was, however, a discrepancy. Although the story unfolded during a torrid interval in July, the photographs showed that the season was late fall or winter. The senior partner of a New York law firm wrote to ask if Wolfe had been "unable to see the trees for the boutonnière." J. T. Reed of Paramount Pictures observed: "This strikes me as being a much more mysterious state of affairs than the one you so adroitly solved." Cornell historian Carl Stephenson minced no words: "I resent my favorite American detective being turned into a boob."

The blooper had been Farrar & Rinehart's. Bundling up a representative selection of letters received, Rex sent them to John Farrar with a covering letter that was but faintly civil: "I've had so many letters similar to the samples enclosed that I'm thinking of asking Farrar & Rinehart to help pay the postage on the replies. I knew darned well those leafless July trees would cause trouble."

Over the signature of Eric Purdon, Farrar & Rinehart sent to all inquirers this explanation:

My hunch was that the photographs probably had been taken not in July because Noel Hawthorne was murdered then, but in February because *Where There's a Will* came out in June. . . . Subsequent clues led me to the right answer. . . . A few days before Noel's death the leaves of all the trees on his sister's estate became the prey to a hitherto unknown species of bug which entomologists have tentatively called *Popillia nazica.* Like the Japanese beetle, it is a pest, and its function is to make total unmitigated blight; attacking only trees, leaving cornflowers, daisies, and rose bushes alone. For some strange reason, the *Popillia nazica* attacked only the Dunn estate and a few of the trees on Park Avenue in New York. All other trees survived. I haven't seen Nero

Wolfe for some time, but I gather he knew of this blight — after all, he follows very closely the news of the botanical world. He therefore took the starkness of the trees into account when he looked at the photographs.

Farrar & Rinehart did not make amends by half-measures.

For *Where There's a Will*, Will Cuppy predicted "a useful future." He had solid ground for his prophecy. The beautiful and accomplished Hawthorne sisters, April, May, and June, with their strange problem — their rich and abruptly deceased brother, Noel, had left a peach to April, a pear to May, and an apple to June, and all the plums ($7,000,000) to his mistress — intrigue us from the start. And they should. Like Lear's three daughters, they are creatures out of myth, with counterparts in folk literature the world over.[14]

Through this period a semblance of the old routine was maintained at High Meadow. In the spring vegetables were planted. Rex made an inlaid chessboard for himself and a puppet theater for his daughters. When he tucked the girls in at night he sometimes told them bedtime stories, which he made up as he went along, and often he sang them a chorus of "Good Night, Ladies." He did not contrive elaborate entertainments for them, as Conan Doyle had done for his children. He would not have done that even if the times had not encroached on his leisure. As a child he had been encouraged to create his own entertainment. He wanted his children to have the same freedom.

That summer Rex campaigned for Roosevelt's reelection. Several times, at campaign rallies, he shared the platform with Eleanor Roosevelt, and in August, at Mrs. Roosevelt's invitation, Pola and he were luncheon guests of the Roosevelts at Hyde Park.

In August, *The American Magazine* carried a piece by Rex entitled "Mystery." Rex ended it on a reflective note, looking to a world beyond war: "Why do normal, everyday people like you and me set about killing one another in the mass murder called war? How can we organize our economic machine to distribute our plenty? What makes grass green? How can we liberate the incalculable energy from a penny's worth of iron? These are mysteries to make your heart beat faster — and, take my word, some day they will all be solved. . . ." In this vision of a world at peace, of resources shared among nations, of nuclear energy harnessed, Rex sought to prophesy the advent of the harmonious society he never ceased to hope for. The terror of nuclear armaments did not then darken that dream.

Early in 1941, when he went to Toronto to address the *Globe & Mail*'s Book Fair, Rex gave a lengthy interview to J. V. McAree. At McAree's invitation Rex named twenty authors whose detective stories he enjoyed. The list held few surprises. He thought E. C. Bentley's *Trent's*

Last Case was overrated and that Edgar Wallace's Mr. Reeder stories were underrated. M. P. Shiel's *How the Old Woman Got Home* was the only crime story he knew "written by a man who used the English language as Shakespeare used it." He made a suggestion. Since the best British and the best American detective stories both found their way to Canada, a Canadian who undertook to combine the best elements of each would "really have something." There is no evidence that Kenneth Millar saw the interview.

To McAree Rex made a surprising admission. "It's Archie," he said, "who really carries the stories, as narrator. Whether the readers know it or not, it's Archie they really enjoy."

And he had a further notable disclosure. The next Wolfe story would take place at a flower show. His mind already was at work on the plot. Yet McAree confided, "At the moment Mr. Stout does not know who the murderer was. Nor . . . has he satisfactorily identified the victim." Thus readers were given a rare look into Rex's mind while it was gestating a new story. In March Rex wrote the story. The next August, as "Death Wears an Orchid," it appeared in *The American Magazine*. As "Black Orchids" it came out in hardcover in May 1942.

Actually "Black Orchids" was the second of the thirty-nine Wolfe novellas Rex would write. The first, "Bitter End," had been written in September 1940. It had been kind of breach birth. In 1939, in *Double for Death*, Rex had built a novel around a detective whom he called Tecumseh Fox. In the summer of 1940 he wrote another Fox novel, *Bad for Business*, which Farrar & Rinehart marked for November release. When it was offered to *The American* for serial publication, however, Sumner Blossom told Rex he would pay double for it if he would turn it into a Wolfe novella. In eleven days time Rex produced for Blossom the changeling he had asked for. As "Bitter End" it was published in Blossom's November issue. *Bad for Business*, still, as originally written, a Tecumseh Fox story, followed it into print in Farrar & Rinehart's *Second Mystery Book,* on 28 November. Because of its vulpine origins, "Bitter End" never was reprinted, in Rex's lifetime, in its lupine reincarnation.[15]

Even if Rex had been tempted to slow his pace when he reached middle life, Lucetta's example would have made him doubt the wisdom of that course. In 1933, when she turned eighty-one, Lucetta had set down for her children some thoughts on the subject of growing old:

Age is not to be determined mechanically by a count of the years which have passed. The true measure of age must be sought in the capacities and potentialities which have been attained and which are available for actualization and development. . . . Each solar cycle brings, not diminution, but an actual access of power, a growth in wisdom, an expansion in sympathy and understanding.

In the years that followed, Lucetta suited her actions to her words. After John's death she had a small house built next to Ruth's at Poverty Hollow. During the winter she lived in New York, with Mary, in an apartment on Morningside Drive. In April, with the first flowers, she arrived at Poverty Hollow. She stayed on till December, when Nature was beyond encouragement.

Ruth dreaded Lucetta's visits to High Meadow. She came home loaded down with bulbs, seeds, roots, and slips. She was eager to try her hand at raising something unfamiliar, even when she ran out of places to plant things. "Rex knew our problem," says Ruth, "but how could he refuse her anything?"

Lucetta followed her own bent — transplanting in full bloom, in drought, in ninety-degree heat — no matter, she never lost a blade of grass. Once she had a room built on her house while the others were away. She got it done when she would have no explaining to do. She was eighty-five when Mary got her driver's license. Mary took her for a drive. "How am I doing?" Mary asked her. "You might go a little faster," Lucetta said. At eighty-five, too, Lucetta still played a highly competitive game of croquet. Her return to rural life marked no slackening of interest in the world around her. She was, as ever, ready for something new. Lucetta was polite but casual about Rex's success as a writer. She did not read his books. "I think she would have liked it better," Ruth says, "if murder wasn't his theme. But she would never have said so."

When Lucetta did not feel well, she ate almost nothing. As she grew older she went in for some inconspicuous fasting. But she had no serious problems of health. In the spring of 1940, however, she did not seem herself. Ruth suspected that the news from Europe upset her. She did not intend to live through another war. Early in July she drew the curtains at her cottage, and turned her back on the garden. She never looked at another flower. Rex came over from High Meadow every few days to see her. He brought bouquets of huge peonies, pink, white, and red. Nothing could tempt her interest. In October they moved her back to the apartment in New York. She stayed in bed. One day she said to Rex, "I suppose I should be ashamed of myself, lying here like a luggard, when I don't really have to." Rex said, "You are doing what you want to do, and that's as it should be." Lucetta smiled and her eyes closed as though she was sleeping. After a time they opened again. "I am going away to another home," she said, "and I think you are all going to be there with me someday."

On 10 December, a Tuesday, at 100 Morningside Drive, at eleven o'clock at night, Lucetta died in her sleep. In the morning Ruth called High Meadow to let Rex know that their mother was gone. Rex was having breakfast. Pola took the call. An hour passed before she could find the words to tell him. Lucetta was buried from the Quaker meetinghouse on Second Street, where she had gone to services since the family came to New York. She was laid out in a blue-flowered dress, the color of the blue sky that hovered over the growing earth she loved.

One day in the spring Rex visited Poverty Hollow and asked Ruth for a perennial. "Just anything," he said, "any favorite of Mother's." "She didn't have any favorites," Fred remarked, "or if she did, no one knew it. Every flower, every person had its own special place. No comparisons. No hurt feelings." Rex took home a moss rose bush. "Superior merit" was the meaning given this flower in the gift books of Lucetta's girlhood.

30

Nero Wolfe Gets Smaller

Rex is to be enormously credited, as a literary person, outside the social political field, taking the positions he did, when he did, and sticking to them.

— JAMES H. SHELDON

On 25 November 1940, on Theodore Granik's "American Forum of the Air," Rex and Ralph Ingersoll, editor of *PM,* a liberal New York daily evening newspaper, faced West Virginia's Senator Rush D. Holt and Representative Melvin J. Maas of Minnesota, ranking member of the Naval Affairs Committee, in a debate on the topic "Shall We Give Full Military Aid to England?" Rex argued that most Americans wanted to help England. Of those who did not, he said, the most dangerous were "a small but influential group of nabobs who want to appease Hitler because they look forward to the day of cheer when they can sell him something." In his opinion, practically and morally we were already at war. "Britain's boys," he said, "are flying our airplanes (paid for) against those who already have crushed freedom on the Continent of Europe and threaten it everywhere." When his arguments sent Holt into a rage, Rex coolly informed him, "Senator, this is not a hog-calling contest."

That same week he had dinner with Whit Burnett and Martha Foley. Their topic was the war and the need to aid Britain, but, typically, Rex took out time to discuss with them a novel about support given by German social scientists to Hitler in his rise to power. The author, George Morlan, was a young instructor at the State Teachers College at Danbury. Rex liked his book and was trying to find a publisher for it. In mid-December, Rex lunched with Morlan. To Rex, Morlan voiced doubts about the United States getting involved in Europe again. "Wouldn't we be playing into the hands of the war profiteers?" he asked. Rex replied, "You don't have to have angels as cooks before you eat cake." "He saw clearly," Morlan says, "when many of us were confused, that if we and our allies had to be completely pure before we defended ourselves against a great evil, there would be no defense."[1]

To Morlan Rex expressed disappointment that Tecumseh Fox had not found the same favor Nero Wolfe had. If he wondered how the third Fox mystery, *The Broken Vase,* due out on 21 January, would fare, his curiosity soon was satisfied. A letter from a Midwestern bookseller said it all: "The chief mystery presented by the latest Tecumseh Fox is outside the covers. A crime has been committed, but by whom? Rex Stout? Farrar & Rinehart? Is Rex Stout bound and gagged somewhere — or (a pleasanter thought) are Farrar & Rinehart? Who wrote *The Broken Vase?* Rex Stout could never, not even in *delirium tremens,* imagine characters so dull or dialogue so *Ladies' Home Journal* as here presented." Rex got the message. The Fox withdrew from the Wolfe's territory. Rex reflected later, "Fox wasn't a created character, like Wolfe. He was put together piece-by-piece and wasn't worth a damn."

On 31 January 1941, the annual meeting of the Baker Street Irregulars was held at the Murray Hill Hotel. Christopher Morley called the meeting to order and, after two "Conanical" toasts were drunk, the twenty-five members assembled were comfortable and benign.[2] Only the principal speaker of the evening, Rex Stout, was not. He had abstained from toasting "Dr. Watson's Second Wife," and must have felt the eyes of the Irregulars upon him. He had no prepared speech text as such, just Morley's two-volume memorial edition of Sherlock Holmes with slips of paper protruding from pages marked for reference the night before. Curiously casual references for what would be a shattering discourse.

Over the next half-hour, Rex gave his address, as indifferent to the groans of his audience as Jonathan Edwards had been when, from his pulpit, he suspended sinners over hell's abyss. His thesis was astonishing. Dr. Watson was a woman: Irene Adler Watson, Mrs. Sherlock Holmes. The minutes of this gathering record that the Stout thesis "threw the meeting into a state bordering upon panic." Reluctantly they conceded that "with profound if unorthodox scholarship, Mr. Stout derived an acrostic from the titles of the tales themselves in support of his thesis." They allowed further: "Mr. Stout also quoted liberally from the Sacred Writings themselves to establish characteristics and foibles on the part of the chronicler which could only be feminine in their nature."

As Rex reached his last sentence, pandemonium broke loose. For a final macabre touch, the minutes relate, "As an after-piece, and to still the turmoil, Mr. Stout obliged by singing 'God Bless Baker Street, My Holmes Sweet Holmes.' "[3]

The next morning, word of Rex's disclosure raced across New York like a tidal wave. H. Allen Smith, reaching Rex by phone at High Meadow, asked for additional information on his amazing discovery. Then Smith broke the story to *World-Telegram* readers. "The world of 1941," he said, "is well accustomed to soul-searing shocks, so we have little hesitancy today in reporting that a startling literary theory has been made public." Smith was right. In certain quarters 1941 would be remembered as the year that began with the Stout hypothesis and ended with Pearl Harbor — two nightmarish happenings.

Rex was ready with his defense. He brushed aside Christopher Morley's theory that Watson was an American. "That is pure bosh," he said. "This Watson woman was certainly not an American." He explained:

My acrostic is not simply an acrostic. . . . There is scientific precision back of it. . . . I have been working out this theory for years. In the daytime I do my regular work with Nero Wolfe, and at night I work on this theory. It is such a complex theory that I may ultimately publish a series of books about it — maybe a whole set of books, bigger than a set of Sherlock Holmes. At the present point I have reached that stage of my investigation in which I am trying to prove that Lord Peter Wimsey . . . is really the offspring of the union between Sherlock Holmes and Irene Watson.

Smith wanted to know what the starting point of Rex's theory had been. "It is simple enough," Rex said. "You find Holmes and Watson together in the evening. All their actions, their conversations, are reported in detail. But they never go to bed. Never is anything said about their going to bed. Now, what would that suggest to you? That they are married, of course." Smith confined his own estimate of Rex's theory to a single final exclamation: "Quick, Watson, the needlework!"

That was just the beginning. The *Saturday Review* carried the address in its 1 March issue. *The New York Times* went farther. It both upheld Rex and identified him as a descendant of the famed English mathematician Isaac Todhunter, presumably to assure readers that he had logic on his side.[4]

In April, Julian Wolff published the Baker Street Irregulars' formal rebuttal under the title "That Was No Lady." Wolff conceded that (even if he was a Wolff) he was taking on a formidable foe. Among the arguments Wolff used to refute Rex was Lestrade's description of Watson as "a middle-sized strongly built man — square jaw, thick neck, moustache. . . ." His clincher was another acrostic compiled from titles of the tales. It read: "NUTS TO REX STOUT."[5]

Even as the fun associated with his Murray Hill address mounted, Rex again was preoccupied with the bitter issue of the war. On 14 February his name was signed to a letter sent to Roy Howard, president of the Scripps-Howard newspapers. Other signers were Robert Sherwood, Leon Birkhead, Cass Canfield, John Farrar, Dorothy Thompson, Alexander Sachs, and George S. Kaufman. Collectively they deplored a Scripps-Howard news item which alleged that the United States army had ordered four and a half million special tags for identifying the American war dead.

That same month John Farrar arranged for Rex to speak to the Dutch Treat Club, a midtown lunch club with a membership of two hundred, including many notables in business, advertising, and publishing. Three hundred people were on hand. "Highlight of my talk," Rex recalled, "was a list of suggestions for a federal cabinet when Hitler and the Nazis occupied the United States." These included: "Gauleiter, Herbert Hoover; Secretary of State, Walter Lippmann; Secretary of War, Charles Lindbergh; Secretary of the Interior, Roy Howard; Secretary of Labor, Walter Reuther; Attorney General, George Sylvester Viereck; Office Boy, Arthur Krock." "Afterwards," Rex told me, "when John and I went to get our coats and hats Charles Norris hauled off to sock me. Since he was a hundred-ninety-pound six-footer, I was glad some of them held him back and I went out whole."

Radio now became increasingly the medium through which Rex carried to the American people his views about the war. On 23 March he was a participant in another of Theodore Granik's "Forum of the Air" debates — this time paired off with William Agar against Colorado's Senator Edwin C. Johnson and Hearst columnist George Sokolsky. The topic was "Shall the Small Invaded Nations Be Fed?" Rex argued that food could not be provided to the invasion victims without prolonging the war. "In the last war," he said, "the food sent to Belgium was of enormous advantage to the Germans."

In April the Fight for Freedom Committee was formed. At the head of the committee stood the Right Reverend Henry W. Hobson, Episcopal Bishop of Ohio, with Senator Carter Glass of Virginia, as honorary chairman, and Mrs. Calvin Coolidge and Francis P. Miller as vice chairmen. As one of the committee's sponsors Rex was brought into close working association with those who had been active in the erstwhile Century Group, including not only Ulric Bell (executive chairman of the FFFC, who, after Pearl Harbor, became deputy director of the overseas bureau of the OWI), but also Robert Sherwood, Peter Cusick, Lewis Mumford, Carl Sandburg, and Alexander Woollcott. Rex ranked with Woollcott and Wendell Willkie as one of the most popular FFFC speakers. Even while traveling extensively for the FFFC, he gave weekly Thursday night broadcasts on NBC. This was the "Speaking of Liberty" program, sponsored by the Council for Democracy and heard coast-to-coast.[6]

Rex's first FFFC speaking engagement came early in the committee's existence — on 24 April 1941 — and the next morning was front-page news in *The New York Times.* It was the committee's reply to a speech Charles A. Lindbergh had made on station WMCA the night before, at the same hour, ten P.M. Lindbergh was an ardent noninterventionist. Rex did not mince words:

I wish I could look you in the eye, Colonel Lindbergh, when I tell you that you simply don't know what it's all about. . . . A desperate war is being fought, and the winners of the war will win the oceans. No matter what we do, we shall be either one of the winners, or one of the losers; no shivering neutral will get a bite of anything but crow when the shooting stops. It would therefore seem to be plain imbecility not to go in with Britain and win.

Rex scorned Lindbergh's futile neutralism: "If we do not see to it that our ships and planes and guns get across the Atlantic where they can fulfill the purpose they were made for, we are saying for all the world to hear, 'You've got our number, Mr. Hitler, you were perfectly correct when you said years ago that Americans were too soft and decadent and timid ever to stop you on your way to world conquest.' " Lindbergh's image was now tarnished:

Every fascist and pro-Nazi publication in America, without exception, applauds and approves of him. . . . Dozens of times in the past year he has been enthusiastically quoted in the newspapers of Germany and Italy and Japan. . . .

Charles Lindbergh is one of the minor tragedies of America. In 1927, twenty-five years old, he was the blue-eyed darling of a hundred million of us, the flaming and indomitable knight of the new element we were conquering, the air. In 1941, thirty-nine years old, he is a middle-aged sourpuss who apparently thinks that we scattered that thousand tons of confetti on him in those glorious days of May because we had found a hero who played it safe, who refused to confront danger like a man.[7]

For himself Rex welcomed the title of warmonger:

The America First Committee is calling people like me, who are convinced that we should go in with Britain now and win, a gang of warmongers. . . . If a 1941 warmonger is a man who advocates that we should immediately send warships and the men we have trained to sail them and shoot their guns, and airplanes and the boys we have trained to fly them and drop their bombs, send them to meet our acknowledged deadly enemy where he is, and attack him and defeat him, then count me in.

In May, Rex enlisted Alexander Woollcott for a "Speaking of Liberty" broadcast set for 19 June. Instead of the usual dialogue, Rex proposed that Aleck talk for eleven out of the thirteen minutes the program was on the air. He said: "I wouldn't propose this to any other guest this side of Shakespeare, for fear of tune-outers and because I love my public, but to the best damn broadcaster in captivity I not only propose it, I implore it."[8]

The plan miscarried. NBC insisted on previewing Woollcott's script. He had none. The broadcast was dropped. Aleck invited Rex up to Bomoseen Lake to revive his spirits. On 2 June Rex wrote him: "NBC stands for Natural Born Clodpates. Thank heavens you have a soul. I'll leave here early in the morning of Tuesday the tenth, arriving at High

Dudgeon, I should think, shortly after noon." Two days of spirited croquet set their world right again. The High Meadow–High Dudgeon Axis was intact.

By June Rex's Plymouth station wagon had seen so much service carrying him back and forth to New York for war committee meetings and speechmaking activities that his reputation for punctuality was at stake. So he junked it for a Cadillac.

On 29 June, under a fifteen-by-twelve-inch color photograph of Rex, in white suit, blue shirt, and red and white checked bow tie, dictating his text to a secretary, the Philadelphia *Inquirer* highlighted an article by Rex entitled "Where They'll Find the Strength of Our Country." A few days before that Lindbergh had said Roosevelt out-Hitlered Hitler. Rex asked now: "How many Americans share Lindbergh's incapacity to perceive any moral or spiritual distinction between . . . a Nation that proclaims the dignity of man and one that savagely asserts and promotes the degradation of man?" Rex appealed to his countrymen to accept the concept of world government — a world union brought about not by Nazi tyranny but by international cooperation.

On 1 August 1941, as spokesman for the FFFC, Rex assured a WMCA radio audience that a majority of the American people now believed that "we should declare war on Germany immediately." He said: "The isolationists and appeasers and defeatists have been thoroughly beaten. . . . Their stock arguments, that this is not our war . . . that Britain is a phony democracy . . . that Hitler is riding the wave of the future . . . that we can lick Hitler alone . . . ," had failed them. With Neronian disdain, he concluded: "The Congress and the people both heard all of those arguments until they were sick of them, and they said 'pfui.' " Only when he spoke of the fear some had of Japan, did Rex's crystal ball go murky. He could not see Japan declaring war on the United States. "With a million men bogged down in China after four years of struggle, an economy on the verge of collapse, and an industry staggering under a load already twice too heavy for it," Japan, Rex thought, had problems enough.

Still astride his dual careers, on 15 July 1941, in "These Grapes Need Sugar," Rex addressed *Vogue* readers on the skyrocketing renown of women detective story writers. Rex recommended that "a law should be passed at once prohibiting females from writing detective stories." He amplified: "In the most frequently recurring nightmare of my boyhood, I was confined in the marsupial pouch of a kangaroo and struggling frantically to get out, and just as I was hanging from the rim, ready to drop, the kangaroo started jumping, and I was afraid to let go. As far as I know, that kangaroo never did stop jumping, with me hanging on, but about that time Freud's first book was published, and my nightmare took the hint and went in for subtlety."[9]

One of his subtle dreams, however, concerned Jane Austen. "No finer novelist than she has ever lived," said Rex.[10] Hence it was a shock to him when he began to dream that Jane "had come back to life and started writing detective stories." But other women offered no threat: "No woman who has never herself committed a murder is capable of believing that anyone ever did commit one, or ever will. . . . Not only is it impossible for her to bypass a thought around her ego, rendering it abstract; it is equally impossible for her to accept a fact as real (if the fact has emotional content) unless she can see a piece of herself in it." Because of this psychological impediment, he said, in detective stories written by women "the dagger is made of suede . . . the blood is raspberry juice." He offered an assessment: Dorothy Sayers's Lord Peter Wimsey is "the most intolerable Galahad in the annals of crime." Mary Roberts Rinehart's detectives are so wholesome they seem likely to take weekends off "to teach their Sunday-school class." Agatha Christie came closest to "creating a detective capable of hounding a murderer to his doom." She made him a foreigner. "That nearly did it, since to an Englishman or woman, foreigners are funny anyway."

The trouble was — well, these ladies could write. While "male geniuses" starved, the distaff scribes were raking in millions. All at once Rex's title became clear. Sour grapes!

In August "Death Wears an Orchid" ("Black Orchids"), the second Wolfe novella, had appeared in *American Magazine*. In *The New York Times* on 21 September, readers found an explanation for the story's brevity. Rex had told Robert Van Gelder that he had, in the past, thoroughly enjoyed writing Nero Wolfe stories:

It was pure pleasure — a game. Then Munich gave me my first bellyache. I'd always been healthy. I became dyspeptic. That's true. I had pains most of the time after Munich, a nervous stomach. I started making speeches, debating those America First fellows, going on the radio to answer them, doing all I could to wake people up to the danger. . . . I'm not dyspeptic any more. The nervousness is all going out, you see, in these speeches. But Nero Wolfe gets smaller, can't keep my mind on him.

In truth, Wolfe was not so necessary to Rex now. His need for an authority figure had dwindled away as his own inward authority grew. Hereafter, when Wolfe returned, Rex would not borrow from the characterization so much as would the characterization borrow from him.

In September, at Lake Mohonk, the New York Library Association held its fifty-first annual conference. On Friday night, 26 September, Schenectady's station WGY broadcast its popular and unrehearsed "Speaking of Books" program from the conference site, over NBC. A transcript of the broadcast was the opening article of the November

1941 issue of the *Wilson Library Bulletin,* which described it as the "high spot" of the conference. The subject of the broadcast was *Out of the Night,* Jan Valtin's best-selling account of his harsh life as a member of the Communist underground in Germany. The book was discussed by Irita Van Doren, Lewis Gannett, and Rex Stout, whom the announcer identified as an "outspoken champion of liberty."[11] A cross-examination of Valtin himself ensued.

Rex had spent a week reading the huge book and found it "a very repellent picture because it's the insides of the minds and hearts of men who have gone back to the barbaric idea that the way to settle the question is by fighting about it." Lewis Gannett jumped in: "Now, wait a moment — you're not speaking for the Fight for Freedom Committee tonight, Mr. Stout." Rex soon took back the advantage. He prized the book but held Valtin's emphasis suspect. He told Irita, "Nearly all of the skullduggery throughout the book is committed by the leaders — either the Gestapo leaders or the G.P.U. leaders — but the rank and file are always pretty good guys. Don't you suspect that?

"My idea," he went on, "is that the percentage of skulduggery among human beings remains just about the same on any level — the rank-and-filers have got the same percentage as the big guys." Gannett countered this argument with the suggestion that rank-and-filers prone to skulduggery naturally rose to positions of leadership. Rex was not reassured: "I think it's a very bad doctrine, Mr. Gannett," he said, "in a democracy."

Valtin was challenged directly by Rex, too. Rex asked him if he considered himself a good Democrat. Valtin said, "I know it is the business of political refugees to be good Democrats." "I know it's good business," Rex snapped, "but are you a good Democrat?" Valtin, who was more a witness against totalitarianism than a champion of democracy, replied, "I believe that having to choose between the American form of capitalism and the Russian form of Communism or the German form of National Socialism, I would say, for all its faults, give me capitalism even if I'm a wage slave under capitalism."

His interlocutors salvaged what they could of the situation. Gannett reminded Valtin that, as the owner of two prosperous farms, he was not a wage slave. Rex offered to swap him broccoli for McIntosh apples.

31

Crusader by Inner Compulsion

We did not seem to meet socially. Probably because I was on a morning newspaper and did my socializing at night, generally in the town's hot spots, and Rex led a more disciplined (I hope) life. Lack of personal contact never cramped the esteem I had for him as the creator of Nero Wolfe and Archie Goodwin. . . . I may be a heretic in that I have an even higher regard and certainly a real affection for Archie than I have for Nero. But I hardly think Stout intended the reader to conceive an affection for Nero, who could be mighty trying. Admiration certainly but I don't think Nero courted affection. Archie is my boy.

— FRANK SULLIVAN

Rex was the nicest angry man I knew in the Hitler period. As chairman of the Writers' War Board he worked in the closest association with my organization, the Fight for Freedom Committee. His anger and brilliance contributed in an extraordinary way to the successful efforts of both the Committee and the Board to alert the country, as a whole, to existing dangers.

— PETER CUSICK

In the early fall of 1941, when the activities of the several groups supporting America's entry into the war were seen to be overlapping, the Fight for Freedom Committee (FFFC) began to explore the possibility of a mass merger. Then George Field came up with the idea of letting the groups keep their separate identities while coming together under one roof, in a building to be called Freedom House. Freedom House would support certain basic objectives. It would promote concrete application of the principles of freedom and disseminate the concepts of freedom. The building itself would symbolize these goals and provide a base from which they could be promoted. Plans went ahead quickly. On 31 October Freedom House was incorporated. Its trustees included Field, Ulric Bell, William Agar, Dorothy Thompson, and Rex Stout.

Thus began for Rex a vital affiliation which would continue unbroken into his ninth decade. Rex would be on hand when, at its formal dedication, on 22 January 1942, Freedom House came physically into existence as a converted residence at 32 East Fifty-first Street. Few alliances were to give him the satisfaction he would get from Freedom House. From the start he found it an admirable instrument through which to champion those principles of conduct he believed in.

Harmony did not always reign within the freedom groups. In that tense autumn of 1941 Rex himself pushed Carl J. Friedrich, a professor of government at Harvard, out of the Council for Democracy. Marshall Shulman, then secretary of the Council's Executive Committee, explains:

Friedrich was the intellectual mentor of the Council; he sometimes alienated people without being aware of it. While not anti-interventionist, he was part of the dominant group in the Council which tried to keep it from becoming polarized on the interventionist-isolationist issue, for the purpose of articulating broadly shared democratic values. Stout was an activist, with little patience for anything but direct action. Both were strong personalities, and the times were such as to heighten personal and political tensions. There were many other well-known people involved — Stephen Vincent Benét, for example, among the other writers — and the Stout-Friedrich relationship was not singular in the complex interplay of personalities.[1]

Of his relationship with Rex, the German-born Friedrich told me: "I didn't like him. He didn't like me. I left not quite voluntarily."[2]

Part of the trouble was that Friedrich opposed organized propaganda activities. "Can the methods of a Goebbels fashion the mind of a new democracy?" he asked. He argued that "nothing less than the corrosion of democracy" would come of such tactics.[3] Rex concluded that Friedrich "despised democracy and apologized for the Nazis." Friedrich dismissed Rex as "an intellectual gangster." "I was a colorful fellow in those days," Friedrich says today, with amusement. Recalling the battle cry of the Creel Committee of the World War I era — "making the world safe for democracy" — Friedrich says now: "Our staunchest democratic allies today are Germany and Japan. I enjoy reminding people of that."

In October 1941, *Cue* magazine caught a sense of the compulsions which impelled Rex. "All through history," Rex told *Cue*, "ambitious single-minded men have tried to build machines to conquer the world. . . . Napoleon's machine wasn't good enough. Now there's one that might be. And it's in the hands of the biggest bastard that ever lived. . . ." Rex then shifted to frank exhortation: "No one can rest now. You can't. I can't. Everything else of importance must be set aside — work, pleasure, family life, everything, until that man and machine are destroyed. Apathy in the face of the world situation is unthinkable. Shout. Write your Congressman. Write the President. Nag. Coerce. Ridicule. Make yourself felt."

"Rex Stout," acknowledged *Cue*, "makes himself felt. He'll talk, nag, ridicule, sting into action anyone who'll listen: an audience of one or 5,000 potential hecklers at a rally. Millions hear him as the interlocutor of 'Speaking of Liberty.' . . ." Yet *Cue* surmised that Rex was "a crusader by furious if reluctant inner compulsion, not by natural preference. . . . What he really wants is to be let alone." *Cue* ended on an enigmatic note: "An interviewer once sounded him out with, 'What question would you ask you, Mr. Stout, if you were I?' Stout removed his tongue from his cheek for a moment. Then put it back. 'Well — you always ask whether a man would rather be Casanova than President. Me? I'd rather be President.' "

Rex was not ready to move into the White House, but he was ready to speak out for the President whenever occasion offered. On 26 November, at an anti-Hitler rally at NYU, he shared the platform with Eleanor Roosevelt. She spoke in her capacity as Assistant Director of the Office of Civilian Defense; he for the FFFC. *The New York Times* reported that, though Mrs. Roosevelt was the next speaker, "the students applauded so long after his speech that Mr. Stout who had taken his seat on the platform, was forced to stand up again in acknowledgment."[4]

Rex was off then to Milwaukee, where he spoke at the home of a beer baron to an audience of sixty German-Americans. He was hard-hitting. His audience grimaced, but took it. On 5 December, with Senator Claude Pepper, he addressed an audience in Providence. The next day the pair traveled on to Boston to speak there. The town was papered with notices announcing that Lindbergh would address a giant America First rally at the Boston Garden on 12 December. Rex made his speech. Lindbergh did not make his. Pearl Harbor brought his campaigning to an irrevocable halt.

On 8 December, *Alphabet Hicks*, Rex's latest detective novel, was published. But with war now formally declared, Rex had no thoughts of shifting his attention back to his writing career. In any case, *Alphabet Hicks* was not the book to do it with. Rex's protagonist, Alfred Hicks, was a brilliant Harvard Law School graduate who had taken up detective work after being disbarred. Even had there been no Pearl Harbor, Hicks still would not have enlisted a large readership. Like Tecumseh Fox, he seemed contrived rather than created. Unlike Wolfe and Archie, he had nothing intimate to say about the author himself. Hicks made one later appearance in "His Own Hand" (1955) and then was allowed to sink from view.[5]

In the fall of 1941 Rex had been approached by Donald MacLaren, an agent of the British Security Co-ordination, working under William Stevenson, the brilliant Canadian who was later knighted for his work as head of the British Intelligence Center in New York and for other wartime activities. The B.S.C. asked Rex to help with an exposé it was preparing which would show how the Nazis were using the money of American consumers, with I.G. Farben as its transmission belt, to help finance Hitler's war. Rex pledged full cooperation. John L. Balderston, an active member of the FFFC, was enlisted to prepare a booklet setting forth the information Stevenson's sources had gathered.[6] Much of the gathering was done by MacLaren, George Merten, and economist Sylvia Porter. When the text was completed, Rex wrote a foreword for it. Then the manuscript was taken to Canada, where it was secretly printed on Camp X presses. As soon as it was ready for distribution, the booklet was smuggled back into the United States.

Merten says: "On the eve of the publication we organized a public meeting in Elizabeth, New Jersey, being near the site of the American Merck Company, one of those involved in close cooperation with the Germans. As the only speaker at the meeting, which was quite well attended, Rex Stout gave an outline of the problems dealt with in the booklet."[7] The speech was given just two days after Pearl Harbor. Though lengthy, it was graphic. Rex knew that his audience was comprised mostly of German-Americans. He said he was sorry that some of them were going to be suspected of disloyalty. "There is nothing more exasperating, nothing that so fills a man with helpless rage and resentment," he said, "as to be made the target of unjust suspicion and the unjust treatment that results from it." He explained why they would be the target of such accusations. Hitler had said: "Germany is wherever a German is." In nearby Linden, Rex pointed out, the General Aniline and Film Corporation, second largest manufacturer of photographic equipment in America, third largest manufacturer of dyes and chemicals, owned by I.G. Farben, was controlled by the Schmitzes and the Duisbergs, who had laid the groundwork for World War II. Rex warned that unless G.A.F. was truly Americanized, Americans, even after Hitler's downfall, would be working still for the sinister German forces that connived for world dominion.

The booklet, entitled *Sequel to the Apocalypse: The Uncensored Story: How Your Dimes and Quarters Helped Pay for Hitler's War*, went on sale in March 1942, its distribution in the United States facilitated by the energetic efforts of Nelson A. Rockefeller, whom President Roosevelt had just appointed Coordinator of Inter-American Affairs. It was described as the work of a mythical "John Boylan." With his name affixed to the foreword, Rex Stout was the only person connected with it who was identifiable. That meant he would bear the brunt of the indignation the booklet provoked. Since he knew that the cause he served was a good one, Rex did not mind in the least. Recalling this undertaking, thirty years later, Sylvia Porter would say, "A great man Rex Stout is indeed."[8]

Rex's foreword stated the hard realities the book implied. Even if the Nazi leaders were killed it would make no difference. The Germans would cheat us out of victory. Rex described "the American lawyers and business men who were selected, between 1923 and 1936, by certain Germans for certain functions" as "supersuckers." This statement brought the expected shouts of outrage. Word carried to Rex that John Foster Dulles was taking steps to sue him for libel. No suit was filed. Events moved too fast.[9]

At twenty-five cents a copy, the booklet sold out quickly. It forced the resignation of Wilhelm vom Rath, the German-born director of G.A.F., and led to the prosecution of the nation's largest drug company, Sterling Products Inc., for giving I.G. Farben an undertaking not to sell goods in Britain, Canada, and Australia. Sterling and three subsidiary companies were fined $5,000 each. *Sequel* also played a role in the seizure of the assets of German-owned subsidiary companies in the United States. The flow of funds was so severely checked that Nazi agents in America found it difficult to operate. Word carried back to Stevenson that the managing director of Standard Oil of New Jersey, which had strong ties with I.G. Farben, had said he would give $50,000 to know who was behind *Sequel to the Apocalypse*. This venture gave Rex the satisfaction of knowing, in the opening days of the war, that he had helped deal Hitler a crippling blow.[10] Greater satisfaction followed swiftly. Rex's good work had not gone unnoticed.

In the ensuing days, Julian "Pete" Street, who headed the Treasury Department's writing staff, asked playwright Howard Lindsay to find some prominent writers who would be willing to promote the sale of war bonds. Lindsay talked over the request with his collaborator, Russel Crouse. Crouse thought that what was needed was a committee of writers. He was willing to serve on such a committee, but he wanted Rex Stout to head it. Lindsay told Rex what he had in mind. Rex agreed to serve but made his acceptance contingent upon three conditions: (1) the committee must be free to run itself, (2) it must be free to support itself in its own way, (3) the choice of those who would serve on it must be left to him. Lindsay accepted all three conditions. On 6 January 1942, Rex met with Pearl Buck, Clifton Fadiman, Oscar Hammerstein II, John P. Marquand, and Russel Crouse at the offices of the Authors' League, at 6 East Thirty-ninth Street, and there the Writers' War Committee, under his chairmanship, came into existence.[11] The group's modest nomenclature reflected its expectations that it would merely run errands for the Treasury Department.

Rex's insistence on reserving to himself the right to determine the makeup of the board quickly stood him in good stead. The board had scarcely come into being when American Communists petitioned for a place on it. Rex was not afraid that the board would find its activities subverted to serve Communist expansionist ambitions in the United States if a Communist joined them. He had been through that ordeal already, with *The New Masses,* and knew he could cope now with any such incursion. He explained: "The chief reason I refused was that I knew a Communist would waste a lot of board time, at meetings, in disputation."

When he assumed chairmanship of the Writers' War Committee Rex realized that he could not continue to live at High Meadow. Accordingly, the painful but necessary step was taken. Pola and he took a seven-room apartment at 55 East Eighty-sixth Street. Barbara and Rebecca moved to New York with them and were enrolled at nearby P.S. 86. For the next four years the Stouts would see little of High Meadow save for occasional weekends.

Even as he was resettling into city life and beginning to fashion a concept of his new duties, Rex honored existing commitments. Late in January he joined Jacques Barzun and Elmer Davis as a guest on Mark Van Doren's popular CBS radio show, "Invitation to Learning."[12] The topic was *The Adventures of Sherlock Holmes*. The four were compatible; all agreed that Holmes belonged among the masterpieces of world literature; and Rex was as ready as the professors were to discuss Holmes's place in the literary milieu that produced him. He had, after all, been over the same ground with Winston Churchill a decade earlier.

Rex had good points to make about Doyle's technique: "The modern detective story puts off its best tricks till the last, but Doyle always put his best tricks first and that's why they're still the best ones." And again: "It is impossible for any Sherlock Holmes story not to have at least one marvelous scene." He left it to his auditors to surmise how his own work had benefited from his exposure to Doyle's.

By expounding a thesis first proffered by Howard Haycraft, Rex made this broadcast relevant to the world crisis then gripping everyone's mind: "I think the detective story is by far the best upholder of the democratic doctrine in literature. . . . There couldn't have been detective stories until there were democracies, because the very foundation of the detective story is the thesis that if you're guilty you'll get it in the neck and if you're innocent you can't possibly be harmed."[13] Rex then made an inevitable point: "In Germany, for instance, there couldn't be a detective story because the officials don't know anything. The amateur 'dick' is the one." This thesis — that officialdom in detective stories is necessarily stupid because justice rests with the people — was Rex's own, and was worth a broadcast in itself.

On a visit to Chicago, in February 1942, Rex met, for the first time, the great Holmesian Vincent Starrett. Friendship was instant. Accordingly Rex obliged when, a few weeks later, Starrett asked him to list his ten favorite detective stories. Rex chose: Collins, *The Moonstone;* Hammett, *The Maltese Falcon;* Van Dine, *The Benson Murder Case;* Sayers and Eustace, *The Documents in the Case;* Chesterton, *The Innocence of Father Brown;* Bailey, *Call Mr. Fortune;* Hart, *The Bellamy Trial;* Crofts, *The Cask;* Christie, *The Murder of Roger Ackroyd;* Innes, *Lament for a Maker.* (In 1951, updating the list, he would add Ambler's *A Coffin for Dimitrios.*) In his covering letter to Starrett, Rex wrote, on

31 March 1942: "Here's that list of ten. Naturally nobody on earth would agree with it, which is what makes democracy the only possible way for men and women to get along."[14]

Five years went by before Rex's list saw print in Starrett's *Books and Bipeds* (1947). But on 13 June 1943, it appeared in Starrett's "Books Alive" column in the Chicago *Sunday Tribune*. In the same column Starrett reminded his readers that Rex, in 1939, had told the editors of *Twentieth Century Authors:* "As it stands now, writing one of the three best mystery stories in the world would satisfy my soul as much as anything else I can think of."[15] Starrett went on: "There may be readers in the Mystery league who think he already has done so, and, while I cannot agree with them, I should have difficulty keeping Nero Wolfe out of, say, the first dozen." Commenting then on Rex's list, Starrett said: "In decency, of course, he could not admit one of his own yarns. So I shall do it for him — the choice is between *Fer-de-Lance, The League of Frightened Men* (what a title!), and *The Rubber Band,* all very close to tops in anybody's list." Starrett noted, too, that Rex had just made his debut in paperback with *The Rubber Band,* "one of his most brilliant and exhilarating performances. Few better mystery stories have been written in our time." Paperback publishers did not know it then, but this was one *Rubber Band* that was going to snap back at them. Rex's appearance in paperback was the start of his personal thirty years' war for larger royalties for authors whose works were reprinted in paperback.

On 5 February 1942, at the Hotel Commodore, Rex addressed the annual meeting of the Authors' Guild, urging one hundred and fifty Guild members present to put their talents at the disposal of his committee. He asked for epigrams, brief essays, and playlets. That seemed a modest enough beginning. A week later, however, listeners found him in a quite different mood at the opening, at Grand Central Palace, of the Carnival for Democracy. Eleanor Roosevelt had spoken to the same audience earlier. For Rex she was a damsel in distress. The week before, on her recommendation, actor Melvyn Douglas and Mayris Chaney, a dancer, had been appointed to the Office of Civilian Defense. An "avalanche of denunciations and catcalls" had greeted the appointments. In Rex's scornful estimate, Pearl Harbor itself had not produced such an uproar. *The New York Times* reported that Rex said we could say "phooey" to any idea of national unity so long as such outbursts were possible. Did Rex say "phooey"? "Of course not," Rex told me, "I said 'pfui.' I neither like the way 'phooey' sounds or looks."

A postscript to the Carnival for Democracy appearance was both amusing and prophetic. In comparison with what Rex expected his own committee to do, the plans other committees were evolving seemed to him inadequate and slovenly. Rhetorically he asked the Carnival audience what the groups serving the Committee for Democracy were doing. He answered his own question: "Pathetically little. They are holding meetings of executive committees and boards. They are preparing to plan to arrange to do something." Never did Rex make more explicit his abhorrence for haphazard organization.

A few months were enough to show Rex that in this war, unlike World War I, he would be doing much more than selling bonds for the Treasury Department. His committee could serve many government and nongovernment agencies. In March, Melvyn Douglas asked the committee to take on some OCD projects and found for it the funds with which to carry them out. Thereafter, for a few months, the committee was content to describe itself as an adjunct of the OCD. That was just as well. The committee had not had from Julian Street the recognition it had expected. Volunteer groups were appearing like toads after a spring rain. Washington did not expect much from any one of them.

In April, with an enlarged membership and an enhanced image of itself, Rex's committee redesignated itself the Writers' War Board and came officially under the aegis of the OCD. Even then its uniqueness was not at once perceived. On 13 May, when Rex joined Clifton Fadiman, William Rose Benét, Eric Knight, and John Kieran in a panel discussion at the New York Times Hall, on the topic "Books Are Weapons in the War of Ideas," the *Times* referred to him only as "chairman of a Writers' War Board cooperating with the government." Two weeks later, when he spoke at the annual dinner of the American Women's Voluntary Services, at the Waldorf-Astoria, and deplored as "dangerous and absolutely false," Herbert Hoover's statement that "plain Fascist economies are needed to win the war," the *Times* merely identified him as "Rex Stout, the author," and noted the surprise of his auditors at the "political" turn his speech had taken. No one suspected that what they were seeing was the chairman of the WWB flexing his muscles. Before Pearl Harbor, Hoover had been an outspoken America Firster. Now that he sought to extend his influence into the war effort, Rex found him a logical target.

In 1971, Robert Thomas Howell, historian of the WWB, would say of the board, "The group represents the best instance of the organized use of writing abilities in a war effort in American history." Of Rex himself, who was to chair the WWB throughout its lifetime, Howell says, "Stout was both the most interesting and by far the most important member." "Much more than any other of us," said Alan Green, "Rex *was* the Board."[16] Even the choice of Elmer Davis as head of the Office of War Information — the official dispenser of United States propaganda in World War II — was made on Rex's recommendation to Robert Sherwood. Davis knew it, too, and he knew Rex could do things he could not do. He called Rex "my Jim Farley."

For four years, the writing efforts of nearly five thousand American writers were mobilized in the service of the United States war effort. During that time Rex often was at his office seven days a week — sometimes even on Thanksgiving Day.[17] Unlike Nero Wolfe, Rex often conducted business right through lunch and dinner. Though his fiction writing ceased, he not only took no salary, he paid the salary of his secretary, Madeline Wallen, and his own travel and entertainment expenses from his own pocket.

A typical week found Rex overseeing the activities of nearly 30 committees (some pursuing several projects) with a combined membership of 124, dealing with 20 requests from 7 government agencies, 12 requests from nongovernment agencies, making daily radio broadcasts on the "Victory Volunteers" radio series, making a sound track for a Treasury Department film, and setting up editorial assistance for *People's War,* a new biweekly. Every major decision the board took cleared across Rex's desk. Sometimes, standing against the board, a minority of one, he put things through by his own magnetism and persuasive energy. In his role as chairman of the WWB, the superb organizing and planning ability which he had developed as the effective head of the Educational Thrift Service manifested itself anew. Added to that was the maturity that came with success, broadened horizons, and a fierce attachment to the cause he served. His deep passion for order, his compelling decisiveness, and all the resources he had developed to win others to his views, seemed now the requisite apprenticeship for this new commitment. He cajoled, he incited, he awed, he compelled. Some were overwhelmed and alienated. To some he was a genius; to others, a scoundrel. For his own part, Rex had great pride in those who served under him. "More than any other group I have ever met with," he told me, "the board members always concentrated on one purpose — getting on with the job."

In Clifton Fadiman, Rex found his ablest lieutenant. Indefatigable, disciplined, and razor-sharp in his own perceptions, Fadiman recognized Rex's awareness and firmness of purpose and his dedication to goals. Reminiscing about Rex, Fadiman told me:

There is nothing saintly about him, he loves and understands the magnificent carnalities of life. But he has an essential generosity of heart which is far superior, in my view, to saintliness. He was for many years my guru. To him, more than anyone else, I owe whatever basic understanding I have of World War II. He understood the Germans long before most of us did. And he knew the significance of the War was to be found in the German character.[18]

Although other assignments removed Pearl Buck and John Marquand from active roles in the WWB, Rex received much immediate help from a score of supporters committed to the board's activities. These included Luise M. Sillcox, Oscar Hammerstein II, Christopher La Farge, Alan Green, Paul Gallico, Carl Carmer, Franklin P. Adams, William L. Shirer, Robert Landry, Jack Goodman, Samuel Grafton, Hobe Morrison, and, later, Ruth Friend.

Rex's expanding role inevitably raised his recognition threshold. That resulted in at least one amusing confrontation. The late Charles Morrison, diffident in deportment and demeanor but a skillful writer, relished the Nero Wolfe stories and admired the man who wrote them, though they had never met. In 1942, Morrison several times saw walking in Central Park a man who he was sure was Rex Stout. One day he stepped into the man's path and said, "It is YOU, isn't it?" "Yes," Rex said. The two men nodded to one another and without any further word between them went their separate ways.

32.

The Lie Detective

I only met Stout once during the war at a lunch and though I have liked many of his books I am afraid I find the meals impossible to appreciate!

GRAHAM GREENE

I hope you are cooking another Wolfe, Rex; I can't get enough of them. They are the best we have, and the best we have had.

— VINCENT STARRETT

In April 1942 Rex had sojourned again briefly in the world of detective fiction. That month, "Invitation to Murder," published as "Cordially Invited to Meet Death," the eleventh Nero Wolfe story, came out in *The American Magazine.* Stout fans also had another reason to be delighted. NBC persuaded Rex to be guest star on Celebrity Theatre. Asked to choose the story to be dramatized, he picked Lawrence G. Blochman's "Red Wine." The program was broadcast on 10 April. Blochman told me: "Rex played Paul Vernier, the plump (but not fat) one-eyed detective who tails a wife-murderer to a rubber plantation in Dutch Borneo and identifies him from among four fellow planters by a gastronomic trick. Rex's performance was highly satisfactory."[1] That no transcription of the broadcast survives is unfortunate. After a fifty-year apprenticeship in Stout family productions, Rex's sole public performance as an actor must be accounted a moment of curious note in the history of the American theater.

The script of a broadcast Rex made to American soldiers overseas for the "Coordinator of Information" on 21 April 1942, saw him trying his own hand at radio drama. There he related that, on his way to a hockey game with a Columbia professor, he had been detoured into a cigar store on Seventh Avenue.

"A chunky broad-shouldered man behind the counter, with his shirt-sleeves pulled above his elbows, finished waiting on a customer and then gave us a look.

"My friend Ryder said, 'Hello, fathead.'

"The man behind the counter said, 'Hello, sap.'

" 'In spite of which,' Ryder said, 'both Americans?'

" 'Okay,' the man said, 'hurrah for America, even including you.' "

When they were alone again, Rex said he had asked Ryder for an explanation. The professor explained that in World War I, Bert, the cigar-store man, had saved his life by making a human bridge of himself across a barbed-wire barrier, in No Man's Land. Bert's heroism had puzzled Ryder because Bert and he were not friends. Later when he tried to thank him, Bert had said, " 'Forget it, sap. You're on my side, ain't you? Hurrah for America, even including you!' " Over the years the phrase had become a password between them. At the end of his talk, Rex repeated Bert's words, hoping, no doubt, that every listener longed to be a human bridge — just like Bert. Morale might have been given a bigger boast had Rex's auditors known that Ryder and Bert were products of his imagination. "I made them up," Rex confessed, miserable in the role of inspirationalist.

The next month brought Rex an opportunity he relished more. On 12 May CBS gave him thirteen minutes to reply to a speech Norman Thomas had made the previous week. Thomas, who had supported the America First Committee before Pearl Harbor, had criticized Roosevelt and the "offenses" against civil liberty being committed in the name of the war effort. He ventured, "It may be a patriotic duty to make, with a view to correcting a fault, the statement that democracy is dying." Roosevelt had said that "bogus patriots" should not be allowed to "pervert honest criticism into falsification of facts." "How does one test 'falsification of fact'?" Thomas had asked. With the incisiveness of Nero Wolfe closing out a case, Rex cited several distortions found in Thomas's own speech, then replied, "It is really very simple, when the man who does the falsifying is as clumsy as he was when he wrote that speech."

Thomas's criticism of the government's "overstaffed and overpaid agencies of propaganda and censorship" drew heavy fire. "We are," Rex said, "fighting the costliest and most destructive war in history, and it is a war of nerves and words as well as a war of planes, tanks, and ships." He cited a *London Economist* estimate that Germany was spending a billion and a half dollars annually on propaganda. He said: "We are spending thirty million; one-fiftieth as much as Germany. We certainly are pikers. . . . If we multiplied it by five . . . we would even then be spending only one-tenth as much as Germany. Which would probably be about right. One free word of a free nation is surely worth ten words of a totalitarian tyrant." Personal pique flavored his next remarks: "As for Mr. Thomas's cheap sarcasm about 'self-satisfying patriots,' I know a dozen or more men who are working in OFF and COI, and without exception they are getting paid considerably less than they formerly earned." He then showed how one pamphlet which Thomas objected to, had, at a cost of thirty thousand dollars, reached eighteen million readers, figuring out to one-sixth of a cent per reader.

In his speech Thomas had wondered if Archibald MacLeish, Librarian of Congress, and Colonel "Wild Bill" Donovan, head of the OSS, ever spoke to one another. Rex wondered who spoke to Thomas — certainly not Laura Ingalls, his fellow worker from America First days, "because she is in jail as a Nazi agent." Certainly not George Sylvester Viereck — "he is also in jail." Rex summed up: "Read almost any sentence of the script of Mr. Thomas's speech, and you find a falsification, a distortion, or a sneer at the people who are fighting or working to win the war — as nearly all of us are. Some of it is clumsy, some of it is subtle, a little of it is plain loony." As a propagandist Rex was at his best when he could have a go at an opponent bare-knuckled. Sentiment was not his forte.

Along with his duties as chairman of the WWB, Rex worked through Freedom House to carry the propaganda war to the enemy. George Field says: "In those days our work together for the common cause was intensive. Rex was never satisfied with half a measure. He contributed his writing talents and his counsel at meetings of our Executive Committee."[2] One of Rex's major undertakings for Freedom House was writing and conducting a network radio series, "Our Secret Weapon," launched in the summer of 1942.

The idea for the series — the "secret weapon" being truth — originated with Sue Taylor White, whose husband, Paul White, was the head of CBS news. Mrs. White, who previously had written soap operas, was an active member of Freedom House. The program was sponsored jointly by Freedom House and Philco. Research for it was done by the CBS staff, under Paul White's direction, with Sue herself serving as Rex's chief researcher. Hundreds of Axis propaganda broadcasts, beamed not merely to the Allied countries but to neutrals, were sifted weekly — some three hundred thousand words — for the materials used in the programs. Rex himself, for an average of twenty hours a week, pored over the typewritten yellow sheets of accumulated data, which carried such headings as "Rome in French," "Tokyo in English," "German to Africa," and made the final selection of materials for each broadcast. Then, using a dialogue format — Axis commentators making their assertions, and Rex Stout, the lie detective, offering his refutations — he dictated to his secretary the script of the fifteen-minute broadcast. Just once CBS tried to interfere. Rex told me: "We all have satisfactions. One of my little satisfactions? In one of the 'Our Secret Weapon' broadcasts, I made a comment on Colonel McCormick. CBS was determined to take it out. I said I'd quit if they did. To hell with contracts. CBS capitulated. That always pleased me. They're so accustomed to cutting scripts as they please."

Rex was paid $1,200 a week for these broadcasts. He gave back half of it to Freedom House. There were sixty-two broadcasts in all. Initially they were aired on Sunday night from seven to seven-fifteen Eastern

War Time. At the end of ten weeks the program shifted to Friday night at the same hour. That remained its scheduled time till the series ended.

Each week, on request, six thousand copies of Rex's script were sent to colleges, secondary schools, army camps, naval stations, and even Japanese-American "relocation" centers. Moreover, the program was shortwaved to the east and west coasts of South America and to the British Isles.

The broadcasts began on 10 August 1942. On 27 September, a Wide World release discussed the logic of refuting Axis lies in broadcasts made to the American people rather than to the people in foreign countries to whom the Axis was beaming them when our monitors picked them up. "It must be brought to their attention," Rex himself explained, "that these monstrous lies are being told. It must be drawn to their attention so they will know how words are killing men in this war as effectively as guns and tanks and bullets." He stressed also a theme he had been promoting through the WWB:

> The American people must be taught the nature of our enemy in order to eliminate the possibility of a premature peace. . . . The chief difficulty to any peace in this world is not the momentary, spasmodic vices of the Nazis but the inherent anti-democratic traits in the German character. We must understand them in order to convince them that the only way to get along in this world is to cooperate with democracy. If we could convince them by giving each of them a copy of the Declaration of Independence, that would be fine. If we can only convince them by killing twenty million of them, we must do that.

Rex said he feared that Hitler would make a peace offer to the world within six months. "Acceptance of such a peace," he warned, "would probably mean another war in another five years." As the lie detective, Rex used the logic of Nero Wolfe and the idiom of Archie — with due allowances for "Pfui," which turned up in the broadcasts every now and again. Indeed, the Wide World interviewer, watching Rex examine, "with patient curiosity," the scripts of the monitored broadcasts, found him quite Neronian.

On 17 August, Rex told his listeners: "Before Adolf Hitler was ever heard of we swallowed their lies hook, line, and sinker." In the same broadcast, he asked, "When the Nazi says we are apt to be attacked now any minute, and the next day says we are not going to be attacked at all, what am I supposed to do, pick the petals off a daisy?" On 23 August, after reviewing the garbled attack of a German broadcaster, Rex said, "He thought he was beaming it to a bughouse." On 20 September, he spoke in pure Goodwinese: "The Germans have no good bets left. They've raked in all the easy pots and from here on they're drawing to inside straights."

When feasible, "Our Secret Weapon" broadcasts were built around one topic. Thus the 12 September broadcast focused on the Axis radios' recent "Hate Roosevelt Week." On 20 September — Yom Kippur — Nazi anti-Semitism was Rex's theme: "If the Jews controlled one-tenth the things they are accused of, the plastic surgeon would be doing a land-office business building up noses that would make Jimmy Durante's profile look like classic Greek." But the tragedy that had befallen European Jews touched him too deeply to be the topic of a jest. "If anybody makes an anti-Semitic crack at a dining-table where I happen to be a guest — or for that matter, an anti-Negro or anti-Catholic or any similar crack — everybody's digestion is apt to be out of kilter by the time I leave the room."

German youth supplied the theme of another broadcast — 27 September. German radio had boasted that German students were examined by the honor system and never cheated. "How the dickens do they know whether the little darlings cheat or not?" Rex asked. "Either they don't know," he said, "or they train the pupils to snitch on each other, and in either case I'll take vanilla." He could deplore the conditioning of German youth. For their elders he had no pity. "I am willing to grant to any grown German one right and one only — " he told a 6 September audience " — the right to a decent burial."

On the first anniversary of Pearl Harbor, *Newsweek* evaluated the series. Rex was described as making "a business of stripping Axis short-wave propaganda down to the barest nonsensicals." CBS was broadcasting the program coast-to-coast. "Although it's hard work," said *Newsweek*, "the lie detective has fun with his broadcasts scoring 'The Great Axis Jabberwocky.' There's no doubt of its success." But *Newsweek* had some bad news for Wolfe fanciers: "The full-bearded Stout . . . says he won't write any more books about his orchid-growing sleuth, Nero Wolfe, 'until the children get hungry.' "[3]

Rex himself had cause for rejoicing. On 22 November he had gotten confirmation that his broadcasts vexed the Germans. On that date Berlin radio said:

A new propaganda organization has been set up in Washington recently, consisting of some thirty-five hundred American writers, headed by Rex Stout, well-known detective story and pulp magazine writer. Rex Stout himself has cut his own production in detective stories from four to one a year and is devoting the entire balance of his time to writing official war propaganda. Now we have the explanation why so many of the war stories released in Washington have so strong a flavor of Chicago gangsterism.

That gibe about the pulp magazines hurt. Rex was proud he had not entered the field of detective fiction by the *Black Mask* route, as Hammett and Chandler had done. Otherwise, he was elated: "Goodness, I hope these little broadcasts I do aren't annoying Dr. Goebbels. I am a man of goodwill. I wish him the best. I hope he is boiled in the very *best* oil — none of that ersatz stuff."

Berlin radio was right on one point. By writing an annual novella Rex kept the continuity of the Wolfe series intact throughout World War II. In August 1942, during a short holiday at High Meadow, Rex wrote "Not Quite Dead Enough." The next August, again at High Meadow, he wrote "Booby Trap." In June of 1944 he went to High Meadow to write "Help Wanted, Male." Soon after V-J day, in the fall of 1945, he wrote his fifteenth Wolfe story, "Instead of Evidence." Archie had just come out of uniform. Once more Rex was back in stride and Wolfe was back in a world in which he could deal with chaos in digestible doses.

"Not Quite Dead Enough" was published in *The American Magazine* in December 1942, but a year passed between the time "Booby Trap" was written and its publication, in August 1944, in *The American.* Thus, though one was available, no Wolfe story was published in 1943, which made it seem, erroneously, that Rex had broken off the series.

By putting his creations to propaganda uses Rex was able to write these stories without feeling he was euchring the WWB out of its full share of his time. "Not Quite Dead Enough" and "Booby Trap" show Wolfe and Archie supporting their country in wartime — Archie as a major in Military Intelligence, Wolfe as a VIP civilian employee of G-2.[4] "Help Wanted, Male" also deals with one of Wolfe's wartime commissions. In the series only these three stories show Rex in his role as wartime propagandist. But nothing more was required. Admirers found Wolfe fiercely loyal to his adoptive country. Although Archie's record of Wolfe's services in this momentous period is meant merely to hint at his full contribution, we are told enough to know that in this great moment of world peril Wolfe responded nobly. We cannot say "saw his duty clearly" because, in a fit of patriotic fervor, Wolfe at first wanted to kill Germans personally.[5] Only when Army Intelligence assigned Archie the task of convincing him that his country could not wait till he dieted and exercised himself back to fitness did Wolfe put his brains to work on the war. Wolfe gives up his leisure, his plants, his privacy, his larder, and his own business for the duration of the war. He takes no pay for his services. He disciplines his palate to make do without the choice viands and other table luxuries still obtainable through the black market. The one extravagance he insists on is gas for his car. The army sees that he gets it.

Rex's desire to catch Wolfe while he was still in the first flush of indignation at Pearl Harbor — and what a loss to us if he had not done so — caused him to forgo his usual practice of setting a story in a time slot corresponding to the period in which it was being written. The events recounted in "Not Quite Dead Enough" take place in March 1942. They were not set down till five months later.

Another project that Rex became involved in during the summer of 1942 reflected his conviction that FDR was the man best fitted to stand at the head of the American war effort. Late in the spring of 1942, Robert Sherwood had come to Rex with a proposal. Thomas E. Dewey, Republican governor of New York, would be up for reelection in the fall. Roosevelt, eyeing Dewey as a likely rival in 1944, wanted to put him out of contention before he could build further momentum. He asked Sherwood to ask Rex to undertake to persuade Wendell Willkie, Roosevelt's Republican opponent in 1940, to run for governor himself. Roosevelt believed Willkie was popular enough for the party to dump Dewey in his favor.

After meeting twice with Sherwood, Rex agreed to help. A committee to draft Willkie was formed then under the joint chairmanship of Rex and Stanley Rinehart. On 30 June they called a press conference at the Hotel Roosevelt, to announce their intentions. The membership of the committee included John Gunther, Herbert Agar, Raymond S. Fanning, Mrs. Ward Cheney, Mary Lewis, John B. Hughes, and Mrs. Harold Guinzburg.

Willkie offered to meet with Rex and Clifton Fadiman over breakfast, in Washington, in his suite at the Shoreham Hotel, to explore the matter further. The meeting lasted four hours. Willkie ended by agreeing to put himself into the race on one condition — that Roosevelt himself, face to face, ask him to do it. Roosevelt backed off. When Rex and Fadiman got his answer, they saw the game was lost and gave it up. For some time afterward, Russell Davenport and others continued to seek popular support for the idea and to importune Willkie to run. But Rex and Fadiman had read Willkie's mood correctly. Dewey took the nomination unopposed, and two years later carried the Republican standard against Roosevelt when he made his bid for a fourth term.

On 21 September Alfred Knopf published *The Illustrious Dunderheads,* an analysis of congressional isolationists containing succinct rundowns on the voting records of 145 congressmen and 28 senators. Frank Sullivan supplied an introduction. Rex was identified as editor. The attribution was undeserved. "Editors at Knopf and Laura Hobson gathered all of it," Rex told me. His chief contribution was an introductory essay, "The Aims of Nazi Propaganda." Here Rex assigned four principal aims to the Nazi propaganda machine: (1) to destroy faith in the elected government; (2) to destroy the faith of the American people in themselves; (3) to divide America; (4) to divide America from her allies. All these goals were being served, he argued, by men now in Congress. The jacket blurb suggested: "Every one of these Congressmen is a patriot; and everyone of them is a dunderhead." Frank Sullivan, branding them "illustrious dunderheads," said nothing about their patriotism, but deplored their stupidity. Rex showed less charity. Elections were in the offing. The idea was to replace congressional isolationists with men who would work with the administration. "The collapse of France," Rex said, "disclosed that some French politicians had been on the Nazi payroll all along." If a man voted like a traitor, then he either was a traitor or a dupe playing into the hands of those whom traitors served. In either case he did not belong in Congress. So ran Rex's argument.

Of *The Illustrious Dunderheads,* Frank Sullivan told me: "The title was supplied by me and I wrote the preface and that was the extent of my contribution. The only reason I had to think that the book hit its mark and did some good was that it elicited a typically virulent attack from Westbrook Pegler."[6]

In October the New York *World-Telegram* expressed its outrage at *The Illustrious Dunderheads* by describing Rex as a "strife promoter and trouble breeder in wartime." In the November elections many isolationists were turned out of office. For Rex that was the only comment that mattered.

33.

Chairman Rex

Anyone can do the public things Rex did, if he has a kind heart and a
generous spirit. But only one man created Nero, the fat man, and Rex and
Nero are king and emperor.

— LEON EDEL

Demands for its services had been so immediate and abundant that the
Writers' War Board had been compelled, in August 1942, to take bigger
quarters — in the Chanin Building at 122 East Forty-second Street. In
its first year it conceived, commissioned, and placed over eight thousand stories, articles, sketches, brief items, radio scripts, and speeches.
Ultimately it was to produce more than three tons of manuscripts. From
the outset, mindful of its origins, the board gave priority consideration
to appeals from government agencies. Indeed, throughout its existence,
eighty-five percent of its efforts were undertaken for such agencies,
though government funding never went beyond a quarter of its total
expenses. Later an accountant figured that the government got materials from the board at one-eighth of one percent of the market price, a
miracle made possible by authors who donated millions of words without pay, and a staff that volunteered its time.[1]

Inevitably much sifting had to go on so that appeals received could
be dealt with in order of merit. Central to this work were the Wednesday meetings. These began at two and often continued until ten or
eleven at night. Rex here introduced a method which had done much
to advance the fortunes of ETS. He would pose a problem and those
present would toss out a variety of suggestions about how to deal with
it.

"Brainstorming" became a standard technique in American business
later. It was, in fact, Rex's personal method for dealing with his own
problems. In later years his son-in-law would describe the process in
these terms: "In approaching a problem, Rex had a very comprehensive
mind — extremely orderly. He would think of as many facets as he
could, then bring them together and proceed in a stepwise orderly
fashion to solve it. Given any kind of a problem he'd approach it this
same way — even problems outside his own sphere of interests." Few
brainstorming sessions ever have had a more distinguished assortment

of brains to call on than did the WWB's Wednesday sessions. The results affirmed it.

In the spring of 1943, the OWI asked the WWB to help promote United Nations Day, on 14 June. Out of the board's response grew some of its most successful marketing techniques, particularly its editorial and house organ services. With OWI assistance, editorials prepared by Rex, Elmer Rice, and others reached 750 newspapers and 2,600 house organs with a total circulation of 20,000,000. By July the board was ready with its own *Brief House Organ Items,* for which the ETS *Gazette* offered a model.

Despite the volume of work, board members did not stay behind their desks. Rex was available for speeches and debates. Others loosely tied to the board, such as John Gunther and Raymond Swing, back-stopped him. In addition the board offered an assortment of speeches which nonaffiliates could deliver. With well-wrought speeches they were able to reach groups which did not share their convictions. "It is surprising," Rex told one joint session of WWB and OWI personnel, "how much you can get in a speech that is contrary to the opinion of the group hearing it and still have the speech accepted."[2]

The women upon whom Rex had daily dependence constituted an extraordinary company. Margaret Leech Pulitzer, a Pulitzer Prize–winning historian, took a role in all major WWB activities, and, with Rex's active cooperation, served as liaison editor for *Transatlantic* magazine, which was published in Britain and helped foster understanding among the Allies.[3] Katharine Seymour, who chaired the Radio committee, and Jean Ellis Poletti, the wife of a former New York governor, supported the board with their writing skills, as did Rita Halle Kleeman. From Luise Sillcox and Frederica Barach the Board got brilliant organizing support. Mrs. Barach's executive ability rivaled Rex's. She perfectly interpreted and even anticipated his wishes. The staff, the mail, the agendas all were under her supervision. As liaison officer of the OCD and later the OWI, she kept up a smooth flow of the business which passed between these groups and assured efficient handling of joint ventures. Yet Mrs. Barach stood in awe of Rex. "He often put in a twenty-hour day," she says.[4] Many of the confident, capable women who appeared in the Wolfe stories after World War II found their genesis in this group.

In September 1942, James M. Landis came in for some hard words from Rex when the OCD, which Landis headed, made lackluster use of a packaged promotion campaign which the board, at the OCD's invitation, had set up to popularize the "V-home" concept — the household geared to cooperate with the war effort. Rex's ire was aroused also by Admiral King, Chief of Naval Operations, in the fall of 1943, when King suppressed three books on the submarine service. The books, written at the navy's behest, had involved a major expenditure of effort on the part of three WWB writers. King was the loser. Thereafter the board took scant notice of navy requests, sometimes burying them in the *Cartoonist's Bulletin,* the board's equivalent of the sports pages.

Dorothy Rodgers, wife of the composer Richard Rodgers, recalls:

I went to work for the Writers' War Board early in 1942 as the chairman of the committee that supplied the War Department with dramatic material (skits, sketches, blackouts, monologues) to be used by the men in the Armed Forces when professional, i.e. U.S.O., entertainment was unavailable. Although the Army, the Marine Corp. and the Coast Guard all used our material, the Navy had rejected it on the grounds that their men were in the habit of seeking their own entertainment when they were on shore leave, and when they were at sea they were there to work. However, the Chief of Naval Personnel, Admiral Randall Jacobs, thought he would be happy to have a brief résumé of all the material we had on hand for him to file. This was an impossible request to fill because some of the material consisted of one or two minute blackouts and it would have taken forever to make a résumé of some 5,000 pieces of material. I went in to see Rex about this problem and to ask him what my answer to the Chief of Naval Personnel should be. Rex, belligerent Quaker that he was, said, "Tell him to go to hell!" I explained that I didn't think I could write such a letter to this high ranking officer and Rex said, "Don't answer it," which advice I followed.[5]

WWB programs could and did work. The Office of Price Administration, for example, credited the board with a major role in reducing to a trickle the amount of gasoline that flowed into the black market. Mark Van Doren's Books for Bonds Committee launched a series of bond rallies, which raised nearly two hundred million dollars. Joseph Wood Krutch's Special Assignments Committee, from a pool of writers which included Pearl Buck, John Dos Passos, and Robert P. Tristram Coffin, supplied several articles weekly to hundreds of newspapers and magazines. An orientation program sent out fifty speakers a month to East Coast service installations. In 1944 Rex and others met with Senator Robert Taft to protest Taft-sponsored legislation which had resulted in narrow censorship, on political grounds, of reading matter sent to servicemen overseas. When Taft did not relent, the WWB launched a campaign of protest. Public sentiment brought modification of the legislation.

The WWB's propaganda effort was not limited to preparation of editorials, speeches, posters, slogans, educational pamphlets, skits, and fund-raising appeals. Fiction writers, playwrights, poets all placed their creative talents at the board's service. At the request of Rex and Clifton Fadiman, Edna Millay wrote her dramatic poem, *The Murder of Lidice,* which told of the slaughter of a Czech town by the Nazis. It got prime radio time. Clifford Odets and Robert Benchley wrote play scripts for armed forces entertainment. Throughout the war years the board supplied several hundred original scripts to thousands of military units. Edna Ferber's *Lifeboat* followed a merchant ship from the start of its construction in inland America to its wartime role carrying supplies to the war zone. Christopher La Farge wrote a story championing the infantryman; Faith Baldwin, a romance which shed benedictions on the air force. Paul Gallico made a special appeal for a neglected specialty in "Bombardier." In this area, in fact, the WWB overextended itself. A novel, 12 short stories, 52 articles, 24 syndicated columns, 3 broadcasts, a handbook, and a song, "I Wanna Marry a Bombardier," which made the Hit Parade, told the story so aptly that the air force was swamped with applications from men wanting to be air cadets, navigators, bombardiers, and tail gunners. Even Inspector Cramer's son (in *Not Quite Dead Enough*, page 74) became a bombardier. The force had to ask the board to desist.

The Women's Army Corps was boosted by scripts prepared by Carl Sandburg, Russel Crouse, Katharine Brush, and Carl Carmer. WAC commander Oveta Culp Hobby said that nothing done by others for her corps came close to the board's contribution. Still, recruitment fell below needs. This uncharacteristic failure piqued Rex, who neither accepted failure nor, in truth, had much experience of it. When he asked John Marquand for his opinion of the problem, Marquand said the corps would get nowhere until it had better officers who could maintain better discipline.[6]

Most of the help Marquand gave the board came in the first eight months of its existence. He got to the meetings every other week. But he saw his role mostly as liaison between the board and the Treasury Department. In May 1942, when it appeared that Julian Street was afraid of the board's autonomy, Marquand had agreed to probe for the board and had invited another Treasury man, Ferdy Kuhn, to confer with them. Marquand told Rex: "I think you can talk to him frankly, always underlining the fact that you are not making any criticism against Pete Street. Pete and Ferdy are old friends and their wives picked daisies together at Vassar, or whatever they do at that institution."[7] Rex handled Kuhn with circumspection and lines of communication were reopened.

Between the two world wars Rex had read a shelf of books on the Germans and conceived a mortal antipathy toward pan-Germanism. During World War II he made full call on this antipathy to shape WWB policy. Most people supposed wars were the work of a few politicians and profiteers. The board, under Rex's prodding, took on a major assignment, therefore, when it sought to convince Americans that blame for Hitler rested on the German people themselves. No one issue involving the board was so controversial.

One of the first things the board did to deepen animosity toward the Germans was to focus attention on book banning and burning in Germany. At Rex's bidding, Stephen Vincent Benét prepared a radio drama which NBC broadcast during prime evening time on 11 May 1942, to mark the ninth anniversary of the major book-burning that followed Hitler's accession to power. Encore broadcasts followed in the United States and overseas, and Farrar & Rinehart published the script as a book. Complementing the Benét material was a second script, "The Nature of the Enemy," prepared by NBC's Orin Tovrov, and released to two hundred and ten stations. Tovrov bore down hard on the theme of collective guilt.[8] Rex himself reinforced this emphasis with talks before the Council on Books in Wartime and the annual convention of the American Booksellers Association.

The success of the May 10th Book Burning Committee was followed up at once. The next month, at the instigation of Alan Green and under Fadiman's chairmanship, the Lidice Committee was formed to arouse, not sympathy, but "the emotion of horror to be followed by the emotion of anger." A second committee, the Lidice Lives Committee, under the general chairmanship of Joseph E. Davies, enlisted as sponsors nearly one hundred and twenty world citizens, including Albert Einstein, Eduard Beneš, Maxim Litvinov, Jo Davidson, William O. Douglas, Carl Sandburg, Thomas Mann, André Maurois, Lion Feuchtwanger, Lord Halifax, and Jan Masaryk, as well as Rex and such dependables as Edna Millay, Lewis Gannett, Louis Adamic, Booth Tarkington, and Carl and Mark Van Doren. The message was sped home. The names of towns and lakes from Canada to Brazil were changed to Lidice. The culminating act of the campaign was Millay's *Murder of Lidice,* which was aired over NBC on 19 October 1942, with Woollcott and Fadiman presiding, and Paul Muni declaiming the lines. Shortwaved to England, and to South America in Spanish and Portugese translations, it stirred a high emotional response. *Variety's* reviewer thought it was "the most eloquent piece of righteous wrath heard on this side of the ocean in the war." It had, he said, "the intensity of a blast furnace." The word *Lidice* became as a synonym for wanton destruction.

Two weeks later, when Rex and Fadiman summed up the work of the Lidice Committee at a P.E.N. Club dinner, they got into a shouting match with Henry Seidel Canby and Arthur Garfield Hayes. The historian and the champion of civil liberties were understandably wary about indicting a whole people. If Hitler was wrong and there was no master race, then it was just as difficult to believe that the German people were collectively tainted. Others, too, were uneasy about the direction WWB propaganda was taking. Rex's old adversary, Carl Friedrich, writing in *The New York Times,* deplored the "highly dramatized and emotionalized messages of hate" which radio was carrying to

Americans everywhere. He advocated a war waged without hatred of the Germans. Without hating them we could rid ourselves of them, like weeds in a cornfield.

In October 1942, Rex was elected president of the Friends of Democracy, succeeding Louis Bromfield. In his new role he was immediately in the news when he spoke at a meeting at the Hotel Pierre on 5 November, pledging an active fight against those advocating postwar friendship with the Axis powers. "If that happens," he said, "we will have the job to do all over again in perhaps twenty years or so." William L. White and Struthers Burt, who shared the platform with Rex, reiterated his views.

Arguing that it was illogical to want to kill Germans unless we hated them, in "We Shall Hate, or We Shall Fail," written for *The New York Times Magazine* at the request of Lester Markel, and published on 17 January 1943, Rex presented a formal rebuttal to Friedrich and those others who had disputed the WWB's nature-of-the-enemy posture. We had to hate those who sought to destroy basic human values:

> The hate I am talking about is a feeling toward the Germans of deep and implacable resentment for their savage attack upon the rights and dignity of man, of loathing for their ruthless assault on the persons and property of innocent and well-meaning people, of contempt for their arrogant and insolent doctrine of the German master race. . . .

Only by following that painful road could we assure restoration of that society in which the values we cherish could flourish:

> There never will be a world in which there is nothing and no one that is hateful. But it can be better than it is if we are sufficiently resolved to make it better. That resolution can be strong enough for its job only if it has emotional maturity and support in an uncompromising hatred for those evils with which there can be no truce, and for the people who are the champions of those evils, or the servants of the champions.

"We Shall Hate, or We Shall Fail" is one of the most closely argued pieces Rex ever wrote. "I worked it over with care," Rex assured me. The admission was unprecedented. His point of view, he argued, had the merits of consistency. What was consistent about British pilots toasting downed German pilots with the words "May the best man win!"? Or about Kentish villagers burying German fliers in swastika-covered coffins? Chivalry and sentiment were absurd when the values of whole societies were at stake, and millions of men and women were being herded into gas ovens or killed by nonstrategic air attacks and targetless bombs.

Letters rebuking Rex poured in to the *Times*. On 31 January, Walter

Russell Bowie, professor of practical theology at Union Theological Seminary, offered a formal rebuttal, "Hate is Moral Poison." Rex replied on 4 February: "There was nothing ugly about the fierce light that blazed in the eyes of Joan of Arc and she called the emotion behind it by its right name, she called it hate." Rex did not object later when Nero Wolfe dismissed the Maid of Orleans as "an inspired hoyden," but here he appears to be her staunch admirer.[9] In the controversy he was engaged in he found her standard useful to march behind.

The day Bowie made his reply, John Haynes Holmes preached at the Community Church on the topic "If We Hate, We Shall Fail!" Holmes contended that Rex Stout, though "patriotic and sincere," was "a public danger" because he did not realize that "the source of heroism is love." If Rex remembered that Joan of Arc also was brought to trial by ecclesiastics, he prudently refrained from pointing up the parallel. The *Times* laid the dispute to rest with a tactful letter from Pearl Buck. Mrs. Buck suggested that some men need to feel a personal, vindictive hatred, to be good soldiers, and that Rex was one of these. Others, she said, had to feel impersonal. Each had to follow his bent.

At the start of "We Shall Hate, or We Shall Fail" Rex acknowledged respect for the consistent Christian who held to the twin imperatives that we must not kill and we must love our enemies — though "human defects and stupidities" made it difficult to attain those ideals. But he thought it "sanctimonious double talk" to split these imperatives, to support one while rejecting the other. He felt Bowie and Holmes ignored this dilemma.

"A man may commit what is undoubtedly a sin, but may himself not be sinful at all," Holmes had said. Perhaps the evildoer behaved as he did because he was "physically depressed, or mentally unbalanced, or stupid, perverted, or ignorant, or . . . dominated by a strange sense of duty." As a writer of crime fiction, Rex already had come to some firm conclusions about the extent of human culpability. He did not agree with William Ernest Hocking, as John Holmes did, that evildoers were merely misfits. Georges Simenon, the creator of Inspector Maigret, would write, in 1960: "For thirty years I have tried to make it understood that there are no criminals."[10] Nero Wolfe wastes no tears on those whom he brings to justice. Rex Stout's views on how to handle the Germans came from no sudden sense of outrage. They were an extension of his views on free will and responsibility as applied to individuals and as illustrated in his detective fiction. When Rex said, "A man who tells you he hates evil but not the doer of evil is kidding either you or himself and in any case is gibbering," Nero Wolfe himself might be speaking.

When Aleck Woollcott had had his gallbladder out at University Hospital, Syracuse, in March 1942, Rex had sent him a note of cheer. What pleased Woollcott most, however, was the salutation, "Dear Nero." Did that mean that Woollcott indeed was Wolfe's prototype? "No," Rex told me, "I said it because I knew he'd like it."

Aleck's illness had taken a valuable man out of the firing line. Thus Rex was delighted when Aleck got back into action in the summer, and in October hosted the Lidice broadcast. In December, when the WWB began laying plans to "dis-celebrate" on 30 January 1943, the tenth anniversary of Hitler's seizure of power in Germany, Aleck agreed to do a piece on the subject for *Reader's Digest.* Rex followed this up with an invitation to Aleck to dis-celebrate further in a panel discussion of Richard Brickner's *Is Germany Incurable?* the discussion to be broadcast nationwide, on CBS's "The People's Platform," on Saturday, 23 January, from seven to seven-thirty P.M. When he called to accept, Aleck, then staying at the Gotham, asked Rex if Pola and he would join him at Voisin's, on the seventeenth, for an intimate prebirthday dinner. He was going to be fifty-six on the nineteenth. At the dinner they had a lively topic. That morning "We Shall Hate, or We Shall Fail" had appeared in the *Times.* Both men savored the prospect of the controversy sure to follow. By the coming weekend the storm could be breaking overhead. That would mean a bigger audience before which to air their views on "People's Platform."

Only one thing dimmed the pleasure of their evening together. Aleck daily was giving ground to arteriosclerosis. Though his weight had dropped sharply from its peak of two hundred and fifty-five pounds, frequent angina attacks had brought him to a state of near-invalidism. Yet he could not wholly forsake his gourmet tastes — certainly not in the presence of the creator of Nero Wolfe. Escargots bourguignonne, a good white wine, lemon-sherry pudding, and a liqueur — he omitted nothing, except a second cup of coffee. "I'm under promise to get back to the hotel alive," he explained.

At noon on 23 January, Woollcott lunched with DeWitt Wallace of *Reader's Digest* and his wife. On his return to the Gotham, he had Jo Hennessey — his faithful "Archie" — send a dozen yellow roses to Mrs. Wallace. At five that same afternoon, novelist Marcia Davenport got a call from Rex. She was needed as a replacement for Dorothy Thompson, who had been felled by the flu. The other panelists, Rex explained, would be Harry D. Gideonse, president of Brooklyn College, George N. Shuster, president of Hunter College, Woollcott, and himself.

Marcia thought she could handle the topic. She was not so sure she could handle Woollcott. In her adolescence she had had several harrowing encounters with Aleck, who had visited her home as the guest of her mother (Metropolitan Opera diva Alma Gluck) and stepfather (violinist Efrem Zimbalist, Sr.). Woollcott specialized in baiting teenagers. His needling of Marcia had continued in the pages of *The New Yorker,* where he wrote corrosive reviews of her books. She knew about his poor health and was afraid he might find her presence exacerbating. Rex told her to stand by. In a few moments he was back on the line. Aleck had no objections to appearing with her on the program. Within half an hour Marcia joined the others at the studio. It was a comfortable setting for Woollcott, the scene of his radio triumphs as Town Crier. Dinner was served in the studio's private dining room, with the mikes in place. Table talk would lead right into the broadcast with only Gideonse, who was in the chair, knowing just when the mikes went live.

Woollcott ate heavily, and when George Shuster said the German people could not be blamed for what the Nazis were doing, roared his protest. Even though this was Rex's cue to reaffirm the views he proffered in the *Times*, for Aleck's sake he tried to move the conversation to a cooler area. Woollcott's color was rising and his tongue getting rasp-edged. He asked for and got a second cup of coffee. As he sipped it, his body stiffened with tension. When he set down the half-emptied cup, Rex slid it out of his reach. Aleck nodded his reluctant acquiescence and seemed to muster his forces to go on. But a change of topics did not help matters. Marcia's books fell under his whiplash. Marcia remembers: "I was no longer my mother's frightened little girl. I told him to forget old scores and stop being beastly and aim his venom at Hitler instead of me." Before Woollcott could coil and strike, the signal was given and the private dinner party became a live network panel show.

On cue, each of the guests gave a brief, provocative response to the panel's topic, "Is Germany Incurable?" Rex held to his hard line. Shuster demurred and so did Marcia. She had to, to keep the panel in balance. But there was the bonus advantage of pitting herself against Woollcott. Possibly she had trouble hating the Germans. She had none hating Woollcott. Thirty-two years later she showed no sign of relenting. She said: "I did not think Aleck Woollcott was gallant or admirable in any way whatever; and I knew him and loathed him for some twenty-five years. He was a monster."[11]

For a while after the broadcast, Marcia used to tell people that she had killed Woollcott.[12] Certainly her antagonism was no balm to the critic's nerves. Rex watched him with growing horror. Woollcott seemed to be in actual pain, but he held to the format of the program and did nothing to suggest a crisis had come. He spoke: "The German people are as guilty of Hitler as the people of Chicago are of the Chicago *Tribune.*" Though he spat the words out firmly, his frame began to vibrate, as if his exertion had shattered him. He seemed to undulate in his chair. He clutched at a pencil and on the paper before him scrawled in large letters, "I'm feeling sick. Carry on."[13] He raised the sheet for Rex and Gideonse to see. When they started to get up, he gestured disapproval with his eyes. The program continued to the halfway point. Rex's distress grew as he watched Woollcott's struggle. He wanted to interrupt the broadcast. "I wasn't as brave about it as Aleck," he told me. Aleck's chair scraped back. He slumped toward the microphone. In an instant the strapping Gideonse had hefted Woollcott from his chair and, bracing him, nearly carrying him, got him from the room. "I'm dying," Woollcott whispered. A nurse's aide took over, and Gideonse, at Woollcott's insistence, rejoined the panel. Immediately after the broadcast, Rex came to Aleck's side. Prone on a couch and all but unconscious, Aleck repeated in his ear, "The German people are as guilty of Hitler as the people of Chicago are of the Chicago *Tribune.*" Four hours later, at Roosevelt Hospital, Woollcott was dead of a cerebral hemorrhage. Before midnight, Paul White, head of CBS news, called Rex at East Eighty-sixth Street to tell him Aleck was gone.

Rex would have carried on as he did even if there had been no Woollcott. Yet, in the days ahead, as strife over his German position mounted, there was comfort in remembering that Woollcott, his would-be Nero, had died upholding him. Rex's twenty-first Wolfe tale, *And Be a Villain* (1948), concerns the death of a panelist during a live coast-to-coast radio show. In two other Wolfe stories, *The Silent Speaker* (1946) and "Fourth of July Picnic" (1958), death strikes as speakers are about to address audiences. In the latter story, after confronting a corpse, Wolfe goes through with his commitment to deliver a speech. Rex made such scenes evocative. As well he might. He knew the drama of such a moment.[14]

34.

Hunting with the Hounds

Rex Stout has done something very rare in his novels. He has created an on-going mini-world, a sealed-off chamber as distinct from our world as Middle Earth. Having his own mirror universe to play with, godlike, gives him a confidence and a field of action the rest of us can only envy from a distance.

Stout is a far better writing craftsman than Doyle, and a much more scrupulously fair *mystery* writer. Beyond that, the Holmes-Watson world was rather smaller and rather fuzzier at the fringes than the Wolfe-Goodwin world; I almost think, for instance, that I would recognize Orrie Cather on the street, and of what secondary Holmes character could one have the same feeling?

— DONALD WESTLAKE

Would YOU Sign This Letter? — a thirty-two page pamphlet exposing German fifth-column activities in the Americas — was published in March 1943. Written by two German-born critics of pan-Germanism, F. W. Foerster and T. H. Tetens, and vigorously endorsed in an introduction signed by Rex Stout and Quentin Reynolds, it documented the WWB's nature-of-the-enemy campaign.[1] One of the pamphlet's targets was Victor F. Ridder, editor and publisher of the New York *Staatszeitung.* On 13 October 1943, the Chicago *Tribune,* reporting on "smear books, especially of the poison pen pamphlet variety," told readers that the outraged Ridder had filed a charge of criminal complaint against Foerster, Tetens, Reynolds, and Stout. Through William L. Chenery, editor of *Collier's,* Reynolds denied ever having seen the pamphlet. He had authorized use of his name because he thought it was a WWB publication. Rex went to see New York County's fire-eating district attorney, Frank S. Hogan, and convinced him that the evidence offered in the pamphlet could be substantiated. Hogan refused to prosecute, and Ridder's counsel was compelled to withdraw the complaint.

On 21 March, in "Books and the Tiger," a review article written for *The New York Times Book Review,* Rex examined several books that did or did not come to grips with the nature of the enemy. He concluded that too few delivered the facts. He took occasion here also to stress the contribution an exact use of language could make toward winning the war. He dismissed the phrase "the war effort" as "infelicitous and repugnant." He said "war job" had more force. Conquered territories were not "German-occupied" but "German-enslaved." Germans did not "execute" civilians, they "murdered" them. The Allies did not "kill" Germans, they "exterminated" them. These verbal substitutions would, of course, bolster the WWB's nature-of-the-enemy campaign.

Rex was advancing the campaign on other fronts too. He inspired a letter onslaught carried out by prominent writers — Maugham, Channing Pollock, Millay, Tarkington, John Gunther — protesting to the press that too many stories favorable to the German people were being published. Together with Paul Gallico and Clifton Fadiman he launched "Operation Radar," a propaganda comic strip which placed stress on collective German guilt. He also made a record, "Are There Any Home-Grown Fascists?" Sent to radio stations throughout the United States, it warned that we would never get "a decent and workable world" if we compromised with the Germans. Rex was nothing if not thorough.

If the nature-of-the-enemy campaign looked ahead to the postwar world, so did some of Rex's other activities at this time. On 8 June 1943, Avon Book Company asked Rex to lend his name and editorial help to a new periodical. In 1942 Avon had acquired paperback rights to *The League of Frightened Men, The Rubber Band,* and *The Red Box* and had found that the books sold well to "a very wide audience." Their *Rex Stout's Mystery Monthly* would be printed in runs no smaller than one hundred thousand copies. Rex consulted with Farrar & Rinehart and on 5 December became the editor of the *Rex Stout Mystery Quarterly,* as it was now called. He had agreed to write an introduction for each issue. The contents, subject to Rex's approval, were to be chosen by a managing editor, Louis Greenfield, one of the Baker Street Irregulars.

This periodical had a short, adventurous life. As a quarterly it appeared twice in 1945, in May and August. In 1946 it came out five times — in February, March, June, October, and December. With its third issue it became the *Rex Stout Mystery Magazine.* With issue number five it became *Rex Stout Mystery Monthly.* With the next issue, for a final title change, an " 's" was added to "Stout." Thus the magazine achieved at long last the identity originally proposed for it. The publishers, however, were better at producing title changes than producing issues. Issue number eight did not appear till May 1947. The ninth and final issue, also dated 1947, was monthless.[2]

As the editor of this magazine Rex refrained from using his position to propagandize on favorite topics. In the October 1946 issue he made an oblique reference to a story "with, heaven help us, five good Germans," but he seemed to be joshing merely, not offering a rebuke. The one true salvo he did fire was aimed at Edmund Wilson. In several essays written in the years 1944–1945, Wilson had dismissed detective fiction as subliterary, ridiculing Christie, Hammett, Sayers, Allingham, and Rex Stout. Wilson confessed, "I rather enjoyed Wolfe himself, with his rich dinners and quiet evenings in his house in farthest West Thirty-fifth Street, where he savors an armchair sadism that is always accompanied by beer." He conceded also that Rex "has created, after a fashion, Nero Wolfe and Archie Goodwin, and has made some attempt at characterization of the people that figure in the crimes." He thought, too, that *The League of Frightened Men* makes use of a clever psychological idea. . . ." But rescission at once ensued: "I had to unpack large crates by swallowing the excelsior in order to find at the bottom a few bent and rusty nails. . . . I even began to mutter that the real secret that Author Rex Stout had been screening by his false scents and interminable divagations was a meagreness of imagination of which one only came to realize the full ghastliness when the last chapter had left one blank."[3]

Rex ignored Wilson's comment but did not forget it. In February 1946, he told *Rex Stout Mystery Magazine* readers about Wilson's problem of getting his high brow caught in the telephone wires when he went for a walk in the country. He expanded on this point later that same year in an introduction written for *Rue Morgue No. 1*, a hardcover collection of mysteries which he coedited with Louis Greenfield:

A good deal of the current irritation in certain quarters with writers of mysteries . . . appears to be based on a resentment of the fact that they do not instead try their hands at another *Hamlet* or *Divine Comedy*. . . . A poet or a philosopher can write about life and death, but only a storyteller can write about *this* life and *this* death. Not only is there no occasion for comparison; there is no basis for one.[4]

Thirty years later, remembering Wilson's scornful dismissal of *The League of Frightened Men*, P. G. Wodehouse said:

I suppose, now that Edmund Wilson is dead, one has to be guarded in commenting on him, so I will merely say that in my opinion he was too pompous and self-satisfied and much too inclined to call any writer whom he did not like "second rate." Somerset Maugham, for instance.

I can't remember if he called Stout second rate, but in every other way he showed his haughty distaste for him and in doing so — again in my opinion — made a fool of himself and revealed his own limitations as a critic. He made it plain that he was incapable of recognizing good writing if the writer was working in a field of which he disapproved.[5]

The nine introductions which Rex wrote for the Rex Stout magazines contain little close critical theorizing of the sort Wilson relished. Yet insights are there. In the October 1946 introduction, Rex wrote:

The establishment in public favor of a Wimsey or a Poirot depends on the plot and narrative of the stories in which they appear. But Homer, even nodding, is still Homer; and Poirot, even on a dull case and doing a routine and uninspired job, is still Poirot. It is actually a pleasure to be with him when he is a little off tone and by no means brilliant; it shows that he is human.

This observation applies as well to Holmes and Wolfe. Holmes in a funk. Wolfe with the sulks. To have neither would be an impoverishment.

Even as Rex continued his weekly Friday night "Our Secret Weapon" broadcasts over CBS at eight-thirty P.M., he began to reach a second and different audience over the ABC network, at the same hour, on Monday nights. At the urging of Himan Brown, Rex had agreed to a summer Nero Wolfe series, "The Adventures of Nero Wolfe." The episodes were thirty minutes long and each story was complete. Louis Vittes was the chief script writer and wrote most of the scripts. None of Rex's story material was used. All characters besides Wolfe, Archie, and Cramer were ABC's own. For the use of Wolfe and Archie, Rex received a weekly royalty. He was not consulted on the scripts, nor did he wish to be. He had no time for that.

Santos Ortega played Wolfe. John Gibson was Archie. Gibson was breezy and Ortega wheezy — indeed, he opened the program with a wheeze, as his signature. One night Rex brought Barbara and Rebecca to the studio to see the broadcast. They were fascinated at the frail Ortega's ability to "sound fat." Rex thought the actors were creditable but winced at the plots. He never listened to the broadcasts.

The series was a success. Sponsored by Williams Shaving Cream, it ran for thirteen weeks, from 5 July to 27 September 1943, when ABC resumed its winter programing. On 18 February 1944 it was revived and continued with the same script writer and cast for another twenty-one episodes. This second run ended on 14 July 1944. Differences between Hi Brown and Edwin Fadiman, who represented Rex's radio, screen, and television interests, as Nero Wolfe Attractions, Inc., prevented its later resumption on ABC. This fact Brown regretted. "Nero Wolfe," Brown says, "is one of the strongest and most successful detective characters in all of fiction."[6]

The series next surfaced early in 1946, on Sundays, on the Mutual Network, with Francis X. Bushman, one-time movie idol, as Wolfe, and Elliot Lewis as Archie. Jergens Lotion sponsored this series, now entitled "The Amazing Nero Wolfe." It signed off on 15 December. The scripts once again were network originals. The humor verged on slapstick. As Wolfe, Bushman seemed pontifical. Ortega's Wolfe had been sardonic. Yet each was, in his own way, commendable. A greater disparity separated the Archies. John Gibson's Archie was both forthright and poised. Too much roughneck showed in Elliot Lewis's version of the role.

For an armed forces rebroadcast of an ABC episode, the announcer had been Peter Lorre. Lorre's long-time partner in crime, Sydney Greenstreet, turned up as the third and last radio Nero Wolfe on an NBC series, "The New Adventures of Nero Wolfe," which Edwin Fadiman produced. This series was launched on 10 October 1950, shifting, at midyear, from Fridays to Sundays. Twenty-five episodes were aired before it ended on 27 April 1951. Rex thought Greenstreet a splendid choice for the role and Greenstreet did, in fact, fill every reasonable expectation. The wryness of Wolfe, for which Archie's drollery is a whetstone, was not felt in the Ortega or Bushman interpretations. Greenstreet caught it. As in the books themselves, interest centered on the characterizations, not the plots. To manage this in a half-hour radio drama was near sorcery. Greenstreet's subtle understanding of his role was responsible.[7]

Gerald Mohr, the gushing Archie who introduced the series with such effusive statements as "My boss is the smartest and the stubbornest, the fattest and the laziest, the cleverest and the craziest, the most extravagant detective in the world," has to be heard to be believed. A brigade of Archies followed Mohr. An angry Herb Ellis. A needling Larry Dobson. An earnest Wally Maher. An assured Everett Sloane. And Wolfe was always so broke he could not even pay the grocer unless he took a case.

The Mutual series also had overflowing introductions: "It's the detective genius who rates the knife and fork the greatest tools ever invented by man . . . the ponderous, brilliant, and unpredictable Nero Wolfe" — but consigned them to announcers, sparing Archie that ordeal. Yet Alfred Bester's dialogue was superb. Bester was an authentic Nerophile, and it showed.

Radio found three outstanding Nero Wolfes, but none of the scripts was perfect. Hi Brown's came closest. Louis Vittes knew the novels and respected the formula within which Rex Stout worked. His Wolfe did not gallivant as the others sometimes did — to satisfy the audience's insatiable demands for action. And Archie often narrated the story. If only Greenstreet had been on Brown's team.

In 1943 Rex's courtroom encounters were not confined to the adventures of his fictional characters. In August he was named, with Leon Birkhead, as codefendant in a million-dollar libel suit brought by Merwin K. Hart of Utica. A Friends of Democracy pamphlet, published in July, had characterized Hart as "an American Quisling." In their defense, Rex and Birkhead argued that Hart had been "a pro-Nazi, pro-Axis propagandist following the Quisling line." The State Supreme

Court ruled in their favor. And on 18 June 1944, the Appellate Court upheld the higher court's judgment.

Rex remembered another incident that took place in the summer of 1943 as an experience much more painful to him personally than Hart's initiation of his suit. He told me: "In August, at lunch with Geoffrey Crowther, editor of *The London Economist,* I argued heatedly about postwar economics, and of course was smothered. . . . I made an ass of myself."[8] Rex had little experience of blundering into error. His vulnerability affirmed the range of his commitments. He could not be thorough in all things.

Yet one of Rex's obligations, at least, was diminishing in urgency. The Axis powers had come to the end of their successes and the propaganda advantage had passed to the Allies. In "Our Secret Weapon" scripts Rex romped as he exposed the efforts of Axis propagandists to hide their growing catastrophe. On 11 June, he said: "Before our soldiers ever get a glimpse of the beautiful Rhine, they will be met with a weird spectacle, a bunch of Germans . . . waving white flags, and shouting, 'Comrade! Hurrah for the Four Freedoms! Brother can you spare a dime?' "[9] On 6 August, Rex told listeners that the Japanese were calling American bombers "coconut harvesters" because all they did was shake the coconuts off the trees during their bomb strikes. "Flying ovens" will follow soon, Rex promised, "delivering the finished product to the Japs in the shape of coconut pie."[10] Amid the gibes, Rex planted an admonition. General Pietro Badoglio had succeeded to power in Italy. That did not mean that democracy had returned to Italy. Nor would a German Badoglio mean a democratic Germany. The true obstacle would remain: "The lust for conquest, the blood-thirstiness, the master race lunacy, of the German people." Rex was holding on tenaciously to his nature-of-the-enemy thesis.

When Italy surrendered and Rome Radio, one of the chief Axis propaganda outlets, ceased broadcasting, the war moved into another phase. At that juncture CBS decided that "Our Secret Weapon" had served its purpose, and the series was terminated. On his final broadcast, on 8 October 1943, Rex quoted several contradictory Axis broadcasts which showed that even the enemy had no idea where Mussolini had set up his government-in-exile. The German radio had reported that Americans intended to exhibit Mussolini in chains, at the Metropolitan Opera House, if they captured him. Rex thought it a pity that visitors in town for the World Series had missed such a spectacle. He ended his sixty-two weeks of uninterrupted broadcasts with a sudden inversion of emphasis. Tokyo Radio had said that week, "The power of the enemy does not show any evidence of decline." The wares Rex had dealt in had been Axis lies. How salubrious it was, he observed now, that the enemy was at last reporting the truth.[11]

Radio, of course, continued to have a claim on Rex's services. On the "Wake Up America" program, on 23 October, he took on the topic "Does Any National Emergency Justify a Fourth Term?" The presidential election was a year in the future, but Roosevelt's critics already were trying to weaken him by ruling out another term for him. Rex stood by Roosevelt. "This, in my opinion," he said, "is a loaded question. . . . It presupposes that a fourth term is an especially bad-smelling and bad-tasting dose of medicine, and we should pinch our noses and gulp it down only if we are awfully sick. But I don't get that." He scoffed at the "mystical danger of continuing any man whatever in that high office beyond an arbitrary fixed period." He saw any limitation on the number of terms a President could serve as "undemocratic . . . an effort to remove a high and important decision from a direct expression of the will of the people, registered by their ballots."[12]

The very next night, such are the spins of fortune's wheel, Rex chatted on amiable terms with the man who had done his best, three years earlier, to deny Roosevelt a third term: Wendell Willkie. The occasion was the presentation, by Willkie, to Walter Lippmann of the first annual Freedom Award made by Freedom House, an award through which Freedom House "was seeking to embody in the person of a man the issue that was of greatest concern to mankind at a given moment of history." Rex had been an originator of the award and was a determining voice in the choice of the recipient, as he would be in the years ahead when the award would be given, in turn (at one of the largest and most perfectly run dinners in any New York season) to Eisenhower, Baruch, Marshall, Acheson, Churchill, Spaak, Brandt, Truman, Johnson, and Warren.[13] Archibald MacLeish confirms that Rex's hopes for the award have been faithfully adhered to: "The awards which Freedom House has made have been awards to men who, in one way or another, and sometimes at great cost to themselves, loved human liberty and acted out of their passion."

In December, as 1943 drew to a close, Rex lay abed with pneumonia. "My temperature was one hundred and five degrees the afternoon the ambulance took me to the Harkness Pavilion," Rex told me. He was hospitalized for two weeks.

His vitality had gone at a dear price. Nineteen forty-three had been for him a year of accomplishments and satisfactions as well as pressures and hard work. On 7 May there had been the heartbreak of Walt's death, at sixty. The gathering at Ridgewood, where five of the family now lay buried, brought with it a new sense of the transiency of human existence.[14]

That year Rex had found his involvement in the Authors' League and the Authors' Guild growing. In November 1942 he had been elected to the Guild Council. A year later he was elected to a three-year term as

Guild president. That same year he was wooed by the League of American Writers. He was a member only briefly when he realized it was a Communist front, and quit on the spot — a fact that got him on the League's hate list. Through the year he continued to chair the WWB, his enthusiasm and zeal giving impetus to its programs on a hundred fronts. And he had done more than forty "Our Secret Weapon" broadcasts. There had been small time for recreation. With Margaret Leech Pulitzer he had gone a few times to sessions of the Algonquin wits. He knew F.P.A. and playwrights Marc Connelly and George S. Kaufman, and liked them. Yet he confessed, "They were all trying so hard to be witty that it was a kind of a bore." Margaret recalled that, usually fuming, Rex took a few minutes every day to read his secretary's copy of the New York *Daily News*. "He wouldn't be seen buying it himself," she said.[15]

Even FDR could not coax Rex to take a night off. At Roosevelt's request Rex made several visits to Washington to confer with him. One day Rex lunched again with him at Hyde Park.[16] But twice he declined invitations to White House receptions.

Behind Rex's back the staff of the WWB tried to relieve him of routine phases of his work. Selma Jerskey Greenstein, a WWB secretary, confessed to Rex in 1971: "I developed a new talent while there — forgery. I used to be able to copy your signature so well that even you didn't know."[17]

In this same period Rex let himself be fingerprinted by the federal government. This was the first time Rex ever had seen fingerprinting done. He did not find the process dehumanizing. Having once collected William Howard Taft's palm prints, he felt he owed the government a set of fingerprints. Yet he doubted that the FBI would find in his prints as much character as he had found in Taft's.

35.

Ideological Racketeer

Come, mark them down with a big black zero
Who don't love Archie, Rex, and Nero.

— PHYLLIS MCGINLEY

In the spring of 1944, Rex helped form the Society for the Prevention of World War III, Inc., a group founded by the Belgian refugee and long-time foe of Nazism Isidore Lipschutz, who, throughout the society's twenty-eight-year existence, would be its chief financial backer. Leon Birkhead, Walter D. Edmonds, Christopher La Farge, William L. Shirer, Booth Tarkington, Mark Van Doren, and Clifton Fadiman agreed to serve as the new society's Advisory Council. Rex himself was chosen as president. As its first official act, leaving no doubt as to why it had been called into existence, the society recorded itself in favor of limiting Germany's economic structure so that it could never begin another war.

On 22 April, acting for the society, Rex placed an ad in *The New York Times* in which he deplored the news that that night a group would meet in Manhattan to form "a so-called council of democratic Germans in this country." For good measure, Rex reprinted the ad in May in the first issue of *Prevent World War III*, the society's monthly bulletin.

The previous January, the journal *Common Sense* had rebuked Rex as the instigator of a campaign to "sub-humanize" the Germans. To *Common Sense* the SPWW3 ad was the last straw. Rex had gone too far. He had launched a "monstrous assault on human rights."[1] In its June issue, *Common Sense* published letters from Henry Seidel Canby, John P. Marquand, Frederick Lewis Allen, Granville Hicks, Alfred Kazin, Quincy Howe, William L. White, Babette Deutsch, Muriel Rukeyser, and Max Eastman, collectively deploring Rex's hard peace policy. Only Struthers Burt, Mark Van Doren, and Elmer Davis upheld him.[2]

Inevitably this powerful indictment led to repercussions at the WWB. The board's working committee asked Rex and Clifton Fadiman to prepare a position paper on the topic "What to Do about Germany." Although the committee was demanding, and the statement was revised severely before it was submitted to the board's Advisory Council,

Dorothy Thompson, then president of Freedom House, immediately protested espousal of the pan-Germanic thesis. In her opinion the SPWW3 had annexed the WWB and was using it for its own propaganda purposes. A showdown was not long in coming.

On 12 June, Mark Van Doren teamed up with Rex to debate with Dorothy Thompson and Louis Fischer at Town Hall, on the topic "What Policy toward the Defeated Reich Offers the Best Guarantee of a Democratic Germany and a Peaceful Europe?" The debate had been arranged by the Committee for a Democratic Foreign Policy, with Quincy Howe moderating, and was anything but peaceful. When Dorothy Thompson suggested that flaws in the social and political structure of the Allied nations, as well as Germany, had brought on the war, a portion of the audience accused her of trying to free Germans of all war guilt. Other segments of the audience believed Rex and Mark were "seeking only revenge and possible extermination of all Germans." Mutual enlightenment did not come that night. But the police did — to quell the uproar.

After the debate Rex went off to High Meadow to write another Nero Wolfe story, "Booby Trap." If Rex, at that point, was seething with hatred for the Germans, he managed to keep it out of his new story. His villains were men who jeopardized the outcome of the war by seeking their own gain. Only one hint about matters currently on his mind was there for the alert reader. Nero Wolfe was reading *Under Cover* by John Roy Carlson (Avedis Derounian), a nature-of-the-enemy exposé of American fascist groups. In *Under Cover* Wolfe would have found this passage to ponder: "I agree somewhat with Rex Stout, chairman of the Writers' War Board: 'The political ethics of the American Communists still are about as low as anything ever observed in these parts, including the Ku Klux Klan.' "[3]

From High Meadow Rex lobbed shots at Dorothy Thompson, which the board gallantly intercepted en route to their target. It suppressed a letter in which he branded her a "German apologist," and refused to act on another in which he called her a "liar." On his return to Manhattan in July, Rex joined the board in hammering out a new statement. With a little semantic tinkering "pan-Germanism" became "the German Will-to-Aggression." Of the sixty-four members of the advisory council, only four objected to this statement on principle — Thompson and Gannett, who found it too harsh; and Ferber and Kaufman, who found it too mild. The August issue of the board's *Bulletin* carried an editorial by Rex entitled "Preparing for 1964," in which he projected an account of German-fomented troubles in the world of the future, if Germany were allowed to regenerate.

On 9 August Dorothy Thompson's syndicated column cited the revolt of Hitler's generals as proof of the existence of the freedom-loving spirit in Germany and, hence, of the bankruptcy of the board's position. A week later, CBS refused to let Rex present the board's view on Edwin C. Hill's opinion program.

On 4 October, learning that the board was ready to release its position paper, Thompson staged her own revolt. "In every word I have published," she said, "I have tried to think of the effect in Germany itself. . . . I have asked myself whether what I wrote would encourage or discourage Germans from standing behind Hitler." She was proud "that Dr. Goebbels has made great efforts to prevent the republication of what I have written." Not everyone had her perspicacity. "Lord Vansittart, Rex Stout and associates, and many others," she lamented, "have been furnishing Goebbels with his most effective propaganda." Rex met this assault with scorn: "To say that an obscure individual named Stout has been furnishing Goebbels with his most effective propaganda . . . is fantastic. Either Miss Thompson is unfit to head an organization I belong to, or I am unfit to belong to an organization she heads. In any case, Freedom House under Dorothy Thompson is no place for me." Rex thereupon resigned his directorship.

Two days later, Dorothy resigned too. She protested that she had not questioned Rex's patriotism. His gesture deflated her, however. She asked him to dinner at 237 East Forty-eighth Street — the handsome brownstone which was the home of her dreams. The only other person present was the Austrian artist Maxim Kopf, her latest husband. At fifty Dorothy was still vital in her sexual magnetism. Would Archie Goodwin have been conscious of it? "Yes, indeed," Rex assured me. But Dorothy had Rex's own magnetism to contend with. It was a standoff. Throughout the long evening they argued, with neither of them giving important ground. Maxie, a man of brawn who cared nothing for issues, sat in a corner, chuckling as they argued and helping them empty three bottles of Dom Perignon. Dorothy assured Rex that her disagreement with him was not personal. She liked him and liked his books. (In fact, her pet name for Michael, the self-willed son she had borne Sinclair Lewis, was "little Nero.") A few days later the two disputants rejoined Freedom House.

In November, with the dust finally settled on the Thompson confrontation, Rex asked the twenty-eight members of the WWB's executive board to produce an agenda the board could concern itself with in the coming year. For twenty-six of them the German problem came first. Thus Rex faced into the final months of the war with an active mandate from his coworkers to continue on course. Later, when the full story was told of the horror of the Nazi concentration camps, the WWB's concern with German culpability made more sense to many. Certainly when Dorothy Thompson protested the Nuremburg trials, her supporters were few. Her biographer, Marion K. Sanders, would conclude, in 1973, "Her concept of the German people as the victims rather than the perpetrators of Nazism was a delusion. . . ."[4]

Even as the WWB's nature-of-the-enemy campaign was being discouraged from one quarter, it was being encouraged from another. In late September 1944, Treasury Secretary Morgenthau had appealed to the board, through Clifton Fadiman, to do what it could to quiet opposition to the plan he had evolved for turning Germany into an economic wasteland after the war.[5] Under fire already for its extremism, the board did not need another cross to bear, but Rex gamely sent off a telegram to Roosevelt in which he warned that reports of dissension over the plan, among members of the President's official family, were discrediting the administration as a source of effective plans for the postwar period. In response, Robert Sherwood, then speech-writing for Roosevelt, came to a board meeting to explain the plan, and Rex was asked to go to Washington to consult further on it. On 5 October, Rex gave the plan a boost on "Town Meeting of the Air," stressing that it was foolish to rebuild Germany economically merely to extract reparations from her. Morgenthau found Rex's presentation "vigorous and convincing" and wrote to tell him so.

Speaking at a luncheon at the Town Hall Club given by the Women's Action Committee for Victory and Lasting Peace, on 11 October, Rex rebuked Henry Luce for a recent *Time* article which characterized the Morgenthau Plan as a policy of hate and vengeance. Luce, he said, was "making it vastly more difficult to deal with the enemy when the war is over." In November, in a WWB editorial — "The Reparations Booby Trap" — Rex deplored the folly of putting Germany on its feet again so it could make good on its assigned reparations.

In just this interval Rex himself had been tripped up by another "Booby Trap" — the novella of that name which had been published on 7 September in *Not Quite Dead Enough*. In October Adelaide Sherer had written to tell him they were in trouble. He had quoted three stanzas of Yeats's "Lake Isle of Innisfree," without a release from Macmillan. Rex wrote Adelaide:

I am an ass. When I was writing "Booby Trap," out in the country, I phoned somebody at Macmillan to ask if it would be all right to quote that poem by Yeats and was told that it would be. But I made no record of the conversation, I don't know the date that it took place, and I don't know whom I talked to. Beat that for carelessness if you can, and let me know which jail I go to.

Rex had entered a season of lawbreaking. On 3 November, under the headline, "Stout Nearly Causes a Riot at Fish Rally," *The New York Times* reported an episode that had happened the night before, in

Monticello, New York. After speaking earlier, at a nearby Democratic rally, Rex had gone to a Republican rally at the Grange Hall. Rex told me: "I was accompanied by a husky six-foot young man who would have enjoyed some activity and his girl friend. They resided there. They knew about me through Friends of Democracy."

When Rex came into the auditorium the meeting was already under way. He took up his station against the back wall of the room and waited. Congressman Hamilton Fish — caricatured in *The Illustrious Dunderheads* as a pompous, frock-coated porpoise dangling on Hitler's fishline — was answering charges that he had abused the congressional franking privilege, to send out Nazi propaganda. "I have been accused of friendship with what are called the Nazis," he said, "I hereby defy anyone to prove it."

That was Rex's cue. In his briefcase he had with him an assortment of statements which Fish had made about the Nazis. "I've got the proof right here," he bellowed. "Do you want me to come up and read it to you?"

"I know you," Fish shouted. "The Dies Committee investigated you. You are a Communist and more dangerous to America than Earl Browder."

"Liar," Rex said.

There was an uproar among the more than three hundred partisan listeners in the audience. They called for Rex's ejection. A policeman came up to him then, told him he was "exciting a riot," and asked him to go. "Mr. Stout," the *Times* observed, "had no opportunity of putting the question and left in high dudgeon."

Rex's editorial for the December issue of *Prevent World War III* gave the Morgenthau Plan a further boost. He urged removal of the equipment of the German chemical and metallurgical industries, in toto, to the devastated countries. That would "restore to Germany's victims at least a portion of that which has been stolen from them; and . . . offer . . . the best possible insurance against any future operations of the German will-to-aggression." In January, Rex's WWB editorial reiterated this view. Actually, however, the board's support of the plan was beginning to break down. On his visit to Washington, Rex had conferred with Morgenthau, at his invitation, for two hours, in his office at the Treasury Building. He came away with some of the misgivings about the plan already voiced by cabinet members Hull and Stimson, and by FDR himself.[6]

Ironically, even as the WWB was pressing its campaign against pan-Germanism, and being denounced for "inverted racism," it was also pressing its campaign on behalf of the number two item on its agenda — racial tolerance in America. These twin goals did not in fact contradict one another. To act to undermine the master race concept in

Germany while racial discrimination in America was left unchallenged would have been hypocrisy.

The WWB's racial justice campaign was no afterthought. Early in the war the board had chosen *Brothers,* a play by black dramatist Langston Hughes, as its script-of-the-month. It illustrated the brotherhood of the races in a time of common danger. Other scripts prepared for radio by Hughes, Eve Merriam, and Fannie Hurst pursued the same theme. Letters on the subject flew between Rex and Lindsay, Crouse, Sillcox, and La Farge. Robert Duffus's "Democracy's Way with a Problem" went out with the board's first batch of editorials. Rex himself took a direct role in promoting distribution of a Signal Corps film, *The Negro Soldier,* which called attention to the black man's contribution to the struggle against the Axis.

In March 1944, when the USO banned *The Races of Mankind,* a pamphlet prepared by Ruth Benedict and Gene Weltfish on the concept of racial equality, Rex set the matter in clear terms before USO president Chester Barnard: *"The Races of Mankind* is an educational pamphlet. . . . The Writers' War Board believes that the suppression of scientifically established facts concerning racial equality tends to the defeat of one of our outstanding war aims. . . . We cannot combat the master race theory in Europe and appease it at home."[7]

To combat Barnard's intransigence Rex conducted a campaign worthy of ETS in its heyday. Letters were sent to more than eleven hundred USO centers around the country. A play script was made of the material and sent to seven hundred schools and radio stations. The controversy the Barnard ban engendered gave a boost to the whole tolerance campaign. Chet Huntley furnished a play script, Robert Landry, an editorial, Helen Hayes lent her name to an article entitled "We Have Racial Equality — Do You?"

Out of one of Rex's celebrated brainstorming sessions came an idea the reverberations of which would carry forward into peacetime. The board's June 1944 *Report* offered this assessment:

Writers play a considerable part in furthering the "old stock" swindle in picking out only Anglo-Saxon names for their attractive characters and marrying them only in Protestant churches and giving them only inferiority-emphasizing relationships to menial Negroes, ignorant working class Catholics, shyster or comic Jews, slovenly if picturesque Mexicans, and so on.

In short, the time seems to have arrived for writers to stop shaking their heads about other people's race bigotry and examine their own very considerable contributions to it. . . .

Although Nero Wolfe was foreign-born, and his team of minor legmen — Saul, Fred, and Orrie — offered the ethnic variation of Jew, Irishman, and Anglo-Saxon (with the Anglo-Saxon the least commenda-

ble of the three, though balanced, of course, by the wholesome Archie
Goodwin, also Anglo-Saxon), Rex was not yet satisfied with his impartial-
ity. Wolfe's newspaper contacts in the early stories had been Bill Pratt
of the *Courier* and Harry Foster of the *Gazette*. Henceforth the contact
man would be Lon Cohen of the *Gazette*. "Since there are more than
two million Jews in New York," Rex told me, "it would be unrealistic
not to have some of the characters Jews." Rex contrived a good mixture
in other areas as well. His dumb cops are by no means all Irish. The most
obnoxious of them, indeed, Lieutenant Rowcliff, is an Anglo-Saxon. His
villains, more often than not, are Anglo-Saxon. Nor can feminists complain. Doyle had found the idea of a woman committing murder unthinkable. Chesterton had been nearly as chivalrous. A full score of the
murders Wolfe investigates are committed by women.

On 16 June 1944 Rex addressed a group of one hundred and nineteen
Radio Guild writers and free-lancers, urging them to use their scripts
to move the nation in the direction of racial tolerance. Again adapting
ETS tactics, the board sent a series of special mailings to those who
asked for further information on techniques to combat prejudice.

High point of the Tolerance Campaign was a one-night show conceived along the lines of the Stout family theatricals gone big-time.
Called *The Myth That Threatens America,* it was staged at the Barbizon
Plaza, 12 January 1945. The cast was a cast such as no producer ever
dreams of assembling. The audience of six hundred was an audience a
producer could dream of assembling only if he had congress with Satan.
These were the people who determined the contents of movies, radio
programs, books, and magazines — the artists, technicians, editors,
writers, and illustrators of the communications and entertainment
media. For them this was a fashion show presenting a new line. All they
had to do if they liked it was to pass the word and it would be in. The
board missed no opportunity to sell them.

Rex opened the show, then stepped aside for John Mason Brown,
master of ceremonies. First came a skit, "Education, Please!" based on
Clifton Fadiman's famous show, "Information, Please!" Four panelists
took part: Moss Hart, Carl Van Doren, Bennett Cerf, and Gypsy Rose
Lee. The substance of the tolerance appeal came out of their exchanges,
without blatancy, without grimness. Well-scripted speeches and clever
songs followed. The audience heard from Avedis Derounian, Christopher La Farge, Margaret Mead, and Eric Johnston, then president of
the United States Chamber of Commerce. Blues singer Benay Venuta
brought the audience to its feet with the "Free and Equal Blues." Oscar
Hammerstein II's "Ol' Man Author," a rewrite of Jerome Kern's "Old
Man River," left them rolling in the aisles. It featured a quartet of
timeworn stage types — Irishman, Jew, black, and Italian — all pleading their cases with that gleeful extravagance that for a century had
made the American stage a major purveyor of bias. Only Brown failed

to catch the significance of this watershed moment in the history of the media in America. At one point he launched into a racist joke, then worked himself free of it with an uneasiness that lent unexpected effectiveness to the arguments the Myth show was designed to unfold.[8]

In a single stroke the WWB had given its message to those who could do something about it, and had shown that it could be done without either rancor or tedium.

The board's realization that true peace could not return to a world torn by racial strife is not remarkable. What is remarkable is that it could pursue this campaign with vigor and success at a time when it was being laid siege to for its German policy. The campaign was not a diversionary tactic on the board's part. It set in motion a machinery that eased pressures which would build later.

36.

A Man of Sovereign Parts

Rex Stout's views on religion or philosophy are unknown to me. But he is, through Nero, a very staunch exponent of the values traditionally upheld throughout Western civilization. Now, when the "Humanities" are under bitter attack, Nero comes into his own, and seems, paradoxically, a more modern and a greater figure than in the 1930's.

— NICOLAS FREELING

Two hours after he greeted the audience assembled at the Barbizon Plaza for the Myth show, Rex boarded an Army Air Force C-54 at a Long Island base and took off for the European Theater of Operations. He had been picked to lead a group of fifteen writers, photographers, editors, and related types on a tour of the war zone in the anxious period just after the Battle of the Bulge. Though the air force, then about to ask Congress for a large appropriation, was hoping for publicity favorable to itself, the touring writers were told to report what they saw. The C-54 was at their disposal for the entire trip and a major and a lieutenant went along to serve as liaison and smooth the way.[1]

The first leg of the journey, with brief stopovers in Labrador, Greenland, and Scotland, took the party to London. In London most of the group elected to stay at the Carlton or the Dorchester. Rex went instead to an air force hotel, reasoning that, since Europe was having its coldest winter in modern times, the air force would have ample heat while the luxury hotels would not. He was quite correct. On one occasion as guests of Air Marshal Tedder, the visitors were taken to see the secret underground Air Force Headquarters, not far from Windsor Castle. Tedder included the castle itself in the tour. It was even colder than the Carlton and the Dorchester. When they entered George III's bedchamber, Tedder told them matter-of-factly, "The king died in this room." Between chattering teeth Marquis Child jittered, "Froze to death, I presume."

During his stay in London Rex dined several times with Herbert Agar, with whom he had arrived on terms of cordial friendship in FFFC days. Agar and his wife, Eleanor Carroll Chilton, one of England's wealthiest women, had a fifteen-room suite at the Dorchester — somewhat warmer, one supposes, than George III's bedchamber.[2]

While the others were in London, Rex, Roger Burlingame, and Child, toured the French battle front. At that time Aachen was under heavy Allied assault. On the bank of the Rhine, Rex stood behind a tree and took a shot at a distant German soldier: "Apparently I missed."[3]

At one point the travelers were near enough to bombed-out Cologne to view the cathedral from across the river, but they did not enter the city. For several days they were in the Vosges Mountains, at an army air force installation fifteen miles east of Epinal. Here Rex learned that the price of fame might very possibly be indigestion. On his arrival, the commanding officer told him that preparations for his arrival had been under way at the mess hall for several days. The mess sergeant knew the Nero Wolfe stories. With a couple of friends he had staged a wild-boar hunt. They had brought in a one-hundred-and-eighty-five-pound boar. With fierce dedication the sergeant had transformed this grisly porker into a calendar of culinary events. On the first day Rex got wild boar's heart for lunch. Dinner was pork chops, gamy but savory. For breakfast, next day — wild boar bacon. Lunch — wild boar ham. The second dinner was a collaboration. A boar roast, seasoned with unknown herbs gathered by local women whose forebears had wrested their secrets from the Vosges centuries before. And so it went.

On 5 February the group moved on to Paris. Even though V-2's then were falling on London every minute and a half, for some of the travelers it was a reluctant parting. Dorothy Cameron Disney's husband was head of the OWI in London. Kay Boyle's husband was there also — an officer in the OSS. Another six weeks of touring lay ahead, however, and left no time for private regrets.

They gave France two weeks. At the Ritz, Hemingway reminisced with Rex about their earlier encounters in Paris, particularly their taxi ride to Chartres. From Paris, the group moved on to Italy. There the winter cold seemed at its worst. "Spending a day along the front lines in the Apennines, in a jeep," Rex told me, "I damned near froze to death. The coldest January and February in nine centuries, they said."

Of the Italian interlude, Rex remembered: "The time in Italy was spent in and near Rome, Naples, and Florence, and nearby posts and headquarters, lunching with generals, talking with and to troops. . . . In Naples I left my fur-lined coat in a command car while I went to lunch with brass, and when I returned the coat was gone. The Air Force did not replace it."

In Rome, Rex met and talked with Thornton Wilder, who, as a lieutenant colonel in United States Air Force Intelligence, outranked Archie Goodwin, a mere major in Army Intelligence. Rex conceded that Wilder merited his rank.

Three weeks later the C-54 carried the party to Africa, where Rex and the others made a whirlwind tour of Libya, Tunisia, Algeria, and

Morocco.[4] At Marrakesh they were domiciled at the same villa that had sheltered Churchill when he had pneumonia after the Casablanca conference. For Rex, who venerated Churchill, to occupy Churchill's suite and sleep in his bed was a high point of the trip.

On the return flight, they had a day at Dakar, Senegal. A seventeen-hour flight followed, to Natal, on 11 March. For twenty minutes Rex did the flying, as senior pilot, for which service Captain George Wells supplied him with a "Pilot's Flight Report," filled out and signed by himself and Gordon Thompson, the navigator. Over the Amazon delta Rex again sat at the controls. The plane touched down in Brazil and Puerto Rico before returning to New York. Thirty-eight years had gone by since Pay Yeoman Stout had visited Puerto Rico aboard the presidential yacht. Even with his confidence and imagination, Rex might have been incredulous had some island sorcerer told him in 1907 that on his next visit he would drop out of the skies as head of a government mission.

While Rex was aloft, negotiating the distance between Dakar and Natal, he was serenely unaware that the Chicago *Tribune* had tried to shoot him down. Entitled "Attacks on the American Press," a cartoon on the *Tribune*'s editorial page on 11 March portrayed, in caricature, "Ex-Rev. Birkhead," "Rex Stout," and "The Foreign-Minded Playboy," as a trio leading three skunks. Birkhead's skunk was tagged "Communist Front Propaganda Sheet." The other two skunks, one labeled "Woodpussy Press," were led by The Foreign-Minded Playboy. Rex, insinuating himself between his two companions, had his right hand on Birkhead's shoulder and his left arm crooked in that of the Playboy. He looked lurid and conniving. He should have looked smug, too, since his Playboy companion was FDR.

Even had leisure afforded, Rex would not have dignified Colonel McCormick's attack with a reply. To reporters who greeted him on his return from the ETO, he had three impressions to communicate. First, he thought it "silly to complain of Americans not appreciating this war to the full." "I thought I had, but I hadn't," he admitted. "You have to see it to have any idea of it." He then put in a word for world government:

We're all telling each other that the world has shrunk and is going to be politically, as well as physically, one world. I had realized it intellectually — but not actually until I'd flown to about twenty different countries as easily as I'd go down to Snyder's Grove for a picnic in the old days.

His third point amplified his second:

This has been said so many times and still no one believes it: It is impossible to see St.-Lô, Aachen, or what one V-2 bomb has done without realizing that another war would destroy everything. There would be no human race left except a few struggling two-legged animals wandering around. We've goddamn got to have an organization for peace or give up.

A caveman analogy which later in the year would develop into "The United Smiths" supplied his peroration:

> The area in which violence is not permitted grows constantly. At first, a caveman's son used to fight his father and try to kill him as soon as he was big enough to wield a club. Then it dawned on them that if they got together they could do a better job of fighting the fellows in the next cave. . . . The trend is bound to continue until it includes the whole planet.[5]

Rex had come a long way from the day he had used a stone to open a gash in Homer Emery's head. Before he would write "The United Smiths," two atomic bombs would fall on Japan. The conditions Rex had postulated on the basis of V-2 rockets now went beyond conjecture. Man had the destruction of the planet within his grasp. World government was no longer merely an ideal. It was a necessity.

The campaign for world government to which Rex would give much of his time and energy in the years following World War II bespoke a concern he was committed to even before there was a WWB. Nine months prior to Pearl Harbor, speaking to a radio audience for the FFFC, he had said, "The time may come — I hope it does, and the sooner the better — when nations will be willing to surrender enough of their sovereignty to permit the establishment of an effective world police." At the international level such a development was as necessary for world peace as racial tolerance was for domestic peace in America. Inevitably it had to be a goal of the WWB.

It was, and thus became the subject of yet another WWB campaign. A first gesture toward international cooperation had been to swap reading materials with the Soviets. Copies of such WWB projects as Benét's "They Burned the Books" were sent to the U.S.S.R. In return the Russians sent back an assortment of their propaganda materials, most of it about as stimulating as old feed and grain reports. The Soviets had not yet heard of human interest. When they ignored Rex's requests for livelier materials, he told them not to send anything else. Once, at the Russian consulate in New York, Rex and Clifton Fadiman sat down with Andrei Gromyko to work out details of a cultural exchange which the Soviets envisaged.

"Some of our writers will come to America. Some of yours will go to the U.S.S.R.," said Gromyko.

"Whom shall we send first?" Rex asked.

"We would like," said Gromyko, "your James Fenimore Cooper and your Jack London."[6]

In May 1943 the Board had prepared the final draft of an eight-point Pledge for Peace which stressed that world organization was the alternative to a third world war.[7] No other activity on behalf of world government more fully engaged the energies of the board. When the campaign at last was launched, 10 November 1943, a front committee of fifty-six eminent Americans, ranging from Albert Einstein to Helen Hayes, was used to boost it. In January 1944 Rex made the pledge the subject of the year's leadoff editorial, "The Bugaboo of Sovereignty." This piece dealt with objections to the pledge. To his disappointment, Rex could not get Eleanor Roosevelt to sign it. And a two-hour session with James B. Conant, in his office in Massachusetts Hall, found the Harvard president firm also in his resolve not to sign. That was Rex's sole visit to the Harvard Yard. While there Rex did not inspect Thayer Hall, the dorm Paul Chapin fell from in *The League of Frightened Men.* "I had other things on my mind," Rex explained.

Some objections to the pledge came from those who did sign it, including John P. Marquand, who argued that cultural and environmental differences keep men around the world from thinking alike. He even surmised that a man's idea of what democracy is might be determined by what he has eaten for breakfast.[8]

During this same period, the Metropolitan Opera Guild offered the board intermission time on its radio broadcasts, for talks on the theme "The Road to Lasting Peace." Under WWB auspices, eight speakers filled spots: Vice President Henry Wallace, Wendell Willkie, Elmer Davis, Archibald MacLeish, Senator Harley Kilgore, Jan Masaryk, Thomas Parran (the United States Surgeon General), and Rex himself, who spoke on 19 February on the topic "Sovereign Rights and Lasting Peace." Rex told his vast audience:

Certainly there can be no world government unless the peoples of the various nations relinquish their external sovereign rights. That is a high and hard demand. The ego of a man is tender and touchy and proud; so is the ego of a people, a nation. But the alternative is simple; which is harder, which is more intolerable, to admit the necessity of relinquishing the external sovereign rights of our nation, or to face the horrible certainty of another war, not far distant, bloodier and costlier than this one . . . ?

In July 1944 a request reached Rex from Henry J. Kaiser, the millionaire industrialist, asking him to supply a name for an organization which he headed which was seeking to foster world government through the UN. Rex suggested "Americans United for World Organization" and the name was adopted. Kaiser then indicated that he wanted two WWB members to serve on his board of directors. At that time none of the members of the WWB was eager to welcome another commitment, even though they all felt Kaiser should be encouraged. To settle the matter they put their names in a hat and drew out two: Rex's and Alan Green's.

In early August, formation of the group was announced. It represented a merger of six groups — including the Committee to Defend America by Aiding the Allies and the Fight for Freedom Committee — plus an agreement to collaborate with eleven other similarly minded groups, including Freedom House. Headquarters were at 5 West Fifty-fourth Street. The group took as its immediate goal the task of persuading the United Nations to form a world organization. Sometime later this group redesignated itself the United World Federalists. Rex was one of its most active campaigners.

On 11 October, reflecting the hopes of the Kaiser group, Rex told members of the Women's Action Committee for Victory and Lasting Peace, at a Town Hall Club luncheon, that the United States and the U.S.S.R., working together in a spirit of mutual trust, could achieve a world peace plan.

The Action Committee luncheon gave Rex his first chance to appear before a television camera. His success was a greater triumph than he himself realized. A year later it occasioned a speech at a television convention at the Hotel Commodore. The technician who had handled the camera at the Town Hall told the Commodore gathering that the assignment had terrified him. Preliminary studies had shown that TV audiences were repelled by the sight of a human face registering the contortions of animated discourse. Rex's beard had been heaven-sent. Even while others spoke, the technician had kept a camera roaming over that beard, exploring every wisp and tendril of it. Viewers were enthralled. The technician got raves. And Rex was remembered as the star of the occasion by viewers and technicians alike.

The last two major campaigns undertaken by the WWB were called to support the Dumbarton Oaks and Bretton Woods conferences, at which groundwork was laid for international cooperation. The board's confusion about the merits of Dumbarton Oaks, however, foreshadowed the dissatisfaction of many of its members with the United Nations. The board's own Peace Pledge had insisted that no nation should be able to secede from the world organization. Dumbarton Oaks did not insist on that. Moreover, it allowed the four major powers the right of veto, and that seemed a weakness. Through the fall of 1944 the board vacillated. To Rex, Lewis Mumford suggested that the board, by going along with the veto, was playing into the hands of the isolationists. Rex had no tradition for changing his stance. The only time he had done so was when Howard Lindsay had convinced him it was inhumane to insist that a man wounded in the service of his country should accept a transfusion from a black donor when his prejudices made the thought abhorrent to him.[9] But Mumford found Rex vulnerable. "I have been wrestling with my soul," Rex told him, "and now agree completely with you. If we settle for Dumbarton Oaks as it now stands we will be participating in another swindle."[10]

To avoid the risk of seeming to want no world organization at all, the board decided to give Dumbarton Oaks qualified support. Thereupon Rex prepared three articles: "Questions and Answers about Dumbarton Oaks," "A Primer for Dumbarton Oaks," and "A Test for Dumbarton Oaks." The first said that while Dumbarton Oaks was no sure-fire panacea for the world's ills, it was "a real start on a set-up that will get us what we want if we work at it." The second article, meant for peace groups, was a simpler version of the first. The third focused on the shortcomings of the Dumbarton Oaks proposals. In March, Archibald MacLeish and Adlai Stevenson sat in on one of the board's meetings. MacLeish was then Assistant Secretary of State, and Stevenson his special assistant. Convinced of the board's sincerity, MacLeish said it was all right for the board to go on urging the creation of a more powerful world organization.

The board found it easier to support the Bretton Woods monetary proposals. It saw that if Congress could not accept this degree of cooperation among nations, the forthcoming conference at San Francisco, to set up a world organization, was doomed. On 25 March, speaking to a nationwide audience on "Report to the Nation," Rex endorsed the proposals. Other speeches, articles, and editorials, exemplifying the board's typical saturation coverage of important issues, carried the message to the nation. Even Orson Welles cut a record for the cause. The following summer the same pattern was adhered to to gain acceptance for the San Francisco Charter. For that campaign Rex at last perfected, as "The United Smiths," his caveman analogy:

In caveman days, the minute Junior got big enough to go after Dad with a club he did so, and Dad was a goner (unless, as often happened, he had got the idea first). But one day some male parent conceived the notion that it might be better for all if, instead of letting nature run its course (father and son have always killed each other so they always will), he and Junior should talk it over and arrange for the United Smiths.

That idea has been spreading ever since . . . there is every reason to suppose it will continue to spread until it covers the globe.

Rex did not have to go back to Cro-Magnon man for this analogy. His struggle to relate to his own father had taught him the value of intrafamilial accord.

When the war in Europe ended in May 1945, Rex lost no time showing that he had not run out of good causes. That month, at a time when his fellow mystery writer, Raymond Chandler, was fuming ineffectually over this same issue, Rex, as president of the Authors' Guild and chairman of its Reprint Committee, sent out letters to two hundred and eighteen important writers, advising them that the twenty-five-cent publisher could and should increase the basic royalty paid them for reprints. A delegation of publishers, led by Random House's Bennett Cerf, promptly waited on him. They went away more alarmed than ever. Robert De Graff of Pocket Books wondered if they couldn't exorcise this new devil by simply bypassing Rex to carry out negotiations with the original publishers themselves. Cerf knew better. "This is something that you will have to settle with Stout," he said. And he said it darkly.

When Rex met with De Graff on 20 June, he held a strong bargaining hand. Many Guild members had signed cards pledging support for the campaign to get increased royalties. Rex also had statistics which showed that annual production of twenty-five-cent reprints would bring the publishers profits of $6,720,000, while total authors' profits would be $600,000. He urged an equal split.

In a "Confidential Interim Report" sent to Guild members on 1 August, Rex said:

> The reprint houses say our figures are utterly cock-eyed. We say we don't think so, and that the only way to prove them wrong is to let us send a certified public accountant, under a pledge of confidence as to details, to inspect reprint house accounts. The idea is abhorrent to them.

He was determined that authors should have a three-cent royalty on every twenty-five-cent reprint sold. "We think we are going to get what we are after," he wrote; "a large increase in the royalties from twenty-five cent reprints. We are more than ever convinced that such an increase is economically feasible." Rex then made a threat publishers would long remember: "If it is not forthcoming, what about the suggestion (made by various writers) that the writers put up the capital for a reprint business of their own, hire competent reprint men to run it for them, and take both profits and royalties?"

In the autumn Rex would be gleeful when Bernard DeVoto, in his *Harper's* "Easy Chair" column, made the reprint cause his own, and sent him an advance copy of the material set to appear in the magazine's December issue.[11] Rex wrote him, on 27 October: "The blast about reprints . . . should singe somebody's hair. If only the hair happens to be on that part of the anatomy where singeing hurts most."

Late in June 1945, when making preparations to reopen High Meadow, Pola and Rex sent an offer of employment to the relocation center set up to find jobs for Japanese-Americans who, after Pearl Harbor, had been placed in detention camps in the Southwest. The government was willing now to relocate these people in the Midwest or the East. The Stout offer caught the eye of Kaso Yasumoto and his wife, Alyce, a young nisei couple, with a son and daughter, Allen and Joy, then just reaching school age. After four years of confinement in a desert camp — with five thousand other Japanese-Americans — at Poston, Arizona, they were enchanted by the thought of life on a New England farm. They asked for the job and got it.

Pola met the Yasumotos on their arrival in New York. No apprehensions they might have had could have withstood Pola's warm and loving nature or the sight of High Meadow in all its June glory. When Rex realized that Kay, as Kaso was called, needed a haircut, he drove him into Danbury, went into a barbershop, and said, "Kay is Japanese-American. Will you cut his hair?" "No problem," said the barber. "Okay," said Rex, "you can cut mine, too." Thus began the seven-year stay of the Yasumotos at High Meadow.[12]

In July, Rex, Alan Green, and Harold Guinzburg went to Washington to see Robert P. Patterson, Under Secretary of War, soon-to-be Secretary of War, at the Mayflower. Their plea to Patterson was that we should not be too easy on the Germans. Harold, just back from Europe, where he had served in the psychological warfare department, was especially eloquent in his pleading. The terror of what had happened in Europe was immediate to him.

That same month the board dealt a staggering blow to those who thought the light of democracy had burned on in Germany through the war years in the person of the Lutheran pastor Martin Niemöller, who had spent eight years in prison because he had stood up to Hitler. Alan Green prepared a WWB editorial in which he questioned the appropriateness of treating Niemöller as a champion of democracy. In World War I Niemöller had commanded a submarine. Later, he had been a Nazi and had supported German expansionism. He broke with Hitler only when Hitler attacked the church. Repeatedly he had volunteered for service in World War II and was proud that his sons had served the Reich. Since his release he had told the press that American-style democracy did not suit the Germans. "They like to be governed," he said; "they like to feel authority." Green's message was quickly taken up by others. Even Eleanor Roosevelt deplored Niemöller as "a dangerous pan-German."

The Christian Century undertook to defend Niemöller. It complained that the WWB "blanket[ed] the nation" with its editorials, that the mischief done Niemöller all stemmed from Alan Green's editorial,

which was shot through with "plain untruths and unwarranted infer-
ences." Sympathetic letters reaching the magazine professed to see at
work once again the fine hand of Rex Stout and his SPWW3.[13] Into this
circle of self-congratulation Rex dropped a devastating bombshell. He
referred *Christian Century* to two articles, one which the magazine
itself carried in June 1939, by Ewart Turner; the other an *Atlantic
Monthly* article written in 1937 by Paul Hutchinson, *The Christian
Century*'s current managing editor. The first article described
Niemöller as antidemocratic and antiparliamentarian. "From 1925 on,"
it ran, "he gave his vote to Hitler." Hutchinson's comments were yet
more devastating.[14] As it ended its period of service, the WWB was
having the last word, after all.

Although activities at the WWB were winding down during the summer of 1945, Rex often was on hand to oversee the work that was being
done.[15]

Late on the afternoon of 14 August, Jean Poletti, Oscar Hammerstein
II, Alan Green, and Rex went to see a British propaganda film, *Colonel
Blimp*, in a screening room on Seventh Avenue, near Forty-seventh
Street. Green remembered:

When we came out, Times Square was crowded. It was V-J Day. The four of
us were starving and couldn't fight our way into any place in the neighborhood.
We struggled cross town to the old Chatham Hotel (Forty-eighth between
Madison and Park). It was ten and the kitchen was closed. We had drinks and
nibbled at peanuts. About midnight, we finally found four empty stools in a
Hamburger Heaven on Madison. There was no deflation of our spirit. V-J Day
hadn't ended our job. The news of Hiroshima reached us during a Board meeting. Then and there we realized that a workable world government was mankind's one hope and that we were going to have to battle for it to get it.[16]

Soon afterward the board had dissolved and reconstituted itself as the
Writers' Board, again with Rex as chairman. Its prime concern now
would be world government and world peace.

In a world at peace, even a peace precariously held, Rex now had
time to think again of his own writing ambitions. In the fall of 1944,
Stanley Rinehart had notified him that John Farrar, then overseas on a
military assignment, was "not returning to the business." The following
summer, Rinehart sought to hold Rex by suggesting that he go on
location in Rome and gather materials for a book on the Catholic hierarchy. A beguiling offer, but a villa in postwar Rome could not compete
in Rex's imagination with the promise of bliss High Meadow offered.
Besides, he thought John might set up on his own and he wanted to
continue with him if he did. Presently, however, John told him he had

come to no decisions and advised him to act in his own best interests.[17]

One day in October Rex and Alan Green found themselves in a cab on Madison Avenue, heading uptown from Authors' League headquarters — at 6 West Thirty-ninth Street. Alan was talking about the advertising agency in which he had a partnership — the Griswold-Eshleman Agency. Harold Guinzburg, president of Viking, had just given them the Viking account. Unexpectedly Rex said: "I'm not going to be published by Johnny any more. Do you think Harold would be interested?" "Jesus Christ, yes!" Alan said. He thought the idea was stupendous. With Rex's approval, he set up a meeting between Rex and Harold. That was all that was required. Rex and Harold were old friends. Harold was an able businessman. Without stirring from his brownstone, Nero Wolfe left Farrar & Rinehart and went to Viking.

Now Viking asked Alan to find out how aware people were of Rex and his rotund detective. Researchers took up their stations outside bookstores in the New York area. "Who is Rex Stout?" they asked. And "Who is Nero Wolfe?" To Alan's surprise, Rex was better known than Wolfe. Yet both scored high. The survey showed also that women knew and liked the books quite as much as men.[18] Moreover, Archie was nearly as popular as Wolfe. His gallantry and derring-do were much admired. Rex was encouraged then to build up Archie. The advice was supererogatory. In 1941 Rex had told J. V. McAree, of the Toronto *Globe & Mail,* that he knew, whether or not his readers knew it, that Archie carried the stories.

Settled in again at High Meadow, Barbara and Rebecca had picked up with their schooling in the Danbury public schools. When they said they needed short poems to declaim for a school recital, Rex gave the job to his muse. Since Barbara missed living near school, as they had in New York City, Rex made that the topic of his first poem.*

For Rebecca, Rex envisaged a disaster which every Penrod in the school must have relished:

> *Morris Street School is on the side*
> *Of a high and sloping hill.*

* The boys and girls come down the street
To school at Lincoln Avenue.
They only have to use their feet,
They live so close — all but a few.

But I live eight long miles away.
Have any of you tried
To walk eight miles twice a day?
Neither have I. I have to ride.

They ought to move Lincoln Avenue
Right near my home, across the street.
Then you would ride, and you, and you,
But I could just go on my feet!

What if it should decide to slide?
I hope it never will.

For if it starts to slide then we
Will be in quite a fix,
Since at the bottom it will be
In the Middle of Route Six!

For Joy Yasumoto, Rex came through with "Like Me":

Some girls are either fat or tall,
But I am not that sort,
In fact I am not big at all;
I'm rather thin and short.

So when I get up to recite
A poem — as you see —
I think I have a perfect right
To make it short like me.

As someone who had been the shortest kid in his class in high school
— and who wore knee pants to prove it — Rex gave Joy the benefit of
his experience. What the poem said was — you can make shortness
work to your advantage, turn minuses into pluses.[19]

With the help of the Yasumotos, the Stouts were quickly settling into
a comfortable mode of life again at High Meadow. From the outset, the
Yasumotos felt that Pola and Rex made them feel part of their family.
For Barbara and Rebecca it was as though they had acquired a brother
and sister and a second set of parents. Pola had to be in New York often,
and in North Philadelphia, where she had opened a mill, and Alyce ran
the house and did the cooking. Kay fell in for a share of Harold's many
jobs — the garden in summer, woodworking in winter, and the usual
indoor chores. They followed no strict working hours. They had Rex's
full trust. They did all the grocery shopping. They were never asked to
account for money spent. Every so often Rex would send Kay to the
bank to draw out $800 or $1,000 in new bills. When guests came —
the Fadimans, the Gallicos, the Cecil Browns, the Greens — at the end
of dinner, Rex would bring them into the kitchen for dessert. He would
see that everyone — and that always included the Yasumotos — was
seated around the large rectangular table where Alyce prepared the
meals. Alyce recalls: "We would have a round-table discussion of world
affairs. We all talked and laughed together. We enjoyed this and learned
so much from these famous people."[20] One year, after Thanksgiving
dinner, Rex put on some Viennese waltzes and the towering Paul Gallico danced several of them with Joy, who was just four feet tall.

As Christmas neared, Rex, with Harold and Kay, would cut a huge
Christmas tree. The Stouts and Yasumotos decorated it together. On

Christmas morning, after breakfast, Pola and Alyce would make egg-nog, then, in the great living room, they would open their presents together, and afterward sing Christmas carols.[21] Dinner, at three-thirty P.M., was followed by more caroling. At Easter, they collected eggs from the chickens, helped the children color them, and then priced them, a nickel up to a quarter. After that Rex and Kay hid them around the court. The children redeemed those they found for the values written on them.

When Pola was not at home, after dinner Rex always played games with all the children. "He would call my children into the dining room," says Alyce, "and they would play Animal, Vegetable, Mineral — Twenty Questions." Every Sunday, rain or shine, all the children were taken to the movies. Once a month, Alyce and Kay were given time off to visit New York City.

The Yasumotos found Rex "very punctual with anything he did." They knew he went to bed at eleven and got up at eight; that before breakfast he applied one hundred and fifty brush strokes to his hair and beard; that after breakfast he went out to check his garden. They knew he liked dinner at exactly six-thirty P.M. and that when the new irises he bought each year bloomed, he would cut one, bring it in, put it in a glass, and look at it long and hard. They knew that when he drove he never took his eyes off the road. They appreciated his interest in good food.

The Yasumotos found Rex as considerate as he was meticulous. When he groomed his beard, he spread newspapers over the bathroom sink to catch the cropped hairs. And when he trimmed his nails, he went out-of-doors to do it. Before going to bed he always emptied his ashtrays. The Yasumotos found Rex passive only if the world situation was not good or if he was about to start writing. Alyce relates: "He always told me to go ahead with vacuuming the house as anything I had to do wouldn't bother him. The only thing that bothered him was people talking. Many times Mrs. Stout would come home from New York and she would come in the kitchen and start to talk, forgetting Mr. Stout was writing. He would holler 'Pola!' She'd talk softly then. Soon after her voice would get louder again and he would stomp on the floor."

While Rex wrote, the children were asked not to play in the court, since it was right below his office. Alyce says: "Always around three o'clock every afternoon, when he was writing, I would bring him his snack — a glass of milk, Uneeda biscuits with cream cheese and jelly, or Brie. He would never hear me come in. He would come down for dinner every evening at exactly six-thirty."[22]

Archie once told Wolfe: "You regard anything and everything beyond your control as an insult." Perhaps Rex Stout did, too. No matter. He rarely felt the sting of such insults.

BOOK VII

Citizen of the World

37.

Under Viking Sail

Nero Wolfe is a massive eccentric of a typically dominating kind in the romantic style; yet he is always subject to reason — and that, I think, is what gives detective fiction its special attraction; power — represented in the omnicompetent detective — is admirable only when it is made to serve justice; if one believes in abstract justice, one sees a sort of hypostasis of justice in reason: and then an incarnation of reason in some admirable figure who is flesh and blood and better than we are but entirely obedient to justice and reason.

— ERIK ROUTLEY

Early in 1946 Pola and Rex gave up the East Eighty-sixth Street apartment. Henceforth a pied-à-terre at 30 Park Avenue would suffice for occasional overnight stays in Manhattan. But Rex's public life had not ended. He still served the Authors' Guild, the Authors' League, the FOD, Freedom House, the SPWW3, and the Writers' Board.[1] And his activities continued to make news. In January the *New Leader* reported:

Rex Stout and his "all-Germans-are-bad" boys are engaged in an organized drive to gag Dorothy Thompson. In this campaign Stout has resorted to character assassination and vituperation, reminiscent of the methods of Fascists and Communists. When Stout says that Dorothy Thompson has "defended German murderers," and "mocked at the sufferings and torture" of Hitler's victims, and that she has written "propaganda in favor of the master race," he simply lies.

After the war was won, Dorothy Thompson had in fact reported that some of the worst atrocities committed in Nazi concentration camps had been committed by the inmates themselves. She reported further that she had found many old friends in Berlin and all had served heroically in the resistance. Lucius Clay, General Eisenhower's deputy in charge of civic affairs in the United States Occupation Zone in Germany, did not travel in the same circles. He told the press: "We haven't modified the nonfraternization order because we haven't found any decent people in Germany." The Writers' Board was glad to credit him.

On 5 February 1946, many newspapers carried a full page ad prepared by the SPWW3. Rex's name headed a list of seventy-nine active members, including Major George Fielding Eliot, Emil Ludwig, Jo Davidson, Mary Ellen Chase, Thomas Craven, Allan Nevins, Sigrid Undset, Louis Nizer, Darryl Zanuck, Walter Wanger, and the usual dependables. The ad offered an eight-point agenda reiterating positions familiar to those who had followed WWB campaigns. These included destruction of Germany's war-making potential, confiscation of German assets, exposure of known Nazis and their supporters, and implementation of the Potsdam decisions.

Five days later, Rex announced that the Writers' Board had forwarded to President Truman a petition containing the signatures of more than a thousand prominent Americans. The petition urged Truman to instruct the American delegates to the UN "to initiate, without dangerous delay," action to transform the UN into a world government empowered to prohibit war and the possession of weapons of mass destruction, and to prohibit as well termination of the membership of individual nations by either withdrawal or expulsion.[2]

On 1 March the Writers' Board launched a boycott against the Chicago *Tribune*'s Sunday literary supplement, terming it, "anti-British, anti-Russian, anti-UNO [UN], anti-everything the world needs and hopes for." Letters were sent out urging the nation's writers to appeal to their publishers not to advertise in the supplement.

For Frederick Lewis Allen the campaign registered as an attack on free speech. Even though he himself disliked the *Tribune*'s stand on the issues, he did not think a newspaper should be boycotted because it disputed the President's foreign policy. To affirm his position, on 3 April Allen wrote to Rex resigning from the board's advisory committee. The gesture was without impact. By then, on its own, the campaign had fizzled. The board learned that it did not have the clout it had had in the war years. The fact is that most writers and publishers, unlike the battling editor of *Harper's*, were too caught up in their own concerns to mount the barricades in behalf of a new cause, however laudable it might seem to the board.[3]

On 4 March, Rex Stout and Clifton Fadiman — as spokesmen for the Authors' Guild and the Authors' League — sent out, under both their signatures, to a select company of eminent writers, copies of a pledge and draft letter which would be sent also to the full membership of the Guild and League if received favorably by those who got it first. The pledge affirmed that the pledgee would sign no contract with any publisher for publication of a book unless the contract either assured the author a ten percent royalty on the reprint edition or left reprint arrangements in his hands. By now many hardcover publishers had gone into the reprint business and were getting a double share of the profits. Rex was adamant. "The Guild," he said, "intends to see this through." Response was immediate. Ernest Hemingway, Sinclair Lewis, Van Wyck Brooks, Kenneth Roberts, James Thurber, Glenway Wescott,

Walter D. Edmonds, Elmer Davis, Louis Bromfield, Frederick Lewis Allen, and Anthony Boucher all signed.

Yet Boucher's reply underscored the difficulties the pledge presented for many writers:

I am happy to sign the pledge and endorse the letter. I'm in an unusually fortunate position to do so, since radio has made me financially independent of book publishing. If I were still a writer living almost exclusively from book contracts, I should probably have qualms and worry about whether such a high resolve could be maintained.[4]

This difficulty deprived Rex of the quick victory he wanted.

That same March, Mark Van Doren took over from Rex as president of the Society for the Prevention of World War III. Rex moved to a seat on the society's advisory council. In the weeks immediately following he was busy writing, but on 6 May, when the Friends of Democracy celebrated its tenth birthday with a dinner at the Waldorf-Astoria, he headed a list of speakers which included Leon Birkhead, Senator Wayne Morse, news commentator Robert St. John, Representative Andrew Biemiller of Wisconsin, and Colonel Robert S. Allen. At the dinner Rex announced that the group had raised $70,000 by inviting people to vote, at $1.00 a vote, for their candidate for the "Ignoble Prize of 1946." Top vote getter was Mississippi's racist Congressman, John E. Rankin. Runners up were Senator Theodore G. Bilbo, also of Mississippi, Colonel Robert R. McCormick, Gerald L. K. Smith, John O'Donnell, and Upton Close.

July 11 found Rex, in the company of Robert St. John, Clifton Fadiman, and Major George Fielding Eliot, visiting the Army Information School at Carlisle, Pennsylvania. There they addressed a capacity gathering of faculty and students on current world issues. *Cavalcade,* the school's newspaper, gave headline coverage to the visit, and, reflecting Nero Wolfe's perennial popularity with servicemen, accorded Rex first place in its ranking of the "distinguished guests."

Autumn brought a fresh spate of activities carried out for Freedom House, the SPWW3, and the Authors' Guild Council. This quickened public role carried over into the new year. On 25 February, at Ridgewood, New Jersey, Rex teamed up with Margaret Bourke-White to discuss the fate of postwar Germany. *The New York Times* radio forum "What's On Your Mind?" supplied the occasion. Ridgewood had been Bob Stout's hometown for a quarter of a century, and the audience, consisting of members of the Ridgewood Women's Club, was glad for the chance to inspect the famous brother of their dynamic local leader.[5] "German industry should be restored," Rex began. Over his audience's gasps, he continued, "but not as German and not in Germany. Practically all the usable industrial equipment in Germany was stolen by them from other countries and should be restored to the countries from which it was stolen." This issue was now waning as a topic of public interest. With world order at stake, Rex still had a terrier's hold on it.

Through the year, Rex dealt with the myriad meetings and projects of the groups he was drawn to serve. Not until the fall did he find himself again in the limelight, and that was on 19 October, when Freedom House gave General George C. Marshall its fifth annual Freedom Award. As Secretary of State, Marshall was then much in the public eye. Nearly eleven hundred prominent Americans gathered in the ballroom of the Commodore for the dinner, making it the largest of the Award dinners to that time. Rex always was a guest at the dais on these occasions, making ample amends with his wit for a nonconformity which saw him dressed in saffron shirts and thorn-proof tweeds while other head-table guests wore black tie. That year a dilemma arose. At the last minute Herbert Bayard Swope, the master of ceremonies, got laryngitis. He implored Rex to preside. To get Rex into a dinner jacket, Pola herself had to intervene.

Although they had taken the man out of the sports jacket, they had not taken the sport out of the man. Rex could be somber for no one — not even Bernard Baruch, the august elder statesman who had received the Award in 1946 and was on hand now to give General Marshall his plaque. When he introduced Baruch, Rex said, "We all know how good Mr. Baruch is at receiving awards. Now let's see how good he is at presenting one." "That was the last time," Rex told me, without repentance, "that anyone ever asked me to preside at one of Freedom House's Award dinners."

The Silent Speaker, Stout's first Nero Wolfe novel in seven years, was begun in March 1946 and finished in April. Thereafter, though he would continue writing for nearly another thirty years, his stories would all be Nero Wolfe stories. He liked Wolfe and Archie. After all, they were an essential part of himself. "During the war years I missed them," he told me. More important, the public liked them too. They were an assured source of income and a guarantee that Rex could live as he chose to. Apparently, also, he recognized the growth in self-esteem he had experienced in the war years and was curious to see how it would manifest itself in his alter ego, Nero Wolfe.

To no one's surprise, *The Silent Speaker* reflected Rex's recent prolonged association with government agencies. The silent speaker was Cheney Boone, director of the Federal Bureau of Price Regulation. Boone is murdered in an anteroom of the Grand Ballroom of the Waldorf-Astoria, minutes before he is to address a dinner of the National Industrial Association, attended by fourteen hundred guests. Reviewers thought Boone bore a curious resemblance to the former director of the

Lincoln School

Rex on presidential yacht Mayflower, *1906*

The Stouts on the steps of their New York brownstone, 1911

Rex, 1916

Fay Kennedy Stout, 1925

The Stout family, 1920

Rex, Joe MacGregor, and Harland Knowlton, Montana, 1926

Rex's first Dolly Varden or bull trout, Montana, 1926

The author of How Like a God, *1929*

Rex pattycaking with Barbara, 1937

Rex and Pola, 1944

Eisenhower signs Universal Copyright Convention, November 1954, with Rex looking on

Rex and his biographer, October 1973 (Photograph © 1977 Jill Krementz)

Office of Price Administration, Chester Bowles (whose initials he shared). And Rex's NIA seemed suspiciously like the National Association of Manufacturers. The Los Angeles *News* complained that the book was "heavily slanted on the political level." The reviewer explained: "Stout hates the man who killed OPA. But he might do better to withhold his intense dislike for the boom-bust crowd to bolster his pamphleteering."[6] In this story Wolfe stalls the denouement to allow the widest possible press coverage for Boone's proconsumer position. Solution of the murder involved pursuit of switched dictaphone recordings, which gives the case a prophetic link with the Watergate era.

In *The Silent Speaker* Charlie, the cleaning man, makes his one and only appearance at the brownstone. Asked what became of him, Rex disclosed: "He stole an orchid and was fired. Archie didn't bother to report it."

The completed manuscript was sent to Harold Guinzberg. Through the years Rex would send his manuscripts to Harold (and, after Harold's death, to Harold's son Tom), who then would pass them along to Marshall Best, Viking's senior editor. Best confined his attentions to the mechanics of publication. "Rex," he said, "submitted the cleanest copy of any author I know." Rex did follow his books through the press, reading proof on them "very promptly and efficiently," says Best.[7]

Viking published *The Silent Speaker* on 21 October 1946. Rex celebrated by finishing on the next day a new Wolfe novella, "Before I Die," which he had begun on 12 October. Here Wolfe, his scruples relaxed now that the war has been won, traffics with the black market to bring choice cuts of meat to his table. By the end of 1946, a pattern was emerging. Rex would write one Wolfe novel and one or two Wolfe novellas annually. With "Before I Die" he began keeping a "Writing Record," something he had not done before. Thus, from October 1946, on we know just when each Nero Wolfe story was written. *Too Many Women* — first entitled "Protect Your Woman" — was begun on 19 March 1947 and finished on 2 May. The record states: "Wrote 1 page 1st day, and 6 full days out. 38 writing days."

When *Too Many Women* was published on 20 October 1947, Isaac Anderson queried readers of *The New York Times Book Review*, "Why does Rex Stout call these books Nero Wolfe novels? Surely Archie Goodwin deserves equal billing with his obese employer." Anderson was a forerunner of the lady who asked a Poughkeepsie bookseller for an "Archie" book. "A Nero Wolfe book?" the dealer wanted to know. "Nonsense," said the lady. "We know who does all the work."

Archie's problem in this book (in which he finds himself, as "Peter Truett," personnel expert, working in an office amid "five hundred" women), is one which Rex, at this juncture of his life, could actively identify with. Not only did he have a beautiful wife, he had two beautiful daughters — one already in her teens.

Barbara and Rebecca remember their relationship with their father as unusual but fair. He never patronized them. He dealt with them always on their own level. He never said do or don't. He wanted them to come to decisions on their own. He rarely discouraged anything. If he was not enthusiastic about some move they contemplated, at most he left them feeling that if they did it, they did it on their own. He was slow to praise. When he did praise, they knew they had merited it. If a problem arose, he would hear it out. Yet if he said no about something, it could not be appealed.

"There were a few choice times," Rebecca admits, "when he laid down the law." Once when Barbara was home from college with a classmate, Rex sent her to her room because she was five minutes late for dinner. None of the family thought the punishment warranted, and they suspected that Rex himself soon regretted it. "Dad never could say he was sorry," Rebecca says. "He would show it, but couldn't say it. One just didn't expect it." He had other crotchets. He liked bright red lipstick and red nail polish on others, but never on his daughters. "He would notice what you wore," Barbara says, "only when he one hundred percent disapproved of it." The girls recall with amusement that when Rex bought himself a box of candy — it was apt to be a five-pounder — he would offer it around and then hide it.

When the girls brought friends home, Rex was careful to make them welcome. "Rex always knew right away whether he wanted to talk to a person or not," Pola said. He never put shy guests through an inquisition. When Alan Green's son Kit was twelve, Rex taught him to play chess. Alan sat in on the lesson. "Rex's acceptance of a young boy on his level was remarkable," Alan said. "No condescension — Rex made him feel an equal."[8]

Barbara and Rebecca took in stride their father's life as a writer. They thought of Nero Wolfe as one of the family. Barbara once told a guest: "My father doesn't support us. Nero Wolfe does." Yet once when Carl Sandburg called and asked Rebecca, "Is Brother Wolfe there?" she replied, "I'm sorry, there's no one here by that name." It all seemed so simple: "Dad spent six or eight weeks a year writing, and that was it." "My father won't retire," Barbara once told Clifton Fadiman. "He has nothing to retire from."[9]

There were good family jokes among them. During the winter of 1946–1947, Rex made his fine Brazilian mauro highboy. When its doors swing open, the startled observer sees that it contains, among other things, an array of superbly wrought birch trays, twenty in all, each able to slide out at a touch, on noiseless runners. A shirt rested on each, fresh and uncrushed — a convenience other men might dream of. Rex wanted it. Rex produced it. To his daughters this highboy has always been Rex's "Sherwood" — because it stands six feet seven, as did his friend Robert Sherwood.

Although Rex did not like holidays because they disrupted routines, for the sake of his family he made the best of them. Polly and Clifton Fadiman and their son Jonathan spent Thanksgiving with the Stouts for better than a dozen years. The Cecil Browns did too, their visits beginning in 1946 and ending only when they moved to Los Angeles in 1959. Brown recalled Rex presiding at the table: "Rex was an expert carver, more like a surgeon with a scalpel, hovering over the bird, asking each person what he or she wanted, and filling the plate. Rex of course did everything with perfection, or at least an effort at it, because that was his quality and his burden."

Rex's friendship with Brown had begun late in 1942, shortly after Brown got back from the Orient, where he had been bombed by the Japanese and "sunk by them in the South China Sea." Once home, Brown came quickly to prominence as a radio news analyst. He owns: "I knew little or nothing about Rex's fame or reputation. What attracted me initially was the precise, refreshing, direct and dogmatic comments he made about current events."

Of Rex as *pater familias* Brown says:

Their friends saw Rex as a demanding husband and father — definitely the lord of the manor. He was repaid with adoration. Pola seemed always ready and eager to submerge her moods and concerns to his needs or demands. To the outsider it looked as though Rex wanted his way all of the time. Yet High Meadow was no medieval fastness. It was a workshop for two remarkably busy, creative people. Pola's workroom was always festooned with great bolts of cloth. Her uncanny sense of color, weave, and texture, reached into every corner of the house. She was always brimming with projects, plans, and activities. The factory in Philadelphia, consultations in New York, lectures, exhibitions, kept her on the road part of every week. She boiled over with enthusiasm for everything she did. While Rex pursued his career she worked well to be a success in hers. Yet she planned and projected nothing without looking to him for advice. She never called him Rex. Her name for him was "Rexlove," and she meant it with all her heart.[10]

Alyce Yasumoto remembers the lord of High Meadow in much the same terms: "Mr. Stout gave us very wise decisions whenever we needed them, yet we always were able to do what we wanted to with our own lives." So much for Rex as suzerain.

Than Selleck, who had delivered both Barbara and Rebecca, was, in Rex's estimation, the best doctor in Danbury, but Rex valued him as a friend even more than as a physician. For a dozen years they got together on Thursday nights at 25 Delta Avenue to play pocket billiards in Than's basement. Afterward they ate apple pie and ice cream and talked till close to one o'clock. Than was the better player, so the odds they played at were 50–70. "I occasionally got fifty before Than got seventy," Rex told me, "but not too often. I was pretty good, though."

A medical background is useful to a detective story writer, as Conan Doyle and R. Austin Freeman unabashedly acknowledged. Even Agatha Christie dated her career from her tour of duty as a hospital aide in World War I, and Simenon has disclosed that he fraternizes chiefly with medical men. Than Selleck was Rex Stout's medical confidant. From him Rex learned what he needed to know about poisons and various medical matters. But he was not the prototype of the middle-sized, short-legged Dr. Edwin Vollmer, whom Wolfe consults when he needs a doctor. At six feet, and weighing one hundred and eighty-five pounds, he was closer to Archie Goodwin's build. There is a Nathaniel in Wolfe's coterie, however — Nathaniel Parker, his attorney, one of the few men with whom he will shake hands. Dr. Nathaniel "Than" Bradford rates a mention in *Fer-de-Lance*.[11]

When in May 1947, the head of the governing board at Danbury Hospital tried to enforce guidelines on medical ethics advocated by the local Catholic bishop, four doctors on the staff, Dr. Selleck among them, opposed him and asked Rex to support their stand. Rex plunged into the fray. He put a full page ad in the Danbury *News-Times*. He followed it up with supporting letters. The issue was decided in favor of the doctors, and the head of the board quit. Rex and Than then went off on a fishing trip to the Miramichi, in New Brunswick. They liked it so well they went there again, for several years running. There, in 1949, Rex would land a prize catch — a thirty-eight-pound Atlantic salmon. Sometimes they fished the northern reaches of the Connecticut River, too. For deep-sea fishing they went out on Long Island Sound. Than had a trap shooting outfit, and Rex also became adept with that.

In the summer of 1947 Rex wrote "Man Alive" — begun 24 July, finished 3 August. No days out. It was published in *The American Magazine* in December. Before its release Rex had another novella finished — "Bullet for One" — written between the seventeenth and twenty-ninth of November, with two days out for Thanksgiving.[12] During the holidays Rex often had a writing project under way. To write in that interval was his way of salvaging time which otherwise would be squandered — as he saw it. Besides, the good feeling he got when he was quit of a book was for him what the holiday spirit would be for somebody else. Rex had a novel and two novellas to show for sixty days' writing in 1947. In 1948 he got out the same amount of work in fifty-five days. He began *And Be a Villain* on 19 March 1948 and finished it on 24 April. Elapsed writing time, thirty-four days.

At one point in *And Be a Villain* Archie says that Wolfe was drawing pictures of horses because he had read somewhere that "you can analyze a man's character from the way he draws horses." Rex told me: "About that time I got in the mail an envelope with a printed return

'Horse Analysis' and a Washington, D.C., address. In it was a 'Horse Analysis' letterhead with the news that if I would send a drawing of a horse by me and two dollars I would get a complete analysis of my character. I did so, and never got a reply. So I don't understand me." Rex concluded by thinking that the sponsors of the venture were taking a census of horses' asses.

"Omit Flowers" was begun on 14 July and completed on 23 July. No days out.

Late in the summer of 1948 Rex and Pola visited Russel Crouse at his house in Massachusetts, at Gloucester, on Ipswich Bay. Then it was back to High Meadow and Nero Wolfe. *And Be a Villain* was published on 27 September. This book opened the Zeck trilogy — Wolfe's death struggle with a master criminal — which would reach its climax two years hence. The trilogy was not preplanned. Rex thought Zeck might be heard from again, but he was not sure.

"Omit Flowers" came out in November. That left Rex's desk swept clean of manuscripts. But not for long. "Door to Death" was begun on 8 December and finished on the nineteenth. One day out. This story, and two others written the next year — "The Gun with Wings" and "Disguise for Murder" — though written concurrently with the Zeck trilogy, would take no notice of Zeck and his harassments.

38.

A Superman Who Talks
like a Superman

Nero is a triumphant Superman detective, the Nero-Archie relationship is done with a merciful absence of sentimentality, the stories fizz along. Rex Stout has given a great deal of pleasure to a great many people, myself included.

— JULIAN SYMONS

Rex found out in 1949, as he had a decade earlier, that world affairs would not let him live the life of man of letters and gentleman of leisure reposing at his country seat. The Korean outbreak was still a year and a half away, but his work for world organization had convinced him that Communism now menaced freedom just as Fascism had a decade earlier. He felt toward the Soviets much as he had felt toward Nazi Germany after Munich — if we were to stop them at all, the time was now. The Friends of Democracy had been founded to fight Communism as well as Fascism. For ten years the Axis powers had absorbed most of the organization's energies. That threat had been repelled. But now, with menacing gestures, the Communist ogre was drawing itself up to its full height. For one example, in the UN, the veto power — which Rex never had liked — had become a potent tool of Soviet statecraft.

The year began amiably enough. On 8 January *The New Yorker* reported that Jules Alberti, founder of Endorsements, Inc. — which specialized in gathering sincere testimonials for advertising clients — had identified Rex, along with Fred Astaire, Humphrey Bogart, Hoagy Carmichael, and Dinah Shore, as one of the "wholesome types" whose help he hoped to enlist gratis. Sincerity and wholesomeness notwithstanding, neither Rex nor Wolfe endorsed so much as a brioche for Alberti.

In mid-January, at Springfield, Vermont, a "Nero and Archie" overture, composed by Rex's long-time correspondent and plant-swapping friend, Alan Macneil, was given its premiere performance by the Vermont State Symphony Orchestra. As Macneil's guests, Rex and Pola were on hand for it. Certainly this was an event of some moment. Sherlock Holmes may have played the violin and written a monograph on the motets of Lassus, but there is no record of a "Sherlock and John" overture, performed by a full symphony orchestra in Vermont, in the dead of winter, in the presence of their creator.

Rex was back in Manhattan in time to preside at the annual meeting of the Baker Street Irregulars in the last week of January. There he received his Irregular Shilling with the investiture of "The Boscombe Valley Mystery."

Trouble in Triplicate, the first of Viking's eleven volumes of Wolfe novellas, came out on 11 February. Publication day found Rex at work on "Grim Fairy Tales," the most closely argued of the five articles he would contribute to the shelf of criticism that deals with the topic of detective fiction. In this article, commissioned by Norman Cousins for the *Saturday Review,* Rex undertook initially to explain why "Sherlock Holmes is the most widely known fictional character in all the literature of the world. . . ." "Sherlock Holmes," he said, "is the embodiment of man's greatest pride and greatest weakness: his reason. . . . He is human aspiration. He is what our ancestors had in mind when in wistful braggadocio they tacked the *sapiens* onto the *homo.*" No subject was of greater interest to Rex. Few men prided themselves more on their exercise of reason. Few men cared less to be dictated to by their emotions.

Looking for an explanation which accounted for Holmes's presence "on his peak," Rex accounted as well for the creation of Nero Wolfe and, incidentally, for Rex Stout himself:

We enjoy reading about people who love and hate and covet — about gluttons and martyrs, misers and sadists, whores and saints, brave men and cowards. But also, demonstrably, we enjoy reading about a man who gloriously acts and decides, with no exception and no compunction, not as his emotions brutally command, but as his reason instructs.

Rex cited Christie, Van Dine, Hammett, and Gardner as writers who understood "this basic principle, this essence, of detective stories." Yet he was surprised to find Dorothy Sayers's Lord Peter Wimsey sleepless on the eve of the execution of a murderer he had run to earth. "A detective story ends," he chided, "when reason's job is done."

Rex contended that the true hero of the detective story is "reason" itself. The detective is not a man but a personified abstraction to which the author assigns a human identity. He then educed that the challenge inherent in creating a ratiocinative hero who is more than a machine explains the success of the series detective. When a writer creates a believable detective, he hangs on to him.

"Grim Fairy Tales" ends on a jesting note. Detective stories get their "enormous audience" by telling "two flagrant lies: that justice is always done and that man's reason orders his affairs." Therein is found the reason why critics discount the genre: "Men love it, desire it, need it, and pay money for it. But they don't really believe it, and they can't be expected to take seriously something they don't really believe."

Of "Grim Fairy Tales" Rex told me: "I didn't give it special attention. I sat down and wrote it. I usually write short pieces longhand — I don't know why — and I probably did that one, but I doubt if I made many changes when I typed it. After twenty-five years I still think it's pretty good." It is indeed. It came together quickly for Rex because it is a distillation of the rationale which governed what he wrote. And it affirms that the detective story was, for Rex, an externalization of his own, given-from-within quest for harmony and order.

On 16 March, Rex began writing *Second Confession.* He finished it on 23 April. Four days out. In *Second Confession* Wolfe tangles with the Communist Party, and Communism itself is dismissed as "intellectually contemptible and morally unsound." A further clash here with Arnold Zeck would prompt the Springfield *Republican* to say, "Ahead can be heard the unmistakable roar of the Reichenbach falls."[1] But *Second Confession* forecast more than a coming crisis in Nero Wolfe's life. It signaled Rex's militant return to the battle lines where forces were joined in the struggle for men's minds.

In 1948, on 19 November, the SPWW3 had sent a lengthy letter to *The New York Times* signed by Rex, Birkhead, Mumford, Mark Van Doren, and fifteen other members, protesting Allied plans to reorganize the Ruhr under German trusteeship, lest the resurgence of German economic power again make Germany a world power and a world menace. On 12 May 1949, as a panelist on the *New York Times* forum "What's On Your Mind?" Rex found himself sharing the platform with two former American military governors in Germany, Charles La Follette and Mack Terry. Their topic was the rebuilding of Germany. Rex deplored American plans to rebuild Germany as "the strongest industrial nation in Europe." He speculated that the United States wanted to "fatten" Germany as an ally in an eventual battle with Russia. "Germany won't help us fight Russia; wait and see," he said. "I predict that the Germans will join the Communists to fight us."

Everyone knew Rex did not believe in a restored Germany. But his strictures on Soviet Communism introduced into his public utterances a hitherto undisclosed emphasis. Behind the scenes Rex had become engaged in an activity which reflected his accelerating concern over the changing world picture. Yet a full account of it lay still some weeks in the future. *Second Confession* already had registered that concern. Like a time bomb the manuscript lay ticking in Viking's vault.

In the spring of 1949, Cord Meyer, Jr., president of the United World Federalists and later an agent of the CIA, had asked Rex to form another writers' board — a Writers' Board for World Government. Rex ruminated, then acceded and acted. His work with the UWF already had shown him where he could best turn for support. On 3 July, the Writers' Board for World Government came formally into existence. On that date the group announced its formation with an "American Declaration of Dependence" — an appeal to more than four thousand American writers to join the board in its efforts to transform the United Nations into a limited world government. "Our only alternative to world war," the declaration said, "is world law. We can get world law only by establishing a world government."

Whatever its claims for being a new organization, the WBWG was, in essence, a revival of the postwar Writers' Board (which had sunk into a spectral existence) with a redefined purpose. Once again Rex was board chairman. Board members were Norman Cousins, Russel Crouse, Clifton Fadiman, John Farrar, Alan Green, Oscar Hammerstein II, John Hersey, Laura Z. Hobson, John Hohenburg, Annalee Jacoby, Christopher La Farge, Margaret Leech Pulitzer, Jerry Mason, Cord Meyer, Jr., Merle Miller, Robert Sherwood, and Ruth Friend (who was the board's executive secretary). The nucleus of the new board — more than half its membership — had either been members of the WWB or had worked closely with it.

As Rex had expected, a board organized to prevent a war did not absorb its members as a board organized to win a war had done. WWB members gave up a full day once a week. WBWG members were not ready to do that. More disappointing was the disinclination of some WWB people to work with the new board at all. Robert Landry saw no point in fostering the hopes the WBWG engendered. "It will be a hundred years," he told Rex, "before any nation, including the United States, will be willing to give up a part of its sovereignty."[2]

Typical of a board under Rex Stout's chairmanship, the WBWG did not sit around "preparing to plan to arrange to do something." Rex proposed that they stage another "Myth" show, this one designed to debunk the notion that a nation can be sovereign and be at peace. The board accepted the idea, and Lindsay and Crouse, Hammerstein, and Sherwood at once began enlisting major talents against an early December target date.[3]

While Rex was pulling together the WBWG and formulating plans for the Myth show, his own life story suddenly was put before the public in terms so extraordinary that even many of his friends began to realize for the first time that Rex was himself a man of mythic dimensions. The presentation came in a two-part profile, written by Alva Johnston, which began appearing in *The New Yorker* in its 16 July issue and finished up the following week. So far as the fortunes of the WBWG were concerned, this twelve-thousand-word appraisal of its chairman came along most opportunely. Rex was portrayed as a wonder man (one of Pola's favorite terms of endearment for him) and as Nero Wolfe's real-life counterpart, "a superman who talks like a superman." Predictably, writers flocked to affiliate with Rex's new board.

In preparation for writing his profile, Johnston had had three searching interviews with Rex, for a total of fifteen hours. Johnston, who followed Rex from Penrod to pundit, seemed awed by his subject and his speculations tended to enhance the legend his factual data propounded. Contrary to rumor, Rex did not edit Johnston's copy before it was set in type.[4]

While the rest of the country was keeping track of Rex Stout's adventures in *The New Yorker*, Rex was on the track of Nero Wolfe. On 16 July he began "The Gun with Wings." He finished it on 28 July. Two and a half days out. Ten and a half days' writing time. The time out was not spent reading Johnston's profile, but in separating iris rhizomes.

In less than four years Rex had written four Wolfe novels and seven Wolfe novellas, nearly doubling the total number of Wolfe stories from what the count had been when World War II ended. He must have been amused, therefore, to find Johnston asserting that Nero Wolfe "has appeared in print infrequently since [World War II] because of Stout's absorption in the work of putting out propaganda for world federation." While Johnston was correct in insisting on Rex's interest in world federation, relatively speaking the curtain was just rising on that phase of his career.

Johnston's profile elicited a postscript from John McNulty, which *The New Yorker* carried in its 20 August issue, together with Johnston's reply.[5] McNulty owned that he was wary about taking on Rex himself, "who, to judge by Mr. Johnston's recent Profile of him, could single-handed out-argue a team made up of Sam Leibowitz, Casey Stengel, and Donald Duck." He addressed himself accordingly to Johnston:

> I say that it is impossible for an eleven-year old boy, Stout or not Stout, to have read twelve hundred assorted volumes of printed matter, especially of such printed matter as must have been in the Stout home fifty-odd years ago. . . . No thrifty Quaker of that time would have handed out good money for a skinny little book of less than four or five hundred pages.

McNulty offered this timetable of "Young Rex Stout's Day":

School	4 hours
Travel time to and from school	2 hours
Sleep	8 hours
Mathematical wizardry	2 hours
Meals	2 hours

Ghost exorcising and such sundries	1/2 hour
Going to church	1 hour
Committing routine annoyances	2 hours
Natural odds and ends	1/2 hour
Total	22 hours
Left for reading	2 hours

As he saw it, to have read 1,200 books in the allotted span, Rex would have had to have read 98 1/2 pages an hour, or about 1.6 pages a minute. And, at that, history and philosophy books, science and poetry. "I simply don't believe it," said McNulty. "Not for 1.6 minutes do I believe it." Johnston replied:

Rex Stout didn't need to be a precocious child to read twelve hundred books . . . he read at the average rate of one book every fifty-four hours. . . . Mr. McNulty errs in supposing that a real reader stops reading because he happens to be doing something else. He is wrong in thinking that it is impossible to read and exorcise a ghost at the same time. . . . A boy bookworm doesn't allow ghosts or school to cut into his reading time.

Johnston cited the persistence of "Dr. Arthur Warren Waite, the bookish murderer, who became incensed when they interrupted his reading to lead him to the electric chair." The controversy died a-borning.

Had Johnston inquired into Rex's current reading habits he might have provided McNulty further astonishments. Not only did Rex read everything Wolfe read — in this period that included books by Catton, La Farge, C. I. Lewis, Hobson, and Gunther — he read dozens of works by "serious" moderns and had definite opinions about them. He thought Arthur Miller "one of the most overrated American writers." Norman Mailer he saw as "a peacock who uses words instead of tail-feathers." Personal acquaintance was no earnest of his approval. Pearl Buck was "a fine person and a good businesswoman," but "a minor writer." He met Robert Frost several times when visiting Mark and Dorothy Van Doren, but he could not get past Frost's ego. He placed E. B. White in the first rank — not because they both were One World-ers — but for his infallible sense of word choice. "He never makes a mistake," Rex said.

Although Rex realized Christopher La Farge was descended from Benjamin Franklin, he never spoke to La Farge of his own descent from Ben's sister Mary. Even without this bond as a contributing factor, during the WWB years close ties of friendship grew between them. When they served together on the WBWG those ties strengthened. On one occasion Rex's advice to La Farge brought a crucial change in La Farge's literary development, as he himself later attested:

In 1949, some months before I began the actual work of writing this novel in verse, *Beauty for Ashes*, you took me to task for overplanning my book in advance. You said then that the chance of achieving greatness, however remote, was diminished in a major work by such too thoughtful planning, because it closed the door to that growth of the work which might be properly expected to come from its own progression. . . .

What came of this was, to me, remarkable. By allowing the book to remain loose in my mind both in detail of plot and of form — form being so great a preoccupation in poetry — I left the book free to grow as it developed in the conception and its execution. Out of this, both in content and in form, came the whole ending, which in turn was made possible by the free development of the parts that had preceded it. . . . You will have to judge of its success or lack of it for yourself. But you should know why I am grateful to you. . . .[6]

Rex could give as well as receive compliments. On 3 August 1949 he wrote to Anthony Boucher:

Fan letter. As you of course know, in England for many years detective stories have been reviewed competently and with discrimination, whereas in this country we have had nothing but — well, I won't mention names. So your pieces in *EQMM* and the *Times* are a relief, a delight, and a big help. Not only do you know what you're writing about, but you also know how to write. I am one of thousands deeply indebted to you.

On 6 September *Second Confession* was published. If Colonel McCormick saw the *Daily Worker*'s review he must have been stunned. There Robert Friedman said: "It was only a matter of time until someone discovered the possibilities in fusing the current anti-Communist drive with the mystery formula. All due credit for the inspiration must go to Rex Stout, a Victor Riesel with a beard who has been hacking out for many years a series of yarns about one Nero Wolfe." *Second Confession* offered "the thrill of the Gestapo chase," said Friedman. He went on: "Which one is the Communist? and then, how about having a Communist who's also a member of a dope-selling racketeer's gang? Too, why not have a second Communist kill the first, alleged Communist? We could go on, but only Goebbels would want us to."[7]

Meanwhile, plans for *The Myth That Threatens the World* were accelerating. A script was prepared by Oscar Hammerstein II, Russel Crouse, Carl Van Doren, Clifton Fadiman, and Phyllis Merrill, with the show itself under Hammerstein's general arrangement and direction. The first performance of this extraordinary production — one of the most distinguished first nights in the history of the New York stage — took place at the Coronet Theatre, Sunday evening, 4 December. The cast included Eddie Albert, Marian Anderson, Brock Chisholm (director-general of the World Health Organization), Russel Crouse, Alfred E. Driscoll (governor of New Jersey), Henry Fonda, Cord Meyer, Jr., General George Olmsted, Robert Sherwood, Clifton Fadiman, Oscar Hammerstein II, and Rex himself, who spoke the prologue. In addition, the audience heard the voice of Carlos Rómulo, president of the General Assembly of the United Nations, who had prepared a special recording for the production, through which he spoke first to Eddie Albert, the devil's advocate of the show, and then to the assembled audience, which consisted of more than a thousand illustrious world citizens, including statesmen from more than fifty nations.

Nothing that could bring distinction to the presentation was overlooked. Recalling the Sunday afternoon before the Coronet Theatre performance, Alan Green told me:

It was a dress rehearsal and they were trying to get the light cues just right for the Carl Van Doren scene — exactly when should the lights come up to reveal the colonial setting and costumes? Out front Oscar Hammerstein, Robert Sherwood, Buck Crouse and Howard Lindsay huddled over the problem. I wonder whether before or since so much theater know-how had been directed to a staging problem.[8]

In his prologue Rex set forth the myth in eight words: "Nations can stay sovereign and stay at peace." He amplified:

Our purpose this evening is not to discredit it, to expose it as a dangerous delusion — history has already done that, again and again, throughout forty centuries. Our purpose is to present the case, or part of it at least, for what we believe to be the only practical substitute. . . . We know that in bygone centuries it may have been of great service to man's soul and conscience; but we think that now, in this shrunken world with its cracked atoms, it is of service only to misery and disaster. . . . But the myth stubbornly persists, and it threatens the world.[9]

Over the next two years, with frequent substitutions (for example, in Hagerstown, Maryland, Norman Cousins took Fadiman's role), under the auspices of the UWF, the Myth show was put on in numerous cities, including Philadelphia, Pittsburgh, Milwaukee, Minneapolis, Chicago, Washington, and Boston. Manhattan had a second performance as well.

After its first performance, the Myth show troupe had been furloughed for the holidays. For Rex there still was time before Christmas to do another Wolfe story. He began "Disguise for Murder" — initially called "The Scarf" — on 12 December, and completed it on Christmas Eve. Eleven days' writing time. Two days out.

His stories were more in demand than ever. Indeed, in the fall of 1949, Farrar & Rinehart had entered into a dialogue with a German publisher, Karl Anders, who wanted to publish the Wolfe stories in Germany, with most of the profits to go to Anders. On 28 December Rex wrote Marguerite Reese of Farrar & Rinehart in terms which suggested that he still was having trouble fitting Germany into his "one world":

> The many earnest and expensive efforts to democratize the Germans, by both British and Americans, having dismally failed. . . . I can't believe it would help much to make an American detective story available to them on terms that would make it in effect a gift. If and when I feel like making gifts of my little literary properties to foreign countries, I shall certainly not put Germany at the top of the list.

If there is anything to Howard Haycraft's theory that the detective story flourishes only in democratic societies, then Rex may have been premature in thinking that democracy had failed in Germany. German editions of his books were arranged for later, on equitable terms, and their sales eventually topped the three-million mark.[10]

39.

Beyond High Meadow

I know Rex Stout is a good man. Anyone who sees the necessity for world
government is good enough for me. I hope he lives forever.

— E. B. WHITE

On 17 January 1950, eight bandits took $1,500,000 from a Brink's office
in Boston. Never had there been a bigger cash holdup in American
history. A day or so later International News Service asked Rex to do
a feature piece on the robbery for national circulation. The temptations
were myriad. But Rex did not make the mistake, as Conan Doyle sometimes did, of assuming the identity of his detective hero. He did not try
to solve the crime. Nor did he lay down ground rules for solving it. He
merely warned against errors of judgment that might impede the investigation. He noted that "rivalry and ill feeling between the Boston cops
and the FBI was out in the open . . . less than a week after the robbery."
Nothing would be accomplished "as long as a cop would rather beat a
G-man than eat, or the other way around. . . ." Fifteen years later, in
The Doorbell Rang, Nero Wolfe would benefit from just such a rivalry.
Right now, however, Rex urged the governor of Massachusetts to appoint an overseer who could bring harmony between the rival law
enforcement teams.

On the basis of what he knew about similar large robberies, Rex
forecast what the probable outcome of the investigation would be, even
if it was carried out prudently. Little if any of the money would be
recovered; few if any of the bandits would be caught and convicted.[1]
He summed up in Goodwinese: "It looks to me like ten to one, with the
owners of the money and the majesty of the law on the short end. I
know long shots sometimes win, but that doesn't prove that people who
back favorites on performance are simpletons."

No doubt to the general relief of Brink's Inc., Rex's adjunctive proposal that "Brink" be added to the language as a "trade term for a
million bucks" did not catch on.

In early April, for a forthcoming Authors' Guild volume, Rex wrote
"The Mystery Novel," another installment of his dicta on the art of
crime fiction. Here he dismissed the compilations of dogma which Ron-

ald Knox, "S. S. Van Dine" (Willard Huntington Wright), R. Austin Freeman, and Dorothy Sayers had propounded. He termed "nonsensical" the ironclad rule that the detective story writer "must play fair with the reader." Not only was it legitimate to conceal the murderer's identity from the reader, he thought it might be fun sometime to withhold the detective's identity. He contended he was competent to talk only about classic detective stories — those in which the detective "is and must be the hero." In such stories, he said, the reader's attention has to be centered not only on the method of the murder, or the identity of the murderer, but on how the detective-hero arrives at a solution. He noted a further complication. While the straight storyteller engages in "designed exposition," the detective story writer works in "designed concealment." He cannot highlight the discoveries the hero makes.

As an addendum to this piece, Rex next produced a jacket essay — "Reading and Writing Detective Stories" — for "J. J. Marric's" (John Creasey's) *Gideon's Day*. After acknowledging that the first detective story he had ever read was "a five-cent paperbound affair — a daring and ingenious exploit of Old King Brady — ," Rex said, "I still can't decide which is more fun — reading them or writing them. The difference is somewhat the same as the difference between watching a baseball game from the grandstand and getting out on the field and playing. To see, from the grandstand, the shortstop make a brilliant play on a sizzler is a delight; but the shortstop's own delight, though surely as keen as yours, is of quite another sort." The look into the creative process which Rex then gave his readers suggested that he favored the player's role over that of spectator.

On 21 April *Three Doors to Death* was published. Meanwhile Rex had been at work for a week on the final volume of the Zeck trilogy — *In the Best Families*. With eight days out for a fishing trip to the Miramichi, it was not finished until 29 May. In this remarkable book, one of the high points of the Wolfe saga, Wolfe deserts the brownstone and sheds much of his excess poundage in preparation for his final confrontation with the master criminal, Arnold Zeck.[2] Incredibily, in pursuit of his goal, he embarks upon a criminal career and infiltrates Zeck's organization.

For those who had followed the saga to this point, Wolfe's voluntary renunciation of his intimate home environment and the comforts it made possible was an event of epoch-shattering consequence. It was as though Jove had come down from Olympus to live as a mere mortal in the fetid slums of the poor. And it called to mind immediately Wolfe's words spoken eighteen months earlier to that spoiled heir to millions, Joseph G. Pitcairn, in "Door to Death." "It would be foolhardy," Wolfe told Pitcairn, "to assume that you would welcome a thorn for the sake of such abstractions as justice or truth, since that would make you a rarity almost unknown. . . ." Now Wolfe himself had done just that. For sake of justice and truth, spurning Zeck's attempts to buy him off, he had accepted the thorn.

Many readers who participated in Wolfe's earlier adventures and knew what this sacrifice on his part entailed were so overwhelmed by it, and so solicitous for his comfort, that they wrote to Rex to tell him that they felt such inner anguish while following the events of this volume that periodically they had had to lay aside the book to muster their spirits before continuing on with it.

Rex himself understood how momentous a move it was for Wolfe to abandon his celebrated sanctuary and the way of life it gave substance to. When Wolfe departed he left standing ajar the front door, which otherwise, save for arrivals and departures, was kept scrupulously bolted. Although normally Rex did not deliberately deal in symbols, he acknowledged that this gesture was meant to carry symbolic meaning. In fact, he saw it as one of his most satisfying touches.[3]

In June, looking about for relaxing chores after his intense writing ordeal, Rex made two nest boxes with a hole size for wrens. Mindful of the loss of pride and initiative that occurs when benefactions are gratuitously supplied, he chalked a price on each wren house — 35 cents. Rex insisted: "In a couple of weeks one of them had been taken and the other hadn't, and I mounted a stepladder, crossed out the 35 cents and put 15 cents. The next day wrens started on a nest in it."[4]

The elation Rex felt in completing the Zeck trilogy seems to have activated a whimsical bent in him. At an afternoon game at Yankee Stadium, he found himself sitting in front of Joe Louis and Sugar Ray Robinson. During the third inning, he bought a bag of peanuts, turned around, and said, "My one great ambition has been to watch a baseball game and eat peanuts being shelled for me by Joe Louis and Sugar Ray Robinson." Sugar Ray said, "Sure, we'll be glad to." And they did.

These playful days were short-lived. On 6 June Merwin Hart, appearing before the House's Select Committee to Investigate Lobbying Activities, insisted that Rex was a Communist. He cited as proof Rex's role in founding *The New Masses*. On 16 June, Rex wrote Representative Frank Buchanan, chairman of the committee, reminding him that he had resigned from *The New Masses* to protest its adoption of the Communist line. "It is ironic," he said, "that one of the many occasions, in the past third of a century, on which I have opposed Communism, should be used by Mr. Hart and others to imply that I was once pro-Communist. . . ." Sunday morning, 25 June, brought the news that South Korea had been invaded by Communist forces from the north. The United States went to war again and once more Rex mounted the barricades.

Through the pages of *Prevent World War III*, Rex spoke out editorially against the North Korean incursion. As chairman of the WBWG he reiterated the need for strengthening the UN's peace-keeping capabilities. As chairman of the FOD, he presented a Special Award of Merit to playwright Arthur Miller for the narration Miller had written for the Italian film *Difficult Years*, then having its premier run at Manhattan's World Theatre. The award hailed the film as the "best dramatization of the impact of totalitarianism on all the citizens of the world." Rex helped Freedom House draft a message to President Truman urging that "Congress should enact legislation to outlaw the Communist Party and all its affiliated agencies and publications." Significantly, the statement affirmed that the forces of subversion could be routed "without using the shotgun of unproven charges and the technique of the smear campaign." Rex saw that the methods of McCarthyism discredited democracy itself. Freedom House did not wish to bundle with strange bedfellows.

When Freedom House revived the "Our Secret Weapon" format, Rex, in conjunction with Leo Cherne, Father George B. Ford, and Harry Gideonse, did a succession of broadcasts unmasking "the big lies" of Stalin. Father Ford, longtime Catholic chaplain at Columbia, and a fighting liberal, was a charter member of Freedom House, and Rex's warm friend. One night, as they were heading downstairs for the broadcast, Rex, coming along behind Father Ford, said, "I'm not sure I like this, going downstairs in the footsteps of a papist." "Listen," responded Father Ford, "I know all about you, and you're more of a papist than I am."[5]

Although he kept to his grinding schedule without complaint, at times Rex found himself wishing world law and world peace might become an instant reality. In reply to a solicitous letter from Adelaide Sherer, he wrote: "I'm fine. I'd be even finer if the Germans and Russians would take a trip to Mars and forget the way back."

On 24 July, against a background of constant meetings and mounting correspondence, Rex began another novella. While he was writing it, he called it "Just in Time." Afterward he changed over to the title "The Cop-Killer." He finished it on 7 August. Three days out. That year, for the first time in four years, there would be no third Nero Wolfe story.

In the Best Families came out on 29 September. With this book the majority of the reviewers seemed to realize that an apotheosis had occurred. Wolfe had taken his place among the immortals. Yet no one said it as well as the Englishman Julian Symons did:

> In the fight to the death between master-detective and master-criminal the most ingenious and unlikely subterfuges are used. . . . All this is very improbable. It is the art of Mr. Stout to make it seem plausible. . . . Holmes was a fully realized character. There is only a handful of his successors to whom that compliment can be paid. One of them, certainly, is Nero Wolfe.[6]

On 10 October, with Sydney Greenstreet in the starring role, NBC launched the final Nero Wolfe radio series. The producer, Edwin Fadiman, was aided by a confidential memo which Rex had prepared for him more than a year earlier — 15 September 1949 — when plans for the series first evolved. Under the heading "Description of Nero Wolfe," the memo read:

Height 5 ft. 11 in. Weight 272 lbs. Age 56. Mass of dark brown hair, very little greying, is not parted but sweeps off to the right because he brushes with his right hand. Dark brown eyes are average in size, but look smaller because they are mostly half closed. They always are aimed straight at the person he is talking to. Forehead is high. Head and face are big but do not seem so in proportion to the whole. Ears rather small. Nose long and narrow, slightly aquiline. Mouth mobile and extremely variable; lips when pursed are full and thick, but in tense moments they are thin and their line is long. Cheeks full but not pudgy; the high point of the cheekbone can be seen from straight front. Complexion varies from some floridity after meals to an ivory pallor late at night when he has spent six hard hours working on someone. He breathes smoothly and without sound except when he is eating; then he takes in and lets out great gusts of air. His massive shoulders never slump; when he stands up at all he stands straight. He shaves every day. He has a small brown mole just above his right jawbone, halfway between the chin and the ear. [Rex had a similar mole.]

A TV producer could not have hoped for more specifics. Nowhere in the saga itself is Wolfe described with such thoroughness.

The memo now proceeded to a "Description of Archie Goodwin":

Height 6 feet. Weight 180 lbs. Age 32.[7] Hair is light rather than dark, but just barely decided not to be red; he gets it cut every two weeks, rather short, and brushes it straight back, but it keeps standing up. He shaves four times a week and grasps at every excuse to make it only three times. His features are all regular, well-modeled and well-proportioned, except the nose. He escapes the curse of being the movie actor type only through the nose. It is not a true pug and is by no means a deformity, but it is a little short and the ridge is broad, and the tip has continued on its own, beyond the cartilage, giving the impression of startling and quite independent initiative. The eyes are gray, and are inquisitive and quick to move. He is muscular both in appearance and in movement, and upright in posture, but his shoulders stoop a little in unconscious reaction to Wolfe's repeated criticism that he is too self-assertive.

Again the memo makes us privy to disclosures the saga withholds.

Under the heading "Description of Wolfe's Office" the memo describes the ground floor of the brownstone:

The old brownstone on West 35th Street is a double-width house. Entering at the front door, which is seven steps up from the sidewalk, you are facing the length of a wide carpeted hall. At the right is an enormous coat rack, eight feet wide, then the stairs, and beyond the stairs the door to the dining room. There were originally two rooms on that side of the hall, but Wolfe had the partition removed and turned it into a dining room forty feet long, with a table large enough for six (but extensible) square in the middle. It (and all other rooms) are carpeted; Wolfe hates bare floors. At the far end of the big hall is the kitchen. At the left of the big hall are two doors; the first one is to what Archie calls the front room, and the second is to the office. The front room is used chiefly as an anteroom; Nero and Archie do no living there. It is rather small, and the furniture is a random mixture without any special character.

The office is large and nearly square. In the far corner to the left (as you enter from the hall) a small rectangle has been walled off to make a place for a john and a washbowl — to save steps for Wolfe. The door leading to it faces you, and around the corner, along its other wall, is a wide and well-cushioned couch.[8]

An accompanying diagram of the office shows that Wolfe's great terrestrial globe stands to the left of the door to the hall, diagonally across from Wolfe's desk. Curiously Rex has put two windows in the wall behind Wolfe's desk — one directly at his back — though this is the wall where the painting of a waterfall (the Reichenbach, Rex surmised) hangs, behind which a secret alcove is located.[9]

On 14 October, George Gallup, director of the American Institute of Public Opinion, published the results of a nationwide survey on mystery writers — the winners of what the institute spoke of as the "Whodunit Derby." Rex placed eighth, being shaded by Gardner, Doyle, Ellery Queen, Poe, Christie, Van Dine, and Mary Roberts Rinehart.[10]

On 2 November Rex presided at the fourth annual UWF banquet at Washington's Shoreham Hotel. Then, in the last days of the year he was Harold Guinzburg's dinner guest. Rebecca West, yesteryear mistress of H. G. Wells, was present. She took Rex into the library to speak with him privately.

Rebecca was an opinion-maker. Rex was an opinion-maker. The armies of many nations were battling in Korea. In the weeks ahead the direction in which events moved could determine the future of the planet itself. There at the brink, Rebecca chose her topic: H. G. Wells. She wanted to hear every detail Rex could recall of that long-ago luncheon at Henry Goddard Leach's, when Wells summoned Rex into his presence to see who the fellow was who was writing to Odette Keun, his French mistress. Lessons in humility are plentiful for those who stand athwart the path of lovers.

40.

King Rex

Homage to Rex Stout. In economy, organization and characterisation he's at the very top of his class. His writing remains as fresh as a green salad, and as pungent as *maquereau moutardé*. Long may his superb cookery whet our appetites.

— Dame Ngaio Marsh

Between 20 January and 1 February 1951, Rex wrote "The Squirt and the Monkey." One day out. In February, Cass Canfield wrote to ask if Rex could see J. B. Priestley early in March. "He said that he was most anxious to meet you," Canfield explained. But Rex was on the road with the Myth show during the British novelist's stay in New York, and the two did not meet. Priestley at least had a new Nero Wolfe book to take home with him: *Curtains for Three* came out on 23 February.

Priestley really did want to meet Rex. In 1959, when he reviewed Rex's *Crime and Again* [*And Four to Go*] for London's *Reynolds News,* Priestley asserted: "My American favourites have long been Rex Stout's Nero Wolfe and Archie Goodwin, not because of the mysteries they solve but because Mr. Stout writes so entertainingly."[1]

Rex's socializing in this period was, in fact, minimal. He husbanded his time, intent on making the best use of it. Rex did go to a large party which the Cecil Browns had in their Manhattan apartment in the winter of 1951. He was popular with Brown's guests, among them Admiral Thomas Kinkaid and Abe Burrows. Brown does not think the detective stories had much to do with it. Rather, "they liked his quick mind, his salty talk, his distinctive beard, and his self-possession. His snapping, brown eyes, his ready smile, and toss of the head beguiled the women even more than his conversation did. They liked his independence of style."[2]

Rex and Burrows already knew one another through their service together on the Authors' League Council. Not long before, at a dinner given by Alfred Knopf, Rex had found himself seated between Knopf and Burrows. Rex said: "When the third or fourth wine was served, a grand claret, Abe took a sip, another one, frowned, and muttered to me, 'Bird droppings?' "[3]

On 29 March Rex began *Murder by the Book*. It was finished on 23 May. Nineteen days out. More than Rex liked. But the salmon were biting.

Among the things Rex managed in April, besides the Miramichi interlude, was an appearance on TV's "Author Meets the Critics." The book was H. Allen Smith's *People Named Smith*. To group Smiths into categories for separate chapters; to pile in hundreds of names; to emerge from this ordeal with a readable book. Herculean labors. Yet Smith had accomplished them successfully, and Rex saw that he had. "Smith," he said, in his summation, "is a master of a difficult trick — transition. He knows how to do it. His transitions in this book are ingenious." "I swear," Smith told me, "I didn't know what a *transition* was. But when I found out later, I was tickled mauve."[4]

The Fourth of July never found Rex at his desk. On that day annually the Stouts gave a bountiful picnic for twenty or thirty guests. The Cecil Browns usually came and the Van Dorens and Marian Anderson and her husband, Orpheus "King" Fisher. Cecil Brown remembers the 1951 gathering. The inimitable British publisher, Victor Gollancz, was there, and Louis Kronenberger, Nickolas Muray, the photographer, and fashion designer Bonnie Cashin, Gilbert Seldes, and Frederick Redefer, a professor of education at NYU. The picnic was spread beneath the massive two-hundred-year-old maple beside the pool. While Pola's exquisite liver pâté whetted appetites, Rex reigned at the grill, basting chickens with his celebrated feather-cluster wand. Pola was everywhere, seeing to the comfort of the guests. Barbara and Rebecca, as was proper to teenagers, "were being helpful, vivacious, petulant, or in whatever mood possessed them at the time." Rex was constantly on duty loading a plate with chicken, potatoes, corn-on-the-cob, roasted in the husk, Kansas style — seeing always that his guests wanted for nothing. The spirit of Snyder's Grove lived on at High Meadow.[5]

"Home to Roost" was begun on 27 July. Even as Rex held himself to his desk to finish this novella on 10 August, with just one day off, other members of his family gathered at Ridgewood to mark Bob Stout's seventy-third birthday. Juanita summed up their feelings in a "flatter-free" tribute. She remembered the happy family gatherings Bob had been responsible for, his support in anxious times, and "his constant ambition and desire to do and be the best in everything he attempted." These were the years for the Stouts to look back with a sense of having done the job well. Rex himself would, in a few months, reach sixty-five, an age at which many men are ready to step aside. Yet who could retire from a commitment to world order and world peace? Certainly not Rex Stout.

On 4 September, Louis Adamic, whose memoirs had suggested to Rex a fitting homeland for Nero Wolfe, was found shot to death in his burning farmhouse in Pennsylvania. Just four words appeared on the sheet of paper inserted in his typewriter: "Now is the time. . . ." A coroner's jury ruled the death a suicide. Adamic's family and friends believed he had been murdered to keep him from completing the book he was working on, which was inimical to Communism. Rex just didn't know. In *Murder by the Book*, which Rex had finished the previous May, several murders are committed to halt publication of a controversial manuscript. Adamic's death gave Rex's book unlooked-for topicality when it was released, on 12 October.

The shortcomings of the publishing industry were a natural topic for Rex to take up at this time. In the postwar years Rex's involvement in the Authors' League had been growing. For several years he had been executive editor of the League's *Bulletin,* through which he promoted copyright revisions and the battle against censorship. On 14 November 1951, at a meeting in the Barbizon Plaza, the League elected Rex president, succeeding Oscar Hammerstein II. On that November day the League annexed Rex. Nearly twenty-five years later he would still be one of its mainstays.

This major commitment to the welfare of writers did not mean that Rex would now reduce his involvement in other activities concerning the welfare of humanity at large. Quite the contrary, he began 1952 with a blast from Freedom House against Senator Joseph McCarthy's demagoguery. General Marshall himself had been traduced by McCarthy, and before the year was out Dwight Eisenhower would be altering campaign speeches to retain McCarthy's goodwill. "Wild exaggerations and inexcusable inaccuracies," said the Freedom House declaration, which Rex had helped to draft, "serve to divide and confuse the country when we should be united in the task of resisting Communist aggression abroad and Communist subversion at home." That same month *The American Magazine* carried Rex's "Nero Wolfe and the Communist Killer" in which Wolfe, even as he exposes an active Communist, disassociates himself from McCarthyism by insisting, "I deplore the current tendency to accuse people of pro-communism irresponsibly and unjustly."

Presiding at the Authors' League Council's meeting on 7 January, Rex took a major role in formulating a statement deploring the reckless blacklisting of writers by *Red Channels,* a booklet published in 1950 by Theodore Kirkpatrick, editor of the magazine *Counter Attack. Red Channels* had linked numerous radio and TV personnel with left-wing causes and had set in motion a major witch-hunt. The League argued that the acceptance or rejection of a writer's work should be decided by its merits, not by his alleged affiliations. At the same time, Rex appealed to Wayne Coy, chairman of the Federal Communications Commission, to call a hearing on the blacklisting of writers by radio and TV stations. He hoped that if the light of reason was brought to bear on the situation, the hysteria would subside.

A second major item on the League's agenda also got press coverage in January. On 30 January, along with Oscar Hammerstein II and John P. Marquand, Rex declared his support of Representative Emanuel Celler's bill revising United States law restricting foreign copyright, so that the United States could join the UN in writing a world copyright convention. They made their appeal to a congressional subcommittee hearing.

Between 20 January and 4 February, with five days out, Rex wrote "This Won't Kill You," a story that would prompt a Toronto *Globe & Mail* reviewer to say: "Mr. Stout's great contribution to contemporary fiction is Archie Goodwin. Nero Wolfe is merely the exotic foil for Archie." In "This Won't Kill You" Wolfe is indeed on Archie's home territory when baseball's "rookie of the year" is bludgeoned to death in the Giants' locker room at the Polo Grounds and Wolfe is asked to find the murderer. Archie is off and running. He confronts Lila, the showgirl wife of one of the Giants. During the game, when the Giants were losing, she had looked happy. Only Archie could deal with the paradoxical Lila. Her mind jumped about so. "That's one reason why Mr. Wolfe can't stand women," Archie tells her. But Lila's reason for liking the Giants' poor showing carries conviction. If the regular players were taken out of play, then her husband would come into the game as a replacement. Archie accepts this explanation. Pleased, Lila takes Archie to see her uncle, a druggist who had asked her husband to fix the game. After narrowly escaping a drenching in acid, Archie returns to the Polo Grounds. In his absence, Wolfe, seated on a leather sofa, has determined both the identity of the murderer and his motives. He reached his conclusions by reason alone and would have verified them much earlier had he not chosen to spite the police by waiting until they had left the scene. Archie furnishes the excitement. Wolfe furnishes the class. "Exotic foil?" Doubtful.

On 13 March, in his capacity as chairman of the WBWG, Rex was scheduled to serve as moderator while Senator Jacob Javits and Congressman Brooks Hays of Arkansas, under the auspices of the UWF, discoursed on "U.S. Foreign Policy: How It Can Win Peace," at the Westchester County Center, at White Plains, New York. Despite a crippling attack of stomach ulcers, Rex made his appearance only to learn that a snowstorm would delay Javits by several hours. Janice Ehrenberg, a member of the White Plains committee, recalls how well

Rex met the crisis: "Through the long wait he recalled, gathered together, exposited, recounted, argued, cajoled, extemporized. I will never forget how his valor, his charm, and presence of mind eased a difficult night." But Janice knew nothing about Rex's ulcer crisis. Rex himself did not know till later that throughout that demanding evening he was hemorrhaging internally.

Triple Jeopardy came out on 21 March. A letter from one reader deplored two of the tales — "The Cop-Killer" and "Home to Roost" — as "those two little stinker anti-Communist stories." By this time McCarthyism had brewed such tensions that even Anthony Boucher said aloud he wished Wolfe would find another adversary. Boucher's protest confirmed Rex's belief that McCarthy helped Communism by making anti-Communism seem reactionary.

Ulcers and hate mail not withstanding, Rex kept his buoyancy of spirit. When Lawrence Blochman, creator of the medical sleuth Dr. Coffee, wrote to wish Rex well as new president of the Authors' League, Rex replied, on 24 March:

It certainly warmed the heartles of my cock (excuse it please, I've been reading *From Here to Eternity*) to get your welcome back. My first endeavor will be to find something to object to, but as you say, that would be a cinch with any organization on earth.[6]

A fishing holiday, spring gardening, and the harvest of spring berries and greens replenished Rex's stamina. On 19 June he began "Dare Base." He completed it on 3 August. Ten and a half days out. "Dare Base" became *Prisoner's Base* when Viking decided that this game of Rex's boyhood was better known outside Kansas by the latter name.

One event that subtracted time from Rex's writing schedule was the departure of the Yasumotos, in July, after seven years at High Meadow. Their families had returned to California. Their children were ready for high school. It seemed time to go. Yet for everyone it was a family separation. The Yasumotos had made their decision in open council with the Stouts. "They all wanted us to stay very badly," Alyce says. "They loved us very much. It was heartbreaking." Later in the summer Rex sent them iris rhizomes for their garden. Every year following, a high point of Rex's birthday would be a call from California from Alyce and Kay and often, after their children were married, the Yasumotos would talk about coming back to High Meadow, to live out their days there.[7]

On 7 August, as president of the Authors' League, Rex jumped into a major labor dispute. Learning that the Screen Writers' Guild was about to strike against the TV Film Producers Alliance, he urged all

League members to withhold scripts from Alliance producers. The strike lasted fourteen weeks but ended with terms vindicating Rex's support of the Guild.

Prisoner's Base was published on 24 October, a record-breaking ten weeks after Rex completed it. Even as reviewers were assessing it, Rex had another story under way. "Invitation to Murder" was begun on 23 October and done by 17 November. Thirteen days' writing time; thirteen days out. Rex did not relish such a fifty-fifty break but commitments were building up again and he had had to learn to move between them. Thus on 8 November, at the Vanderbilt, he had presided at the dinner session of the Fifth Annual Meeting of the UWF's New York branch and spoken on plans to strengthen the UN.

In "Invitation to Murder" Archie undertakes to discover whether the sister of Herman Lewent has been murdered by one of the three female predators who serve her crippled husband, Theodore Huck, as housekeeper, nurse, and secretary. Lewent himself is a self-admitted incompetent, easily manipulated by women. His father accordingly had left him dependent upon his sister's generosity for income. Now he is dependent on Huck — a chancy arrangement, since Huck seemed likely to fall soon under the complete dominance of one of the three predators, Mrs. Cassie O'Shea, Sylvia Marcy, or Dorothy Riff.

When Archie visits the Huck household, his most immediate problem is to learn which of the three women has the inside track with Huck. All three, as Wolfe presently will note, are "young, smart, alive to opportunity." Archie is fascinated by Mrs. O'Shea's hip movements, by nurse Marcy's constant cooing, and by Riff's calculating guile. "I know how his mind works," says Dorothy. Sylvia affirms her compatibility by wearing a dress to match Huck's shirt.

The plot deepens when Lewent is murdered. Archie, finding that he is too susceptible to feminine wiles to be objective, uses a ruse to bring Wolfe to the scene. "The fault is Mr. Goodwin's," Wolfe says, "on account of a defect in his makeup he has botched his errand here so badly that I was compelled to intervene." He is a god come down from Olympus to undo the folly of an erring emissary. He continues: "I suspected that he was so thoroughly bewitched by one of those women that his mental processes were in suspense." Wolfe thereupon follows through with a remarkable demonstration of his own immunity to feminine wiles. He shows, with inexorable logic, why the three women cannot have killed Lewent. The list of suspects is narrowed to Paul Thayer, Huck's nephew, who is so agreeable that readers readily exempt him from suspicion, and Huck himself. Huck indeed is the guilty man. From his high-powered wheelchair he had carried out the murders of both his wife and her brother: the first, to keep secret his affair with Mrs. O'Shea; the second, to keep Lewent from learning the truth about his sister's death. Infatuation has put reason to rout.

At the end of the story, with great presence of mind, Mrs. O'Shea dissociates herself from Huck's act. Riff and Marcy likewise plead noninvolvement, Riff even to the extent of returning to Huck a ruby-studded watch. The others, who had received identical gifts, do not relinquish them. They are not stampeded to that degree. Once again, men have had their emotions exploited for feminine gain. Chaucer had said women excelled at three things, "weeping, weaving, and lies." Wolfe would agree.[8]

As well as writing detective stories, Rex was musing about them. In his introduction to *The Later Adventures of Sherlock Holmes,* a de luxe, three-volume Macy edition, published in 1952, he discoursed on the literary offenses of Conan Doyle. He now had the status to do this, since more and more he was being accorded a place beside Doyle. Unlike Mark Twain, who detailed James Fenimore Cooper's literary offenses to repudiate his art, Rex's intention was to show that the magic of the Holmes stories transcended plot to depend on "the grand and glorious portrait" of Holmes himself. Doyle's mistakes seemed to enhance that portrait.

In "Wisteria Lodge," the governess, Miss Burnet, was "rescued with no trouble at all by an 'excited rustic,' " for just one reason: "she would be needed to clear up details for Holmes and the police." In "The Devil's Foot," Sterndale throws a distinctive red gravel at Tragennis's window, even though ordinary substitutes are available. Without this gravel Holmes could not have solved the case. In "The Disappearance of Lady Frances Carfax" Holmes wires the landlord at Baden for information concerning Dr. Shlessinger's left ear, although Watson already has supplied that information. And so it goes. In this same story, the lawbreakers give Holmes the slip, despite his best efforts. "This is extraordinary and even scandalous," Rex said, "but is it actually a defeat?" He did not think so.

Rex was fascinated with that quality in Holmes for which Middle English supplies the word *daunger* — that personal authority which maintains others in a position of awesome respect toward one. "We are not supposed to reach real intimacy with him. We are not supposed to touch him." Yet, "that is one of the thousand shrewd touches in the portrait of the great detective . . . stoked in quite casually, without effort or emphasis. . . ."

Just how Doyle's shrewd touches combine to bring Holmes to life remains a mystery. Rex concluded: "No one will ever penetrate to the essence and disclose it naked to the eye. For the essence is magic, and magic is arcane."

In Rex's appreciation of Doyle's art, we find valuable guidelines for understanding Rex's own art. He saw the necessity of making Wolfe a man rich in human contradictions. Wolfe's eccentricities surpass those of Holmes. At times he is childish in his moods. He shuts his eyes more often than Holmes does to "moral issues." More than once he "arranges" for the suicide of a culprit, to save himself the bother of a courtroom appearance. Yet, withal, even as Holmes is, he is "grand and glorious."[9]

41.

Watch Out for Rex Stout

My only recollection of Rex Stout is total recall regarding that weird beard. Maybe it is different now, but when I met him in 1954 it all grew underneath his chin and was trained to grow upward and forward and then curl back down again. Strange, strange.

— JOHN D. MacDONALD

On 18 January 1953, the playwright Maxwell Anderson wrote to *The New York Times* suggesting that the Authors' League had unleashed general confusion by defending all radio and television writers listed in *Red Channels* — the guilty and innocent alike. He urged that the League set up a board to sift them out. "Every American Communist," he said, "is a traitor to his country and has forfeited the right to be heard." Rex, on 25 January, reminded Anderson that he himself had been present the year before when the League had drafted a statement of its position and had supported it. That statement continued to be League policy. As much as he deplored Communism, Rex would not use his office as League president to create a Star Chamber. He was still sailing his course between the Scylla of McCarthyism and the Charybdis of Communism.[1]

In general, almost as though he had been overtaken by the mood of Eisenhower's "placid decade" (a suggestion he would have loathed), Rex's chief preoccupations during much of 1953 were of a domestic and literary kind. On 31 January, he gave away his daughter Barbara, a student at the Parsons School of Design, when she married Donald E. Maroc, of Hammond, Indiana. Don was recently out of the marines. The ceremony and reception were at High Meadow.

Early in February, after a quick visit to Manhattan to participate in an Authors' Guild panel held to promote National Book Week, Rex wrote "Diary of a Plant Detective," for *House & Garden*, to set the record straight about his houseplants. He had no rooftop greenhouse, no orchids. He spent only ten dollars a year on houseplants. These he kept in "the passageway," a glassed-in corridor connecting house and garage. Unlike Nero Wolfe, he was fond of geraniums, especially scented ones. He owned that his plants sometimes posed problems which stymied him. Wolfe no doubt has insoluble problems too. But he does not broadcast the fact.

Of his scented geraniums — apple, apricot, nutmeg, and lemon — Rex said: "I keep them at strategic spots where I frequently pass, and every time I go by I get a good whiff of their fresh and pungent fragrance. . . . They all smell good even before breakfast, which is my acid test for odors." Rex once had three hundred rex begonias, and kept them blooming through the winter. They needed more time than he could spare. "One fall," he told me, "I said goodbye and let the frost take them."[2]

Among his plants Rex placed, here and there, for variation, a bowl of hyacinths or narcissus, a tricolor maranta, a coral ardista, or cacti, "for punctuation." His occasional orchids did not prosper. Perhaps he expected too much of them. Perhaps they expected too much of him.

Between the eleventh and twenty-fifth of March, Rex wrote "The Zero Clue." Ten days' writing time. Five days out. This tale finds Wolfe seeking the murderer of Leo Heller, a probability expert. To identify his killer, Heller has left a mathematical clue. Wolfe puts his analytical powers to work while Heller's clients, fearful that their secrets will be made public, writhe in anguish. There is Susan Maturo: "When I start to talk about it, it sticks in my throat and chokes me." When Susan pounds on Wolfe's desk, Archie is solicitous for Wolfe. "A woman cutting loose," he says, "is always too much for him." There is John R. Winslow, to whom Wolfe has to say, "Please, Mr. Winslow, don't bounce like that. A hysterical woman is bad enough, but a hysterical man is insufferable." And Mrs. Albert Tillotson, a plump matron who looks like "a woman-hater's pin-up and lies fiercely and absurdly and with the expectation of being believed." Agatha Abbey is an "executive-type" female. She is "cool and composed and in command" and has "a controlled, thin, steely voice." She has made her way by renouncing her own sex, a fact still less palatable to Wolfe than a display of feminine faults. Agatha tells Wolfe: "There are six female tigers trying to get their claws on my job right now, and if they all died tonight there would be six others tomorrow." She hates women with a bitterness which comes from denying her nature. Wolfe says pityingly: "The wretch. The miserable wretch. Her misogyny was already in her bones; now her misandry is too." Even the murderer himself is a man of obsessive enthusiasms. Despite the irritability such distractions engender, Wolfe gives himself low marks for not at once deciphering Heller's clue.

Publication of "The Zero Clue" — as "Scared to Death," in *The American Magazine* in December 1953 — occasioned an unusual correspondence between Rex and Norbert Wiener, the father of cybernetics, at MIT. On 1 December Wiener wrote Rex:

I am a great admirer of detective stories in general and of yours in particular. If I were to meet either Nero Wolfe or Archie Goodwin I would recognize them at once. . . .

Nevertheless, dear sir, I have a bone to pick with you. In "Scared to Death" your corpse is an alleged probability expert. . . . Let me tell you that Mr. Leo Heller is a fraud and that it would not take one-tenth the insight of Nero Wolfe to find that out in three minutes. . . . Mr. Heller is able to astonish a hardheaded bookie by batting 1.000. This means that he has been confining his effort to what would be very nearly a sure thing . . . or that he has had an extraordinary run of luck . . . or else that he has been pretending to use probability methods where he really has other sources of information. . . . In the first case, people as astute as I should expect his employers to be would have a sufficiently good smell of his results without employing Mr. Heller at all. . . . As between the second and third cases, the probability, a priori, of such a long run of luck is so small as to make the last supposition, that Mr. Heller is a swindler, by far the most humanly probable. This is a possibility which should not be missed by Nero Wolfe. . . . You will therefore accept may deepest sympathy at having been taken in by such an utter fraud as the adipose Nero.

Rex replied on 5 December:

It is so great a pleasure and honor to get a letter from the renowned cyberneticist that I wouldn't care if the bone to be picked were the femur of a brontosaurus. . . .

What happened is obvious. You like detective stories, but when you came upon one that presumed to deal with your specialty you reacted typically. You resented the author's insolent trespass into your personal meadow, and you were indignant. You wanted to denounce the author as a brash ignoramus, but that impulse was vetoed by your courteous and compassionate nature, so you resorted to a subterfuge. Instead of attacking the author, a warm-blooded creature who could suffer, you went after a fictive bozo named Nero Wolfe. . . .

I say pfui. . . . I claim that Mr. Wolfe — I am not sufficiently intimate with him to call him by his first name, as you seem to be — is a real smart cookie. At one point in the story that prompted your letter he called Heller a charlatan. At another he called him a quack. At still another he called him a humbug. He spoke of his "claptrap" and "hocus-pocus."

Indeed, as I proceeded with the report of that affair, I was invaded by the disturbing suspicion that Mr. Wolfe regards all probability tycoons as imposters and racketeers. I assure you that I do not share that uncharitable view. For you, as a most eminent one, I feel the profoundest admiration, with, I must confess, a lamentably vague notion of what it is I am admiring. But by gum I stick to it; I do admire you.

Wiener wrote back on 7 December, giving way gracefully:

You can not only take it, but you can dish it out. May I hope that the fact that we have not met will not prove to be too permanent, for I really would enjoy tracing the fierce detective story to its lair.

For the present, I am preparing to leave the country on the nineteenth of this month for a six weeks' flying visit to India. If I do not end up on the burning ghats of Benares or shipped in a cool layer of ice for transmission home, may I hope that sometime after I return early in February we can get together and open our souls?

The proposed meeting never took place. But the two prodigies who had, each in his own way, bridged the gap to maturity, in a sense had opened their souls to one another and were delighted with what they saw.

In April, with Alan Green's son Steven as his on-campus equerry, Rex lectured at the University of Connecticut.[3] On 12 May he began *The Golden Spiders*. He finished it on 1 July — seventeen days out. (The Miramichi again.) While Rex was catching salmon, his review of Joseph Wechsberg's gustatory memoir, *Blue Trout and Black Truffles*, appeared in *The New York Times Book Review*. Wechsberg's mouth-watering tour of Continental restaurants got five stars: "This fine book makes it clear that the spirit of *la grande cuisine* is the spirit that is essential to any human performance that deserves to be called grand."[4]

When Merle Miller visited High Meadow in 1950, he decided he liked the area and asked Rex to find him a house. Rex told him that his neighbor Kurt Rahlson wanted to rent for a year. That suited Merle and he moved into the Rahlson house. In 1953, he became Rex's permanent neighbor when he bought a few adjacent acres and put up his own house. Since Miller had become president of the Authors' Guild and Rex was president of the parent body, summit meetings involving League and Guild now became a simple matter. Only one thing irked Miller: the sureness of Rex's pen. His own books took him a couple of years to write. From his house he could see the lights at High Meadow flickering like party lanterns. Rex no doubt was taking his ease. "He writes sixty days a year, no more, no less," Miller complained to Lewis Nichols. "I get so damned mad — and jealous — when I think of that."[5]

Rex, as guru, also heard that summer from Egmont Arens. Arens was writing a detective novel built around their old friend, Casanova, and wanted to avoid pitfalls. Rex saw one: "Can you get a guaranty that none of Casanova's natural great-great-grandchildren will sue for libel?"

On 27 September Rex began work on "When a Man Murders." He finished it on the twentieth anniversary of the start of the series, 18 October, again splitting the interval down the middle — eleven days' writing, eleven days out. Thus, when *The Golden Spiders* was published on 26 October, its successor already was on hand. What Rex was doing during those eleven days when he was not working on "When a Man Murders" was soon explained. In an interview with Lewis Nichols, published in *The New York Times* on 15 November, Rex talked about his work schedule: "Something comes along like the World Series and those days are immediately out." Merle Miller could take meager comfort from another of Rex's disclosures to Nichols: "The plots come when I'm shaving, watering the plants, puttering around. Sometime I think of them for three weeks, sometime for three days. . . . When I sit down at the typewriter I'm pleasantly surprised, and sometimes shocked, to find four-fifths of it is already there."

Before he began writing a story Rex would create a certain state of readiness. The decision to write a story had to be taken before a story idea came. Once that happened, he moved to the setting and asked himself what might happen in that setting. He selected the most interesting of the ideas that occurred to him, then asked himself questions about it. Why would a visitor conceal a paper in one of Wolfe's books? Why would someone want to kill a college president with a poisoned golf club? "The answers come right along," Rex assured me. "You have your plot. You write." Mark Van Doren supplied a further insight: "Rex told me it was easy to plot a detective story — just know what happened and then reveal or suppress just as much as you need to on the way. Easy haha."

Rex knew the ages and occupations, as well as the names, of the six or eight most important characters. He knew who would be killed, who would do the killing (usually), and why. Sometimes he let the material simmer for several weeks. He would not be consciously working on it, but said, "I suspect that while I'm doing other things, I think about it. If you keep the main facts firmly in mind, and don't let anything contradict you, you can move around freely." When he was planning a story he let his family know, but he did not really have to tell them. During this period of gestation, he became quieter, less relaxed to talk to. He was off with his characters — "out in the distance" — even more out of things than when he was actually writing.

From the moment he chose the names of his characters Rex had a sense of the fitness of the names he had chosen. But he did not foresee the turnings of the plot, nor how a story would end. "I know pretty much what my main characters are like," he told me, "but beyond that I just have to wait to see what comes out of the typewriter." He thought the characters themselves wrote most of the story. He explained: "I make up maybe one-third of the things people say and do in the stories I write, but I have nothing to do with the rest." Sometimes he was surprised at something Wolfe said or did, and might ask himself, "Would he do that, say that?" Then he saw that Wolfe knew more about it than he did, and questioned it no further.

All the Wolfe stories were written in the little L-shaped office in the service wing. "I can't leave myself any room to wander around," Rex assured me. "I can't stand distractions. I never even look out the window when I write."

Until the last years of his life, Rex composed on a typewriter. "My feeling for my typewriter," he told me, "is like a carpenter's feeling for his saw and plane and chisel." He was convinced machines take on characteristics of their users. He felt he did not have adequate rapport with a machine shared with someone else.

In his day count, Rex never counted days he was away from his desk, although he conceded that, at such times, bits of dialogue, turns of phrase, and twists of plot came into his head. He did not scribble them down to remember them. They were there in his head when he needed them. Some days writing went more easily than on others. He had no writing streaks, yet, as he neared the end of a story, his pace often accelerated. His maximum output for any one day was twelve pages. He was as sure as he was deliberate. "The initial draft has always been the only draft," he told me, "with an original and two carbons." He did no revision whatsoever. At the most, he interpolated a phrase. He seldom did that much.

While a book was in progress, Rex lived it every minute of the day. "It bothers me to be interrupted when I am in any act whatever," he explained, "but I try not to make faces."

Before going to his office Rex might show Harold some odd jobs that needed doing — sanding a board, moving an asparagus bed — but for the most part he hardly spoke to anyone. During those days he rarely received guests, rarely accepted dinner invitations. "When I have, I wasn't really there," he said. "My mind wasn't free. I was off with my characters, wherever they were. I wasn't bad company, but not very entertaining. . . . I'm a one-job man," Rex confessed. "No matter what I'm doing, by God that's what I'm doing and nothing else. When I'm writing a story, if a leg falls off a chair I don't give a damn. I will later, but not while I'm writing." While he was writing, trifles could bother him — a piece of lint on the carpet, a partly opened drawer — "But not for long," he told me, "because I attend to them at once."

Slipups are rare in the Wolfe stories. No system of double-checking prevented them. For that, Rex's phenomenal memory sufficed. Not only did he not reread the earlier stories when he began a new one, he did not even reread a story he had just written. He told me: "Writing a story is like touching off an explosion. When it's happened, there's no use going around looking at the debris." He was not afraid he would spoil a story if he undertook to revise it. He said further: "My reason for not revising was (and is) that it would have been hard work, including retyping. If I had to revise in order to make the stories publishable, I would have."

Rex offered two reasons to account for his ability to get, on first try, the story he wanted. He took pains to put everything in its proper place.

And he enjoyed writing. He was not impressed by writers who say they suffer over their art. "The 'sort of agony' stuff," he said, "is a pose." But he did not insist that his methods were superior to those of other writers. "Facility has nothing to do with quality," he told me. "The amount of output depends upon your work habits, your knowledge of people and places, your command of words." Writing at the rate of a page an hour and brooding about those pages for weeks before he began to write, and day and night while he wrote them, Rex did the work of revision in his head.

"No editor can tell you anything about the content or production of my stories," Rex said. "None of them, either at Viking or at Farrar and Rinehart, has ever suggested changing a sentence." Nor was the matter of his stories ever suggested to Rex by anyone. He never used ideas sent to him by readers. "They never seemed right," he told me. Nor did he discuss what he was writing with anyone while writing it. "I have never felt that I needed to," he explained. Occasionally he would stuff a shoe box with money, or ask his son-in-law to lie on the floor, so that he could judge how much of one or the other would occupy a given space, but if anyone wanted to know what was going on he would have to wait till the book was done. As each page came from his typewriter, Rex placed it face down on the desk beside him. So far as he was concerned, he was done with it. He did read carefully the galleys and the page proofs.

While a novel was under way, Rex was a teetotaler. He was always able to predict the exact time when he would finish a story — "Saturday, the twenty-third, at four-twenty-seven P.M." To his family it would signal the completion of his task when Rex would appear at the predicted hour and mix himself a tall whiskey. "Drinking," he said, "would fuddle my logical processes." So, presumably, he did not leave as much of the work to his subconscious mind as he alleged. While he was writing, smoking fell under no similar interdiction. At a typical writing session he might smoke two Gold Label Barcelonas. That was all he leaned on. Sometimes, though, he leaned on his publishers for help with a title. The title was not there at the outset. Nor did he find it till he was well along into the story. When it came to him, he worked it into the text, rather than finding it there.

In December 1953, at Marjorie Hillis Roulston's house, Rex, as president, presented the Authors' League's 1953 "Encouragement for Good Reading" award to Seymour Siegel, director of station WYNC, for its "Festival of Books" broadcasts the previous spring. Rex was as conscientious in seeing through these ceremonial duties as he was in wrestling with the big issues.

In December also, Rex was interviewed by free-lancer Rochelle Girson. After making a plea for world government, Rex, in an unprecedented volte-face, jiggled the hands of the doomsday clock. "I certainly realize that democracy has got to triumph," he said, "and if it can only do it by violence, then I am for that. Even if there is only one democrat left and he mutters, before he dies, 'Well, we licked them,' I'm for him." This grim "better dead than Red" pronunciamento may be read as an augury of Rex's resolute stance as a hawk through the long years of war in Southeast Asia.[6]

Rex began 1954 with his usual full schedule of activities. In January, after a seven-year absence from the field, he made a spectral reappearance as editor of a mystery magazine. This time it was the *Nero Wolfe Mystery Magazine,* published by Hillman Publications and announced as a bimonthly. In all, three issues appeared. In addition to the January issue, there was a March issue, and one in June. As supervising editor, Rex supplied an introduction for each issue. In the March issue, although it was a commodity he himself had shunned ever since he had written *Under the Andes,* he spoke a tolerant word for the preposterous: "Peddling the preposterous in fiction is by no means paltry per se. It depends on whether the reader feels himself gagging or whether he swallows it with pleasure. A list of the most successful peddlers of the preposterous would include Stevenson, d'Annunzio, Melville, Dumas, Tolstoi, Dickens of course — it would fill a fine library." A lot of Rex's boyhood passions were on the list.

In the June issue Rex pinpointed the one characteristic all detectives share in common:

They are all inscrutable. That is the one iron rule which is apparently never to be violated. The elegant and erudite Philo Vance, and the tough and rough Sam Spade; both are inscrutable.

If sometimes you find this universal conformity to an ancient pattern a little tiresome, don't blame the creators of the detectives. Don't shoot the piano player; he is doing his damnedest under the circumstances. The conformity is the result, not of an epidemic whim afflicting the writer, nor of any sinister combination in restraint of trade, but of the inevitable pattern of the stories. . . .

Each issue of the *Nero Wolfe Mystery Magazine* contained ten short tales, a Wolfe novella, and a "Criminal Crossword Puzzle" prepared by the crossword editor of *The New York Times,* who was Margaret Farrar, John Farrar's wife.

On 16 January 1954, Rex shared the platform with Canadian Supreme Court Justice Ivan Rand and Arthur Goodhart, master of University College, Oxford University, at the closing session of a conference, "Community Security vs. Man's Right to Knowledge," arranged in observance of Columbia University's bicentennial. Rex reminded his audience that dissent must not be mistaken for treason, that the writer must be judged on sincerity and intent.

Along with sincerity an author needs income. That was Rex's topic two days later, at the Barbizon Plaza, at a joint meeting of the Authors' Guild and the Mystery Writers of America. There Rex urged the three hundred writers present to support a new campaign on an old issue. Publishers still were splitting reprint royalties fifty-fifty with authors. Rex thought that that should be stopped. After all, even agents only got ten percent. He also thought publishers should stop getting a cut of the royalties on magazine serial rights, dramatic rights, and movie rights. This would cease, he said, if only two hundred big-name writers would stand together on the issue. Raymond Walters, Jr., was not amused when he reported Rex's remarks to *Saturday Review* readers a month later. Rex's "benign-looking beard," he warned, "ought not deceive any embattled publisher."[7] Rex did not let this issue die here. There would be more to follow.

"Die like a Dog," begun on 28 January, was finished on 10 February. The winter snows affording welcome isolation, the story was done with only four days out.

On 27 February formation was announced of a national committee to seek early congressional ratification of the Universal Copyright Convention. Sixty-five Americans prominent in the literary, educational, and communications fields made up the committee's membership. Rex and Douglas M. Black, president of the American Book Publishers Council, were named cochairmen.

There are some things that executive ability cannot help with. On 3 March, Barbara Stout Maroc was at High Meadow when she went into labor. Only Rex was at home. Barbara says, "It was the only time in my life when I felt I was more in control than Dad was. He was as attentive as anyone could be and saw that I was on the way to the hospital with no delay. But I could see he wanted me to get somewhere else where he wasn't." Rex came through this ordeal with his dignity bruised but his vanity gratified. Barbara gave birth to a daughter — Lizbeth. While Rex had at last been initiated into the league of frightened men, he was now also a grandfather.

On 26 March, *Three Men Out* was published. By 5 April Rex had started another novel, *The Black Mountain*, the only story in the saga to transport Wolfe to Montenegro, where he had passed his early life. Of the seventy-nine days that passed between the time Rex began the book and its completion, on 22 June, he took forty-two days out — an unprecedented interlude of truancy. The garden was partly to blame. And fishing the Miramichi. Perhaps, to put Montenegro's mountainous terrain in his mind's eye, he had gone to look at the Laurentians.

He told me he had not. Nor is there evidence to suggest that he halted work because he had reached a sticking point. Rex Stout had no place in his life for sticking points.

In a "Warning" prefacing *The Black Mountain,* Archie explains that he is re-creating conversations spoken in tongues he is unfamiliar with. This Twainian notice was not an afterthought. Rex told me: "Knowing what the problem would be, I wrote that before I started writing the story."[8] A similar disclaimer, prepared by Archie, appears as a foreword to *Too Many Cooks.*

During World War II, Harvard University historian Bernard DeVoto had served on the WWB's Advisory Council and loaned the board the full weight of his pen. Rex and DeVoto soon were on a Rex and Benny basis — an intimacy hastened by DeVoto's admiration for Nero Wolfe. When, in 1944, Edmund Wilson scoffed at Rex and at detective fiction in general, DeVoto had shown instant resentment. He wrote Rex: "Not that I felt that you needed defense from anyone or that anyone needed defense against Edmund Wilson, but purely to satisfy an impulse that has been itching my fingers for a long time, I devoted part of the December 'Easy Chair' [DeVoto's *Harper's* column] to being as snooty as possible about Wilson's *New Yorker* piece." Early in 1954 DeVoto decided to do a long "Easy Chair" piece on Wolfe.[9] In preparation he reread all the Wolfe stories and asked Eric Larrabee, at *Harper's,* to cruise along West Thirty-fifth Street in a taxi, looking for likely brownstones. At the same time DeVoto let Rex know that he would welcome amplifications. None was forthcoming. Rex's rule was to let the stories speak for themselves. DeVoto's request may have gotten Rex started on *The Black Mountain,* a cornucopia of new disclosures about Wolfe's early life, although Rex told me that it did not.

On 8 May, DeVoto sent his completed manuscript — "Alias Nero Wolfe" — to Rex for reading.[10] He wrote: "This is a small sin to come from so long a labor, but it's the best I can contrive in my *Harper's* space. I hope it will open up an opportunity to do something longer, for I have a notebook full of stuff I would like to use. I've got enough, for God's sake, to make a book. . . . If I've made any gross error or said anything you find offensive, let me know. I can always make changes in the galleys."

DeVoto was unaware that Rex was working on a new book which would augment substantially the data he had compiled. Rex thought it best not to tantalize him with the news that the book was under way. Nor did he care to tamper with DeVoto's article. On 19 May, he wrote: "I am in no condition to appraise the piece or even comment on it. That an eminent man of letters took the time and trouble to assemble the data and put these eight pages of manuscript together so inflates my self-esteem that I am beyond hope. Sure, you were just having fun, but wasn't Sainte-Beuve having fun when he wrote the *Causeries?* It's wonderful."

As "a member in good standing of the American Historical Society," DeVoto reviewed the discrepancies and contradictions in the Wolfe stories. He concluded that they were intentional. Sometime between 1913 and 1916 Wolfe had been "involved in an episode of so desperate a nature . . . that connecting him with it must be made forever impossible and his true identity must forever be concealed."

In *Too Many Cooks* (1938) Wolfe had said that he was not a native-born American. Yet in *Over My Dead Body* (1939) he told Stahl, an FBI agent, that he had been born in the United States. Taking it as "an inescapable assumption that a professional detective tells the truth about himself when interrogated by the FBI," DeVoto decided that Wolfe, for calculated reasons, had lied in *Too Many Cooks*. Although even in 1939 Wolfe and Archie already were able to savor with amusement the pomposity of the FBI men who visited the brownstone, Wolfe's challenge to the Bureau still lay a decade in the future and DeVoto may be forgiven for not anticipating it. Rex told me that even in 1939 Wolfe was irked by the FBI's consuming curiosity about the private business of law-abiding citizens. In consequence, Wolfe felt under no constraint to tell the truth about himself when interrogated by Stahl. There was, however, another reason for Wolfe's contradictory statements about his place of origin. Rex explained: "Editors and publishers are responsible for the discrepancy. . . . In the original draft of *Over My Dead Body,* Nero was a Montenegrin by birth, and it all fitted previous hints as to his background; but violent protests from *The American Magazine,* supported by Farrar & Rinehart, caused his cradle to be transported five thousand miles. I suppose I should have fought more valiantly for his true nativity, even perhaps have organized a Montenegrin Natal Liberties Union; but I got tired of all the yapping, and besides it seemed highly improbable that anyone would give a damn, or even, for that matter, ever notice it."[11]

DeVoto's speculations about Wolfe's childhood friendship with Marko Vukcic also are seen to be deficient when placed beside disclosures made in *The Black Mountain.* Yet DeVoto did not err seriously. He went as far as unaided reason could take him.

In putting forward his thesis that Wolfe must keep his true identity hidden, nowhere is DeVoto more plausible than when he speculates that the name Nero Wolfe is itself an alias suggested by the name of Wolfe's ancestral homeland, Montenegro, with its towering mountain landmark which Italians call Monte Nero. One wonders why DeVoto did not speculate further on the name Vukcic, which in Serbo-Croatian means "little wolf," or build on his conjecture "that in some way Archie's birth and childhood are related to the mystery of Wolfe's life, or have some bearing on it."[12]

In May the paperback issue surfaced again. On 8 May Bennett Cerf reported in his "Trade Winds" column in the *Saturday Review* that paperback sales were slumping. Each month half of them came back to the publisher, yanked to make space for new titles. In six months' time guarantees had shrunk by seventy-five percent. This information imparted, Cerf gave Rex his attention: "It pleases Mr. Stout to believe that a publisher makes a sinful fortune out of every piece of trash he sponsors, while the author is fobbed off with a miserable pittance." Cerf recalled that, as a member of the committee of publishers which had visited Rex in 1946 to discuss reprint royalties, he had found "that Rex had no interest in examining mere statistics. He preferred to huff and puff up and down the office [like the wolf(e) in the story of the *Three Little Pigs?*], threatening to steer his authors' committee into publishing paperbacks itself if we didn't grant his full demands then and there."

Cerf saw a way of dealing with Rex's latest threat. "The unkindest cut existing paperback publishers could inflict upon Rex Stout and his committee," he said, "would be to actually assist them in setting up shop instead of trying to dissuade them. Let them learn the facts the hard way."

Rex replied on 19 June. He said he had been visiting the Gaspé and had just seen Cerf's comments. (In fact, most of the time he had been at High Meadow, working on *The Black Mountain*.) "I have great admiration for Mr. Cerf as a joke collector," cooed Rex, "but as a reporter he seems to have some flaws." Returns were nearer to twenty-five percent than fifty percent, he said, and guarantee shrinkage, except for a few big titles, was more like ten percent than seventy-five percent. As for Cerf's assertion that Rex believed publishers made "a sinful fortune" out of "every piece of trash" they sponsored, Rex replied, "If it is true that I believe such bosh I am of course an ignorant jackass, so I beg Mr. Cerf to tell me how he learned that I believe that. I have never said or written anything that could possibly be so construed. Can it be that Mr. Cerf has started to write his own jokes?"

As for Cerf's contention that Rex cared naught for statistics, Rex countered: "It was the statistics I had collected, which the hardcover publishers could not impugn, that caused Mr. Cerf and other publishers to realize how bum a deal they had made with the reprint houses. It was the statistics I had collected that revealed the fantastic incompetence of the hardcover publishers as businessmen."

Rex closed with an offer to duel Cerf with his own weapons. "I'll bet Mr. Cerf the price of a year's subscription to the *Saturday Review*," he wrote, "that I can write a column about him and reprints that will be funnier than the one he wrote about me and reprints."

Cerf fumed but could say nothing. Sometime later he brought out a joke book in which he included, complete with illustration, an apocryphal story about Rex. He said that Rex, riding on a crowded subway train, was dismayed once when a diminutive passenger hung onto his beard when he could not reach the overhead strap. Strangely enough, according to Cerf, Rex did not relish this dependency.

At Christmas, in 1955, Rebecca Stout, along with a group of friends, was invited to a dinner party at Cerf's house. Over the soup Cerf asked her if she was related to Rex. She identified herself further. Although Rebecca herself dined heartily at the Cerf board, Bennett did not seem to enjoy the rest of the meal.[13]

At Christmas, in 1964, seeking to cheer a few publishers he knew, the humorist H. Allen Smith sent each of them a framed photo of a tenantless stable. From front to back throughout, generous mounds of horse manure were visible. Smith captioned the photo, "Annual Convention, Authors' League of America." He also sent a copy to Rex, promising that, if a hearing resulted, he would "stand before the assembled members of the League, and with eyes cast downward and chin-a-tremble, say, 'I am the only true horse turd in this room.' " Rex wrote back: "I'm old fashioned, and the only art that appeals to me is the representational, so I love that photograph . . . but I'm a little uncertain about the one in the far left corner. Could it possibly be Bennett Cerf? They sneak in sometimes."[14]

Rex did more than teach Cerf that a ready wit is to be prized above a full joke file. He told me: "A few writers demanded a better split and got it; I was one of the first. Many established writers now get more than half of the paperback income. I get two-thirds, and any paperback arrangement must have my approval, and I have a voice in negotiations."

One disruption in Rex's routine while writing *The Black Mountain* can be credited to the UWF. The UWF's annual banquet, held on 6 June 1954, at the Waldorf-Astoria, was a major cultural event. Oscar Hammerstein II prepared and directed the entertainment. Vermont's Senator Ralph Flanders and Norman Cousins spoke. To commemorate the occasion, Rex had the WBWG prepare a souvenir journal for national distribution. Contributors included Robert Sherwood, Ogden Nash, Cleveland Amory, Christopher La Farge, John Hersey, Herblock, Elmo Roper, and Bill Mauldin. Rex's own contribution, "The Opposition: All Flavors," sketched quick, deadly profiles of the "loudest and most active" critics of world federalism — the warmonger, the two-hundred-percent American, the Communist, and the champion of the status quo. "We've got enough hydrogen bombs right now to win it in forty-eight hours, if we use them right," confides the warmonger. "I myself had a forefather who was a notary public during the revolution, and that's why I love America!" insists the patriot. Rex reserved his heaviest scorn for the Communist — as the archcritic of world federalism: "Its real purpose is the destruction of the people's democracy of the Soviet Union and the extinction of the Russian people.' "

In the year ahead, the appointment of a Supreme Court justice would be held up while the United States Senate debated whether or not he was "soft" on world government. And Dag Hammarskjöld himself would say that the world was not yet ready for it. The movement would slacken. But a few more skirmishes for that golden ideal still lay in Rex's future.

In June, alone in his workship, Rex caught his fingers in an electric saw. Harold sped him to Danbury Hospital. The tip of the third finger of his left hand was mangled and dangling. He lost three-eighths of an inch of it. The adjacent fingers were merely scraped. Did he keep his composure throughout the incident? "Of course," Rex assured me.

On 16 August Rex wrote to Juanita DeBrock thanking her for a solicitous letter: "Now that's what I call a perfect letter. It had news (about your new home), sympathy (for my sawed fingers), and a dash of tonic for my vanity (your neighbor with a dog named Nero)."

On 23 September, Rex began writing "The Next Witness" and had it done on 13 October. Eight days out.[15] That same month "The Town I Like — Brewster, New York," illustrated with Dick Dodge watercolors, was published in the *Lincoln-Mercury Times* — a friendly, first-person piece in which Rex spoke in the character of a long-time native of Brewster. He was glad that the residents had not "slicked up Brewster . . . to a concrete-and-chromium Commutania." He had bought the materials for his house from Brewster folk and had expected to be taken because, he said, "First, I was an alien, another big-city man who had got his claws on a parcel of the township's acres. . . . Second, I was a political freak, a man with a sizable income but a Democrat. . . . Third, I was going to build a house with a flat roof and a court enclosed on three sides." To his pleasant surprise, they had treated him "simply swell." He then sketched several Brewster men.

The Brewster piece suggests that Rex had under observation a Spoon River or Winesburg, Ohio, where things had gone — right.

At the Mayflower Hotel, in Washington, D.C., on 16 October, Rex was master of ceremonies at a benefit dinner for the Cancer Fund. A score of mystery writers, including Georges Simenon, Manfred Lee and Frederic Dannay (Ellery Queen), Anthony Boucher, Leslie Ford, Pat McGerr, Lawrence G. Blochman, and Harold Q. Masur, joined with him to help put the dinner over. Beforehand, seated behind a long line of card tables for the afternoon, at Kann's Department Store, they autographed books for an admiring public. Between signings, Dannay asked

Rex where he got the name "Nero Wolfe." Rex outlined the O-E theory, which Alexander Woollcott had propounded. Nero and Sherlock have the same vowels in the same order; so do Wolfe and Holmes. Rex thought he might have set up the parallel subconsciously. Dannay thought it all went back to P-o-e.[16]

Two weeks later, on 5 November, Rex was back in Washington for the signing of the Universal Copyright Convention. The Senate had ratified it on 25 June. The House passed the necessary implementing domestic legislation on 29 July. On the night of 18 August, it had cleared the Senate. The Convention provided that each member nation would offer the same copyright privileges to foreign nationals that it guaranteed to its own citizens. Coming after fifty years of struggle, it was a major victory for American authors. On 27 August Rex had sent out a jubilant "Victory Notice" to the members of the Authors' League. It was their victory.

Yet Rex could take personal satisfaction in it too. He could remember sitting with Twain and Tarkington, at Delmonico's, in 1909, feeling curious but helpless, while the two literary behemoths bemoaned the copyright situation. Perhaps his subconscious had programmed him then to do something about it. Behind the scenes, as president of the Authors' League, Rex had worked without letup, instigating letter and telegram campaigns, and arranging personal appearances at congressional hearings. One of the chief foes of the bill had been the A.F. of L. American domestic copyright law had a notorious Manufacturing Clause, which specified that no book or periodical in the English language could be copyrighted in America unless it was printed from type set here. Typographical and other unions affiliated with the International Allied Printing Trades Association did not want to see that changed. Yet the United States could not give effect to the Convention unless it was. As late as 11 August, Nevada's Senator McCarran, had, on that account, stalled passage of the bill. The session seemed in danger of passing into history without action being taken. Rex saw to it that "a flood — or anyway, a colossal trickle" of wires and phone calls was sent to Washington from 14 to 18 August. They supplied the margin of victory. When the news reached them at the League office on the night of the eighteenth, the austere Luise Sillcox grabbed Rex's hand and told him feelingly, "I must be dreaming. I've watched this fight, and been in it, for forty years, and I just can't believe it."

Rex was asked to stand at President Eisenhower's side as he signed the legislation into law. "Now you can sell more copies of *Crusade in Europe*," Rex said when the President handed him the pen he had used. Ike grinned and answered, "We don't have to sell more of *that.*"

In the October-December issue of *The American Writer* Rex summed up the history of the struggle that had led to final enactment of the Convention. The victory, he knew, belonged to those who had carried on the battle from the founding of the League, in 1912. He recalled Booth Tarkington's major effort, over forty years, in behalf of this cause. He wondered if John Stout would have been proud that what his former pupil, Booth Tarkington, had launched had been completed with the help of his son, Rex Stout.

With this victory Rex did not cease to work for copyright revision. During the next twenty years, revision of domestic copyright law took much of his attention. Between 1964 and 1966 alone, he made eight appearances before congressional committees to clarify provisions fundamental to this legislation. Rex had been dead nearly a year when President Gerald Ford signed into law the final version, on 19 October 1976, but his part in the victory was commemorated by the Authors' Guild with its presentation of the first Rex Stout Award, on 14 January 1977, to Representative Robert W. Kastenmeier, of Wisconsin, for his part in steering the legislation through Congress.

Rex did not send Bernard DeVoto a copy of *The Black Mountain* until it was published on 14 October. If DeVoto was annoyed that Rex had held back so much information in the spring, he did not show it. On 5 November he wrote Rex:

This is all very stimulating and exhilarating and exciting and informative and all that, and I am lost in my usual envious admiration. Nevertheless, these fascinating new revelations embody an *a fortiori* which has the most serious implications. I should be saddened and chagrined if my research, which was conducted in the purest spirit of devotion, were to make trouble for Mr. Wolfe, but it has been published and is on the record. Mr. Stahl's promotion was doubtless for merit and he is much too efficient an officer to have forgotten that in October, 1938 Mr. Wolfe told him that he was born in the United States.

I soothe my anxiety with the reflection that many revelations remain to be made and that unquestionably this apparently sinister tangle will be unsnarled. I await them eagerly and I hope yet to see Mr. Wolfe calling on Mr. Cramer for assistance as apparently he will have to do.[17]

What a canny forecast of *The Doorbell Rang!* How shrewd a surmise! DeVoto attested his loyalty with one further statement: "Some time ago Elmer Davis wrote me asking if I could tell him whether Archie remained irresistible to women. I told him that he was a bigoted Baker Street Irregular and should have more faith."

DeVoto was right when he concluded that "many revelations remain to be made." Regrettably, he would not be there to relish them. The next November, at fifty-nine, he was dead of a heart attack — stricken, in a way reminiscent of Woollcott's death, in a New York television studio.

42

The King in Action

Montenegro is about the same size as Peru if you take away Lake Titicaca. With a population of only two hundred thousand, give or take a Serb, it produced Nero Wolfe.

The U.S.A. has about two hundred and ten million, many of whom are literate. And what did we come up with? Sigmund Spaeth.

Peru hasn't done well either.

— HENRY MORGAN

The Carey-Thomas Awards for creative book publishing were given to the winners by *Publishers Weekly,* at the Hotel Roosevelt, at a Twelfth Night luncheon in 1955. Rex had been one of the prize jurors. His place at the table was next to Louise Bonino, juvenile editor of Random House. A certificate of honorable mention given to Miss Bonino for the Landmark series stated that the series had originated with "that shy and diffident publisher, Bennett Cerf." The phrasing was not Rex's.[1]

Rex soon was back at High Meadow, snugly snowed in, writing "Immune to Murder," which he began on 21 January and finished on 3 February, with two days out. In this story Wolfe visits an estate in the Adirondacks which has "three miles of private trout fishing." Rex told me: "There was a mile or so of such a stream on the River Farm, the La Farge property in Saunderstown, Rhode Island, with lots of trout, and I fished it a couple of times with Kipper."

In *The Black Mountain* Nero Wolfe breaks off reading Elmer Davis's *But We Were Born Free* to set out in search of a murderer. In February 1955 Davis got to the book. "Thousands of people," Davis wrote Rex on the twenty-third of February, "would never have heard of *Born Free* if it were not for you and Nero. My thanks to you both; I don't blame him for putting it back in the bookcase half-finished when he had to find the killer of his daughter and his best friend. Thanks also for giving me more pleasure than I have had out of the Black Mountain since the Merry Widow."

Rex's gesture was not unprecedented. Mark Van Doren recalled: "Rex told me once that he likes to mention his friends in his stories — a book they have written, for instance, or something they have done.

This is plausible because Nero reads everything and seems to know everybody."[2]

In April Rex started *Before Midnight.* Distractions were few. Begun on 14 April, it was finished on 20 May. Five days out. Rex's spirits always were up when he finished a book. That was just as well. A battle was in the offing.

At the invitation of Janice Ehrenberg, a UWF supporter, Rex had agreed to address the Parents Association at P.S. 24, in Riverdale, New York, on Wednesday evening, 25 May, and to dine with the Ehrenbergs beforehand. His topic would be "Atomic Peace."

Janice was worried about what to feed her guest. She remembered that on his visit to White Plains in 1952, Rex was following an ulcer diet. What do you give a gourmet with a duodenal ulcer? Rex sought to reassure her: "My diet isn't quite as limited as it was that evening at White Plains. The only thing I must absolutely deny myself is uncooked bark from oak trees less than two hundred years old." She tried her hand at a *boeuf bourguignonne.* When she botched it she made a last-minute switch to a roast and a rich lemon dessert. Rex enjoyed that, and the wine and the cordials. The evening was off to a good start. Before the night was done, however, Janice had further reason to be thankful Rex's ulcer was quiescent. After Rex spoke, he held a question period. The night was hot and the questions desultory until a man in the back of the hall, Benedict Rapport, said he had a question.

As a matter of fact Rapport, chairman of the Americanism committee of the local American Legion Post, had several questions. How could Rex reconcile his prediction that hydrogen warfare would destroy the United States and/or Russia, when the radius of destruction of a hydrogen bomb was at most two miles? Why would Russia feel compelled to join a world government when Russia and China together had more people than the United States and its dependable allies had? When the chair objected to Rapport's bellicose tone, Rapport let loose a torrent of allegations. Wasn't it true that the UWF was on the Attorney General's list of subversive organizations? Wasn't it true that Rex himself had been affiliated with four subversive organizations? Rex waved his notes menacingly above his head. "No," he thundered, "and I condemn you for such a statement." Rex had a *déjà vu* feeling. It was the Ham Fish evening reversed.

Even as Rapport unleashed his attack, catcalls and boos rose from every corner of the hall. At a nod from the P.A. president, Mrs. Julian Koock, her husband grabbed Rapport by the arm and hustled him out. The Riverdale *Press* gave the story front page space on 2 June — under the headline "PEACE TALK ENDS IN 'WAR.'" The *Press* also published two letters, one from Janice Ehrenberg, the other from Benedict Rapport, setting forth opposing accounts of what had happened. Janice pointed out that the UWF not only had never been declared subversive, but that President Eisenhower himself had commended the group's efforts for the cause of world peace. Rapport deplored the misguided zeal of those who had invited to Riverdale "speakers whose records of affiliations render questionable the motives behind the opinions which they express."

The next week, the *Press* again gave the story front-page space. Norman Cousins had offered to come to Riverdale to explain the aims and purposes of the UWF. Seven letters continued the controversy. In their midst appeared Rex's picture, captioned "Rex Stout — Storm Center."

On 11 June, Leon Racht gave the story a full column on the editorial page of the New York *Journal American.* Under the leader "Subversive Front," readers were told, "Stout in Riverdale Rhubarb." In "ritzy Riverdale" an American Legionnaire, the father of two, had suffered a "shameful ejection" when he "challenged paper-backed fictioneer Rex Stout on his political background." Rex was "the goat-bearded Stout," who was "currently on a world-government kick," and the UWF "the propaganda outfit dedicated to a world super-state which would destroy national sovereignty." The column then reviewed Merwin Hart's charges about Rex's subversive affiliations. "How much of the hogwash he dishes out as front man for the United World Federalists do these parents assimilate and pass out to their children?" asked Racht.

Since Racht suggested that local propagandists were using the Riverdale *Press* "to knock his [Rapport's] brains out," the *Press* had one of its reporters interview Rex. In the interview, given front-page space on 16 June, Rex told Joe Fitzpatrick: "I am an American and a good American. . . . The information contained in Racht's article has been disseminated by the Legion and they know damn well it's false. No evidence to support any of the charges has ever been produced." Rex then systematically struck down the charges. He was not on the advisory committee of the Hollywood Writers Mobilization. He did not contribute to the League of American Writers. He had nothing to do with the "Dinner for the Century of the Common Man." In a separate release, the UWF explained that the only piece by Rex published by the League of American Writers had been an attack on anti-Semitism. And the League had pirated that.

In the same issue of the *Press,* a letter from Rapport insisted that Rex was trying to sell the "country down . . . the Volga River." But an editorial disclosed that Rapport and the county commander of the Legion had met with Courtland Hastings, chairman of the New York State branch of the UWF, and discovered that they had areas of concurrence.

As copies of the *Press* became available, Janice Ehrenberg sent them to Rex. On 20 June he wrote to her:

A virus that loves me a lot more than I love it has kept me so limp and useless for three weeks that I haven't even sent you a line to thank you for your communiques from the battle line. You may be sure that they have been devoured and much appreciated. . . .

The chief effect of the Battle of Riverdale on me personally has been an adjustment of my vocabulary. After that extremely pleasant visit at your home I would have said (formerly) that I felt *en rapport* with you and your husband and the boys, but now I'll have to find another phrase for it.

Rex loathed puns. Riverdale had not unsettled him that much. It must have been the virus. The Ehrenbergs closed the episode by scheduling a meeting on atomic annihilation. Nobody came.[3]

On 15 June, Viking published *Full House,* the first of its eight Nero Wolfe omnibus volumes.[4] The poker term would be a feature of the series. It suited Archie's idiom. Moreover, continuity titles help sell books.

If the omnibus did not speed Rex's convalescence, then a review of the book done by Charles A. Brady for the Buffalo *Evening News* did. In any assessment of Wolfe scholarship, Professor Brady's review must be counted a major step in according the series recognition as literature.

Of contemporary crime fiction writers, Brady thought that "for serious consideration" the field narrowed to "only those two very different artists, Rex Stout and Raymond Chandler." Then he reduced the company to one. "Without being at all old-fashioned — in fact he strikes a neat balance between tradition and innovation — Stout is more the traditionalist than Chandler. In the long run he will also have, I think, greater staying power." Of Wolfe, Brady said: "He speaks in ponderous Johnsonese that can be extraordinarily witty. To tie up this fat bundle of fruity mannerisms Stout resorts to the tried and true old trick, borrowed from the comedy of humors, of characterizing through salient gesture and personal peculiarity." As an epigrammatist, Wolfe was to Brady "the La Rochefoucauld among fiction's great detectives."

Of Archie, Brady said: "If Nero Wolfe is traditional all through, the rasping-minded Archie Goodwin is an innovation. His citified Huck talk — I think it is fair to describe Archie as speaking Huckleberry Finnish — counterpoints Wolfe's rolling periods, and is, in its different ways, as successfully witty."[5] Between the thirteenth and the thirtieth of August, Rex wrote "A Window for Death" — twelve days' writing; six days out.

On 24 September, at Denver, President Eisenhower suffered a coronary occlusion. During the first stages of his convalescence, doctors would not let him read. Reading records were substituted. On 1 October, the press reported that the first records played for Ike were *Vengeance Valley*, by his "favorite Western author — Luke Short," and *Prisoner's Base*, by Rex Stout. As a fellow Kansan, Ike probably would have been at home with Rex's original "Dare Base" title.

In the fall of 1955 Rebecca began her freshman year at Bennington. Rex had not insisted that Rebecca attend college. He left the choice to her. And now he put no pressure on her about the way she managed her life and her allowance. Nonetheless, periodically she let him know how she stood. One such report brought a reply, on 1 November, that any daughter would have cherished:

My entire auditing department admires and applauds the clarity and thoroughness of your financial accounting, and your recording is much appreciated and will be properly filed; and if you want to continue with such full itemization because you think it's a good idea that will be fine, but there is no law requiring it.

One thing you didn't include in the account is the actual total of the checks you have drawn against your bank account, but the balance must be somewhat below $100, so I'm sending the bank a check for $135 to be deposited to your credit.

I was surprised to find no entry of gin or marijuana on your list, but I suppose that was covered in the item "General stuff $2.00."

I miss you around here. . . .

On 12 November, he wrote again:

I'm thoroughly conversant with the first report from your Bennington teachers. It's not bad at all, though it of course has room for improvement, as Heaven does too, no doubt. Particularly I like the way each of them suggests specific ways for you to get more out of the courses, and since a hint to the wise is sufficient, and since you are certainly wise, the future looks bright! Congratulations.

If Rex and Rebecca were speaking across a generation gap — she was eighteen; he was sixty-eight — it didn't show.

The Wolfe stories continued to reach the public promptly. *Before Midnight* came out on 27 October. "Immune to Murder" was in the November issue of *The American Magazine,* and "Die like a Dog" and "The Next Witness" had appeared there also, in recent issues. Bernard DeVoto would have considered this flood of new Wolfe material an ample response to his appeal to Rex, made the previous November, to "please absent yourself from idleness and hurry on with the next one." But DeVoto had died on 13 November. His death was followed just a few hours later by Robert Sherwood's. Two cherished friends, dead suddenly in their fifties. Yet Rex could not weep for those who had given to life so much more than they had taken from it.

On 7 December, Moss Hart became the new president of the Authors' League. At Moss's behest, Rex stayed on as vice president.

43.

More than a Duke

Rex Stout has many times the vigor of the average human. He always has
had. Once Frances and I went to look at Rex's iris at its height and Rex took
us down the steep grade in front of his house to see some especially prized
flowers. He bounded down ahead of us. We admired. Rex bounded back up.
We trudged. We were both some years younger than Rex and still played
a good deal of tennis. When we got back to the house that day, Rex went
into a steep rock garden, leaping from crag to crag to point out plants. We
stood and watched, wistfully. . . .

— RICHARD LOCKRIDGE

On 6 January 1956, Rex presided at the annual dinner of the Baker
Street Irregulars. Rex's presence always lent its own excitement to the
occasion. Among themselves his fellow mystery writers now referred to
him as "the king" — his title by right as well as by Rex. No one now
thought he was "only a duke." To those assembled for this meeting,
Edgar W. Smith, editor of the *Baker Street Journal*, read some of the
letters and telegrams received. Five years later, when Smith died, Rex,
in "The Case of the Politician," recalled that night:

One of the telegrams saluting the BSI effusively and paying homage to Sherlock Holmes, was signed by a certain nationally prominent politician. Edgar's
reading of that telegram was a subtle revelation of his essential character and
spirit. His manner, his tone and inflection, were urbane and not supercilious,
courtly but not condescending, sophisticated but not pert, contemptuous but
not rude. . . .
Edgar knew . . . that the telegram was an empty pretense to a shared enthusiasm in furtherance of a political ambition. . . . But Edgar didn't say so. He said
nothing. He merely picked up the telegram, read it, and let it drop to the table.[1]

Rex's tribute to Smith did not mention the name of the man who paid
hollow tribute to Holmes. Who was it? I asked him. "Richard Nixon,"
Rex told me.

After the BSI dinner, Rex was immediately at work on "Too Many
Detectives," taking out just one day between 13 January, when he
began it, and 24 January, when he finished it.

A National Authors and Dramatists Assembly, to celebrate the forty-fifth anniversary of the founding of the Authors' League, was first proposed by William L. Shirer early in 1955. Rex appointed a League committee, under the chairmanship of Elizabeth Janeway, to follow it up, and sent out questionnaires to League members. More than seven hundred favored an assembly. When Moss Hart succeeded Rex as president, he pressed the matter further, appointing Rex and Russel Crouse as cochairmen of the assembly committee. Hart had tried without success to get Rex's permission to do a Nero Wolfe play. Even so, he was fond of Rex and was enthusiastic about his plans. Crouse and Rex drew up a three-day program. As Rex wrote to John Marquand, on 12 March 1956, "Details have already been sufficiently discussed to show great promise of an interesting and useful three days, even to me — though I dislike conventions on principle and am congenitally skeptical about them." In the same letter, he mentioned that Elizabeth Janeway, John Hersey, and he himself each had pledged five hundred dollars toward the expenses of the undertaking. Though notably parsimonious, Marquand came through with another five hundred.

The assembly was fourteen months off. No matter; Rex and Crouse schemed in earnest for its success. The committee serving under them consisted of Margaret Cousins, Clifton Fadiman, Jacques Barzun, Dorothy Fields, Alan Lerner, Richard Rodgers, and Herman Wouk. Rex found Fadiman quite as indispensable as he had been as a member of the WWB. And Barzun matched his dedication and industry. To insure the stamina of his committee, Rex saw to it that they met around a well-laden table. Margaret Cousins says: "We used to meet in the Library or some private suite at the St. Regis Hotel. Rex ordered the dinner personally and chose the wines. Here I ate some of the gourmet dinners of my life and had my first education in fine wines."[2]

Another responsibility Rex assumed at this time was chairmanship of the Authors' Guild's membership committee. Under Rex this committee took on great significance. Sending out annually several hundred individual letters to members and nonmembers, Rex increased Guild membership and got for the Guild the funds it needed to survive and to develop its programs and campaigns.

For *The Mystery Writers' Handbook*, published by the MWA in 1956, Rex wrote "What to Do about a Watson." Rex here scoffed at the "modern hybridizers" who saw the detective story as "a sex-and-gin marathon." His concern was with a Watson's role in "the true detective story." He admitted that a Watson could be "a devil of a nuisance," but was convinced his usefulness outweighed his drawbacks. The detective himself was the hero. The steps that led him to his triumph were therefore central to the story. The best way to divulge them without giving away their significance was through a Watson. Rex noted that at times things must be held back in a detective story. If the author is the narrator and holds something back, readers may accept it, but will resent it. For a Watson, carrying this feat off can be a cinch. "That's where a Watson," said Rex, "is a jewel and a blessing."

Three Witnesses came out on 10 March. On 16 April Rex began *Might as Well Be Dead*. With just a week out, it was done by 23 May. At least one interruption explained itself. On 17 May Barbara gave birth to her second child, Reed. Rex now had a male descendant.[3]

In May, too, "A Window to Death" was published in *American Magazine:* the thirty-first Wolfe story to appear in *The American,* it was also the last. The magazine ceased publication soon thereafter. That was the beginning of the end for the Wolfe novellas. The short story market was shrinking. Over the next six years Rex would write another nine novellas, but three of these — "The Rodeo Murder," "Poison à la Carte," and "Murder Is Corny" — would go into hardcover with no beforehand magazine publication at all. Although Rex publicly had endorsed Doyle's view that the shorter form suited the detective story best, his novellas had been written to accommodate the magazines. When the magazines no longer wanted them, he stopped writing them. Did he believe the short form more functional? "No," he told me, "I was just talking." Yet Rex's alliance with the magazines had been a happy one. In many busy periods of his life if publishers had not settled for a novella he would have written nothing and many of Wolfe's finest moments would have gone unrecorded. Indeed, when the novella market disappeared many did go unrecorded. At eighty-nine Rex said he still would be writing them, and fairly often, if the demand had persisted. Because of fuller characterization, Charles Brady adjudged the novels superior to the novellas. Anthony Boucher preferred the novellas. Rex conceded that he stripped down the novellas to meet page limitations: for example, in the novellas Wolfe's current reading seldom is mentioned. But the pace never seems hurried in consequence. Nor do the novels seem padded. There everything merely ripens on a grander scale and there is time for intimacy.

In June, Rebecca and her roommate at Bennington, Emily Cram, whom Rex dubbed "Cindy," set out on a cross-country automobile tour. Anxious to give Rebecca the advantages of his own experience as a cross-country motorist, Rex had the old Plymouth station wagon reconditioned. Then he built a roof rack, a platform with air mattresses to go inside, and two boxes which fitted under the platform, in which to stow gear. Anything they needed, he supplied. Anything unnecessary, he vetoed. Why two flashlights when one would do? The trip got the same thorough planning he had given his own packing in trips. He even mapped the route. But he held his advice to a minimum. Sleep under lights at motor inns was one recommendation. There was a jocular warning, too. Don't drive more than twelve thousand miles. He also lined up post offices along the way, so that they would have letters waiting for them, and gave Rebecca five hundred dollars in traveler's checks, for expenses. And a baseball bat for warding off attackers.

In Springfield, Illinois, the Plymouth sprang an oil leak and the engine burned out. When Rebecca called Rex, he offered no reproaches. He apologized because the car had delayed them. He wired money for repairs. In Topeka the travelers visited the house at 900 Madison. The owner knew that Rex Stout had lived there, and showed them through. (In 1966 the house was demolished by a tornado. A Holiday Inn now stands on the spot. The same tornado sheared off the roof of the East Eighth Street house; abandoned now, it is slated for razing.)

As they pulled up the drive at High Meadow, at the end of August, the girls saw that they had gone exactly 11,980 miles.

In the August heat Rex kept himself amused writing "Christmas Party," at first entitled "License to Kill."[4] Begun on 19 August; finished on 4 September.

On 6 September Rex was the featured speaker at the weekly luncheon meeting of the Danbury Lions Club. He warned that protests raised by highly placed members of the American Legion, the D.A.R., and the V.F.W. were slowing the drive for world government. "Ninety-five percent of their membership do not realize what is going on," he said. Yet their influence was pervasive. In the past, Eisenhower and Stevenson had advocated world law. If they did that now, they "would be hissed and booed and called Communist-lovers." Rex had not forgotten Riverdale.

Rex found that the Soviet Union's attitude deepened the plight. The current Soviet leaders were "no different from Stalin." He saw no hope that Russia would "change its way and become peace-loving." While nations clung to their sovereignty there would be no world peace.

A presidential election was heating up and that took some of Rex's interest, too. It also occasioned a mild rebuke to J. Donald Adams of *The New York Times Book Review*. Adams wanted to affix Rex's name to a statement supporting Eisenhower and Nixon. Rex wrote back: "Since I am for Stevenson and Kefauver, I must decline the invitation extended in your letter of September 21st. Has *The New York Times Book Review* come out for Eisenhower and Nixon? If not, I question the propriety of using the letterhead of that publication for a partisan political letter."

Eat, Drink, and Be Buried appeared, under Rex's editorship, on 18 October. The twenty stories had a common theme, which Rex had chosen. In each "the route of murder is the gullet." Another feature is a statement from each author — prudently placed at the end of each story — in which the author identifies the story's strongest and weakest

points. Stanley Ellin implied that Rex had intimidated him. To quote
Ellin quoting Rex: " 'If any contributor regards his story as without a
weakness,' added Mr. Stout, thoughtfully picking apart the petals of a
priceless orchid as he spoke, 'who does he think he is, Shakespeare?' "

In his introduction, Rex once more set down his long-cherished views
on the artistic fruits of discipline:

> The indictment of mystery stories as "formula stuff" is poppycock. You might
> as well call Petrarchan sonnets "formula stuff" because they adhere to a pre-
> scribed rhyming scheme. John Milton and Edna St. Vincent Millay both faith-
> fully held to the scheme; and the writers of the stories in this cover faithfully
> held to the theme, but observe the wide variety in approach, treatment, devel-
> opment, and emphasis.

Eat, Drink, and Be Buried was more than an anthology. It chided the
detractors of the detective story and upheld a thesis.

Might as Well Be Dead came out on 21 October. On 28 October, Rex's
review of *My Lord, What a Morning* — Marian Anderson's autobiography — commanded the front page of the *Herald Tribune*'s book section.

Nero Wolfe made his debut as a comic strip on 26 November. The
strip ran weekdays and Sundays, and appeared in numerous Midwestern newspapers.[5] The stories were written by comic-book writer John
Broome and drawn by Mike Roy. Broome's Wolfe was not a shut-in. The
series did not pit him against the monstrous misfits whom Dick Tracy
regularly confronted, but at least one adversary was a mechanical man.
Few true Wolfe fans can have followed the series, which made less of
an effort than radio had to catch the spirit of Rex's stories. Yet it ran for
several years. Rex let it happen, to help a friend. It brought him no
income. He never read it.

On 6 December Rex began work on another Wolfe novella, "Easter
Parade." With his holiday stories Rex perversely showed his contempt
for holidays by mixing holiday seasons, writing about Easter at Christmas, and about Christmas on Labor Day. With these stories he departed
from his customary practice of setting a story in the period in which he
was writing it. "Easter Parade" also was the first story Rex started in one
year and finished in another.

A compelling reason accounted for the twenty-three days Rex took
out before "Easter Parade" was finished on 8 January. On 11 December,
Rex's youngest sister, Betty, had ended her life with an overdose of
barbiturates. Betty had never married and, through the years, as a
nurse, had spent most of her income on charity cases. Fiercely independent, she accepted no help from other members of the family. At
sixty-six she realized her working days were nearly over. For her, the

choice was a choice to continue her freedom. When Ruth and Mary came to remove Betty's things from her apartment, Mary found in the closet a pair of high-heeled shoes, curiously alone among her practical oxfords. "I think she never wore them," Mary said, "but I think she wanted to wear them."

For the funeral the family once again gathered at Ridgewood, New Jersey. Afterward, at the Ridgewood Country Club, where Bob was president, they met for dinner and discussion. Bob and Rex had not sat down together in twenty-eight years. Now they shared a common concern — to console Mary, whose capacity for empathy had always been so great.

A sense of transiency touched all five surviving siblings. But Rex, at least, had reason to believe his life had not yet run its course. His duties had continued to multiply. On 15 March he had been elected treasurer of Freedom House, succeeding Cass Canfield. In November he became chairman of the Authors' League Fund. These were sensitive posts which made a heavy call on his abilities. He functioned in them so well he would still hold them at eighty-nine.[6]

44.

Master of Mystery

I take pleasure in writing herewith a few lines on Rex Stout. I only regret my lack of originality but, outside the writing of novels, I am completely lost.

Rex Stout is one of the most attractive persons I have ever met. What struck me in him, at the beginning of our acquaintance, was his natural kindness towards everyone. His contribution to the detective novel is, I am certain, of great importance. He created a character who becomes a kind of friend for every reader. A little manic, and a little grumpy, but whom one always looks forward to meeting in another novel. Not to mention his cook who prepares extraordinary menus to make any gourmet's mouth water.

You see . . . my text doesn't come up to much. I have written it with all my sympathy, my friendship and admiration for Rex Stout.

— GEORGES SIMENON

In January 1957, Marion Wilcox solicited from Rex recipes for a dinner meeting of the Syracuse Rex Stout Fan Club. To Marion, whom he had come to think of as his quintessential fan, Rex wrote on 28 January: "It sounds to me as if the SRSFC is now about big enough to be a pressure group. If so, I hope Katherine Sullivan doesn't use a pressure cooker for the dinner on March 22nd. I don't like pressure cookers and neither does Fritz or Mr. Wolfe." This time Rex declined to answer questions about the books on the theory that "once a question is answered it is no longer interesting," an argument that betrayed Rex's admiration for Lewis Carroll. Yet, for Marion, he relented. "Is there a woman who comes in to clean? Good Lord, no. A man comes in to clean, and some day he is going to . . . but I'll save that for a story I have in mind."

"The Christmas-Party Murder," published in *Collier's* on 4 January, has Wolfe, at one point, perusing Herblock's *Here and Now*. On 4 February Block wrote Rex: "One thing about the demise of *Collier's* — it ended in fine style, with the cover proudly proclaiming a 'Nero Wolfe thriller.' And a thriller it certainly was; but I don't think anyone else could have got the added special thrill that I did when I came to the lines about *Here and Now!*"[1]

Another holiday story, "Fourth-of-July Picnic," was begun on 9 March and finished on 22 March. Writing time, nine days. Rex wrote no other Wolfe story in so brief a span.

On 24 March Rex reviewed Henry Goddard's *Memoirs of a Bow Street Runner* for *The New York Times Book Review*. Goddard was a bona fide private detective of the Victorian era. As early as 1835 he had identified a culprit (a butler, no less) by an improvised "ballistics" test. His initiative alone assured him Rex's approval.

In late March, television cameras moved into High Meadow to do an hour-long documentary on Rex and his personal world. The passageway came under the camera's eye, as did the great sunken living room, the kitchen where Rex prepared his popovers and *oeufs au beurre noir,* and his office, and the rolling acres, which, even in winter, were soothingly symmetrical. Topekans saw the program the night of 16 April. David Overmyer and his sister Amy watched it. With them was Rex's old classmate, Tinkham Veale, jailed with him when they strung up their victory banner in 1902.[2]

That same day Rex's "Easter Parade," complete with photos posed by professional models, was published in *Look* magazine's Easter issue. *Look* had paid $30,000 for this twenty-five-thousand-word story — the largest sum Rex had received up to that time from a magazine for a single work.

Three for the Chair was published on 3 May.

On Sunday afternoon, 5 May, Rex joined five youngsters, ages eleven to fourteen, at the Du Mont Telecenter, on East Sixty-seventh Street, for a *New York Times* Youth Forum discussion on the topic "Do Allowances Help Youth Learn Money Values?" The *Times* identified Rex as "a founder of the Educational Thrift System, by which thousands of students save at school." Rex gave his age as "more than fifteen." Rex's questions cut right to the issues: "When one parent refuses you money do you go to the other?" "When a child is thrifty does it reflect the practice of his parents?" The young panelists leveled with him freely. In his summing up Rex showed he had not forgotten the lessons inculcated by ETS, or what it was like to be an adolescent: "An allowance should not cover food, clothing, and other necessities. . . . The amount of an allowance should depend on what it is used for and on whether or not a child can handle it intelligently."

The next day, the Authors' League's first national assembly at last convened. Headquarters was the Biltmore, where four hundred and twenty-six writers registered for bare-knuckled discussions on contracts, copyrights, and censorship, and for a wide-ranging series of panels, which featured Lillian Hellman, Elizabeth Janeway, S. J. Perelman, Mark Van Doren, Anthony Boucher, Oscar Hammerstein II, Theodore White, Bruce Catton, and John Mason Brown. Rex had done a prodigious amount of paperwork setting up these panels in advance, and formulating contingency plans to cover sudden illnesses and absences. He was one of the assembly's four hosts, the others being William L. Shirer, Moss Hart, and Oscar Hammerstein II.

On Tuesday morning Rex chaired the "Book Markets and Contracts" panel. Panelists included Anthony Boucher, Pete Martin, Richard Lockridge, Bentz Plagemann, and Osmond Fraenkel. Rex's role in landing Boucher was typical of the trouble he went to to assure the assembly's success. Boucher wanted to come, but it meant traveling from Berkeley to New York. When he capitulated, in mid-March, Rex wired him for "three names to discuss science fiction in order of preference." Ray Bradbury had dropped out. Boucher's three candidates each declined. The search resumed. Pete Martin agreed to talk on ghostwriting. Boucher then had to be asked, in mid-April, to talk both on mysteries *and* science fiction. "All it means," Rex said, "is that you will speak for eight hours instead of four." Boucher accepted the assignment.[3]

On the third and last day of the assembly, a general session met at the Helen Hayes Theatre. The topic was censorship. The speakers were Howard Lindsay, John Vandercook, Mark Van Doren, Oscar Hammerstein II, and Rex. Rex made a disconcerting disclosure: "I had the first thoughts I had that the censors would consider vile after reading a story in *The Youth's Companion.*"

On 16 May, Rex started *If Death Ever Slept.* He finished it on 19 June. Just three days out. On one of those days — 10 June — he attended a meeting of song-writers, playwrights, actresses, cartoonists, and novelists at the Waldorf-Astoria. The group included Otto Harbach, Helen Hayes, W. C. Handy, Arthur Schwartz, Paddy Chayevsky, Al Capp, Abe Burrows, and Oscar Hammerstein II. They issued a joint statement protesting radio and television monopoly groups which gave broadcast preference to the music in which they had a financial interest. RCA Victor and Columbia were owned by broadcasters. Broadcast Music, Inc., controlled more than two-thirds of all the music publishing firms in the United States.

Rex would follow up this matter later by appearing before a Senate communications subcommittee, chaired by Senator Pastore of Rhode Island, urging it to report out a bill divorcing radio and television station licenses from interests in music publishing and recording companies. He charged that broadcasters discriminated in favor of the music of Broadcast Music, Inc. He said:

Certainly those granted licenses do not have the right to act as arbiters in the selection of what is to be heard by the listening public. . . . To lose one freedom is to endanger all other freedoms. . . . Every creative work that utilizes words is a potential target for absorption by these same broadcasters under existing conditions. . . . What can prevent the broadcasting interests from buying up book publishing firms, magazines, and every other kind of medium for the writer of words?

Here was a censorship of a new and heinous kind. Ideological censorship was insupportable, but in the struggle for men's minds it was at least understandable. Commercial censorship was waged for the control of men's pocketbooks. That was both outrageous and sinister.

The morning following the Waldorf-Astoria symposium, on a radio broadcast, Rex, along with Helen Hayes, Anita Loos, Oscar Hammerstein II, and George S. Kaufman, paid tribute to W. C. Handy. Handy, then nearing the end of his life, was present in a wheelchair.[4] Rex told me: "Helen Hayes was absolutely nasty to Handy. Just nasty. And I've always hated her ever since. Very unfairly, because almost certainly — it was eleven o'clock in the morning when we did the radio thing — she hadn't been up that early for thirty years and was completely out of sorts. So I was completely unfair to blame her, but I did. I just resented it to beat hell."

Temperament of another sort caught Rex off guard a few days later. He entered his regular barbershop in Danbury to find a fractious five-year-old battling his mother. He did not want to get his hair cut. "Let the barber cut your hair," Rex instructed the boy. "Then you'll look nice and your mother will be happy." The boy took him in, then snapped back, "Why don't you cut the hair on your face and make *your* mother happy?"

With his daughters Rex had better rapport. At the end of June Rebecca's professors, including Howard Nemerov (who soon would forsake the classroom to wear a poet's laurels), had forwarded close-of-term reports extolling her growth and achievements during her time at Bennington, and expressing confidence in her potential. To celebrate Rex struck off a gleeful quatrain:

> *Nemerov, Fowlie, Dorner and Soule*
> *Are brainy when they my daughter extol.*
> *They know my daughter is nobody's fool —*
> *Nemerov, Fowlie, Dorner and Soule!*

Between the fifth and fifteenth of August, Rex wrote "Murder Is No Joke." One day out. He now left himself free of writing commitments for the remainder of the year.

In late September, because Warden Harold E. Hegstrom asked him to, Rex visited Danbury's federal prison, ate dinner with the prison population, and spoke to the men afterward on the topic "What a Locked-up Man Can Do That a Man at Liberty Can Not Do." He scored with his audience and went away pleased to learn that Wolfe and Archie had no enemies on the other side of the bars, even though they had put a few people there.[5]

If Death Ever Slept was published on 25 October. The book is memorable on several counts. Wolfe is offstage much of the time. Archie is in his best form. Industrial espionage gives Rex the chance to take potshots at business chicanery. Wolfe solves a double murder, but has to call a second assembly to do it. And Archie leads a double life, as "Alan Green," to the astonishment of the real Alan Green, who first knew about it when he read the book. A detailed timetable gives readers the opportunity to behold Rex's meticulous record-keeping. For his own use, Rex made just such a timetable for each of his books.

If Death Ever Slept brought a letter from Jack Jarrell, whose father, Frank Jarrell, city editor of the Topeka *Daily Capital* in 1900, had been a good friend of the Stouts. Jack told Rex he was delighted to find Jarrells aplenty in *If Death Ever Slept,* and rather hoped Lois Jarrell would prove to be the murderer, since Lois was his wife's name and he could imagine the jolt it would give her. Rex answered: "As you know by now, Lois Jarrell was not the culprit. I would never make a poet a murderer, not even a spasmodic female poet. Surely it is possible that Otis Jarrell [another character in the book] is your uncle, and if so I hope he leaves you a couple of million in his will."

To Marion Wilcox, Rex, on 4 November, sent a timetable of his own recent activities:

Since getting your letter of September 19th I have (a) visited my daughter at school at Bennington, (b) eaten a meal with, and made a talk to, the 582 inmates of the Federal prison at Danbury, (c) gone to bed for a week with the flu, (d) watched four World's Series games at Yankee Stadium, (e) chaired two meetings of the Authors' League Council, (f) chased twenty-nine deer, including five fawns, from my garden, (g) spent two weeks in the Gulf of Mexico catching kingfish, (h) had a return engagement with the flu, and (i) worried a total of thirty-three hours about Sputnik.

Rex then answered several questions for Marion:

No one teaches the parakeets to talk; NW will not permit it. I think George Sanders might be a pretty good Archie. . . . The piano in the front room is played by only two people: Fritz Brenner and Saul Panzer. Fritz's repertoire consists of three Chopin preludes, Debussy's "Golliwog's Cakewalk," "Malbrouck s'en va-t-en guerre," and "Believe Me If All Those Endearing Young Charms." Saul plays almost anything, but mostly he improvises.[6]

The thought that Wolfe is sometimes a captive audience to presumably energetic renditions of "Believe Me, If All Those Endearing Young Charms," "Golliwog's Cakewalk," and "For He's a Jolly Good Fellow" boggles the mind.

On Rex's seventy-first birthday, Rebecca got a phone call from her boyfriend, Bill Bradbury. She had left her parents' car at Bennington, and Bill, a student at Bates, had offered to drive it home. He was now in Keene, New Hampshire. He had run into an ice storm and the car had gone into a tree and had been demolished. Pola waited until the next day to tell Rex. It did not matter about the car, Rex said, so long as Bill was all right. He reflected further: "I've never carried collision insurance, so what I've saved covers the loss." Bill wanted to square it with him. Rex said no, and that was final. Nor did he ever refer to it again.

On 21 December, Pola's and Rex's silver wedding anniversary, Rebecca came home again, for the holidays. She spent the day nearby, cooking and baking with Alice Ruffles, at the Ruffleses' farm house. Barbara could have no role in the day's doings. She was at Danbury Hospital where, just five days before, she had given birth to a second son, Christopher.

Once the repast was ready, Rebecca's job was to get it back to High Meadow without Rex and Pola knowing about it. Polly and Mel Evans came to her rescue. They agreed to invite the jubilarians out for an anniversary cocktail. Polly had been Clifton Fadiman's first wife. Pola and Rex were fond of her, and she and Mel had been married in the big living room at High Meadow.

After an hour, Polly and Mel found an excuse to go back with the Stouts to High Meadow. When they pulled up the drive, fifteen couples stepped into view to greet them. In their midst was Marian Anderson, singing an Italian canzona. Rex liked to be caught unaware about as much as Nero Wolfe does. But he was very pleased. Rebecca says, "He talked about it a lot afterwards."

And Four to Go was published on 14 February 1958. It appeared that, to reduce "Murder Is No Joke" to the size of the other novellas in the volume, Viking editors had excised several thousand words from the original version, for when it was published as a three-part serial in the *Saturday Evening Post* (after publication of *And Four to Go*), it was considerably longer. But Viking was not culpable. The Viking version is the original version. Rex wrote a longer version of the story for the *Post*, because *Post* editors asked him to do that and paid him well for doing it. No other Nero Wolfe story has a similar history.

The incident was a fortunate one. A close comparison of the two texts makes the reader privy to the functioning of Rex's creative processes in a way otherwise not possible with a writer who did all his revision work in his head. In comparison, even "Bitter End," as a radical redaction of *Bad for Business*, teaches us little.

Among those whom Rex met at the Book Reviewers Convention in Manhattan in February 1958 was Victor P. Haas of the Omaha *World Herald*. Haas was fascinated by Rex's "personal trademark": his "rather absurd white beard which begins beneath his chin and goes far enough to hide the second button on his shirt." He was astonished when Rex told him he wrote for only sixty-eight days a year and was trying to reduce the number to sixty-five because "two hundred ninety-seven seems so untidy." Haas gravely concluded: "Though he doesn't write anything even remotely resembling literature his stories are competent and (more often than not) exciting."

Rex began another novel on 1 March. The working title was "Murder of an Unmarried Mother." Rex finished it on 24 April, then entitled it *Champagne for One.* Thirty-four writing days. Still more remarkable was the three-week hiatus in Rex's work schedule. He had been to Florida.

A new Wolfe omnibus, *All Aces,* was published on 15 May.

While Rex's career was moving, Pola's was, too. At the Exposition des Arts Décoratifs, in Paris, in 1925, she had won prizes in hand looming — prophetic awards. By 1958 she was one of the top designers of wool fabrics in the United States, and the best package designer anywhere. Between 1940 and 1945, designing Annuals and Perennials for Botany Mills, Pola had shown America's capacity to carry on free of European fashion influences. In 1946, underwritten by eight leading manufacturers, she set up in North Philadelphia her own textile mill, a venture she pursued with great energy over the next eight years. In 1949, the International Wool Secretariat, at Paris, asked her to design a wool and worsted composition for its London exhibition. The Queen Mother came to view her work and congratulated her on the brilliance of her conceptions. In August that year, as Eleanor Roosevelt's guest, she discussed textiles and apparel with Mrs. Roosevelt before a nationwide radio audience.[7] She was called upon to create fabric collections for Dior, Mainbocher, Norell, Trigère, Irene, Adrian, Monte-Sano & Pruzan, Anthony Blotta, and Jo Copeland. She conducted seminars at Cornell, Syracuse, Florida State, Texas Christian, Tobé-Coburn School for Fashion Careers, Philadelphia College of Textile & Science, and Harvard University. Exhibits of her textiles were held at the Philadelphia Museum School of Art, where she also lectured, at the Museum of Contemporary Crafts, and the Fashion Institute of Technology in Manhattan. (The latter exhibit ran a full year.)

Now on 4 June 1958, Pola was recipient of an award from the Philadelphia Museum School "for the distinction she has brought to her profession." Corecipients of awards on this same occasion were sculptor Jacques Lipschitz and designer Norman Norell. Though Rex joined Norell for lunch, neither realized that the other had been born in Noblesville, Indiana, in adjacent houses on Cherry Street, and that between them they constituted Noblesville's whole claim to fame.

What Rex did with words, Pola did with threads. Her fabrics were as sincere as herself. She wanted people to wear clothes that were comfortable, that expressed the world they lived in and their life-style. She wanted them to wear clothes that expressed native American ideals, designs and fabrics that expressed the character of each region. She wanted good design for the masses. She urged an underlying harmony

— coordinated designs — so that a woman's wardrobe could have a basic unity even as it allowed for plentiful variations in texture and pattern. Her thrust was always positive: "The mainstream moves constantly, if sometimes slowly, in the direction of better taste." She sought to bring young people into her work. In their fresh vision she saw the hope of the future.[8]

"Poison à la Carte," a novella, was begun on 26 June and finished on 10 July. Three days out. The story totaled seventy-two pages in typescript. By the preference of his editors Rex's later novellas were longer than those done earlier for *The American Magazine*.

On 5 July, the *Saturday Evening Post*, bringing to a close its three-part serialization of "Murder is No Joke" (here entitled "Frame-up for Murder"), gave readers a "Keeping Posted"–eye view of Rex. For the *Post* Rex projected his idea of Utopia — a tent alongside the grandstand in Yankee Stadium. Within he could engage in "cabinetmaking, playing chess, and arguing with somebody about something." Outside he could garden, cook on a grill, and watch "some ball team, no matter which, whaling the daylights out of the Yankees."[9] A fantasy, contrived of course to give Rex a chance to sneer at the Yankees.

The Summer 1958 issue of the *Bulletin of the Authors' Guild* carried Rex's "Cinderella Paperback." A dozen years before he had conjectured that the postwar years might see as many as 120,000,000 paperbacks published annually. The figure had proved modest. In 1956, the actual number was 253,229,000. Erle Stanley Gardner alone had had a sale of 75,000,000 in paperback. But authors were getting just a penny a copy on the first 150,000 sold. The trade publishers got as much as the authors did. Rex hit out: "The publisher's plea that he must have half the paperback royalty in order to survive is not a claim in equity; it is an appeal for bounty." Rex found that more than three-fourths of the net worth of the ten biggest paperback houses had been accumulated from profits. They could double the royalties paid and still prosper. He had a further rebuke for the trade book publishers. They had frowned on the efforts of Guild and League to get authors an increase in paperback royalties. Since they were "quite satisfied" with what they were getting, an increase should go wholly to the writers. If total royalties jumped from two to four million, then three should go to the authors. He meant it. "This Cinderella," he said, "is not a fairy tale."

As the days of summer shortened, Rex wrote his third Wolfe story of the year: "Method Three for Murder." Begun on 21 August. Finished on 3 September. One day out. This story would not appear in print until the *Saturday Evening Post* carried it as a three-part serial beginning on 30 January 1960.[10]

In 1958, Rex became the fourteenth president of the Mystery Writers of America, succeeding Margaret Millar, the wife of Kenneth Millar

("Ross Macdonald"). MWA presidents serve one term only. The post is honorary, but Rex took it "to keep an eye on the MWA." As president, he presided over publication of the first issue of *Sleuth Mystery Magazine,* an MWA-sponsored venture, which appeared in October. Rex greeted the fledgling readership with a confident editorial: "What of the writers? Will having a share in a magazine give a fillip to their ingenuity and felicity? Will A's plots be a little more adroit, or B's characterizations a little sharper, or C's atmosphere a little more electric? I really think they may be. Without forfeiting any of the old incentives a new one has been added, and mystery writers are human." Was *Sleuth* a ploy — a hint to publishers that writers at last were ready to take things into their own hands? Apparently not. It never had a second issue.

Champagne for One came out on 24 November. With the praise of reviewers still sounding in his ears, Rex began "Eeny Meeny Murder Mo" — his fourth Wolfe story that year — on 15 December. The writing period spilled over into the new year. The story was finished on 5 January. Thirteen writing days. Nine days' truancy.

For Rex, as mystery writer, 1958 had been a peak year. In mid-April the MWA had affirmed this by awarding him an Edgar and acclaiming him, at the society's annual dinner, a "Grand Master of Mystery."

Of the seventy-two Wolfe stories, only "Bitter End" has a more curious history than "Counterfeit for Murder." Rex began "Counterfeit for Murder" on 22 January 1959 and finished it on 11 February — eighteen days' writing time; three days out. Then he had second thoughts about it. On 6 March he began a second version of the story. He finished it on 31 March — seventeen days' writing time; nine days out. In the first version Hattie Annis is killed at the outset, Tammy Baxter is Wolfe's client, and a battery of T-men, behaving like FBI men at their rudest, invade the brownstone. In the second version, Tammy is the victim, and Hattie shines. Only one T-man shows up, and he is well behaved. Rex's unprecedented decision to write a second version of this story was vindicated by the results. Anthony Boucher described Hattie as "the most entertaining client to visit West Thirty-fifth Street in some time." Readers everywhere agreed. The acerbic Hattie all but runs off with the story. She owes a good deal to Alice Todhunter. Never has a mystery writer revived a corpse to better advantage. No wonder Rex could not let her stay dead.

This episode was unique in the whole span of Rex's writing history. "Counterfeit for Murder" is the only story Rex ever rewrote because he was dissatisfied with the first version. Later he could not recall why he had done it. Yet clearly, in the twenty-three days that elapsed between finishing the first version and starting the second, something had happened that drove him back to his desk. There is one probable explanation. Rex had spent much of that interval with his former neighbor Than Selleck in Florida, on Paradise Island, near St. Petersburg, where

Than had gone to live in 1957, after he had a coronary. The vacation had been a full one. "Every morning," Rex remembered, "when the weather permitted, which was about nine times out of ten, Than and I went out on the Gulf in his boat and returned in time for supper. Fishing, chiefly for mackerel and kingfish. I caught a forty-seven-pound king."

Fishing and boating did not provide his only recreation on this visit. "On a long, level, open stretch of road" Rex accepted Than's invitation to open up the throttle on the Selleck Cadillac. When the speedometer read 118 mph, both agreed that the car had had an adequate testing.

But Than had played too hard on their mutual holiday. When Rex got back to High Meadow word awaited him that Than had died of a second heart attack.

For Rex, work was the best therapy for emotional trauma. He was hardly prepared to begin at the beginning with a new story, but he could rework the one that lay on his desk. That perhaps is part of what happened, but surely he was not pleased anyway with the first version of the story. Rex Stout did not redo anything he had done already to his satisfaction.

Even before he became treasurer of Freedom House and a member of its executive committee, Rex had been an active and vocal member, a sharp and useful critic of all Freedom House programs in their developmental stage. As treasurer he found that the task of preparing promotional literature and fund letters fell exclusively to him. In 1957, with the inauguration of Freedom House/Books USA, he assumed responsibility as well for the separate appeals sent out for that program. Freedom House/Books USA supplied reading matter presenting American culture and institutions favorably to individuals and organizations in foreign lands. Rex continued to prepare its releases and appeals up to the time of his death.

As chairman of the Authors' Guild Council in this same period, Rex reigned with a becoming assurance which swept away objections before they could take shape. Edward Mabley, asked once by Rex to assume the chair in his absence, protested that he had never chaired a meeting before and was not to be relied on. "Nothing to it," Rex told him. "If one of your rulings is challenged simply pound on the desk and say 'Not according to Roberts' *Rules of Order!*' "[11]

Actress Florence Eldridge adds her own observation about Rex's resourcefulness in debate. She had seen him preside at meetings of the WWB and the Authors' League. She says: "I admired his technique in a discussion of closing his eyes in apparent slumber when it was his adversary's turn to present *his* case."[12]

Rex began *Plot It Yourself* on 20 May 1959 and completed it on 2 July. Thirty-four working days. Ten days away from his desk. A modest interruption considering the preparations going on around him. Rebecca was graduated from Bennington on 27 June. On 28 June, at High Meadow, she married William Wyatt Bradbury. Bill was the son of Judge Harry Bruce Bradbury, of the probate court of neighboring New Milford, and of Bianca Bradbury, who wrote children's books. The judge performed the marriage ceremony. It was an outdoor wedding and the gardens at High Meadow were at the height of their June radiance. The ceremony took place in the croquet court, as traditional a place in Stout-Todhunter history as memory could supply, and Marian Anderson sang "He's Got the Whole World in His Hands." A wedding feast worthy of Nero Wolfe at his most Lucullan followed the ceremony. With characteristic individualism, Rex had had an extra table set up in the empty swimming pool, which hung on the hillside like a tilted oval grotto, supplying a cameolike setting for those who gathered there. Bill and the ushers wore white jackets and dark pants. Ever his own man, Rex wore dark pants and a bright red sports jacket.

Both his daughters had found husbands. Now, at seventy-three, Rex seemed quit of the immediate responsibilities of fatherhood. But life had some intricate plotting to do and several chapters still to go before that would be true.

Rex began "The Rodeo Murder" on 17 September and finished it on 14 October. Seventeen writing days; eleven days out.

Plot It Yourself was published on 30 October. This tale pitted an association of authors and dramatists against the book publishers. That had to have been fun for Rex. Wolfe is more human here than ordinarily. He even enlists the services of Dol Bonner, the lady detective who had shone briefly in *The Hand in the Glove*. British reviewers thought the story among Rex's best. *The New York Times* agreed. But for country papers and small burgs, the plot seemed too complex.

As the end of the year approached, Barbara, with her three small children, came to live at High Meadow. Her marriage with Don Maroc was ending. At seventy-three Rex faced the prospect of raising a second family. If he had to, then he would. That was the way Rex Stout handled life.

45·

The Best We Have

I think I have read everything Mr. Stout has written about Wolfe and Goodwin, and I have a standing offer for second-hand copies of *Too Many Cooks:*
it is more comfortable to give them to people than to know who has stolen
mine, which happened three times before I learned that trick.

— M. F. K. FISHER

Rex Stout is a great citizen of the world and storyteller.

— JOHN CARDINAL WRIGHT

"Death of a Demon" was begun on 26 January 1960, the day the action
of the story itself begins.[1] During the first five days Rex wrote twenty-
three pages.

On Sunday, 31 January, Rex rested. During the ensuing week he
wrote another twenty-three pages of "Death of a Demon," quitting
early on Saturday to go over to Ridgefield with Pola to have dinner with
the Samuel Graftons. Rex and Grafton, the columnist and publisher,
had worked together in the Authors' League since 1950 and had become good friends. Sam had been awed in Junes past when he had seen
Rex's iris in full bloom at High Meadow. That fact prompted him now
to an act of deviltry. On the afternoon of Rex's visit Grafton had a
commercial florist deliver several dozen hothouse irises. At dusk he
stuck them into the snow banks lining his own drive. Under the flood-
lighting Rex got a plentiful view of them as he entered Grafton's
grounds and made his way up to the house. Says Grafton: "I shall never
forget his outraged 'I'm a son of a bitch!' as he stepped out of his car.'"

Grafton got full value out of this hoax because he understood Rex. He
said: "The big thing about Rex Stout to me is that he always asserts and
maintains mastery over his environment. Rex shapes the world he
wants to live in. He shapes it morally as well as physically: People who
win his nod hate Fascism, believe in reason, act on the basis of principles. His novels are major diatribes against cynicism and pretense. His
villains are almost always pretentious characters, whom he has a marvelous time exposing."[2]

Taking out another two Sundays (with the Marocs established at High

Meadow, Sunday had become a family day for Rex), and a Tuesday (when he had to be in New York), Rex finished "Death of a Demon" on 16 February. "The subconscious is not a grave, it's a cistern," Wolfe tells a lady client in this story. But once again, Wolfe's quarry is not the subconscious, but a bona fide villain, and he brings him down with his usual impeccable powers of reasoning.

The story done, Rex again was ready for a Florida holiday. At Polly Evans's suggestion, Pola and he went to Sanibel, the island sixty miles south of St. Petersburg and four miles off the coast, to which Anne Lindbergh, in 1955, in *Gift from the Sea,* had given fame. Pola and Rex, in their long walks, enjoyed gathering shells along the tidewrack. Sanibel was said to be the best shell beach in the United States. Rex could well believe it, yet he marveled that Poe had become an expert in conchology. The convolutions of the human mind interested him more than the spiraling imbrications of gastropods.

At Sanibel, Rex also enjoyed the coastal shore drives, in sunlight and in moonlight, at speeds well under 118 mph. As a driver, Rex handled a car with all the ease he attributed to Archie. To the end of his life he would retain his driver's license and occasionally get behind the wheel for short runs. He admitted to no accidents, though his family suspected he had had a few dents hammered out with dispatch so that no evidence of them would be apparent. "Rex drives with the arrogance that goes with perfect assurance," Alan Green said.[3] The only tickets he ever got were for speeding — that is, when he failed to talk his way out of them. Cecil Brown remembers Rex as a "frighteningly fast driver who kept things in command." When a highway patrolman stopped Rex once on the Merritt Parkway, Brown sat there stunned while Rex explained, with animation, that he was an ornithologist, that he had spotted a Ross's gull — then an unprecedented bird visitor in New England — and had been racing to keep it in view. "Fascinated by the gall of the man," Brown says, "the officer bought it, and gave him no ticket."[4]

On 29 April *Three at Wolfe's Door* was published. While others were reviewing it ("some of the best entertainment in the mystery business," "a feast of reason"), Rex was reviewing Vincent Starrett's *Private Life of Sherlock Holmes* for *The New Republic.*

"How many novelists are there, let alone crime novelists, who give unfailing pleasure by the sheer quality of their writing and the conversations of their characters?" asked the London *Tablet* when *Too Many Clients* was published. This reaction was typical. Rex began *Too Many Clients* on 6 May and completed it on 22 June — thirteen days out; thirty-five days' writing time. Archie here is at his funniest and most visible. Maria Perez is the liveliest foreign girl to appear in the series since Anna Fiore in *Fer-de-Lance,* and the late Thomas Yeager —

who maintained what Wolfe refers to as "a bower of carnality" in one of New York's worst neighborhoods — is a superb portrait of the businessman type that Rex despised.[5]

With Barbara and her babies now under Rex's roof and under his care, by every reasonable reckoning the heightened tempo of life at High Meadow ought to have told on his nerves and on his capacity to concentrate. It did not. He simply made the necessary adjustments and went on.[6] He even went along with a stunt photo for the *Saturday Evening Post*'s forthcoming publication of "Counterfeit for Murder" (which the *Post* called "Counterfeiter's Knife"), showing him surprised at his desk by Chris, age three, in Superman costume, and Reed, four and a half, in Western togs, both drawing a bead on him with six-shooters.[7]

Too Many Clients came out on 28 October. On 5 December Rex started "Kill Now—Pay Later." With just seven days out, including Sundays and Christmas Day, he finished it on 29 December.

John Stout had known C. F. Menninger well. May Stout had served with him in the Homeopathic Society. Thus Rex was doubly pleased when, in February 1961, C. F.'s son Karl, cofounder and now director of Topeka's Menninger Clinic for psychiatric care, wrote to him, saying,

My wife and I passed the January *Saturday Evening Posts* back and forth to one another especially in order to read your short story, "Counterfeiter's Knife." She remarked to me that I ought to write you a letter telling you that I am a long time fan of yours and a great admirer of Nero Wolfe — whom I am said by some of my less kind friends to resemble in certain aspects, the less desirable points, of course — but I lay awake at night and wonder how to hire Fritz away from him.[8]

On Sunday, 2 July, Rex and Pola were guests at a cookout at the home of Brewster friends, actress Glenda Farrell and her husband, Dr. Henry Ross. H. Allen Smith also was there. That morning Ernest Hemingway had shot himself in Ketchum, Idaho, and the wires were hot with the news. Of what ensued, Smith says: "We sat at a picnic table and I talked about Hemingway (unfavorably) while Rex kept questioning me about the techniques involved in writing humor, demanding that I give him examples of word-twistings and hyperbole and bassackward phrasing and other things, most of which I didn't understand."[9] Rex was not being heartless. He had his own idea of outdoor men — Joe MacGregor, Harland Knowlton — going back to his holidays in Montana.

On 23 April Rex began *Deduction for Death*. He finished it on 5 June. Twelve days out; thirty-two days' writing time. When Viking balked at the title on the grounds that it gave away the motive — murder for tax benefit — Tom Green, Alan's son, supplied a new one, *The Final De-*

duction. By late July, the book was on its way through the press, slated for publication on 13 October. At that juncture, in a capricious moment, Alan got hold of the color proofs of the jacket. These proofs then were complete as to front, spine, and back, but both flaps were blank. First Alan had the art department airbrush the *u* in *Stout* into an *o* so that the front of the jacket was perfect save for the slight error of "Rex Stoot." Next he had this brief blurb printed on the front flap:

"The fact is," says Nero Wolfe at the conclusion of this brilliant case, "the man was dead all the time. His wife had killed him. The ransom note was merely a device to pay herself half a million dollars and claim an income tax deduction on it."

And Nero, of course, was right. Hence the beautiful double meaning of the title: *The Final Deduction.*

The back flap was imprinted with a portrait of Abraham Lincoln, with Rex's name under it — implying that all bearded men look more or less alike. Beneath the photo the text read: "Mr. Stout is the undisputed master of the modern mystery novel, now that Alan Green has stopped writing them. And if Stout doesn't buy the above qualification then I say to him, 'Me Barzun, you vain.' Jacques Barzun."[10] The expense incurred by the art department for this production was about two hundred dollars — cheap at the price.

On Saturday, 11 August, Rex and Pola drove to Westport for dinner with the Greens. A goodly number of guests were on hand: Marshall Best, Norman and Ellen Cousins, Clifton and Annalee Fadiman, and William Harlan Hale and his wife, Jean. At dinner Rex found the hoax jacket laid at his place. He laughed till the tears sprang down his cheeks, then sent the jacket around the table for the others to share.[11]

The joke was good enough to export. Harold Guinzburg was in the Maritime Alps recuperating from surgery. Alan sent him a duplicate of the jacket and had the satisfaction of knowing it amused him. Guinzburg died on 18 October, just five days after the book itself was published. Wolfe fans were Harold Guinzburg's debtors. Like John Farrar he had had the prudence to let Rex shape the world of Nero Wolfe as his creative instincts decreed. Author, publisher, the public, the genre — all benefited from his good sense.

On 1 December, Rex opened his *New York Times* to find a 4 × 7 layout placed there by Viking. His picture; the caption "HAPPY BIRTHDAY REX!" — then this affirmation: "We enthusiastically join your world of friends in celebrating this, your seventy-fifth birthday. We warmly salute your rich contributions to the enjoyment of readers everywhere. We gratefully acknowledge your long years of service to America's writers, in whose interests and for whose freedoms you have so stoutly labored."

To celebrate Rex's birthday, Pola and the girls bought new dresses and asked him to take them to Sardi's for dinner. He grumbled but gave in. He even wore a dinner jacket.

At Sardi's the doorman told him they would have to eat upstairs in the Belasco Room. Inwardly fulminating, Rex boarded the elevator. The first thing he saw when they disembarked was a panoramic collage of photographs of Rex Stout — extending from his boyhood to the present. That had been Pola's project. What he saw next had been the work of many individuals. Waiting in the Belasco Room, for his birthday dinner, were one hundred and eight remarkable people. Their collective friendship for Rex had brought them together. Some of these friendships went back nearly fifty years. Rex saw before him, encapsulated in affection, much of the history of his life in New York.

Among those slated to give "Aspects of Rex" speeches — whom Alan Green, chairman of the dinner committee, dubbed "minutemen" because each had a minute and a half to speak — were Egmont Arens, Lewis Gannett, Sumner Blossom, Russell Crouse, Samuel Grafton, Dorothy Fields, Norman Cousins, Mel Evans, Clifton Fadiman (by recording), Marian Anderson, Julian Wolff, Peter Cusick, Father George Ford, Alan himself, and Pola. Arthur Schwartz was master of ceremonies. John Hersey would give the keynote. Other guests included Frederica Barach, Marshall Best, Leo Cherne, Orpheus Fisher, Ruth Friend, Tom Guinzburg, Howard Haycraft, Peter Heggie, Selma Hirsh, Elizabeth and Eliot Janeway, Irwin Karp, Howard Lindsay, Florence Eldridge and Fredric March, Merle Miller, Ann Petry, Jean and Charles Poletti, Margaret Pulitzer, Dorothy and Richard Rodgers, William L. Shirer, Luise Sillcox, Howard Taubman, Mills Ten Eyck, Jr., Pauline Trigère, Joan Kahn, Charles Van Doren, Irita Van Doren, and Glenway Wescott.

The meal was one Nero Wolfe would have eaten without qualms: Turtle Consommé Prisoner's Base. Cheese Straws On the Wind. Veal Bercy Fer-de-Lance. Risotto At Wolfe's Door. Green Beans In the Best Families. Rolls Full House. Zabaione Ice Cream-Cake Trouble in Triplicate. Vin Mersault Before Midnight. And Liqueurs Final Deduction.

Arthur Schwartz began with a letter from Moss Hart. Norman Cousins spoke. Dorothy Fields spoke. The praise flowed on. The penultimate word rested with John Hersey: "More than any other writer, and with more success, Rex has worked for the human condition of his fellow writers. There were times when the Guild was pretty nearly broke and Rex endorsed the notes of the Guild against his own bank account. Luise Sillcox says: 'He never could *not* let us do the things that had to be done.'" Hersey then presented Rex with a gold-plated silver Tiffany bowl.

Now Rex spoke:

An hour ago, while looking around, a lot of thoughts in succession popped into my head, and one of them was, why, good heavens, it isn't possible that all of these people here love me, is it? I asked myself then which I would want most if I could have either your love or respect, but not both. I decided I would want your respect. The reason for that is you have to earn respect. Love is a matter of luck. . . . That to me is the most important single fact about tonight. I realized there wasn't a single person in this room that does not have my respect. If I'm proud of myself tonight, it's for that reason — that the people who came together to make me happy about my seventy-fifth birthday are all people whom I can respect, and thank God for that. . . . A little warm honor and love is a damned nice thing to have around. And if you brought it along for me tonight, I'll take it.[12]

To Father William McEntegart, a Jesuit priest in India, with whom Rex carried on the most extended and metaphysical correspondence of his lifetime, Rex wrote soon afterward: "Last month, seventeen of my oldest and dearest friends talked about me into a microphone for about an hour and none of them mentioned Nero Wolfe or Archie Goodwin. That probably has some significance, but I have no idea what."[13]

During Moss Hart's first term as president of the Authors' League (1955–1959), Rex, as a working vice president, had eased his burdens. Selected for a second term, in 1959, Hart appealed to Rex to stay on the job. Rex stayed. Then on 20 December 1961, Hart died of a coronary and Rex found himself, at seventy-five, just where he had been a decade before — president of the Authors' League. This time a full eight years would go by before Rex withdrew again to the office of vice president. By then, an Authors' League without Rex Stout in one of the two top posts had become unthinkable to its membership. Rex remained on as the League's vice president till the day of his death.

"For the past quarter century, Rex Stout, in a very real sense, has been the Authors' League," said Cleveland Amory in 1973. "He is a marvelous person. I love him for what he is — the ablest, finest man imaginable. Among other writers he stands out like the Washington Monument. He towers above us all."[14]

46.

A Majesty's Life

In America we take for granted the two pillars of our work — freedom of the press and security of copyright — when in fact the rats are always gnawing at them. And we are very laggard about combining our efforts to achieve minimum bargaining conditions. We tend to be self-absorbed loners.

Rex Stout is a spectacular exception. His sense of responsibility for the community of authors is extraordinary. He has inspired many to follow his example. I am one. I'm grateful to Rex Stout for teaching me to give time, effort, and money to the defense and betterment of our literary profession.

— HERMAN WOUK

Rex began *Gambit* on 10 February 1962. Working at a steady pace, with just two days off, by 24 February he had written four chapters. He then laid the manuscript aside for twenty-six days to make what had become his annual pilgrimage to Florida. This time, as guests of Pola's friend Pat Waters — whose husband was a Midwestern newspaper magnate — Pola and he discovered Captiva, Sanibel's lesser-known, equally lovely, neighbor. In that era Northern youngsters were not yet running around with *Sanibel* and *Captiva* stenciled on their T-shirts. A visit to the islands was a visit to an unsullied environment. Rex and Pola liked Captiva well enough to repeat their visit the next year.

The only part of these holidays Rex did not like were visits to the local country club with their hostess. Rex said: "I don't like the awful people you find in such places. They're no damn fun. The fact is, I've never met any man who had lots of money that I could stand. They just aren't human. There's something about a great deal of money that does that to people."[1]

During the last nine days of March, Rex added another thirty-two pages to *Gambit*. One day off. In April he took off eleven days but still managed to get ninety-five pages written, including a surprising ten on 23 April. The final seven pages were written on 1 May.

On 29 April Rex had written nothing. On that date he gave the principal address at the annual conference of Rotary International, District 721, at Grossinger's in the Catskills. The title of his talk was "It Isn't True." His topic: *Webster's Third International Dictionary* (1961). Rex's name had not been linked before with *Webster's Third*, but its permissiveness assured his disapproval. When *Gambit* came out in

October, his readers would find ample proof of that. The book opens with Nero Wolfe, seated before the fire, yanking pages by the fistful from *Webster's Third* and thrusting them into the flames. Like Wolfe, Rex had been a charter subscriber. Of his copy, Rex told me: "I encased it in wire netting, wired it to the end of an aluminum pole, soaked it in kerosene, set fire to it, and burned hornets' nests." Thus he rid himself of the sting of both.[2]

When *Consumer Reports,* in the fall of 1963, published a favorable estimate of the dictionary, written by Allen W. Read, a Columbia English professor, Rex protested. On 4 November, Consumers Union's assistant director wrote to Rex to set him straight: "When Consumers Union chooses consultants in any field . . . it is our policy to choose experts in the particular area. . . . We have had a good deal of comment from readers. Much of it has been like yours. On the other hand, scholars in the field of language appear to agree with Professor Read's definition of the function of a dictionary." She then quoted yet another English professor, thinking this would skewer Rex: "It is important to have the evaluation of such works made on the grounds of their merits in the tradition in which they are composed, rather than on hysterical feelings of outraged gentility." She closed with a few thoughts of her own: "The pedants in this case seem to be among the critics of the *Third International.* It is they, the critics, who are insisting on authority for propriety in their dictionaries, while the scholars seem to be able to take the flow of language in stride. . . . Consumers Union was not stepping out of its role in appealing to scholars in the field."

Rex's answering letter gave no ground:

Every sentence in your letter of November 4 is either misleading or untrue. "When Consumers Union chooses consultants in any field . . . it is our policy to choose experts in the particular area." That is precisely what CU did not do in its evaluation of the *Third International.* The avowed purpose of a CU report on a product is to inform consumers on its usability. Professors of English are "experts" only in linguistic history and theory; they are not *ipso facto* experts on the value of a dictionary to users of it. In preparing a report on frozen fish CU does not take professors of dietetics as its sole experts.

Rex did not pause to savor his pun. He went on:

"Consumers Union was aware that in the case of dictionaries there would be likely to be differences of opinion between the professionals in linguistics and the lay users of these volumes." 1. Nonsense. "would be likely to be"? There *were* differences of opinion. They had been widely publicized, and surely CU was aware of it. 2. The phrase "lay users" is again nonsense. Mark Van Doren, Howard Taubman, Clifton Fadiman, John Steinbeck, Allan Nevins, John Hersey, William Shirer, Lewis Gannett, all of whom disagree with your "experts," (and I can name dozens of others), are not lay users, they are professional users.

They are certainly better qualified as expert appraisers of the usability of a dictionary than a group of linguistic pedagogues.

". . . hysterical feelings of outraged gentility." That silly phrase should have warned you that the professor was completely disqualified as an objective expert. The reaction to the *Third International* by the professional writers I have named, and by many others, does not come from "hysterical feelings of outraged gentility." It comes from their reasoned conclusion that an expensive tool offered for their use in their profession is inadequate, mal-functioning, and untrustworthy.

"Consumers Union was not stepping out of its role. . . ." Of course it was. I think it would be wise for you to admit the misstep instead of trying to justify it by special pleading.

As Wolfe would say — Satisfactory.

In July 1962 another new book was to catch Rex's eye but would produce quite different feelings. Viking's Tom Guinzburg was reading the unpublished manuscript of Ian Fleming's newest James Bond thriller, *On Her Majesty's Secret Service,* when he came upon a passage which found Bond visiting his Chief — the inscrutable M:

M began to fill a pipe. "What the devil's the name of that fat American detective who's always fiddling about with orchids . . . ?" . . .

"Nero Wolfe, sir. They're written by a chap called Rex Stout, I like them."

"They're readable," condescended M. "But I was thinking of the orchid stuff in them. How in hell can a man like those disgusting flowers?"[3]

The early 1960's was host to a James Bond mania. In a short while sales of Fleming's novels on the dashing British agent had topped the twenty million mark. Accordingly, when Guinzburg sent Rex a Xerox copy of Fleming's comments, Rex wrote Fleming, thanking him for his gesture. Fleming wrote back, suggesting that they have Archie and Bond visit back and forth in one another's books.[4] Rex demurred: "Bond would get all the girls. And that would bruise Archie's ego." Fleming later told Guinzburg: "Rex Stout has one of the most civilized minds ever to turn to detective fiction."

In July, the Lockridges published their fiftieth thriller, *The Ticking Clock.* To mark the occasion the Mystery Writers of America awarded them an Edgar. The presentation and celebration took place in the library of the St. Regis Hotel. The only bodies found in the library on this occasion were those of warm friends, who looked on with thorough approval while Rex bestowed the award. Events had moved a long way since the day when Frances wondered how Rex could afford such green grass.

"Blood Will Tell" was begun on 4 August and finished on 29 August.

Rex took off seven days, plus fractions of other days, so that his estimate of total working days reduces to sixteen.

While Rex was writing, Pola was in Denton, Texas, at Texas Woman's University, where, for the fourth successive summer, she was chief designer-consultant to Dr. Edna Brandau's workshop in textiles and apparel. Press coverage on Pola's work was tremendous. Her lectures were spreading a new gospel in the Southwest.[5]

Throughout World War II, Rex, as chairman of the WWB, had found novelist Upton Sinclair instantly obliging. For the seven War Loan drives Sinclair, at Rex's invitation, wrote compelling letters, which, given mass circulation, stimulated buying. In June 1944, when the Hungarian government ordered the destruction of all Jewish books, Rex had wired Sinclair: "REQUEST STATEMENT FROM YOU DESIGNED AROUSE RESISTANCE SUCH ACTIONS WHICH CAN BE SHORT WAVED TO HUNGARY AND REST EUROPE SOONEST POSSIBLE." Sinclair obliged with a statement so eloquent it was widely circulated in America, too.

Sinclair had been a founder of the Authors' League. When in August 1962, he renewed his membership, at eighty-four, Rex was delighted. On 6 September he sent him a word of warm greeting, to which he appended this notation: "I know of your nomination for the Nobel Prize. I am of course one of the signers of the nomination, and I am going to write a few letters — not as a favor to you, but as a service to American literature."

On Saturday, 8 September, Rex and Pola were dinner guests of the Van Dorens, at Falls Village. Rex shared with Dorothy a love of Jane Austen. Of Jane, Rex told me: "She chose and handled words without the slightest attempt to assert their importance as 'literature.' She made no pretensions of any kind. She sustained suspense without strain better than any other writer of fiction."

On this visit Rex peppered Dorothy with questions. What did Jane read? Were the Austens in good circumstances? Did Jane believe in God? Dorothy did some sleuthing and mailed the results to Rex on the tenth. Yes, Jane had read *Tom Jones* and Boswell's *Johnson*. The Austens had several servants and ate well. And — "At least by the time she died, she certainly believed in God — you old anti-clerical you! A proper English High Church god, and I rather think nothing else had ever occurred to her."

On his visit Rex had brought along a prepublication copy of *Gambit*, due out on 12 October. Dorothy wrote: "Mark sat up till 2:30 finishing *Gambit*. . . . I should like a new one at least once a month, not to put too much pressure on you."

In 1960, the Belmont Raceway in New York inaugurated, for the

Baker Street Irregulars, its Silver Blaze Stakes, which has been run each September since then. Rex and Pola were in faithful attendance the first five years. In 1962 and again two years later, Rex presented the trophy to the winning jockey.

That same fall of 1960, when the Fashion Institute of Technology, in Manhattan, ran a retrospective exhibit of Pola's fabrics, Rex was on hand for the opening. Eleanor L. Furman, a director of the institute and a Wolfe addict, admits that, for her, the prospect of meeting Rex dwarfed every other aspect of the evening. When Pola introduced Rex to her, she was not disappointed. "I had," she said, "the lovely feeling that he was just the way he should be."[6]

Although he had had a full and busy year, Rex began a new novel — *The Mother Hunt* — on 17 December. Nearly a third of the book — fifty-nine out of one hundred and eighty-five pages — was written in the waning days of the old year. He took off just three days. Christmas was a full working day, during which he produced six pages, to match his Christmas Eve output. New Year's Eve he worked three-quarters of a day, producing four pages. In the first weeks of the new year, the book was his most pressing business. He wrote the final two pages on 9 February. Actual writing time, thirty-seven days. Twelve and a half months would go by before he would write again.

In a letter to Rex sent on 4 May 1962, Edna Ferber had made copyright revision her topic: "President Kennedy has shown more interest in writers and writing in the first year of his presidency than all our presidents have shown since, and including, Washington. I think that the Authors' League must be more vocal about this and I say this as one who — as you know, shrinks from publicity, dislikes public scenes and is a congenital non-joiner." An earnest tribute ended the letter: "You have been of enormous help in sustaining the Authors' League these many past years, and I admire you for it, as you well know."

Rex replied on 7 May: "Our recommendations to the Register of Copyrights are only a small part of our effort on revision of the copyright law. We have conferred frequently with other organizations and have gained their support for extension of the term of copyright to life plus fifty years. Last week several of us went to Washington and saw some key people, and we are maintaining contact with them; and when the time comes for Senate and House hearings on the bill we shall be there with all the strength and persuasion we can manage."

Rex's efforts did not stop there. In his January 1963 tax message to Congress, JFK urged adoption of an income-tax-averaging provision which would assure "fairer tax treatment of authors." On 20 February, Rex submitted his own tax message to Congress, a statement to the House Ways and Means Committee asking for essential changes in federal tax provisions which would benefit authors. Rex argued: "The author's tax problem is not simply a matter of 'fluctuating income.' Though attributed solely to the year of receipt, for tax purposes, it often was the result of writing done over a period of two years or more." Such "bunched income" averaged over three years would ease the tax burden of the writer. He stressed the needs of the individual: "Often the fruits of one book may have to provide the funds on which he must draw for four, five or even more years, not only because one book takes a long time to write but because his investment of time, talent, and money in a particular book or play may be a total loss if it is a financial failure. This means that the successful book must carry the author for that much longer a period of time."

Rex believed our national culture was impoverished by our tax laws: "Many writers now forgo . . . free-lance writing for the security and higher income they can obtain writing as employees of motion picture companies, television networks, and advertising agencies." Recourse to such havens, he believed, was a form of prostitution. He continued:

The great works in our literature and theater have been created by free-lance writers — self-employed authors writing books and plays they believed in. . . . Tax assistance that will increase the incentive to the author to forgo the security and rewards of employment for the risks and hazards of independent writing, will enable more writers to devote themselves to the kind of writing that is of greatest value to our culture.

Rex himself did not take years to write a book. He did not produce failures. No year passed which did not bring him new writing income. Yet he knew that the lot of most writers differed from his own and he fought hard for them. Those who were privy to Rex's methods for dealing with the hundreds of appeals which reached the Authors' League Fund each year were astonished at his insight, his thoroughness, and his fairness. He understood the legitimate woes of authors, and he gave help where it was most needed, and no priest in his confessional held more firmly in his bosom the identity of those who came to him for help than Rex did the names of those he aided through the fund.

On 12 April 1963, Norman Cousins had a seven-hour visit with the Russian premier, Khrushchev. Cousins says Rex supplied one of his portfolios: "Rex, as president of the Authors' League, empowered me to look for a solution to the copyright tangle we had with the Soviet Union. He authorized me to suggest that any copyright agreement start fresh, free of past liability."[7] Cousins came away convinced the matter had moved closer to solution. Two years later, Rex told Harry Gilroy, a *New York Times* reporter: "Our discussions with Soviet writers and publishers over several years, as well as official contacts, have made plain that only a political decision, such as the one on patents, will be effective." A decade later, a solution still was pending. For Rex, that was a personal misfortune as well as a public disappointment. On 14 March 1971 the London *Sunday Times* would report that, next to Agatha Christie, more of the work of Rex Stout had been "rendered into Russian than that of any other living foreign writer."

Now established as America's foremost detective story writer, Rex was a natural choice to supply an introduction for an album of Sherlock Holmes records narrated by Basil Rathbone, which was released in April 1963. As usual, Rex had no trouble finding new things to say about the inexhaustible subject of Holmes. "Holmes," he said, "is a man, not a puppet. As a man he has many vulnerable spots, like us; he is vain, prejudiced, intolerant; he is a drug addict; he even plays the violin for diversion — one of the most deplorable outrages of self-indulgence." Yet Holmes has a shining virtue which routs all his shortcomings: "He loves truth and justice more than he loves money or comfort or safety or pleasure, or any man or woman. Such a man has never lived, so Sherlock Holmes will never die."

And Rex was in demand, of course, to talk about his own detective hero. On 19 April, in *Life*, in one of his rare appearances outside the saga, Archie Goodwin discussed "Why Nero Wolfe Likes Orchids." Archie knew just how far he could go without giving offense. Through Archie's eyes we spy on Wolfe without feeling we are either intruding or offending.

Archie reports on Wolfe's dealings with a Cymbidium hybrid. Each year it produced just one little flower, "off-white, the size of a dime, hidden down in the foliage." Once Archie saw Wolfe scowling at it and muttering, "Confound you, are you too timid or too proud?" Conversely, to a bench of gaudy Miltonias, in their moment of fullest bloom, Wolfe said, "Much too loud. Why don't you learn to whisper?" Rex's sister Mary often had rebuked Nature in just such terms.

Archie owns to an insensitivity which makes it impossible for him to feel things with the same intensity Wolfe feels them. He tells us what he has observed and then stands aside, leaving it to us to conclude that we are better equipped to appreciate Wolfe than this poor boob Archie. With our finer sensibilities we thus see ourselves subtly established as respected members of that intimate household.

Some problems Wolfe poses are insoluble to both Archie and the reader. Wolfe's reason for cutting a particular flower on a particular day is one such mystery. When Archie put the question to Wolfe, Wolfe's answer was a reminder to him and to us that the mind of a genius has nooks and crannies which others cannot penetrate: "The flower a woman chooses depends on the woman. The flower a man chooses depends on the flower."[8] Woman is subjective; man, objective. How does that explain why Wolfe might choose a resplendent orchid one day, and a subdued one the next?

Wolfe spends four hours a day with his orchids. Clients must accommodate themselves to this schedule. Rex does not use the orchid schedule to gloss over gummy plotting. Like the disciplines the sonneteer is bound by, the schedule is part of the framework he is committed to work within. The orchids and the orchid rooms sometimes are focal points in the stories. They are never irrelevant. In forty years Wolfe has scarcely ever shortened an orchid schedule.

Rex conceded: "My knowledge of orchids derives from a book, *American Orchid Culture*, published in 1927 by A. T. DeLaMare Company; and the catalogue of Jones and Scully Inc. of Miami, Florida. I have never met an orchid grower and have never read up on orchids."

On 20 March 1963, David Overmyer told Rex in a letter: "The Stouts are as a legend in our family. I believe we regard them as an eternal part of our spiritual life. . . . In the event we should not meet again on this sphere, how about getting together some place up around the Pleiades, and sitting down at a table that Phidias carved and getting drunker than Hell on the Nectar of the Gods?" In July, David's sister Amy died. Rex wrote David on 18 July: "In your letter of March 20th there was a clause: 'In the event we should not meet again on this sphere. . . .' I didn't like that possibility at all and rejected it. But now Amy's death is one more reminder that we can't reject sad possibilities offhand. . . . You say the Stouts are a legend in your family, and so are the Overmyers in ours. . . . In those far-off days there must have been something psychic, or spiritual (or you pick a word), in our relations that we were not aware of at the time. I can't spot it even now, in retrospect, and I don't think anyone could. But there it was, and still is, and always will be."

The death of Amy, who had baby-sat him in his first year, supplied an appropriate moment for Rex to cast a nostalgic eye over the past, but for Rex a moment quite sufficed for excursions into nostalgia. His thrust was always into the future. The past was inalterable. The future was malleable.

On 28 July, at Marian Anderson's nearby Marianna Farm, where Pola had a studio, Rex went to a lawn party which netted the Freedom Fund of the Danbury Chapter of the NAACP more than $3,000. Other guests included Fredric March and Florence Eldridge, Edward Steichen, Roy Wilkins, and Manfred Lee of the Ellery Queen partnership. Ignoring the ninety-degree heat, Rex and Manfred found a quiet spot beneath the green and white striped canopy where they sampled punch and hors d'oeuvres, reviewed the current state of crime fiction, and posed for the Danbury *News-Times.* The sight of Ellery Queen and Nero

Wolfe with their heads together raised an intriguing question in some minds. Who was consulting whom?

That same week Rex had a letter from John T. Winterich, the *Herald Tribune* book editor, concerning a monograph Winterich was preparing on New York University's Fales Collection — a research library built around the novel in English, the detective story included. Winterich found the proofreading of detective stories habitually bad. He was delighted, therefore, to find that a comma omitted in the first printing of *The Mother Hunt* was supplied in the second. He wanted to know who had caught the error, and he wanted permission to quote Rex's answer in his monograph. Rex wrote him on 30 July:

That now-you-see-it-now-you-don't comma at the end of the first line on page 98 of *The Mother Hunt* is too much for me. Of course it was in the manuscript — as you say, without it the sentence is gibberish. It was missing in the galley, and I inserted it. In the book it was missing again. Then more books were printed, and the comma was there!

I suspect automation. I believe that as automation broadens its field inanimate objects will reject human control and do as they please. Not only commas; door knobs, cups and saucers, can openers, shoe strings . . . and of course words. All the wonderful words that have served us so well.

That damned comma is merely one of the vanguard.[9]

When *The Mother Hunt* was ready to appear, Rex sent Mark Van Doren an advance copy. On 6 September Mark replied: "Thank you for one of the best. Maybe *the* best, considering Mrs. Valdon, whom I find myself liking as much as Archie did. You know, of course, that Archie's in danger." Van Doren had a point. Archie has many girl friends in the saga, but Lucy Valdon is the only one he goes to bed with while on a case. This episode would worry a lot of readers.

By mid-November Rex was sorting out the first inklings of a new story. He planned to start work on it in December.[10] Perhaps he meant to follow up here Archie's infatuation with Mrs. Valdon. If he did, then his intentions were obliterated by his preoccupation with the events of the ensuing days. Shortly after noon on 22 November, Barbara burst in on him as he read the *Times,* to tell him JFK had just been shot in Dallas. He followed the events of the tragedy on television. He was watching on Sunday morning when Ruby killed Oswald. In the weeks ahead, the pulse of events as the nation adjusted to the tragic loss of its young president and to Lyndon Johnson's entry into the White House fascinated Rex.[11] Not until 21 February was he able to settle down to writing another book.

The featured review in the *Times Book Review* on 2 February was Rex's review of William M. Kunstler's *The Minister and the Choir*

Singer. Kunstler's book concerned the Hall-Mills murder case, which took place in New Jersey in 1922 and is known as "the most bungled murder mystery in modern times." Kunstler had his own theory about who had killed the Reverend Edward Wheeler Hall and Eleanor R. Mills, the choir singer Hall had romanced, but to Rex the solution of the crime was of less interest than the police procedure associated with it. Kunstler had set down a "fascinating account, fully documented, of sustained official ineptitude, surely never surpassed anywhere." "From now on," Rex proposed, "when a writer of detective stories is accused of overdoing the nonfeasance, misfeasance and malfeasance of officers of the law, he can merely lift his brows and say, 'Read William M. Kunstler's *The Minister and the Choir Singer.*'"

Rex agreed with Vincent Starrett that Conan Doyle had prepared "a brilliant analysis of the facts" in the Slater case and had presented them in "the veritable accent of Holmes, talking to the faithful Watson." But, unlike Doyle, Rex did not try to assume the identity of his sleuth for purposes of solving actual crimes. He received frequent appeals to run culprits to ground but acted on none of them — not even a commission from a Fall River, Massachusetts, reader to establish the complicity of Richard M. Nixon in the Watergate break-in and cover-up.

In a full-page assessment, on 5 March, the New York *Post's* David Murray drew out Rex on Wolfe. Said Rex: "Wolfe really goes right back to Edgar Allan Poe. . . . I'm just as fascinated by this man now as I was when I first started writing about him. If I weren't I'd stop doing the stories." He knew of no deliberate link between Wolfe and Holmes. "If it's there," he said, "it's purely unconscious."

Rex finished his new novel, *A Right to Die,* on 7 April. Thirty-five writing days; twelve days out. Fresh from this accomplishment, over lunch at Chambord's he interviewed David Cornwall (John Le Carré) for *Mademoiselle.* In a few months time, Le Carré's *Spy Who Came in From the Cold* had sold more than a quarter of a million copies. He could have been a pompous subject to deal with. To Rex's great satisfaction, he found Le Carré "utterly without pose or pretension." In "The Man Who Came in From the Cold," Rex reported on the encounter.

In July Rex spent ten days in bed with pneumonia. Pearl Buck wrote him, "Just remember, I can't do without you." Her letter was one of hundreds that conveyed the same message. What choice had he? At seventy-eight, here was a clear mandate for him to go on.

Rex did not have long to wait before heavy new burdens were thrust upon him. On 12 September *The New York Times* reported a schism within the Authors' League. The dramatists wanted the League reorganized to give separate existence to their Guild and the Authors' Guild. Representatives of the respective groups thrashed out the matter. Reorganization was agreed on, and the members voted approval.

Beforehand they had received from Rex a statement pointing out that "in effect, dramatist members have been paying not only the entire cost of League activities but also a portion of the cost of the Authors' Guild activities." Indeed, even though only one in seven active members was a dramatist, $211,638 of the $257,179 paid into the League in 1963 had come from the dramatists.

By an adroit use of compromise, Rex had led the League through a crisis which could have destroyed it. In point of fact, Rex himself had sponsored the separation to keep the complicated affairs of the dramatists from dominating the League's agenda to the virtual exclusion of the concerns of the nondramatists.[12] Disaster still was possible; the 2,285 active Authors' Guild members were reduced to a budget less than one-fifth of what their working capital had been. As chairman of the membership committee, Rex moved at once to restore solvency by mounting a recruitment drive which, at eighty-nine, he would still completely direct — even to writing each piece of correspondence sent out for this purpose by the Guild — with laudable results.

During the reorganization period, while Rex was president of the League, Pearl Buck was president of the Guild. Both wanted to preserve the Guild, and they met frequently. Rex knew much more about committee work than Pearl did and he enjoyed putting her down. Once, however, the advantage was hers. He said something about certain things being ridiculous, "like a widow writing a book about her widowhood." "Not my book, Rex," Pearl said quietly. Rex had forgotten that Pearl's *A Bridge for Passing* (1962) was just such a book. Generally, however, Rex and Pearl got on well. They appreciated one another. Pearl was not the kind of lady whom you embraced and swung around and gave a big kiss to, but Jean Wynne, the Guild's membership secretary, remembers that Rex would do that to Pearl — not when everyone was around, but when she was leaving — and Pearl did not protest.

A Right to Die was published on 22 October. The courage with which Rex dealt here with the theme of racial justice recalled Wolfe's earlier statements on that theme in *Too Many Cooks*. Another fact linked the two books. Paul Whipple, Wolfe's black client in *A Right to Die*, had been, as a youth, a key witness in *Too Many Cooks*. He was now a middle-aged man. Wolfe and Archie were still no older than they had been in 1938. By literary legerdemain, Rex carried the feat off.

Shortly after publication of *A Right to Die*, Rex received word that he had been elected to the advisory council of the National Committee against Discrimination in Housing — a welcome indication that the sincerity of his plea for racial justice was recognized.

After Ian Fleming died, on 12 August 1964, *The New York Times Book Review* had asked Rex to review Fleming's posthumous children's book, *Chitty Chitty Bang Bang*. Rex's review was in the *Times* on 1 November. While Rex was enthusiastic — "I'm going to run the risk of reading Mr. Fleming's book to my grandchildren, aged 5, 7, and 10. It will create difficulties, but why not live dangerously?" — one phrase in the review was self-deprecating: "If I understand children at all, which I admit is doubtful. . . ." Rex's uneasiness was not a pose. Bill and Rebecca had separated. Perhaps he asked himself if his own example of competence had given his daughters false expectations of general all-around resourcefulness in their spouses. His was a hard act to follow. But the girls still were young. Experience hastened the coming of maturity, and they soon had their lives again on a firm track. The Bradburys were reconciled. A happy marriage lay ahead for them. And Barbara married Than Selleck III, who, as well as becoming Rex's son-in-law, became, like his father (Nathaniel Junior), and his grandfather (Nathaniel Senior), before him, Rex's friend and physician.

BOOK VIII

A King's Ransom

47

A Fish at Wolfe's Door

He has been a great favourite of mine for many years now, and unlike most detective-story writers he can be read over and over again. Some of the works of his old age — notably *The Doorbell Rang* — are among his very best. Rex Stout is a remarkable man.

—J. B. PRIESTLEY

Rex began *The Doorbell Rang* on 18 December 1964. The first day he wrote one page. The next day, Saturday, he added four. He wrote nothing on Sunday, two pages on Monday, three each on Tuesday and Wednesday, two on Christmas Eve. He wrote nothing on Christmas, nine pages on the two days following, took off the next three days, then wrote two pages on New Year's Eve. After that the tempo quickened. During the first week of the new year he wrote twenty-seven pages. Thereafter he took off just six days until the book was finished, on 6 February. During the last nine days alone, he wrote fifty-six pages, including eleven on the last day. Virtually a third of the book was written in that brief span. Rex could never recall having such "fun" writing a book. To Pola, the twinkle in his eye at dinner confirmed it.

The manuscript went in the mail at once to Viking. Back came a wire from Tom Guinzburg: "MUCH THE BEST BAG JOB YOU HAVE EVER DONE." Certainly *The Doorbell Rang* was Rex's most audacious book. In it Wolfe's adversary is the FBI and its august director, J. Edgar Hoover. The manuscript now circulated among a few close friends. Their excitement confirmed Viking's estimate. No doubt about it, the tempo of Rex's life was about to quicken. Unconcerned, he picked up with his usual routine.

As its contribution to the National Book Award festivities, on Tuesday morning, 9 March, the Authors' League held a panel discussion to explore relations "between authors and reviewers." At the Biltmore, Rex presided over a panel of seven writers: C. D. B. Bryan, Muriel Resnik, Edward Albee, Ralph Ellison, Barbara Tuchman, Jerome Weidman, and John Cheever. At the start each panelist had two minutes to speak to the topic "What I Think of Book Reviews and Book Reviewers." Since the audience comprised "most of the book reviewers of the nation," none of the speakers took a strident tone. Weidman came closest to saying what all were thinking: "The relationship between the reviewer and the writer is the same as that between a knife and a throat." Rex closed the discussion with a rhetorical question: "Have any reviews of any of your books made you a better writer?" The only possible answer was "yes." That was said for Master Manners. Rex told me: "I pay no attention to them. Most of them are badly written."

On 11 March the Authors' League reelected Rex to another term as president. He was unopposed.

On 12 March, at Miami Beach, at St. Francis Hospital, four months short of his eighty-seventh birthday, Bob Stout died, after a four-year bout with cancer. At midday, when the news reached Ridgewood, flags were lowered to half-staff.

The Presbyterian service took place on Monday afternoon, with burial in Valleau Cemetery, where seven other Stouts lay buried. Only Juanita and the three siblings who had settled as neighbors in rural Connecticut remained: Ruth, Mary, and the squire of High Meadow.

Rex did not attend the funeral at Ridgewood. He lay abed at High Meadow, stricken with double pneumonia. Despite a raging fever, he refused hospitalization. His physician son-in-law Than Selleck hovered over him. That helped. Spring beckoned. That helped, too. When newsman Bill Ryan visited Rex in late April, he found him ensconced in a wing chair before the windows in his mammoth living room. "I didn't expect anyone was ever going to write anything more about me — except maybe in an obituary column," Rex told him. Yet his booming basso belied these expectations. He blasted publishers: "Most book publishers are jackasses." Agents came off worse: "Agents on the whole, with very few exceptions, are absolutely worthless people."[1]

Rex was irked that critics dismissed detective stories as frivolous:

Dostoyevski . . . read Poe and he used the same framework when he wrote *The Brothers Karamazov*. It's a hell of a good detective story. How silly it is to say today that any book is "just a detective story." Great writing has to have two factors: To create people just as real to the reader as any people he's ever known, and then to make a comment on human behavior. It doesn't make any difference what kind of framework you use. . . . I don't think that Ernest Hemingway ever made important comments on anything. He was a silly kid up until the day he died. He was a hell of a writer though. Jim Cain . . . made important comments. And Dashiell Hammett, in *The Glass Key.* . . .

He spoke of his own writing: "I love writing. I love to feel the pieces going together. I love to monkey with words. You want an expression on a face and you want to give the reader a distinct impression in two or three words. It's a hell of a lot of fun."

Others, too, acknowledged Rex's handling of words. On 21 April, Indiana University gave him, in absentia, a special citation "in recognition of his more than fifty volumes about the fictional detective Nero Wolfe."[2]

On 26 May congressional hearings began on revision of the 1909 Copyright Act, which Rex had heard Twain and Tarkington deplore when he lunched with them as a lad of twenty-two. Now, at seventy-nine, Rex himself was keynoter at the hearings, leading a delegation which consisted of Elizabeth Janeway, John Hersey, Herman Wouk, and Irwin Karp. Together, Rex noted, they represented the interests of five thousand authors and dramatists.

With more justification than they could have credited, Rex reminded Congressman Kastenmeier, chairman of the subcommittee, and the others present, that he had "talked about revision of the copyright law now since before any of you gentlemen were born. . . ." He had two points to put across. First, he thought jukebox operators should pay performance royalties. Second, he believed educators should not be allowed to copy copyrighted works indiscriminately.[3]

With that visit Congress was by no means quit of Rex's attentions for 1965. On 5 September *The New York Times* would carry a letter over the signatures of Rex Stout, Elizabeth Janeway, and Sidney Kingsley, respective presidents of the Authors' League, Authors' Guild, and Dramatists' Guild. Congress, importuned by the Authors' League, had passed corrective legislation which kept authors over sixty-five from losing retirement benefits because people continued to buy books they had written before they reached that age. This, they suggested in a pointed reference to White House fetes honoring writers, meant more to authors than "banquet and bouquet" did. The letter then called on Congress to enact legislation, currently pending, which would confirm the right of authors to establish retirement funds.

A second group declaration which Rex put his name to at this time — Freedom House's statement "The Silent Center Must Speak Up" — drew Frederick Redefer's fire. "If every statement we make must be screened as to whether Communists have made the same statement," he wrote Rex, "I really think we are back in the days of Senator McCarthy. Have you thought about this?" Rex's answer came from a kiln hotter than Redefer's.

But Rex's mood was wholly amiable when, on Friday night, 21 August, he joined Marian Anderson in a "Conversation" at the Joyce Memorial Library, in neighboring Brookfield. Marian was then about to set forth on her farewell world tour. From her Rex drew salient facts about her career as a singer — how and where she studied, where she had sung, some of her experiences along the way. Being equally skillful in putting himself out of the picture and putting his subject at ease, Rex led the shy Marian to the same state of composure she knew when they sat at leisure in the court at High Meadow.[4]

Royal Flush, the fourth Wolfe omnibus, came out on 6 September. Though it tended to get postscript notices in reviews of *The Doorbell Rang,* which was published on 8 October, it was welcomed. "Rex Stout," said one reviewer, "has no trouble in making his work unique in a field in which a prodigious number of books is published."

Saturday night, 19 September, Rex was the principal speaker at the final meeting of the National League of American Pen Women's North Atlantic regional conference. In her introduction, Pauline Bloom, New York State president, explained that her earlier correspondence with Rex had elicited this reply: "Since it is not a felony for a speaker to stray from his subject, 'Creative Women I Have Known' will do just fine. . . . I'll be there — hungry!" Rex gave full measure — Virginia Woolf, Edith Wharton, Katherine Anne Porter, Amy Lowell, Willa Cather, Gertrude Stein, Katherine Mansfield, Elinor Wylie — a dazzling galaxy. "I'm an old guy," Rex explained, "and I've really known a lot of them!" Then he came to grips with a topic more germane to the immediate interests of the Pen Women than the triumphs of bygone women writers: "The Xerox people, who are building a thirty story building which they intend to occupy themselves, now have 15,000 employees and expect to have 40,000 within five years . . . they hope that in ten years all authors will go to Xerox with their work."[5] In parting, Rex dropped a hint about what was to come — *The Doorbell Rang:* "It's created a helluva stink about the FBI and J. Edgar Hoover."

The idea of writing *The Doorbell Rang* hit Rex while he was reading Fred J. Cook's investigative report, *The FBI Nobody Knows.* Rex thought it would be fun for Wolfe to give Hoover his comeuppance. Wolfe's client, Mrs. Rachel Bruner, had been so taken with Cook's exposé she had bought ten thousand copies and sent them to members of the government, from cabinet rank on down to state representatives. The remaining copies had gone to publishers, bankers, network executives, newsmen, educators, and law enforcers. The FBI had replied with a program of harassment. Wolfe deals with the problem by flushing out the FBI in one of its borderline operations. And, for final sweet revenge, he leaves Hoover himself standing on the front stoop of the brownstone, his jabs at the doorbell unanswered — a Henry IV humbled at Canossa.

Cook's first knowledge of what Rex had done came in late August. He was working on a new book when a copy of *The Doorbell Rang* came in the mail. Rex had inscribed it: "August 20 — 1965 —/To Fred Cook/ with admiration, esteem, and many thanks for priming my pump/Rex Stout." Cook told me: "I thought to myself, 'Well, isn't that nice, but I wonder what the devil it's all about?' " He put the book aside and went back to his typewriter. At lunchtime, his daughter picked up the book. "Dad," she said, "did you notice what the little man on the cover is reading?" Cook stared. Nero Wolfe was reading *The FBI Nobody Knows.* "Well, I'll be damned," he said. An exchange of letters followed. Rex presently helped Cook regain the rights to a children's book he had written for a series the Britannica had jettisoned. But the two men never met.[6]

In mid-September, Caskie Stinnett sought out Rex for a comprehensive interview on the book for the New York *Herald Tribune*'s *Sunday Magazine.* Stinnett was impressed that the book contained no disclaimers designed "to soften the author's attitude toward the FBI." Rex had stood his ground, confronting the Bureau with "the positive figure of Wolfe, imperious at times, contemptuous, vigorously assertive, sometimes posturing and pugnacious, sometimes bleak and inconsolable. But never apologetic."

Rex was more than ready to confront the implications of his book. He thought it childish that the FBI wrapped itself in the American flag and adopted the assumption of infallibility. He was not afraid of reprisals against himself for challenging the agency's image.[7] "Several of my friends who have read the book feel that the FBI will let out a scream of outrage," he said, "but they won't if they have any sense at all. It's really a very outrageous outfit." Viking's lawyers had checked to make sure there was no FBI man named Wragg in the New York office, but otherwise were showing no anxiety. Rex recalled for Stinnett his own single encounter with the FBI. About 1950 an agent had visited High Meadow to ask Rex questions about a friend. When the agent asked if the man he was inquiring about read *The New Republic,* that did it. Rex said: "I wouldn't talk to him anymore. I will not cooperate with a subversive organization, and to censor or restrict what a man reads is subversive. I got so damned mad, I put him out."[8]

Stinnett wanted to know if "the big fish" standing on Wolfe's doorstep at the end of the book was Hoover himself.[9] Rex said, "In my opinion, it is. Hoover is a megalomaniac, although I detest that word. He appears totally egocentric, and in addition to other things he is narrow-minded. I think his whole attitude makes him an enemy of democracy. . . . I think he is on the edge of senility. Calling Martin Luther King the 'biggest liar in the world,' or something like that, was absurd. He is getting sillier and sillier. . . ."

Rex told Stinnett he thought the FBI had obtained an advance copy of *The Doorbell Rang.* He added: "They say the FBI does such things as root through your garbage to see if you're eating food or putting out liquor bottles that would suggest you're living beyond your means. If my garbage is tampered with, I can never be sure whether it's the FBI or whether it's raccoons. It's accessible to them both." Rex did not tell Stinnett that a set of galleys of the book had been stolen from Viking's office even before the book was set up in page proofs. He assumed they were procured for Hoover.

In Stinnett's wake came Haskel Frankel of the *Saturday Review*. Rex told Frankel: "I didn't think of *The Doorbell Rang* as an attack on the FBI while I was writing it. I hadn't the faintest idea of attacking. Have you ever read a Sherlock Holmes story? Did you consider it an attack on Scotland Yard? Now I'm beginning to think that the book may lead people to stand up and speak out against the FBI." He was amused at the prospect of coming under FBI surveillance. "It is conceivable to me that the FBI might tail me or tap my phone because of this book. I think it is wonderful. I've written so often about ditching tails. I'd like to try to do it." He grew serious: "In a democratic country, J. Edgar Hoover is a completely impossible person to be in a position of authority. . . . I've been asked if I know what kind of man he is. . . . I got my first idea from the newspapers years ago when I read that he frequently went to the races with Senator McCarthy. I was astonished that a man — Hoover — whose function it is to preserve and uphold the law would take as a social companion a man who was so obviously a threat to the very basis of democracy." Rex ended the interview with a whimsical threat. "I've written a lot of stories in which the New York police and the D.A. of Westchester County have done questionable things but it's never kicked up the dust like this one. I may stick with the FBI for a few more years if it makes people buy books. The FBI certainly has asked for it."[10]

Perhaps Rex meant it too. Leo Rosten, who had been Deputy Director of the OWI during World War II, recalls a get-together with Rex soon after *The Doorbell Rang* came out:

We were having cocktails before a luncheon meeting, chatting quite informally, as writers will, and he mentioned some amusing episode involving the FBI. . . . I proceeded to tell him of an experience I had had with two FBI men who came to see me in their "field survey" of a distinguished American I knew, who was being considered for a high government post. Rex's eyes twinkled and he encouraged me to go on, adding little details and offering offbeat characterizations. And when I had finished, he broke into laughter, lit a cigar, and looked at me with amusement. "What's so funny?" I asked. Rex replied, "You have given me the first four chapters of my next book."[11]

In a *Books* interview, Rex spoke of what he saw as the real threat inherent in the FBI:

The FBI has enough in its files to wipe out democracy in this country. Now, do I personally think Hoover will use his power to do something like that? No, I don't think so. But the *potential* is there, and any potential is a threat. . . . If I were President, I'd appoint a commission to go through all the FBI files carefully, and destroy every single bit of information that doesn't pertain to U.S. national interests *right now*.

The pileup of interviews continued. Rex told the UPI's Margaret Bancroft that the FBI had said Hoover had "no comment" on the book. "They are smart men," he conceded. "If the FBI raised hell it would just help sell the book." But Hoover did not quite hold his tongue. John Rains, in his column, "Rains' Patter," in the 14 November edition of the Goldsboro, North Carolina, *News-Argus,* reported that Hoover had written him, saying,

It is not true that we review all scripts pertaining to the FBI. In those cases where we do extend such cooperation, we do so in the belief that the public is entitled to an accurate portrayal of our jurisdiction, practices and activities. I might add that this is a factor which is completely lacking in *The Doorbell Rang,* for if a special agent ever conducted himself as depicted in Mr. Stout's book, he would be subject to immediate dismissal.

In October, Rex was interviewed on the "Today Show." On 15 November *Publishers Weekly* reported that Viking had 30,000 copies of *The Doorbell Rang* in print, double the bookstore sales of earlier Wolfe mysteries.

In the Ridgefield *Press* Ruth Stout reviewed *The Doorbell Rang.* "To me," said Ruth, "there's something unappealing about publicly praising one's family or one's country. . . ." On that account she never reviewed Rex's books. But with the FBI as Wolfe's target, she was willing to make an exception. She thought it was high time that an agency that engaged in "illegal wiretapping, bugging of offices and residences, and monitoring of people's mail" was rebuked. And she was glad her brother had done it. Presently two FBI men visited her at her isolated farmhouse, to ask her about her politics. "Do you believe in God?" one of them asked her when he was leaving. "I guess I'm an atheist," Ruth said. "Have you thought about what's going to happen to you?" persisted the agent. "I know what's going to happen to me," Ruth said. "I've left my body to the Yale Medical School. Perhaps they'll learn something so that the blind may see, or the lame walk. Good day, gentlemen!" The agents were slack-jawed as she swung shut her door. Then she called Rex and told him about the visit. "He was eaten up with envy," she said.

With *The Doorbell Rang* many readers saw suddenly that the dual careers of Rex Stout were not mutually exclusive. He was not a champion of civil liberties who also wrote detective stories for profit or diversion. The Wolfe saga all along had served him as a vehicle for stringent social commentary. In *Over My Dead Body* Wolfe says, "An

International Banker is somebody who when held up on the street, would hand over not only his wallet and jewelry but also his pants, because it wouldn't occur to him that a robber would draw the line somewhere."[12] In *Too Many Cooks*, Wolfe shows his abhorrence of racial prejudice; in *The Golden Spiders*, his disgust with immigration quotas. And so it went. Rex's use of a highly sensitive target merely drew attention to what he had been doing all along. Many reviewers now reassessed the Wolfe epic and cited its relevance to Rex's other commitments.

The Doorbell Rang did not bring the Wolfe saga some new quality it had hitherto lacked. Quality had been there from the outset. What it did bring to the series was expanded recognition. It was discovered by a heavenly host of readers who before had been unaware of it. On Rex, it conferred a new status. What had been recognized and valued in him all along by readers who stood close to him, was now recognized by a much wider readership. Of more immediate consequence, *The Doorbell Rang* launched him on the busiest year he had known since the turbulent days of the WWB.

With the dust settling, Rex gave thought to which commendation pleased him most among the many *The Doorbell Rang* had brought him. He chose a letter he got from Howard Lindsay as his favorite: "Thomas Jefferson thanks you. Thomas Paine thanks you. John Adams thanks you. And, humbly, I thank you, too."

That autumn the world said farewell to another controversial American. Henry Wallace, former Vice President of the United States, had died on 18 November. Toward Wallace, however, Rex had feelings of goodwill. Robert Sherwood had introduced Rex to Wallace in 1942. Since then the two men had been friends. Although Rex had found Wallace, as a political thinker, "a strange mixture of horse sense and naïveté," he had found the man himself "extremely likable and good company." In 1950, Wallace bought a one-hundred-acre farm at North Salem, fifteen miles from High Meadow. There he lived out his last years. He supplied Rex with some of his high-yield hybrid corn, and Rex found it amusing to accept for it the plaudits of his conservative neighbors, and then tell them where it came from.

Meantime, as a defender of the social order, Rex was being heard from on a new war issue. A front-page story in *The New York Times* on 29 November revealed that Freedom House had released a statement which argued that while those who opposed the government's Vietnam policy had a right to speak, those who supported it had an obligation to shout. The statement, said the *Times*, "has been signed so far by 104 national figures, among them Richard M. Nixon, Dean Acheson, General Lucius Clay, James B. Conant, Douglas Dillon, and Rex Stout." On 5 December the *Times* carried a full page ad from Freedom House calling for blanket endorsement of the United States commitment in Vietnam. Rex had helped phrase it. His name appeared among the signers. The ranks of hawks and doves still had not formed, but Rex was certain of his hawk stance and, in the years ahead, would stay anchored to his perch, scornful of all inducements to leave it, no matter how cogently they were presented.

The day the ad appeared, Herbert Mitgang called Rex to task in crisp terms. He thought the statement "volatile and political" and deplored its call for "an end to free debate" on the government's Vietnam policy. Rex shot back: "There is nothing in the Freedom House statement that even suggests let alone calls for, 'an end to free debate.' You should know that I wouldn't dream of signing any statement that did, since I love to debate, even with men for whom I have a warm regard, like you."

Recalling this episode later, Mitgang said: "William Shirer and I, who felt strongly against the Vietnam war, once questioned Rex's use of the Guild's name in this connection. Rex got up on his high horse — and he had one that stood many hands tall — and took it personally. We assured him that we were addressing ourselves to the issue rather than to the man we all admired." Mitgang, in fact, delighted in Rex's autocratic style: "I see him at meetings: He would sit there in a tan sports jacket from the pocket of which would protrude a row of cigars. It always reminded me of a bandolier of machine gun cartridges."[13]

Liberals and conservatives alike were confused by what seemed Rex's contradictory stances. Even as he upheld the administration's hard-line policy on Vietnam, he rebuked the FBI. In Hollywood, actor John Wayne read an abridged version of *The Doorbell Rang,* and wrote Rex: "Have always enjoyed your Nero and Archie, but I read your story in the April issue of *Argosy.* Goodbye." The *Daily Worker*'s Joseph Brandt read the book and forgot all about *The Second Confession.* "Stout," he reported, "has Nero Wolfe take on a new, modern, up-to-date, contemporary heel, the FBI agent."[14] The *National Observer* saw the book as "little more than an anti-FBI diatribe." San Francisco's *People's World* commented: "It simply isn't done. Like Albert throwing custard pie at Queen Victoria, it's unimaginable . . . heartwarming."

One thing brought together Rex's seemingly disparate positions, his fierce commitment to human freedom. To him, anyone who jeopardized that freedom, whether FBI agent or Communist, was reprehensible.

Rex Stout had protested the execution of Julius and Ethel Rosenberg, on 19 June 1953, both before and after their deaths. He did not find creditable the testimony which identified them as the spies who had handed over America's atomic secrets to the Russians. He had welcomed the chance, therefore, when Edward M. Keating, editor of *Ramparts,* invited him, in November 1965, to prepare a three-thousand-word critique of *Invitation to an Inquest*, a book by Walter and Miriam Schneir, which deplored the role the FBI played in the Rosenberg trial.

Rex's article, "The Case of the Spies Who Weren't," was presented as a Nero Wolfe mystery.[15] The introductory page proffered an illustration, showing a paperback Wolfe story — following the standard Bantam format — carrying this new title. The cover blurb described Rex as the "author of the most ingenious, most deeply satisfying mysteries being written anywhere in the world today." An explanatory statement from Archie prefaced the article:

> For three hours last evening I sat at my desk taking notes. Nero Wolfe, my employer, in his oversized chair at his desk, and Rex Stout, my literary agent, in the red leather chair, who had been a dinner guest, were talking about a book that had just been published by Doubleday — *Invitation to an Inquest*, by Walter and Miriam Schneir. Around midnight Wolfe asked how many pages of my notebook were filled and I told him twenty-seven.
>
> He frowned at me. "Much too much. It must be less than three thousand words or Mr. Keating will not publish it. Contract it. Cramp it." I frowned back. "You cramp it. Or Stout. Let him earn his ten per cent. Dictate it."
>
> They both said no. Nothing doing. I fought them for five minutes and lost. So this cramping job on their verdict on that book is mine.

Here were two rarities: a Wolfe-Archie dialogue occurring outside the canon; a summary — recorded by Archie — of a conversation which had taken place between Nero Wolfe and Rex Stout, the only record ever made of an actual visit to the brownstone by the master of High Meadow.

In a brief introduction to the Wolfe-Stout minutes, Archie stressed that Wolfe and Rex had not reconstructed imaginatively the Rosenberg case to arrive at their conclusions about it: "All I can do is report some of Wolfe's and Stout's conclusions, based not on any speculations or polemics by the authors but on the corroborated and documented record submitted by them." A grave Archie makes this statement. In the report itself he does not relax his mood. Not a single wisecrack intervenes. The business he was engaged in was too important for that.

Wolfe, quite as much as Rex, condemned the process which had led to the condemnation of the Rosenbergs. Three people had supplied the testimony which made the case against them — Harry Gold, David Greenglass, and Elizabeth Bentley. Gold had since admitted that he perjured himself. Greenglass, Ethel's brother, had been described by his own wife as a pathological liar. In a subsequent case, Elizabeth Bentley's "status as an incorrigible liar" was established to the satisfaction of the courts. The true culprit behind the Rosenbergs' conviction was, said the Schneirs, the FBI itself. Archie, as he begins his summation, is Neronian in his eloquence: "In this extraordinary pageant of mendacity and perversion, the palm must be awarded to the FBI."

Wolfe's conclusions are provocative. The FBI had conferred with Gold, before the trial, for a total of nearly a thousand hours. It had manufactured his testimony for him. There had been no "contact or connection between Harry Gold and David Greenglass before the FBI cooked one up." The photographer, Schneider, who identified the Rosenbergs from the witness box, had had a previous look at them when he was smuggled into the courtroom by an FBI agent. Before, during, and after the trial, J. Edgar Hoover had issued statements meant to inflame the public mind. He had acted as a character witness for Elizabeth Bentley, assuring the Senate Internal Security Subcommittee that her word was reliable. Evidence that could have cleared the Rosenbergs was in the FBI files and kept there, by Hoover's expressed wish, so they could not escape the fate he had chosen for them. Wolfe and Rex saw just one possible way of accounting for the tragedy of the Rosenbergs.

Impelled by a fierce and terrible delusion — one which he was able to implement fully through the awesome machinery of his formidable agency — J. Edgar Hoover had sent the Rosenbergs to their deaths.

Though it was not widely noted, "The Case of the Spies Who Weren't" was a much sharper attack on Hoover and the FBI than *The Doorbell Rang* had been. For readers of the saga, here was important evidence placing it in the mainstream of Rex Stout's commitment to universal order realized through the expression of democratic ideals.

When Rex reached his eightieth year, on 1 December 1965, Jacques Barzun, then dean of faculties and provost of Columbia University, remembered the occasion with a scholarly monograph on the Wolfe saga. Of Archie, Barzun wrote: "If he had done nothing more than to create Archie Goodwin, Rex Stout would deserve the gratitude of whatever assessors watch over the prosperity of American literature. For surely Archie is one of the folk heroes in which the modern American temper can see itself transfigured."[16] Barzun saw Wolfe as "a portrait of the Educated Man," a man whose "penetration of motive owes as much to his knowledge of literature as to his natural shrewdness." He enjoys "telling people to their face what he thinks of their mental and moral confusion. . . ."

While drollery suffuses Barzun's tribute, a scholar's earnestness imbues his final estimate of the sage and the saga:

In this sublime duet of Don Quixote and a glamorized Sancho Panza who go tilting together against evil, there is no mystery, nothing but matter for admiration, edification, and (if desired) self-identification. The true mystery is in their inspired creator, Rex Stout. Not two characters alone, but a palpable atmosphere exists in that brownstone house on West Thirty-fifth Street. And what sinewy, pellucid, propelling prose tells those tales — allegories of the human pilgrimage. . . .[17]

Barzun's tribute to "Rex Stout's cosmos" lifted Wolfe scholarship to a new pinnacle. What Brady proposed, Barzun fulfilled. The Wolfe saga had been given official recognition as literature, and American literature had a cult figure who shared full status with Holmes. Rex could take up his reign and rule.

48.

Champion of Justice

Rex Stout, Nero Wolfe, and Archie Goodwin have no greater admirer in all mysterydom than

ELLERY QUEEN

From Sarasota, Florida, where she had moved from Syracuse, New York, Marion Wilcox, Rex's quintessential fan, wrote at Thanksgiving, 1965, to assure Rex that her devotion to the Wolfe cult remained constant. Marion's latest queries brought an answer from Rex on 4 December: "Archie would probably deny it, but I suspect that on the rare occasions that he sits on Wolfe's chair he has a feeling he is making a concession. As for Wolfe's approval, that concerns him only in professional matters, never in personal ones."

Like Mark Van Doren, Mrs. Wilcox wondered if Lucy Valdon was going to put to rout the admirable Lily Rowan and lead Archie to the altar. "Marry Lucy Valdon, or anyone, no," said Rex. "It may be that there have been and are, incidents in his relations with Lucy which he has not mentioned to Lily Rowan, but I am not Paul Pry. In my relations with Archie I avoid giving him an opportunity to tell me to mind my own business."

In this same season an interviewer and a photographer from *Life* visited High Meadow. A Stout spread appeared in *Life*'s 10 December issue. The opening page was occupied by a 9 1/2 × 11 1/2 photo of Rex rising out of the center of an apple tree, the ground beneath strewn with a wagonload of apples. Whether or not Rex was the transgressing Adam or the tempter himself perched amid the branches of this ravaged tree of knowledge, *Life* refrained from saying. The title of the article, "Nero Wolfe Takes on a Surprising Villain," promised more discussion of *The Doorbell Rang*, but Rex was growing weary of that topic and dispatched it in a trice: "The FBI syndrome will collapse when J. Edgar dies. Hoover has what I call a self-made halo. The next man won't have it so good." This exercise in foreknowledge accomplished, he spoke then of living, writing, and thinking.

Rex explained that complications in his stories were arrived at "by a curious sort of reasoning process that happens more or less by itself."

He illustrated. "In *The Doorbell Rang,* I knew that the bullet wouldn't be found in the room, but I didn't know why. Later, when it turned out that the FBI took it, I was delighted."

What did Rex himself believe in? "Belief means faith," he said, "and there's only one damn thing in the world I have any faith in. That's the idea of American democracy, because it seems to me so obvious that that's the only sensible way to run human affairs."

Mark and Dorothy Van Doren were visiting High Meadow when the *Life* team arrived and were photographed with Rex in the passageway amid begonias and apple geraniums. It was a good meeting place.[1]

In addition to being Rex's birth month and marriage month, December, through the years, had become a month of melancholy milestones. Emily Todhunter died on 19 December 1906. Lucetta had died on 10 December 1940. Sixteen years later, on 11 December, Betty died. Now, in 1965, on 15 December, Juanita, in her eighty-fourth year, died at Toledo, Ohio. The family had thought of Juanita as the most conventional of the Stouts. A family friend described her as "conforming but not very." Most of her married life, Juanita had lived in Queens. Both her daughters were already married when her husband died in 1952. She lived alone and content till 1963, when severe depression overcame her. The girls — Virginia (Mrs. Millard Pretzfelder, who lived in Port Clinton, Ohio) and Juanita Merle (Mrs. Walter DeBrock, Maumee, Ohio) — rallied to her support and, at last, in 1964, Juanita agreed to come live with the DeBrocks. Death came at Flower Hospital, after a brief illness — the only hospitalization in Juanita's long lifetime. Of the nine Stouts only the fifth, sixth, and seventh, Ruth, Rex, and Mary, were left.

On 7 January 1966, the Baker Street Irregulars met at Cavanagh's Restaurant to celebrate Sherlock Holmes's one hundred and twelfth birthday and to honor Rex Stout. A high point of the dinner gathering was Thomas M. McDade's "First Conanical Toast," drunk to *"The Woman"* — Pola Stout:

> *For here is The Woman, our toast for today,*
> *Pola the beautiful, witty and gay. . . .*
> *She has found the one king who could equal her art,*
> *That Bohemian Rex who so well did his part,*
> *That we now toast "Fair lady, won by Stout heart!"*[2]

Rex's eightieth year was off to an exuberant start. Indeed, he gave added assurance of that. On 27 January he began *Death of a Doxy.*

In his first week at work on the new novel Rex averaged four pages a day. Then, on 4 February, he learned that Lewis Gannett, his friend for forty-six years, had died the day before. Through Lewis he had met Pola. Too many friends were dropping off. Perhaps it bothered him. On 4 February he worked just half a day. During the first eight days he had written thirty-one pages. For the second eight-day period, the number dropped to twenty-two; and to fourteen for the third. After another week, Rex's rhythm returned. During the final twenty days, with just one day off, he wrote eighty-three pages — fully half the book.

The time was not far distant when almost every issue of *The New York Times* would carry the obituary of someone whom Rex had been associated with and respected. In the months ahead Russel Crouse and Egmont Arens would die — hard losses. Rex later told me: "I have never attended funeral or memorial services except for my mother and father and brothers and sisters. I doubt if it matters to the dead people and I prefer to sit at home and remember them. Death is so universal and routine that I have never been much impressed by it. The conventional attitude to death is based on conceit."[3]

On 1 February, William Baring-Gould, Creative Director of *Time* magazine's circulation and corporate education departments and author of *Sherlock Holmes of Baker Street*, sent Rex a proposal. He wanted to write *Nero Wolfe of West Thirty-fifth Street*. Over the preceding "three or four months" he had reread all the Wolfe tales. "I know how much you prize Nero Wolfe and Archie Goodwin as characters," he said, "and I can only say that all I know about them I have learned from your own writings. So they — and Cramer and Saul Panzer and the rest — would certainly be depicted as you have created them." Rex wrote him on 8 February: "Certainly, verily, sure thing, decidedly, forsooth, (or, as that damned radio commercial says, but of course), the answer is yes. I am honored and flattered. A whole book! I have no idea how many people will buy it, but that risk is for you and the publisher. For me, there is no risk at all."

Baring-Gould was no stranger to Wolfe scholarship. In *Sherlock Holmes of Baker Street* (1962), he contended that Wolfe is the natural son of Holmes and Irene Adler, a thesis advanced first in 1956, in the *Baker Street Journal*, by John D. Clark, in his article "Some Notes Relating to a Preliminary Investigation into the Paternity of Nero Wolfe."[4] Clark had said his thesis emerged from his ruminations on Bernard DeVoto's proposal that Mycroft Holmes might have been Wolfe's father. DeVoto's conjecture, in turn, originated much earlier with Christopher Morley, who had proposed to Rex (to his pleasant astonishment) that Holmes's corpulent and sedentary brother, Mycroft, may unconsciously have served him as a model for Wolfe.

When Edgar W. Smith, editor of the *Baker Street Journal*, invited Rex to edit Clark's article prior to publication, Rex, on 14 June 1955, replied: "As the literary agent of Archie Goodwin I am of course privy to many details of Nero Wolfe's past which to the general public, and even to scholars of Clark's standing, must remain moot for some time. If and when it becomes permissible for me to disclose any of those details, your distinguished journal would be a most appropriate medium for the disclosure. The constraint of my loyalty to my client makes it impossible for me to say more now."[5] If Baring-Gould expected to have this information communicated to him, he was destined to be disappointed. After a few letters and a luncheon meeting with Rex, he realized he was on his own. Rex told him: "Any further disclosures about Wolfe must come through Archie, in the books, not through me. Artistically it would be a mistake to do otherwise."

At the annual meeting of the Authors' Guild, at the Barbizon-Plaza, on 23 February, Merrill Pollack, then senior editor of W. W. Norton, described Norton's plan to give increased royalties to authors of "runaway" hits in paperback and its practice of year-end bonuses to authors. *Variety* reported that the news brought Rex to his feet. He thought this latter move a more important precedent than improving the royalty rates on successes. For book publishers to "declare in" the creators of the books was "heart-warming."[6]

On the night of 23 February, President Lyndon B. Johnson received the annual Freedom House Award. For the dinner, held in the Grand Ballroom of the Waldorf-Astoria, fifteen hundred guests were on hand. Outside, four thousand peace picketers gathered to protest the administration's Vietnam policy; three hundred policemen, a third of them in dinner dress, were there to deal with the protesters. Johnson arrived escorted by Chief Justice Earl Warren, Solicitor General Thurgood Marshall, UN Ambassador Arthur Goldberg, and Senator Robert F. Kennedy. All had flown up from Washington with him on Air Force One. Ignoring the chanting of the mob — "Hey, hey, LBJ. How many kids did you kill today?" — Johnson entered the hotel and was greeted by Roy Wilkins and C. Douglas Dillon, the other speakers of the evening. Johnson's speech, his first full statement on the administration's Vietnam involvement since the Senate had begun its inquiries two weeks earlier, was the lead story in *The New York Times* the next morning. In it Johnson pledged no "mindless escalation" of the war.

Rex Stout said once that he had the mind of a bookkeeper. He did in fact handle most problems in bookkeeping fashion. He lined up facts as though they were figures, made the necessary deductions, and totaled what was left. In his opinion, the resultant answer could not be impugned. As a writer he was served well by this habit. When he wrote, he proceeded not recklessly but with caution. As a result, on first try, he produced a finished manuscript. For a work of the creative imagination, Rex's methods of procedure were feasible. After all, as a storyteller he could be as innovative as he liked. Yet in human relationships and in judging world problems, this across-the-board consistency did not always function with the same efficiency. A writer invents the facts he utilizes and can work with what invention supplies. Human relationships and world problems often are shaped by elusive elements which may show themselves reluctantly or develop slowly. Rex did not know how to extricate himself from a position he took which subsequently proved untenable. This was true even of issues of transitory importance.

But at least such matters, after a time, ceased to matter. If Rex met with opposition, however, when he took a stand, he at once geared himself for a battle unto death. Thus, because of business differences, he remained estranged from his brother Bob for thirty-five years. In 1965, several weeks before his death, Bob called Rex seeking a reconciliation. Still inflexible, Rex refused to take the call. Even the ill-advised reader who wrote Rex to task him on a point of grammar or word usage was likely to get a stinging reply, scoffing at his logic, though Rex had, in fact, erred.

When a position he took was disputed, Rex bristled like a porcupine. The LBJ Award dinner constituted such an occasion for Rex. He had made the decision to support the administration's war policy. For him, at that time, it was a logical sequel to earlier steps he had taken. We had to give battle to Hitler after Munich. We had to give battle to North Korea after it invaded South Korea. Therefore we had to give battle to North Vietnam after it invaded South Vietnam. Rex was in the fight to the finish.

The siegelike atmosphere in which Lyndon Johnson had had to deliver his speech stirred Rex's fighting blood. Johnson and the men he had brought with him, by virtue of their roles in government, were to Rex the very embodiment of the democratic ideal of law and order. Rex could not sympathize with the mob that opposed Johnson or with the views that caused that mob to gather. Moreover, he saw this protest action as an attack on the integrity of Freedom House, the sponsor of the award dinner. Freedom House had been championing human freedom and human rights since before most of these protestors were born. What was the source of their superior wisdom?

Eventually, perhaps, Rex might have been appealed to by the logic which enabled others to reverse themselves and repudiate the war, if he had not passed through that tempestuous night. But he did experience it and the revulsion he felt sealed him hermetically into a position which he never thereafter relinquished. He occupied that position so openly and so vehemently that he could not abandon it without bitter humiliation. In time he would be like the monkey who put his hand through a small aperture to pick up an orange. He could not extricate his hand without letting go of the orange. And he would not relinquish the orange. As time went on, Rex became increasingly exasperated with the multiplying follies of those who prosecuted the war in Vietnam. But he would not reverse himself. This stubborn consistency ultimately led to a major illness that nearly cost him his life. Even so, his grip on his orange never relaxed.

At the Washington *Post*'s Book and Author Luncheon, at the Statler Hilton on 29 March, Rex, as the featured speaker, made censorship his topic. On 22 March the Supreme Court, by a five to four vote, had upheld Ralph Ginzburg's conviction on obscenity charges. Rex found the decision "ridiculous." He said: "The Authors' League of America is not in favor of dirt, but it is in favor of having writers free to write what they want and to find a publisher." The morality of literature was the concern of "the parent and grandparent, rather than the cop and the legislature."

In the days that followed, Rex, Sloan Wilson, and others founded the Committee to Protest Absurd Censorship, "to protest censorship and the conviction of Ralph Ginzburg." Anthony Boucher was one of many writers who wrote to Rex then putting themselves at the committee's disposal.

Committee or not, Rex did not delegate to anyone his thinking about the issue of censorship. Eventually, in June 1971 Sloan Wilson wrote to Rex to suggest that the committee issue a statement saying that Ginzburg (who was to begin serving his sentence in mid-July) was being jailed "for making a bad joke" (Ginzburg had sought to mail promotional materials for *Eros* magazines from Intercourse and Blue Ball, Pennsylvania). Rex demurred. "We don't think a man should go to jail for anything he wrote or published, no matter what, and I think the stress on the 'bad joke' switches the attention from that basic point."[7]

When, in March 1967, *Arts in Society,* a journal published at the University of Wisconsin, sent Rex a questionnaire on censorship, his answers were spirited. "Since I believe that censorship does not 'belong within the province of the law,' " he said, "I deprecate the statutes under which the actions were brought against Ralph Ginzburg, Edward Mishkin, and *Fanny Hill.* The decision of the Supreme Court regarding Ralph Ginzburg, holding that the publications were not in themselves obscene but that the advertising of them made them so, was ridiculous."

Arts in Society reported that R. G. Collingwood deplored censorship on the grounds that the artist must be free to function as the guardian of society's consciousness. Rex dismissed this argument: "He says 'The artist must prophesy . . .' No one can be permitted to dictate any 'must' for the artist. It is not true that 'Art is the Community's medicine for the worst disease of the mind.' It may be, or it may not be. Sometimes art is a carrier of a disease, but it is still art." To substitute one tyranny for another was not freedom even when it was done in the name of freedom. That was not the answer *Arts in Society* expected, but it was instructive. Rex did not let *Arts in Society* off lightly. He had two questions of his own: "Who chooses or appoints the censor? Who will censor the censor?"[8]

Asked presently by Don Bensen, then Pyramid Books' editor-in-chief, if he thought limits should be set on what can be published, Rex's answer showed that his thinking on censorship was all of a piece:

> You might say, look at all these writers, using all these four-letter words on every page. Do I like it? No. Offensive? Sure. But for so many years writers couldn't use these words at all, no matter how much sense they would have made to the story, to the atmosphere, that now the damn fools are just using too many of them, and not being sensible about it. But that's no reason to bring the law in on it.[9]

Happily, not all of Rex's involvements in the spring of 1966 called for heavy decision-making. When their admirers gave a welcome-home dinner for the New York Mets, in the Hilton, on 14 April, Rex was there. Knowing of Rex's love for baseball, Tom Guinzburg had taken a table for ten. Besides the Guinzburgs and the Stouts, the party included Alan and Gladys Green, Monica McCall (Graham Greene's agent), and Cork and Sheila Smith. Cork handled Stout's material for Viking. The day following — the opening day of the baseball season — the New York *Post* gave front page space to a photo of Rex and a ten-year-old, Andy Eichmann, standing side by side, cheering on the Mets. Since the look of rapture on Rex's face was identical with that of his companion, the obvious message was that Rex Stout was as young in heart as a ten-year-old.

Rex finished writing *Death of a Doxy* on 17 April — thirty-nine days in production.[10] The public that had applauded *The Doorbell Rang* would not be disappointed.

On 18 April, Rex was interviewed by an editor from *P.S.* magazine. Rex, happy perhaps to be quit of another book, was in an ebullient, reckless mood. He told the interviewer that Wolfe was six feet tall; that his nose was regular in size, neither a beak nor a pug; and that "He drinks bottled beer and goddamn it, I think he drinks Prague beer, though I hate to say it because it's behind the Iron Curtain." He said further, "It is thought that *he* murdered his wife. It's never been recorded, but, as I say, it's *thought* that he murdered his wife." He did concede, in a curious runaway-horse analogy, that both Wolfe and Archie sometimes said and did things that surprised him.

Asked if Archie ever had fallen in love, Rex said:

> In the sense that the poets and most storytellers mean when they say "fallen in love," no. He has, during the course of these stories, probably screwed somewhere between fifteen and twenty girls. I suppose he has. But he has sense enough to know that the most boring thing you could possibly write about is

an act of sexual intercourse. Hell, you might as well write about a guy blowing his nose. I just don't believe that the poets have put a false veneer of romanticism on what leads up to or surrounds the sexual act. I don't think that it's phony at all . . . these are the most interesting things about sex, the thousands of things that lead up to it, and the things that come after it.

The interviewer expressed surprise that Henri Soule, who had died on 27 January, had willed J. Edgar Hoover a gold watch — evidently honoring him as a gourmet. "There's never been any indication as far as I know," Rex said, "that Soule was a man of judgment of taste or intelligence or anything else. He was just a great cook. . . . Of course, whenever you have reason to strongly dislike somebody, it's awfully hard to think anything well of him at all, and therefore, quite naturally, I suspect that Hoover really didn't know a goddamn thing about food, but that he knew Le Pavillon was the place to go in New York. I would hate to think that J. Edgar Hoover has a really discriminating palate. What an awful thought!"

On the night of 22 April, while attending an MWA dinner in Manhattan, Rex felt a sudden onset of weakness. Pola drove him back to High Meadow. The next morning, hemorrhaging internally, he was admitted to Danbury Hospital, as his son-in-law Than Selleck's patient. He was given three units of whole blood, and his condition stabilized. The following day, bleeding was brisk and he was transfused four additional units of whole blood. The source of the hemorrhaging was identified as an ulcer in the superior aspect of the duodenum. An adjacent ulcer crater confirmed that he had, in the past, gone through a similar crisis undetected. On 1 May he was well enough to go home. The workup also had established the presence of chronic bronchitis and obstructive pulmonary emphysema. These were problems Rex had lived with for some time. Ignoring them, he went back to his usual full schedule.

By mid-May Rex was well enough to permit himself a Todhunterian guffaw when Pola's longtime friend, radio commentator Lisa Sergio, wrote to ask him how she should go about making Social Security payments on royalties received. "Do ask someone to let me know," said Lisa, "if you are too busy committing another murder to write yourself."

In late May the University of Oregon joined a lengthening list of colleges and universities when it invited Rex to donate his personal papers to its library. Rex answered: "When I feel that it is time for me to decide where to send my stuff one point for Oregon will be my memory of the six-pound steelhead I caught on the Rogue River."

On 2 June, Rex again became a grandfather, when Rebecca gave birth to a daughter. At Rebecca's and Bill's invitation, Rex named the newcomer — Rachel.

In the summer of 1964, Rex had appealed to Moscow to show clemency to Valery Tarsis, a Soviet writer then under restraint. Tarsis now sought Rex's further help. In July 1966, Yugoslavian writer Mihajlo Mihajlob was arrested by the Tito government after announcing plans to publish a journal advocating multiparty socialism. Would Rex intervene? Yes, indeed. Rex at once formed an ad hoc committee for Mihajlob's release. Yugoslavian freedom fighters now had another reason for admiring the creator of their compatriot, Nero Wolfe.

Despite the committee's efforts, Mihajlob was given a three-and-a-half-year prison sentence. After his release, in 1971, Mihajlob would write Rex:

> I did not know until now that you also took part in the effort to help me. . . . Although numerous interventions and appeals from all around the world did not shorten my prison term . . . these appeals helped me to win the status of political prisoner. I had the opportunity to follow the press, read countless books and write. . . .
>
> I thank you once more and I am begging you to forgive me that by circumstances I could not do this before.

On 11 August, Rex sent a memo to the City Trust Company of Bridgeport. His current balance was off by $4,129. An assistant vice president assured him he had $4,129 less in his savings account than he thought he had. Rex's answer blew the bank sky-high: "It won't do. Apparently your new bookkeeping machine juggles balances by whim. Maybe it has fun doing that, but, like Queen Victoria, I am not amused."

Rex's lifelong talent for bookkeeping had not deserted him. A banner headline greeted readers of the Connecticut *Sunday Herald* on 11 September: "Claim $52-a-Week Teller Stole from 'Nero Wolfe.' " One of the tellers at the City Trust Company, a twenty-one-year-old runner-up in a local phase of the Miss America beauty contest, had been nibbling away at Rex's account and at that of a local church. The total embezzlement, before Rex sounded the alarm, had reached $16,000. The FBI had moved into the case. The *Herald* was happy to report: "The FBI agents are treating the girl with extraordinary kindness. They allowed Danbury police to make the arrest and have left the prosecution to State's Atty. Otto J. Saur." Had disposition of the case rested with the FBI, would the agency have pinned a medal on the girl who had peeled off $4,129 from the account of the author of *The Doorbell Rang* and "The Case of the Spies Who Weren't"?

Wolfe would scarcely take notice of a mere case of embezzlement. Disporting himself in the Neronian manner, Rex soon turned his back on the bank theft incident to occupy himself with a crime of a magnitude worthy of his mettle. He read *Rush to Judgment,* Mark Lane's dissenting analysis of the Warren Commission's report on President

Kennedy's assassination, and gave it a favorable notice. An early mail brought a rebuke from Rex's Freedom House ally George Field. Field thought Rex had shown a want of judgment in siding with Lane. Rex's reply to Field was sharp:

> If the devil himself writes a book, and the publisher sends me an advance copy, asking for a quotable comment if I think it deserves one, and I read it and find it is a good job, I shall certainly say so. Also I regard *Rush to Judgment* as a useful contribution to a necessary controversy.... Veracity or integrity, either of Warren or of Lane, is not at issue. The issue is the record, made and published by the Warren Commission itself, in its Report and the 26 volumes of testimony.
>
> I'm not mad, but my brows are up.

Back came Field's reply, suggesting that if George Field, in the WWB years, had commended "a book written by a supporter of Adolf Hitler," Rex would have raised ructions. "Twenty-three years ago," Rex wrote back, with visible pique, "I did praise a book written by a supporter of Mussolini and Hitler — a book of poems by Ezra Pound."[11] Dismayed, Field replied that he had reacted to Lane's book as he did because he suspected it was "politically motivated" and designed "to undermine confidence in our democratic processes." He assured Rex of his continued affection. Rex let the matter rest there.

That August, Rex's knuckles were rapped again. *Death of a Doxy* brought in a protesting letter from a retired Methodist bishop, Herbert Welch, then nearing his one hundred and fourth birthday. The venerable bishop was troubled by "the climate of the book." "The picture," he said, "is painted all in black. Is that fair? Is that worthy of the Rex Stout who is a public servant, a man dedicated to making this world a better place to live in?" The bishop's letter uplifted Rex's spirit. Octogenarians seldom find themselves on the junior side of a generation gap.

In England, however, publication of *Death of a Doxy* would occasion a brilliant review by Edmund Crispin, in the *Sunday Times.* "Crispin" is the British composer Robert Bruce Montgomery. As Crispin, he is one of the masters of modern British crime fiction.

> The effect of Rex Stout's Nero Wolfe stories [Crispin wrote] is cumulative rather than immediate.... After six stories or so you're beginning to be hooked; after twelve, you are hooked; and after twenty-four, you join the considerable band of far from softheaded people who can gossip happily for hours about the details of the menage in the old brownstone on West Thirty-fifth Street, details by this time so encyclopaedic and thoroughgoing that the Holmes-Watson menage on Baker Street, in comparison, is reduced to the sketchiest of shadow-shows....
>
> The prose of Archie Goodwin reveals Archie himself to perfection.... Addi-

tionally, Archie's lucid, sardonic mind is the perfect medium through which to study Wolfe.

On first acquaintance Wolfe seems simpler than Archie, more of a parcel of conventional humors — lazy, misogynistic, self-indulgent, Johnsonian . . . egotistical and a glutton. But better knowledge discloses a far-from-conventional tough stoicism verging on bleakness, as when in *Death of a Doxy* an impertinent doctor comments that Wolfe is overweight. "Wolfe nodded. 'Seventy pounds. Perhaps eighty. Death will see to that.' "

Discussing Wolfe as a champion of human rights, Crispin might be speaking of Rex himself:

Wolfe is a Liberal in politics, but so nearly a Jeffersonian that nowadays no Liberal Party anywhere would dream of countenancing him for a single moment. And in the last analysis it's perhaps this that makes him so formidable: he is prepared to do battle with the entire resources of the State, if not only his interests are threatened but even his comforts. In a world where most citizens regard such battles as lost even before begun, Wolfe is a citizen who still wins them, and would regard it as wholly contemptible to refuse their challenge, let alone delegate the fighting to some organization.[12]

Rex made a morning appearance, on 22 September, on the Teaneck, New Jersey, campus of Fairleigh Dickinson University to address an Arts and Letters Forum on the topic "The Evolution of the Modern Mystery Novel."

On 25 September, in the New Haven *Register,* interviewer Tom Golden said that Rex had told him that he had "never made a serious sacrifice in any respect."[13] Yet, to his friends, Rex's four-year voluntary exile from High Meadow, during World War II, seemed a substantial sacrifice.

When Rex agreed to speak at the Houston *Post*'s Book and Author Dinner on 30 September, the *Post*'s Marguerite Johnston phoned him beforehand, at High Meadow. In *Death of a Doxy* Wolfe had removed More's *Utopia* from his bookshelf when he concluded that More had lied about Richard III. Marguerite wondered if there was a story there. There was. Like Wolfe, Rex had spent a week investigating the matter, using Josephine Tey's *Daughter of Time* as a prompt book. "Everything I find supports her position," Rex said. He went on: "Wherever Richard III is, he can't care a hell of a lot now. But we should. . . . *The worst lies* are those that twist facts."

The night prior to the dinner, Rex was guest of Camille Bermann, manager of Maxim's in Houston. In Bermann's "wine cellar" — actually an ample room on the second floor of Foley's garage — he had had set up, among his numerous wine bins, a large round table, laid for nine. He bowed as Rex entered. "Latour '29," Rex said at once, falling into the indicated mood. Bermann nodded and the two men vanished among the bins. A bottle of vodka, encased to the neck in a solid block of ice, was produced. "Real Polish vodka?" Rex said, letting himself be impressed. "You know, my wife is Polish." He grew jovial. "A lot of people have referred to me as that goat-bearded writer, but I've never seen a goat with whiskers like mine."

They sat down to dinner — lobster bisque, fillet of red snapper with fresh artichoke hearts and mushrooms, a rack of lamb, and, for dessert, brandy freeze. The wines pleased Rex — for example, the white wine, Meursault Clos des Perrières 1961. "I wish I could say right away what it is," he said. "What is it?" Bermann allowed himself the hint of a smug grin.

Many readers have wondered if Rex could cook. Few have wondered if he brought a gourmet's appreciation to a fine meal. Camille Bermann concluded that he did. Thew Wright, a New Haven lawyer with whom Rex had grown friendly after Wright defended a few men who had had charges brought against them by the McCarthy committee, offered this account of Rex as a gourmet:

> Rex's love of good food and good wine is obvious in his books. What may not be so obvious is his supreme talent for enjoyment of both in the old-fashioned way which has all but vanished from this earth. I can cite an occasion when he lingered with me and my wife over a gourmet dinner which she had prepared for him and a bottle of Château Laffitte which I had pawned my last possession to get for him, no less than four hours, and enjoying each morsel and each drop right down to the end. . . . He makes the process of eating and drinking a luxurious experience, and the appropriate concomitant to the entertaining conversation which is one of his great talents and delights.[14]

His Fairleigh Dickinson talk had found Rex thinking anew about the nature of the detective story. His thoughts on that subject found their way into the address he gave on 30 September at the Shamrock Hilton in Houston, before an audience of five hundred and seventy-five, including Pierre Salinger, who had been JFK's press secretary.

The first essential of a detective story is that "it must realize what it is," Rex said. He explained that if he were picking a cast for an ordinary novel from the audience, he would first introduce them as characters, hint at their emotional conflicts, then develop those conflicts and finish up with a murder — as he had done in *How Like a God*. A detective story reversed this normal pattern: "The most exciting thing must happen by page twenty. The interest of the story focuses, not on the conflicts, but on the detectives, not on people, but what the detective is finding out about those people."

Rex picked up then with a topic to which Salinger's presence gave further interest: "If you write detective stories you get interested in the process of detection, in fiction and in real life. . . . I have never found any case where the performance was handled as badly as in the Warren Commission Report. Any American citizen interested in the proper functioning of American democracy must spend some time studying this case. It didn't get a competent and complete investigation."

Rex would continue to speak out on this topic. When Rex and Pola, together with Rebecca West and her husband, Henry Andrews, were the guests of the Thew Wrights, at their Greenwich Harbor house, on 22 October, the Wrights were treated to a virtuoso performance. Thew says:

> Rex sat at one end of the table, and Rebecca at the other. The subject under discussion, beginning with the meat course and continuing past the champagne, was the Report of the Warren Commission. . . . Both were highly critical of the Report and the investigation. The argument flashed back and forth over the heads of the rest of us like summer lightning, each telling comment preceded by "But *dear* Rebecca . . ." and "But really, *dear* Rex . . . !"[15]

A second book dealing with real-life crime engaged Rex's notice that fall. On 29 October his review of Gerold Frank's *The Boston Strangler* appeared in the *Saturday Review*. The strangler case was a million-dollar introduction into the vagaries of human nature. It was these that fascinated Rex, not the murders themselves. He was intrigued by the characteristics of the would-be informants and amateur sleuths who surfaced in this case. Yet the murderer himself was the leading oddity. After first knotting his strangling apparatus — some piece of apparel — and then garroting his victim, he tidily looped it into a bow. That detail beguiled Rex, as did the disclosure that the actual killer, when caught, explained that he did this because it had been his practice to tie into bows the cords on the casts worn by his crippled daughter, "to make her feel pretty." In the details he singles out in Frank's book Rex gives us a practical lesson in how his own mind worked.

On 12 November, as Rex's eightieth birthday approached, David Overmyer sent felicitations from Topeka. Rex wrote back on 17 November: "Yes, you have let me alone and I have let you alone, but all the time I know you are there and you know I am here — so many years! Somehow there is a simple sureness about it — that's what makes it so fine a pleasure to get word from you. If we were together for a day, what the hell would we talk about?" The letter was in longhand — an especial mark of Rex's affection.

Jean Loth, Eastern story editor of Columbia Pictures, visited Rex on 14 November. He wanted permission to make a Nero Wolfe movie. Rex was laid low that day with "a king-sized headache." He doubted if he was even coherent. No bargain was struck. Rex thought it doubtful that a bargain would have been struck in any circumstances. He still did not like the movies.

December first, Rex's birthday, brought a flood of tributes. James T. Farrell's was typical: "May it come to pass that you will receive greetings, felicitations, and salutations for many years to come. For your colleagues, you have done much." The tone was biblical, as though Farrell was addressing a prophet. He would have said that he was.[16]

Nineteen sixty-six had been for Rex a year of bursting concerns — despite the illness that had invalided him in the spring. Yet there was the ever-present reality of the ulcer diet. There were days when the diet did not wholly take care of the problem. He was not altogether himself. He had announced that he would begin his next novel on his eightieth birthday, but the day passed, and the month passed, and no start was made on it. Rex had a right to relax his pace. "There was no outside difference that he was not fifty-five," says Robert Landry.[17] Yet he was in fact eighty. When it chose now, Nature could apply pressure.

49.

The One and True Paradigm

He knew his name and was a kingly President. At luncheon meetings of the
Council, he would first have a double scotch, just to limber up his parliamen-
tary procedure. His secret was that he knew every nook and cranny of
League history; no fast ones went past Rex. Can a beard twinkle? His did.

— JOHN HERSEY

At the first of the year, in 1967, William Baring-Gould rendered a state-
of-the-manuscript report on *Nero Wolfe of West Thirty-fifth Street.* The
book was all but done. He promised Rex that he would send the completed manuscript to him in another few weeks.

On 4 February Rex underwent a gastrectomy and vagotomy at Danbury Hospital to end his long ulcer ordeal.[1] Even while surgery was
under way, Dorothy Van Doren was putting together thoughts for him
to read in convalescence:

If you must have an operation for an ulcer, you've got a nice day for it. Blue
skies, melting snow, and mild sun. Think about things like this instead of your
uncomfortable insides, and how pretty the annual bed will be, how big and
shiny the eggplant, how fat the grapes. . . . Please get well & don't think about
anything; because I need another book.

The day following, Mark himself wrote: "Pola just called to give us the
good news: no more ulcer. We are delighted and relieved — so much
so that we'd have telephoned you if Pola hadn't said a note would be
better. Since your tubes are not speaking tubes, that is understandable.
Lie there meekly, dear man, and get well soon."

Unaware that Rex had undergone surgery, Baring-Gould sent him
the "top carbon" of his manuscript on 9 February, exactly a year and
a day after Rex had given him authorization to proceed. He was "standing by to make any additions, subtractions, or revisions you may want
to suggest." When he did learn of Rex's hospitalization, he wrote again,
saying: "I hope you will read it when you damn well feel like it." In fact,
Rex still had the manuscript when Baring-Gould, at fifty-four, died
suddenly of a stroke, on 10 August.

By late May Rex was ready to deal with interviewers again. Richard

S. Lochte II spent an afternoon with Rex on the twenty-seventh.[2] Crime fiction was his topic. Had Rex achieved his ambition to write one of the greatest mystery novels? Rex said: "No writer ever knows where his work stands." Of Dashiell Hammett, Rex commented:

Hammett's *The Glass Key* is a more pointed and profound, a deeper commentary on certain aspects of the behavior of the human male, than anything Hemingway ever wrote. The things that were bothering Hammett's hero were exactly the same things that bothered Ernie all his life. And I think Dash did a better job of dealing with them. . . . Hammett never got the kind of encomium Chandler did. And that's silly. In my opinion, Hammett deserved it a lot more.

Impatient when no Wolfe book appeared that spring, New York's park commissioner, Robert Moses, himself seventy-nine, wrote Rex, asking, "Where is Nero Wolfe? His fans and aficionados demand his return." Moses believed in affirmative action. He used the next two pages to outline a plot for a new Nero Wolfe story, hoping that that would get Rex started on one. Other fans have outlined whole plots. Rex never found one he could use.

After a writing pause of nearly twenty months, Rex began work on *The Father Hunt* on 29 October 1967. He felt ready to write, and he was ready. Although Pola was making preparations to invade Israel in mid-December, as the guest of Ruth and Moshe Dayan — to teach textile designing to Israeli artisans — Rex held to his desk, averaging four pages a day up into early December, when planning sessions for Pola's ten-week incursion finally absorbed him.

Of four days Rex missed writing prior to 5 December, three had been spent in Manhattan on business. On the thirteenth he saw Pola off. The next day he was back on schedule. Between the fourteenth and the twenty-sixth he wrote the final fifty-one pages, taking time off only on Christmas Eve. Writing time, forty-four days.

In *The Father Hunt* Archie allowed himself a wistful aside which many readers would instantly interpret as a confidence made to them by Rex Stout himself. Archie said: "Before long the day will come, maybe in a year or two, possibly as many as five, when I won't be able to write any more of these reports for publication." Reviewers alluded to this passage in horror. That Archie should cease to write was unthinkable. Yet Rex was being neither fey nor maudlin. He was eighty-two. He accepted his mortality. In another few years he would be gone.

Rex's age seemed to be in J. B. Priestley's thoughts when he wrote to Rex in the new year: "May I congratulate you, as a fan of Nero Wolfe and Archie Goodwin for many years now, on the wonderful way in which you have kept these two going? But may I suggest also that there is one story you really must write now, and that is the story of how they first met?"[3] Rex vetoed this suggestion. "Nonsense," he told me; "I could have done it twenty years ago — now it would be an artistic blunder."

Priestley apparently was not thinking in terms of a summary report, because he offered Rex a caution too: "In *A Right to Die* you made what seemed to me the mistake of introducing an element of real time. These heroes of our modern legends must live in a different time from ours, and so appear ageless." Rex thought Priestley was right about that.

While Pola was away, dinner invitations poured in — a grave hazard for a reputed gourmet who is following an ulcer diet. On Sunday, 21 January, Rex lunched with the Alan Greens at Westport. All went well. On 28 January, he wrote Pola: "My internal arrangements are doing fine, with a slow but sure improvement week after week. I even bought a pound of pork sausage at the pork store and had it for three meals, broiled, and my insides thoroughly approved. I haven't cooked oatmeal once since you left." Rex went to the Goodmans' to dinner on 3 February, and had lunch with the Van Dorens at Falls Village the day following. He did not like so many breaks in his routine. "I'm going to the Derecktors' for lunch next Sunday," he told Pola on 6 February, "and that will do me for a while."

He had other news too: "I now find, to my amusement, that *The Father Hunt* left the writing bug quite active in my system, and I'm thinking of starting another book around March 1st. I even have the plot already started in my head. I may go ahead with it; after all, the outdoors is no great temptation in the months of March and April, and all summer long I wouldn't have to be looking forward to doing a story in the fall."

He offered a further insight into factors determining his writing periods: "There are three important meetings late this month (Authors' Guild Annual Meeting February 20th, Authors' League Annual Meeting February 27th, and Freedom House Annual Meeting February 28th), so I'll have all that behind me on March first.[4] It would be more fun to write a story in March and April than it was in October and November and December because I feel a lot better. So I may do it."

Pola returned home on 27 February, laden down with clippings touching on her visit. The morning of Pola's departure, Moshe Dayan put into her hand some brass medallions he had had struck the previous night. They were replicas of an ancient Jewish symbol — the hand of friendship. Back again at High Meadow, Pola slipped one onto Rex's key ring.

Pola was not home long before she saw Rex poring over articles on Labrador retrievers. Bonnie, their redbone coonhound, had died while she was away and Rex was lonesome for a dog's companionship. He was pleased to read that Labradors have the best developed brains of any dog. So they bought a year-old Labrador bitch, Czarna. Rex told Pola:

"We started with a dog named Czarna. Let's finish with a dog named Czarna."

"Czarna was as attached to Rex as Rex would let a dog become attached to him — more so than he had been to Bonnie, or Lucky, Bonnie's predecessor," Pola told me. The family was amused at one of Czarna's tricks. At night she slept outside Pola's door. When Pola was away, Czarna transferred her vigil to Rex's bedroom door. "I don't let a dog sleep in my bedroom," Rex explained.

In late March, Don Bensen interviewed Rex. With Bensen, Rex went deeper into the process of creation: "The whole situation came to me in one concept . . . Archie, Wolfe, the house, and so on." He showed an interesting sense of priorities. Occasional discrepancies did not disturb him: "It's just not worthwhile to be precise about details that aren't factors in the plot. There are other essential matters to bother about." To answer Bensen's questions about contemporary fiction, Rex gave a small speech: "Most of what are called writers of serious fiction now seem to be convinced . . . that life itself is unacceptable. Well, I certainly do not believe that life is unacceptable. . . . I have no interest in most so-called serious fiction now, not because it deals with some people who are unpleasant and unhealthy but because it assumes that everyone is unpleasant and unhealthy. The hell with it."

That spring Rex supplied the *Reader's Digest* with a jacket essay for *Modern Classics of Suspense:*

Ever since Homer first spoke the tale of Achilles and the fall of Troy, storytellers have been reciting tales — in print; and the best ones may bow to Homer but need not apologize to him. They know what Shakespeare knew, that "an honest tale speeds best being plainly told." They know that in a tale that speeds best there must be thrills for the reader not only in what happens next but in how it happens and who makes it happen.

Thus he described guidelines to which he himself adhered.

In late May Rex wrote to Juanita Merle, his favorite niece: "Here we are, with lots of flowers in the garden to look at and smell — and out in the world plenty of ructions to deplore. But what the hell, I've been deploring ructions for eight decades." As time passed, Rex was coming more and more to think of High Meadow as a Neronian brownstone within which the order he sought prevailed and wherein he stood apart from disorder outside, which it was improbable that he could banish.

Within his own domain Rex continued to function well. When *The Father Hunt* came out on 28 May, Lewis Nichols looked in on Rex. He told readers of *The New York Times Book Review:* "He is no creaking elder statesman, mouthing halting reminiscences in his beard. . . . On that day . . . he was doing the following: thinning peas, spacing strawberry runners, picking eleven quarts of strawberries, cutting chives and putting up wire fence to keep the deer at a distance. It was a thoroughly exhausting day for a visitor, who felt a hundred."[5]

In June, *Esquire* magazine asked Rex if he could persuade Wolfe's chef, Fritz Brenner, to write a piece on the care and feeding of Nero Wolfe. Although Rex found Fritz amenable, readers had to wait till the *Nero Wolfe Cookbook* was published, in 1973, to get a glimpse of the Brenner prose style. In late June Rex had a gallbladder attack. Than Selleck counseled elective surgery. Rex entered the hospital on 5 July and was back home, minus a gallbladder, on 10 August. Recovery was routine but plans to write the *Esquire* piece were dropped. Gourmet cookery did not seem a proper topic for a man on a restrictive diet.

During his convalescence Rex had the pleasure of reading a lengthy new contribution to the body of critical commentary growing up around his work. The article, "Homicide West: Some Observations on the Nero Wolfe Stories of Rex Stout," published in *English Studies,* in Amsterdam, in the summer of 1968, was forwarded to him by the author, Mia I. Gerhardt, a professor at the University of Utrecht. Professor Gerhardt found it difficult to believe that the nonbookish Archie can write as well as he does. One wonders if she would object to Huck Finn on the same grounds. She had no other quibbles, however. She commended Rex's success in managing Archie so that, even as he invites our admiration of and confidence in Wolfe, he "puts him on a human level." She praised Rex's unique device of "double timing." The stories take place in a changing world, yet the protagonists never grow older. She said: "It is fascinating to observe the little adjustments by which he manages to keep it up. . . . As a literary expedient it is not absurd at all."

Central to Gerhardt's critique of the stories was her need to know if Wolfe's literary character is "acceptable in itself." She concluded that it ·is and that interplay between Wolfe and Archie contributes to that result. Like Barzun, she placed their partnership in the Quixote-Panza tradition. Even their linguistic byplay is Quixotic. Though flattered, Rex did not think the comparison could be pursued too far. He told me: "Wolfe isn't a phantasiast, and Archie wouldn't ride a donkey."

Gerhardt also recorded an alteration in the Wolfe-Archie relationship that had gone undetected by others: "If in the earlier stories Nero Wolfe often seems rather pompous, and Archie somewhat obtuse, this soon changes; Wolfe's self-confidence becomes less assertive, while Archie gains in finesse and wit."

In her estimate of secondary characters in the saga, Gerhardt puts the regulars in formalized roles recalling "the technique of the old *Commedia dell' Arte.*" Verbal skill rescues them from the mundane. Expert use of Balzac's "returning-characters" device, which sees them, like repertoire players, now in a supporting role, now taking a lead, adds to their lifelikeness. Characters invented for particular stories, even those briefly observed, are "nicely picked out." Inconsistencies in the stories were no problem to Gerhardt. Rex refused to be "the captive of his own text." Like a river correcting its course, he resorted to such changes "to improve certain features as he goes along." An instance would be Orrie Cather's tendency to grow younger and handsomer as the series progresses. Even what appear to be authentic blunders (for example, a picture of the Washington Monument being substituted for the waterfall picture, in "Booby Trap,") were excused by Gerhardt on the grounds that exact parallels offer in *Don Quixote.*

Gerhardt's study of the saga led her to conclude that "on the level of literary craftsmanship, a writer of sound detective stories can bear to have his devices examined along with those of the great masters of the craft of fiction." Her inquiries gave new solidarity to Wolfe scholarship. Thus we find German critic Helmut Heissenbüttel writing in 1971: "Erich Franzen called my attention to Rex Stout. Franzen himself considered Stout to be the one and true paradigm of the detective story."[6]

Rex wrote Professor Gerhardt on 5 September: "I pursed my lips only twice; at 'the house is only apparently lived in . . . ,' and at 'Now this is humbug' — Nero Wolfe's reviewing Rowse's dating of *Cymbeline.* '. . . just one book on the desk.' Of course there were many books about Shakespeare on the shelves, but, having read them, would NW have to consult them about a controversial point like the dating of *Cymbeline?* I wouldn't."

After drawing this surprising parallel, Rex resumed, with uncharacteristic humility, "But these are trifles. In addition to the pleasure your compliments and your wit gave me, I got hints. For instance, your comments about 'flat' and 'round' characters. Your application of Forster's distinction to my characters made me consider whether I have done acceptably what I intended to do. For that consideration I shall not do any reading of my books (I never do), but when I write another one — starting next month — your comments will certainly be an item in my mental luggage." Possibly Rex's later, fuller characterization of Rowcliff and Cather show him acting on this resolve. He did not think so. "I was paying her a compliment," he told me. "Any storyteller worth his salt would like to have all his characters round."[7]

On 3 October, acting for the SPWW3, Rex wrote Secretary of State Dean Rusk, urging that the United States supply adequate arms to Israel. On 16 October, Deputy Assistant Secretary of State Rodger P. Davies (assassinated in 1974, while ambassador to Cyprus) wrote Rex to advise him that President Johnson, on 9 October, had asked for supersonic aircraft for Israel "in such numbers as may be necessary to provide Israel with a deterrent force capable of preventing future Arab aggression and to replace losses suffered by Israel in the 1967 conflict."

On 9 November, Marion Prilook reminded Danbury *News-Times* readers that Rex soon would be entering his eighty-third year. In a telephone interview Rex told her he had another book under way. Marion asked: "Would you like us to come and get a new picture of you, or shall we use one we took in 1965?" Said Rex: "I'd prefer it if you used one of me when I was twenty." "We got the message," said Marion; "Rex Stout doesn't feel a day over twenty."

That was not quite true. On 20 September Rex had started writing the book he had hoped to begin in March. The book was not finished until 7 February 1969. The working title had been "Dead Dude." Later Rex changed it to *Death of a Dude.* For this book Rex preserved no daily writing record. He explained, in a succinct, wry notation: "Many interruptions, including World Series and a broken back. Writing time not calculable."[8] In November he had slipped on the living room stairs.[9] Stubbornly he refused to have his injuries evaluated. In January, when the pain began to abate, he agreed to have X rays. He had fractured the fifth vertebra. His back never felt right again. Stairs remained a permanent difficulty.

50.

A Man Who
Gloriously Acts and Decides

In that pantheon which includes Sherlock Holmes, Lord Peter Wimsey, and Hercule Poirot, it's certain that Nero Wolfe will have an honored place, although there may be some difficulty in finding a seat sufficient for his corpulence. I'm not so sure, however, that they will always find him congenial company. I can imagine Wolfe, eyes half-closed, listening to the pompous Holmes, the polished Wimsey, and the dandified Poirot, and interrupting with an earthy "Pfui!"

— VERMONT ROYSTER

Although Richard Nixon took office as President of the United States in January 1969, many lycanthrophiles agreed with Marion Prilook that the news that Viking would release William Baring-Gould's *Nero Wolfe of West Thirty-fifth Street* on 27 January was "infinitely more interesting than the cabinet appointments to a new administration." Harold C. Schonberg described the book to *New York Times* readers as the *terminus ad quem* of Wolfe scholarship. "Here," he said, "starts the canonization of Nero Wolfe, the most discussed and admired private detective of modern times." In *The Nation,* Max Byrd wrote: "Rex Stout has restored great sleuthing to the country that, properly speaking, discovered it. And in matters far more subtle than geography, he has *Americanized* the genre." Wolfe and Archie, as Byrd saw them, "belong to that great American company of buddies, spiritual kin to Huck and Jim, Ishmael and Queequeg."

For *Time* magazine, "If there is anybody in detective fiction remotely comparable to England's Sherlock Holmes, it is Rex Stout's corpulent genius, Nero Wolfe. . . . All the stories abound in the qualities that have made Wolfe's creator . . . one of the few detective writers with a wide appeal to the serious fiction reader. Stout serves up lean, lucid prose, masterly narrative construction, intricate yet gimmick-free plotting."

The *Saturday Review*'s Patrick Butler was so stunned by Baring-Gould's imprudent calculations showing that Wolfe was seventy-eight — "three years older than J. Edgar Hoover" — and that Archie was pushing fifty-eight — "only seven years this side of Medicare" — he could progress no further in his estimate of the book.

Wolfe fanciers were glad to have the book. Yet most had hoped for more. The book had a "rough-draftish flavor." Rex's own comments are significant. He told me: "He had my assent, but the book was not done with my active cooperation. His liking for the stories pleased me. And I liked him. But I didn't think he was a very good writer and I still don't." When Marion Wilcox expressed dismay at some of Baring-Gould's conjectures, Rex told her, "As for Baring-Gould's remarks about Nero Wolfe's past, they are mostly just guesses, so who cares? Not you or me."[1]

The hardcover edition sold six thousand copies. Book club and paperback editions put total sales well over the one hundred thousand mark.

On 16 February, Viking took a full-page ad in *The New York Times Book Review* to announce a "Mammoth Nero Wolfe Quiz Contest" designed to promote Baring-Gould's book and a new Wolfe omnibus, *Kings Full of Aces,* scheduled for release on 24 March. Contestants had four questions to answer — three of which showed a knowledge of Wolfe, the other, a knowledge of Archie. Top prize was a picnic hamper stuffed with gourmet treats. There were twenty-five second prizes — Nero Wolfe books. Certificates of membership in the West Thirty-fifth Street Irregulars would go out to the first five hundred to send in their entries. The word "Mammoth" was, of course, mischievously placed. It referred to Nero Wolfe and not to the contest, which was not that ambitious an undertaking.

In three weeks, 612 entries were received from 28 states; an additional 2 came in from Vietnam. Of these, 243 had the right answers. Alan Green, whose advertising agency ran the contest for Viking, drew the 26 winners, by lot, from among the correct entries. The top prize went to David G. Hanes of New Jersey. Philip Paley, a corporal in Vietnam, was one of the second-prize winners.

Rex, at the most, allowed the contest to happen. He did not enjoy such Madison Avenue promotional charades (as readers of *Before Midnight* could verify), but he saw them as a necessary evil and learned to bear with them. With motion pictures, radio, and television, however, he showed no inclination to compromise.

After hearing five minutes of a radio tape of "Murder in the Rain," with Sydney Greenstreet portraying Nero Wolfe, Rex said he could take no more. He liked Greenstreet. The script he found impossible. Once he previewed a TV Nero Wolfe pilot film. "It was terrible," he told me. Rex saved his greatest tirades for television: "I despise television. It exhausts and debilitates creative writing talent. For years I have refused all offers from movie and television producers, and shall go on refusing. I wouldn't trust either of those media with Jack and the Beanstalk if I had written it. In the contracts for two Nero Wolfe movies forty years ago, I insisted on excluding radio and television use."

During the last decade of his life Rex rejected more than fifty offers from movie makers and TV producers who wanted to follow up Perry Mason's success with a Nero Wolfe series. Some of the sums quoted ran into seven figures. Rex was not impressed. He told me, "That's something my heirs can fool around with, if they've a mind to." One offer suggested Orson Welles and Darren McGavin as Wolfe and Archie; another, Welles and Bill Cosby.[2] Lorne Greene has been proposed for the Wolfe role. And Raymond Burr. One 1972 offer was from a TV producer who wanted Zero Mostel to do Wolfe and Dick Cavett, Archie. "Nuts," Rex said. "The only actor whom I would have liked to see doing one of my characters," he told me, "was Charles Laughton as Nero Wolfe." Yet he conceded that Bogart, as a young man, could have been Archie. When Paul Newman was suggested as Archie, Rex merely cocked an eyebrow.

Television did bring Rex income nonetheless. In 1964 a Nero Wolfe story was pirated by German television. Rex protested and was paid $3,500 in settlement. And in 1968, for $80,000, he allowed Italian TV to produce twelve Nero Wolfe stories. He agreed only because he would never see them. In May 1968, the Italian magazine *Epoca* discussed the forthcoming series. Wolfe was described as having "a vast number of admirers in Italy." With obvious affection, *Epoca* went on to describe Wolfe as "a mountain of flesh." Readers wanted to know what Rex himself was like. *Epoca* had reassuring words: "Just like Nero Wolfe, he hates it when he has to leave his country house in Connecticut. Unlike Wolfe, he did not marry a female poisoner: his wife is an affectionate companion."

On 21 February 1969, Italian television began broadcasting a first group of weekly Nero Wolfe programs — each in two episodes. These, in order of appearance, were *Veleno in sartoria* [*Poison at the Tailor Shop*] (*The Red Box*), *Circuito chiuso* [*Closed Circuit*] (*If Death Ever Slept*), *Per la fama di Cesare* [*For Caesar's Fame*] (*Some Buried Caesar*), *Il Pesce più grosso* [*The Too-Big Fish*] (*The Doorbell Rang*). The second series — *In the Best Families, Too Many Cooks,* "Murder is Corny," *Where There's a Will, The Rubber Band,* "Counterfeit for Murder," *Gambit,* and *The Final Deduction* — followed several weeks later. The role of Wolfe was played by Tino Buazzelli, who soon became the plump subject of many pictorial interviews. Archie was played by Paolo Ferrari, a lean, earnest fellow who looked like Dana Andrews.

The name Nero Wolfe has magic in Italy. When the cover of *Grazia,* on 18 August 1974, announced in inch-high letters the presence within of "Nero Wolfe e l'orchidea rosa" ("Easter Parade"), the issue was exhausted the second day of sale.

Late winter 1969 found Rex handling with ease his usual full schedule. He had completed his third term as president of the Authors' League, but continued as vice president. On 29 March he was in Washington for a Washington *Post* Author and Book Luncheon. On 23 April he gave an address to P.E.N. Two days later he went to the MWA's annual awards banquet. There was one disquieting bit of news. Mark Van Doren was in the Torrington Hospital after suffering a coronary occlusion. But Dorothy sent positive news: "I spend every day with him. The doctors say he is doing fine. I thought you would be touched to know that when he is not eating or sleeping he — and I, too — are reading Nero Wolfes, one after another. He says you are better than ever."

In early August, Alfred Bester, an editor of *Holiday*, undertook a long interview with Rex, at High Meadow, spread over two visits.[3] Bester found that Rex let his cigars go out when engrossed in conversation. He found that Rex's current preference in beverages was "a horrendous mixture of Earl Grey tea and grapefruit juice." He learned that Rex was soon to be a grandfather for the fifth time. He found him, in conversation, "all interest and tolerance," the last of a vanishing breed. When Rex told him, "My mornings are just God-awful. I'm not miserable and unhappy; I'm just not alive yet. I'm in a fog," Bester replied, "That seems to have a familiar sound." "Yes," Rex agreed, "it does sound like Archie Goodwin, doesn't it?"

Rex wanted to know if Bester read the underground newspapers. When Bester said he read them with horror and disgust, thinking of the kind of person who read and enjoyed them, Rex said: "Nothing should horrify you." He offered a pattern to follow: "It's like the story about the two psychiatrists who pass in a corridor and one gooses the other. The guy who's been goosed turns around indignantly. Then he shrugs and says, 'What the hell, it's his problem.' " Rex volunteered: "Life on the whole is wonderful, but there are a lot of things wrong with it. That a nasty little poop like Wagner should write such beautiful music — it just isn't fair."

On 8 August Bester wrote to ask Rex to do a piece on orchids for *Holiday*'s forthcoming "Exotica" issue. "It doesn't have to be an expert piece or an informative piece or anything like that," Bester said, "just Rex Stout on orchids, whatever you feel or think about them." In the same letter, Bester said he had been rereading *Death of a Doxy* and had paused over a passage that spoke of the differences between imagination and invention. "Is there a difference?" Bester asked.

In his reply, on 11 August, Rex consented to do the orchids piece. Then he took up imagination and invention, the bait that drew his quick reply: "You know damn well there's a difference. Imagination is plastic power; invention is aggregative and associative power. Imagination creates; invention contrives. Dickens had imagination; Bernard Shaw had only invention. Merely semantics? No no no."

As he received them, Rex inscribed for Pola the first copy of each of his books. On 5 November 1931 he wrote in *How Like a God:* "To Pola/Who having everything else/might as well have this too." On 21 March 1933 he inscribed *Forest Fire:* "To Pola,/I write it in this book/instead of on the skin of my body,/but it means the same thing." For *The League of Frightened Men,* on 15 August 1935, Rex wrought a quatrain:

> *To Pola, hoping as to be*
> *Her wonder man, her radiant hero;*
> *Oh let her, pray, discern in me*
> *Archie's strength and wit of Nero.*

For *The Rubber Band,* on 13 April 1936, Rex struck off a jocose inscription: "To Pola/with love, and a promise to give her/all the royalties on this book/after the first 100,000 copies." (A dangerous gesture; by 1972, paperback sales alone, of *The Rubber Band,* reached 316,808.) In *Too Many Women,* on 20 October 1947, Rex wrote: "Too many?/To me all the women in the world/would not be enough without you." And so the inscriptions went.

For Pola, on 20 August 1969, in *Death of a Dude,* a book which took Montana for its locale, Rex now wrote: "It was thirty-seven years ago that you,/a dudine, and I, a dude,/were horseback in Montana — " (a reference to their marriage on horseback).

In the good August weather Rex spent several hours each day working in his garden. On the afternoon of 12 August he came around to the garden court to greet me on my arrival from Lexington, Massachusetts. Then he brought me inside, where he fixed me a Jack Daniel's old fashioned and made for himself one of his grapefruit juice and Earl Grey concoctions.

"You were five hours on the road from Boston? Explain yourself!"

"I don't have Archie for a chauffeur. I'm a slow driver."

"Well, at least you didn't run over any of my iris coming up the drive."

"On Wednesday afternoons I sideswipe only cattleyas."

"You're out of luck. I don't have an orchid on the place."

Our topic that day was the Wolfe saga.

Do you intend to fill in the gaps Archie's left in reporting Wolfe's history?

No. I decided long ago not to trespass on Archie's prerogative of reporting on milieu, character, and events.

The times advance but Wolfe and Archie are immune to age. You effect a kind of miracle. . . .

Those stories have ignored time for forty years. Any reader who can't or won't do the same thing should skip them. I didn't age the characters because I didn't want to. That would have made it cumbersome and would seem to have centered attention on the characters rather than the stories. The thing that has interested me most has been the story. Whether that is what has interested people most I don't know. But I don't give a damn; that's what has interested me most.

Why did you make Wolfe a recluse?

Other people's detectives seemed so busy — they ran around so much.

Do you object to sex and violence in detective stories?

Sex and violence, like all other items of human behavior, are acceptable and desirable in a detective story if they are essential to the story.

Do you set any limits on what a writer can say?

I believe there should be no legal restrictions whatever on freedom of expression, except when words become acts, as in libel.

What are the advantages of using a first-person narrator to tell the Nero Wolfe stories?

The big one which Poe saw and used. Since in a detective story the reader must not be inside the detective's mind, third-person omniscience is impossible, and the best way to avoid it is to have someone else tell it.

Simenon says he is able to take up more serious subjects in his Maigret stories than he can in his "straight" novels. Do the Wolfe stories open the same opportunity to you?

Sometimes the plot and characters necessarily involve such subjects (as in *A Right to Die*), but I never "take up" one. My only conscious purpose is to write a good story. Of course, writing about such a subject can be a source of satisfaction to me.

Anthony Burgess says that those who write series detective stories are artists — like Wodehouse and Faulkner — building a world. Do you agree?

Depends on the writer. Doyle or Simenon, yes; Christie or Gardner, no.

Do you think the best novels have a moralistic or exegetic tone?

That debate is as old as Aristotle. Morality may be a consideration in the "usefulness" of a novel, but not in its merits as a work of art.

In your stories you seem to get inside your characters — to think as they think. Do you possess, to an unusual degree, the ability to understand another's point of view?

To an unusual degree, yes.

Do you form reliable impressions of people based on the manner, rather than the matter, of their speaking?

Yes. Often.

Why do you invent names for cars, liquors, rugs, guns, locks, fishing tackle rather than using brand names?

A character's liking for a Heron car or Ten-Mile Creek bourbon cannot be impugned.

Your culprits always capitulate plausibly. Do you take care to see that they do?

Everything in a story should be credible, but one of the hardest things to believe is that anyone will abandon the effort to escape a charge of murder. Therefore it is extremely important to "suspend disbelief" on that. If you don't, the story is spoiled.

More than two-thirds of the Wolfe stories begin on a Monday or Tuesday. Why?

The reason for that is that I started at the typewriter on a Monday or Tuesday or because I wanted to have four or five days for action before the weekend came.

What have you to say to those critics who argue that by portraying the police unsympathetically you encourage disrespect for law enforcers?

I am much kinder to the police than most writers of detective stories. My two main police characters, Cramer and Stebbins, are neither stupid nor brutal, and, judging from letters I get from readers, they are likable.

Eighteen Wolfe stories report on cases that fall in March and/or April. Another nine occur in August. What's behind this seasonal preference?

By putting a story in the season in which I was writing it I avoided the chore of producing a snowstorm in June.

Do some episodes in your books please you more than others?

There are certain episodes in certain stories which I think are better handled than others — for example, the carton-of-milk scene in *The Doorbell Rang.* I think I wrote that very well. I think that's done just the way such an episode should be done. The best-written episode is that one in which every word pertains to and is essential to, the action, but not a word beyond that — when the whole action is given as it should be, but nothing extraneous, not even one word, gets in.

Your novellas give no sense of an author pressed for space. Is that by conscious design?

It's deliberate. Any good storyteller should know whether a plot idea is right for a given length.

Is a novella easier to write than a novel?

In a way, short fiction is harder to write than long. An unnecessary page in a long novel doesn't hurt it much, but one unnecessary sentence in a three-thousand-word story spoils it.

Raymond Chandler and Ross Macdonald are addicted to similes. You avoid them. Why?

They don't suit my style and method. In most fiction more than ninety percent of them are merely flourishes, and usually not good ones. They often impede and they nearly always intrude.

Wolfe has yet to encounter a perfect murder. Do you think you could commit one?

Yes.

Wolfe only once is reported eating beef. Why?

I have no idea; he must eat tons of it.

He eats tons of shad roe too. Is shad roe his favorite dish?

No. I wrote many of the stories in the spring, when shad roe is in season. I like it, so Wolfe got it.

What beverages does Wolfe drink at meals?

At breakfast, coffee or cocoa. At other meals he drinks almost nothing — occasional tiny sips of Schweppes tonic. After, coffee. He doesn't drink wine with his meals because drinking liquids with meals interferes with the taste of the food.

Has Wolfe read La Rochefoucauld's Maxims?

Given the first three words of any of them he could probably finish it.

Is Wolfe an atheist or an agnostic?

An agnostic.

If Wolfe became incapacitated midway in a case, is there anyone you'd trust to take over for him?

I wouldn't mind if Maigret finished it. Simenon and I have many readers in common. Why not? We're both good storytellers, and some of our characters would bleed if you made a cut.

What person or persons within your range have been a source of Archie's idiom?

The source of "Archie's idiom" was and is everything I have heard people say, and I suppose to some extent what I have read. Those are the sources of everything I write or say.

Did Archie hang up the picture of Sherlock Holmes that is found over his desk, or did Wolfe put it there?

I was a damn fool to do it. Obviously it's always an artistic fault in any fiction to mention any other character in fiction. It should never be done.

May we take it as settled that Lily sleeps with Archie?

I should think anybody would except "an unravish'd bride of quietness."

A reader once advised you to kill off Lily. Are you apt to?

I would tackle a tiger bare-handed to save her from harm.

Saul Panzer was in business before Hitler's panzers were. Did it bother you at all that Saul bore a name that brought Hitler and his doings to mind to many readers?

A little. It still does, a little.

Did you inspect West Thirty-fifth Street after it became Wolfe's address, to see if it was appropriate?

I walked, once, from Fifth Avenue to the river.

Do you think of the brownstone as an actual presence in the stories?

Yes.

Why do you think readers prefer Wolfe to be in his brownstone, rather than somewhere else?

That's a very comfortable house. People like to be comfortable, that's all. They don't like to be jerking around.

Would you consider leveling the brownstone by fire to give the series another high point?

Too much trouble. I'd have to rebuild it.

Do you have a good opinion of Fowler's Modern English Usage?

The first time I read it I decided I must have written it in my sleep.

How about Brewer's Dictionary of Phrase and Fable?

I'm on my second copy. I wore out the first one.

Do you think Bunyan's and Woolman's plain style influenced your prose style?

Yes.

A lady critic says: "Rex Stout's style is so elegant, it is a real pity that his language isn't." Any comment?

She might as well say, "His features are elegant but his face isn't."

Agatha Christie has written a book in which she kills off Hercule Poirot. Do you have similar plans for disposing of Wolfe?

Certainly not. I hope he lives forever.

How would you feel if someone wanted to continue the Wolfe series after you laid aside your pen?

I don't know whether vampirism or cannibalism is the better term for it. Not nice. They should roll their own.

What do you think of those critical articles that link your work to Cervantes and Twain?

There's no man who doesn't enjoy reading well-written complimentary remarks about things he has done; if there is, he's no relative of mine.

What about fan mail from the multitudes?

Much too much, since courtesy requires that letters be acknowledged. Much too little, since self-esteem is a glutton.

Have you read The Catcher in the Rye?

A good writing job, but nearly all writing about adolescents is adolescent. The great exception is *Huckleberry Finn.*

What's your opinion of Portnoy's Complaint?

Terrible trash. I've got a better title for it: *Penrod Revisited.*

Where does Chaucer stand among your preferences?

In the first rank. I tried *The Canterbury Tales* first, in Middle English, in my teens, and it was a real battle. Never finished it. Tried it again in my forties and fifties and loved it. Tried Neville Coghill's translation and rejected it. I have the facsimile of the Kelmscott Chaucer by William Morris, and often spend an evening with it.

What moves you to write?

Oh, now come. You know damn well that the roots of any man's motivations are so deep in his subconscious that all answers to that question are phony.

A lady I know says she's sure you have a secretary who writes all your books. Comment?

The name is Jane Austen, but I haven't the address.

Phil Casey of the Washington *Post* arrived at Danbury to interview Rex in August 1969. He phoned High Meadow to make sure Rex was up to a visit. Rex told him: "I'm expecting you and I expect to be here. I have heard nothing from St. Peter."

"Stout," Casey said, "is a straightforward man, pantingly ready to say exactly what he thinks on any and all subjects." Rex, he learned, loved life, but not in the Schweitzerian sense: "I thoroughly approve of life. Not reverence for life. I approve of life itself. I have no quarrel with nature. People are always saying something is unnatural. How can it be unnatural, if it happens? If a man makes love to fourteen women in one night, it may be astounding, it may be debilitating, but it's not unnatural." To these comments on life, Rex would later provide me with a coda: "The most basic fact about life is death . . . the most usual act for creatures to keep alive is to kill some other creature . . . to speak of *sacredness of life* is idiotic . . . a guy will sit down and eat a big beefsteak and then talk for an hour about sacredness of life. Ridiculous."

Rex ended his interview with Casey on a light note. He spoke of his metaphysical sparring partner, Father McEntegart: "Last time I wrote him I signed myself S.J. too. My S.J., I told him, was for 'still jaunty.'"

On 2 September Rex was a guest on Dick Cavett's TV talk show. He felt curiously depleted of energy and did not come across with his usual force. When one is eighty-three, jauntiness is, after all, an elusive quality.

In mid-October Rex sent along to Alfred Bester the piece Bester had commissioned for *Holiday:* "Do Orchids Have the Right to Privacy?" Here orchids merely served Rex as a device for an opening gambit. His true topic was man's penchant for violating the privacy of everything in nature from orchids to outer space. In man's invasion of the privacy of the atom, he suggested, the grandest irony of all may have been reached. The result might be "not the improvement of our lot but its finish." But the consolations of philosophy had come to him in old age. "We have certainly had a lot of fun," he said, "and, having danced, we shouldn't complain if we must pay the piper."

To Dorothy Beall, who was promoting a cookbook to raise funds for the Joyce Memorial Library, in neighboring Brookfield, Rex supplied a preface, on 15 October. Since it would be absurd to suggest that he had tried any substantial number of the 781 recipes contained in the book, he centered his vision on the "Miscellaneous Suggestions" given at the end of each chapter. On those new to him he offered this unorthodox tally:

Promising, must be tried	36
Possible, worth a try	22
Doubtful	15
Preposterous	9

He didn't think that that was a bad score: "Suppose that in the next half a year I try all of the 36, and half of them prove out, and as a result 18 of the things I eat taste better. Not many books have as good an excuse as that."

That same fall, when the League for Mutual Aid was making preparations to celebrate its fiftieth anniversary, Herman Singer, editor of the *Anniversary Journal,* petitioned Rex for a short statement detailing his personal reasons for joining the League. On 22 October Rex supplied a blithe answer: "I joined the League for Mutual Aid many years ago because Roger Baldwin told me to. I have continuously supported it because I share its objectives, approve its methods, and admire its conduct."

Rex became a grandfather for the fifth time on 2 November when Rebecca gave birth to her second daughter, Lisa, at South Bend, Indiana, where she and Bill then were living. The last member of the family to have been born in Indiana was Rex himself. Rex claimed he left there before his first birthday because he did not like Indiana politics. Rebecca told Rex that Lisa could not see that they had improved any in the eighty-three years that had intervened. Before the year was out the Bradburys moved to California.

In November, as president of the SPWW3, Rex wired President Nixon affirming support of the hard-line policy Nixon had enunciated on 3 November in a speech on Vietnam. Back came a personal letter from Nixon, dated 5 December, thanking Rex for his support, and insisting, "The confidence and understanding you have shown will do much to strengthen our efforts to achieve the just and lasting peace that all of us desire." Vietnam made strange bedfellows.

At the start of November Rex began experiencing the first of an epic series of blinding headaches which, during the two years that followed, robbed life of nearly all pleasure and meaning for him. On 31 October he had begun writing *Please Pass the Guilt.* The first day he wrote six pages. The next day, stricken with an excruciating headache, he could write nothing at all. Throughout his life Rex had been mostly immune to headaches. Now one headache quickly followed another. Through November and December he was unable to write. When he tried to pick up with the book again in January, he began by writing two pages on the fourteenth.[4] But efforts to bully himself back to health by holding himself to a given number of pages on the days he wrote were not getting the results he looked for. With sixty pages completed, he stopped work on 10 February. On the fourteenth he entered Danbury Hospital for tests.

As word of Rex's illness spread his mail increased. Typical was a cheering letter from fellow mystery writer Donald Westlake: "So far as I remember, Nero Wolfe has never had to leave the house to go have a check-up in a hospital. I should think it would make him irascible. (I can see half the book.)" But Rex was too ill to move Wolfe into a hospital bed, however apposite that might prove to be.[5] Not until 1 June did he try to take hold again. Then he wrote Juanita Merle:

> When your February 7 letter came (and the book) I had already been fighting chronic recurring headaches for two months, and a week or so after your letter came I went to the hospital. During my seven weeks there they took 854 tests or maybe it was 896, and still didn't know what caused the headaches — and neither did I. I still don't know, after being home for nearly two months, but at least they have let up a lot and I am digging into the stack of accumulated mail. . . . Anyway, there are a lot of flowers outside and the iris has started to bloom, and I am expecting to resume on a book before long, so what the hell.

But Rex did not match bravura with performance. When he did not have a headache, he was afraid he was going to have one. Than Selleck found Rex a vexatious patient. He had to explain to Rex in painstaking detail the generic names of medicines and the logic that lay behind various courses of treatment. Informed, Rex would go ahead with the treatment. Kept in ignorance, he was capable of rejecting it altogether.

Those close to Rex wondered if his mind set had something to do with his headaches. He had begun to wear eyeglasses in his fifties — "to see telephone numbers" — and his left ear had begun "signing off" in his late seventies, but no encroachments of age were apparent otherwise. The onset of illnesses at seventy-nine meant a serious period of adjustment for him. He was no longer able to walk up his hill as rapidly as he liked. He was not accustomed to being dictated to by his body. Hitherto his mind had dictated to it.

There was a further problem. On the issue of the war in Vietnam he found himself increasingly isolated. One night, when Norman Cousins and Alan Green were guests at dinner, Rex said that Communist countries were monolithic. "They're not building monoliths like they used to," Alan rejoined. As soon as he made the remark he regretted it. But the damage had been done. Rex was irate. He was not accustomed to seeing his table set on a roar at his expense. He bellowed his dissent. His color altered so dramatically that Pola grew alarmed. In the days that followed she called several of Rex's friends, asking them to avoid the war as a topic when they talked with him. That had become her own strategy. She was a dove herself. She had never previously disagreed with Rex on a key issue. She would not hurt his pride now by putting herself openly in opposition to him. Apart from that, since his mind was shut against every viewpoint except his own, opposition would only rile him. She did not want to see him upset. Indeed, Than suspected that latent misgivings Rex may have had about the tenability of his stance on Vietnam might be generating his headaches. Either that, or they were triggered by his dismay that those who stood with him on the issue were fast dwindling in numbers. Under the circumstances, prudence decreed that the topic be avoided.[6]

Thoughts of the garden, which ordinarily would have been gathering force as spring neared, gave Rex no pleasure. He kept to his room and his bed. This would be the pattern of his life for more than eighteen months. "I was nothing for a year and a half, with goddamn headaches," he said later. To his family it seemed as though the magnificent man they had known was collapsing into ruin.

In Rex's room Pola hung a gift from Indiana's Hamilton County Historical Society — a copy of the society's Fifth Annual Historical calendar. Each month had its own six-by-eight etching. The etching for May was of "Rex Stout Birthplace, Noblesville." The caption read: "Rex Stout, author of the famous 'Nero Wolfe' detective stories, was born in this house in 1886." Rex wondered if the town of his birth had discovered him in the year of his death.

When Rex came home to High Meadow from Danbury Hospital, Nancy Timms, twenty-two, a graduate of Becker Junior College, was hired to give him part-time secretarial assistance.[7] If he was to have any peace of mind, inroads would have to be made on the mountain of mail that had accumulated. Nancy came three afternoons a week, between three and six, when Rex felt at his strongest. During the first weeks she found him in pajamas and bathrobe. She sat in his bedroom with him while he dictated brief letters. Even things on his bedside table, a short distance away, had to be fetched for him. Often he spoke about his unfinished book. He wanted to get back to it, but he would never touch a pencil if he did not feel right. By six he was always exhausted.

One of the letters Rex had to deal with was from Calvert Distillers.

Calvert offered $4,000 for a story of 1,500 to 2,000 words in which Rex would mention Passport Scotch. If he liked scotch, he would be sent a supply. Rex refused the offer. His headaches were not a factor. "It would have been prostitution," he told me.

Another letter, received in mid-May, was from Mary Stout. At eighty-two, Mary was in frail health and a shut-in in her mother's cottage at Poverty Hollow. But she found comfort in Rex's books. "I do hope you are finishing your book," she coaxed. "I could use another Nero Wolfe story." On a few days Rex did try to write, now for the first time putting a story down in longhand. There were long lapses as he wrote — he needed time to pull his thoughts together — but when he put something down, it was right. As always had been his practice, he changed nothing.

Meanwhile, the world had not forgotten him. In January the British Crime-Writers Association had named Rex recipient of its coveted Silver Dagger Award for *The Father Hunt,* chosen as "the best crime novel by a non-British author in 1969." At a ceremony in May, the late publisher Sir William ("Billy") Collins accepted the award on Rex's behalf. In *The Tablet* Anthony Lejeune said: "The most famous ratiocinative detective of all, of course, is Nero Wolfe. His creator, Rex Stout, is now well into his eighties, but *The Father Hunt* shows no sign of a flagging pen or an enfeebled mind. On the contrary, it's as good as any he's written."

When Jerome Weidman succeeded Rex as president of the Authors' League, Rex had assured him his duties would not be onerous. On 5 June 1970 Weidman wrote Rex:

> For years I have heard people saying there is nothing to this business of being President of the Authors' League. All you need is a goatee and an assistant named Archie to write your jokes. Maybe so. I don't know. I have no goatee, and my assistant is named Peggy, and her jokes raise welts, and maybe that is why I miss you so much. Will you please for God's sake get off your you know what and come back? You may have forgotten our deal. I have not. I said I would go into the bullpen and throw a few until your elbow got better on condition that you remain as vee pee and come back as prez. Rex, boy, where are you?

At eighty-four few men are importuned to take on major responsibilities. No doubt about it, the world was letting go of Rex reluctantly. To know that he had not labored in vain was itself a tonic.

In an average year Rex received fifteen hundred pieces of fan mail. While he was ill, the flow quickened. From Garson Kanin came a copy of his latest book, inscribed, "To our leader — the one and only." From London, Dr. George Sacks, assistant editor of *The Lancet,* disclosed his longtime addiction to Stout. So did the Marquess of Donegal and the Maharajah of Indore, an extraordinary range.

There was a letter from William Dement, Professor in Psychiatry at Stanford University School of Medicine, who said that when his son was born, he sent his wife a bouquet with a message which read "Satisfactory." Another came from the senior consulting physician in a West Pakistan hospital — Dr. Najib Ullah — who described the Wolfe stories as "the best detective stories *ever* written by *anybody.*" From Texas came a letter from Dr. James Kennedy, who admitted that for years, using a general physical examination as his cloak, he had been asking patients to try to raise one eyebrow at a time — Archie-fashion. Though he never had found anyone who could do it, his faith was not shaken. Nor should it have been. Rex could do it.

After Rex's defense of Richard III in *Death of a Doxy,* the Richard III Society made him an honorary member. On the 485th anniversary of Richard's death, 22 August 1970, the Society published the following obituary in *The New York Times:* "PLANTAGENET — Richard, great king and true friend of the rights of man, died at Bosworth Field on August 22, 1485. Murdered by traitors and, dead, maligned by knaves and ignored by Laodiceans, he merits our devoted remembrance." The author of the anonymous notice was Rex Stout.

In September 1968, in "The Truth about Nero Wolfe," Bruce Kennedy had told *Baker Street Journal* readers that on 22 June 1966 Rex had.written him saying, "Since the suggestion that Nero Wolfe is the son of Sherlock Holmes was merely someone's loose conjecture, I think it is proper and permissible for me to ignore it." But the Baker Street Irregulars were reluctant to quit their unorthodox alliance with Wolfe. Kennedy suggested another set of parents for Wolfe: John Watson and Mary Morstan. That set the pot boiling. In December, in "Holmes, Wolfe, and Women," Barbara Paul reinstated Holmes as Wolfe's father. Thereupon, in "Like Father, Like Son?" Andrew Peck identified Watson as Wolfe's — mother! There the matter rested until September 1970 when, in "Dr. Handy's Wild-Eyed Man," Jonathan Sisson theorized that Holmes sired Wolfe by Lizzie Borden when she visited Baker Street, in 1890.[8] The murder of the elder Bordens followed their discovery that Lizzie had borne Nero.

When Nancy Timms came up to High Meadow on 1 December, she learned that it was Rex's eighty-fourth birthday. In her car she had a huge yellow paper chrysanthemum, which her students had made. She brought it in to Rex. He gave it a place of honor in his office until spring arrived and his own gardens came to life again.[9]

51

Nero Equals Archie

The best and truest thing I can say about Rex Stout is that, for me (apart from Sherlock Holmes) he is the only detective-story writer who is not only consistently readable but consistently re-readable.

— GILBERT HIGHET

The London *Sunday Times* had said in March 1971 that in the Soviet Union more of Rex Stout's works were in print than of any other American writer. For a start, theorizing that these Stout books had propaganda value because they exposed flaws in capitalist society, the Russians had published *The Doorbell Rang, Too Many Cooks,* and *A Right to Die.* When these proved popular others followed. But even as the *Sunday Times* was reporting Rex's popularity with Russian readers, in the *Literary Gazette* Soviet critic Gogo Anjaparidze was raising a cry of alarm. "Most detective fiction," he protested, "defends the foundation of capitalist society — the 'sacrosanct' right of private property — and expresses warm feelings toward the propertied classes. Do you call this exposing capitalist society?" Despite Anjaparidze's concern, Soviet readers yearly would grow more avid for detective fiction, and the list of Nero Wolfe books available to Russians, Poles, Estonians, Latvians, Lithuanians, Rumanians, Bulgarians, Hungarians, and Yugoslavs steadily would lengthen. Increasing numbers of readers behind the Iron Curtain would ponder the motivations of the affluent Nero Wolfe, who relinquishes his comfort, suffers the rebukes and harassments of others, and endangers his life to uphold ethical standards, remedy social abuses, and see that the ends of justice are served, even when men of power and means must be humbled to bring about that result. No Soviet writer could attack with impunity the head of the KGB. In America, Rex Stout could lay the director of the FBI under severe reprimand, and go unpunished.

During the last decade of his life, Rex received many letters from Iron Curtain countries, from readers wanting more of his books. If Gogo Anjaparidze was right, then the popularity of books which defended the foundation of capitalist society was growing steadily in the Communist world. Although those editions of his books which circulated in the Communist countries were unauthorized and brought him no income,

Rex accepted that fact without great perturbation. He was glad that his ideas were reaching readers behind the Iron Curtain. That itself was a form of recompense.

Yet, as a champion of authors' rights, he was not wholly reconciled to this piracy. "Pola," he said one day, with a wry grin, "I must have a lot of royalties accumulating in Poland. Let's go there and spend them." His business eye, of course, did not dim. In the spring of 1971, Thew Wright told him he was quitting his law practice and would write mysteries for a change. Said Thew, "I have decided to make use of a catchy pen name — Rex Stout." "Go ahead," Rex answered. "I'm in favor of anything that will bring in more royalties to Rex Stout."[1]

Others also realized that Rex's name carried clout. In April, William Morris, editor-in-chief of the *American Heritage Dictionary*, came to Rex with a proposal. Morris had just been made editor-in-chief of the new *Harper Dictionary of Contemporary Usage*. Would Rex join the dictionary's Usage Panel, a group of one hundred and thirty-six writers and editors who used language well and would be willing to be polled on various points of controversy? On the Usage Panel, Morris assured him, Rex would be playing "an important part in recording the standards of usage respected by today's foremost writers." Rex approved of the project and joined the panel.[2]

On 21 September, after a summer marred by more headaches, Rex entered the Harkness Pavilion of the Columbia-Presbyterian Medical Center in Manhattan for evaluation of his problem by Dr. Arnold P. Friedman, a ranking authority on headaches. Friedman concluded that Rex's headaches were muscular-vascular in origin. After ten days Rex came home, freed of headaches. In the ensuing months he found that the siege had lifted permanently. His ordeal had ended as abruptly as it had begun.

After his illness, the first major interview Rex gave was to *The New York Times*'s Israel Shenker, who visited High Meadow in late November, on the eve of Rex's eighty-fifth birthday. Rex acknowledged that, at his age, you could experience "a mealy self-satisfaction when you compare what you've done with what other people have done." Yet contentment was undercut by dismay. He was uneasy about his growing "inability to be concerned about things not close at hand." He rebounded: "It's much easier for me to excuse myself for not being concerned about somebody else's problems because I have a right to be dead now anyway." That comment led him into comments upsetting to Pola and to Stout admirers who read the Shenker interview. Rex told me he was developing a line of thought rather than speaking intimately of his own wishes. But the rasp of recent suffering gave to his words an edge that carried conviction:

How pleasant it would be — at sixty-two or seventy or seventy-five — if a man with a healthy attitude toward life and his own death could arrange a really pleasant end.

There seems to be something in the nature of the human animal that makes it difficult for him to hear the very word "death." If you ask me, that's pretty dirty and it accounts for so much of the misery of life. People's attitudes are so morbid that they consider suicide immoral. That's the unhealthiest and most contemptible attitude people can have, and I think we should be bitter about letting death make such jackasses of us. I'm eighty-five now, and I could have such a pleasant time deciding on the day and the arrangements for my own quitting, but the feeling of moral turpitude is so strong that my wife and daughters won't allow me to be happy. It annoys me that I'm not allowed to do a thing that would give me so much pleasure and so much satisfaction.[3]

May Stout had been a second mother to Rex and the others. Her death by suicide and, later, Betty's death by suicide, had made both Ruth and Rex fiercely defensive about suicide. It seemed as though to repudiate it would be to condemn those whom they had loved. Could that have been the outlook Lucetta evolved when her sister Clara took her own life?

A few days later, in the San Francisco *Chronicle,* Charles McCabe pointed out a parallel between Rex's views and those of Montaigne, who found it natural, in old age, to "enter into a certain loathing and disdain of life" and to deplore the hubbub others raised as they saw a loved one slipping away. "A good man deserves more than a decent burial," said McCabe. "He deserves a decent death." Rex found this view reasonable. For him, McCabe's invocation of Montaigne was irresistible.

When Ruth Stout read Shenker's interview, and notwithstanding medical problems of her own, she wrote Rex one of her piquant letters:

If in a moment of doubt, you wonder if you have ever done anything worthwhile for anybody, here is one thing you've done for me. Strangely enough, lying here with shingles, I find that reading bores me — even Dostoyevsky. Well, believe it or not, Nero & Archie never bore me. I read nothing but your books, but very, very slowly, because I want them to last. I read a sentence, close my eyes, then read another. But don't feel too sorry for me — I'm not really as desperate as all that sounds. In fact, I'm not desperate at all. Now to my favorite — *The Doorbell Rang* — [4]

In the weeks that followed, Rex's interest in life quickened again. When the Shenker interview was mentioned by callers and correspondents, Pola could see Rex was displeased with himself for having let himself be interviewed when he was not feeling well. To me, Rex expressed himself on the subject in these terms: "To be in terror of the unknown is one thing, but to be in terror of something that is absolutely certain to happen is so damn silly. My attitude toward suicide is not based on a personal inclination. I could see myself in that situation but, God knows, I haven't come within a thousand miles of it yet. I love life. I don't want to die. But to have a constant dread of death — such a waste of nervous energy. My Lord!"

With the headache ordeal behind him, life was expanding again in meaning for Rex. Presently, when Nancy Timms arrived for her secretarial stint, she would find him dressed and sitting in his favorite corner on the living room plateau, by the unused fireplace. He kept the abandoned manuscript in view on the table next to him. No one spoke to him about it. He had it there to remind himself that there was work to be done.

In December, Rex had an electric chair-lift installed to take him to and from his upstairs office. Nancy was there when it came and he insisted that she ride up and down on it. He was not embarrassed by his dependency on it. He needed it. He accepted it. That was his way. Yet he did scheme to get those around him to use the lift too. He knew the joy Archie felt in springing up the stairs while Wolfe had his bulk carried aloft in his private elevator. He missed that independence. When others rode the lift he felt less isolated by his infirmities. "Does it make you feel more Wolfean to have your own elevator?" I asked him. "I don't feel 'Wolfean,'" he snapped.

In the days that followed, Nancy saw that Rex was prone now to bestir himself when some item needed fetching. He was gaining daily in stamina. She found him easy to be with. "That would be logical," he would say when she said she didn't know something he asked her about. "He would never let me feel stupid when I made a mistake," she said. "He would remind me that he had sixty years' experience on me."

Nancy was amazed she could work so well with a man sixty-two years older than she was. "Despite all his years of experience," she said, "he is a very down-to-earth person to talk with. He's a warm, friendly person. When I'd be leaving he'd say, 'Goodbye, darlin',' and throw me a kiss." Once he asked her if she could recite the alphabet backward. To his surprise, she could. Nancy didn't know then that Julie Jaquette, in *Death of a Doxy,* could perform this same feat. And that Rex could too.

In the fiftieth anniversary issue of the *Authors' Guild Bulletin* — February-March 1972 — the Guild president, Herbert Mitgang, wrote:

We are dedicating this special anniversary issue of the *Bulletin* to Rex Stout, our longtime leader, inspirer, chairman of the membership committee, holder of numerous public service offices, distinguished writer, and friend. If authors and dramatists could confer official honors instead of only a few kind words, Rex would receive the Medal of Freedom from grateful writers and colleagues. The records show that when President Eisenhower signed the Universal Copyright

Convention, Rex Stout, John P. Marquand and Herman Wouk stood watch for the Guild. Rex has continued to stand watch for creators everywhere. No wonder he comes from an Indiana town called Noblesville.

The March issue of Indiana University's *Library Newsletter* also was interested in Rex Stout. It recalled, with warm approval, Nero Wolfe's destruction, in *Gambit,* of Webster's *Third International Dictionary.* Delighted to find other admirers of Wolfe's "verbal captiousness," Dean Fraser, chairman of the Department of Microbiology, wrote to the *Newsletter*'s editor, Neil S. Boardman, lauding Rex as "the best contemporary writer of detective stories," and urging that Indiana give him an honorary degree. In May, Boardman published a lengthy piece of his own recommending Rex for a degree. Rex appreciated Indiana's goodwill but uniformly declined honorary degrees. He explained, "They are given so promiscuously that they are meaningless."

In February Rex had again picked up work on *Please Pass the Guilt.* Writing in longhand, he found no great difference in the results, but each page was a day's work. He was thankful to reach the bottom of the page. As pages accumulated, Nancy began typing them. At Rex's suggestion, she triple-spaced. He expected to go from this version to a final, double-spaced version. The precaution proved superfluous. As usual, first time around he got the story down the way he wanted it.

He wrote in pencil — minuscule script, on lined paper. Sometimes he even wrote up the sides of the pages. Nancy frequently got two typewritten pages to his one written one. He did not dictate any part of the book, though rumors would circulate that he did. Nancy always worked from his manuscript copy.

At first he had no title. It was just "the book." "Then all at once," Nancy said, "in a letter he was writing to you, he spoke of it as *Please Pass the Guilt* — and from that time on, that was it."[5] "A couple of times he asked me if I thought it was up-to-date," Nancy said. "I told him it was fantastic." When April came, Rex put the book aside for the summer. For the first time in several years he was interested again in his garden.[6]

In March, Nancy had told Rex she was going to be married in May. "If you quit smoking, I'll go to your wedding," he said. That surprised her because at the start of every work session, he always offered her one of his cigars. At his insistence now, she brought her fiancé, Darrell Lutrus, to High Meadow to meet him. Rex asked him his nationality. When he said Lithuanian, Rex held forth knowledgeably on Lithuania. Then he found out Darrell was an angler, and fishing became their topic. Rex knew all about that, too. When Darrell was leaving, he found he had locked his keys in his car and came in to the house for a coat hanger. Rex went out to watch him open his car with the hanger. That was something Rex didn't know anything about. "When I'm feeling better," he told Darrell, "I want you to show me how you did that."

Marlene Dietrich wrote Rex early in July. She was a Wolfe fan. She excoriated the German translations: "They try to copy the jargon of Archie — frightful." Archie intrigued her: "I know how he looks. A bit like Burt Bacharach, but *taller*. If I were young and a man, I could play Archie better than anyone."[7] Barbara and Than came to dinner that night. Twice during the meal Rex drew a furious look from Pola by addressing her, "Marlene . . . eh, that is, Pola. . . ."

On 11 July Rex and Harold went over to Poverty Hollow to see Ruth and Mary and to partake of Ruth's fricassee and dumplings — Rex's first social visit away from High Meadow in almost three years. For a side dish, Ruth served soybeans from her celebrated garden.[8] Rex never had grown soybeans. In the middle of the meal he left the table to go out to the garden to see them growing.

Through the summer Nancy Timms continued to help Rex with his correspondence. During broadcasts of the Fischer-Spassky chess match, they worked in the lower living room. With the aid of a magnetic chessboard, Rex followed the match on television, moving his chessmen to the same positions. Between moves, he dictated letters. He would turn off the sound, then turn it on to get the move. Once they lost track of moves and Rex had to wait till next morning to find out what he had missed. Sometimes when Nancy was leaving, Rex would go off to the garden with her and load her down with chives and shallots.

In October Rex picked up again with *Please Pass the Guilt*. The tempo of the work accelerated. He found writing a welcome alternative to thinking about the presidential campaign then unfolding. When McGovern dropped Eagleton as his running mate, Rex's faith in him sank to zero. Archie shared Rex's reaction. When I sent him greetings for his birthday, on 23 October, Archie wrote back to me: "Thank you very much for your good wishes. I need them right now because I'm crabby. I like to vote and I don't see how I can next week, for a jerk like Nixon or a sap like McGovern. Nuts." When Barbara and Than held a house party to raise funds for McGovern, Ruth came, and Mary sent a check. Pola came too, and auctioned off a bracelet she had had since girlhood. At the end of the evening the buyer restored it to her. The party raised $4,000 for the campaign. Only one thing had been lacking to make the evening a triumph. Rex had stayed home.

After the election, thinking it unlikely that he could survive four more years of Nixon, Rex updated his will. For this project, he relied on two lawyers — "Irwin Karp for his technical knowledge about writers' income and property, and Clark Hull of Danbury for his knowledge of Connecticut law." Hull was then lieutenant governor of Connecticut.

On 10 December, at seventy-eight, Mark Van Doren died of a heart attack. Despite his practiced forbearance, Rex felt the wrench of parting. "With Mark gone," he told me, "my old and dearest friends are about cleared out." On 20 December he wrote to Dorothy Van Doren: "Of course Mark was yours, but he was ours too. I didn't fully realize while he was alive how highly I esteemed him and how much I loved him. He would have understood because he came close to understanding everything."[9]

"Archie," Mark said, in July, five months before his death, "is Rex himself. They are identical in brightness, in cockiness, in learning, in hatred of sentiment, in directness and sharpness of speech. I often hear Rex talking between Archie's sentences, or for that matter in them." He probed the ambience of Nero Wolfe's world:

The sameness of the settings — the house, the plant room, the front stoop, the front door with its chain, the office with its chairs . . . the priceless operators who come and go with highly specific assignments (Saul Panzer *et al.*), the ever-present Inspector Cramer and the burly Sergeant Stebbins . . . you would think all this sameness would wear thin, but it doesn't. Reason: the intelligence of Archie who is Rex, and the brilliance of Rex when it comes to telling stories. . . .

There are times when Nero equals Rex. . . . As a matter of fact there are plenty of correspondences between him and Wolfe. . . .

Rex is a perfect writer — economical, rapid, free of cliché. Epigrammatic, intelligent, charming. What else? That's enough.[10]

In December, Nicaragua issued twelve stamps commemorating twelve fictional detectives. Only four living authors — Agatha Christie, Georges Simenon, Ellery Queen (Frederic Dannay), and Rex Stout — were honored by having their creations chosen. Wolfe's likeness appeared on a twenty-five-centavo stamp, his creator's name in prominent view on the spine of a book beside Wolfe's portrait. Archie got a mention on the licking side of the stamp.

The writing went on. Through December Nancy walked up in snowstorms to leave off or fetch pages. With each visit Rex gave her an increasing number of pages. Sometimes she could scarcely believe how many he had for her. His new stamina impressed her. Now he could work till six-thirty P.M. and show no strain. She was amazed to see how little revision was needed. A phrase here. A word there. That was all.

On the afternoon of 26 January, Rex finished the book. Viking was jubilant. Alan Green's reaction said it all. "For Rex to write of the youth revolution as freely and convincingly as he does in *Please Pass the Guilt* is amazing," he said. "It's one thing to know about it — another to write about it."

Alan had a further reason to rejoice. Rex had told him he was dissatisfied with *Death of a Dude*. He did not think it was a good book. He had wanted *Please Pass the Guilt* to be a better book, one with which the saga could end forcefully if no further volumes should follow. Alan thought Rex had done what he set out to do. *Please Pass the Guilt* was published on 24 September. Reviewer opinion upheld Alan's judgment. Many reviewers, realizing that Rex soon would be eighty-seven, read the book as the final episode in the saga. They were glad to find Wolfe secure in his brownstone, his wits intact, his resourcefulness undiminished. Like the figures Keats contemplated on a Grecian urn, Archie and Wolfe could live forever in our memories, awaiting another summons to service.

In *The New York Times Book Review* Frank Jellinek pronounced a verdict — "Wolfe solves cases by reasoning and deduction rather purer than Sherlock Holmes" — and issued an invitation — "Nearly forty years of detection from the old brownstone is long enough to have established a canon which should now merit the sort of studies devoted to the sacred writings of Dr. Watson."[11] Never before had *The New York Times* given a full page to a Wolfe novel. Jellinek's judgment had been free of qualifying reservations. Rex understood its significance. He had beaten the odds. He had lived long enough to know that his Nero Wolfe stories would be read and revered for generations to come.

52.

Sage of High Meadow

Rex Nero Wolfe Stout has given me many hours of pleasure and psycho-therapeutic sedation. In keeping with the spirit of the times, I am prepared to accept bids now from any of the drug companies who might wish to use an advertising slogan, "Dr. Karl Menninger states that next to Nero Wolfe, *our* hypnotic arsenal is the best in the business." What worries me is the double entendre here; they might think that a book which puts people to sleep is a dull book. Far from it. I want a book that's so exciting that I fall to sleep in spite of it. That's what Rex Stout supplies. In the night I work out a solution and sleep peacefully.

— KARL MENNINGER

While Rex was writing the last pages of *Please Pass the Guilt* his mail brought surprising news. James Marvin, director of the Topeka Public Library, announced that the library was undertaking to bring together, for its new Topeka Room, the world's most complete Rex Stout collection. "I wish I had known about it in 1903," Rex said, and went back to work.

Several weeks later Rex again heard from Topeka. This time the news was disquieting. Stricken with heart failure, David Overmyer had died at a Topeka hospital on 26 March. On his desk he had left unfinished a letter he had been writing about his boyhood days with Rex Stout. David's early ambitions had been realized. His vast murals graced the ground-floor rotunda in the State Capitol at Topeka and a dozen other state buildings in Kansas. Now he was gone. For Rex, the tie with Topeka that had lasted longest had been broken.[1]

On 24 April Robert Cromie came to High Meadow to tape a television interview with Rex for his Chicago-based "Book Beat" program. Would Rex keep on with the Wolfe series, Cromie wanted to know. The question was an awkward one, but Rex had a way of making people forget how old he was. He made the best of the situation. "I understand," he said, "I've been told (this is a rumor), that after you're cremated it's pretty hard to write stories."[2] David Overmyer's loss seems to have made Rex keenly aware that the race was almost run. His age still was much in his thoughts when the portrait photographer Jill Krementz came by to photograph him for her gallery of famous authors. "How old are you?" he asked. "Thirty-three," she said. "My God," said Rex, "there isn't a generation gap between you and me — there are two!"

More and more Rex enjoyed being alone. To ambitious correspondents, he wrote: "In my ninth decade I forgo the pleasure of making visits or receiving visitors." Yet mentally he was not retreating from life. Pola found his perceptions deepening with age. Speculations entertained over long years were coming to fruition. Family intimacy attained a new richness. At Rex's suggestion, a housekeeper — Hortensia Noel, a West Indian — was found so that Pola could pick up again with projects in designing which she had dropped during the period of Rex's illnesses. A gentle, sparse woman, nothing like the hulking black woman who showed up to clean Wolfe's brownstone in *Please Pass the Guilt*, Hortensia understood the punctilious nature of the master of High Meadow and was never a moment off schedule in serving his meals. She owned mystification, however, that Rex sometimes lingered two hours over lunch when he ate alone. She concluded that he got lost in thought. Her unobtrusive competence pleased him. One day he came into the kitchen. "Hortensia," he said, "don't you ever drop *anything?*"

Rex's personal habits remained much what they had been. He told me: "Since I built High Meadow I've gone to bed regularly at eleven o'clock. I sleep with the windows open. I require about nine hours' sleep a night — yes, like Archie. I never took naps the first eighty-three years. I do now sometimes, but don't like to because it takes me a full hour to get awake after only a one-hour nap. All my life it has taken me about fifty-two seconds to be sound asleep; it still does." Rex still got up at eight-fourteen and brushed his hair and beard before breakfast.

For thirty-five years Rex smoked a pack of cigarettes a day. He told me: "In 1948 I quit smoking cigarettes with little difficulty. In 1958 I started smoking cigars, and haven't quit." During most of that time he smoked Gold Label Barcelonas — forty cents each. In 1973, after I mentioned to him that some of his friends thought his Barcelonas smelled like five-cent stogies, he switched to Monte Cruz — ninety cents each. "They are," he assured me, "the best I can find anywhere." Rex's letters were always impregnated with the smell of cigar smoke till June of 1975, when he finally gave up smoking for good.

Dr. Than Selleck, Jr.'s, death in 1959 had halted Rex's career as a sportsman. There had been little in it to excite the *Guinness Book of Records* because Rex had always felt exercise should come as the byproduct of other meaningful activities. Among spectator sports, baseball alone had absorbed him: his baseball knowledge was encyclopedic. In 1964 he stopped going to games. Thereafter he followed baseball on TV. He relented in his detestation of that medium even to the point of hailing the advent of color TV because it enabled him to see fast grounders better. His interest in chess lasted too. At eighty-seven he still played chess by mail with Samuel Grafton. He considered himself an orthodox player but sometimes allowed himself an unconventional move. One night in April 1973, his son-in-law, Than Selleck, beat him at chess. Than had never done that before. Even though it was eleven o'clock, Rex asked for an instant rematch — with Than using the same opening he had used before. Than gave no quarter. But Rex went to bed a winner.[3]

After a four-year lapse, Rex went back to gardening that spring. Gone were the days when he could shame Richard and Frances Lockridge, darting over slope and gully while they came panting behind him. But he found a way to cope. He bought a golf cart. With that as an energy resource he could double his gardening effort without exhausting himself. "He stoops by the hour," Barbara said, "stoops and doesn't move an inch while he's working in one spot. I don't know how he does it." Rex was not impressed. "I work in the garden from eleven to twelve and from two to five," he said. "Formerly, I worked about double that." He told me: "It's a goddamn nuisance that physically I've had to let up a lot, but mentally not at all. The result is that my mind works a lot faster than my tongue will. I used to be a pretty good talker, but not any more. My tongue doesn't work well enough. The mind does." I asked him if he had found a pet name for his golf cart. He gave me the sort of answer I would have expected to get from Nero Wolfe: "I *don't* give names to machines." As far as I could see, his tongue was working well enough.

I had come in June so I could see the iris blooming. I had come from New York, where I had gone to tape interviews with some of his friends.

"I'm glad you got out of New York with a whole skin."

"I did. Everything went okay. I found some of those people easier to interview than I thought I would."

"Whatever you do, if you do it with conviction it will be accepted."

We talked about human affairs and human destiny:

Are we closer to world government than we were twenty-five years ago?

We are closer either to world government or to the final blowup, and toss a coin.

Do you think we have to adopt a policy of triage, directing aid only to those countries with the greatest prospects of survival?

Unless and until an effective worldwide effort is made to reduce and keep reduced the number of people on earth, all humanitarian feeding of people in hungry countries and all efforts to prolong the span of human life do more harm than good. Of course my sympathies and instincts deplore and reject that statement, but my intelligence insists on it.

Do you believe in capital punishment?

Yes. With qualifications, of course. Furor about abolishing capital punishment is jejune. It's childish.

Do you believe in ameliorative evolution?

No. It would be nice work if we could get it.

Are you a deist, agnostic, or atheist?

An agnostic.

Do you believe there is a cosmic intelligence in the universe?

A superhuman force of some sort? Obviously there is one. The things that make up the universe — they're there. We didn't create them.

Do you believe in an afterlife?

Improbable, right to the edge of absurdity.

Do you think most men would be better off without a church affiliation?

Depends on the man. The function of revealed religion is to meet a need, and evidently I don't need it. I might if I live long enough.

Do you see man as mechanistically determined?

Don't know. No one does. But I'm not a follower of Spencer. If man is mechanistically determined, the causes and impulses are so unimaginably numerous and complex that they can never be charted, so what difference does it make? The mechanics and their complications are infinite, never to be discoverable, so you can't box me (or anyone) in.

Have you ever tried meditation as an avenue to new perceptions?

I meditated once for about three minutes, but nothing happened.

When did you cease to think of yourself as a Quaker?

At eleven or twelve I became an agnostic. In a way I still think of myself as a Quaker, which may sound silly but isn't. Quaker background and influence must be an essential part of me. But I don't know in what way.

Who is your favorite philosopher?

Professionals, Protagoras. Amateurs, Montaigne.

In A Right to Die, *Wolfe says: "Probably no man will ever corral truth, but Protagoras came closer to it than Plato." Do you agree?*

Yes. And I had a letter afterwards from a professor of ancient history at Cornell, who said that he agreed with Wolfe.

Simenon says it's a mistake for him to deal in abstract ideas, however simple. Is that true of you, too?

A "mistake," no. But when, in contemplation or conversation, I am on an abstraction, I soon find myself on a particular, a specific, an instance.

Judge Learned Hand said he had faith in "the eventual supremacy of reason." Do you?

No, and I certainly wouldn't wish such a fate on posterity.

In Please Pass the Guilt *Archie says: "One of my basic opinions is that people who take things for granted should be helped to a better understanding of democracy." One of yours, too?*

Yes. I would qualify it, but there are damned few statements I wouldn't qualify.

What do you think of efforts to revive Indian culture in America?

Nothing is more futile than efforts by Indians to continue to act like Indians, except perhaps efforts by Christians to act like Christians.

What do you see as some of the benefits of a life lived close to Nature?

I can speak only with reference to myself. With a Napoleon, a James Boswell, or a Bob Dylan, I doubt if there would have been any. With me, obviously it helps to see trees and grass and birds frequently, I have no idea why. During the twenty-one years I lived in New York I always could — across the street from Morningside Park, across the street from Central Park, and at the three addresses in Greenwich Village never more than a three-minute walk from Washington Square. The three and a half years that I had an apartment in New York during the war it was at Fifty-five East Eighty-sixth Street, a two-minute walk to Central Park. Obviously the sight of trees and grass and birds is a real need for me, but I don't know why. I could do a pretty good panegyric on it, but it would be just a writing stunt.

What are your views on nudity?

In favorable circumstance — the milieu, the kind of body, good weather, the audience, the intent — nudity is wonderful. People in nudist parks must be pathetic creatures.

A French philosopher said: "Marry a woman who makes good conversation. In time everything else goes, but the conversation stays till the end." Your comment?

Just talk. Rather good talk, but just talk. I talk a little, too, for instance: "Never marry a woman until you have seen her eat an egg sandwich with her fingers and drink from a bottle."

Have you accepted "Ms."?

I hate it. I think women should have something for that purpose that doesn't indicate their marital status, but I just do not like the look or sound of "Ms." I refuse to use it, but I suppose I shouldn't. I don't like "chairperson" either, but I can't suggest a good alternative. I wish women would accept "man" as a term covering both sexes, but I don't blame them for not wanting to.[4]

If the choice was yours, what period of history would you like to live in?

This one.[5]

What has been the happiest period of your life?

From 1889 to 1973.[6]

What do you want most to be remembered for?

If I say A, it's sort of a disservice to B. If someone asked you which fruit you liked best, how could you say oranges when you remembered how you liked apples? How could you say apples when you remembered how you liked pears? The trouble with that question is that it creates negatives.

The thing I'd most like to be remembered for . . . the stories I've written. I could say the time and trouble and expense I went to in fighting Hitler and Hitlerism, but God, there were so many people who did that . . . there aren't so many people who've written my stories . . . only I wrote those — a lot of other people have written some damn good stories, but they didn't write mine. One reason I would pick the stories is that a man would like to have what he feels is a firm estimate of the status, and the standing, and the worthiness of the work he's done — a writer or a painter would, of course — and the trouble with that goddamn desire is that the basis on which a decision can be made he can never apply . . . to base it on your own estimate is goddamn nonsense, just worthless. My own estimate is pointless, doesn't mean anything. The estimate of the critics — doesn't mean a goddamn thing. Readers, and letters received, give some indication. The only real indication of the standing of the stories I've written can't be known for another fifty or sixty years.

Of the things you've done in your life, what are you proudest of?

That I have helped more than I have hurt. Don't ask me for documentary evidence.

What makes you angry?

The abrogation of human rights, injustice, hypocrisy, waste.

Will your remains be cremated?

My will says to cremate and scatter the ashes in my garden here. The cadaver is merely matter that has served its purpose. It is refuse, debris. What remains that still has life and meaning is in the hearts and minds of people — or, of course, something that was produced by him or her.

Can Watergate be thought of as a real-life detective story of breathtaking dimensions — one in which the culprit, the master criminal, is the President of the United States himself?

Yes, indeed.

The next morning Rex handed me a sheet of labels on each of which he had written his name together with an apparently arbitrary word. One read, "harsh/Rex Stout," another, "rude/Rex Stout," another, "crude/Rex Stout." "Paste those in your Wolfe books," he said. "Another Rex Stout mystery?" I asked. "If you think so," he said. I figured it out the next day. If the labels were arranged in a certain sequence the words read, "I come to pluck your berries harsh and crude,/And with forc'd fingers rude . . . ," from the opening lines of Milton's "Lycidas."

That summer Rebecca and Bill spent July at High Meadow, their first visit East in two years. One afternoon Rebecca went blackberrying. When she came back with a pail of berries, Rex asked her what she meant to do with them. Before she could answer, he volunteered, "A blackberry pie would be delicious." She made him one. In two days he ate the whole of it, having it at breakfast, lunch, and dinner till it was gone.

"Stout's vast detective, Nero Wolfe, became fat in the most delectable way — he eats like Lucullus," Alan Green told *Saturday Review* readers on 29 January 1972. Green promised them that the *Nero Wolfe Cookbook* would be "served up" soon by Viking. When the cookbook did appear, on 8 August 1973, Rex said in his introduction, "Barbara Burn's name should be on the title page. The comments and explanations in italics are all by her, as well as the final wording of most of the recipes. . . . She also tested, or supervised the testing of, many of the dishes." That latter role called for some heroism. Barbara confesses: "The corn fritters alone took about fifteen testings, though that was partially because I just like corn fritters a lot. It took me at least a year to lose those extra pounds from testing the recipes."[7]

Some of the recipes, especially those in *Too Many Cooks,* had originated with the late Sheila Hibben, for many years *The New Yorker*'s food authority. Rex had paid her two thousand dollars for them. Together they had tested them, some several times over. As her recipes suggest, Sheila Hibben was not the product of a country kitchen. One January day when she came out to High Meadow for a cooking session, Rex fetched her from the station. As they rode along, she commented: "The country is so wonderful like this, without all those goddamn leaves obstructing the view." Sheila was one of the few women Harold Ross liked.

The *Cookbook* contains more than two hundred and twenty-five recipes. Mrs. Vail's baked beans is not among them. In a book which includes recipes for Cassoulet Castelnaudary and Eggs Boulangère there was no feasible way of extending gourmet status to New England baked beans. Asked what recipe he would recommend to a condemned man who wanted to eat his last meal from the *Cookbook,* Rex chose Roast Pheasant. Barbara Burn concurs but suggests the inclusion as well of the fatally attractive corn fritters (no problem to someone soon to be dead), Avocado Todhunter, and, for dessert, Green Tomato Pie. Not every dish Rex relished is found in the *Cookbook.* Asked what items he would most like to find in a gourmet gift package, Rex said: "First, fresh Beluga caviar. Second, fresh Beluga caviar. Then *pâté de foie gras,* Bar-le-Duc jelly, black walnuts, turtle soup."

On 9 August, in a full-page illustrated article in *The New York Times,* John Hess greeted the newest Stout volume as "the year's most forgivable gimmick cookbook." Although Hess opined that Simenon's Madame Maigret set a better table than Wolfe, he refrained from suggesting that Maigret's superior fare made him a superior detective.

In "Alimentary, My Dear Watson," Nelson W. Polsby, in the August

Harper's, noting Wolfe's indifference to delicacies offered in Manhattan itself, came to a painful conclusion: "Wolfe suffers from a mild case of culinary anti-Semitism." In sorrow more than anger, he added: "This is truly anomalous in the palate of a practicing liberal of the heart and head, as Wolfe clearly is." *Newsday's* Robert Wiemer advised readers to treat the book "as another novel in the series." He further proposed that Stout fans organize themselves into "the Rusterman's Regulars." "The purpose of this organization," he said, "will be to enjoy food cooked in the Brenner style, to enjoy conversation in the Wolfe style, and to enjoy ourselves in the Archie Goodwin style."

Rita Delfiner interviewed Rex for the New York *Post* one afternoon in late August. Rex spoke of the advantages of being eighty-six: "In one way it's more fun to look at pretty girls than when you're in your fifties. Because when you're in your eighties, you can look at a pretty girl with appreciation without aspiration." Rita asked if she simply must have an atomizer to apply the dressing to Wolfe's avocado-on-nasturtium-leaves salad. "Better buy one," Rex said.

Readers wondered how Rex could eat as Nero Wolfe eats and reach eighty-seven. Of course he did not. He never had. In later years he became almost ascetic in his diet. "Without his being aware of it," Pola told me, "his routine of eating changed much much more as he grew older." Rex told me, "I take one vitamin capsule a day because Pola thinks I should." Much of what he ate came from his own garden. He scorned health foods. "They are," he said, "misnamed, ill-born, and ill-bred."[8]

One longtime friend who would have liked the *Cookbook* never saw it. The day before the book was published, Maxwell ("Mac") Kriendler died at Mount Sinai Hospital. Rex had known Mac since "Fight for Freedom" days and had served with him on the board of Freedom House. Mac's famous 21 Club, an elaborate brownstone at 21 West Fifty-second Street, had been the site of many of the board's dinner meetings from the founding of Freedom House. On his visits to Kriendler's brownstone, Rex did not feel he was dining at West Thirty-fifth Street. Nor did he feel as much at ease as Wolfe feels on visits to Rusterman's. "I don't like places," he said, "where most of the customers have come only to be seen there."

The week the *Cookbook* appeared Rex signed a contract that would keep fifty-four of his titles in print till 1980. That meant he had more books in print than any other American author, living or dead.[9] His sales already had gone past the one hundred million mark. In England alone, more than ten million copies of his books had been sold since 1954. In that same period, 2,567,966 had been sold in Germany, 1,801,897 in Italy, and 177,093 in Sweden. Moreover, in August a Paris publisher would contract to bring out new editions of twenty-four titles in France, where Stout sales always had been brisk. In 1972, contracts had been signed to publish the stories in Greek and Hungarian. Nero Wolfe now could be read in twenty-six foreign languages, including Spanish, Dutch, Hebrew, Flemish, Portuguese, Singhalese, Czech, Danish, Finnish, Japanese, Norwegian, Slovenian, Serbo-Croat, Polish, Hindi, and four different Russian languages. The foreign titles sometimes are droll: for example, *Los Amores de Goodwin (The Silent Speaker); Ce bébé est pour vous (The Mother Hunt); Ein dicker Mann trinkt Bier (Fer-de-Lance).* Rex took no role in choosing these titles.[10] He told me: "I am not interested in any of the details of the foreign editions of my books, and only glance briefly at the copies I receive." Yet in his office he kept copies of each of them. The Ceylon edition of *The Golden Spiders* did delight him. He was told that no other detective story had ever been translated into Singhalese.

Along with the *Cookbook* and *Please Pass the Guilt,* in 1973 Viking brought out *Three Trumps,* its sixth Nero Wolfe omnibus. When an eighty-seven-year-old author publishes three books in six months, that's news. *Publishers Weekly* thought so and gave two pages to Rex in October. Seven of Jill Krementz's soul-searching photos — including one of Rex at work in his office — made the article eye-catching. To John F. Baker, who supplied an interview to accompany the pictures, Rex said, "No man my age writes books."[11]

Originally a young woman from *Publishers Weekly* had gone to High Meadow to gather material for the magazine's tribute to Rex. Rex found her abrasive. "Do you like the way you let Nero exploit Archie Goodwin?" she asked. His visitor, Rex decided, was "a leftist-activist of some variety."

"What are you talking about?" he growled. "Archie Goodwin exploits Nero Wolfe."

"Oh, you're just trying to be funny," the Ms. said.

"Not at all. Archie Goodwin would have no trouble at all getting along without Nero Wolfe. He'd have a real good time. Nero Wolfe would have a devil of a time getting along without Archie."

In the summer of 1973, a new book began taking shape in Rex's mind. Watergate supplied him his theme. By October he had the first three chapters in his head. In November, sitting in his bentwood rocker on the living room plateau, he wrote a few pages. Then he laid the manuscript aside. He had reached a sticking point.

53·

Hip Hooroy, You Bearded Boy

Rex Stout was one of God's angry men. He was prolific with his talent, profligate with his energy, passionate with his convictions; a loyal friend, an unforgiving enemy and a total, complete "original."
They better keep things in order in Heaven or Rex'll raise hell.

— DORE SCHARY

We were such fans of Rex Stout. He brought us enormous pleasure and excitement. I think we have read everything he ever wrote — including *A Family Affair*. And now we have just been told that he is dead. Our hearts are heavy.

— ALFRED LUNT AND LYNN FONTANNE

As he advanced into his ninth decade, Rex narrowed the number of publications he went to for world news and current opinion. His chief resource remained *The New York Times*, which every day he read from first page to last. He owned: "I subscribe to eleven magazines, but don't read them much, except *Time, The New Yorker,* and *Sports Illustrated.*" On 4 February 1974, Rex cocked an eyebrow when *Sports Illustrated* carried a letter from "Rex Stout" analyzing the declining performance of the Philadelphia Flyers' Rick MacLeish. Rex did not follow hockey, and had not written the letter.

Stout apocrypha on a more spectacular scale appeared just two weeks later in the Washington *Post.* On 18 February, the *Post* gave half its editorial page to "18 1/2 Missing Minutes; A 'Nero Wolfe' Mystery," a short story by Lawrence Meyer. In Meyer's story, at Wolfe's bidding, Archie brings Richard M. Nixon from White House to brownstone to give an account of the eighteen-and-a-half-minute erasure on the tape of his 20 June 1972 conversation with H. R. Haldeman. Wolfe's interrogation points to Nixon's involvement in the Watergate cover-up. Rex did not know beforehand of Meyer's stunt. When he saw it, he commented: "Nero Wolfe wouldn't use 'perpetrator,' and he would never use such a cliché as 'strains the imagination.' But on the whole it's a pretty good job."

Reorganization in 1964 had reduced the membership of the Authors' Guild to 2,285. As chairman of the membership committee, Rex pushed recruitment with such vigor that the tally by 1969 stood at 3,252. When a mere sixty were added to the rolls in 1971, Rex, unwilling to allow that his illness took momentum from the drive, reminded members that 1971 had been a recession year. Working with the Guild's Jean Wynne, who came out to High Meadow several times a year to go over each stage of the program with him, he then redoubled recruitment efforts. At the annual meeting, in February 1974, the Guild's executive secretary, Peter Heggie, was able to announce that membership had topped 4,000. Rex showed his satisfaction by setting 5,000 as the new target number.[1]

Meanwhile Rex was making a contribution to a drama being enacted in Maine. At Westbrook, a women's college in Portland, the student council had voted to allow male visitors to remain overnight in the dorms. Westbrook's president, James Dickinson, rejected the plan. That night successive delegations of students rang his doorbell. Dickinson wrote Rex an account of what ensued: "After an exchange of views with them, Mrs. Dickinson and I stopped answering the doorbell. We sat like Wolfe and Archie at the end of *The Doorbell Rang* and I paraphrased Wolfe — 'Let them get sore fingers.' "[2]

To Andrea Vaucher, who, undeterred by February snows, sought him out for an interview, Rex said of himself: "I would describe my 'life-style' today the way I would have sixty years ago. I do the things each day that either interest me or need to be done. That's always been my 'life-style.' There are two basic reasons for doing anything — one, because you want to and two, because you need to."

Having received letters from a Methodist bishop, Herbert Welch, and from Leland Stark, the Episcopal Bishop of Newark, Rex told me he seemed to have progressed further with Protestant churchmen than with the Catholic hierarchy. Then a laudatory letter, dated 21 February 1974, was received from John Cardinal Wright, a member of the Vatican Curia.[3] Rex was impressed: "So we've got a cardinal, and a tiptop one. I glow." Then, with Holmesian speculativeness, he added, "Do you suppose there's any chance that His Holi — . . . no, I guess not."

In mid-April Rex revealed to me the unique fate of the novel he had halted work on the previous November:

> I've scrapped an idea for a story after writing a few pages — something I had never done before. The idea was murder of an electronics expert because it was suspected that he was going to disclose that he had been paid $10,000 to alter some of the Nixon tapes. I suspended proceeding until I could decide if it was believable, and now of course it isn't. It's obvious that the altering was bungled and therefore wasn't done by an expert (I think Nixon did it himself because Haldeman probably would have done a better job). So I'll monkey around the garden until I get a usable idea.

I asked Rex if Lawrence Meyer's unwitting incursion into the same area for his Wolfe parody had shorted his circuitry. He said it had not.

Please Pass the Guilt was published on 1 May in England. The Manchester *Guardian* marked the event with a full-page interview secured by Raymond Gardner on an April visit to High Meadow. Gardner had arrived to find Rex ailing with a bellyache, and cursing loudly at his discomfiture: "If my stomach wants to act up this way I'll fool it by putting nothing in the goddamn place. That'll show it. . . . When our insides try to discipline us we have to discipline them, by God, to show who's in control." He sounded like General George C. Patton.

Solicitous for his host, the British visitor got quickly down to cases. Where did Rex get his characters from? Rex told him:

> I never make up characters. I never contrive them. I know damn well that if I bring someone into a story — I don't care if it's just a man carrying a ladder — unless I'm interested in him then the reader can't be. So if I'm tempted to make up a character just to save time I wait till I get there and let him make up his mind what he's like. Now that sounds funny; impossible even. But any half-ways decent storyteller knows that as far as possible you let the characters make the decisions.[4]

Gardner came away feeling he had been dealing with Archie, not Wolfe. The Rex Stout of his interview had breezy American ways. Gardner conceded that Rex knew how to brew a proper cup of tea, but found Rex more bracing than tea. He even rebuked *The New York Times* for saying that Simenon's Maigret eats better than Wolfe. "Nonsense," he insisted. "The Wolfe/Brenner diet is altogether more stimulating than *cuisine bourgeoise.*" Prudently he refrained from speculating on the origins of Rex's bellyache.

Long the target of Colonel McCormick's editorial tirades in the Chicago *Tribune*, Rex saw the wheel come full turn when the *Tribune*, on the last Sunday of July 1974, presented its "Book World" insert as a "Special Rex Stout Issue."[5] Along with reviews of *Triple Zeck* — the newest Wolfe omnibus — and the *Cookbook*, by Nelson Polsby and John Hess, it contained an interview conducted by Timothy Dickinson and Rhoda Koenig, a reflective appraisal of Wolfe by the *Tribune*'s Sunday editor, Robert Goldsborough, a Nerophile Quiz, a photo of Rex, a silhouette of Wolfe, and, here and there, blocked off and set in italics, thumbnail tributes from a dozen other writers, including fellow Hoosier Kurt Vonnegut, Jr.

In August Rex found another Wolfe story taking shape in his mind. "It's the best plot I've ever thought of," he told me. But he had no intention of starting it while the garden continued to provide him with chores. Other matters kept him from writing, too. He had been following with intense interest the events that led up to the resignation of Richard Nixon. He said, "I can't ever remember more interesting things happening than are happening now. Except for personal things, I never in all my life have had such a feeling of relief as I'm having about Nixon. My God, he was a dangerous man. He was unquestionably the greatest danger that ever occurred to American democracy."

In early September Rex gave this tally of Wolfe's current reading: "Three books about the impeachment of Nixon, including the final report of the House Judiciary Committee. Two books about the impeachment of Warren Hastings. Two books on the trial of Charles I. Of course making comparisons." By mid-October, there was a slight shift in direction: "Wolfe is reading everything he can get his hands on about Richard Nixon, trying to decide how such a monumental jackass reached eminence in a democracy." He spoke of the novel in prospect: "I haven't turned my mind loose on it, but I probably shall do so soon, now that we've had heavy frost." Those close to him wondered if Wolfe's current reading, which Rex Stout tended to duplicate, would be a resource for the new book. He seemed to be closing in, from another direction, on the theme abandoned the previous April.

The signals were up. Rex was getting ready to write again. Before he began work, however, he received one last visitor: Colin Graham, who had just arrived from England to direct the Metropolitan Opera's first production of *Death in Venice* and had written ahead asking to see him.

"I was curious to meet the man who directed a hundred operas at Covent Garden," Rex told me. On his visit Graham revealed that he was writing a book-length critique on the Wolfe saga. He did not realize that he was the last outsider Rex would receive. Finding Graham a satisfactory note to end on, Rex rang down the final curtain on that phase of his life.

Rex was pleased with the sudden upsurge of interest in his works. He was flattered that Graham wanted to do a book on his stories. He was mystified too. He told me: "The books I've written have something in them that makes them distinctive. Obviously, or there wouldn't be all these goddamn articles and things, and I wouldn't get all these letters. I don't know whether its the characters, the ingenuity of the stories, something about my basic attitude toward people and life that comes out in them. I don't know what the hell it is. I'm afraid I'll never know while I live."

On Tuesday night, 5 November, John Farrar died at his home in Manhattan.[6] The year had swept away many old friends — Margaret Leech Pulitzer, Jean Poletti, and Ed Fadiman, who had died of injuries sustained in a car crash. Rex first knew of Farrar's death when he read about it in *The New York Times,* on the seventh. One way to pay tribute to John was to perpetuate the things he believed in. Rex, in fact, was already doing that. John had launched the Nero Wolfe series. Rex had another Wolfe novel under way. He had begun writing it the previous afternoon.

By 23 November, writing in a minuscule hand, Rex had accumulated forty pages of manuscript. I offered to discontinue my weekly questionnaires while he was writing. Rex protested: "Send them. I won't let things pile up while I'm writing a story. I pay bills even more promptly than usual. But the answers will be short; some may even be brusque."

On the twenty-eighth, Barbara and Than, with their sons, Chris and Reed, joined Rex and Pola at High Meadow for Thanksgiving dinner. Rex gave himself a holiday. Asked what Nero Wolfe was reading currently, he said: "Nothing, because Archie won't let him. They're on a case." The following Sunday Rex entered his eighty-ninth year. Through the day there were phone calls from well-wishers. Earlier in the week there had been calls from would-be interviewers. Wanting to conserve his energy for writing, Rex begged off.

Since the three surviving Stouts had entered their eighties, verses had flown among them on their birthdays — a revival of the family fun they had had writing and producing home theatricals. When Mary turned eighty, in September 1968, Rex wrote her:

> *Eighty years! I knew that you*
> *Would face it, not evade it;*
> *And what you write is very true —*
> *I know; because I've made it.*

When Rex reached eighty-five, Ruth cheered him in similar terms:

> *If you are gay, or if you're sad*
> *Time doesn't stop — it goes.*
> *Well, eighty-five is not too bad.*
> *Take it from one who knows.*

Rex thought that that rated a reply:

> *No, eighty-five is not too bad,*
> *And also not too tough;*
> *But here now says this veteran lad:*
> *It surely is enough.*

> *Oh-oh and oops; that's much too rough*
> *To get me into heaven —*
> *Saying that eighty-five's enough*
> *To a girl of eighty-seven!*

The allusion to an afterlife gave Ruth her theme for the year following:

> *When you have got to eighty-six —*
> *Well, I admit, you're in a fix.*
> *But think of those at eighty-eight*
> *Standing there at heaven's gate.*
> *Heaven or hell — whichever one*
> *Might even be a bit of fun.*

She signed herself "The Optimist." Rex's reply matched her mood:

> *If eighty-eight is not too late,*
> *Then eighty-six is early.*
> *So hip hooroy, you bearded boy,*
> *And hip hooroo, you girlie.*

Told that his friends were betting he would touch one hundred and twenty-five, Rex said, "I will *not* go on to one hundred and twenty-five, I hope. Good Lord, I would weigh about eighty pounds. I now weigh twenty pounds less than I weighed for sixty years but feel as if I were all still here. Nonsense."

On his birthday, Rex kept to his writing schedule. Seated in his bentwood rocker by the always-unlighted fireplace, his back to the window, but with the light pouring in from the court, he added two and a half pages to the book. Pola had bought a quart of Mumm's Cordon Rouge, Brut, but held off opening it till after dinner, when Barbara and Than were able to come by for a visit. "To drink so much champagne ourselves," Pola exclaimed, "our heads would have been swimming!"

Early in December Rex phoned Nancy Timms Lutrus to ask if she would be interested in typing his new story. "Wonderful," he roared when she said she would love to. She picked up the first forty pages on the afternoon of 3 December. When Rex gave her the manuscript, he said, "If you lose it, I'll have to write it over. And I'm not sure if I'd shoot myself, or you, or both of us." Nancy told him, "If that happened I'd shoot myself for you." Rex wanted to be brought up to date on Nancy's activities. They talked, too, about Nixon and Watergate. "He said something very important to me when we finished our conversation," Nancy told me. "He said, 'I'm glad you're the one that's twenty-seven, and not me.' "

Nancy could see no change in Rex's writing methods since *Please Pass the Guilt:* "Same size writing, same lined paper (also I'm using the same exact typing he likes). Even the same margins. Some little additions (not really changes). The only different thing was he wrote me a little note on the side of the paper — he wanted me to try setting up a part on a separate piece of paper first." Rex's handwritten manuscripts always were done on lined paper. Once when Georges Simenon showed him one of his manuscripts, Rex was astonished to see that, though the paper was unlined, Simenon's script was not a fraction out of line.

Nancy had found Rex healthy and happy and pleased with the new story. When she began reading it she could see why. "He doesn't need to ask me if it is contemporary enough this time," she said. "It couldn't be any more up-to-date and he knows it. I just love all of it. He constantly has so many good sharp lines that I laugh out loud while I'm typing it." His forty manuscript pages ran to fifty-one in typescript.

On 21 December Rex called Nancy to say he had another forty pages ready. "Of course you know who the murderer is?" he said, when he saw her. "No," she said.

Nancy brought back the second batch of fifty-one pages on 30 December. "He wondered," she said, "why I typed the second group faster than the first. I got so involved in the story and so excited that I guess my fingers got the point and typed even faster."

Rex took careful note of what Nancy was wearing and, if it was something he had not seen before, asked about it. On 30 December she was wearing a new navy blue nylon jacket that her husband had given her for Christmas. "We made a thorough examination of it," Nancy related, "except for the hood, which has fake fur on the edge. We didn't talk about *that.*"

When Rex had a third of the book written, he began to think of it as *A Family Affair.* While writing he followed a strenuous regimen. He wrote each afternoon. After dinner he napped from seven-thirty to nine, then got up and wrote till midnight. No one had to wake him; he roused himself. As this work advanced, he got an intestinal upset. In the past he had never written when he felt unwell. He hesitated this time, then said to Pola, "If I write, then I may forget it." And he went back to writing. He had forty-one pages for Nancy on 4 January. He then wrote fourteen more pages, finishing the book with a characteristic sprint on 6 January.

Nancy saw that the book held firm to the end. Yet she paused over one closing passage. Cramer twirls Wolfe's huge terrestrial globe. He explains that in doing this he has given in to an age-old impulse. Then he says, "I've never mentioned that this is the best working room I know. The best-looking. I mention it now because I may never see it again." He has threatened to revoke Wolfe's license. Ostensibly he is talking about that. But there is a valedictory ring to his words. Rex Stout seemed to realize that he, too, had made his last visit to the brownstone on West Thirty-fifth Street.

Nancy brought the final typed pages to High Meadow on 16 January. The next day, Rex mailed the manuscript to Viking.

In *A Family Affair,* Wolfe is plunged into a case engendered in the dark womb of Watergate. Violence erupts in the brownstone itself, the refuge where Wolfe, by choice, has remained agreeably immured during most of the past fifty years. Eventually the clues lead Wolfe away from Watergate, back through his own portals, to confront a villain who is an extension of himself. Within his own close circle Wolfe discovers corruption. When he makes this discovery, he does not condone at the brownstone a cover-up he could not tolerate at the White House. He is not a hypocrite. He recognizes that the reign of justice cannot come to pass in society-at-large if justice is not insisted on at the familial level. Painful though the decision is for him, he purges his family of its taint. The last lesson Wolfe teaches us is the greatest lesson Rex Stout learned from life. For sake of truth and justice we must be prepared to receive the thorn.

At the close of *The Doorbell Rang*, Wolfe left J. Edgar Hoover standing on the front stoop of the brownstone, his door shut against him. When he has wanted to, Wolfe always has shown the world his back. In *A Family Affair* Wolfe arrives at a new sense of man's mutual interdependence. When Watergate climaxed in the resignation of Richard M. Nixon, Rex said, "We all are to blame. We didn't fight hard enough for the things we believe in."[7] At the end of *A Family Affair* the front door of the brownstone is shattered, reminding Wolfe that our responsibilities carry beyond our own threshold. We may shun the reality of evil. In the end, it will seek us out. Wolfe does not flinch from this truth. When Cramer charges him with responsibility for the death of Orrie Cather, Wolfe says:

"I won't challenge your right to put it like that. Of course I would put it differently. I might say that the ultimate responsibility for his death rests with the performance of the genes at the instant of conception, but that could be construed as a rejection of free will, and I do *not* reject it. If it pleases you to say that I killed him, I won't contend."[8]

Wolfe agrees in essence with the great colonialist Perry Miller's avowal that "the mind of man is the basic fact in human history." How man uses that mind will determine the future of humanity and perhaps the future of the planet itself.

"There is," says Leon, the renegade priest in Graham Greene's *Honorary Consul,* "a sort of comfort in reading a story where one knows what the end will be. The story of a dream world where justice is always done."[9] Leon is speaking of the English detective story he is reading. In *A Family Affair* justice prevails. Wolfe does his duty and cleans his own house. But something is changed for good and always. Wolfe is compelled to realize that we cannot isolate ourselves from the rest of mankind. The tide of chaos has reached our doors.

Alphabetically *A Family Affair* stands first among the seventy-two Nero Wolfe stories, in a sense closing the cycle. The cycle could not end on a more solid note.

After Rex finished *A Family Affair,* he told me, "I'm a little concerned that Orrie Cather's implication might be too obvious too soon." It is not. In *Death of a Doxy,* and earlier, Orrie had been guilty of misconduct, but he had been assigned no major criminal role. Somehow you think he is in the clear again. Mary Stewart speaks for all readers of the saga when she says: "At the end of the book, and *only* then, you realize that you had seen it coming. You should have seen it coming long ago." Rex's artistry did not fail him. He did not disappoint those expectations which caused a first printing of twenty thousand copies of *A Family Affair* to be sold out before publication day.

During Rex's eighty-ninth year death would reap a great harvest among friends acquired through a long lifetime — Elizabeth Schnemayer, Maude Snyder, Julia Sanderson, Lawrence Blochman, Paul Ruffles, Alan Green, Fredric March, Amy Vanderbilt, Kathryn Dreher, Katherine Gauss Jackson, James Sheldon, P. G. Wodehouse.[10] As the tally mounted, Pola found him serene yet pensive. He told her one evening, "I think my father would be pleased at the way we are ending our life together. We have had the same love, same dependence, same feeling for one another, all these years." His parents' marriage had been a shambles. By offering his own successful marriage in reparation, Rex, at the close of his quest for a consequential life, was making his final bid for his father's good opinion.

Their marriage had, in fact, been a happy one. Joan Kahn, of Harper & Row, who knew Rex before there was a Nero Wolfe in his life and knew Pola before there was a Rex Stout in her life, found both Rex and Pola "remarkably pure in heart." Joan conjectures that Pola's devotion must have been a tremendous resource for Rex.[11]

Pola explains: "We always respected one another. He let me be me." She never felt that Rex expected her to Americanize her ways to fit into his world. Barbara would enjoy calling her "my Continental mother." Indeed, her accent persisted. Rex never sought to correct it. On the contrary, he learned many Polish expressions from her and was apt to use her language for the salutations and intimate terms of endearment that passed between them. His gifts to her were always aesthetic gifts — jewelry often — for many years a brooch. One year, however, he gave her a nude statuette of the Egyptian goddess Hathor for her New York studio. The next year, in a rare episode of absent-mindedness, he duplicated the gift. His daughters did not let him forget the slip. It was one of the few things they ever had on him.

To the astonishment of Lina Derecktor, when her friends gave her a surprise birthday party, at her home in Katonah, New York, on 29

March 1975, there was Rex seated among the guests — "serene, majestic, smiling in such an amused way." She ran forward and threw her arms around him. She knew how seldom he came down "off the hill" now and guessed rightly that it had been years since he had gone out for a social evening other than within his immediate family circle. For an old friend, Pola had passed a miracle.[12]

Rex began the planting season with his usual confidence. At the end of April he was working in his garden, with Harold, "two or three hours" each day. He thought he could do better. "It has been too damned cold and windy," he explained. "Soon it will be more." In mid-May he decided to add another dozen irises to his collection. But at the end of May he was attacked by a pervasive nummular eczema and stopped going out-of-doors. "The itching is intolerable," he told me, "and keeps me occupied most of the day and night." Even then, however, he estimated the odds of beginning another Nero Wolfe novel the coming November — "If I get rid of the eczema, and I hope and expect to, even money."

Not until mid-June was an antihistamine found — Periactin — which was effective in stopping the torment. Even this remedy exacted a price. Rex said: "The Periactin twisted my nerves into a knot that is stubborn. But it's more bearable than the damned itch." In mid-July he disclosed: "The itch is gone and the nerves are in order, but I haven't resumed garden work." He was, in fact, beset with graver encroachments. Several months earlier he had become sightless in his left eye. During the period of the eczema he had lost entirely the hearing in his left ear. Now in the long, hot dog days, his breathing became labored. Than Selleck had an oxygen tank placed beside his chair to support him when the attacks were at their most acute.

On 18 August I called Rex to set a time to go over the final pages of the manuscript of the biography, which he had been reading through the spring and summer as the chapters came from my typewriter. "Come tomorrow morning," he said, "there's a fifty-fifty chance I'll still be breathing."

Rex was alert and cheerful for the visit. Seated in the durable bentwood rocker, by the fireplace, he spoke with vigor. But he had a new consciousness of age. "I just don't see anybody," he said. "I don't want to. It takes energy. The necessity at eighty-eight of pretending that you're only fifty-eight — and it *is* a psychological necessity; you just can't help it — well, to *hell* with it. I'm not interested in the effort. I'd much rather stay here and look around at things and read books. I haven't got the energy. I'm on the slide."

He ate an ample lunch: chicken salad, a sliced boiled egg, a pale Rhine wine. He said he had reread *Emma* recently. He showed me a bookcase of Honduras mahogany which Harold and he had made in

March, to hold his new *Britannica* and the two volumes of *Who's Who.* He chortled when he opened a letter from Marlene Dietrich and read that the president of France, Valéry Giscard d'Estaing, is an avid reader of the Nero Wolfe stories.[13] Next, he sang a chorus of "O Careless Love," to give me an idea of the lyrics and, as he pointed out, the limitations of his singing voice.

Then, with a curious surge of energy, Rex suddenly mustered himself to speak to me about publishers. He spoke with the vigor and conviction of a man in his prime. Pola was as astonished as I was as the words flowed trippingly from his tongue: "One of the first things you have to learn, if you haven't already learned it, is never hesitate to tell a publisher to go to hell. Don't think publishers won't take that. You're damn right they'll take it. With a publisher you should always begin with the assumption that you're practically tied up with a moron, and proceed on that basis. The chief reason for that up until now has been this — all publishers have loved to regard themselves as important intellectual and aesthetic people. But they are under a constant necessity of running a profitable business, of being — a good businessman. And the two just don't go together. The result is that many many times what a publisher does or says is just a lot of goddamn nonsense, because he hasn't made the necessary effort to combine those two requisites of a good publisher.

"A good publisher should have excellent taste, excellent judgment, and great knowledge of what has been published before. Also he should be a good soap salesman. Well there aren't many men who answer that description, you know. Goddamn few. The most famous that I know of was Alfred Knopf. Alfred Knopf could. He had both of those attributes. But very few publishers do.

"John Farrar was very knowledgable, and also not a bad businessman. Stan Rinehart was a very good businessman but really knew very little about the rest of it. I remember a dinner party at Stan Rinehart's house once, where there were, I don't know, a dozen of us at the table, and we were discussing the Nobel prize. And I said, 'No, it would be all right sometime for O'Neill, the dramatist, to get a Nobel prize, but this year they should not have given it to O'Neill. If they wanted to give it to an American they should have given it to Theodore Dreiser.' Well, John Farrar knew immediately exactly what I meant and why. And Stan Rinehart hadn't the slightest idea why I had said that. Most publishers are like Stan. So handle them rough."

The remaining hours of the afternoon were given over to an appraisal of the manuscript. At the end of that session Rex took time to go through an album of baseball cards with my eleven-year-old son, Jay, gravely consulting with him on the plan he followed in arranging them, and on the Red Sox's chances for winning the pennant. He gave Jay a hug when I took their picture together. As always, his rapport with youth was superb. When we left in the early evening, he came along with us as far as the plant passageway. We paused to look at an orchid. He said it was a *Brassocattleya Calypso*. It was blooming a second time for him. Finally he was making headway with orchids. He clasped my hand in a firm grip. I bussed him on the cheek. "Your paternal blessing . . . ," I said. He grinned and said, "Why, of course. . . ."

I wondered if I would see him again. I was not hopeful. On his dresser, in his bedroom, I had counted thirty-eight separate medications. Pola said he was taking twenty pills a day.

Rex had been weighing the idea of letting himself be interviewed on the ABC "AM America" television program, in late August, as part of the promotion buildup for *A Family Affair*, due out on 8 September. "If I do," he told me, "it'll be kind of a swan song, of course." He did not make the broadcast. Instead, he entered Danbury Hospital. His medications had created problems of fluid retention. Complications extended in several directions. Any one of six ailments carried a lethiferous threat. The powerful machine was at last giving out. Rex, as usual, insisted on a full account of the problems he faced and of methods for dealing with them. When he knew where he stood he asked that no extraordinary measures be taken to prolong his life. His immediate problems were regulated and he was kept comfortable. He read *The New York Times* every day and sometimes worked the crossword puzzle. Barbara brought him a copy of the newly published *A Gang of Pecksniffs* by H. L. Mencken.[14] He read it through — the last of the avalanche of books he had dealt with in his long lifetime. A copy of Agatha Christie's *Curtain*, on his bedstand, lay unread. In August he had been looking forward to it. But not now. He was happy to be quiet. His mind remained alert but he preferred to rest and do nothing.

Rex came home to High Meadow at the end of the first week of October. He sat in his rocker again on the living room plateau and sometimes would walk to the kitchen nearby, or to his bedroom. His fine woolen shirts, made from Pola's spectrum fabrics, kept him snug against the chill of a week of rains. He knew time was running out. "It's all right," he told Rebecca; "I've had my money's worth." To Pola, in a final surrender of masculine logic to feminine good sense, he whispered a conclusion he had reached long years before: "You don't need me to tell you what to do. Rely on your intuitions. They are good and will carry you through."

During the weeks of crisis, Pola, with no thought of herself, had spent much of her time at the hospital. The strain told. Physically used up, she at last had to share her vigil with Rebecca and Harold. And now Ann Johnston, the nurse who had attended Bernard Baruch in his last illness, joined the household, to see after Rex's medical needs.

Sometimes Rebecca read his mail to him. "I am 'holding the thought' for you," Grace Overmyer wrote. "I know you will remember that your mother used to say that." For Marion Wilcox he inscribed two copies of *A Family Affair*. For the Stout collection, at the Topeka Public Library, he inscribed another. He talked to Rebecca about the biography and passed along bits of information to be included in it. On television he followed the most exciting World Series in years. On the night of 21 October he told himself he would watch the game until the fourth inning. This was the breathtaking sixth game, won by the Red Sox at twelve thirty-three in the morning, when Carlton Fisk homered in the twelfth inning. Rex watched till the end. He thought it was baseball at its finest. Yet he was glad when long-denied Cincinnati took the series the next day. He had never wavered in his loyalty to the National League.

On Friday, 24 October, Rex seemed well enough for Rebecca to fly home to California. Barbara came over to be with him. Ann Johnston would be there, as usual, each night. Harold was within easy call. And so was Alice Wallace, who had succeeded to Hortensia Noel's role as cook and housekeeper.

Than Selleck was at High Meadow throughout the day on Sunday, and in the evening Barbara and he were joined by Barbara's two older children, Liz and Reed, and Peter Driscoll, Liz's current beau. Throughout the afternoon, Rex had kept his place in his bentwood rocker, on the living room plateau. His mind continued clear. "You know how my will reads," he told Than. "Scatter the ashes in the garden." To Than he owned that it distressed him to realize our bodies serve us with increasing inefficiency as we grow older, and at last break down. He seemed to be drifting out of reach of those frail supports holding him to life.

For his dinner Barbara and Than decided Rex should have those things he had a special fondness for. With daughter, son-in-law physician, and the three young people sharing in his meal, Rex, in good cheer, supped that night on Beluga caviar, *pâté de foie à la strasbourgeoise*, and white Burgundy (Montrachet) brought to him by Rebecca on her recent visit.

Before bedtime, Rex spoke to Than of the *Phaedo* of Plato, and of the account given there of the dignified end of Socrates, who knew he had come to the close of his days and, among friends, chose, without perturbation or bitterness, the moment of his exit. Rex knew that the *Phaedo* offered considerations on immortality which every future generation has relied on to strengthen its belief in an afterlife, but he did not espouse them. Plato's endorsement of the Pythagorean doctrine of transmigration of souls, and his account of the soul condemned to return in the body of a fox or a wolf, held no attraction for him. He stated anew to Than his belief that the measure of our immortality is given in the quality of the life we have lived. The contribution made by a worthwhile life extends our existence. Beyond that, nothing is certain.

To Than, Rex's mood seemed the mood of Socrates. Rex understood that he had come to the bottom of the cup of life and he was making his peaceful farewells. Than decided to stay on with him through the night. For a time, in his room adjacent to the plant passageway, where a cymbidium had put forth a single, majestic bloom, Rex slept peacefully in the fine American walnut bed he had built years before. At five-thirty in the morning, his life signs began to ebb. At eight, with his grandson Chris looking on, he died in Than's arms.

Plato ended the *Phaedo* with the words "Such was the end, Echecrates, of our friend, whom I may truly call the wisest and justest and best of all the men whom I have ever known." Rex Stout was such a man. And there are many men alive who would say so. But Rex neither expected nor desired that. If the good he had done lived on, to him that would have seemed the fullest of rewards and the most valid of eulogies. He looked for nothing more.

In midmorning, Than drove to Poverty Hollow to tell Ruth that Rex was gone. "That's all right," Ruth said, at ninety-two comforting her comforter. "If he wasn't himself what was the use of his staying around? He wouldn't have liked it." She told Than she would break the news to Mary. With Mary, empathy ran deep. Ruth said she would find a way of telling her that would help her bear up. Than knew she could manage it. Yet, twenty-four hours later, after the whole world knew that Rex Stout was dead, Ruth still was trying to think of a way to tell Mary. Stoicism is hard to apply when you have lost someone you have known and loved for eighty-nine years.

Radio and news programs across the world had begun broadcasting the news of Rex's death in midevening, Monday night — "The American Conan Doyle is dead," CBS told its listeners at eight o'clock. The next morning, Alden Whitman's tender obituary was front-page news in *The New York Times* — "Rex Stout, Creator of Nero Wolfe, Dead." On the ABC Evening News, Harry Reasoner told a nationwide television audience:

The news today was as usual full of politicians and other movers and shakers. But the odds are overwhelming that when historians look at the bright blue late October of 1975 the only thing they will keep about the 27th is that it was the day Rex Stout died and the 28th was the day the death was reported. Rex Stout was a lot of things during his eighty-eight years, but the main thing he was was the writer of forty-six mystery novels about Nero Wolfe and Archie Goodwin. A lot of more pretentious writers have less claim on our culture and our allegiance.[15]

That same day, the latest issue of *Time* appeared on the newsstands. It carried a review of *A Family Affair,* which lauded Rex's "elastic, contemporary mind" and his capacity "to confound the actuarial tables."[16]

A rainstorm was lashing the hill when Rex's ashes were brought back to High Meadow on Thursday. At noon, Saturday, Allhallows' Day, Harold Salmon scattered some of them in the garden where Rex and he had worked together during forty-five summers. Under thinning clouds, the gray light of the lingering storm had given way to lambent sunshine. All Souls' Day dawned fair. That morning — on a day when the dead anciently have been kept in remembrance — Pola went alone to the foot of the great white oak that shelters the slope below the croquet court. There Rex and she had exchanged their first kiss. In that place she secreted some of the ashes under the sod. Barbara and Than carried the remaining portion back to West Redding. In the sacramental dusk of that Indian summer day, Than scattered this last unction of ashes over the raddled earth where, in April, daffodils would bloom.

Notes

In the Beginning

1. In *Might as Well Be Dead* (1956) Rex wrote: "Paul Herold had a three-inch scar on his left leg, on the inside of the knee, from a boyhood accident. . . . It had made him 4F and kept him out of war" (p. 8).

1. Rootstock and Genes — The Stouts

1. "I've never been much interested in genealogy, but you've found out that my great-grandfather seven times removed, John Stout, lived, in Shakespeare's time, at Burton Joyce, in Nottinghamshire, just sixty miles from Stratford-upon-Avon. Quite possibly he saw him, or heard him speak. I'm sorry I didn't find that out a long while ago. It would have been fun all my life to know that." RS

2. Morgan Edwards, *Materials Toward a History of the Baptists in Jersey*, Philadelphia, 1792. Henry C. Green and Mary W. Green, *Pioneer Mothers of America*, Philadelphia, 1912, III, 388–391. John T. Cunningham, *Colonial Heritage*, vol. 3, no. 7 (November 1972): 2. Margaret O'Connell, *Jersey's Story*, Chicago, 1958, pp. 30–32. Claude D. Stout, *Richard and Penelope Stout*, Palmyra, Wisconsin, 1974. Published in the author's ninety-fourth year. Deborah Crawford, *Four Women in a Violent Time*, New York, 1970. Wayne D. Stout, *Our Pioneer Ancestors*, Salt Lake City, 1944, pp. 19–20. Conversations and correspondence with Deborah Crawford, Admiral Herald F. Stout, Professor William Giffin, Indiana State University, and Professor Francis Jennings, chairman of the History Department, Cedar Crest College, Pennsylvania, supplied further clarifications.

3. *Encyclopedia of American Quaker Genealogy*, ed. William Wade Hinshaw, Ann Arbor, 1936–1946, 5 vols. *Carolina Quakers*, edited by Seth B. Hinshaw and Mary Edith Hinshaw, Greensboro, South Carolina, 1972. Herald F. Stout, *Stout and Allied Families*, Dover, Ohio, 1951. Correspondence with Ernest H. Stout, genealogist, Trenton, N.J.

4. Loren Scott Noblitt and Minnie Walls Noblitt, *Down the Centuries with the Noblitts, 1180–1955*, Greenfield, Indiana, 1956, pp. 51–55. Asked if he thought he had any characteristics passed down to him from his Huguenot forebears, Rex said: "See my trilogy on genes."

5. George Pence, "Makers of Bartholomew County," *Indiana Magazine of History*, 22 (1926): 70–73. John A. Keith, "History of Bartholomew County," *Illustrated Historical Atlas of Bartholomew County*, 1879, pp. 6, 14. See also "Excellence in Indiana," *Architectural Forum*, August 1962; "The Town that Architecture Made Famous," *Architectural Forum*, December 1965; "An Inspired Renaissance in Indiana," *Life*, 17 November

1967; "The Athens of the Prairie is a Rare Architectural Oasis," *New York Times,* 22 March 1970; "Athens on the Prairie," *Saturday Evening Post,* 21 March 1964; "Design for Belonging," *Saturday Review,* 21 August 1971.

6. Brant and Fuller, *History of Bartholomew County,* Chicago, 1888, pp. 258, 575. B. F. Bowen, *Biographical Record of Bartholomew and Brown Counties, Indiana,* 1904, p. 125.

7. Willa Swengle to JM, 12 July 1974. In 1975, Grace Overmyer and Margaret Salb located the grave of Regina Swengel [sic] at Reddington Cemetery, near Seymour, Indiana. The inscription on the headstone reads: "Regina Swengel/D. January 10, 1875/86 years. 5 mo. 29 da."

8. John Wallace Stout, then twenty years old, was serving in Mexico with the U.S. Infantry — Company F, Indiana Infantry — when his nephew and namesake was born on 8 April 1848. On 20 April he wrote from Napaluca to his friend William Harrison Terrill, Jr., an editor of the Columbus *Gazette:* "While I write my pen *curls* up with the most devout reverence, indignation, respect and esteem for your *loving kindness* and *extraordinary* activity in writing letters and sending papers. . . . I have had the pleasure of *not* receiving a paper from you or anybody else since the 1st of January last; neither have I had the *dis*pleasure of receiving a letter from you since 1847!!!"

A second letter, sent from Brazos, Santiago, 3 September 1848, to Terrill, finds J. W. in poor health, but still droll and flippant:

> Two Jackasses were appointed 2d and 4th Sergeants by Capt. FitzGibbon. When the men protested that it was their privilege to choose their own officers, FitzGibbon thundered: *"By God, I have appointed the two sergeants and that is sufficient!"* Let any man, when I come back (if I ever do), talk to me of FitzGibbon's "kindness, generosity, goodness, and love for his men, and his disinterested benevolence" and I will knock him down if I am able. . . . I could tell that about Capt. F. that would *lower* him so in the estimation of the people of B[artholomew] C[ounty] that the inspired pen of the Angel Gabriel could not bring him into notice. . . .

R. E. Banta, in *Indiana Authors and Their Books, 1816–1916,* Crawfordsville, Indiana, 1849, says the Cincinnati *Gazette,* 7 December 1876, called attention to "a spirited and very racy account of the services of the Fourth Indiana [Regiment] while serving in Mexico," written by J. W. Stout. No copy is extant. J. W. may not have had the makings of a propagandist of the stature Rex Stout, his grandnephew, reached in World War II, but this sole writer on the Stout side of the family, had a liveliness when expressing himself that the creator of Archie Goodwin relished when I showed him these letters.

9. Accounts of Stout's mill appear in notes given to Rex Stout by his first cousin, Clarence Wickersham, in 1916, and in issues of the Seymour *Weekly Democrat,* dated 20 January 1881, 3 March 1881, 19 January 1882, and 2 February 1882. The destruction of the mill was reported in the Seymour *Daily Republican* in issues appearing on 22, 26, and 27 February 1912, and in the Indianapolis *News,* 27 February 1912.

2. Rootstock and Genes — Todhunters

1. Colonel John F. Todhunter, Bures St. Mary, Suffolk, England, Todhunter family historian.

2. George E. McCracken, *The Welcome Claimants Proved, Disproved, and Doubtful*, Baltimore, 1970, pp. 426–427. Gilbert Cope, *Genealogy of the Smedley Family*, Lancaster, Pa., 1901, pp. 117–119. Gilbert Cope and Henry Graham Ashmead, *Chester and Delaware Counties*, Pennsylvania, New York, 1904, pp. 49–50. Francis S. McIlhenny, Jr., and Mrs. Virgil Lindstrom, officers of the Hoopes Family Organization.

3. Cordelia Todhunter Ballard, *The Todhunter Family in America*, Wilmington, Ohio, 1947. *The History of Perry Township*, 1882, pp. 776–777. Hinshaw, *Encyclopedia of American Quaker Genealogy*, V, "Ohio."

4. *Dill's History of Fayette County*, 1881.

5. Thomas Wright, *The Life of Daniel Defoe*, London, 1894, pp. 26, 237, 348; John Robert Moore, *Daniel Defoe: Citizen of the Modern World*, Chicago, 1958, pp. 10–11. Wright thought that Elizabeth (1700–1782) was Defoe's niece. Moore rejects this claim. Elizabeth's grandson was named Daniel Defoe Job in token of Elizabeth's claim of kinship to Defoe.

6. Information supplied by Elizabeth Ellis Miller from the genealogical papers of her uncle, Howard Ellis; and George Robinson, Washington Court House, Ohio.

7. The original of Reverend Richard Lanum's letter is owned by Mabel Barrett Todhunter, Clara's niece.

8. The original of Daniel McNeal's letter is owned by his great-granddaughter, Adda Burnett Meyer.

9. John Frederick Dorman, Fellow, American Society of Genealogists.

10. Ballard, *The Todhunter Family in America;* Howard Ellis papers; family sources: Mabel Barrett Todhunter, Willis Todhunter Ballard, Elizabeth Ellis Miller, Adda Burnett Meyer, Burnett Meyer, Natalie Stout Carr. Frank Rhoades Ambler and Mary Grace Ambler, *The Ambler Family of Pennsylvania*, Jenkintown, Pennsylvania, 1968. Carl Van Doren, *Jane Mecom: The Favorite Sister of Benjamin Franklin*, New York, 1950, pp. 21–27. Bernard Fay, *Franklin: The Apostle of Modern Times*, Boston, 1929, pp. 75–77, 114, 124. Others who assisted me in these inquiries were William B. Willcox, editor, The Papers of Benjamin Franklin, Yale University; Whitfield J. Bell, Jr., librarian, American Philosophical Society; L. Bancel La Farge; Professor Frances S. Childs.

3. Cabbages and Kings

1. Irene Miller, President, Hamilton County Historical Society; James T. Neal, editor, Noblesville *Daily Ledger;* Margaret R. Campbell, Terre Haute, Indiana; Bud Ayres, Greenfield *Daily Reporter,* Greenfield, Indiana.

2. Thomas L. Kelsay, Hydrologic Specialist, U.S. Weather Bureau, Indianapolis.

3. Pola Stout to JM, 28 October 1972.

4. Natalie Stout Carr to JM, 10 December 1972.

5. Family sources: Ruth Stout, Mabel Todhunter, Elizabeth Miller, Todhunter Ballard. Wilmington sources: Esther Doan Starbuck, Martha Jo Gregory, Tom J. Hunter, editor, Wilmington *News Journal.*

6. Mabel Todhunter, Esther Starbuck; Kathryn E. Williams, historian, Clinton County Historical Society; Professor Willis H. Hall, Department of History, Wilmington College.

7. Opal Thornburg, *Earlham: The Story of the College, 1847–1962*, Richmond, Indiana, 1963. Grade records and memoirs provided by Opal Thornburg, Earlham College Archivist, including manuscript reminiscences of Benjamin F. Trueblood, and William W. Thornburg, enrolled at Earlham, 1869–1872. Memoir of Alice Todhunter Burnett Bradley, prepared by her daughter, Adda Meyer, 22 September 1973.

8. John Stout was already familiar with Earlham. In October 1869, his only sister, Mary Ruth Stout, had married William Bailey Wickersham, who had graduated from Earlham in 1867.

9. In his files Rex had one of the original wedding announcements. It reads:

Married
July 22, 1875

John W. Stout   Lucetta E. Todhunter
Elizabethtown, Ind.   New Martinsburg, Ohio.

The names of the principals were elegantly set forth in Modified Old English Wedding Text. The use of modest Roman, Light Roman Italic, and French Roman types elsewhere in the announcement nonetheless produced a sense of restraint conforming in every way to strict Quaker norms. In arriving at this judgment I am grateful for the assistance of Robert Boyd, manager, Social Engraving Department, Shreve, Crump & Low Company, Boston, and John Black, vice president, Excelsior Engraving, Crane & Co., Inc.

4. John and Lucetta

1. Memoir, Adda Meyer.
2. Amy Overmyer to the Stouts, December 1940.
3. Rex also found it fascinating that Sophia took snuff.
4. Ruth Stout to JM, June 1972, October 1973, August 1974, August 1975, June 1976. See also: Ruth Stout, *As We Remember Mother*, New York, 1975.
5. Hiram Erastus Butler, *Solar Biology*, Applegate, California, 1888. Oscar was born on 4 July 1848. According to Butler, Oscar was sensitive, loving, and kind, and persevering if he did not have to work under the direction of others.

5. Stout Traits — Todhuntery Ways

1. Adel F. Throckmorton, *Kansas Educational Progress, 1858–1967*, Topeka, 1967, pp. 8–12. For this volume and much information relating to John Stout's career in public education in Kansas, and the schooling and daily life of his children there, I am indebted to John W. Ripley, editor of the *Bulletin of the Shawnee County Historical Society*. Ripley's *Legacy of Sam Radges*, Topeka, 1973, is a perfect introduction to Topeka in the years when the Stouts lived in Kansas.

Zula Bennington Greene, columnist for the Topeka *Daily Capital*, several times brought problems of Stout research to the attention of Topekans.

2. Young David was not his father's namesake. Hicks, his middle name, was the maiden name of his mother, Alice Hicks Overmyer.
3. Unpublished memoir prepared by J. Robert Stout in 1963, and made available to me by his daughter, Natalie Stout Carr. Henceforth cited as JR's Memoir.
4. Juanita Merle DeBrock to JM, 1 December 1974.

6. Everything Alive

1. For much of the information on the history of Wakarusa, I am indebted to Tom Muth, Assistant Director of the Topeka Public Library, and Curator of the Stout Collection. Wayne E. Corley, *County and Community Names in Kansas*, Topeka, 1962, p. 77. According to Mary E. Jackson, in *Topeka Pen and Camera Sketches*, Topeka, 1890, Wakarusa meant "big weeds." The stream was sluggish, and on its banks Jamestown weeds and sunflowers grew to great heights. Bill Weir, "Name Intrigues, but Wakarusa's History Quiet," *Topeka Journal*, 20 November 1954. The Wakarusa War, a confrontation between slave and free-soil elements, took place on 26 November 1855, east of the present town, which was not platted until 1868. Twelve hundred "ruffians," bent on attacking Lawrence, were persuaded to disband without bloodshed, by Governor Wilson Shannon. According to Major A. M. Harvey, who wrote *Trails and Tales of Wakarusa*, Topeka, 1917, "nothing important ever happened in Wakarusa." See also: "Wakarusa Industries," *The Bulletin of the Shawnee County Historical Society*, 31 (December 1958): 54–55; "A Visit to the Other Wakarusa," Wakarusa *Tribune*, Wakarusa, Indiana, 15 July 1959; Bessie Moore, "Two Townships in 1861," *Bulletin of the Shawnee County Historical Society*, 35 (June 1961): 69–70; A. T. Andreas, *History of the State of Kansas*, Chicago, 1883, pp. 531, 596–598; James L. King, *History of Shawnee County, Kansas and Representative Citizens*, Chicago, 1905, pp. 52–53; *The Kansas Historical Records Survey*, Inventory of the County Archives of Kansas, no. 89, Shawnee County, Topeka, 1940, pp. 16–19; John Thomas VanDerlip, *Wakarusa Whispers*, Wakarusa, 1917.
2. Mary Emily Stout, fourth daughter of Lucetta and John Stout, was born 28 September 1888. Mary Stout died 20 August 1977.
3. See also Rex's introduction to *The Game of Croquet, Its Appointments and Laws*, by Horace Scudder, edited and augmented by Paul Seabury, New York, 1968, pp. 7–8.
4. In part II of "Alias Nero Wolfe," a profile of Rex Stout published in *The New Yorker*, 23 July 1949, Alva Johnston says the pig belonged to Rex (p. 36). It was Walt's pig.
5. For this anecdote I am indebted to Frances Bellman Cox, longtime secretary to J. Robert Stout.
6. JR's Memoir.

7. Hackberry Hall

1. A large atlas always lay within arm's reach. Unlike Nero Wolfe, Emily Todhunter had no terrestrial globe.

2. *How Like a God,* New York, 1929, p. 4.
3. Nancy Timms Lutrus.
4. Oscar B. Todhunter, "Brazil: Discovery and Settlement," *The Earlham-ite,* June 1890, pp. 205–209. Oscar B. Todhunter, "Is It a New Science?" *The Earlhamite,* April 1891, pp. 147–151.
5. "We saw a good deal of our Uncle Oscar, and liked him." RS
6. John James Bradley, but always known to everyone as "J. J."
7. Memoir, Adda Meyer.
8. Cordelia Todhunter Ballard's son, Willis Todhunter Ballard, or "Tod," as he was known to the family, would be a powerful exemplar of Todhunter stamina and writing competence. Stricken with polio as he entered his teens, Tod resolutely dubbed himself "Hooks" to describe his crippled condition, and continued on with his education, graduating with honors from Wilmington College in 1926. He then began writing for *Black Mask* magazine and soon became a pivotal author in the *Black Mask* school, which Joseph T. Shaw, the editor of *Black Mask,* formed around Dashiell Hammett. Jim Anthony, the Super Detective, and the Phantom Detective were among Tod's productions in this period. He describes much of it as "formula writing." With the aid of a dictaphone he sometimes turned out forty pages in a day. Tod was in on the discovery of Raymond Chandler. When Chandler submitted his first detective story, "Blackmailers Don't Shoot," to *Black Mask,* late in 1933, Shaw passed it along to Tod for his assessment. Tod liked it and Chandler joined the *Black Mask* team. See Frank MacShane, *The Life of Raymond Chandler* (New York, 1976), p. 49.

   "Blackmailer's Don't Shoot" was published before *Fer-de-Lance,* the first Nero Wolfe story, was published. That is not significant. The Archie Goodwin tone did not show itself in Chandler's writing until he wrote "Goldfish," his tenth story. "Goldfish" appeared in *Black Mask* in June 1936. By then Archie Goodwin was well established.

   In the late 1920's Tod Ballard married Phoebe Dwiggins, daughter of the cartoonist Clare Dwiggins. Since that time Tod and Phoebe Ballard have written, between them, one hundred and fifteen novels, some inde-pendently, some in collaboration. They also scripted fifty movies and teleplays and wrote more than one thousand stories. Some of Tod's novels feature a tough-guy detective who shares attributes in common with Archie Goodwin.

   In *Plot It Yourself* (1959) Rex may have had Aunt Cordelia Ballard in mind when he created the resourceful executive secretary of the National Association of Authors and Dramatists, Cora Ballard. But Cora also resem-bles Luise Sillcox, the executive secretary of the Author's League. See *Plot It Yourself,* p. 52.
9. Elizabeth Miller to JM, 16 October 1973.
10. Margaret Egan Todhunter to JM, 7 October 1972; 11 March 1974.
11. "The Chautauqua salute was rendered by standing and waving handker-chiefs — a gesture to express love and admiration." Mabel Todhunter to JM, 14 October 1972.
12. *Too Many Cooks* (1938), pp. 166–167. Here, Wolfe, addressing a black youth enrolled at Howard University, said: "I remind you that Paul Lau-rence Dunbar said 'the best thing a 'possum ever does is fill an empty belly.'" Surprised, the young man asked him, "Do you know Dunbar?" Wolfe answered, "Certainly, I am not a barbarian."

8. Mr. Brilliance

1. "Populist Party Name History," Topeka *Daily Capital*, 20 May 1972.
2. Topeka *Daily Capital*, 22 August 1897.
3. Unpublished memoir prepared by David Hicks Overmyer, 2 November 1972.
4. Hoke Norris, Director of Public Relations, Chicago Public Library, to JM, 13 August 1974. See also Norris's *The Treasures of All Knowledge*, Chicago, 1972, pp. 5–6, and Carl B. Roden, *Thirty-seventh Annual Report*, Chicago Public Library, 1908–1909, p. 13. In 1871, as acting librarian and secretary to the library's board of directors, William Bailey Wickersham had set up Chicago's first public reading room. He was secretary both to the library and the board until his death in 1908.
5. "Who's Who — And Why," *Saturday Evening Post*, 19 October 1935, p. 87.
6. JR's Memoir.
7. Several years later, Vinewood Park, an amusement area, opened in this locale. The Stouts, then living in Topeka, visited it often. To the children it seemed a foretaste of paradise. "I went there many times, to drink root beer and ride the merry-go-round." RS
8. Memoir, David H. Overmyer.
9. Ruth Stout to JM, 13 August 1974.
10. Grace Overmyer to JM, 17 February 1974.
11. The late Maude Beulah Snyder as recently as 1973 had a clear recollection of her parents discussing this feat at the time it happened.
12. "I read much of Pope in my teens, and I still spend an hour with him now and then (especially the *Dunciad* and the *Imitations of Horace*) because he was the wittiest versifier who ever lived. Just as Wagner was a nasty little man who wrote beautiful music, Pope was a nasty little man who wrote perfect verse." RS
13. "I was ten or eleven when I first read Montaigne. Probably what so strongly attracted me (though of course I didn't know it then) was that he is 'sceptical without being negative and humorous without being satiric' [Hazlitt]." RS
14. "I tried Trollope three different times, and I found him dull three times. Of course I put him above C. P. Snow. I loved *Jane Eyre* in my teens, but later I found that the Brontë girls were unreadable." RS
15. Memoir, David H. Overmyer.
16. Ruth Stout to JM, 31 May 1972.

9. Know-It-All in Knee Pants

1. Kathryn E. Williams supplied the original newspaper clippings on Clara Todhunter's suicide and funeral.

    The heroine of *The Rubber Band* (1936) is Clara Fox. Like Clara Todhunter [foxhunter] she is plunged into a crisis as a result of the theft of funds. Her wits are equal to this ordeal, however, and she emerges unscathed. Thus Rex rewrote family history.
2. JR's Memoir.
3. Elizabeth Schnemayer to JM, 20 October 1972.

4. JR's Memoir. JR's daughter, Natalie Stout Carr, says her father often recalled, over the years, his mother's thoughtfulness in covering him with her shawl that night. Bob's children suspected Lucetta knew he was awake and carried on her discussion about family finances in his hearing to appeal to his generosity.
5. In 1965, Ruth appeared on nationwide television, on "I've Got a Secret." Her secret was that she had smashed a saloon with Carry Nation, in 1901.
6. Ruth Stout to JM, 14 June 1976.
7. School records supplied by the indispensable John Ripley.
8. Memoir prepared by Helen McClintock, 1973.
9. For the background to this game I am indebted to Tom Muth, another indispensable Topekan.
10. Grace Overmyer, in 1976, still had the playbill for *Repentance*, a play which the children gave at the Stouts' house on 24 February 1900. Printed in green ink, it was prepared, at no cost, by one of Juanita's beaux, a young man learning the printer's trade.
11. Otis Skinner costarred in this production with Ada Rehan. Cornelia Otis Skinner to JM, 12 February 1974.

10. Dramatic Interlude

1. Juanita Lord to Ruth Stout, 18 November 1972.
2. "I have never had any career goal other than writing. Probably that was why I was named Class Poet." RS
3. "I had saved up for months to buy the graphophone and records." RS
4. A. G. Goodwin became Topeka's chief of police in April 1905.

11. The *Mayflower* Years

1. JR's Memoir.
2., "It was the most grievous experience of my life. I could have bit nails." RS
3. *Autobiography of William Allen White*, New York, 1946, p. 361.
4. *Golden Remedy*, New York, 1931, p. 34.
5. Rex first had mango ice cream in Havana. In "A Window for Death" (1956), the purchase of mango ice cream leads to murder.
6. Julia Sanderson Crumit to JM, 27 May 1973. While on tour in the spring of 1907 Julia visited Rex's mother and sisters in Indianapolis. On 1 September 1907, shortly after Rex left the navy and returned to the Midwest, she married famed jockey James "Tod" Sloan, who had worn the colors of England's Edward VII. In 1901 Sloan had been banned from racing for betting. George M. Cohan's *Little Johnny Jones* (1904) was based on Sloan's story. In this musical Jones (Sloan), standing on a London dock watching his friends sail for America, introduced Cohan's famous song, "Give My Regards to Broadway." Julia divorced him in 1913.
7. Juanita and Walter were married on 3 October 1906. Juanita's closest friend, Susan Rodgers Durant, pawned her own diamond ring so that she could loan Walter the money for a wedding trip to Manhattan, Kansas. Susan Rodgers Durant to JM, 18 November 1972.

Walter, born 30 October 1886, was Rex's age. Juanita was twenty-four on 12 October 1906.

8. "I qualified as some kind of a gun pointer somewhere but doubt if it was on the *Illinois*. I was probably trying my hand at fiction." RS

9. Topeka *Daily Capital*, 10 January 1907. In the Kansas City *Post*, a few days later, Barney Sheridan wrote, in an editorial captioned "A Loss to Kansas":

> A veritable Saul fell in Kansas when David Overmyer died. He was an idealist and a champion of human rights. In him were combined the gladiator, the orator, and the actor. He was original, contradictory, and courageous. Genius is always inconsistent and talent ignores consequences. Mr. Overmyer never looked back. The intensity of his devotion to the right as he saw the right made him changeable. . . .
>
> Mr. Overmyer was a student and scholar of the Topeka bar. Often he overshot the heads of both court and jury, but he never failed to touch the heart, no difference how dry the question or how weak the case. Next to Ingalls he was a master of the English language.

In David Overmyer Rex Stout found many attributes worth emulating.

10. Vice Admiral David H. Bagley, Chief of Naval Personnel, procured for me Rex's full dossier from the navy's storage depot at Pittsburg, Kansas. By a curious turn of fortune the navy located its records depot in the very town Rex went to, to enlist, in 1905. Vice Admiral David H. Bagley to JM, 26 October 1972.

1 2 . Logic and Life

1. In *Murder by the Book* (1951), Rex shows a marked antipathy toward lawyers. See also Edward S. Lauterbach, "Wolfe and the Law," *The Armchair Detective*, January 1970, 3:2, 164.

2. Natalie Stout Carr says that her father, in later years, even though Rex and he had been long estranged, remembered Rex's solicitude in this interval, always insisting that he owed his survival to Rex's thorough nursing care.

3. At this time Rex was working as a stablehand at Durland's Riding Stables.

4. At eighty-eight Rex reenacted the process, producing copies of each of his palm prints, for his biographer. "A messy process," he commented.

5. Memoir, Adda Meyer.

6. For another dozen years, Dr. Harding was a tempestuous presence in Topeka life. In 1912, in a joint press interview with her father (who that day was celebrating his eighty-eighth birthday), she denounced a local Methodist minister, Dr. Loveland, for his attack on the tube skirt. "Nothing on earth," said Dr. Harding, "is more unsightly than the average man's legs." In 1915, she offered herself as a Democratic candidate for Congress. The *Journal* greeted her as "A self-vaunting damsel named Harding/Whose vaunting ambition needs guarding." In 1917 she was hauled into federal court for battling the draft law. She died in 1920, at sixty-two, shortly after being chosen as Socialist candidate for the U.S. Senate. In keeping with her wishes her funeral services were conducted by two women friends.

13. A Brownstone in New York

1. Jacques Barzun, *A Birthday Tribute to Rex Stout,* New York, 1965, p. 5.
2. Ruth was so certain the others, through inadvertence, would acquire a New York accent she periodically asked them to repeat after her the phrase, "The girls must buy skirts on Thirty-third Street."
3. Unpublished memoir prepared by Ruth Stout.

14. Literary Apprenticeship

1. "I carry three kinds of insurance: fire and theft on the house and contents, automobile, and workmen's compensation. I have never carried life insurance because I refused to bet that I would die sooner than I should." RS
2. Grace Overmyer to JM, 8 September 1973.
3. Memoir, David Hicks Overmyer.
4. See Rex Stout Checklist for relevant bibliographical data. Ruth also had a poem, "Three Kisses," accepted by *The Smart Set.* The magazine offered her two dollars in payment. "All right," she wrote back, "but I do think I ought to get at least a dollar a kiss." She was paid three dollars.
5. On 10 September 1930, Sheila wrote Rex:

> I make a point never to read the books my friends write, but the other day down on Cape Cod I found myself alone with *Seed on the Wind* and I haven't been able to disentangle myself yet from the cyclone of impressions it produced.
>
> It is a swell book and I wouldn't be surprised if you and Lucretius and Pierre Louys and the rest are more or less right about love being a superimposed vice — probably brought in with Christianity — and having very little to do with the real business of love-making.

6. Unpublished memoir prepared by Ruth Stout.
7. Did Ed Carlson and Archie Goodwin share traits in common? "Yes. They both ate soup with a spoon." RS
8. Eugene Manlove Rhodes (1869–1934), who had been a cowboy in New Mexico for twenty-five years, was best known for his historical novels utilizing a western background: e.g., *Good Men and True* (1911), *West is West* (1917). At his own request Rhodes was buried at the summit of San Andres Mountain "forty miles from nowhere."
9. Sam Moskowitz, ed., *Under the Moons of Mars,* New York, 1972; see "A History of 'The Scientific Romance' in the Munsey Magazines, 1912–1920," pp. 291–433. Ron Goulart, *Cheap Thrills: An Informal History of Pulp Magazines,* New Rochelle, New York, 1972.
10. Juana Lord never acted on Rex's advice. But Grace Overmyer did. In 1920 Grace moved to New York and stayed there for forty-seven years before returning to Topeka in 1967. During that time she published three books — *Government and the Arts* (1939), *Famous American Composers* (1944), and *America's First Hamlet* (1957). In 1976, at ninety, Grace completed a life of Antonin Dvořak. She died 30 December 1976.

11. In the summer of 1915, for *Smith's Magazine,* Rex wrote three short stories — " A Little Love Affair," "Art for Art's Sake," and "Another Little Love Affair" — built around a virago, Maria Chidden, and her brother, Robert. Maria keeps a boarding house. Robert is her drudge — his subjugation so nearly complete that he wears Maria's cast-off underwear. Utimately he rises up and squelches her. The Chidden trilogy is memorable as Rex's exclusive attempt at producing series characters before launching the Wolfe saga.

12. In 1910, when he was working as a bookkeeper with the Milbury Atlantic Supply Company, a mutual interest in music led Rex to form a friendship with Roy Larossa, an Italian youth who worked in the packing room. Rex told me: "Roy lived with his parents and brothers and sister in an apartment on Lafayette Street, in Manhattan. His father had been a boyhood friend of Caruso's in Naples, and the friendship had continued. I was a guest at that apartment one Saturday afternoon in late September in 1910 (about a dozen people were there), and for a full two hours Caruso fried squash blossoms in the kitchen and brought them in to us. Part of the time he would clown, pretending his English was worse than it was — then he'd make fun of German lieder. He was continually singing snatches of things just to hear himself."

Louise Homer (1871–1947) sang with the Metropolitan Opera Company from 1900 to 1919, and again in 1927. See Anne Homer, *Louise Homer and the Golden Age of Opera,* New York, 1974.

15. Underground Novelist

1. Robert W. Fenton, *The Big Swingers,* Englewood Cliffs, New Jersey, 1967.
2. Philip José Farmer, *Tarzan Alive,* New York 1972. Farmer's genealogical table of Tarzan's lineage alleges that Tarzan's grandfather and Nero Wolfe's grandmother were brother and sister. That would have been an interesting point for Burroughs and Rex to have thrashed out when they met, in 1914. Farmer's table was reprinted in *Esquire,* April 1972, p. 131.
3. Moskowitz, in *Under the Moons of Mars* (1972), refers to *Under the Andes* as "extraordinarily vigorous and well-written," p. 361.
4. Rex was introduced to *oeufs au beurre noir* at the Brevoort.

16. The Heart Has Reasons

1. Rex could offer no explanation for this. Perhaps it was a carry-over from his initial success as a writer-chiromancer.
2. *All-Story Weekly Magazine,* 11 April 1914, 13 pp.
3. *All-Story Weekly Magazine,* 11 April 1914, 8 pp. Bob earlier had submitted "Windows of Darkness" to another magazine. When it was rejected, he shoved it in a drawer of his desk and forgot about it. When Tad found it there, a couple of years later, she resubmitted it, on her own, to *All-Story,* where it was accepted.

4. *All-Story Cavalier Weekly,* 8 August 1914, 9 pp.
5. "Ownership," *All-Story Weekly,* 7 April 1917, 8 pp.

17. Crime Fiction

1. Moskowitz, *Under the Moons of Mars,* p. 316.
2. "Their Lady" may have been published in 1912. No copy of it has come to light. *All-Story* editors twice credited Rex with its authorship, once in notations accompanying "Warner & Wife," 27 February 1915, and again, in notations accompanying "Justice Ends at Home," 4 December 1915. In addition, beginning on 16 May 1914, during *All-Story*'s serialization of *A Prize for Princes,* Rex was thrice credited with having written "Their To-Day." "Their To-Day" probably had read "Their Lady" in a hasty script and had been misread by the compositor. Since the plot of "Their Lady," as Rex reconstructed it from memory, is markedly similar to the plot of *Her Forbidden Knight,* conceivably "Their Lady" may merely have been Rex's original title for that novel. It suits it well. Rex did not trust his memory on that point.
3. In *Not Quite Dead Enough* (1944) Archie says, "If Helen of Troy were alive today, she'd be a cashier in a Greek restaurant," p. 12. Even in 1915 Rex thought Helen was a rapid calculator.

18. Melons and Millions

1. Walter Hugh (called Junior), was born 25 April 1909; Juanita Merle (called Sister), was born 21 May 1910; Roger Wallace was born on 21 April 1913. Juanita's last child, Virginia Sands, was born on 4 November 1919. Walter Stout's adopted daughter, Ruth, also had the middle name of Merle. Walt and Juanita both liked that name when they were children and decided then to give it to their own daughters.
2. Fay says: "My name is correctly spelled Faye but I have never used that version. I don't like it. And yes, I have two middle names. Faye Mary Margaret Kennedy. The two middle names were after my two grand-mothers."
3. Was Rex a virgin when he married Fay? "Of course not; I was thirty years old. I told chastity goodbye at seventeen." RS
4. Bob told Frances Cox that he had kept Rex locked in his room at the Schenley until he had worked out the full ETS plan of operation. Rex said this never happened. Fay agrees: "Locking him in a room at the Schenley is absurd. Rex worked out all the forms and the general operation of ETS, but not under duress."

   Rex's files contained much of the data needed to understand how the Educational Thrift Service operated, developed, and prospered. Fifty years later, Rex's memory of the operation still was replete and exact and he supplied frequent clarifications. I am indebted also to Natalie Stout Carr and her husband, Wallace Carr, to Frances Cox, Charlotte Foucart Boyle, Helen May Iooss, Juanita Roddy DeBrock, Ruth Stout Johnson, Mrs. Harry Donovan (whose husband bought ETS from Bob Stout around 1940), and Fay Kennedy Koudrey, all of whom actively served on the ETS team, for a sense of the day-to-day functioning of ETS, and of the spirit which assured its success.

5. "For fifty years I have had my personal scratch pads made of goldenrod-colored paper." RS. All the notations Rex made before he began writing a novel were made on a few of these sheets, which measure 8 1/2 × 5 1/2.
6. JR's Memoir.

19. Pied Piper of Thrift

1. Rex did not find it remarkable that he climbed Pike's Peak in his book first.
2. On a visit to Glendale, in *Murder by the Book* (1951), Archie comments: "I got up and crossed to a window to look out at the California climate. I would have thought it was beautiful if I had been a seal" (p. 143).
3. Ruth Stout, unpublished memoir.
4. "MacArthur was an interesting combination of skills and stupidities." RS
5. During this period Theodore Dreiser was living at 165 West Tenth Street, an old three-story frame building with tiny balconies. Fay's friends Joe and Mary Coffey lived in the same building, next door to Dreiser. Rex and she often dropped by to visit them. Fay says: "Joe had a dog. He and Dreiser built a fence between the tiny galleries. The dog jumped over it one way, and crawled under it the other. So Dreiser laughed and said to forget the fence." Fay Koudrey to JM, 13 May 1974.
6. Helen May Iooss to JM, 19 September 1974.
7. Charlotte Foucart Boyle to JM, 8 August 1972.
8. "I had no qualifications as a judge of conductors. I merely knew that I enjoyed and understood the music much better when Toscanini conducted." RS
9. They also ate at the Jumble Shop of West Eighth Street, and at Chambord.
10. While in California, Ruth took an airplane ride with a barnstorming pilot — her first flight. At her insistence, he flew the plane upside down, to show that he could do it. Satisfied, Ruth never flew again.
11. Fay and Egmont shared back-to-back birthdays, Egmont on 15 December, Fay on 16 December, a fact which contributed an added interlude of merrymaking to the two families in the holiday season.
12. Carpentier and Rex Stout both died on 27 October 1975.
13. *Joseph Conrad: A Psychoanalytic Biography*, Princeton, 1967, p. 307; see also pp. 291–316.
14. Borys Conrad, *My Father: Joseph Conrad*, New York, 1970, pp. 33–34.

20. Civil Libertarian

1. Natalie Stout Carr to JM, 9 December 1972.
2. Bob and Rex came up to Saranac to see to the funeral arrangements. Donald was buried in one of several plots Bob had bought at Ridgewood, New Jersey. Soon afterward Bob had May's body brought on from Denver and reinterred there also.
3. Morris Ernst to JM, 21 March 1973.
4. Scott Nearing to JM, 12 November 1972.

5. Letter in Arens Collection, George Arents Research Library, Syracuse University. *Playboy* was published intermittently between January 1919, and June 1924. Between July 1921 and February 1923, no issues appeared at all. In all, only nine issues appeared.
6. *It's Me Oh Lord,* New York, 1955, pp. 398–399.
7. Rex had them framed and hung them in the hall, outside his office, at High Meadow, where they still are.
8. One of these sets is on Nero Wolfe's bookshelves, in his office. Rex had a set on a shelf in his bedroom — the only books he kept in his bedroom.
9. *Rex Stout Mystery Magazine*, No. 3, February 1946.
10. Though Scott several times proposed to Ruth, she always refused him. At ninety, Ruth said of Scott, who then, at ninety-two, was touring Red China: "The things he's been saying lately, I'm glad I never married him."
11. "In the sense that I can articulate its premises and conclusions, I understand the theory of relativity. But I cannot digest it, as for instance I have digested the Second Law of Thermodynamics." RS
12. Mrs. Egmont Arens to JM, 8 February 1977.
13. *Beards: Their Social Standing, Religious Involvement, Decorative Possibilities, and Value in Offense and Defence through the Ages,* New York, 1949. Jacket essay by Rex Stout.
14. Lawrence Pope to RS, 18 April 1966.

21. His Own Man

1. "Because I knew and liked Art Young I gave them some money to start the magazine." RS
   In *Writers on the Left,* New York, 1961, Daniel Aaron says:

   > In the light of subsequent charges that the Communist Party controlled the magazine from the start, the following facts cannot be too strongly emphasized: 1) the overwhelming majority of the organizing committee were liberals or independent radicals; 2) the sponsors of the magazine clearly intended to keep it free of any party label; 3) the directors of the Garland Fund knew this when they granted the appropriation [p. 100].

   See also pp. 96–102.
2. Rex donated the office furniture too. An additional $4,500 was raised from other sources.
3. The Garland Fund was, as well, the mainstay of *The New Masses.*
4. Scott Nearing to JM, 12 November 1972.
5. Roger Baldwin to JM, 26 February 1973.
6. Morris Ernst to JM, 21 March 1973.
7. In the early days of *The New Masses* Ruth had sold the magazines on the sidewalk in front of lecture halls, while Scott Nearing was lecturing. Sometimes she brought along an overnight bag containing a nightgown, in case she was arrested. She never was.
8. The Fifth Avenue Playhouse, which opened as a legitimate theater in December 1925, was on the ground floor. It became a film theater in 1926 and remained one until 1974, when it was taken over by the Parsons School of Design.
9. Norma Millay to JM, 15 January 1976.
   "O'Neill wrote a lot of trash, but *A Long Day's Journey into Night* is

the best play written by an American. . . . We have had no playwright of the stature of Twain or Melville." RS

10. John Munn Hanford did the surgery.

11. In 1920, in Clearfield County, Pennsylvania, Rex had gone quail hunting as the guest of another baseball immortal, Christy Matthewson. Chief Meyer accompanied them.

12. Rockwell Kent, *It's Me O Lord*, New York, 1955, p. 414.

13. *Not Quite Dead Enough*, New York, 1944, p. 91; *Might as Well Be Dead*, New York, 1956, p. 69. See also *Prisoner's Base*, New York, 1952, p. 8; and *The Mother Hunt*, New York, 1963, p. 75.

22. Expatriate Novelist

1. He also spent a day on Salisbury Plain, inspecting Stonehenge, enticed by Hardy's utilization of it in *Tess of the D'Urbervilles*.

2. Chesterton once wrote a story called "The Dagger with Wings." Rex later would write one called "The Gun with Wings." At Beaconsfield Chesterton built a house, which he called Top Meadow, and there he lived out the remainder of his days.

3. Various interviewers have reported that Rex debated word usage with Oscar Wilde during his sojourn in Paris. Rex told me: "Of course I never met Oscar Wilde. He died in 1900. One day long ago a man bragged about knowing more about Wilde than he could possibly have known, and to check him I told him I had met Wilde in Paris in 1928, and he didn't challenge me. Since then I have tried a dozen or more people with it, and have never been called, till you called me."

4. Whit Burnett, *The Literary Life and the Hell with It*, New York, 1939, p. 93. Alvah C. Bessie later would be drama critic of *The New Masses*. In 1938 he went to Spain as a member of the Lincoln Brigade. Bessie's writing career also would take a turn toward crime fiction. The protagonist of his *Bread and a Stone* (1941) is a murderer.

5. *The Literary Life and the Hell with It*, pp. 95–98.

6. *Waylaid in Boston*, New York, 1953, p. 9. See also Elliot Paul, "Whodunit," *The Atlantic Monthly*, 168 (July-December 1941): 37.

7. Tragic news from home may have quickened in Rex the resolve to get on with the serious business that had brought him to Paris. On 18 January, in New Jersey, his nephew, Walter Roddy, Jr., had run the family car into an abutment in a rainstorm. The steering wheel passed through his chest, killing him instantly. The day following the accident, Bob gave the Roddys a new car, his way of telling them that, however difficult it was, they had to pick up again with the business of living.

8. José Luis Castillo-Puche, *Hemingway in Spain*, New York, 1974, pp. 158–159, 203, 228, 360.

9. Karl Menninger to JM, 12 April 1973. "I didn't dabble with psychiatry in those stories; I dabbled with people. I know almost as little about psychiatry as psychiatrists do." RS

10. D. Joy Humes, *Oswald Garrison Villard: Liberal of the 1920's*, Syracuse, N.Y., 1960, pp. 59–61.

11. Encouraged by Ruth to follow his own bent, Fred, in the course of the thirty-one years of their marriage, became one of the foremost woodturners in the United States.

12. *How Like a God,* New York, 1929, p. 178.
13. One reader had no quarrel with *How Like a God.* Rex himself. Vanguard sent him six copies. A week later Rex wrote back: "I have already read and enjoyed three copies and look forward to enjoying the remaining three." For this story I am indebted to the perdurable Evelyn Shrifte, fifty years with Vanguard.

    Rex's working title for this book had been "Stairway to God."

23. Squire of High Meadow

1. When Paul died early in 1975, Rex commented: "Paul Ruffles is gone. A good life. A good neighbor. Good neighbors help a lot."
2. Scott Nearing says: "The closer men live to the rhythm of Nature, the greater their stability and poise, and sense of oneness with life." Rex said of that: "It depends on the man. Some men trying to live 'close to the rhythms of nature' would be bored stiff. Among those I know I could name twenty offhand."
3. Lawrence G. Blochman to JM, 16 August 1973.
4. Frank Morley to Morley Kennerley, 16 September 1930.

    Rex was one of the few people whom Christopher Morley invited to call him "Kit," the name his brothers, Felix and Frank, called him by. Frank Morley recalls: "Meetings at which I happened to be present were as arranged by brother Kit and Rex themselves and largely dominated by them. . . . I can certainly verify the warmth of the friendship between Rex and my brother at the time when I observed it." Frank Morley to JM, 17 February 1974. Felix Morley concurs. Felix Morley to JM, 27 February 1974.
5. "Havelock Ellis left instructions that his copy of *Seed on the Wind* was to be sent to me after his death, and I have it (with his bookplate)." RS

    On 1 December 1966, the novelist James T. Farrell wrote Rex: "I first read you in Paris in 1931, the woman who is a baby farm. It is good."
6. Naomi Mitchison to Morley Kennerley, 20 January 1931.
7. Carvel Collins to JM, 16 November 1973. See also Joseph Blatner, *Faulkner: A Biography,* New York, 1974, II, 1093, 1141.
8. In the summer of 1972, a forty-five-year-old actuary, married but childless, advertised in a Philadelphia newspaper for a woman who would bear him a child. He offered "$10,000 fee plus expenses for an 18-month period, plus educational scholarships and fringe benefits." A Boston woman who said she had "three children by two fathers and that all of her youngsters were beautiful" applied for the job. Neither the actuary nor the would-be mother had read *Seed on the Wind.* See Ken O. Botwright, "Philadelphia Man Extends Pregnancy Search to Boston," Boston *Globe,* 11 August 1972.

24. A Literary Farmer

1. James Henle to Rex Stout, 4 May 1931.
2. Morris Ernst to James Henle, 12 May 1931.
3. James Henle to Rex Stout, 12 May 1931.
4. *Golden Remedy,* New York, 1931, pp. 104–105.

5. *Golden Remedy*, p. 137.
6. *Golden Remedy*, p. 224.
7. Egmont Arens to Rex Stout, August 1931.
8. *Golden Remedy*, p. 282.
9. Egmont Arens to Rex Stout, 5 October 1933.
10. Born with a caul, Pola was an object of awe to the villagers of Stryj, in the period of her childhood. They believed her to be a child of destiny. When she passed along the street, people reached out to touch her, hoping some of her good fortune would communicate itself to them. Pola was a student at the University of Lemberg when she decided to enroll in Hoffmann's school. She ran away to Vienna, where she worked as a milliner and slept on a park bench for six weeks to save money for tuition. During her four years in Vienna she worked for Sigmund Freud and mended a Gobelin tapestry for him. Pola remembers being introduced to Rex at a ball, in 1926, when she first arrived in the United States. She remembers, too, that she was wearing a red dress. Rex did not recall that encounter when she reminded him of it later.

25. Stout Fellow

1. For this information I am indebted to Margaret and John Farrar. For much of the correspondence touching on the books which Rex published through Farrar & Rinehart, I am under obligation to Marguerite Reese and to her associates at Farrar & Rinehart, Beruta Lukshis and Mary Laychek, who assisted me in my search.
2. "Durham rhymes with hurrum." RS
3. Vrest Orton to John Farrar, 27 December 1932.
4. In 1934, Rex's first wife, Fay Kennedy, married Vladimir Koudrey [Koudriavsky], a tall blond Russian, a former Soviet Commissar of Army Supplies and the stepson of the Russian revolutionary leader Leonid Krassin. Koudrey was a friend of Ruth Stout's, and Fay met him at Poverty Hollow, where he had built a hut in one corner of Ruth's fifty acres. Koudrey wanted to write his memoirs. Ruth helped him with his English and typed his manuscript for him. Yale University published it, in 1937, as *Once a Commissar*. Koudrey died of a cerebral hemorrhage the following year. He was forty-three. After her marriage to Koudrey, Fay studied art. She relates: "Vladimir and I spent a year in San Francisco, during which time I worked very hard at my painting. When we came back to New York I was given a one-woman show in the Weyhe Gallery, one of the best in New York at the time. John Sloan liked my pictures, which helped. The show was arranged by Carl Zigrosser, who was later on the board of directors of the Museum of Modern Art. Adolph Dehn's comments on my pictures helped me, too."

   At eighty-five Fay still was painting vigorously at her home in Escondido, California. She died of a stroke 24 June 1977.

   Pola was quick to assert her primacy as chatelaine of High Meadow. On a visit to a Brewster butcher shop, she listened in astonishment while her new husband described to the butcher the cut of meat he wanted. "Rex," she exploded, "I am the woman of the house!"
5. *Forest Fire*, New York, 1933, p. 53.
6. *Forest Fire*, pp. 174–175.

7. Julian Symons to JM, 6 February 1974.
8. Rex Stout to Marguerite Reese, 31 December 1948.

26. Lazy Bloodhound

1. 20 February 1963. Statement reprinted under heading "Authors League Backs JFK, Asking Fairer Tax Treatment for Writers," *Publishers Weekly*, 11 March 1963, pp. 27–29.
2. *The Further Rivals of Sherlock Holmes,* ed. Sir Hugh Greene, New York, 1973, pp. 102–103. Concerning *Fer-de-Lance* John Farrar wrote JM, in November 1973:

> I remember trying to sell the idea of doing this one into a movie to Jacob Wilk (of Warner Brothers?) when we were walking along the boardwalk at Atlantic City. He was interested in our version of wonderful plot, but when he discovered that fer-de-lance was a snake, he said no. Snakes were not popular in movies of that day when Nelson Eddy and Jeanette Macdonald were all the rage.

3. Duddington Pell Chalmers, the detective-hero of John T. McIntyre's *The Museum Murder* (1929), has been suggested as Wolfe's prototype. The only thing they have in common is their obesity. A more likely candidate is Gerald Verner's Superintendent Budd, "the stout detective," who is fat, lazy, graceful on his feet, prone to shut his eyes while thinking, and "not susceptible to feminine beauty." Budd appears in a series of novels by Verner. *Sinister House* (1934) may record his first appearance. By then, of course, Stout had created Wolfe. Another candidate to consider is Fatso, a detective who appears in several short tales written by Ford Madox Ford.

   Of Wolfe's office inquisitions, David G. Kamm, chief trial attorney for the Office of the Prosecuting Attorney in Kent County, Michigan, remarks: "The technique of the denouement in the office is so skillfully used that it operates as a substitute for the trial, and it allows Rex Stout very subtly to place the capstone on the individual personalities in a far more exciting atmosphere in which the participants are not hidebound by decorous, deadly judicial procedure." David G. Kamm to JM, 4 March 1974. Innovation, not imitation, was Rex's strong suit.

   Of changing a character's name while a work was in progress, Rex said: "I think I could with no difficulty, but I never have. I name the principal characters before I start writing. In *Please Pass the Guilt* I called a character Browning. That wasn't a good name. I don't know why I called him that. It's not right."

   Did Rex see Wolfe as a grotesque? "Of course not. Webster on 'grotesque': 'A clown or a person in fantastic disguise.'" RS

   Was *Fer-de-Lance* written on a typewriter? "Yes. On an Underwood that I bought new in 1920. My first typewriter was a used Underwood that I bought in 1912 for $16.50. I bought another Underwood in 1937. My fourth one, still with me, I bought in 1956. My desk when I wrote *Fer-de-Lance* was an old battered table, pine, painted. It's now in the tool house, in the garden." RS to JM, 19 August 1975.
4. Gilbert W. Gabriel, "Mystery on High Meadow," *Saturday Review of Literature*, 18 September 1937, p. 6.

5. Alfred Bester, "Conversation with Rex Stout," *Holiday*, November 1969, p. 39.

6. Alva Johnston, "Alias Nero Wolfe — II," *New Yorker*, 23 July 1949, p. 36.

7. Johnston, p. 30.

8. Margaret and John Farrar to JM, November 1973.

9. Marshall Best to JM, 24 July 1972.

10. Mark Van Doren to JM, 6 July 1972.

11. Jacques Barzun to JM, 16 June 1972.

12. "Archie's not so hidden wish to shoot a book out of Nero Wolfe's hand is a not uncommon son versus father fantasy." B. Frank Vogel to JM, 15 July 1976. See *Before Midnight*, p. 159.

13. "There was such a picture — small, about ten by sixteen, on the wall of our bedroom in Kansas. I don't know who put it there." RS

14. "I have always been a milk drinker and still am, but not with AG's persistence." RS

15. "There's nothing about southern California I like. North of San Francisco there are wonderful spots." RS

16. "He merely dislikes bells; he would hate chimes." RS

17. The gold bookmark was a gift from Barbara and Than.

18. Periodically Rex gave me fuller reports on Wolfe's reading than it was feasible to introduce into the novels. On 28 June 1969, Rex said Wolfe had been reading *"Histories* by Polybius, *Colloquies* by Erasmus."* On 28 December 1971, Rex said: "Nero Wolfe recently read *My People* by Abba Eban, and *The Works of Existentialism*, edited by Maurice Freedman. He dogeared the latter. He is about half way through Macaulay's *History of England."* On 3 September 1973, Wolfe was reading Gilbert Murray's translation of Euripides. Rex said on 29 January 1974, "Wolfe is reading *Your Mirror to My Times* by Ford Madox Ford, *Fable of Man* by Mark Twain, and *Plain Speaking: An Oral Biography of Harry S. Truman* by Merle Miller." After he passed safely through the ordeal recorded in *A Family Affair*, Wolfe followed a comfortable, almost nostalgic, reading program. On 15 February 1975, he was reading Nat Shaw's *All God's Dangers,* and rereading some of Sainte-Beuve. On 30 April he was reading "Coleridge on Shakespeare and the new biography of Samuel Johnson." On 24 July Rex said Wolfe was "mostly rereading classics." Rex himself completed a rereading of Jane Austen's *Emma* at this time. And so did Wolfe. That is the last we know of Wolfe. Rex did not speak again of his activities. Nero Wolfe, last seen in the company of Jane Austen. Who could wish to disturb that scene?

19. "What neuter pronoun have we for 'him or her' or 'he or she'?" RS

20. "I don't think it has been recorded, but I suppose NW's parents belonged to the self-governing national church of Montenegro." RS

21. How would Rex have felt had someone hung up the phone on him in a huff? "No one ever has, but since that's what I would often like to do, I'd probably sympathize with him." RS

22. What did Rex think of electric blankets? "One of science's greatest contributions to happiness." RS

23. Once, when Pola gave new bills to a New York cabbie, the man said to her, "Hey, you're like another customer I had today. Old gent with a neat beard and a booming voice. Paid me in new bills, too." "Where did you take him?" Pola inquired. "Thirty Park Avenue West." "I thought as much," Pola said. "That's where I live and he's my husband."

27. Mystery Monger

1. "I seem to remember Charles being very interested in the character of Nero Wolfe. I always regretted I did not get to play Dora Chapin." Elsa Lanchester (Mrs. Charles Laughton) to JM, 6 December 1974.
2. This phrase was printed on the program prepared for the surprise dinner given Rex by more than a hundred friends, at Sardi's, on his seventy-fifth birthday.
3. Carvel Collins to JM, 18 November 1973.
4. "Biggers is not an awfully good writer. The conversations aren't well done. What I like about the Charlie Chan books is that there's some damn good detective work in them. He's a really good detective, that Charlie Chan." RS
5. Farrar & Rinehart sent an orchid to each New York reviewer the day *The League of Frightened Men* was published.

   In *The League of Frightened Men* the protagonist, Paul Chapin, is injured when he falls from Thayer Hall, a freshman dormitory in the Harvard Yard. There is such a dormitory in the Yard. Rex chose Thayer as the site of the disaster because he had in mind Judge Webster Thayer, the judge who presided, with disastrous results, in Rex's mind and in the minds of many of his contemporaries, at the Sacco and Vanzetti trials.

   Rex got the idea of having Chapin fall from a Thayer ledge while crossing between entries from a photograph of Harvard's celebrated Billy the Postman (Theodore Parmelee Prentice) crossing between entries on a ledge at Weld Hall (also in the Yard), in the 1870's. Prentice did this daily, to avoid having to go downstairs and up again, when delivering mail. Prentice's stunt was much admired by Harvard students. In 1878, D.K.E., the Hasty Pudding, and the Institute of 1770 (later combined), elected him to membership.
6. Egmont Arens to Rex Stout, 31 March 1934.
7. Morris Ernst to JM, 21 March 1973.

28. Commander over the Earth

1. As a person and as a writer how important did Rex think it was to have a sense of humor? "Requisite, imperative, indispensable." RS
2. *The Bedroom Companion*, New York, 1935, p. 36.
3. "Over the years I have written forty or more verses like these just for the fun of it, never for publication. I don't know why I kept only these; I hope not because they are the best of the lot. Just so-so, I would say." RS
4. Rex sang this song for me, in good voice, on 19 August 1975. JM
5. Rex did not make a formal study of the fashion and textile industries for these stories. "I used what I had learned in conversations with Pola." RS
6. Rex's respect for Pola's integrity is reflected in his own preferences. He disliked synthetics. He disliked double knits. He wore only cotton pajamas.

   In *Red Threads* the murder happens on the seventh day of the seventh month, in 1937, which was the seventh anniversary of the death of the creator of Sherlock Holmes, Sir Arthur Conan Doyle — a detail put there for the alert reader, since Rex does not mention Doyle in the book.

   Of greater interest to Stout readers is the identity of the detective in this novel: Wolfe's sometime antagonist, Inspector Cramer. Here, without Wolfe's intervention, Cramer solves the Doyle-day murder.

7. *The Rubber Band,* New York, 1936, p. 183.
8. *The Red Box,* New York, 1937, p. 178.

    Rex had to battle to get a contract for *The Red Box,* but not in the usual sense. On 12 June 1937, he reported to William Sladen of Farrar & Rinehart that his parrot (actually a macaw, Nero) apparently had stolen the contract, because he could find it nowhere. On 18 June, Sladen sent a replacement copy, recalling, gingerly, that he once had been bitten by a parrot belonging to Stanley Rinehart's father. On 21 June Rex returned the signed contract with the notation, "I fooled the parrot this time. Here it is." On 22 June, a secretary filed it, with the solemn notation: "Contract No. 3757. Mr. Stout's parrot ate the original copy."
9. *The Red Box,* p. 200.
10. *What Became of Jane Austen?* p. 114.
11. Karl Menninger to JM, 22 May 1973.
12. Sir Hugh Greene to JM, 19 January 1974.
13. Lionel Tiger, *Men in Groups,* New York, 1969. Robert Ardrey, *The Hunting Hypothesis,* New York, 1976, pp. 91–96. For bonding alliances Rex did not have to go outside his own experience. There had been his father's lifelong friendship with David Overmyer; and his own friendship with David Hicks Overmyer, and his good and rewarding friendships with Wallace Whitecotton, Ed Carlson, Egmont Arens, Mark Van Doren, Harold Salmon, Lewis Gannett, Christopher Morley, Clifton Fadiman, Alan Green, Christopher La Farge, George Field, Robert Sherwood, Nathaniel Selleck II, Samuel Grafton, Norman Cousins, and Oscar Hammerstein II. These alliances had been for him a source of strength in the courageous ventures he often undertook through much of his lifetime.
14. *Witness,* New York, 1952, p. 218. The luncheon with Ruth took place in 1926. The other guest was Harry Freeman, brother of Joe Freeman, a founder of *The New Masses.*
15. Richard Lockridge to JM, 1 October 1972.
16. Egmont Arens to Rex Stout, 31 July 1936.
17. Gabriel, "Mystery on High Meadow," pp. 5–6.
18. On 1 February, Whit Burnett had dropped by to enthuse with Rex over a spectacular aurora borealis which had blazed in the skies the previous night. Rex had missed it. Burnett remarked: "It was the only thing in his neighborhood that Rex had ever missed." To save face, Rex took Whit on a tour of his barnyard. His goats were going to have kids. Two of his Buff Orpingtons had won first prizes at the last Danbury Fair. *The Literary Life and the Hell with It,* p. 151.
19. Gabriel, "Mystery on High Meadow," p. 6.

29. King's Gambit

1. Rex's obituaries would applaud him for keeping Wolfe "almost always aloof from politics." See the Boston *Herald American,* 28 October 1975, p. 12.
2. *Too Many Cooks* is one of the finest Wolfe stories. It is the closest thing to a locked-room mystery that Rex wrote. Accounting for his failure to work in this area, Rex said: "Since the interest is focused on one spot, Nero

Wolfe would have to go there, and he wouldn't like that."

3. Lily Rowan, Archie Goodwin's steady girl friend, first enters the saga in
Some Buried Caesar (1939). Did Rex agree with the reader who said Lily's
given name is ironic? That Lily is, in fact, a loose woman? "No. Of course
I don't know his definition of 'loose woman.' If he merely means a woman
who had probably slept with a man or men she wasn't married to, certainly. I thought the name Lily Rowan was right for the kind of person
I had in mind. There was no other conscious reason for the name of any
characters in my stories." RS

Rowan is another name for the mountain ash — a tree which, in Scotland, is thought to ward off evil. Rex sneered at the reader who suggested
that Lily's surname was meant to recall lewd puns on "mountain ass," a
regional term for a loose woman.

4. Albert Benjamin III to John Farrar, 6 April 1938.

The *Too Many Cooks* slipcase supplement, containing the menu of the
"Living Issue Luncheon," an introduction by Nero Wolfe, and thirty-five
Nero Wolfe recipes, was made up in a limited edition of a thousand copies
and has since become one of the most sought-after items of Stoutiana. In
recording Jerome Berin's recipe for Saucisse Minuit, Rex disclosed that
Berin had recently been "killed by a Fascist bomb in Barcelona, where
he had gone to fight for the Loyalists and the freedom of the Spanish
people. . . ."

5. Albert Benjamin III to JM, 3 July 1974.
6. The decision was taken dispassionately. "I experienced no epiphany. I
have always been antiepiphany." RS
7. Publishers have asserted: "Rex Stout thinks *Double for Death* 'the best
detective story I ever wrote.' " Rex told me: "I don't think *Double for
Death* is the best story I ever wrote; I think it is the best detective story,
technically, that I ever wrote."
8. *Over My Dead Body* contains an allusion to "Corsini the great Zagreb
fencing master." Was there a Corsini? "No. I supplied the name." RS

With *Over My Dead Body*, Rex had produced eight books in three
years. Rex remarked in 1973: "Eight books in three years? I'm surprised
but not impressed. I must have needed money for something."

9. Adamic cites Tennyson's lines commending the Montenegrins:

> O smallest among peoples! rough rock-throne
> Of Freedom! warriors beating back the swarm
> Of Turkish Islam for five hundred years.

The Native's Return, New York, 1934, pp. 129–130.

10. Adamic describes the Montenegrin male as tall, commanding, dignified,
courteous, hospitable. He is reluctant to work, accustomed to isolation
from women. He places women in a subordinate role. He is a romantic
idealist, apt to go in for dashing effects to express his spirited nature. He
is strong in family loyalties, has great pride, is impatient of restraint. Love
of freedom is his outstanding trait. He is stubborn, fearless, unsubduable,
capable of great self-denial to uphold his ideals. He is fatalistic toward
death. In short, Rex had found for Wolfe a nationality that fitted him to
perfection.

11. When Fadiman reviewed *How Like a God* favorably, in 1929, Rex and he
had not yet met.

12. For information covering this phase of Rex's activities I am indebted to

Barry Bingham, Herbert Agar, James Sheldon, and, most especially, Colonel Francis Pickens Miller and George Field. See Francis Pickens Miller, *Man from the Valley: Memoirs of a 20th-Century Virginian*, Chapel Hill, 1971, pp. 87–109.

13. George Merten to JM, 15 September 1972. See also H. Montgomery Hyde, *Room 3603: The Story of the British Intelligence Center in New York during World War II*, New York, 1962, pp. 125–126. And William Stevenson, *A Man Called Intrepid*, New York, 1976.

14. In *Over My Dead Body* (p. 93), Archie makes a remark which suggests that Cramer is Irish. In *Where There's a Will* (1940), Wolfe says Cramer's first name is Fergus. In *The Silent Speaker* (1946) Cramer's initials are given as L. T. C. When Rex wrote *Where There's a Will* did he think of Cramer as Scottish? "I didn't think of Cramer as a Scotsman. To me he is just Inspector Cramer." RS

15. Typical of the jests Rex Stout implants in his stories for the delectation of attentive readers is Tecumseh Fox's momentary adoption, in this novel, of the alias William Sherman. Fox is allied in other respects with the Civil War hero General William Tecumseh Sherman. Just how, the student of history knows best. See "Bitter End" in *Corsage*, ed. Michael Bourne, Bloomington, Indiana, 1977.

30. Nero Wolfe Gets Smaller

1. George K. Morlan to JM, 30 June 1973.

2. In addition to Morley those present included Howard Haycraft, Edgar W. Smith, Mitchell Kennerley, the James Keddies, father and son, Louis Greenfield, and Dr. Julian Wolff.

3. For eyewitness accounts of the impact that Rex's paper had on the Baker Street Irregulars, I am indebted to Julian Wolff and James Keddie, Jr.

   In his office, at High Meadow, Rex, for many years, had a sixteen-inch-high full-figure statuette of Sherlock Holmes, the gift of the man who made it. Although Rex cherished it, he could not remember the name of his benefactor.

4. Rex was not related to Isaac Todhunter, despite his own mathematical prowess and that of his cousin, Alice Todhunter's grandson, Professor Burnett Meyer, a member of the mathematics department at the University of Colorado.

5. Wolff's article was published in Edgar Smith's *Profile by Gaslight*, New York, 1944, pp. 166–172.

6. Herbert Agar to JM, 27 September 1972.

7. The parade that welcomed Lindbergh home from Paris, on 13 June 1927, in New York City, went past Rex's penthouse. "With a dozen or more guests, Fay and I saw it from our balcony at 66 Fifth Avenue." RS

8. Alexander Woollcott Papers, Houghton Library, Harvard University, 21 May 1941.

9. Notwithstanding his attachment to his mother, Rex told me he had no such dreams.

10. "I used to think that men did everything better than women, but that was before I read Jane Austen. I don't think any man ever wrote better than Jane Austen." RS

11. Irita Van Doren later urged Rex to do a column for the *Herald Tribune.*
Rex declined. "I wouldn't touch that kind of writing with a ten-foot
ballpoint." RS

31. Crusader by Inner Compulsion

1. Marshall Shulman to JM, 24 March 1975.
2. Carl Friedrich to JM, 11 February 1975.
3. As late as March 1944, in the *American Journal of Sociology* 49:424,
Friedrich made an oblique attack on Rex, asserting that the WWB was
"permeated with" people who exemplified the "pro-fascist mentality."
4. *New York Times*, 27 November 1941.
5. "His Own Hand," was published first in *Manhunt*, April 1955, and reprinted as "By His Own Hand," in *Eat, Drink and Be Buried* (1956), an
anthology edited by Rex. There Rex commented:

> I still think it was a neat and original idea. A writer creates a fictional character
> and makes him famous, and in time the writer identifies with his character. And
> when a movie actor becomes identified with the character by the public, the writer
> regards it as an intolerable usurpation and is driven to remove the actor by killing
> him.

Rex based this plot on a situation reported to him by Frederic Dannay,
in 1954, when they were making a joint appearance at Kann's Department Store in Washington, D.C. A radio actor portraying Ellery Queen
identified with the part to the point where he opened a charge account
under the name of Ellery Queen. Later, another actor portraying the part
on television began making lecture appearances as Ellery Queen. Since
there were two Ellery Queens already — his creators, Manfred Lee and
Frederic Dannay — obviously four Queens made an ample hand. Lee and
Dannay got rid of their interlopers short of murder. Queen reported these
episodes in "Over the Borderline," in *In the Queen's Parlor*, New York,
1957, pp. 146–148. Frederic Dannay to JM, 15 September 1975; 18 December 1975.
Like Alphabet Hicks, Erle Stanley Gardner's Donald Lam is a disbarred
lawyer. Like Archie, Lam is first-person narrator, legman, and wise-
cracker. He also is attractive to women. His partner, Bertha Cool, is in
some ways a female counterpart to Nero Wolfe. She is stout, yet light on
her feet. She is a heavy eater. She will not drive her own car. An unhappy
marriage has left her wary of the opposite sex. Donald and Bertha made
their first appearance in 1938, postdating Wolfe's first appearance by four
years but anticipating the advent of Alphabet Hicks by three years. In
Pass the Gravy (1959), Donald Lam meets a girl who is an avid reader of
"stories of Nero Wolfe by Rex Stout" (p. 16).
6. William Stevenson, *A Man Called Intrepid*, New York, 1976, pp. 279–285.
7. George M. Merten to JM, 15 September 1972. Dr. James H. Sheldon sent
me the original text of this hard-to-come-by speech just a few days before
he dropped dead, on 16 April 1975, while addressing the United Nations
Association of the United States.
8. Sylvia Porter to JM, 3 October 1972.
9. As an attorney for the New York law firm of Sullivan and Cromwell, John
Foster Dulles made semiannual visits to Berlin in the 1920's and early

1930's. In 1934, Dulles and his wife attended a Walter Gieseking concert with Adolf Hitler, as Hitler's personal guests. Dulles admitted representing International Nickel and American Radiator, both of which had cartel connections, but insisted that he had no ties with their foreign subsidiaries. His biographer, John Robinson Beal, says that Dulles "never had anything to do, directly or indirectly, with the great German chemical firm, I.G. Farben." *John Foster Dulles,* New York, 1957, pp. 83–85.

On 30 November 1975, columnist Jack Anderson reported in the Washington *Post* that he had found in his examination of newly accessible State Department files that Rex Stout was described there as "a tool of Comintern agents" because of his role in promoting *Sequel to an Apocalypse.*

10. Miller, *Man from the Valley,* p. 109; Hyde, *Room 3603,* pp. 124–127.

11. Of Marquand's stories about his Japanese sleuth, Mr. Moto, Rex said: "Well conceived and well told, but the characters never warm up."

12. "The Adventures of Sherlock Holmes," in *The Second Invitation to Learning,* ed. Mark Van Doren, New York, 1944, pp. 236–251. A copy of this volume was loaned to me by Professor Van Doren.

13. Howard Haycraft, "Dictators, Democrats, and Detectives," *Murder for Pleasure,* New York, 1972, pp. 312–318. On 1 November 1972, Haycraft wrote me:

> The original version was written in white heat on the day World War II broke out [1 September 1939]. *The Saturday Review of Literature* printed it as a guest editorial [7 October 1939]. Rex may have expressed similar ideas, unknown to me; it would certainly have been in character for him to have sensed the relationship. I should certainly be happy to share the credit with Rex.

"Howard was there first." RS

14. In 1973, on 5 May, Rex again updated the list. It now read: "The Murders in the Rue Morgue," *The Hound of the Baskervilles, The Moonstone, Daughter of Time, The Maltese Falcon, The Brothers Karamazov, Strong Poison, The Murder of Roger Ackroyd, The League of Frightened Men,* and "one of a dozen or so Maigrets." A significant change was Rex's choice of one of his own books for the "favorite ten."

15. *Twentieth Century Authors,* ed. Stanley Kunitz and Howard Haycraft, New York, 1942, pp. 1354–1355, describes Rex as one of the "most active and successful mobilizers of public opinion in World War II." An updated biographical sketch appears in *Twentieth Century Authors,* ed. Stanley Kunitz and Vineta Colby, New York, 1955, pp. 963–964.

16. Alan Green to JM, 23 March 1973.

17. Archie Goodwin said once that Wolfe, from behind, looked like a float in Macy's Thanksgiving Day parade. Rex did take out time during the years in Manhattan to bring Barbara and Rebecca to this parade every Thanksgiving.

18. Clifton Fadiman to JM, 18 August 1972.

32. The Lie Detective

1. Lawrence G. Blochman to JM, 5 March 1974.

2. George Field to JM, 5 August 1972.

3. *Newsweek,* 7 December 1942.

4. Did Rex give much thought to making Archie a major? Why not a captain

or a colonel? "No. Why must there be a why not?" RS
5. *Not Quite Dead Enough,* New York, 1944, p. 19.
6. Frank Sullivan to JM, 5 October 1972.

33. Chairman Rex

1. An Ann Arbor microfilm print of Robert Thomas Howell's 557 page dissertation, *The Writers' War Board: Writers and World War II,* done as Professor Howell's Ph.D. thesis at Louisiana State University, has been a major resource in tracing the history of the WWB. Howell interviewed many board members and searched the one hundred and forty-three boxes in the Manuscript Division of the Library of Congress, in which WWB records are stored. He has, as well, given valuable direction in correspondence with me.
2. "Report to Date on the Activities of the Committee on Speeches and Speakers," 6 November 1943, Container 13, WWB Records, Manuscript Division, Library of Congress. See Howell, p. 103.
3. Margaret Leech Pulitzer earned two Pulitzer Prizes in History, the first for *Reveille in Washington* (1941); the second for *In the Days of McKinley* (1959). Geoffrey Crowther, editor of the *London Economist,* edited *Transatlantic* in London. Margaret Leech Pulitzer to JM, 22 March 1973.
4. Frederica Barach to JM, 22 March 1973.
5. Dorothy Rodgers to JM, 29 November 1972.
6. John Marquand to Rex Stout, 28 June 1943. The Marquand letters are at Houghton Library, Harvard University.
7. John Marquand to Rex Stout, 1 June 1942.
8. Orin Tovrov to JM, 12 January 1974.
9. *Might as Well Be Dead,* New York, 1956, p. 107.
10. "Nonsense. Of course there are criminals by definition." RS
11. Marcia Davenport to JM, 14 April 1975.
12. Marcia Davenport, *Too Strong for Fantasy,* New York, 1967, pp. 302–304.
13. "I knew Aleck was in serious trouble. Otherwise he would have written, 'I AM ILL.' Aleck was fussy with words." RS
14. See Samuel Hopkins Adams, *A. Woollcott: His Life and His World,* New York, 1945; Howard Teichmann, *Smart Aleck: The Wit, World and Life of Alexander Woollcott,* New York, 1976; Edwin P. Hoyt, *Alexander Woollcott, The Man Who Came to Dinner,* New York, 1968. Woollcott and Rex were nearly exact contemporaries, having been born just fifty days apart. Yet Rex told me that fey feelings did not enter into the impressions Woollcott's death made on him. Rex never felt insecure about anything.

34. Hunting with the Hounds

1. The cover carries in small type, just above the title, the words "To Prevent World War III," words Rex would find a later use for.
2. Exercising an editor's prerogative, Rex enlisted two WWB stalwarts to contribute to the *Mystery Monthly.* Christopher La Farge's "Three Cups of Tea" was in the May 1947 issue, pp. 107–116. Alan Green's "Sea-Scape" was in the final issue (1947), pp. 62–81.

3. Edmund Wilson, "Why Do People Read Detective Stories?" *A Literary Chronicle, 1920–1950*, New York, 1952, pp. 324–326. Wilson also wrote a hostile review of *Not Quite Dead Enough, The New Yorker*, 14 October 1944.

4. *Rue Morgue No. 1*, New York, 1946, p. ix.

5. P. G. Wodehouse to JM, 3 July 1972.

6. Himan Brown to JM, 1 December 1972.

7. Greenstreet had not undertaken a sustained radio role before. He was then seventy-one, and dying of Bright's disease. He said he found the part "colorful and away from the usual run of whodunits."

8. Rex liked Crowther in his role as editor of *Transatlantic Magazine.*

9. "Our Secret Weapon," No. 45, 11 June 1943.

10. "Our Secret Weapon," No. 53, 6 August 1943.

11. "Our Secret Weapon," No. 62, 8 October 1943. In announcing the end of the series, Rex's sponsor, the Philco Corporation, commented: "Rex Stout has been more than a match for the whole Axis propaganda machine from Berlin to Tokyo."

12. To the end of his life Rex opposed limiting a President's term in office.

13. Rev. George B. Ford to JM, 3 July 1972.

14. What attributes did Walt and Archie share in common? "Wearing pants and eating three times a day." RS

15. Margaret Leech Pulitzer to JM, 22 March 1973.

16. "I went to the White House four or five times by appointment during the war — once to try to sell FDR on world government. No sale." RS

17. Selma Jerskey Greenstein, 2 December 1971.

35. Ideological Racketeer

1. "The War Guilt of Fadiman Kip," *Common Sense*, 13 (January 1944): 34.

2. "The Shame of American Writers," *Common Sense*, 13 (May 1944): 187; "Writers' War Board," *Common Sense*, 13 (June 1944): 206. In this interval Rex also was the target of a *Daily Worker* attack. In mid-March 1945, although he himself was out of the country on a government mission, and took no part in the decision, Rex's alignments were affirmed when his fellow directors at Freedom House voted 13–1 to reject a $5,000 gift made by Earl Browder, on behalf of the Communist Political Association (as the Communist Party in America then designated itself), for Freedom House's Willkie Memorial Building. Browder's donation was the only one of thousands made which was accompanied by a press release from the donor. Through it, Browder sought to annex Willkie as a fellow traveler. When the board's decision was announced, Herbert Bayard Swope, as spokesman, said of the Communist Political Association, "You cannot associate with that body without taking on its odor." A month later, the Party expelled Browder as a deviationist. On Rex's return, he acclaimed the board's decision. It paralleled exactly his own policy in rejecting Browder's help with the WWB, in 1942. See Aaron Levenstein and William Agar, *Freedom's Advocate*, New York, 1965, pp. 75, 83–85.

3. *Under Cover*, Cleveland, 1943, p. 520.

4. Marion K. Sanders, *Dorothy Thompson: A Legend in Her Time*, New York 1973. Sanders says also: "In the outline for her memoirs Dorothy wrote, '1949 — Began Decline.' "

5. Fadiman to JM, 2 November 1972.
6. "It was patently irrational and unfeasible." RS
7. Rex Stout to Chester Barnard, 14 March 1944.
8. For a copy of the script and for details concerning the production, presentation, and tour, I am indebted to Mrs. Oscar Hammerstein II, Ruth Friend, and Alan Green.

36. A Man of Sovereign Parts

1. My account here is enlivened by the recollections of Rex, Kay Boyle, Dorothy Cameron Disney, Marquis Child, Carol Brandt, and Beatrice Blackmar Gould. Edward L. Burlingame, nephew of Roger Burlingame, shared with me notations in his late uncle's journal which helped fix a timetable for the day-to-day progress of the tour.
2. Herbert Agar to JM, 27 September 1972.
3. In 1974 Rex told me he regretted his poor marksmanship on this occasion.
4. Kay Boyle and Roger Burlingame left the group before the end of the tour, irked by the behavior of a few of their number who "were dealing heavily in the selling of American currency to officers in our armed forces." "Rex's reaction," says Kay, "was as indignant as my own." To meet his obligations, he stayed with the tour.
5. New York *Post*, 18 May 1945.
6. "Since I don't know the Russian language I'm not qualified to judge Chekhov as a writer. What gets me is his ability to communicate his amazing understanding of the imponderables in human character and conduct." RS
7. The Pledge for Peace urged the founding of a world government the member states of which would "give up forever the sovereign right to commit acts of war against other nations." It also called for the creation of an international police force to keep peace.
8. John Marquand to Rex Stout, 14 June 1943; John Marquand to Rex Stout, 23 June 1943.
9. "Howard convinced the WWB with a three-page letter. The vote agreeing with him was unanimous." RS
10. Howell, *The Writers' War Board*, p. 469, quoting Rex Stout to Mumford, 19 October 1944. Container 88, WWB Records.
11. *Harper's*, December 1945, pp. 505–509.
12. Alyce Yasumoto to JM, 14 September 1973.
13. "Why Attack Niemöller?" *Christian Century*, 62 (12 September 1945): 1031–1032.
14. *Christian Century*, 62 (21 November 1945): 1290.
15. Barbara J. Benjamin, who had a summer job with the board that year, says:

> I remember the times Rex would mysteriously disappear without telling anyone where he was going — and then return to the office with his beard a darker color than it had been when he left. We always felt that he never knew that we knew he dyed it — but we did. I also have lovely memories of him bringing us his own enormous home grown peaches — and even bringing an occasional orchid to the office.

Barbara J. Benjamin to JM, 2 July 1973.

16. Alan Green to JM, 24 March 1973.
17. John and Margaret Farrar to JM, 18 April 1973.
18. Is it probable that Archie is the hero of the series to many lady readers? "More than probable, certain. Judging from letters I get from women of all ages, to about four-fifths of them." RS
19. "I wrote nine or ten like these for our daughters and the Yasumotos to recite in school." RS. Those who insisted that Rex, as propagandist, wrote with a pen dipped in vitriol might have been nonplussed had they learned that he was now occupied in producing verses for grade schoolers, including sansei children just emerged from wartime detention camps.
20. Alyce Yasumoto to JM, 25 April 1973.
21. Rex thought children have a more normal childhood if they grow up as part of a large family. He was upset when his daughters got so many gifts at Christmas that they wearied of opening them.
22. Alyce Yasumoto to JM, 25 April 1973.

37. Under Viking Sail

1. Rex was on hand when the permanent headquarters of Freedom House, the Willkie Memorial Building at 20 West Fortieth Street, was dedicated on 8 October 1945, the first anniversary of Willkie's death.
2. *New York Times,* 11 February 1946.
   Alan Green recalled Rex's initial assessment of Truman: "We went to Kip's [Clifton Fadiman's] New York apartment on the night of April 12th 1945. FDR had died that afternoon. Rex and Pola were there. We'd come together out of shared shock and sorrow. Someone — maybe I — was bemoaning the inexperience of Truman taking over. 'He'll do all right,' said Rex. 'He's a sound little guy and he's tough. The office will make the man.' "
3. Darwin Payne, *The Man of Only Yesterday: Frederick Lewis Allen,* New York, 1975, pp. 210–211.
4. Anthony Boucher to Rex Stout, March 1946.
5. Not only had Bob founded the local Community Chest and built the Red Cross Chapter House, he was then in his twentieth year as president of the North Jersey Trust Company and deep into his commitment to raise eleven million dollars for the Valley Hospital. The community was proud, too, of Bob's son, Jay. A captain in the Air Force, Jay had come through World War II with a chestful of medals.
6. As a pioneer consumer advocate himself, Rex held Ralph Nader in high esteem.
7. Marshall Best to JM, 24 July 1972.
8. Alan Green to JM, 23 March 1973.
9. Clifton Fadiman to JM, November 1972.
10. Cecil Brown to JM, 8 January 1974.
11. *Fer-de-Lance,* New York, 1934, p. 120.
12. "Bullet for One" features murder on the bridle path, in Central Park. Did Rex approve of horseback riding in the park? "For horse lovers, fine. For show-offs, pfui." RS

38. A Superman Who Talks like a Superman

1. "When I wrote *And Be a Villain* I didn't plan, or even consciously contemplate, subsequent appearance or appearances of Zeck, but I suspect my subconscious thought he would show up again. When I wrote *The Second Confession* I must have felt he would appear again, but I had no idea how or when." RS
2. Robert Landry to JM, 19 March 1973.
3. Ruth Friend to JM, 17 November 1972. Ruth Friend says: "Without Rex's great qualities of leadership, nothing would have been done. He knew when to cajole or to bully. He spent a tremendous amount of time in the office, keeping all our accounts in the most meticulous fashion, and writing the letters, making the calls that needed his extra touch."
4. "Alias Nero Wolfe — I," *The New Yorker*, 16 July 1949, pp. 26–41; "Alias Nero Wolfe — II," *The New Yorker*, 23 July 1949, pp. 30–43.
   "Johnston offered to let me read it in advance, but I declined with thanks." RS
5. *The New Yorker*, 20 August 1949, pp. 52–58.
6. What writer would Rex have been willing to pay a comparable compliment to? "E. B. White." RS
   La Farge's letter, written on 26 July 1953, began:

   What I am going to say in this letter, I have already said to you. But I have wanted for some time to write it to you, so that it might become if you choose, a more permanent part of your personal archives. What happens to the work of any artist ultimately is too hypothetical to be worth predicting. But even though the chance of survival in interest should be but one in ten thousand, it is worth that chance to tell you what I feel.

   How could a biographer not feel tender regard for Christopher La Farge?
   Rex thought La Farge's phrase "that growth of the work which might be properly expected to come from its own progression" particularly fine.
7. *The Daily Worker*, 19 October 1949.
8. Alan Green to JM, 13 February 1974.
9. After the performance the board presented Rex with a framed metal replica of the ticket of admission. It read: " 'The Myth that Threatens the World'/Coronet Theatre/230 West 49th Street/Sunday Evening December 4th/8:30 sharp/Admit Rex Stout/who thought of it in the first place."
10. Has postwar Germany turned out better than Rex expected it to? "Maybe." RS

39. Beyond High Meadow

1. Less than $60,000 of the Brink's loot was recovered. All of the robbers were apprehended, tried, and convicted, however, after one of their number, Joseph ("Specs") O'Keefe (cheated out of his share of the stolen money), turned state's evidence and informed on the others.

2. In *In the Best Families*, Wolfe, after losing eighty pounds, says he looks like "a sixteenth century Prince of Savoy named Philibert." Was there such a prince? "I think I saw a picture of him in the Louvre, but I'm not sure. I may have made him up." RS. Perhaps the portrait Rex saw was of Emmanuel-Philibert Tête de Fer, 1528–1580, duc de Savoie, who married the daughter of François I of France, or of Philibert II Le Beau, 1480–1504, also duc de Savoie. What happened to Wolfe's orchids while he was off chasing Zeck? "Hewitt had them and returned them to Wolfe." RS

3. Was the open door in *In the Best Families* meant to be symbolic? "Yes. It is symbolic. I agree that it's subtle. One way to put it is that Wolfe was removing from the house what the closed door had guarded from intrusion, but it could be said several other ways and each reader could choose for himself." RS

4. At one point in *Where There's a Will*, Archie incredibly describes Wolfe as "zooming around like a wren building a nest."

5. Rev. George B. Ford to JM, 18 July 1972.

6. Julian Symons, Manchester *Evening News*, 5 April 1951; Sir Hugh Greene to JM, 1 February 1974.

7. At what age was Archie fixed in Rex's mind? "I like thirty-four." RS

8. Does the brownstone stand flush to adjacent brownstones? "There is a space on the east side, none on the west." RS
    Could someone break through the west wall? "Yes. I must alert Archie." RS

9. Rex received so many queries about the floor plan of the brownstone that eventually he had one printed up, which he sent to all inquirers.

10. Frederic Dannay (Ellery Queen) and Eleanor Sullivan, managing editor of *Ellery Queen's Mystery Magazine*, pulled this information from their files for me.

40. King Rex

1. J. B. Priestley, 19 July 1959. Of Priestley, Rex said: "Priestley is a competent and readable writer."

2. Cecil Brown to JM, 8 January 1974.

3. Abe Burrows to JM, 12 January 1974.

4. H. Allen Smith to JM, 26 January 1973.

5. Cecil Brown to JM, 8 January 1974.

6. Letter loaned by Lawrence G. Blochman.

7. Alyce Yasumoto to JM, 14 September 1973.

8. Not quite. "Nero Wolfe doesn't think women are good liars." RS

9. "The pretense that Holmes and Watson existed and Doyle was merely a literary agent can be fun and often is, but it is often abused and becomes silly. My 'never knowing more about Archie and Wolfe than what Archie chooses to tell' is not a pose; it is a necessary barricade. In letters from everywhere I have been asked thousands of questions about NW and AG. If I started answering them, where would I stop? If scholars of the future are interested in them, that will be fine, no matter what they say about me." RS

41. Watch Out for Rex Stout

1. The League neither defended nor condemned the individual views of its members.

2. In 1955. Years later the jackets of his books still insisted that he had three hundred house plants.

3. Alan Green remembered:

> On the train on our way to Hartford where we would be met and driven to the University of Connecticut, where we were jointly speaking on behalf of UWF, Rex said he had an idea for a plot for his next NW. Then (totally unlike him — he never discusses his plots in advance) he outlined a premise and a middle. "But Rex," I said, "That's the line Christopher Bush used in his *The Perfect Murder Case* back in the thirties." Rex seemed astonished, expressed his gratitude and we talked of other things. I still rather think he was having me on.

Alan Green to JM, 4 April 1974.

4. "A Rich and Varied Menu," *New York Times Book Review*, 24 May 1953.

5. "Talk with Merle Miller," *New York Times Book Review*, 10 October 1954.

6. Did Rex subscribe to the view "Better dead than Red?" "No. A slogan is a weapon, not an argument." RS

7. "Another Author's Gripe," *Saturday Review*, 20 February 1954.

8. Rex could sympathize with Archie. He spoke only English.

9. The previous spring, when Representative Carroll D. Kearns entered comments in the *Congressional Record* that were meant to identify DeVoto as a Communist or Communist sympathizer, citing his friendship with Rex as one proof of this, DeVoto had written letters to both Representative Emanuel Celler and Representative Kearns repudiating Kearns's attack on Rex. Before drafting these letters he corresponded with Rex on the subject to be sure he had his facts straight. Kearns had reiterated the hoary charge that Rex was an editor of *The New Masses*. *The Letters of Bernard DeVoto*, ed. Wallace Stegner, New York, 1975, pp. 189–192.

10. Absentmindedly DeVoto gave his article the same title — "Alias Nero Wolfe" — that Alva Johnston had given his two-part *New Yorker* profile of Rex, in 1949.

11. Rex Stout to Basil Davenport, 15 March 1940. This remarkable letter is now in the possession of Peter Stern, a dedicated student of the Wolfe saga.

12. "Vukcic rhymes with Book-sitch." RS

13. Cerf closed one column with the admonition, "Watch Out for Rex Stout." "His liking for me was about as thin as mine for him." RS

14. Rex Stout to H. Allen Smith, 31 December 1964. See also H. Allen Smith, *Desert Island Decameron*, New York, 1945, p. 13.

15. Rex once told an interviewer that his own favorite among his novellas was in *Three Witnesses*. "I don't remember saying that. If I did, I probably meant 'The Next Witness.'" RS

16. "The Great O-E Theory," *In the Queen's Parlor*, New York, 1957, pp. 4–5.

17. This letter and other DeVoto papers in the DeVoto Collection at Stanford University were made available to me by Avis DeVoto.

42. The King in Action

1. "Except for the gravy a few writers get, which is fine, book awards are meaningless." RS
2. Mark Van Doren to JM, 6 July 1972.
3. Janice Ehrenberg kept a complete file on "the battle of Riverdale" and turned it over to me. I salute her.
4. An earlier omnibus, *The Nero Wolfe Omnibus*, was published by World Publishing Company, in 1944. It contained *The League of Frightened Men* and *The Red Box*.
5. Charles Brady to JM, 12 February 1974. Declining to comment on Brady's remarks, Rex said: "A writer who evaluates another's estimation of his works, except for his own files, is an ass."

43. More than a Duke

1. *Baker Street Journal*, June 1961, pp. 82–83.
2. Margaret Cousins to JM, 1 November 1975.
3. Don Maroc, Barbara's husband, was then sales manager for Pola Stout, Inc., which had its designing studio at 455 West Thirty-fourth Street.
4. In "Christmas Party" Rex mentions Bill Gore for the last time. Bill, along with Saul, Fred, and Orrie, had been used by Wolfe, through the years, for special assignments. Why did Rex drop Bill? "It wasn't deliberate. Apparently he bored me." RS
5. Roy Hunt, Richard Lochte, Mike W. Barr, and Mike Nefenbacher procured for me a representative selection of the Nero Wolfe comic strips.
6. In 1956, one of Rex's friends presented him with a verse tribute. To the best of Rex's recollection, the friend was John Steinbeck. Illustrations placed at the end of each line of the poem were a Steinbeck trademark. Mrs. Steinbeck assures me that her husband was "a great fan of the Nero Wolfe stories," but she "simply is not sure" whether the poem was written by Steinbeck. Mrs. John Steinbeck to JM, 17 June 1975. We reproduce the text:

A Poem for Parlous Times

There's Nixon,
   And Dixon,
      And Yates,
And Dulles's [*sic*] — Alan and John.

There are bombs and bacteria
And pervasive hysteria
And *putters* all over the lawn.

We're scared to wake up in the morning
And wouldn't feel safe to go out
If we couldn't say —
As we do every day —
Thank God for the presence of Stout!

Here's to Archie, and Nero, and Rex
May they thrive like the gourd vine of yore

And the Stout whiskers bristle
Like the proverbial thistle
While Nero keeps feasting and Wolfe's at the door.

44. Master of Mystery

1. Later, Block met Pola at Sardi's and sent home with her a note to Rex, affirming his admiration for him and his works. In the final Nero Wolfe book, *A Family Affair* (1975), Wolfe peruses an inscribed copy of Herblock's *Special Report*. While Rex was writing *A Family Affair*, Herblock had sent him an inscribed copy of *Special Report*, a collection of Richard Nixon cartoons.

2. David Overmyer to Rex Stout, 17 April 1957.

3. Correspondence supplied by Phyllis Boucher.

   In 1970, J. Francis McComas edited a Boucher Memorial anthology, *Crimes and Misfortunes*. The contents were donated by the authors and the royalties went to the Mystery Writers of America, in Boucher's memory. Rex contributed "Bullet for One." He introduced it with this commentary:

   > Years ago this story solved a problem for me and caused Tony a lot of bother. The Authors' League of America had made me chairman of a committee to organize a three-day National Assembly of Authors and Dramatists to be held in New York, and I was having a devil of a time getting firm commitments for the sixteen panel sessions. I called Tony long-distance to tell him that I wanted and needed him on the panel on Freedom to Write. He said no, he couldn't make the trip, and then he said, "Well . . . damn it. . . . I just read your story 'Bullet for One,' and I like it so much that I suppose I'll have to. . . . All right, I'll come."
   > When Tony said he liked a story, he really meant it.

4. Handy died on 28 March 1958.

5. "He can work free of many unwanted interruptions, e.g., answering the telephone." RS

6. The eighteenth-century French nursery ditty "Malbrouck s'en va-t-en guerre" is sung in the English-speaking world as "We won't go home until morning," with the second verse, "For he's a jolly good fellow."

7. Mrs. Roosevelt told Pola that FDR read and enjoyed three or four Nero Wolfe novels.

8. Pola's friends and admirers are legion, but I must thank especially Edna Brandau for the bulging files she supplied me and Gay Simpson for her memoir on Pola as an artist and a friend.

9. *Saturday Evening Post*, 5 July 1958, p. 90.

10. "Poison à la Carte," written prior to "Method Three for Murder," appeared in hardcover in 1960. In 1968 it was published in the April issue of *Ellery Queen's Mystery Magazine*.

11. Edward Mabley to JM, 5 July 1973.

12. Florence Eldridge to JM, 27 August 1972.

45. The Best We Have

1. In eleven of fifty-five Wolfe tales for which he kept a writing record, Rex placed the start of the action within three days of the day he started writing. In another six the action begins within a week of the day he started writing.
2. Samuel Grafton to JM, 29 May 1973.
3. "I am *not* an arrogant driver." RS
4. Cecil Brown to JM, 8 January 1974.
5. Young, foreign women are likely murder victims in Rex Stout's novels, including his last novel, *A Family Affair.* Usually they have a secret.
6. Adjusting to heartbreak was a Stout trait that year. On 23 August death had taken Rex's longtime friend Oscar Hammerstein II. "Oscar never missed a meeting of the WWB, through the whole of its existence," Rex said. The records of the board bear him out (Howell, *The Writers' War Board,* pp. 26–27). On Thanksgiving Day, Fred Rossiter, Ruth's husband, died. Ruth called High Meadow to tell Rex. Rex and the family were in the midst of dinner. "Everything is under control," Ruth said. "Finish your dinner, then call me back and we'll talk about it."
7. *The Saturday Evening Post,* p. 94.
8. Karl Menninger to Rex Stout, 8 February 1961.
9. H. Allen Smith to JM, 26 January 1973.
10. Alan Green received an Edgar from Mystery Writers of America for *What a Body!,* New York, 1949.
11. Alan Green to JM, 5 March 1974.
12. Pola Stout provided a tape of the evening. Jack Mahoney, Director of Audio-Visual at Boston College, transferred it to cassettes for me.
    Mark Van Doren gave me a copy of his verse tribute. It reads:

> To Rex this toast, while Archie shuts his eyes
> And dreams of sandwiches and Fritz's pies,
> And milk, and girls that take him by surprise.
>
> To Rex this altogether serious word
> Of how he hoped to stop World War the Third,
> And so far does, for it has not occurred.
>
> He thought of it before the Second ended.
> The German fence, he said, would not be mended
> Till what was true was told, and what pretended.
>
> So Rex and his Society made known
> Mankind's then greatest danger. All alone
> They labored, turning over every stone
> Till all the ground was clear, and light poured in
> As even now it does — lo, on Berlin!
> To Rex a long good life, and peace within.

13. Rex Stout to Rev. William McEntegart, S.J., January 1962.
14. Cleveland Amory to JM, 19 September 1974.

46. A Majesty's Life

1. Rex had no desire to winter in the West Indies. He gave two reasons: "One, because I like the four seasons. Two, because most of the people you are with in those places are not at work, and people not at work are irksome."

2. "I have no idea what the size of my vocabulary is. Of course I would rather use a thousand words well than a million poorly. I doubt if I have ever failed to look up an unfamiliar word when I met one. In recent years I haven't added too many words. I guess you don't take on new words in your eighties. I could use 'stonewall.' " RS

   Did Rex ever have a word ruined for him by some unpleasant association? "Yes. 'Gay,' for instance." RS

   "How does the word 'fanzine' strike you?" he was asked, when in 1974, Lee Poleske, of Seward, Alaska, launched a "Nero Wolfe Fanzine." "It doesn't," Rex replied.

   "Detente?" "As a word, fine. As a policy, full of cracks." RS

3. *On Her Majesty's Secret Service,* New York, 1963, pp. 142–143.

4. Ian Fleming to Rex Stout, 18 July 1962.

5. Gay Simpson, fashion editor of the Dallas *Morning News,* was at High Meadow once when a patronizing guest turned to her and said, "Whatever do people in Texas talk about?" Before Gay could come back with a reply, Rex squelched her inquisitor with the withering retort, "Oil!"

6. Eleanor Furman to JM, 20 February 1974.

7. Norman Cousins to JM, 20 March 1973.

8. "Why Nero Wolfe Likes Orchids," *Life,* 19 April 1963, p. 108.

9. John T. Winterich, *The Fales Collection: A Record of Growth,* New York, 1963, pp. 17–18. Rex Stout to John T. Winterich, 30 July 1963.

10. In late December John Barkham hailed Rex in the *Saturday Review* as "the doyen of American mystery writers." The phrase was widely circulated after that. Both Rex and his venerable correspondent, Rev. William McEntegart, S.J., found the phrase, as a compliment, meaningless.

11. Rating our Presidents, Rex said: "In the first rank I put only Washington and Lincoln. Of recent Presidents, on a percentage scale, I rate Truman 74, Ike 47, LBJ 61, JFK 53." Rex had not voted for JFK. He was afraid he might be priest-ridden. That year he voted for no one.

12. "Rex presided over the long and complex discussions and arrangements for the reorganization which produced a very effective new form of relationship that gives each Guild complete independence in its field, yet permits complete cooperation on the matters of common concern to both authors and dramatists. The new structure has functioned extremely well." Irwin Karp to JM, 22 February 1974.

47. A Fish at Wolfe's Door

1. "I recall the scorn Rex once poured on my head for having a literary agent. What did I want *that* for? Everyone could and should manage his own business affairs and know to the last penny — etc. etc. He managed all *his* own literary business — subsidiary rights, serial, translations, anthology etc. etc. — What did I mean letting anyone take 10% off me for something *anyone* could do (anyone with half a brain, he implied). It was

a magnificent tirade — commanding awe, if not emulation." Barbara Tuchman to JM, 14 March 1973.

In 1960 Hillman Books published *The Rubber Band* under the title *To Kill Again*. Rex dedicated this paperback edition to "RS, my literary agent." I asked him who RS was. "Rex Stout," he told me.

Irwin Karp confirms Rex's competency as a businessman: "Rex is one of the few authors who had the foresight not to include television rights in a contract authorizing a motion picture version of one of his early novels. To its chagrin, the film company had to come back and negotiate with him again — as all companies should — for permission to show the film on television. Most authors who sell film rights see nothing of the profit the company makes when it licenses television broadcasts." Irwin Karp to JM, 2 February 1974.

2. Robert W. Mitchum, Director of the Indiana University Writers' Conference, to JM, 27 October 1972.

3. Copy supplied by Peter Heggie and Jean Wynne. Irwin Karp says: "Rex was active in the campaign for the Copyright Revision Bill. The League was primarily responsible for inserting the life-and-fifty year term in the Bill, a clause which terminated assignments of copyright after thirty-five years and returned rights to the author, and several other major provisions." Irwin Karp to JM, 2 February 1974.

Of Rex's joint appearance with Elizabeth Janeway, John Hersey, Herman Wouk, and Karp himself, before a House Judiciary Subcommittee on 26 May 1965, in behalf of copyright revision, Karp says: "Rex's testimony was very lively and quotable. And for me — at one point — embarrassing. Rex was holding forth with great confidence on some technical point, and then turned to me and said 'Am I right, Mr. Karp?' — and I was obliged to tell Rex and the Congressmen on the dais, that I regretted to inform him he was wrong. Undaunted, Rex plowed on."

I am indebted also to John Hersey for background concerning this appearance before the Subcommittee. John Hersey to JM, 8 August 1975.

Rex never got so caught up in the big issues that he forgot individuals. In 1961, at the age of seventy-three, after serving the Authors' League for forty-one years, Luise Sillcox retired to a farm at Hartford, Vermont, because of ill health. At Rex's suggestion, the Directors voted to continue her salary. Rex visited her in Vermont to see after her needs. She died on 28 June 1965.

4. For the details of this appearance I am indebted to Dorothy Beall, chairman of the Friends of the Brookfield Library.

5. "This situation is now worse than ever." RS, August 1975.

6. Fred J. Cook to JM, 11 September 1972; 6 January 1974; 14 January 1974; 13 August 1975. And see Fred J. Cook, *The FBI Nobody Knows*, New York, 1964; and Harry and Bonaro Overstreet, *The FBI in Our Open Society*, New York 1969.

7. Rex told Stinnett that he was "on speaking terms with three members of the New York State Police, and God how they hate the FBI." Rex told me: "Harold Salmon's son (Harold, Jr.) was a state trooper for several years, and I met a couple of his colleagues."

8. "The subject of the field survey was Jake Baker." RS

9. "The big fish" was one of Rex's favorite terms of disparagement. During the Riverdale crisis, he used it also to describe the national director of the National Americanism Commission of the American Legion.

10. *Saturday Review*, 9 October 1965, p. 54.

11. Leo Rosten to JM, 28 February 1974.
12. *Over My Dead Body* (New York, 1940), p. 156.
13. Herbert Mitgang to JM, 19 March 1974.
14. On 30 November 1965, under the heading "Nero Wolfe Finds FBI Agents Are Demonic Doorbell Ringers," F. O. Eberhart wrote in *The Daily Worker:*

> Somewhere in the files of the Federal Bureau of Investigation, a new or perhaps updated dossier must read along these lines: "Rex Stout — established subversive, active in World War II for the defeat of Fascism, chairman of a front organization, Writers' Board for World Government, had held or still holds office with various egghead groups such as the Authors' Guild and Authors' League of America, wears a beard obviously cut in imitation of Ho Chi Minh (this may also relate to domestic peace movements): author of a scandalous novel designed to put the FBI in ill repute."

Eberhart wrote further: "Stout himself would no doubt disclaim any immortal spot for himself in literature, but he is entitled to an award for being the first popular writer to burst the FBI bubble. . . . Sic 'em Nero!"
15. This format was an afterthought. Originally the article was written as a review.
See "The Rosenberg Case," *Commentary,* June 1966, pp. 9–10; a letter from Rex Stout to the editor of *Commentary,* protesting Alexander M. Bickel's review of *Invitation to an Inquest* in *Commentary's* January 1966 issue.
16. "Jacques Barzun and I have discussed Archie Goodwin several times. He is sure he knows more about him than I do." RS
17. *A Birthday Tribute to Rex Stout,* New York, 1965, p. 8.

48. Champion of Justice

1. "We were there because Rex wanted us to be." Dorothy Van Doren to JM, 29 August 1975.
2. *Baker Street Journal,* March 1966, p. 23.
3. In later years Pola never spoke to Rex about the death of friends. Rex said the news did not upset him. Pola thought that it did.
4. *Baker Street Journal,* January 1956, pp. 5–10. See also Edmund Wilson's 1945 essay, " 'Mr. Holmes, They Were the Footprints of a Gigantic Hound!' " reprinted in *A Literary Chronicle: 1920–1950,* New York, 1956, p. 351; Bernard DeVoto, "Alias Nero Wolfe," *Harper's,* July 1954, p. 15; William S. Baring-Gould, "Meeting in Montenegro: June 1891," in *Sherlock Holmes of Baker Street,* New York, 1962, pp. 207–212.
5. *Baker Street Journal,* January 1956, p. 11.
6. Abel Green, "Authors' Guild's Hero-Publisher," *Variety,* 2 March 1966.
7. Rex Stout to Sloan Wilson, 5 July 1971.
8. *Arts in Society,* Spring 1967, p. 295.
9. Don Bensen, "An Exclusive Interview with Rex Stout," *Writers' Digest* (May 1968), p. 57.
10. In this book Wolfe makes a further tangential inquiry into Hoover's role in the Rosenberg case.
11. Rex's praise of Pound was qualified. "Ingenious choice and handling of words. Third-rate cerebration." RS

12. Edmund Crispin, "Archie, Your Notebook," London *Sunday Times*, 4 June 1967.
13. "I meant I never wasted time regretting a sacrifice, so it wasn't 'serious.' " RS
14. Thew Wright to JM, 1 March 1974.
15. Thew Wright to JM, 1 March 1974.
16. In 1947 Farrell paid Rex the compliment of adapting one of his titles for his book *The League of Frightened Philistines.*
17. Robert J. Landry to JM, 19 March 1973.

49. The One and True Paradigm

1. The surgeon was Joseph B. Cherry.
2. Richard S. Lochte II loaned me the cassette tapes containing the interview.
3. J. B. Priestley to Rex Stout, 20 February 1968.
4. Nineteen sixty-eight was Rex's last full year as president of the Authors' League.
5. *New York Times Book Review,* 14 July 1968.
6. Helmut Heissenbüttel, "Spielregeln des Kriminalromans," in *Der Wohltemperierte Mord; zur Theorie und Geschichte des Herausgegeben von Viktor Zmegac,* Frankfort, 1971, pp. 204–205.
7. "A character who is thought out is not born; he or she is contrived. A born character is round, a thought-out character is flat." RS. "Readers seldom give a damn what characters 'illustrate,' or whether they illustrate anything. The reason they are more interested in my characters than my plots is that the characters seem real to them and engage their emotions and concerns just as 'real' people do. Most characters in stories don't do that. I haven't any idea why and how I have created characters who do." RS
8. The scene in *Death of a Dude* in which a man tells a woman her breasts are "milk-fake" repeats a scene found in *Forest Fire,* p. 40. Rex told me that, contrary to his usual practice, he refreshed his memories of Montana before writing *Death of a Dude* by rereading *Forest Fire.* Other parallels between the two books are also apparent.
9. A flight of four steps. Through the years Rex often had astonished guests by jumping over the side of the banister when halfway down these steps. He was not stunting when he fell.

50. A Man Who Gloriously Acts and Decides

1. To an admirer, Brian Richter, Rex wrote on 1 September 1970: "I have no idea why or how I chose the name Nero Wolfe for him. As for the notion that he was sired by Sherlock Holmes, I don't believe Archie Goodwin has ever mentioned it."
2. "A black Archie would have of course been possible, but I didn't consider it, and why should I? The complications caused by a black Archie or a black 'member of the team' would of course be interesting but sometimes handling them would be a problem, and it wouldn't make the stories any

better, so why bother?" RS. At the end of *A Right to Die* (1964), Wolfe's black client, Paul Whipple, tells him: "We were discussing the trial, Mrs. Ault, and we got talking about you, and she said, 'I wish he was a Negro.' " To this Wolfe replied, "If I were, Mr. Goodwin would have to be one too." Concerning that, Archie says: "I haven't bothered to take that apart. As I said, I gave up long ago trying to figure how his mind works." Here is a crux for future Wolfe scholars. Is Wolfe claiming kinship to Archie? Is Rex acknowledging that Wolfe and Archie both are aspects of himself?

3. Alfred Bester supplied a complete transcript of his interviews. The transcript includes much material not used in the version published in *Holiday*.

4. Rex Stout to JM, 15 January 1970.

5. "Since Nero Wolfe is housebound anyway it would be pointless." RS

6. Where did Rex ultimately think blame should be placed for the collapse of South Vietnam? "Pass it around. Probably chiefly on Thieu, obviously incompetent. The men we sent to do the job [meaning the leaders, especially Westmoreland] weren't up to it. Westmoreland did nothing right." RS. Even prior to the general rout of the South Vietnamese forces, Rex came to believe that American aid should cease because it was "not being well or effectively used."

7. Rex Stout to JM, 31 August 1970: "A girl who looks like Petrarch's Laura is doing my scrawling for me."

8. Lizzie Borden's only visit to Europe took place in 1890.

9. Nancy Timms Lutrus re-created for me many of her moments with Rex. She is a good observer and has a good memory. And she does look like Petrarch's Laura.

On 15 December 1970, Rex wrote to me: "Christmas was once a jolly affair. It must have been nice, so by gum if we pretend hard enough — "

51. Nero Equals Archie

1. Thew Wright to Rex Stout, April 1971.

2. *The Harper Dictionary of Contemporary Usage,* ed. William and Mary Morris, was published in October 1975. There Rex told readers: "Changes made by the genius and wit of the people are inevitable and often desirable and useful. Those imposed by ignorant clowns such as advertising copywriters and broadcasters are abominable and should be condemned by all lovers of language" (p. xviii).

3. *New York Times,* 1 December 1971. Rex's speculations on death predated the Shenker interview by some years. In 1969 he accepted membership on the advisory councils of both the Euthanasia Society of America and the Euthanasia Educational Fund. Although not active in the movement, he contributed "modest sums" for its support.

Customarily Rex told interviewers to suppress adverse comments he might make about living writers, yet with Shenker he relaxed his guard. Rex had said that he found John Updike's title, *Rabbit Redux* "pretentious." Of E. B. White he had said: "When you're with E. B. White you're with the best American writer, not in the sense that he's written great things, but he understands the fitness of words. . . . He never makes a mistake." Rex was sorry that this latter comment got into print. White was too. On 11 December 1971, he wrote Updike: "Writers usually take their worst shellacking from other writers like the one you and I took from Rex Stout the other day when he said you were being pretentious with the title Redux and that though my stuff didn't amount to much I never make a mistake. Wait till Belle catches up with Stout." *Letters of E. B. White,* ed. Dorothy Lobrano Guth, New York, 1976, p. 631.

4. Ruth Stout to Rex Stout, 4 December 1971.

5. Rex Stout to JM, 23 May 1972: "The title of the book temporarily on the shelf is *Please Pass the Guilt.*"

6. Of Rex in this interval, Alan Green told me: "After Rex got over his long siege of headaches he called me one day, referred to the bridge problems in the *Times* and asked, 'What's "vulnerable" mean?' I told him and then asked how he could have been reading the column without knowing that basic fact. 'Oh, I used to play pretty good auction and I managed to figure out the problems fairly well.' What a man!" Alan Green to JM, 4 April 1974.

7. Marlene Dietrich to Rex Stout, 7 July 1972.

8. Ruth Stout's garden books include her best-selling *How to Have a Green Thumb without an Aching Back* (1955); *Gardening without Work* (1961), and *The Ruth Stout, No-Work Garden Book* (1971).

9. Dorothy Van Doren, who preserved this note, shared it with me, with Rex's approval. Thoughtful notes from Dorothy to Rex during his last illness were a major source of comfort to him.

10. Mark Van Doren to JM, 7 June 1972.

11. *New York Times Book Review,* 11 November 1973.

52. Sage of High Meadow

1. David also painted the official portraits of the presidents of Kansas State University. Information supplied by Grace Overmyer.

2. In May 1973, Robert Cromie provided me with the full transcript of his "Book Beat" interview, which was not released on television until the following autumn because the Watergate hearings monopolized viewing time in June. Shown then, nationwide, it brought in an avalanche of letters from friends and readers elated to see Rex, at eighty-seven, in fine fettle, his wits and sense of humor intact, his spirits irrepressible.

3. Early in June 1975, I asked Rex if Wolfe still played chess. He answered: "Not now. He used to, mostly with Marko Vukcic. He keeps up fairly well on current games." Archie, of course, kept up with poker. Of a new book on poker, Rex said, in November 1973, "Archie found it readable and on the whole sound, but thinks it unnecessary to apologize for, or defend, the check-and-raise on a cinch tactic. Of course it is often resented, but so are many other poker ploys that are legitimate."

4. Did Rex think modern liberalism had swept past him in his old age? "Modern liberalism has many faces and angles. I neither accept nor reject all of anyone else's conception of it; I roll my own. I don't think anything has 'swept past' me." RS

5. How did Rex think the United States should cope with the oil price boosts of the OPEC nations? "Probably the only quick solution would be to send fleets of aircraft carriers with bombs, and that is politically impossible. I

think that both politically and economically the world is in the worst and most dangerous mess of modern times. Of course what makes it the most dangerous is the bomb." RS

In acknowledgment of the energy crisis has Nero Wolfe lowered his thermostat to sixty-eight, even though he prefers the temperature in his office to be seventy-two? "Yes, but he cheats." RS

6. Was there anything Rex would like to have done in his life that he had not done? "One: play a piano well with no audience — at the top would be some Chopin preludes with a couple of Beethoven sonatas. Two: catch a thirty-pound mahseer on light tackle in the foothills of the Himalayas. Three: get up in the summer months early, to see the sunrise. Four: spend a weekend with Sappho." RS

7. Barbara Burn to JM, 2 July 1973.

Are meals introduced into the Nero Wolfe stories for atmosphere, or dramatic relief, or are they meant to be functional? "In such a menage there had to be meals, so why not make them interesting?" RS

8. "My favorite breakfast dish has always been oatmeal with plenty of sugar and cream." RS

9. "I don't know if you think that kind of information is suitable for a biography, but there is no law against bragging." RS

10. "A number of the paintings of René Magritte (1898–1967), the internationally famous Belgian painter, are named after titles of books by Rex Stout." Harry Torczyner to JM, 24 May 1974. Torczyner, who was Magritte's attorney, is also Georges Simenon's attorney.

11. Did Rex enjoy life more after forty than he did prior to that age? "Yes, because my time (our most precious possession) has been completely under *my* control." RS

53. Hip Hooroy, You Bearded Boy

1. "Rex single-handedly increased the Guild's membership at a breathtaking rate. This reflects his skill as an administrator, a hell of a lot of energy, and his talent as a letter writer. And he is a good writer of letters, sharp and to the point. He can say it better, in fewer words, than most people around." Irwin Karp to JM, 2 February 1974. At Rex's death Guild membership stood at 4,400.

2. James Dickinson to JM, 27 February 1974.

3. John Cardinal Wright to JM, 21 February 1974.

4. "The Guilt on the Gingerbread," Manchester *Guardian*, 4 May 1974, p. 8.

5. How might we account for the current popularity of detective stories? "People are thirsty for stories about people who do something besides suffering and whining and chewing their cud." RS

6. Rex paid tribute to John Farrar in a pithy phrase: "Good company, good talker, good friend, intelligent, good judgment about books and writing."

7. Rex did not give Richard Nixon's successor high marks. On 28 May 1975, he told me, "I do not intend to support Ford in 1976."

8. *A Family Affair*, New York, 1975, p. 151.

9. *The Honorary Consul*, New York, 1973, p. 247.

10. When Rex learned of Wodehouse's death, on 14 February 1975, he said: "He always used the right words, and nearly always used them well. As

an entertainer he was unsurpassed. While apparently being merely playful he often made acute and subtle comments about human character and behavior."

In 1973, when I told Wodehouse that Pola Stout was uneasy about a passage in *Please Pass the Guilt* (a passage which spoofed the feminist movement), because Rex seemed, uncharacteristically, to be stunting there with words, Wodehouse offered prompt reassurance: "I am sorry it upset Mrs. Stout. I wasn't at all disturbed by the Women's Lib parts. Do tell her so if you think it will please her." P. G. Wodehouse to JM, 30 October 1973.

11. Joan Kahn to JM, 25 September 1972.
12. Lina Derecktor to JM, 10 May 1975; and earlier letters dated 12 April and 25 April 1975.

Afterward Lina told me: "Pola's constantly widening horizon, her abiding interest in young and old, with emphasis on young, creates an atmosphere of rejuvenation, wherever she is. Rex's environment is geared entirely to him. Pola sees to this superbly. Since things outside himself are ordained for his sustenance and support, his priorities can find expression, he can reserve his strength for what is important to him. What a comfort it must be to have someone nonjudgmental, nondemanding, when life is closing in."

13. See Auberon Waugh, "Can Valéry Giscard d'Estaing Save Western Civilization?" *Esquire*, August 1975, p. 59.
14. H. L. Mencken, *A Gang of Pecksniffs: And Other Comments on Newspaper Publishers, Editors, and Reporters*, ed. Theo Lippman, Jr., New York, 1975.
15. Harry Reasoner to JM, 7 November 1975. Reasoner provided me with a copy of his script.
16. "Notable — *A Family Affair*," *Time*, 3 November 1975, pp. 94–95.

On 9 December 1975, the Authors' Guild Council wrote Pola: "We still believe in the divine right of Rex. . . . Rex proposed; Rex disposed — and we loved him for it."

At the Annual Meeting of the Authors' League, on 26 February 1976, John Hersey said:

> In the entire history of the Authors' League, no single member has ever given so much lifetime and passion to the cause of the rights and well-being of writers as Rex Stout did. . . . He *was* a noble man. His strength . . . lay in the deep-seated values he held to in human dealings — his decency, his generosity, his burning sense of justice — and yes, strange as it may sound, his humility. And if his salads of debate were seasoned with both imagination and mischief — well, that was what made being around Rex such very good fun.

Authors' Guild Bulletin, March-May 1976, pp. 11–13.
In the London *Sunday Times*, Edmund Crispin's "Ave Atque Vale" saw Rex peaceably domiciled in paradise:

> Rex went to Paradise:
> That was only fair.
> Puffing Gilbert met him first,
> And led him up the stair.
> Allingham and Sayers,
> Wilkie and Sir Arthur,
> Stood with Edgar at the top,
> Creators of the slayers:

While those who prowl to seek them out,
  Philip, Perry, Peter,
Poirot and the others bowed
  To welcome Stout —

Took him to a brownstone house.
  Archie let them in:
Nero surged out of his chair,
  Huge and wise as sin:
Set him on the yellow chair,
  Rang the bell for beer,
Sent out to the Precinct
  For Cramer to be here.
Fritz smiled at Lily Rowan,
  Lily smiled at him;
Theo Horstmann scratched his head
  — Saul looked grim,

For Nero Wolfe was speaking now:
  'Here is not for you,
Scholar, sailor, banker, gardener:
  Go somewhere new.'
So they showed him a wooded height,
  And there he built a home
Twin to one in Tunis —
  There he turned the loam
For strawberries and irises;
  And there he lives for aye,
Where simple flowers, not orchids,
  Fling their perfume to the sky.

Copyright © 1976 by Times Newspapers Limited ("with apologies to Janeites and to the shade of Rudyard Kipling"—E.C.)

The last words Rex wrote were for a blurb for Hilda Simon's *Private Lives of Orchids,* Philadelphia, 1975. On 19 August he told me: "I wrote: 'If I were an orchid I would be proud to be in this beautiful book. Since I am merely a man who likes orchids, I am proud to own it.' They liked that quote. Naturally. Why wouldn't they?"

A Rex Stout Checklist

Early Publications

POETRY:

"In Cupid's Family," *The Smart Set*, November 1910, p. 58.
"Cupid's Revenge," *The Smart Set*, June 1911, p. 140.
"The Victory of Love," *The Smart Set*, October 1911, pp. 49–50.

NOVELS:

Her Forbidden Knight. All-Story Magazine. In five parts, August through December 1913 (107 pages).
Under the Andes. All-Story Magazine, February 1914 (139 pages).
A Prize for Princes. All-Story Weekly Magazine. In five parts, 2 May through 30 May 1914 (163 pages).
The Great Legend. All-Story Weekly. In five parts, 1 January through 29 January 1916 (147 pages).

SHORT STORIES:

"Their Lady," 1912. Unlocated.
"Excess Baggage," *Short Stories*, October 1912, pp. 26–32.
"The Infernal Feminine," *Short Stories*, November 1912, pp. 88–91.
"A Professional Recall," *The Black Cat*, December 1912, pp. 46–50.
"Pamfret and Peace," *The Black Cat*, January 1913, pp. 49–56.
"A Companion of Fortune," *Short Stories*, April 1913, pp. 112–117.
"A White Precipitate," *Lippincott's Monthly Magazine*, June 1913, pp. 730–734.
"The Pickled Peace," *The Black Cat*, June 1913, pp. 46–56.
"The Mother of Invention," *The Black Cat*, August 1913, pp. 27–33.
"Méthode Américaine," *The Smart Set*, November 1913, pp. 129–134.
"A Tyrant Abdicates," *Lippincott's Monthly Magazine*, January 1914, pp. 92–96.
"The Pay Yeoman," *All-Story Magazine*, January 1914, pp. 186–192.
"Secrets," *All-Story Weekly*, 7 March 1914, pp. 208–216.
"Rose Orchid," *All-Story Weekly*, 28 March 1914, pp. 876–883.*
"An Agacella Or," *Lippincott's Monthly Magazine*, April 1914, pp. 465–473.
"The Inevitable Third," *All-Story Weekly*, 25 April 1914, pp. 886–892.*
"Out of the Line," *All-Story Cavalier Weekly*, 13 June 1914, pp. 218–224.
"The Lie," *All-Story Cavalier Weekly*, 4 July 1914, pp. 859–864.
"Target Practise," *All-Story Cavalier Weekly*, 26 December 1914, pp. 133–141.
"If He Be Married," *All-Story Cavalier Weekly*, 16 January 1915, pp. 762–768.
"Baba," *All-Story Cavalier Weekly*, 30 January 1915, pp. 351–356.
"Warner and Wife," *All-Story Cavalier Weekly*, 27 February 1915, pp. 222–242.
"A Little Love Affair," *Smith's Magazine*, July 1915, pp. 615–626.
"Art for Art's Sake," *Smith's Magazine*, August 1915, pp. 757–764.

*Published under the pen name "Evans Day."

"Another Little Love Affair," *Smith's Magazine*, September 1915, pp. 1241–1252.

"Jonathan Stannard's Secret Vice," *All-Story Weekly*, 11 September 1915, pp. 236–242.

"Sanetomo," *All-Story Weekly*, 25 September 1915, pp. 717–723.

"Justice Ends at Home," *All-Story Weekly*, 4 December 1915, pp. 260–293.

"It's Science that Counts," *All-Story Weekly*, 1 April 1916, pp. 468–478.

"The Rope Dance," *All-Story Weekly*, 24 June 1916, pp. 561–570.

"An Officer and a Lady," *All-Story Weekly*, 13 January 1917, pp. 610–616.

"Heels of Fate," *All-Story Weekly*, 17 November 1917, pp. 688–695.

Later Publications

NOVELS 1929–1975:

How Like a God, Vanguard, 1929.

Seed on the Wind, Vanguard, 1930.

Golden Remedy, Vanguard, 1931.

Forest Fire, Farrar & Rinehart, 1933.

The President Vanishes, Farrar & Rinehart, 1934.

Fer-de-Lance, Farrar & Rinehart, 1934.

The League of Frightened Men, Farrar & Rinehart, 1935.

O Careless Love, Farrar & Rinehart, 1935.

The Rubber Band, Farrar & Rinehart, 1936.

The Red Box, Farrar & Rinehart, 1937.

The Hand in the Glove, Farrar & Rinehart, 1937.

Too Many Cooks, Farrar & Rinehart, 1938.

Mr. Cinderella, Farrar & Rinehart, 1938.

Some Buried Caesar, Farrar & Rinehart, 1939.

Mountain Cat, Farrar & Rinehart, 1939.

Double for Death, Farrar & Rinehart, 1939.

Red Threads, in *The Mystery Book*, Farrar & Rinehart, 1939.

Over My Dead Body, Farrar & Rinehart, 1940.

Bad for Business, in *The Second Mystery Book*, Farrar & Rinehart, 1940.

Where There's a Will, Farrar & Rinehart, 1940.

The Broken Vase, Farrar & Rinehart, 1941.

Alphabet Hicks, Farrar & Rinehart, 1941.

The Silent Speaker, Viking, 1946.

Too Many Women, Viking, 1947.

And Be a Villain, Viking, 1948.

The Second Confession, Viking, 1949.

In the Best Families, Viking, 1950.

Murder by the Book, Viking, 1951.

Prisoner's Base, Viking, 1952.

The Golden Spiders, Viking, 1953.

The Black Mountain, Viking, 1954.

Before Midnight, Viking, 1955.

Might as Well Be Dead, Viking, 1956.

If Death Ever Slept, Viking, 1957.

Champagne for One, Viking, 1958.

Plot It Yourself, Viking, 1959.

Too Many Clients, Viking, 1960.

The Final Deduction, Viking, 1961.
Gambit, Viking, 1962.
The Mother Hunt, Viking, 1963.
A Right to Die, Viking, 1964.
The Doorbell Rang, Viking, 1965.
Death of a Doxy, Viking, 1966.
The Father Hunt, Viking, 1968.
Death of a Dude, Viking, 1969.
Please Pass the Guilt, Viking, 1973.
A Family Affair, Viking, 1975.

NOVELLAS 1940–1964:

"Bitter End," *The American Magazine,* November 1940, pp. 47–51, 127–147.
"Black Orchids," in *Black Orchids,* Farrar & Rinehart, 1942.
"Cordially Invited to Meet Death," in *Black Orchids,* Farrar & Rinehart, 1942.
"Not Quite Dead Enough," in *Not Quite Dead Enough,* Farrar & Rinehart, 1944.
"Booby Trap," in *Not Quite Dead Enough,* Farrar & Rinehart, 1944.
"Help Wanted, Male," in *Trouble in Triplicate,* Viking, 1949.
"Instead of Evidence," in *Trouble in Triplicate,* Viking, 1949.
"Before I Die," in *Trouble in Triplicate,* Viking, 1949.
"Man Alive," in *Three Doors to Death,* Viking, 1950.
"Omit Flowers," in *Three Doors to Death,* Viking, 1950.
"Door to Death," in *Three Doors to Death,* Viking, 1950.
"Bullet for One," in *Curtains for Three,* Viking, 1950.
"The Gun with Wings," in *Curtains for Three,* Viking, 1950.
"Disguise for Murder," in *Curtains for Three,* Viking, 1950.
"The Cop-Killer," in *Triple Jeopardy,* Viking, 1952.
"The Squirt and the Monkey," in *Triple Jeopardy,* Viking, 1952.
"Home to Roost," in *Triple Jeopardy,* Viking, 1952.
"This Won't Kill You," in *Three Men Out,* Viking, 1954.
"Invitation to Murder," in *Three Men Out,* Viking, 1954.
"The Zero Clue," in *Three Men Out,* Viking, 1954.
"When a Man Murders," in *Three Witnesses,* Viking, 1956.
"Die like a Dog," in *Three Witnesses,* Viking, 1956.
"The Next Witness," in *Three Witnesses,* Viking, 1956.
"Immune to Murder," in *Three for the Chair,* Viking, 1957.
"A Window for Death," in *Three for the Chair,* Viking, 1957.
"Too Many Detectives," in *Three for the Chair,* Viking, 1957.
"Christmas Party," in *And Four to Go,* Viking, 1958.
"Easter Parade," in *And Four to Go,* Viking, 1958.
"Fourth of July Picnic," in *And Four to Go,* Viking, 1958.
"Murder is No Joke," in *And Four to Go,* Viking, 1958.
"Poison à la Carte, in *Three at Wolfe's Door,* Viking, 1960.
"Method Three for Murder," in *Three at Wolfe's Door,* Viking, 1960.
"The Rodeo Murder," in *Three at Wolfe's Door,* Viking, 1960.
"Death of a Demon," in *Homicide Trinity,* Viking, 1962.
"Eeny Meeny Murder Mo," in *Homicide Trinity,* Viking, 1962.
"Counterfeit for Murder," in *Homicide Trinity,* Viking, 1962.
"Kill Now—Pay Later," in *Trio for Blunt Instruments,* Viking, 1964.
"Murder Is Corny," in *Trio for Blunt Instruments,* Viking, 1964.
"Blood Will Tell," in *Trio for Blunt Instruments,* Viking, 1964.

SHORT STORIES 1936–1955:

"It Happened Last Night," *The Canadian Magazine*, March 1936.
"A Good Character for a Novel," *The New Masses*, 15 December 1936, pp. 17–18.
"Tough Cop's Gift," *Christmas Annual*, Abbott Laboratories, 1953, 5 pages.
"His Own Hand," *Manhunt*, April 1955, pp. 49–61.

NOVELLA COLLECTIONS:

Black Orchids, Farrar & Rinehart, 1942.
Not Quite Dead Enough, Farrar & Rinehart, 1944.
Trouble in Triplicate, Viking, 1949.
Three Doors to Death, Viking, 1950.
Curtains for Three, Viking, 1950.
Triple Jeopardy, Viking, 1952.
Three Men Out, Viking, 1954.
Three Witnesses, Viking, 1956.
Three for the Chair, Viking, 1957.
And Four to Go, Viking, 1958.
Three at Wolfe's Door, Viking, 1960.
Homicide Trinity, Viking, 1962.
Trio for Blunt Instruments, Viking, 1964.

OMNIBUS VOLUMES:

The Nero Wolfe Omnibus, World, 1944.
Full House, Viking, 1955.
All Aces, Viking, 1958.
Five of a Kind, Viking, 1961.
Royal Flush, Viking, 1965.
Kings Full of Aces, Viking, 1969.
Three Aces, Viking, 1971.
Three Trumps, Viking, 1973.
Triple Zeck, Viking, 1974.
Wolfe Pack, Bantam, 1971.

EDITED VOLUMES:

The Illustrious Dunderheads, ed. Rex Stout, with an introductory essay. A. A. Knopf, 1942.
Rue Morgue No. 1, edited by Rex Stout and Louis Greenfield, with an introduction by Rex Stout. Creative Age Press, 1946.
Eat, Drink, and Be Buried, edited by Rex Stout, with introduction. Viking, 1956.
The Nero Wolfe Cook Book, by Rex Stout and the Editors of The Viking Press, 1973.

ARTICLES:

"So You're Going Out for a Record," *The Bedroom Companion or A Cold Night's Entertainment* (New York, 1935), pp. 13–21.
"Love Among the Editors," *The Bedroom Companion or A Cold Night's Entertainment* (New York, 1935), pp. 179–186.
"Who's Who — And Why," *The Saturday Evening Post* (26 October 1935), pp. 86–87.
"Mystery," *The American Magazine*, August 1940, p. 164.
"We Mystery-Story Writers Don't Kid Ourselves," *Publishers Weekly*, 28 December 1940, pp. 2312–2314.
"Watson Was a Woman," *Saturday Review*, 1 March 1941, pp. 3–4, 16.

"Where They'll Find the Strength of Our Country," *Philadelphia Inquirer's* "Everybody's Weekly," 29 June 1941, pp. 1, 5.

"These Grapes Need Sugar," *Vogue's First Reader* (New York, 1942), pp. 421–425.

"We Shall Hate, or We Shall Fail," *The New York Times Magazine*, 17 January 1943, pp. 6, 29.

"Books and the Tiger," *The New York Times Book Review*, 21 March 1943, p. 11.

"Sense or Sentiment," *Prevent World War III*, May 1944, p. 3.

"Dear Dorothy Thompson," *Prevent World War III*, October 1944, p. 3.

"An Editorial," *Prevent World War III*, December 1944, p. 3.

"Why Some People Grow Vegetables," *House Beautiful*, April 1947, p. 123.

"Grim Fairy Tales," *Saturday Review*, 2 April 1949, pp. 7–8ff. Reprinted as "Crime in Fiction" in *Writing for Love or Money*, ed. Norman Cousins (New York, 1949), pp. 118–126.

"Nero Wolfe's Creator Looks at $1,500,000 Robbery" [Brink's Robbery, Boston, Mass., 17 January 1950], International News Service, February 1950.

"The Case of the Lacking Law," *The Friend: A Religious and Literary Journal*, 2 November 1950, pp. 131–132.

"Diary of a Plant Detective," *House and Garden*, October 1953, pp. 186–187.

"The Opposition, All Flavors," *The 1954 Federalist Annual* (New York, 1954).

"The Town I Like — Brewster, New York," *Lincoln-Mercury Times*, September-October 1954, pp. 1–5.

"At Last We Belong," *The American Writer*, October-December 1954, pp. 3–5.

"Let's Take the Mystery Out of Cooking," *The American Magazine*, August 1956, pp. 33–36, 62–63.

"What to Do about a Watson," *The Mystery Writer's Handbook* (New York, 1956), pp. 161–163.

"Cinderella Paperback," *Writers Roundtable*, edited by Helen Hull and Michael Drury (New York, 1959), pp. 112–119.

"The Case of the Politician," *Baker Street Journal*, June 1961, pp. 82–83.

"Why Nero Wolfe Likes Orchids," *Life*, 19 April 1963, p. 108.

"The Man Who Came in from the Cold," *Mademoiselle*, July 1964, pp. 61–63.

"The Case of the Spies Who Weren't," *Ramparts*, January 1966, pp. 30–34.

"Censorship," *Arts in Society*, Spring 1967, Madison, Wisconsin, p. 295.

"The Mystery Novel," *The Writer's Book*, ed. Helen Hull (New York, 1950), pp. 62–67.

"Do Orchids Have the Right to Privacy?" *Holiday*, September-October 1970, pp. 19–21.

"Forewarning from Rex," *Authors Guild Bulletin*, February-March 1972, p. 3.

FOREWORDS, INTRODUCTIONS, PREFACES, JACKET ESSAYS:

Sequel to the Apocalypse by John Boylan [John Balderston]. (New York, 1942). Foreword by Rex Stout, p. 1.

Would YOU Sign This Letter? by F. W. Foerster and T. H. Tetens (New York, 1943). Introduction by Rex Stout and Quentin Reynolds, pp. 1–2.

That Man in the White House: You and Your President by Frank Kingdon (New York, 1944). Afterword by Rex Stout, pp. 177–178.

Beards: Their Social Standing, Religious Involvement, Decorative Possibilities, and Value in Offense and Defense Through the Ages by Reginald Reynolds (New York, 1949). Jacket Essay by Rex Stout.

Gideon's Day by J. J. Marric [John Creasey] (New York, 1950). Jacket essay by Rex Stout.

The Later Adventures of Sherlock Holmes (New York, 1952), 3 vols. Introduction by Rex Stout, pp. v-xi.

The Stories of Sherlock Holmes read by Basil Rathbone (Caedmon Records, April 1963, TC1172). Introduction by Rex Stout.

French Cooking for Americans by Louis Diat (Philadelphia, 1966). Foreword by Rex Stout, pp. 7–8.

The Game of Croquet, Its Appointments and Laws by Horace Elisha Scudder. Edited and augmented by Paul Seabury (New York, 1968), Foreword by Rex Stout, pp. 7–8.

Modern Classics of Suspense (New York, 1968). Jacket essay by Rex Stout.

The Brookfield Cookbook edited by Dorothy Beall *et al.* (Brookfield, Connecticut, 1969). Preface by Rex Stout, p. iii.

Great Stories of Mystery and Suspense (New York, 1977). Jacket essay by Rex Stout.

FUGITIVE VERSE:

"On My Bashfulness," *The Bedroom Companion, or A Cold Night's Entertainment* (New York, 1935), p. 36.

"Apologia Pro Vita Sua," *The New York Times*, 21 August 1935.

BROADCASTS IN PRINT:

"Jan Valtin Explains," *Wilson Library Bulletin*, November 1941, pp. 213–223. Rex Stout with Stephen Gannett, Irita Van Doren, and Jan Valtin.

"The Adventures of Sherlock Holmes," in *The Second Invitation to Learning*, ed. Mark Van Doren (New York, 1944), pp. 236–251. Rex Stout with Mark Van Doren, Elmer Davis, and Jacques Barzun.

REVIEWS:

"Learning What It Means to Be a Negro," New York *Herald Tribune*, 25 May 1947. *Kingsblood Royal* by Sinclair Lewis.

"A Rich and Varied Menu," *The New York Times Book Review*, 24 May 1953. *Blue Trout and Black Truffles* by Joseph Wechsberg.

"Cooking with Sauce," *The New York Times*, 19 September 1954. *The Art of Eating* by M. F. K. Fisher.

"A Great Singer's Self-Portrait," New York *Herald Tribune*, 28 October 1956. *O Lord What a Morning* by Marian Anderson.

"He Got His Man," *The New York Times Book Review*, 24 March 1957. *Memoirs of a Bow Street Runner* by Henry Goddard.

"Genesis of a Detective," *The New Republic*, 9 May 1960. *The Private Life of Sherlock Holmes* by Vincent Starrett.

"Was the Murderer in the Jury Box?" *The New York Times Book Review*, 2 February 1964. *The Minister and the Choir Singer* by William M. Kunstler.

"Ages 9 to 12: Stories Past and Present," *The New York Times Book Review*, 1 November 1964. *Chitty Chitty Bang Bang* by Ian Fleming.

"A Murderer's Milieu," *Saturday Review*, 29 October 1966. *The Boston Strangler* by Gerold Frank.

Interviews:

Anon., "Topeka Boy Cruises with President," Topeka *Daily Capital*, 13 January 1907. One photo.

Anon., "Writings of Ex-Topeka Boy Wins Approval N.Y. Editors," Topeka *Daily Capital*, 4 May 1913. One photo.

Gilbert W. Gabriel, "Mystery on High Meadow," *Saturday Review*, 18 September 1937, pp. 5–6. Two photos.

J. V. McAree, "Detective Fictionist Discusses Colleagues," Toronto *Globe & Mail*, January 1941.

Robert Van Gelder, "An Interview with Mister Rex Stout," *The New York Times Book Review*, 21 September 1941.

Anon., "People of the Week — Rex Stout," *Cue Magazine*, 1 November 1941. One photo.

Anon., "Rex Stout," *Twentieth Century Authors* (New York, 1942), pp. 1354–1355.

John Bainbridge, "Rex Stout: The Quaker Who Is Heckling Hitler," *Look*, 23 February 1943.

Mary Braggiotti, "On Nero Wolfe's Pay Roll," New York *Post*, 16 May 1945.

Alva Johnston, "Alias Nero Wolfe," Part I, *The New Yorker*, 16 July 1949, pp. 26–42; Part II, *The New Yorker*, 23 July 1949, pp. 30–43.

Anon., "Rex Stout," United Press Release, 6 August 1949.

Taylor Glenn, "Books and Authors," Bridgeport *Sunday Post*, 14 October 1951. One photo.

Lewis Nichols, "Talk with Rex Stout," *The New York Times Book Review*, 15 November 1953.

Rochelle Girson, "Stout Claims Characters Must Live for Authors, Too," *Evening Citizen*, Ottawa and elsewhere, 9 January 1954.

Anon., "Rex Stout," *Coronet*, February 1956. Three photos.

Victor P. Haas, "Bookman's Notebook," Omaha *World Herald*, 4 March 1956.

Jane Allison, "Man of Mystery," Indianapolis *Star Magazine*, 14 April 1957. Two photos.

Anon., "Mr. Stout's Idea of Fun," *The Saturday Evening Post*, 5 July 1958, p. 90.

Beth Stewart, "Rex Stout, Besides Writing Nearly 50 Books, Is Also a Brilliant Mathematician," Danbury *News-Times*, 30 January 1960. One photo.

Anon., "Mystery Writer Reaches for the Sky," *The Saturday Evening Post*, 28 January 1961. One photo.

Jim Neal, "An Illustrious Son," Noblesville *Republican Ledger*, 1 December 1961.

Anon., "Nero Wolfe's Creator Finds Fun in Writing," Rochester *Democrat and Chronicle*, 11 May 1962.

John Barkham, "Rex Stout's 38-Day Wonders," New York *Herald Tribune*, December 1963.

David Murray, "Nero Wolfe," New York *Post Daily Magazine*, 5 March 1964.

Bill Ryan, "Rex Stout Reflects Two of His Creations," May 1965, syndicated newspaper column.

Larry Vershel, "What Makes Rex Stout Tick?" Danbury *News-Times*, 14 August 1965.

Anon., "The FBI in Fact and Fiction," *Books*, October 1965.

John T. Winterich, "Private Eye on the FBI," *Saturday Review*, 9 October 1965, pp. 54–55. One photo.

Margaret Bancroft, "Rex Stout: Why Is FBI Sacrosanct?" UPI dispatch, 3 October 1965.

Caskie Stinnett, "Rex Stout, Nero Wolfe and the Big Fish," New York *Herald Tribune*, 10 October 1965. One photo.

Lewis Nichols, "Nero Wolfe," *The New York Times Book Review*, 24 October 1965.

Gerald Nachman, "Nero Wolfe vs. the FBI," New York *Post*, 3 November 1965.

Jim Neal, "Rex Stout Authors Another Nero Wolfe," Noblesville *Republican Ledger*, 6 November 1965.

Ann V. Masters, "Rex Stout, Nero Wolfe, and FBI," Bridgeport *Sunday Post*, 28 November 1965. Three photos.

Anon., "Author Rex Stout vs. the FBI," *Life*, 10 December 1965, pp. 127–132. Five photos.

Arthur Pottersman, "G-Men Are after Me, Says the Man Who Made Nero," London *Sun*, 10 February 1966.

Anon., "Author of Nero Wolfe Heads Lunch Guest List," Washington *Post*, 20 March 1966.

Anon., "An Interview with Rex Stout," *P.S.*, August 1966, pp. 20–26.

Tom Golden, "Rex Stout: He's His Own Man and Nero Wolfe," New Haven *Register Sunday Pictorial*, 25 September 1966. Four photos.

Marguerite Johnston, "Rex Stout Combats a Lie Firmly Embedded in History," Houston *Post*, 26 September 1966.

Marion E. Prilook, "Rex Stout Marks 80th Year with New Nero Wolfe Story," Danbury *News-Times*, 1 December 1966.

Richard S. Lochte II, "Rex Stout," Chicago *Daily News*, 30 September 1967. One photo.

Gerald Kloss, "Crime Pays for Rex Stout," Milwaukee *Journal*, 15 February 1968. One photo.

Don Bensen, "An Exclusive Interview with Rex Stout," *Writer's Digest*, May 1968, pp. 53–57, 86–88. One photo.

Lewis Nichols, "Nero's Creator," *The New York Times Book Review*, 14 July 1968. One photo.

Marion E. Prilook, "Wolfe a Thinker — And So Is Stout," Danbury *News-Times*, 9 November 1968.

John J. McAleer, "Rex Stout Writing Number 70 at 83," Boston *Globe*, 20 August 1969.

Phil Casey, "Rex Stout is Alive and Arguing in Fine Fashion," Washington *Post*, 5 October 1969. Three photos.

Alfred Bester, "Conversation with Rex Stout," *Holiday*, November 1969, pp. 39, 65, 67. One photo.

Richard S. Lochte II, "Who's Afraid of Nero Wolfe?" *The Armchair Detective*, July 1970, pp. 211–214.

Roger Roddy, "Scope," *Pennysaver Publications*, 1970.

Israel Shenker, "Rex Stout, 85, Gives Clues on Good Writing," *The New York Times*, 1 December 1971.

Barbara Burn, April 1972. Unpublished Viking house memo (10 pages).

John Sopko, "Stout, 86, Finds Reading Thin," Bridgeport *Telegram*, 1 December 1972.

Steve Koppman, "Rex Stout Writes on at 86," Danbury *News-Times*, 11 February 1973.

Robert Cromie, "Book Beat" TV broadcast. Taped 24 June 1973.

Rita Delfiner, "At Home with Rex Stout," New York *Post*, 25 August 1973.

Mike Bourne. 18 July 1973. *Corsage*, 1977.

Jeanne Lesem, "Rex Stout Cooks Up Stories and Meals," UPI dispatch, 20 September 1973.

John F. Baker, "Rex Stout: 'No Man My Age Writes Books,' " *Publishers Weekly*, 29 October 1973, pp. 28–29.

John J. McAleer, "Sales Top 100 Million — and Nero Wolfe May Go On Forever," Boston *Globe*, 12 January 1974. One photo.

Andrea Vaucher, "Octogenarian Tells of Lifetime of Writing," White Plains *Reporter Dispatch*, 18 February 1974.

Irene DeBrock, "Novelist Rex Stout Has Kin in County," Forsyth County *News*, 27 February 1974.

Graham Lord, "A Hero All Over the World: The Super Sleuth Who Solves Crimes from Home," London *Sunday Express*, 28 April 1974.

John J. McAleer, "Rex Stout Greets the Wolfe Pack," *Views and Reviews*, Spring 1974, pp. 25-27.

Raymond Gardner, "The Guilt on the Gingerbread," *The Manchester Guardian*, 4 May 1974.

Timothy Dickinson and Rhoda Koenig, "And Now a Word or Two with the Master," Chicago *Tribune Book World*, 28 July 1974. One photo.

Bobby Ray Miller and Donald G. Burns, "Never in the Summer, Nero Wolfe Creator Says," Rochester *Democrat and Chronicle*, 21 October 1974. One photo.

Selected Criticism:

Bernard DeVoto, "Alias Nero Wolfe," *Harper's Magazine*, July 1954, pp. 8ff.

Charles A. Brady, "Stout Wittily Proves He's Master of New 'Detective Style' Fairy Tale," Buffalo *Evening News*, 25 June 1955.

John D. Clark, "Some Notes Relating to a Preliminary Investigation into the Paternity of Nero Wolfe," *Baker Street Journal*, January 1956, pp. 5-11.

Jacques Barzun and The Viking Press, *A Birthday Tribute to Rex Stout* (1 December 1965), 15 pages. Brief biography by Judith I. Churnus.

Thomas L. Stix, "Six Characters in Search of an Author," *Baker Street Journal*, March 1966, pp. 28-29.

Edmund Crispin, "Archie, Your Notebook," *London Sunday Times*, 4 June 1967.

Mia Gerhardt, " 'Homicide West': Some Observations on the Nero Wolfe Stories of Rex Stout," *English Studies*, August 1968, pp. 107-127.

Bruce Kennedy, "The Truth about Nero Wolfe," *Baker Street Journal*, September 1968, pp. 154-155.

Barbara Paul, "Holmes, Wolfe, and Women," *Baker Street Journal*, December 1968, p. 208.

Andrew Jay Peck, "Like Father, Like Son?" *Baker Street Journal*, March 1969, pp. 42-43.

Francis Hertzburg, "A Preliminary Study in the Literature of Nero Wolfe," *The Mystery Reader's Newsletter*, April 1969, pp. 11-13.

William S. Baring-Gould, *Nero Wolfe of West Thirty-fifth Street* (New York, 1969), 203 pages.

Anon., "Stout Sleuth," *MD*, June 1969, pp. 253ff.

Edward S. Lauterbach, "Wolfe and the Law," *The Armchair Detective*, January 1970, p. 114.

John J. McAleer, "The Baring-Gould Chronology," *Mystery Reader's Newsletter*, June 1970, p. 36.

Robert A. W. Lowndes, "The Wolfe Saga Reconsidered," *Startling Mystery Stories*, February 1971, pp. 4-7, 120-128.

Thomas D. Waugh, "The Missing Years of Nero Wolfe," *The Armchair Detective*, October 1971, pp. 16-18.

D. F. Rauber, "Sherlock Holmes and Nero Wolfe: The Role of the 'Great Detective' in Intellectual History," *The Journal of Popular Culture*, Spring 1973, pp. 483–495.

Jon Tuska, "Rex Stout and the Detective Story," *Views and Reviews*, Spring 1974, pp. 28–35.

Robert Goldsborough, "The Fattest, Classiest, Brainiest Detective of Them All," Chicago *Tribune Book World*, 28 July 1974, p. 3.

W. Bruce Hepburn, "Fat Man's Agony," *The Practitioner*, June 1976, pp. 726–728.

David Anderson, "Creative Order in Rex Stout," *The Mystery Nook*, August 1976, pp. 1–6.

Marvin Lachman, "The Real Fourth Side of the Triangle," *The Mystery Nook*, August 1976, pp. 11–13.

Judson C. Sapp, "Nero Wolfe 'On the Air,'" *The Mystery Nook*, August 1976, pp. 19–20.

Frank D. McSherry, Jr., "Rex Stout as 'Editor,'" *The Mystery Nook*, August 1976, pp. 21–23.

Guy M. Townsend, "The Nero Wolfe Saga: The Early Years," *The Mystery Nook*, August 1976, pp. 31–41.

Donald L. Miller, "The Nero Wolfe Saga: Three at Random," *The Mystery Nook*, August 1976, pp. 61–62.

John McAleer, Introduction to *Justice Ends at Home* by Rex Stout, New York, 1977, pp. vii–xxvi.

Alternate Titles of Rex Stout Books:

Alphabet Hicks/The Sound of Murder
And Be a Villain/More Deaths Than One
And Four to Go/Crime and Again
Black Orchids/The Case of the Black Orchids
Eat, Drink, And Be Buried/For Tomorrow We Die (ed. by Stout)
Fer-de-Lance/Meet Nero Wolfe/Point of Death
The Hand in the Glove/Crime on Her Hands
In the Best Families/Even in the Best Families
The League of Frightened Men/Frightened Men
Mountain Cat/The Mountain Cat Murders/Dark Revenge
Plot It Yourself/Murder in Style
Prisoner's Base/Out Goes She
The Red Box/The Case of the Red Box
The Rubber Band/To Kill Again
Some Buried Caesar/The Red Bull
Where There's a Will/Sisters in Trouble

Alternate Titles of Rex Stout Novellas and Short Stories:

"Black Orchids"/"Death Wears an Orchid"
"Christmas Party"/"Christmas Party Murder"
"The Cop-Killer"/"Cop Killer"
"Cordially Invited to Meet Death"/"Invitation to Murder"
"Counterfeit for Murder"/"Counterfeiter's Knife"

"Death of a Demon"/"The Gun Puzzle"
"Die like a Dog"/"The Body in the Hall"/"A Dog in the Daytime"
"Disguise for Murder"/"The Affair of the Twisted Scarf"/"Twisted Scarf"
"Fourth of July Picnic"/"The Fourth of July Murder"/"Labor Union Murder"
"His Own Hand"/"By His Own Hand"/"Curtain Line"
"Home to Roost"/"Nero Wolfe and the Communist Killer"/"Nero Wolfe Devises a Stratagem"
"Invitation to Murder"/"Will to Murder"
"Murder is No Joke"/"Frame-up for Murder"
"The Next Witness"/"Last Witness"
"Rodeo Murder"/"The Penthouse Murder"
"The Squirt and the Monkey"/"The Dazzle Dan Murder Case"/"See No Evil"
"This Won't Kill You"/"This Will Kill You"/"The World Series Murder"
"Tough Cop's Gift"/"Cop's Gift"/"Nobody Deserved Justice"/"Santa Claus Beat"
"A Window for Death"/"Nero Wolfe and the Vanishing Clue"
"The Zero Clue"/"Scared to Death"

Acknowledgments

The nature of the debts I have incurred in the course of conducting more than three hundred hours of taped interviews and maintaining a correspondence that is contained now in twelve hundred and eighty folders, in five filing cabinets, prohibits a meticulous accounting of specific obligations. Rex and Pola Stout were, of course, my starting point. Pola's collection of clippings and photos, which she turned me loose among when I began work, gave me my first clear realization of the magnitude of my task and, as well, of the delights that it would hold. Rex's annual letters of introduction, inviting the recipients to "include warts" when they communicated with me about him, were a guarantee that useful information would flow to me in a constant stream — and sometimes in a torrent — through the whole period of my research. In addition, Rex's two hundred and sixty-three letters to me, written between our frequent summit conferences at High Meadow, made him my most prolific and valuable correspondent.

Many helpers — Ruth Stout, Barbara Stout and Nathaniel Selleck III, M.D., Rebecca Stout Bradbury and William W. Bradbury, Alan Green,* Lawrence G. Blochman,* Mabel Todhunter, Esther Doan Starbuck, Mark Van Doren,* Natalie Stout Carr and Wallace Carr, John W. Ripley, Thomas J. Muth, Frances Cox, Alfred Bester, Elizabeth Vogel, Eleanor Sullivan, Julian Wolff, Burnett Meyer, Peter Heggie, Jean Wynne, Leonard Sussman, and David Anderson — were on instant call, always eager to communicate or seek out information needed to keep the work moving forward.

There is no easy way to list the foremost achievers among those who supported me in my work. I owe too much to too many for that. I have set up categories of helpers. That arrangement is one of only limited adequacy. The scope of the information and insights those who helped me have provided reaches in too many directions for me to focus their contributions. But let it be said that each is cherished as much for encouragement given and goodwill shown as for documents recovered, books loaned, photographs unearthed, letters shared, memories recalled, and specific answers given to specific questions.

The existence of the Wolfe Pack cannot go unexplained. It consisted of members of Rex Stout's readership scattered from Farsund, Norway, to Katoomba, Australia. It included teenagers and nonagenarians, churchmen and switchboard operators, microbiologists, anthropologists, and housewives, UN interpreters, orchidologists, an FBI administrator, an erstwhile CIA agent, a Manxman, a Montenegrin, and a member of the exiled Yugoslavian nobility.

These people volunteered to serve as listening posts around the world. Little was written or said about Rex Stout and his books during the seven years the biography was in progress that did not find its way into my files as a result of the zeal of the Wolfe Pack. That service offers a true measure of the esteem and respect which Rex, Wolfe, and Archie everywhere inspire.

*An asterisk means the person mentioned is now deceased.

A. FAMILY HELPERS:

Pola Stout, Barbara Stout, Nathaniel Selleck III, M.D., Rebecca Stout Bradbury, William W. Bradbury, Ruth Stout, Mary Stout,* Fay Kennedy Koudrey,* Lizbeth Maroc, Reed Maroc, Christopher Maroc, Natalie Stout Carr, Wallace Carr, Winona Stout Bruder, Donald Stout, Juanita Merle Roddy DeBrock, Virginia Roddy Pretzfelder, Millard Pretzfelder, David DeBrock, Irene DeBrock, Ruth Stout Johnson, Mabel Todhunter, Mary Millicent Todhunter Milner, Adda Burnett Meyer, Burnett Meyer, David Hicks Overmyer,* Grace Overmyer,* Margaret Salb, Elizabeth Ellis Miller, Willis Todhunter Ballard, Rex Todhunter,* Margaret Egan Todhunter, Willa Swengel, Wilson Shannon Daily, Frank H. Cox, Roger Roddy.*

B. SCHOLARS:

American Philosophical Society, Whitfield J. Bell, Jr.; Briarcliff College, Dean Walter Chizinsky; California State University, San Jose, Richard VanDerBeets; University of California, Davis, Max Byrd; Canisius College, Charles Brady; Cedar Crest College, Francis Jennings; Columbia University, Jacques Barzun, Marjorie Hope Nicolson; University of Edinburgh, Owen Dudley Edwards; European Center for Nuclear Research (CERN), Lew Kowarski; University of Hawaii, Leon Edel; Howard Payne College, Allen Billy Crider; Kutztown State College, James H. Tinsman; University of Massachusetts at Salem, Robert Briney; New York University, Carroll Newsom, president emeritus; Notre Dame University, Carvel Collins; University of Pennsylvania, Herman Beerman, M.D.; University of Pittsburgh, Robert F. Whitman and Marina von Neumann Whitman; St. John's University, Richard Harmond; St. Olaf's College, J. Randolph Cox; Southeastern Massachusetts University, Richard Reis; Southern Illinois University, Donald L. Brehm; Tarleton State College, Joseph R. Christopher; Trinity College, Hartford, Richard P. Benton; Westbrook College, James Dickinson, president; University of Wisconsin, E. N. Feltskog; Yale University, Donald Kagan, William B. Willcox, Robin Winks.

C. EDITORS AND PUBLISHERS:

Albert Benjamin III, Donald R. Bensen, George Berryman, Marshall Best, Sumner Blossom, Jon Breen, Jan Broberg, Barbara Burn, Cass Canfield, Lianne Carlin, Donald Carmony, Mark Carroll, Steve Clarkson, Cyril Clemens, Sir William A. R. Collins,* Norman Cousins, Robert Cromie, Norman Goldfind, Thomas Guinzburg, Deryck Harvey, Iwan Hedman, Sandy Henschel, Allen J. Hubin, Tom J. Hunter, Joan Kahn, Herbert Kenny, Fred Klein, Rhoda Koenig, Steve Koppman, Ellen Krieger, Frank V. Morley, Arthur H. Motley, James Neal, Michael Nevins, Luther Norris, Jon Tuska, Mollie Waters; and J. Randall Williams III and Llewellyn Howland III, my tutelary divinities at Little, Brown, and their loyal aides Elisabeth Humez and Nancy Ellis.

D. WRITERS AND OTHER ARTISTS:

Eric Ambler, Kingsley Amis, Cleveland Amory, Isaac Asimov, Mike Avallone, L. Fred Ayvazian (Fred Levon), Faith Baldwin, Theodore Bernstein, Elizabeth Coatsworth Beston, Abe Burrows, James M. Cain, John Dickson Carr,* Marc Connelly, Fred J. Cook, Deborah Crawford, Frederic Dannay (Ellery Queen), Dorothy Salisbury Davis, L. Sprague deCamp, Marlene Dietrich, Anne Homer Doerflinger, Michael Dorman, Mrs. Davis Dresser (Helen McCloy), Mignon G. Eberhart, M. F. K. Fisher, Nicolas Freeling, Euell Gibbons,* Joe Gores, Samuel Grafton, Colin Graham, Graham Greene, Sir Hugh Greene, Howard Haycraft, W. Bruce Hepburn (James Balfour), John Hersey, Gilbert Highet, Edward

Hoch, Elizabeth Janeway, Elsa Lanchester, Mary J. Latis and Martha Hennissart (Emma Lathen), Richard Lockridge, Robert A. W. Lowndes, Alfred Lunt* and Lynn Fontanne, Miriam Lynch, David McCord, Mrs. George S. McCue (Lillian De La Torre [Bueno]), Phyllis McGinley, John D. MacDonald, Archibald Mac-Leish, Dame Agatha Christie Mallowan,* Fredric March* and Florence Eldridge, Dame Edith Ngaio Marsh, Harold Q. Masur, Kenneth Millar (Ross Macdonald), Margaret Millar, Arthur Mizener, R. Bruce Montgomery (Edmund Crispin), Henry Morgan, Joyce Porter, J.B. Priestley, Erik Routley, Vermont Royster, Lisa Sergio, Georges Simenon, Cornelia Otis Skinner, H. Allen Smith,* J. I. M. Stewart (Michael Innes), Mary Stewart, Jean Stubbs, Julian Symons, Lawrence Treat, Barbara W. Tuchman, Louis Untermeyer, John Updike, Gore Vidal (Edgar Box), Robert Penn Warren, Hillary Waugh, Jerome Weidman, Donald Westlake, E. B. White, Herman Wouk, Leslie Charteris, Max Wilk.

E. CHURCHMEN AND MEN IN GOVERNMENT:

Anthony Eden, first earl of Avon;* the Honorable Hubert H. Humphrey, Senator from Minnesota; the Honorable Thomas P. O'Neill, Jr., Speaker of the House; John Cardinal Wright; the Right Reverend Leland Stark.

F. LIBRARIANS, MEMBERS OF HISTORICAL SOCIETIES AND ASSOCIATIONS:

Bedford (Massachusetts) Library, Elizabeth Dowling; Boston College Libraries, F. Clifford McElroy, Marilyn Grant; Chicago Public Library, Hoke Norris, Sylvia Polovich; University of California at Los Angeles, University Library, George Chacon, Edith M. Moore; Cleveland Public Library, Lillian A. Clark; Earlham College, Lilly Library, Opal Thornburg,* J. Arthur Funston; Guilford College Library, Treva W. Mathis; Harvard University Libraries, Rodney G. Dennis, Caroline Jakeman, Herbert Kleist; Hofstra University Library, J. Terry Bender; Haverford College Library, Barbara L. Curtis; Indiana State Library, Helen S. Morrison; Indiana State University Library, Martha E. Wright; Indiana University Library, Thomas Glastras, Elfreda Lang; Lexington (Massachusetts) Public Library, Robert Hilton, Gladys Killam; Library of Congress, Norman J. Shaffer; New York Public Library, Paul Myers; Noblesville Public Library, Helen M. Couch; Norfolk (Virginia) Public Library, Lucile B. Portlock; Occidental College Library, Jane Guymon; Seymour (Indiana) Public Library, Mildred Graves; Stanford University Libraries, Patricia J. Palmer, Swarthmore College, Friends Historical Library, Eleanor Mayer, Nancy F. Speers; Syracuse University, the George Arents Research Library, Carolyn A. Davis; University of Texas, Humanities Research Center, F. W. Roberts; Topeka Public Library, James Marvin, Tom Muth; Wilmington Public Library, Sarah Crestle, Martha Jo Gregory.

Bartholomew County (Indiana) Historical Society, Frances Schaefer; Hamilton County (Indiana) Historical Society, Irene Miller, Nell Roberts; Indiana Historical Society, Caroline Dunn, Mrs. Lawrence Gerlach; Historical Society of Pennsylvania, Nicholas B. Wainwright; Shawnee County (Kansas) Historical Society, John W. Ripley; Wilmington (Ohio) Historical Society, Kathryn E. Williams.

G. GENEALOGISTS:

Frederick Dorman, Fellow of the American Society of Genealogists; Seth B. Hinshaw; Colonel John J. McAleer, Deputy Director, Criminal Investigative Command, United States Army; Michael McAleer, Archivist, Microfilm Division, Mormon Records, Salt Lake City; Janet McCrosky, Springfield (Ohio)

Genealogical Association; Francis S. McIlhinney, Jr., president, Hoopes Family Organization; George A. Robinson, Washington Court House (Ohio) Genealogical Society; Ernest Stout; Admiral Herald F. Stout; Colonel John Todhunter, Bures St. Mary, Suffolk, England.

H. FRIENDS AND ASSOCIATES OF REX STOUT — PRE–WORLD WAR II:
Roger Baldwin, Alvah C. Bessie, Charlotte Foucart Boyle, Stuart Chase, Opal Davids, Mrs. Frank Donovan, Susan Rodgers Durant,* Morris Ernst,* Margaret and John Farrar,* Ruth Gannett, Helen May Iooss, Helen McClintock,* Norma Millay, Helen and Scott Nearing, Mrs. Lawrence Pope, Marguerite Reese, Alice Ruffles, Paul Ruffles,* Mary and Harold Salmon, Julia Sanderson,* Elizabeth Schnemayer,* Zoltán Sepeshy,* Maude B. Snyder,* Fred Swenson, Charles Wilson, and Alfred A. Knopf.

I. FRIENDS AND ASSOCIATES OF REX STOUT — WORLD WAR II ERA:
Herbert Agar, Mathilde Arens, Frederica Barach, Barbara Benjamin, Barry Bingham, Kay Boyle, Carol Brandt, Himan Brown, Marquis Child, Peter Cusick, Marcia Davenport, Walter D. Edmonds, Polly Evans, Clifton Fadiman, George Field, Carl Friedrich, Paul Gallico,* Harry Gideonse, Beatrice Blackmar Gould, Alan Green,* Gladys Green, Selma Greenstein, Dorothy Hammerstein, Laura Z. Hobson, James Keddie, Jr., Robert Landry, Dorothy Cameron Disney MacKaye, George Merten, Francis Pickens Miller, George Morlan, Lewis Mumford, Sylvia Porter, Margaret Leech Pulitzer,* Richard and Dorothy Rodgers, William L. Shirer, Marshall Shulman, Frank Sullivan,* Orin Tovrov, Julian Wolff. Others who illumined this period are Anna Lou Ashby, Carl Brandt, Jr., Edward L. Burlingame, Thomas Howell, L. Bancel La Farge, Armitage Watkins, and Christina Marquand Welch.

J. FRIENDS AND ASSOCIATES OF REX STOUT — POST–WORLD WAR II:
Gloria Amoury, William S. Baring-Gould,* Dorothy Beall, Ruth Bishop, Phyllis Boucher, Edna Brandau, Cecil Brown, Ernestine Gilbreth Carey, Bonnie Cashin, Leo Cherne, Margaret Cousins, Edith Deen, Lina Derecktor, Avis DeVoto, Reverend George B. Ford, Ruth Friend, Eleanor and Sylvan Furman, William W. Goodman, Katherine Gauss Jackson,* Irwin Karp, Margaret Adams, Mrs. Alan Macneil, Edward H. Mabley, Karl Menninger, M.D., Herbert Mitgang, Robert Moses, Leo Rosten, Howard Rusk, M.D., Dore Schary, James Sheldòn,* Gay Simpson, Mrs. John Steinbeck, Leonard Sussman, Howard Taubman, Mills Ten Eyck, Dorothy Van Doren, Ira Wallach, Thew Wright, Alyce and Kaso Yasumoto.

K. THE WOLFE PACK:
Cheryl Althoff, Herbert C. Arbuckle, Mike W. Barr, Charles F. Black, Peter E. Blau, Michael Bourne, Jeffrey Burnoski, Virginia Cancelliere, William J. Clark, Florita Cook, Joe Diamond, Sylvia Doff, Grace and Carroll Dunham, Al Feltskog, Malcolm Ferguson, Al Germeshausen, Martin Halperin, Lucille Hesse, John Harris, Stacey Holmes, George C. Hoyt, Jr., Roy Hunt, Frank Jellinek, Katherine A. Johnson, David Kamm, Irene Keegan, Anthony Klancar,* Anita and Kenneth Kulman, Steve Lewis, Richard Lochte II, Orin MacFarland, Frank McSherry, Lewis Martin, Sally Ann Martin, Walker Martin, Elizabeth Morris, Robert H. Morris, Lee Peleske, Ken Pierce, Judson Sapp, Arriean Schemer, Danny Kaye Sizemore, George Smith, Ray Stannich, Ernest and Milton Starr, Donna Steinkrauss, Peter Stern, Karen Tweedy-Holmes, John D. Vining, B.

Frank Vogel, M.D., Rose Vogel, Marion Wilcox, Bengta Woo, Lavender Wood-thorpe, and Ann Marie Maloney, peerless leader of the pack.

Special notes of thanks are due to my research assistant, David Anderson, who performed a thousand research tasks with unfailing cheer and exactitude; to Elizabeth Vogel and Joseph Kilbridge, who gave the typescript a close critical reading and disputed error where they found it; to deans Thomas F. O'Malley, S.J., and Donald J. White of Boston College, for a timely sabbatical and faculty research grant; to my chairman, Paul Doherty, who allowed me to develop courses in Literary Biography and in Crime Fiction and Folk Myth, so that my vocation and avocation were fruitfully allied; to my three daughters, Mary Alycia, Saragh, and Seana, and my three sons, Jay, Paul, and Andrew, who relinquished a part of their childhood to support their father's illusion that he had six secretaries; and to my wife, Ruth, who, when Leon Edel asked her whether she was married to me or to Rex Stout, unhesitatingly answered "Rex Stout."

And, finally, a loving word for "Plummy" — P. G. Wodehouse — who knew that Rex Stout, like himself, had created his own cosmos, and in the realm of the gods which he occupied accorded Rex coequal status. Plummy never ceased to encourage me in my labors. He was glad to know Rex's biography was taking shape. Impelled no doubt by the conviction that a god cannot be introduced by a mere mortal, when past ninety he wrote his foreword for it.

Index